ROBERT W. WHITE received both his undergraduate and graduate training at Harvard University and has spent more than thirty years there in a range of capacities: Chairman of the Department of Social Relations, Director of the Harvard Psychological Clinic, and Professor of Clinical Psychology. During this time Dr. White has been distinguished for his many contributions to the fields of clinical psychology and personality.

NORMAN F. WATT received his Ph.D. from The Ohio State University. He then served as a post-doctoral fellow in mental health at the Federal Institute of Technology in Zurich, Switzerland, following which he was Assistant Professor and then lecturer in Clinical Psychology at Harvard University. Presently Dr. Watt is Professor of Clinical Psychology at the University of Massachusetts.

THE ABNORMAL
PERSONALITY

ROBERT W. WHITE
HARVARD UNIVERSITY

NORMAN F. WATT
UNIVERSITY OF MASSACHUSETTS

FOURTH EDITION

THE RONALD PRESS COMPANY · NEW YORK

Library of Congress Catalog Card Number: 72-97149
PRINTED IN THE UNITED STATES OF AMERICA

Preface

Our purpose in this book is to write about abnormal people in a way that will be valuable and interesting to students new to the subject. A first course in abnormal psychology is not intended to train specialists. Its goal is more general: it should provide the student with the opportunity to whet his interest, expand his horizons, register a certain body of new facts, and relate what he learns to the rest of his knowledge about mankind. The value of a course in abnormal psychology is not limited to those who plan to become professional workers with troubled people. We try here to present the subject in such a way as to emphasize its usefulness to all students of human nature.

This Fourth Edition of *The Abnormal Personality* is distinctly a child of its own time. Abnormal psychology has undergone revolutionary changes since the first publication of this text. At that time, when mental hospitals were largely custodial, when research on somatic causes was in doldrums, when shock methods were just coming into use, when group psychotherapy looked like a dubious shortcut, and when mental health received only feeble public interest and financial support, the chief breakthrough for abnormal psychology was the psychoanalytic treatment of the neuroses, with the light this cast on personal development and unconscious motivation. The most drastic happening in subsequent years was the revolution in public attitudes whereby mental health became a popular cause and a community responsibility. Concurrently, mental hospitals began to be transformed into therapeutic milieux, shock treatment was perfected but then substantially displaced by tranquilizing and antidepressant drugs, and research on somatic causes moved strongly ahead, especially with respect to behavioral genetics and brain biochemistry. Group psychotherapy expanded widely, behavior therapy and family therapy rose to established places, and the generality of the medical or disease model, so long traditional in explaining abnormal behavior, was effectively challenged. Psychoanalytic thinking moved toward ego psychology, producing among other things the socially oriented concept of ego identity, and the cumbersome analytic technique began to give way to innovations branching out in all directions. To be a child of its time, a book on abnormal psychology must be responsive to all these developments.

The attainment of this goal clearly entailed a rethinking of the whole subject as it had been presented in previous editions. If chapter headings have often been retained, what appears under them is in most cases substantially different, with long sections that are wholly new. The new atmosphere can already be scented in the two introductory chapters. The past does not change, but our historical introduction illustrates the principle that each age rewrites history to emphasize present concerns. In the clinical introduction three of the five cases are new; two of the subjects were not born when the first edition went to press. These cases differ most importantly from those they have displaced in that they show the social embeddedness of disordered behavior and the complex social operations involved in attempts at treatment.

The next three chapters pursue the theme of adaptation. The adaptive process is first presented descriptively, then related to fundamental principles of learning and cognitive organization, after which we examine the special effects of anxiety on the learning process and develop the concept of protectively burdened personalities. The two chapters (4 and 5) on the development of personality are intended to give an account of normal growth while showing at each point how development can go astray. To the extent that disordered behavior represents faulty adaptive habits, these three chapters provide a foundation for its understanding.

The neuroses are presented not as diseases, with sharp distinction between symptom and underlying cause, but as miscarriages in meeting the difficulties of living. We retain, however, the concept of constitutional vulnerability, especially for such radical forms as the obsessional and hysterical disorders. Two chapters on psychotherapy follow immediately. We count it an educational blunder to postpone treatment to the end of the book, as if description of disorders were a goal in itself regardless of what can be done. The chief methods of psychotherapy, including behavior therapy, have all arisen out of treating neuroses, even though wider applications have later been made. Dealing with the subject at this point is therefore historically appropriate; it is also of service in directing attention to possible treatment for each of the disorders discussed in subsequent chapters. There is a great deal of new writing in the two chapters on psychological treatment.

The next three chapters (9–11), expanded from a single earlier one, deal respectively with delinquency, drug dependence, and sexual disorders. These troubles have in common the acting out, rather than the suppression, of certain impulses, and they share the theme of conflict with the law. Delinquency and drug use, increasing sharply in recent years, have caused widespread public alarm which has led to increased effort both in treatment and in research. With special force these chapters exemplify the social embeddedness of the behavior we call abnormal.

In the remaining chapters on specific varieties of disorder (12–16) we have somewhat tipped the balance from psychological to somatic components. The disease model should be eliminated, in our opinion, only where it is inappropriate—not everywhere. Reflected in these chapters is the recent progress of research on genetics, which has proved to be decisive for certain forms of mental retardation and suggestive as regards other kinds of disorder. We also describe those advances in brain physiology which, if not yet a breakthrough, are possibly headed in that hopeful direction.

In the final chapter the problem of disordered behavior is allowed to expand again to its full social dimensions. In keeping with current trends, the chapter is organized around the idea of community mental health and of care by means of community mental health centers. Treatment, care, and prevention call for social effort and social organization. Part of the work must be done by professionally trained people, but they cannot do it all. They can be effective only in a favorable climate of public opinion which shows itself in provision of facilities, volunteer service, public and private financial support, and dedication to a social order conducive to sound human growth.

It is a pleasure to express our gratitude to Dr. Donald Peterson and Professor Joachim Meyer for permitting us to use their case material. Special thanks are also due to Drs. Margaret Riggs, Sheldon Cashdan, George Levinger, Norman Simonson, and Richard Louttit, who have helped in several ways, and to students too numerous to mention individually who read and criticized some of the new sections. And we are much indebted to Mrs. Sally Ives, who typed and retyped several drafts of a good part of the book, searched for obscure library references, and served as a general editorial assistant. We are especially indebted to Michael Weissman for preparing a very thorough Index.

ROBERT W. WHITE
NORMAN F. WATT

Marlborough, New Hampshire
Amherst, Massachusetts
January, 1973

Contents

**1 HISTORICAL INTRODUCTION: ORIGINS OF ABNORMAL
PSYCHOLOGY**   **3**

The Subject Matter of Abnormal Psychology. Evolution of Attitudes
Toward Disordered People. Mental Disorders Considered as Diseases
of the Brain. Beginnings of Psychopathology: The Study of Hysteria.
Freud's Basic Discoveries. Psychological Conceptions of Treatment.
Present Outlook.

**2 CLINICAL INTRODUCTION: EXAMPLES OF DISORDERED
PERSONALITIES**   **45**

Introduction to the Cases. 1. An Adolescent Maladjustment: Walter
Lilly.   2. An Adolescent Mental Breakdown: Kathi Hermann.
3. Chronic Multiple Disorders: Benton Child.   4. A Progressive Brain
Disease: Martha Ottenby.   5. A Persistent but Unsuccessful Criminal
Career: Bert Whipley.   Conclusion.

3 THE ADAPTIVE PROCESS   **90**

Meaning of Adaptation. Main Features of Adaptive Strategy. Relevant Principles of Learning. Recovery from Frightening Experiences.
Defense Mechanisms. Protectively Burdened Personalities. Varieties
of Unadaptive Outcome.

4 DEVELOPMENT OF PERSONALITY: EARLY CHILDHOOD   **134**

Dependence and Deprivation. Early Growth of Competence. Discipline and Self-Control. Aggression and Its Management. The Family
as Environment for Growth.

**5 DEVELOPMENT OF PERSONALITY: LATER CHILDHOOD
AND ADOLESCENCE**   **167**

Mental Development and Education. Social Development: Relations
with Groups. Social Development: Intimate Relations. Sexual Development. Self and Ego Identity. Generativity. Life Patterns:
Workable and Unworkable.

6 THE NEUROSES   202

Anxiety States. Phobias. Obsessional Neurosis. Dissociated Conditions. Conversion Hysteria. Problem of the Choice of Neurosis.

7 PSYCHOTHERAPY: INDIVIDUAL METHODS   238

Nature of Psychotherapy. Behavior Therapy. Psychoanalysis. Other Forms of Psychotherapy. Choice of Patients for Psychotherapy. Results of Psychotherapy.

8 PSYCHOTHERAPY: GROUP METHODS   286

Family Therapy. Psychodrama. Group Psychotherapy. Encounter Groups. The Therapeutic Milieu.

9 DELINQUENCY AND CRIMINAL BEHAVIOR   311

Professional Crime. Juvenile Delinquency. Psychopathic Personality. Society's Response to Crime.

10 DRUG DEPENDENCE   340

Smoking. Psychoactive Drug Dependence. Chronic Alcoholism.

11 SEXUAL DISORDERS   373

Varieties of Sexual Disorder. Disorders of Sexual Performance. Homosexuality. Disorders of Sexual Aim. Conclusion.

12 PSYCHOSOMATIC DISORDERS   396

Emotion and Bodily Changes. Gastro-intestinal Disturbances. Cardiovascular Disorders. Bronchial Asthma. Problem of Symptom Placement. Implications for General Medicine.

13 SCHIZOPHRENIC DISORDERS   429

Kraepelin's Varieties of Schizophrenia. The Process-Reactive Dimension. Disorganization in Schizophrenic Thinking. Schizophrenia in Childhood. Psychodynamic Aspects of the Disorder. Somatogenic Aspects of the Disorder. Treatment of Schizophrenia.

14 DEPRESSIVE AND MANIC DISORDERS   479

Depressed States. Manic States. Nature of Depressive and Manic Disorders. Psychological Aspects. Problems of Classification. Somatic Aspects. Methods of Treatment.

15   INJURIES AND ABNORMAL CONDITIONS IN THE BRAIN   507

Varieties of Pathological Process. Effects of Localized Cortical Injury. General Effects of Abnormal Conditions in the Brain. Brain
Dysfunction in Children. Epilepsy. Mental Changes and Disorders
of Old Age.

16   MENTAL RETARDATION   548

Down's Syndrome (Mongolism). Phenylketonuria (PKU). Cultural–
Familial Retardation. Other Forms of Retardation. Conclusion.

17   COMMUNITY MENTAL HEALTH   574

Size of the Problem. Community Mental Health Centers. Developing Facilities for Mental Health Care. The Manpower Problem. Prevention of Disordered Behavior. The Citizen's Contribution.

NAME INDEX   604

SUBJECT INDEX   611

THE ABNORMAL
PERSONALITY

1

Historical Introduction: Origins of Abnormal Psychology

Abnormal psychology was once considered to be a remote province of knowledge, explored only by a few specialists. As such it played no more than a minor part in man's thinking about his own nature. Today it contributes richly to the training of professional workers, especially psychiatrists, psychologists, social workers, teachers, and ministers, whose duties bring them in frequent contact with troubled people. More than this, it occupies a respected place among general college courses, for it is seen to be capable of making a significant contribution to all thinking about human problems and the human quest for a better way of life. Abnormal personalities are not mysteriously set apart from the normal. Their various peculiarities are often simply exaggerations of what is to be found in every human being; their problems may represent unfortunate outcomes of processes we all use in seeking to lead our lives. They are therefore well suited to enlarge our understanding of personal development as a whole. If we know what can go wrong with adaptive behavior, we are the wiser in making it go right.

When we set ourselves to examine the field of abnormal psychology we can proceed in two ways. We can look into the history of the subject and discover how it came to be what it is today. This method offers distinct advantages over an immediate plunge into facts and current problems. Science generally advances in a disorderly fashion. At any given moment the greatest activity occurs at three or four isolated points, the location of which is

3

determined by temporary urgency, by newly discovered techniques, or even by fashion. It is easy to get lost in the details and preoccupations of current research, and the best protection against doing so is to anchor our study firmly in the framework of history. By turning up the facts in the same order in which they confronted past investigators one can better appreciate the really basic difficulties which tend to impede understanding, and one can more readily keep the whole subject in place in the larger context of human affairs. On the other hand we could begin our study in a quite different way: by making a clinical survey of the facts that constitute the subject matter of abnormal psychology. We could examine a series of cases illustrating the kinds of things we shall be studying in more systematic form throughout the book. The clinical method has the advantage of realistic vividness and of proceeding in the right direction from fact to theory. The advantages of each method are in fact so great that in this book we shall use them both. This chapter contains an *historical introduction* to abnormal psychology; the next one will provide a *clinical introduction*.

THE SUBJECT MATTER OF ABNORMAL PSYCHOLOGY

At the present time the province of abnormal psychology can be roughly described as the study of *disordered personal reactions* to life and its circumstances. When we say *disordered* we have in mind people whose lives in some way go astray, so that they find themselves frustrated, unhappy, anxious, baffled in their deepest desires, misfits in their society; or, in the most serious instances, people who get so badly out of touch with surrounding life that we call them insane. When we say that the disorder lies in *personal reactions* we intend to limit the field more closely by excluding what may be called the external reasons for frustration and sorrow. Accidents, bereavements, ill health, war and other disasters, unemployment and poverty, lack of opportunities, unfair social barriers, and a hundred other external circumstances may stand in the way of happy and effective living. These obstacles are tremendously important, but it is not the task of psychology to study them in their own right. They are already claimed for other fields of knowledge such as medicine, public health, and especially the various social sciences. To all such circumstances, however, the individual makes a personal reaction. Even to a disease affecting his own body each person reacts in a way that is peculiar to himself. It is at this point, where the personal reaction begins, that we cross into the province of psychology, and we reach the subprovince of abnormal psychology when we concentrate on disorders in the personal reaction.

To illustrate what has just been said let us take the example of unemployment. A man may become unemployed through no fault of his own, purely as a result of economic forces over which he has no control. This external circumstance evokes in him some kind of personal reaction. The professional task of the social scientist is to understand the economic forces which brought about the unemployment; that of the psychologist begins with the personal reaction. Unemployed people react to their misfortune in a variety of ways. Many of these ways it would not occur to us to call disordered or abnormal. Unhappiness and discouragement, indignation and bitterness, seem well justified by the circumstances. Attempts to understand the situation and to change it by organized action seem well adapted to the problem as it stands. Certain people, however, behave in more extreme and peculiar ways. One man may take the blame entirely upon himself, declaring that his misfortune is a well-deserved punishment for his own sin and worthlessness. Another may believe that his former employers formed a conspiracy to throw him out of work and are even now trying to poison his food and take his life. A third may become extremely shy, hiding from his neighbors even when they too are unemployed, convinced that everyone holds him in contempt because he is no longer able to support his family. Still another may decide to shoot the President: this indeed is no fanciful example, for in 1932 a hungry unemployed man fired at the President-elect at a public gathering and killed another public official who was standing nearby. These people, we say, are acting in a very peculiar fashion. Their personal reactions are so little warranted by external circumstance, or so poorly designed to achieve desired results, that we cannot avoid considering them disordered. Factors within themselves are contributing disproportionately to their behavior. Abnormal psychology is the study of these disordered and disproportionate personal reactions.

EVOLUTION OF ATTITUDES TOWARD DISORDERED PEOPLE

If one undertook today to make a list of disordered personal reactions bothersome enough to suggest the need for psychological help, the result would be a bulky catalogue. In the course of time we have learned to see in this light a great many forms of behavior which were earlier taken to be moral problems belonging in the realm of volition. If people were unhappy, anxious, and irritable, if they were unduly boastful and self-centered, if they did not get along well with their family and friends, if they wasted time and took to drink or drugs, they were likely to be censured and told to mend their ways. The idea that such difficulties in living might be strongly rooted, resistant to change, and in need of scientific study and professional help has had widespread acceptance only in recent years. It makes its way into the history of abnormal psychology only in the course of the present century.

Quite the opposite is the case with the severer forms of mental affliction. Here we can observe a distinct evolution of attitudes in Western society from medieval to modern times. Insanity is described in some of the earliest scientific writings. The insane, with their obvious unfitness to take care of themselves and their inconvenience and occasional danger to others, have always managed to establish some kind of claim on public attention. The early history of abnormal psychology is thus the history of attempts to understand insanity.

For the most part this history is a discouraging tale of isolated observations which never grew into a body of tested knowledge. The Greek physician Hippocrates, somewhere around 460 B.C., did his best to bring insanity into the fold of medicine by pronouncing it a disease of the brain and treating it like other diseases. In the writings of the great medical men from Galen in the second century to Weyer in the sixteenth, and of the great observers of human nature such as Vives and Montaigne, one finds many shrewd observations on the nature of insanity, much sympathy for the lot of its victims, and a disposition to seek humane methods to restore tranquillity of mind. Indeed the history of mental disorders reveals many surprising anticipations of what we now like to regard as modern attitudes and modern discoveries. But these prophetic voices of the past cried in the wilderness of an unenlightened, unconcerned public opinion. They were all but powerless to effect the social change upon which any systematic study of the insane was dependent.

One fact overshadows all others: there were no real hospitals for the mentally ill until the very end of the eighteenth century. There were no organized institutions to embody the humane feelings of those few enlightened minds that recognized the nature of mental disorders. This meant that there was no proper opportunity to build up an adequate knowledge of the subject, no chance to accumulate hospital records and compare large numbers of cases. Science could advance but little until suitable institutions were created, and institutions could not be created until public opinion was ready to support them. It was no accident that mental hospitals came simultaneously with the American and French Revolutions. They sprang from the same slowly growing sense of the rights and needs of the less fortunate.

The Insane as Social Outcasts

Before the establishment of hospitals the mentally disordered were treated as outcasts and hardly distinguished from criminals. The community felt responsible for them only to the extent of preventing them from troubling their fellow men. Some of the less troublesome wandered about the countryside, begging and stealing their food and finding shelter in barns and pigsties. Others were thrown into prison where, side by side with criminals, they lived amid revolting filth, often chained, always at the mercy of their keepers. In 1785 a French physician described the situation as follows:

Thousands of deranged are locked up in prisons without anyone's thinking of administering the slightest remedy; the half-deranged are mixed with the completely insane, the furious with the quiet; some are in chains, others are free in the prison; finally, unless nature comes to their rescue and cures them, the term of their misery is that of their mortal days, and unfortunately in the meantime the illness but increases instead of diminishing.[1]

Even those rare physicians who interested themselves in lunatics recommended severe and violent treatment. According to one medical authority of the seventeenth century:

> Discipline, threats, fetters, and blows are needed as much as medical treatment. Truly nothing is more necessary and more effective for the recovery of these people than forcing them to respect and fear intimidation. By this method, the mind, held back by restraint, is induced to give up its arrogance and wild ideas and it soon becomes meek and orderly. This is why maniacs often recover much sooner if they are treated with torture and torments in a hovel instead of with medicaments.[2]

Toward the end of the eighteenth century and even during the nineteenth there were many physicians who advocated harsh discipline for excited patients. Even the great American pioneer in psychiatry, Benjamin Rush, who in other respects advanced the cause of humane treatment, described in 1812 "terrifying modes of punishment" for refractory patients, recommending "pouring cold water under the sleeve, so that it may descend into the armpits and down the trunk of the body," or, if this failed, deprivation of food and threats of death.[3]

Hard as was the lot of the insane a century and a half ago, it had nevertheless undoubtedly been worse in earlier times. In the Middle Ages, and indeed in all but the most enlightened periods of human history, it was generally believed that the insane were possessed by evil spirits. Some malignant demon was supposed to be inhabiting the body of the victim or to be directing his lunatic behavior from without. During the fifteenth and sixteenth centuries this general belief reached its extreme development in the institution of witchcraft, borrowed undoubtedly from primitive pagan sources but by this time thoroughly absorbed into Christian theology. What gave to the witchcraft trials their peculiar ferocity was the belief that the accused person had surrendered body and soul to the devil and made a solemn pact to do his evil work. For someone to be possessed was thus not merely a personal misfortune; it put the whole community in great moral danger. Witches, great numbers of whom would now be classed as psychologically disordered persons, were hunted, captured, tried in court, sometimes tortured to obtain confessions, and if found guilty were publicly burned. Such happenings were not at all uncommon.

Judges were called upon to pass sentence on witches in great numbers. A French judge boasted that he had burned 800 women in 16 years on the bench;

---

[1] J. Colombier, quoted by G. Zilboorg and G. W. Henry, *A History of Medical Psychology* (New York: W. W. Norton & Co., Inc., 1941), p. 316.

[2] T. Willis, *ibid.*, p. 261.

[3] B. Rush, *Medical Inquiries and Observations upon the Diseases of the Mind* (Philadelphia: Kimber & Richardson, 1812), p. 180.

600 were burned during the administration of a bishop in Bamberg. The Inquisition, originally started by the Church of Rome, was carried along by Protestant Churches in Great Britain and Germany. In Protestant Geneva 500 persons were burned in the year 1515. Other countries, where there were Catholic jurists, boasted of as many burnings. In Treves, 7,000 were reported burned during a period of several years.[4]

The Insane as Sick People: Pinel's Reforms

It was thus a step forward when the notion of demon possession gave place to the notion that the lunatic was merely a public nuisance to be kept out of the way. As we have seen, however, the benefits were at first not very great; the mentally disordered were still outcasts and were still subject to brutal inconsideration. This was the situation which toward the close of the eighteenth century at last began to stir the public conscience. As is usually the case, reform was in the air and cannot properly be attributed to a single individual. But the figure of Philippe Pinel (1745–1826) stands out above his contemporaries, and his experiences well illustrate the social movement that was under way. Pinel was a physician and scholar who lived most of his life in Paris, who gradually centered his interest on mental disorders, and who found a golden opportunity to carry out his progressive ideas when in the first years of the Revolution he was made physician-in-chief at the Bicêtre, a hospital chiefly populated by the mentally deranged. His progressive ideas sprang from a rare sympathy for the insane and a persistent, discerning attempt to understand them. "The mentally sick," Pinel declared, "far from being guilty people deserving of punishment, are sick people whose miserable state deserves all the consideration that is due to suffering humanity. One should try with the most simple methods to restore their reason." [5]

Pinel's first step was to remove the chains and fetters with which most of the patients were bound. This required permission from the Commune, and the president came in person to talk with the patients and assure himself that no political enemies were concealed among them. Greeted by shouts and the clanking of chains, his attempts at conversation answered only by curses and execrations, the president is reported to have asked Pinel, "Citizen, are you mad yourself, that you would unchain such beasts?" To this Pinel replied, "It is my conviction that these mentally ill are intractable only because they are deprived of fresh air and of their liberty." [6] Permission was granted, and Pinel proceeded with his experiment. While in some cases no great benefits resulted, there were numerous instances in which patients hitherto considered dangerous and completely unmanageable became calm and reasonable when released from restraint and treated with

[4] W. Bromberg, *The Mind of Man: The Story of Man's Conquest of Mental Illness* (New York: Harper & Row, 1937), p. 61.
[5] Quoted by Zilboorg and Henry, *op. cit.*, pp. 323–24.
[6] R. Semelaigne, *Les grands aliénistes français* (Paris: 1930), Vol. I, p. 41.

kindness. Some who had been incarcerated half a lifetime were shortly discharged from the hospital with their health restored. But above all Pinel showed beyond any doubt that a large mental hospital could be safely and beneficially conducted with a minimum of mechanical restraint.

This was Pinel's most dramatic action, but it was only the beginning of the reforms which laid a foundation for the psychiatry of the future. Soon after the experiments at the Bicêtre he was transferred to the larger Salpêtrière hospital where he applied himself to a huge task of reorganization. He began to train attendants so that they should be something better than guards, and he tried to give the patients the benefit of comfort and a healthful routine. Of enduring importance was his introduction of the psychiatric case history and the systematic keeping of records. This arose from his habit of observing patients closely and taking careful notes. Before his time it often happened that no one remembered when or for what cause a patient had entered the hospital. Obviously it was impossible to build up a sound knowledge of mental disorders until Pinel's custom of making records became an established practice. It was only in a well-regulated hospital, moreover, that methods of treatment could be properly explored, different methods compared, and results followed and verified. Pinel himself completed in 1801 a treatise on the nature and treatment of mental disorders, based largely on his own hospital experience. In the introduction he portrays the new role of the physician as he himself enacted it.

The habit of living constantly in the midst of the insane, of studying their habits, their different personalities, the objects of their pleasures or their dislikes, the advantage of following the course of their alienation day and night during the various seasons of the year, the art of directing them without effort and sparing them excitement and grumbling, the gift of being able to assume at the right time a tone of kindness or of authority, of being able to subdue them by force if methods of kindness fail, the constant picture of all the phenomena of mental alienation, and finally the functions of supervision itself—the combination of all these must give an intelligent and zealous man an immense number of facts and minute details usually lacking in the narrow-minded physician unless he has taken a special interest during fleeting visits to asylums.[7]

This was indeed the dawn of a new day both for the mentally disordered and for man's whole understanding of his own nature.

The ideas behind Pinel's reforms began to spread slowly through the Western world. At last the public mind was beginning to be ready to receive them. In England William Tuke, a wealthy Quaker merchant, founded in 1796 the York Retreat where amidst quiet country surroundings kind and gentle methods of treatment were put into effect. Yet it was another fifty years before the policy of non-restraint became established in England, and even later in other countries. Naturally it was slow work to

[7] P. Pinel, *Traité médico-philosophique sur l'aliénation mentale* (Paris: J. A. Brosson, 1801), p. 15.

secure reforms that entailed greater expense, but it is surprising to realize the force of opposition within the medical profession itself. When Gardiner Hill, around 1840, was fighting to promote the policy of non-restraint and demonstrating in his own Lincoln Asylum that the plan really worked, other British medical men pronounced it the "wild scheme of a philanthropic visionary," indeed "a breaking of the sixth commandment," and asserted that "restraint forms the very basis on which the sound treatment of lunatics is founded." [8] Not until 1857 could it be reported that non-restraint was generally accepted in British hospitals.

The Insane as Public Charges: State Hospitals

To provide a sufficient number of hospitals for the mentally disordered was itself a major crusade. Here the contribution of the United States was particularly noteworthy. Several hospitals were opened early in the nineteenth century to embody the new humane principles: the Friends' Asylum at Philadelphia in 1817, McLean Hospital in Massachusetts in 1818, Bloomingdale in New York in 1822, and the Hartford Retreat in 1824. By 1840 there were fourteen mental hospitals in the United States capable of accommodating altogether something like 2,500 patients. But the census of the same year showed over 17,000 insane, of whom scarcely more than 5,000 were supported as public charges.[9] The great mass of the mentally ill were still without benefit of treatment, public support, or proper accommodations. The correction of this state of affairs was one of the many reform movements which spread through the country toward the middle of the last century. It was set in motion largely by Dorothea L. Dix, a Massachusetts schoolteacher who on her own initiative began to investigate the almshouses, jails, and private homes where the pauper insane were kept. In 1843 she presented to the Massachusetts legislature a memorial describing in detail what she had seen: insane persons "confined in cages, closets, cellars, stalls, pens . . . chained, naked, beaten with rods, and lashed into obedience." [10] The success of her petition marked the beginning of a long, remarkably effective career. Miss Dix personally investigated conditions throughout the United States, presenting reports and arguing with state legislators, until she had become the chief moving force in the founding or enlarging of more than thirty state hospitals. She afterwards extended her activities to Scotland and England, and her tours of inspection in most of the countries of Europe carried her influence still farther afield. Few people today remember how much the modern system of state hospitals owes to this indomitable worker. Her influence was in no small measure responsible for the trend revealed in the following figures. In 1840 the mental

8 Bromberg, op. cit., p. 105.

9 A. Deutsch, The Mentally Ill in America (Garden City, N. Y.: Doubleday & Co., Inc., 1937), p. 232.

10 D. L. Dix, Memorial in Behalf of the Pauper Insane and Idiots in Jails and Poorhouses Throughout the Commonwealth (Boston: Monroe & Francis, 1843), p. 4.

hospitals of the United States housed 2,561 patients, this being 14 per cent of the estimated number of insane in the country. Half a century later, in 1890, the mental hospitals housed 74,028 patients, this being 69 per cent of the insane in the country.[11] The neglected lunatic of previous centuries at last stood a good chance of finding proper shelter, food, and medical attention.

The Mental Hygiene Movement

By 1900 the care of mental patients had greatly improved, but there was still much to be accomplished. A vivid picture of conditions in that year can be found in the autobiography of Clifford W. Beers, who later inaugurated the mental hygiene movement. As a young man of twenty-four, recently graduated from college, Beers became depressed, attempted suicide, and for the next two years saw the inside of three different mental hospitals from the point of view of a patient. After returning to health he wrote the story of his illness in *A Mind That Found Itself* (1908), a book destined to achieve a tremendous influence toward the understanding of mental disorders. Beers admitted that he was a difficult patient. During the latter part of his illness he was elated, arrogant, dictatorial, doubtless exceedingly irritating to those in charge, and inclined at times to create rather violent scenes. Considering this, and comparing his treatment with what was meted out in earlier centuries, his care was a model of patience and forbearance, yet he was choked and thrown to the floor, kicked and spat upon, kept lightly clad in a cold cell, bound painfully tight in a straitjacket, and treated with childish displays of temper by the attendants, as when his holiday dinner was snatched away because he dallied over it. It is perhaps not surprising that the attendants displayed shortcomings; the first training school for mental nurses in this country was then not quite twenty years old, and the practice of hiring untrained guards was still widespread. On the doctors' part, what we miss is not so much a lack of humanity as a lack of insight and of that attitude which makes it possible not to be irritated by the patient's refractory behavior. In small and useless ways Beers was thwarted and thereby infuriated. His clothes were withheld, he was denied pencil and paper, and once he was even forbidden to collect some harmless corncobs that happened to strike his fancy. Moreover, there was practically no attempt to study his mental processes or to understand how the illness came about. "It was upon the gradual but sure improvement in my physical condition," Beers wrote, "that the doctors were relying for my eventual return to normality." [12]

Beers and his book became the agents of another forward stride in the evolution of attitudes toward disordered personal behavior. In 1909 Beers established the National Committee for Mental Hygiene, later expanded to

11 Deutsch, *op. cit.*, p. 232.
12 C. W. Beers, *A Mind That Found Itself* (Garden City, N.Y.: Doubleday & Co., Inc., 1931), p. 73.

international dimensions, having in view three main purposes: (1) to alter the widespread popular belief that mental disorders were incurable and that they carried a stigma of disgrace, (2) to improve those conditions in mental hospitals which Beers's own experiences brought so clearly into the open, and (3) to encourage the early recognition and prevention of mental disorders through the establishment of child guidance clinics designed to study and treat problems of behavior before they grew to more serious proportions. The reponse to these intended enlightenments seemed at first very slow. Mentally disordered people continued to be regarded as baffling and sinister, best handled by removal from the community and consignment to the care of specialists. Hospitals were given better support, but not enough; child guidance clinics were opened, but not in sufficient number; and funds for research continued to run in a trickle compared to those available for the study of other human ailments. Even as late as 1950 most supporters of mental health still regarded their movement as the Cinderella of the medical world. Few would have predicted the abrupt change of status that was about to take place.

Community Mental Health

No doubt it was simply the final stage of an evolution that had long been under way, but when the change came in the 1950's it went forward with revolutionary speed. Mental health sprang into the position of a major public concern. All at once it became the object of large government programs, substantial financial support, and enthusiastic volunteer service in the community. Social historians have the intriguing task of explaining this burst of interest and relating it to other contemporary social movements. The resulting state of affairs would perhaps strike Pinel, Tuke, and Miss Dix like a dream come true, but it should be noticed that the revolution went far beyond their goals and in certain respects entailed a change of direction. When the Joint Commission on Mental Illness and Health, authorized by Congress in 1955, submitted after long study its final report in 1961, it discouraged further building of mental hospitals and recommended instead that major support be thrown to the establishment of community mental health clinics. The objective was set at "one fully staffed, full-time mental health clinic available to each 50,000 of population." [13] Obviously it will take a long time to reach such a goal, but the number of community mental health centers has increased rapidly, and this pattern of health care presently commands substantial public approval.

Implicit in this plan is recognition that disordered personal behavior is embedded in the community and should be treated there as far as possible. The mental hospital continues to have its use for acute and severe disorders requiring specialized or extended treatment, but it is no longer to be a

[13] Joint Commission on Mental Illness and Health, *Action for Mental Health* (New York: Science Editions, Inc., 1961), p. xiv.

remote institution into which people are shunted as soon as their behavior becomes bothersome to others. The ideal of community mental health is to have available, at a single center close to home, the whole spectrum of resources that can be brought to bear to alleviate disordered behavior, including emergency services, outpatient facilities, consultation, social service, family counseling, and preventive measures to the extent that these are discovered to be possible. Any such plan requires strong community support. It implies acceptance of mental health as at least in part a responsibility of the community, not just a job for doctors. There is work here for the citizen as well as the specialist.

MENTAL DISORDERS CONSIDERED AS DISEASES OF THE BRAIN

In the early stages of scientific study progress consists largely in ordering and classifying the facts. Not until this preliminary step has been accomplished is it possible to develop hypotheses and put them to any kind of crucial test. Because of the absence of hospitals, records, and facilities for observation, the study of mental disorders lingered long in the first stage. During the twenty-three centuries from Hippocrates to Pinel there were thousands of attempts to make a satisfactory classification. But Pinel himself, when writing his treatise in 1801, felt that the time was not yet ripe for sharp distinctions and clearly defined categories. He preserved only the little that was common to the earlier attempts and contented himself with distinguishing four large groups: mania, melancholia, dementia, and idiocy.

With the establishment of hospitals and the taking of systematic records, a wealth of facts began to accumulate. Examples of insanity became available in large numbers. To understand this rich experience, to arrange and organize the facts in some intelligible fashion, became for the curious scientist an increasingly urgent problem. But the difficulties proved at once to be enormous. "Mental disease," Pinel remarked, "appears greatly to tax the attention of good observers because it presents itself to us as a mixture of incoherence and confusion." [14] By their very nature the phenomena seemed to defy understanding. Moreover, the really good observer was likely to be baffled by the wide range of individual differences. "When one has seen many insane people," wrote one of Pinel's contemporaries, "one can recognize that there are as many differences among them as there are personalities among individuals whose minds are healthy. It is therefore really difficult to make up classes of diseases which would not prove fictitious." [15]

The Somatogenic Hypothesis

About the middle of the nineteenth century there was a strong revival of Hippocrates' original belief that mental disorders were diseases of the brain.

[14] Pinel, op. cit., p. 1.
[15] Fodéré, Traité du Délire (Paris: 1817), quoted by Zilboorg and Henry, op. cit., p. 392.

Underlying and essential factors were to be looked for in conditions affecting the central nervous system. This way of looking at the problem was strictly in accord with the general outlook of medical science which constantly sought to establish the bodily conditions and tissue changes responsible for illness. Because it looks for the *genesis* of the trouble in the body or *soma,* this theory is commonly called the *somatogenic hypothesis.* Representative of the trend toward somatogenesis was the German psychiatrist Griesinger (1817–1868) who recognized no distinction between neurology and psychology and who considered a diagnosis valid only when it specified a physiological cause. In France the same tendency was illustrated by Magnan (1835–1916) who gave his most careful attention to disorders associated with very obvious bodily conditions such as alcoholic intoxication, paralysis, and the changes accompanying childbirth. In 1857 a major treatise was published by the French psychiatrist Morel (1809–1873) whose thinking was organized around the theory of degeneration: briefly stated, that mental disease was the result of hereditary neural weakness. These workers and many others who accepted their premises believed that when the brain and the human constitution revealed their secrets the riddles of mental disorder would be solved.

But to make the brain and the human constitution reveal their secrets soon proved to be a long campaign. Only the gross anatomical divisions of the nervous system—cerebral hemispheres, cerebellum, medulla oblongata, spinal cord, and peripheral nerves—were known in the first half of the nineteenth century. More precise localization of functions began only in 1861 with Broca's discovery of a center controlling speech. The mapping of cortical areas was accomplished between 1870 and 1900, but is still a matter of some dispute. Of similarly recent date is our knowledge of microscopic structure. Not until 1889 did improved microscopy disclose the existence of the synapse, thereby showing that each nerve cell and its fibers formed an anatomically separate unit. Thus before 1900 only the very grossest abnormalities of brain structure could have been perceived. Griesinger, Magnan, Morel, and their followers had little sound knowledge at their disposal. The confidence in somatogenesis was based more on faith than on facts, and was reasoned out by analogy with the rest of medical practice.

Notwithstanding these difficulties, the somatogenic hypothesis was a great advance in the understanding of mental disorders. It demanded a search for essential causes rather than a preoccupation with surface phenomena. It called upon methods long used with success in the study of bodily ailments. There was a long-standing tradition, recognized even by Hippocrates, that each separate disease had a characteristic *beginning,* a typical *course,* and a typical *outcome.* Each disease, furthermore, was represented not by a single symptom but by a typical pattern of symptoms or *symptom-complex,* which might vary in detail from one case to another yet still signify a common underlying disorder. If one could show that certain symptoms frequently occurred together, that they made their first appearance in some fairly regular way, that they ran a typical course which led to a typical outcome, then one was probably well on the way toward isolating a specific disease produced by a specific condition of the brain. Let us examine this method in action, choosing what is probably its greatest triumph in the field of behavior disorders.

The Discovery of General Paresis

One of the most creditable chapters in the modern history of medicine was the discovery of general paresis. This disorder, alternatively called *dementia paralytica* or *general paralysis,* was first clearly described in 1798 by Haslam, who noticed among patients at the Bethlehem Hospital a frequent association of delusions of grandeur, dementia, and progressive paralysis. Haslam was unable to carry his observations further than this; he simply recognized a common association of symptoms, a *symptom-complex,* and thus set apart certain patients from the undifferentiated mass of the insane. He characterized these patients as follows:

> Speech is defective, the corners of the mouth are drawn down, the arms and legs are more or less deprived of their voluntary movements, and in the majority of patients memory is materially weakened. These patients as a rule fail to recognize their condition. So weak that they can hardly keep on their legs, they still maintain they are extremely strong and capable of the greatest deeds.[16]

A few years later, in 1805, a French physician, Esquirol, who later succeeded Pinel at the Salpêtrière, observed that patients having this symptom-complex never recovered; deterioration and paralysis progressed fairly rapidly to a fatal outcome. Esquirol thus called attention to a typical *course* and a typical *outcome.* It is worth noting that such observations, necessarily extending over a period of time, could scarcely have been made except under the conditions of hospital care and record keeping that Pinel had but lately established in Paris.

As experience increased, so that reliance could be placed upon statistics, it became clear that general paresis occurred in men about three times as often as in women. The *time of onset* was found to be rarely earlier than the age of thirty or later than fifty. The *mode of onset* proved particularly baffling. Attempts to reconstruct the patient's history generally showed an insidious beginning marked at first by barely perceptible abnormalities of behavior. Only after a period of time did this behavior come to be sharply at variance with the patient's previous mode of living.

The identification of the organic disorder proceeded slowly at first, handicapped by the prevailing ignorance of brain structure and brain function. In the first half of the century post-mortem examination of paretic brains showed something to be wrong with the tissue. Various writers

---

[16] J. Haslam, *Observations on Insanity* (London: F. & C. Rivington, 1798), p. 259.

spoke of irritation, inflammation, and degeneration, these being hardly more than guesses. Around 1860 improved microscopy revealed an excessive growth of connective tissue in the cortical substance together with a widespread destruction of nervous tissue. The cause of these changes still eluded observation, and the next forward step came with the help not of the microscope but of the case history. In 1894 Fournier showed from various statistical studies that a history of syphilis was obtained in 65 per cent of paretics, as compared with 10 per cent in other mental illnesses. He offered the hypothesis that general paresis had its origin in syphilitic infection which, even though apparently cured, had in some way invaded the tissues of the brain.

At first it seemed a weakness in this theory that histories of syphilis were not obtained in all cases of general paresis. In answer to this objection it was pointed out that correct histories of previous syphilis are by no means easily obtained; patients have strong motives for concealing the indiscreet sexual adventures that led to infection. A bold experiment by Kraft-Ebing in 1897 greatly strengthened the theory of syphilitic origin. Nine paretic patients who denied previous infection were inoculated with the syphilitic virus. None of them developed syphilis. This surprising immunity constituted proof that the patients, despite their denials, had once been infected and had subsequently recovered. Further evidence accumulated during the next fifteen years as a result of newly discovered laboratory methods for recognizing syphilis. The blood and the cerebrospinal fluid of syphilitics can be made to show highly characteristic chemical reactions, and these reactions were now demonstrated with great regularity in paretic patients.

The final step, sufficient to dispel any lingering doubts about the origin of the disorder, came with the discovery of the syphilitic infectious agent in the brain tissue of paretic patients. This infectious agent, a minute organism known as *Treponema pallidum,* was not identified as the cause of syphilis itself until 1905, but the search for it in nervous tissue proceeded thereafter without delay. In 1913 Noguchi and Moore found *Treponema pallidum* in the nerve-cell layers of the paretic cortex, thus at last accounting for the tissue destruction recognized but not explained nearly a century earlier. The essential cause of general paresis now stood fully revealed, and the way was opened for preventive measures and for research on methods of treatment.

This is the kind of story of which medical science is rightly proud. Careful observation, patient research to which hundreds of workers contributed, the constant development of more refined techniques which carried the investigation forward in unexpected ways, led at last to the discovery of underlying causes and thus to the possibility of prevention and treatment. Zilboorg weighs the accomplishment in the following words:

It proved a blessing for hundreds of thousands of unfortunates suffering from a syphilitic infection which had not been properly cured and which had become invisible for a period of years, only to reappear in the form of a devastating disease of the brain and spinal cord—a disease which was destructive to the whole personality of the individual and was invariably fatal. Studies in serology and empirical therapeutic efforts, stimulated and made possible by the discovery of the nature of general paralysis and its cause, had finally reduced substantially the number of fatal outcomes, increased the number of recoveries, and, what is most important, led to rational preventive measures which at least in some countries (Scandinavia) almost entirely eliminated general paralysis as a disease.[17]

Similar stories could be told for other varieties of disorder, notably those connected with senile changes and those dependent upon metabolic deficiencies. But since it is our purpose here to sample the main trends and grasp the persistent problems, rather than to set forth an exhaustive history, we can be satisfied with the example of general paresis, postponing until Chapter 15 a systematic consideration of the somatogenic disorders.

Kraepelin's Outlook on Mental Disorder

The culmination of the idea that mental disorders are physical diseases, analogous in every respect to ailments that have no mental symptoms, occurred in the work of Emil Kraepelin (1855–1926), the German psychiatrist whose great textbook, passing through eight editions from 1883 to 1913, stamped its impression deeply on subsequent psychiatric thinking. Building on the observations of predecessors as well as his own, he tried to accomplish for all mental disorders what was being done so brilliantly with general paresis. He tried to achieve a sifting, sorting, and grouping of mentally disordered patients in order to bring out the typical symptom-complexes and the typical patterns of onset, course, and outcome which distinguished one disease from another. If patients could be properly classified according to certain regularities in the symptoms and course of their illness, if one could thus correctly name and distinguish the different disease entities, then the energies of research could be bent toward finding the specific bodily condition responsible for each disease.

Kraepelin brought to this task a genius for combination and classification. His work was carried out in large hospitals, with large numbers of patients, and with extensive hospital records—a proper culmination of Pinel's reforms. He was in tune with the objective scientific trend of his times. The work of Pasteur and Lister had prepared the way for the understanding and mastery of infectious diseases. Remarkable triumphs in clinical medicine were occurring all around him; within a short space of time a great many varieties of bodily disease had been isolated and clearly defined. The growing resources of the physiological laboratory were constantly at his disposal and he followed with keen interest all developments along this line. As a result his conception of the possible bodily aspects of mental disorder was far richer than the original notion of a defect or injury in the brain. In addition to gross destruction of nervous tissue, such as occurred in general

[17] Zilboorg and Henry, *op. cit.*, p. 399.

paresis, he was aware of the possible effects of metabolic changes, improper bodily economy, and disorders of the endocrine glands.

Thus oriented and equipped, Kraepelin studied large quantities of case histories. He examined not only the story of each illness and its course while the patient was in the hospital but also the history of the patient's previous life, and he followed the histories of patients who were discharged from the hospital. In this way he was able to establish regularities concerning the symptoms and course of disease. Discounting individual variations, he sorted out what was common to numerous cases and arrived at classifications. Working along these lines, he came to the conclusion that in addition to the entities already recognized there were two major mental diseases: *manic-depressive psychosis* and *dementia praecox* (now generally called *schizophrenia*). In forming the first of these two disease entities he drew together the excited, elated conditions (mania) and the melancholy, depressed states (depression), showing that in many cases these moods succeeded each other in the same patient. As had been done with paresis, he here isolated a symptom-complex having a typical beginning, course, and outcome. The symptom-complex was centered around abrupt changes of mood and did not include signs of deterioration such as defects in gait, speech, and memory. The onset was sudden rather than gradual; the course was periodic rather than steadily progressive; the outcome was spontaneous recovery though with a strong likelihood of future recurrence. Each of these points emphasized the fundamental difference between manic-depressive psychosis and general paresis. Dementia praecox represented an even larger synthesis of previously recognized disorders. Kraepelin felt justified in making this combination because all the subvarieties, outwardly rather different, had two central features in common: they all showed an early onset and they all progressed in the direction of incurable dementia. Here was a disease that had its onset earlier than either paresis or manic-depressive psychosis. Its course was progressive rather than periodic, and its outcome was complete dementia, not including, however, paralysis and early death.

Progress in understanding these two mental disorders was urgently needed. Together they included nearly two thirds of the patients in mental hospitals, claiming nearly two thirds of the doctors' effort and time. Kraepelin postulated that manic-depressive psychosis was caused by an irregularity in metabolic function. Because the disorder seemed to run in families he assumed that the metabolic irregularity was based on some kind of hereditary defect. In the case of dementia praecox he proposed the hypothesis that the sex glands were at fault, producing an unfavorable chemical state which affected the nervous system. He justified this guess by pointing out frequent associations between the onset of the disease and changes in sexual function: the changes of puberty, menstrual irregularities, childbirth, and the involution period. He thus applied the type of reasoning that prevailed in general medicine and searched for the causes of disorder where any physician would look for them: in tissue changes, endocrine disturbances, hereditary peculiarities; in short, in some specific derangement of the bodily economy.

Unfortunately these classifications and theories did not lead to the happy culmination that occurred with general paresis. After many decades of research there is still no certainty about the somatic bases of either manic-depressive disorders or schizophrenia. This does not necessarily mean that such bases do not exist; it may testify simply to the difficulty of disclosing them. The physiology and biochemistry of the nervous system have proved to be enormously complex. Nothing as simple as gross destruction of brain tissue, nothing as unitary as metabolic irregularity or faultily working sex glands, is likely to come to light as the sole somatic villain in either of the major mental disorders. It is worth pointing out that the somatogenic view of a disorder accomplishes nothing in the way of treatment so long as the cause is hypothetical and has not actually been discovered. In an historical study Bockoven has shown that rates of recovery at mental hospitals declined during the nineteenth century while the view was gaining ground that mental patients were suffering from somatic disorder.[18] As Clifford Beers had observed, the typical mental hospital around 1900 was simply a place of custody where little was done beyond keeping patients in good physical condition. It is possible that therapeutic leverage was weakened by thinking of patients merely as medical problems rather than as burdened people who might profit from personal interest, encouragement, and a sympathetic environment.

In recent years, however, recovery rates at mental hospitals have begun to improve, in some places sufficiently to reduce the number of occupied beds. In considerable part these gains have come from somatic rather than psychological methods of treatment. Curiously enough, these methods have been hit upon almost by accident; they do not represent the logical application of a somatic theory, nor have they contributed much to the development of such a theory.

Discovery of Treatment Through Shock

In 1929 Manfred Sakel hit upon the idea of using insulin shock as a means of treating schizophrenia. He had been working with morphine addicts, using insulin routinely to effect a mild lowering of the blood-sugar level. In certain cases a standard dose occasionally had a stronger effect, throwing the patient into shock or coma. Sakel noticed that this experience sometimes created an apparent improvement in the confused mental state of his addicts, so he tried the same experiments with confused schizophrenics. The results were sometimes impressive. Even after the first treatment, and more durably after several, confused patients became more lucid and more responsive to people around them. Sakel was insistent that the temporary

18 J. S. Bockoven, *Moral Treatment in American Psychiatry* (New York: Springer Publishing Co., Inc., 1963).

gains achieved by insulin shock needed to be consolidated by appropriate psychotherapy. In this he was not always followed by later workers, some of whom convinced themselves that shock treatments alone were sufficient. Sakel's discovery, made incidentally in the course of other work, illustrates both the stumbling nature of scientific advance and the crucial importance of imagination on the part of the scientist. Insulin shock treatment was not derived from a well-developed thesis about somatic events. Quite the opposite: there is still no generally accepted theory of how it works.

Overdosing with insulin is not the only way to produce shock, and other methods, less time consuming and less disagreeable for the patients, were shortly brought under investigation. Most widely used was *electroshock,* a procedure introduced in 1938 by Cerletti and Bini in Italy. The technique consists of attaching electrodes to the head and passing controllable electrical currents through the brain. The resulting shock differs considerably from the coma produced by insulin, and the method has proved most successful with manic and depressed conditions rather than schizophrenia. In contrast to an insulin treatment, which requires several hours under constant nursing care, electroshock takes but a short time. Current is applied for only a few seconds; the patient immediately loses consciousness and there is a brief but violent convulsive reaction of his whole body. As he awakens, his mind is apt to be cloudy and his memory disturbed, but these impairments are not of long duration, and in favorable cases there follows considerable relief from distress.

To give a person a severe shock would hardly seem on the face of it a sensible way to go about curing a mental disorder. Shock methods, especially electroshock, nevertheless enjoyed a period of great popularity during the 1950's. It became apparent that these methods did not usually produce permanent cures nor lower the rates of readmission, but even a temporary lifting of the sufferings of mental disorder must be reckoned a great gain. The popularity of shock treatments, however, proved to be somewhat fleeting. Insulin shock is today rarely used, only as a method of last resort, and electroshock is usually reserved for what has proved to be its most effective service, the relieving of severe depressed states.

Treatment by Means of Drugs

On the heels of treatment through shock came the discovery that mental disorders responded favorably to tranquilizing drugs. Chlorpromazine and reserpine seemed to have a beneficial effect especially upon patients who were agitated, anxious, and confused. As their feelings became more calm, their thinking became less peculiar and their relation to other people more intelligible, sometimes to the point that psychotherapy could be undertaken for the first time. Treatment with drugs is by no means perfect. Any preparation strong enough to produce a real tranquilizing effect is likely to have other effects, some of which may not be desirable. The control of these side effects is a major research problem as different drugs are compounded and tested. In spite of these difficulties, drug therapy is currently in widespread use.

There is no reason to suppose that drugs, any more than shock methods, touch the fundamental causes of disorder or fortify the patient against relapse. Admitting that these particular physical methods are palliative rather than fundamental, we must nevertheless assign them a significant place in history. They have built new hope in the minds of workers whose interests lie in physiology and biochemistry. They have also given a tremendous boost to the morale of workers in mental hospitals. At last something can be done besides keeping patients comfortable and waiting for nature to take its upward or downward course. The use of drugs seems at last to have stemmed the tide of constantly growing hospital populations. In addition it has helped to produce great improvements in the care of mental hospital patients, making it possible, for instance, to reduce drastically such measures as physical restraint and seclusion. Pinel's mission in striking the chains from the insane has only now come close to its goal.

It is disappointing that these methods have contributed so little to scientific understanding. They are used because they give beneficial results, but how they do so—the actual mechanism of change—has not been satisfactorily illuminated. In the appropriate later chapters we shall examine those research advances which may, or may not, end by putting substance under Kraepelin's disease model of the major mental disorders.

BEGINNINGS OF PSYCHOPATHOLOGY: THE STUDY OF HYSTERIA

The Psychogenic Hypothesis

In contrast to the somatogenic hypothesis, which holds that disordered personal reactions have their genesis in somatic or bodily disturbances, the psychogenic hypothesis attributes causative significance to psychological processes. We can give it a crude first statement, to be much refined in later sections of the book, by saying that disordered personal reactions occur because the patient's thoughts, feelings, and strivings are disturbed. His somatic processes, even his brain and central nervous system, may be working in an entirely normal fashion; it is the content of what he feels and imagines that throws his personal reactions into disorder. We can begin to speak of *psychopathology* at the point where ideas or some other psychological processes are held responsible for disordered behavior. Pathology means the science of disease processes; psychopathology deals with those disorders which have their origin in psychological processes rather than tissue or chemical dysfunction.

The psychogenic hypothesis won its way into modern medicine through the study of hysteria. In its early stages this study was much assisted by the use of hypnotism, which itself offered an interesting trial ground for the psychogenic point of view. Hypnotism first became widely known through the activities of an Austrian physician, Mesmer, who set up a flourishing practice in Paris shortly before the French Revolution. Hundreds of patients were cured of diverse ailments by attending Mesmer's magnetic sessions, as they were called. Mesmer's methods were highly theatrical, but they inspired serious investigation. His followers very quickly discovered all the main phenomena of hypnotism as we know them today. They showed that a hypnotized person was highly responsive to whatever was suggested. For instance, he could apparently be made to see things which were not there (positive hallucinations) or not to see things which were there (negative hallucinations). Parts of his body could be temporarily paralyzed and made insensitive to touch and pain. He could move about, answer questions, talk and think clearly, but upon awakening have no recollection of what had transpired. Some of these curious phenomena were valuable in effecting cures. If a patient complained of aches and pains, for instance, these might be made to disappear by suggestion in the hypnotic state, so that the patient would wake up magically cured, remembering nothing of the process.

By what mechanism were these striking changes produced? Mesmer explained them by supposing that an invisible fluid passed between himself and the patient, influencing the patient's body in a distinctive fashion. By analogy with the action of magnets he christened this influence *animal magnetism,* and his writings on the subject show that he considered it a strictly physical process. A commission appointed to investigate his activities made a number of careful experiments which contradicted his theory. The commissioners showed that the phenomena supposed to be produced by magnetism occurred only if the patient knew he was being magnetized, and they drew the conclusion that the demonstrable effects were obtained through "the excitement of the imagination." At that time this conclusion had the effect of discrediting Mesmer, but it was actually an alternative hypothesis for explaining the observed facts of hypnotism. One of Mesmer's pupils aptly put the question: "If Mesmer had no other secret than that he was able to make the imagination exert an effective influence upon health, would he not still be a wonder worker?"[19] A later follower, Bertrand, reasoned that hypnotism "served merely to render conspicuous and to amplify phenomena dependent upon the working of the general laws of imagination, expectant attention, and desire."[20] This was a fully psychogenic hypothesis, seeking to explain hypnotic behavior by appeal to psychological processes.

[19] Quoted by P. Janet, *Psychological Healing, a Historical and Clinical Study,* trans. E. and C. Paul (London: Allen & Unwin, 1925), Vol. I, p. 161.
[20] *Ibid.,* p. 157.

Charcot's Study of Hysteria

The reported therapeutic successes of hypnotism become less surprising if we make the assumption that considerable numbers of the patients who sought this treatment suffered from the form of disorder known as *hysteria*. This disorder, known even to the ancients, manifests itself in a large variety of symptoms many of which have an outward resemblance to organic diseases. Prominent in nineteenth-century descriptions of hysteria are symptoms such as partial or total blindness, impairments of hearing, and paralyses of hands, arms, legs, even a whole side of the body, usually accompanied by anaesthesia of the same parts. Symptoms of this kind could easily be interpreted as results of local injury to the nervous system. Occasionally patients would have convulsive attacks ("hysterical fits") that resembled epileptic convulsions, and it was not uncommon to find gaps and peculiarities in memory suggestive of possible brain disorder. In retrospect it can be seen that if hypnotism cured nothing but hysteria it might still gain the reputation of curing almost anything.

In 1878 several severely incapacitated hysterical patients came to the attention of J. M. Charcot, a distinguished neurologist in Paris. Charcot himself had never practised hypnotism, but some of his assistants at the hospital became interested in the subject and experimented with the patients. One day they showed their chief some remarkable facts. Before his eyes they demonstrated that by means of hypnotism it was possible to produce artificially all the typical bodily symptoms of hysteria, and afterwards to remove them again. By hypnotic suggestion a patient's perfectly healthy arm could be rendered paralyzed and anaesthetic; Charcot himself, examining the patient, could not tell the difference between this and a natural hysterical paralysis with anaesthesia, except that it disappeared upon further suggestion. The whole array of hysterical symptoms could be brought into and put out of existence at whatever speed and in whatever form one chose. How could the nervous system do it?

Challenged by this discovery, Charcot set to work to investigate hysterical symptoms. Clearly they were not caused by local injury to the nervous system. He tried to discover how the symptoms started, and found that the circumstances were often peculiar. One patient, for instance, was in a street accident during which, so he thought, a carriage ran over his legs. At the hospital both legs remained paralyzed for months, but as a matter of fact the carriage had not even touched the patient. A young girl stepped lightly out of bed one morning only to find her left leg paralyzed in a rigid clubfoot position. Charcot examined many such cases: the initial circumstances were never sufficient to account for the symptom. The disappearance of symptoms also occurred in a strange fashion. Sometimes a paralysis would end abruptly during a moment of emotional excitement. Sometimes it could be removed by hypnotic suggestion. Charcot discovered that Mesmer's claims were partly justified: the young girl with the clubfoot paralysis was cured after a strenuous series of hypnotic sessions.[21] Again it appeared that symptoms were capable of migration. Paralysis might shift spontaneously from one side of the body to the other. One of the most startling discoveries was that the hysterical symptom might cease to operate when the patient was inattentive or asleep. Janet, a student of Charcot's, told of a man paralyzed in both legs who was addicted to walking in his sleep. He often climbed out on the roof and had to be rescued by the attendants with extreme care because his legs became totally paralyzed the moment he was awakened.[22]

Probably the most significant of Charcot's discoveries was that hysterical symptoms often made what we might call anatomical nonsense. Sometimes a patient would have a paralyzed hand with anaesthesia which stopped at the wrist, thus including roughly the area that would be covered by a glove. Such an anaesthesia is anatomically impossible in the sense that no conceivable nerve injury could produce it. The arm is supplied by three main nerve trunks extending down into the hand. Injury to any one would involve only part of the hand and would affect part of the arm as well. Injury to the center in which the three paths join would produce an anaesthesia including the whole arm and shoulder. The glove anaesthesia therefore is a perfect example of anatomical nonsense which strikes the final blow at a somatogenic hypothesis for hysteria.

How, then, does a glove anaesthesia come into existence? We can see that there is an oddly mental character to this seemingly physical symptom. The area of anaesthesia corresponds to the idea one has of the hand as an anatomical unit. The first patient's paralysis likewise corresponds to an idea he had that a carriage ran over his legs. But we must beware of jumping to the conclusion that these patients are simply putting on a conscious act. Mental origins do not necessarily mean conscious or voluntary origins. That patients often had no conscious idea about their symptoms was testified in many ways. Sometimes examinations revealed an area of anaesthesia, or perhaps even a blindness of one eye, of which up to that moment the patient had been totally unaware. The most telling fact, however, which absolved hysterical patients from conscious deception, was that sometimes the symptoms made perfect anatomical sense. There were cases, for example, clearly hysterical and curable by suggestion, in which paralysis of the entire right side was accompanied by disturbances of speech. One certainly could not suppose that in 1880 clinical patients of slight education had an idea about the location of the speech centers in the left cerebral hemisphere and the control by this hemisphere of the right side of the body.

[21] J. M. Charcot, Œuvres Complètes (Paris: Lecrosnier & Babé, 1890), Vol. IX, pp. 462–78.

[22] P. Janet, The Major Symptoms of Hysteria (2nd ed.; New York: The Macmillan Co., 1920), p. 28.

Janet's Conceptualization

Charcot left the problem at this point. The symptoms of hysteria were mental, yet not wholly mental; they were psychological, yet mixed up in a puzzling way with bodily processes. The attempt to capture this paradoxical quality in a theory was made by Pierre Janet, who during the 1890's began to publish his acute observations of neurotic patients. Janet was fascinated especially by changes of memory in hysteria, and he described with great care the phenomenon of *somnambulism,* in which the patient's memory seemed to be curiously divided. The patient would act for a time under the complete dominance of a single set of ideas, with no recollection of the rest of his experience or sometimes even of his identity. Janet's classic example was the case of Irene, a young woman whose memory was normal except that she had forgotten the recent death of her mother. Every so often, suddenly becoming oblivious to everything around her, she would act out with vivid gestures and frantic expressions of grief the harrowing scene at her mother's deathbed; equally suddenly she would go on calmly doing whatever she had been doing before, the dramatic interlude completely forgotten. Janet was particularly impressed by the forgetting. "Things happen as if an idea, a partial system of thoughts, emancipated itself, became independent, and developed itself on its own account," he wrote. "The result is, on the one hand, that it develops far too much, and, on the other hand, that consciousness appears no longer to control it." [23]

To understand such facts Janet adopted the concept of *dissociation.* This concept was designed to account for the pathological separation between systems of ideas that normally would interpenetrate and influence one another. In hysteria, as Janet conceived of it, the personality lost some of its normal organization. Certain systems fell out of the hierarchy, so to speak, and escaped from the governing influence of the self. Janet believed that the concept of dissociation applied equally to the bodily symptoms of hysteria. If a patient was unable to walk it was because the organized system of images and sensations which functioned during walking had become dissociated from the rest of the personality. Charcot's patient who believed himself run over by a carriage had a dissociated idea that his legs were paralyzed, and this idea, simply because it was dissociated, became overdeveloped—like Irene's drama of grief—and actually controlled the motility of his legs. Dissociation occurred not only to systems of memories but to natural subsystems of the neural mechanism.

True to the confusingly mixed character of hysterical symptoms, Janet's explanation hovered between the somatogenic and the psychogenic. He allowed that dissociation was more likely to occur in people who were fatigued, anxious, and worn out by their problems. He implied that the

[23] *Ibid.,* p. 42.

splitting off of a system of ideas might serve to avoid unbearable pain or a conflict of irreconcilable motives. This put him on the edge not only of a psychogenic explanation but of a psychodynamic one, in which systems of ideas were driven apart, so to speak, by the force of conflicting urges. But it impressed Janet that dissociation occurred importantly only in certain patients, those customarily classified as hysterics. Other people cannot split up their memories and neuromuscular systems, no matter how strong the inducements. Janet dealt with this difficulty by the further hypothesis of an hereditary weakness or *constitutional vulnerability*. Hysterics, he concluded, were burdened by an innate tendency toward dissociation, a weakness of capacity to maintain the organization of self under conditions of stress. It fitted this interpretation that hysterics were often described, apart from their symptoms, as impulsive, childlike, self-dramatizing people who tended to lose themselves in each passing experience.

Janet's thinking was not confined to hysteria. He was a careful observer of another large class of so-called "nervous disorders," characterized by irrational fears, obsessive ideas, and compulsive actions or rituals that often interfered greatly with patients' lives. As people, these patients made a decidedly different impression from hysterics. Far from forgetting the unpleasant, their minds were full of ruminations, doubts, conflicts, anxieties, and attempts to solve everything intellectually. Janet called this whole category of neurosis by the name of *psychasthenia,* and he postulated behind it a constitutional vulnerability of an entirely different kind. In this way he made a classification for the chief "nervous disorders"—the *neuroses*—much as Kraepelin had done for the more severe mental disorders—the *psychoses*.

Breuer and Freud's Theory of Abreaction

A different way of looking at hysterical symptoms had been developed in the meantime by a Viennese physician, Joseph Breuer, who shortly enlisted the collaboration of a younger colleague, Sigmund Freud. From 1880 to 1882 Breuer had under treatment a curious and difficult case of hysteria. The patient, a girl in her early twenties, was bedridden for several months with a long array of symptoms. Both legs and the right arm were paralyzed, sight and hearing were impaired, the neck muscles were uncomfortably contracted, there was a persistent nervous cough, and at times speech became difficult. Besides these largely somatic afflictions there were frequent alterations of mental state: confusions and a dreamy condition which Breuer called "absence." During her periods of "absence" the girl often mumbled to herself as if her thoughts were busy. Breuer took note of her words and later, during hypnotic sessions, repeatedly gave them back to her. In this way she was led to reveal the fantasies that occupied her in her dreamy states. When she had unburdened herself of these fantasies she felt relieved, and awakened from the hypnosis temporarily much improved.

Presently Breuer discovered that under certain circumstances a symptom might be permanently removed. If during hypnosis the patient could remember the situation in which the symptom began, and if the accompanying emotion was freely and fully expressed, the symptom would disappear for good. Breuer found that the paralysis of the right arm had its origin during a painful period when the patient was nursing her father through his protracted last illness. One evening she dozed off at her father's bedside and had a nightmare: a huge black snake was attacking her father and she tried in vain to fend it off with her right arm. She awoke terrified, freed her arm which was over the back of the chair, and hastily suppressed her feelings lest her father perceive her fear. When the patient not only recalled this forgotten incident but also experienced fully the emotion she had so forcibly suppressed, her paralysis disappeared for good.[24]

In the course of time this patient was completely cured. The process was always the same: recovery during hypnosis of some drastic incident in which emotion had been suppressed, full and dramatic expression of the emotion, permanent disappearance of the symptom that had been laid down on that occasion. The release of suppressed emotion—of "strangulated affect"—was the core of Breuer's discovery, and received the name of *abreaction*. Reviewing this case some years later, Freud set forth the theory in the following words.

. . . We are forced to the conclusion that the patient fell ill because the emotion developed in the pathogenic situation was prevented from escaping normally, and that the essence of the sickness lies in the fact that the imprisoned emotions undergo a series of abnormal changes. In part they are preserved as a lasting charge and as a source of constant disturbance in psychical life; in part they undergo a change into unusual bodily innervations and inhibitions which present themselves as the physical symptoms of the case.

You see that we are in a fair way to arrive at a purely psychological theory of hysteria, in which we assign the first rank to the affective processes.[25]

This theory was not only more purely psychological but also more psychodynamic than the one proposed by Janet. The dissociation of memories and bodily movements from conscious control was interpreted always in dynamic terms—in terms of a conflict of forces between emotions pushing for expression and other motives pushing them back. The personality did not, in this interpretation, fall apart; it was pushed apart by strong conflicting forces. Every symptom expressed conflict and became intelligible when the circumstances of conflict could be recovered.

---

[24] J. Breuer and S. Freud, *Studies in Hysteria*, trans. A. A. Brill (New York: Nervous & Mental Disease Publishing Co., 1936), pp. 26, 27.

[25] S. Freud, "The Origin and Development of Psychoanalysis," in *An Outline of Psychoanalysis*, ed. J. Van Teslaar (New York: Modern Library, Inc., 1924), pp. 30, 31.

FREUD'S BASIC DISCOVERIES

After his study of the Breuer case it seemed clear to Freud that hysteria could be cured by the release of pent-up emotion. The therapeutic problem was to secure abreaction so that the energy of strangulated feelings might come to normal expression instead of "spilling over" into bodily symptoms. Abreaction, however, could not take place without recall of the original pathogenic situations, and these seemed often to be completely forgotten. In the Breuer case it was necessary to enlist the aid of hypnosis in order to bring forward the crucial memories. Freud began to use this method with his neurotic patients, but he soon became discontented with hypnotism. Many patients were insusceptible to hypnosis, and even with good subjects the results seemed uncertain and transient. Freud began to look elsewhere for a technique of abreaction.

The Method of Free Association

At first glance the method he hit upon seems hardly a method at all. Instead of requiring the patient to talk about some particular subject, Freud asked him "to abandon himself to a process of *free association,* i.e., to say whatever came into his head, while ceasing to give any conscious direction to his thoughts."[26] He was told that he must report all that occurred to him, resisting any temptation to choose among his thoughts. His only obligation was to communicate everything in the order of its occurrence and to make no attempt to supervise the course of his associations in the interests of logic, decency, or conventionality. To the extent that patients could actually do this, Freud reasoned, their thoughts would be guided by the imprisoned feelings that needed abreaction, and the entrance of these feelings into conscious experience would be hastened.

It was perhaps unfortunate to call this process *"free association."* It is free from many conventional restraints, but it is not free in the sense of being an idle wandering of fancy. Freud himself declared that "free association is not really free." In the first place, all the associations have to be communicated to a listener. The reveries have to be made public, which at once brings into play all of one's desires to make sense, to be logical, and to put up a good front. Under these circumstances it is by no means an easy matter to tell everything that drifts through one's head. In the second place, the patient is suffering from a neurosis and has come to the physician in order to be cured. This circumstance dominates the whole situation and exerts an influence upon the course of the associations even when the patient makes no conscious attempt to control them. Freud probably put the matter too strongly when he claimed that nothing will occur to the patient that is not somehow related to his neurosis. But the

[26] S. Freud, *The Problem of Lay-Analyses* (New York: Brentano's, 1927), p. 25.

therapeutic purpose is always present and constitutes the most consistent factor influencing the train of thought.

Resistance and Repression

The adoption of free association led to Freud's next discovery. His patients found it impossible to obey the fundamental rule of telling everything.

The patient tries in every way to escape its requirements. First he will declare that he cannot think of anything, then that so much comes to his mind that it is impossible to seize on anything definite. Then we discover with no slight displeasure that he has yielded to this or that critical objection, for he betrays himself by the long pauses which he allows to occur in his speaking. He then confesses that he really cannot bring himself to this, that he is ashamed to; he prefers to let this motive get the upper hand over his promise. He may say that he did think of something but that it concerns someone else and is for that reason exempt. Or he says that what he just thought of is really too trivial, too stupid, and too foolish. I surely could not have meant that he should take such thoughts into account. Thus it goes, with untold variations, in the face of which we continually reiterate that "telling everything" really means telling everything.[27]

If driven from these simpler tactics the patients found more complicated ways of resisting the fundamental rule. They might embark upon elaborate arguments about the theory and soundness of the procedure. They might show an eager curiosity to be instructed in such a way that they might practice it alone in the privacy of their own rooms. They might even begin to act out toward the physician various anxious and hostile feelings set off by the task of associating. In countless ways Freud's patients showed a strong resistance against telling everything.

Resistance does not go on forever. In the course of time a patient, perhaps after hours of circling around the topic, becomes able to bring forth memories and painful feelings about some earlier event in his life. Often the patient is surprised that an experience now so clearly recalled has been so long forgotten. It was on these observations that Freud based his theory of repression. Strong forces evidently prevented the patient from remembering certain emotionally charged experiences. Freud reasoned that these same forces, which now opposed the entry of the forgotten ideas into consciousness, must have been responsible for their original banishment. He called this original process *repression*, and considered it to be attested by the observed facts of resistance.

Freud next asked himself why such a process should occur. He came to the conclusion that repression was a device whereby the personality is protected from unbearable pain. In all his cases it appeared, after the forgotten material had been recovered, that in the original situation a

[27] S. Freud, *A General Introduction to Psychoanalysis* (New York: Liveright Publishing Corp., 1920), pp. 249, 250.

wish had been aroused which conflicted sharply with the person's other desires, especially with his "ethical, aesthetic, and personal pretensions." The appearance of such a wish in consciousness created sharp and painful conflict which was solved by repression. The ideas which were the bearers of the wish were ejected from consciousness, for practical purposes forgotten, although such forgetting was very different from the ordinary fading of neutral memories. Painful conflict was avoided, but at a cost. The wish itself could never be wiped out in this way; blocked from direct expression, it discharged itself instead into the various symptoms of neurosis. When the physician tried to call up the repressed memories in order to withdraw the energy of the wish from symptom formation he was met by the full force of the ethical, aesthetic, and personal pretensions which originally found the wish intolerable.

Anxiety and Defense

For a while Freud's attention was absorbed in studying the banished urges as they crept back into consciousness. Here he made important discoveries about human motivation. Motives could influence behavior even when they were not conscious, he found, and it was typical of human strivings to generate a great deal of internal conflict. But the concepts of unconscious motivation and conflict did not by themselves yield a atisfactory theory of neurosis. It was necessary to find a specific point oɪ difference between normal conflicts effectively solved and neurotic conflicts solved only by crippling symptom formation. Gradually Freud turned his attention from the banished urges to the forces in personality that were responsible for the banishment. His interest became centered on defensive activities. With the same sensitivity that had enabled him to infer the existence of unconscious wishes, he now began to understand the unwitting evasive tactics whereby patients protected themselves from mental pain.

In 1926 Freud published an important work, *Inhibition, Symptom and Anxiety*,[28] in which he assigned to *anxiety* the central place in the theory of neurosis. Repression, he concluded, is one of several *defense mechanisms* directed against the emergence of impulses that would carry with them unbearable anxiety. If urges were merely at odds with adult ethical, aesthetic, and personal pretensions, the conflict would not require such drastic measures. The urges responsible for neurosis represented a greater danger, portending disaster and evoking panic. This suggested that the conflicts had first occurred in early childhood, when fear of parental punishment, desertion, and loss of love can easily be of panic proportions. Freud thus arrived at a much needed clarification of his theory: he now saw neurosis as the outcome of attempts to avoid severe anxiety through

[28] Translated by H. A. Bunker with the title *The Problem of Anxiety* (New York: W. W. Norton & Co., Inc., 1936).

the use of desperate and primitive defense mechanisms such as repression, mechanisms that prevented a later discriminating solution of the conflict. The resistance observed during treatment could now be understood as a fight against the emergence of anxiety. Abreaction of imprisoned emotions was not a correct statement of the goal of treatment. The crucial thing was to bring into awareness the anxiety that had become associated with certain urges, so that its force could be reduced.

The Importance of Sexual Strivings

While he was still concentrating on the nature of suppressed wishes, Freud convinced himself that neurotic misery was closely linked to sexual needs. Particularly in cases where fatigue was a prominent complaint— a variety of neurosis called *neurasthenia*—he found grave disturbances in the patient's current sexual life. In his own words: "The more I enquired into such disturbances (bearing in mind that all men conceal the truth in these matters) and the more adept I became at persisting in my interrogations in spite of denials at the beginning, the more regularly did pathogenic factors from sexual life disclose themselves, until there seemed to me little to prevent the assumption of their general occurrence." [29] This much he obtained from direct inquiry, but the use of free association presently led to discoveries far more startling. In patients with all varieties of neurosis, including hysteria and the obsessive-compulsive states, the same thing happened again and again: the associations led back into the patient's past until "experiences were finally reached which belonged to his infancy and concerned his sexual life; and this was so even when an ordinary emotion, not of a sexual kind, had led to the outbreak of the disease. Without taking into account these sexual traumas of childhood it was impossible to explain the symptoms, comprehend their determination, or prevent their return. After this, the unique significance of sexual experiences in the aetiology of the psychoneuroses seemed incontestably established." [30]

The words just quoted were written in 1905, the same year in which Freud produced his monograph, *Three Contributions to the Theory of Sex*. In 1905 the ideas advanced in his monograph were considered extremely radical and were quite generally met by shocked repugnance. The claims to which Freud was led by the free associations and recollections of his patients can be summarized in the following statements. (1) The sexual need is active in infancy and to a lesser extent throughout childhood. (2) It is more diffuse in its nature than the adult need, consisting of a variety of "partial impulses" not strongly dominated by genital excitation, showing itself in such actions as thumbsucking, display of the naked body, inquisitiveness about the bodies of others, masturbation, pleasures connected with anal excretion or retention, and anything

29 S. Freud, *Collected Papers*, trans. J. Rivière (London: International Psychoanalytic Press, 1924), Vol. I, p. 273.
30 *Ibid.*, p. 275.

else that yielded pleasurable stimulation of sensitive or erogenous zones of the body. (3) The sexual need is not innately attached to any particular objects, the choice being accomplished by learning; in childhood, therefore, members of the family and playmates of either sex may become its objects. (4) It is subject to an active campaign of adult disapproval which tends to encourage repression. (5) The childhood history of sexual experiences, fantasies, and repressions exerts a powerful effect on sexual behavior following the strengthening of the urge at puberty. Both the methods of satisfaction and the object choices must be revised if the person is going to advance to a normal adult sexual life.

From these ideas Freud went on to a massive generalization, the *libido theory,* in which he gave sexuality the predominant position among human energies and attributed to it a regulating role in the whole course of development. This arbitrary step led to discord in the psychoanalytic movement. Fortunately, it also led to the careful observation of other motives likely to become sources of anxiety. Alfred Adler, for instance, heard a different theme in the free associations of neurotic patients. Everywhere he noticed the subtle workings of a striving to dominate, degrade, and triumph over others. He came to believe that the ruling motive in neurosis was a *striving for superiority,* directed, however, toward dominating the household by being ill. Adler was convinced that at heart the patients felt weak and inadequate: they suffered from anxious *feelings of inferiority* for which illness was an attempt at *compensation.* "The exemptions and privileges of illness and suffering give the patient a substitute for his original hazardous goal of superiority." [31] Karen Horney, who also started with Freud's methods, attached special importance to *aggression,* an urge that in early childhood becomes easily linked with anxiety because of its effects on parents. Even more than sex, Horney believed, aggressive behavior begets anger and hostility in parents which awaken great fears in the child and may precipitate disastrous defensive measures, so that future assertiveness is paralyzed.[32]

These formulations enlarged the range of motives that had to be considered important not only in neurosis but in all of human behavior. They unseated sex from the conceptual throne on which Freud had put it, but they did not cancel his shrewd observations of the extensive part played by sexual strivings in human life. Nor did they supplant the idea that anxiety is the core of the problem of neurosis.

Psychodynamics

Pathways of discovery often start in unexpected places and proceed through strange twists and turns. What began as a search for a better way of treating neurotic patients led Freud in the end to a radically changed

[31] A. Adler, *The Practice and Theory of Individual Psychology* (New York: Harcourt Brace Jovanovich, Inc., 1929), p. 23.
[32] K. Horney, *The Neurotic Personality of Our Time* (New York: W. W. Norton & Co., Inc., 1937), chap. 4.

view of human nature. His method of treatment, which he named *psychoanalysis,* evolved into a prolonged and exhaustive exploration into the patient's emotional life. Over months and over years, always through use of the basic method of free association, memories and feelings were recovered that finally reached back into early childhood and constituted a detailed biography of the patient's emotional development. The picture of human nature that emerged differed greatly from the conventional one of Freud's time. The conscious self, with its pride, its declared values, and its civilized virtues, began to look like a shaky superstructure beneath which surged the instinctual drives, the satisfaction of which Freud interpreted to be the true goal of living. Freud came to see the conscious self as largely a system of defenses, distortions, and self-deceptions. It came into existence through the child's training for acceptable civilized behavior as this was understood by the parents and the surrounding culture. In neurotic patients the plan for socialization had conspicuously miscarried. The anxiety generated by training had produced so great a constriction of instinctual urges as to be incompatible with health. But instincts could not be wholly suppressed, and their clamor for outlets could be detected not only in neurotic symptoms but in dreams, fantasies, inadvertent behavior, errors, and slips of the tongue.

Because of this emphasis on forces—motives and wishes—Freud's theory of personality is called *psychodynamic.* Few theories of behavior dispense altogether with motivational concepts such as drive, but other schools of thought give relatively greater prominence to learning, perception, and intellectual development. Freud's interest was drawn to the forces; his genius lay in penetrating the conscious level and disclosing beneath it the play of wishes, anxieties, and defenses. It was here, he reasoned, that one confronted the true springs of behavior, the forces that under certain circumstances produced neurosis but were in any event the authentic causes of all behavior.

Psychodynamic theory, in Freud's version or its several modifications, was destined for a large career. Before long the new insights were being extended to an increasingly wide range of problems. The psychodynamic element was sought in delinquency, criminal behavior, chronic alcoholism, drug addiction, sexual deviations, and many other serious social problems. The question usually asked—what had happened to a person to make his behavior disordered—was amplified by asking what he was trying to do, how his behavior might be seen as an expression of unconscious motivation. The psychodynamic aspect was also sought in the more severe mental illnesses, especially the manic-depressive and schizophrenic disorders. It was even looked for in ailments of a clearly physical character such as ulcers, high blood pressure, asthma, skin diseases, arthritis, and migraine headaches. Some of these somatic troubles, it appeared, deserved to be called *psychosomatic:* the physical disorder was the end result of chronic psychological stress, and its recurrence could not be prevented unless the patient's conflicts and anxieties were liquidated.

Psychodynamic interpretation was presently extended to problems outside the traditional realm of abnormal psychology. As an example we may take difficulties in school work. School failure had always been attributed to inadequate mental equipment, faulty methods of study, or a lamentable lack of the will to work. These causes are not to be lightly dismissed, but sometimes it comes out that the student's effort has been blocked by disordered personal reactions arising out of his relation to family, friends, and teachers. Perhaps he wastes hours brooding over social failures, sex, or the unjust actions of teachers and parents, or perhaps he dashes from one thing to another in an attempt to forget these problems. Even when failure is restricted to one subject, such as reading or arithmetic, the disability can occasionally be traced to a clustering of anxiety-laden associations around a particular mental operation. Failure sometimes occurs, in short, either because school work has an unconscious personal meaning that invests it with anxiety or because anxieties elsewhere in the pupil's life drain his energies away from study.[33]

Extensions of this kind eventually brought psychological thinking into direct contact with social science. The personal meaning of school work has been shown to vary with social class and with parents' interest in upward mobility.[34] Sociologists, too, have shed new light on school failure; the *psychogenic* story cannot be complete unless the *sociogenic* story is also told. Nowhere is this more apparent than in the extension of psychological thinking to such traditionally social problems as alcoholism, drug use, and delinquency. Chronic use of alcohol and other drugs can be considered a disordered personal reaction in which the drugs are used to relieve frustration, anxiety, or some other form of distress. Yet the availability of drugs and the social sanctions surrounding their use—things which differ a great deal in different parts of our society—clearly influence the choice of this particular method for relieving frustrations and anxiety, and treatment will not proceed far if it ignores the social situation. In like fashion, cases of delinquency can often be illuminated by psychological study, but the social environment must be carefully considered both in explaining the delinquent behavior and in trying to change it. The student of abnormal psychology cannot avoid becoming to some extent a student of society.

The importance and wide range of Freud's ideas make him a monumental figure in modern intellectual history. His own writings touched upon anthropology, history, the study of religion, and the psychodynamic analysis of works of art. His influence spread widely into the social sciences and humanities, having an especially marked effect on literature. He contributed to a revolution in child training and in attitudes toward sex. It is never safe to attribute revolutions to one person; they must be in the air, so to speak, before individual voices are truly heeded. But the widespread

[33] See especially G. H. J. Pearson, *Psychoanalysis and the Education of the Child* (New York: W. W. Norton & Co., Inc., 1954).

[34] A. B. Hollingshead, *Elmtown's Youth* (New York: John Wiley & Sons, Inc., 1949).

current interest in openness and warmth in human relations, in authenticity of feelings, and in breaking down the hypocrisies, evasions, and subtle cruelties that result from inept socialization, is in harmony with Freud's outlook and probably owes a great deal to his influence.

Freud's discoveries thus led far beyond the original problem of treating neuroses. But we must now return to that theme and sketch the evolution of ideas about the nature of psychological treatment.

PSYCHOLOGICAL CONCEPTIONS OF TREATMENT

When a psychogenic hypothesis is adopted, the treatment of disordered behavior comes to be seen as a problem of psychological influence. If a patient's troubles have sprung from his thoughts, habits, feelings, and strivings, it is these that must become the object of change. Accustomed as human beings are to exhorting one another to behave in acceptable ways, the idea of psychological influence is familiar, but the conditions under which it works prove to be anything but simple. Exhortation, by no means always effective with normal people, is useless in affecting the strange ideas and behavior of the mentally disordered, and nothing is accomplished by urging an hysteric to snap out of his paralysis or telling a victim of obsessions to stop thinking in circles. The influence that one person can have upon another through conversation and social interaction is decidedly limited. Yet it is just such influence that constitutes the operative principle of psychological treatment.

Suggestion

Hypnotism won its place as a method of treatment because it seemed to magnify this influence. Hypnotized patients, drowsily relaxed in what was called a "trance," seemed uncommonly ready to act on whatever ideas were proposed. Under these circumstances the hypnotist could sometimes put an end to an hysterical symptom by what was hardly more than a command. A patient might be told, for instance, that when he awoke his legs would no longer be paralyzed and he would walk with ease. Much repetition and several sessions were usually required to produce a lasting result, but success was frequent enough so that during the second half of the nineteenth century hypnotic clinics flourished in various parts of the Western world. Hypnotism became for the time being the popular treatment for nervous disorders.

Mesmer's theory of hypnotism had been strictly somatogenic. Influence was presumed to be conveyed through animal magnetism, which was considered to be essentially a physical force. When this was shown to be impossible, a search began for an adequate psychological explanation. The most distinctive concept that emerged was *suggestion*. In a technical sense suggestion means a specific form of influence different from conveying information, reasoning, persuading, exhorting, and commanding, all of which appeal to us at the ordinary alert level of mental functioning. Suggestion, it was hypothesized, worked at a subconscious level. Much was made of the notion, called *ideo-motor action* by William James, that ideas tend to go straight over into appropriate action if other considerations do not interfere. The relaxed hypnotic state came to be understood as one in which other considerations were silenced, criticism laid aside, and trustful compliance made total. Under these circumstances ideas proposed by the hypnotist affected the patient's behavior just as if they had started in the patient's mind.[35]

Suggestion was not considered to be an abnormal phenomenon. We are influenced all the time by perceptions that do not enter the focus of attention; we constantly perform acts without deliberate thought. Hypnosis simply magnified a normal process. To many workers it seemed probable that hysterical symptoms came into being through suggestion and could thus readily be removed by the same means. The patient who believed a carriage had run over his legs was the victim of an automatic process whereby the idea produced the appropriate motor paralysis without the intervention of conscious judgment; it was not surprising that the symptom could be relieved in the same way. In retrospect the view seems justified that hypnotic clinics had their largest success with hysteria and were less effective with other types of neurosis. Suggestion sometimes worked wonders, but it was by no means universally successful.

Persuasion

As an automatic process of influence, involuntary as far as the patient was concerned, suggestion was not to every therapist's liking. Some workers argued that if the patient's own effort were not enlisted in his cure he was left unprotected against recurrence of his trouble. Around 1890 a Swiss psychiatrist, Paul Dubois, revived an older tradition of psychological treatment under the name of *persuasion*. When used in treating neuroses, this method involves more than the persuasions of everyday life. It entails the careful development and use of the personal relation between therapist and patient. Persuasive therapeutics typically began with a sympathetic exploration of the patient's problems, conducted without haste, in the course of which the physician could demonstrate his deep interest and concern for his patient. The success of treatment depended upon the patient's assurance of this concern and confidence in the doctor's wisdom. "Our aim must not be to make the patient stupidly suggestible," wrote Dubois, "but to restore to him his power of self-mastery. Our only weapon must be encouraging

---

35 The history of hypnotic treatment and the theory of suggestion is described in detail by P. Janet, *Psychological Healing: A Historical and Clinical Study,* trans. by E. and C. Paul (London: George Allen & Unwin, Ltd., 1925), Vol. 1, part 2. See also W. James, *Principles of Psychology* (New York: Holt, Rinehart & Winston, Inc., 1890), Vol. 2, chaps. 26–27.

conversation." [36] Gradually the patient was urged to believe that his symptoms originated in his mind, that he could safely disregard them, and that a bold, active, useful life was within his reach. To the extent that the patient embraced this philosophy of commitment, as we would call it today, he would move into a new kind of life, involved with other people and real enterprises, that would leave little room for preoccupation with self and symptoms.

Methods of this kind, sometimes described as "medical moralization," became common in the early 1900's following a decline in the popularity of hypnotism. They reflected an optimism and an outspoken moral earnestness that today seem unsophisticated. Furthermore, the exclusive reliance on such a commonplace process as encouraging conversation is bound to seem unimpressive in an age accustomed to miracles of specialized technology. But it is hard to reject the argument made by Jerome Frank that in all methods of psychotherapy, even the most sophisticated, there is an inescapable element of persuasion.[37] Even if nothing is said about behaving differently, something is inevitably implied. The therapist may sedulously avoid comments of a censorious nature and try to keep his own preferences out of the conversation; but it is clear that in the end he is against the irrational anxieties, defenses, and symptoms that make for neurosis, and in favor of a more free and healthful pattern of life. Patient and therapist alike know that change is desirable; the whole point of their relation is to produce it. Thus it is likely that even when persuasion is kept out of the foreground it plays a significant part in all kinds of psychological treatment.

Psychoanalysis

As we have seen, Freud's thinking about therapy took a different direction. Convinced at first that he had to liberate imprisoned affects, concluding later that the central task was to reduce the anxiety connected with repressed instinctual urges, he attached great importance to bringing unconscious feelings and wishes into awareness. Good results, he believed, could not be expected unless the trapped instinctual energies responsible for symptoms could be brought into the open and expressed in reasonable and appropriate ways. Suggestion, in his view, might remove a symptom without changing the conflict of forces responsible for it, thus encouraging either recurrence or the development of another symptom. Persuasion, with its appeal to noble sentiments and social values, might simply strengthen the forces of repression and further strangle the instinctual urges. The route to health lay for Freud in uncovering what had been repressed and learning not to fear it, after which the patient was freed to direct his own behavior as he saw fit.

---

[36] Quoted by P. Janet, *Psychological Healing, op. cit.,* Vol. 1, p. 101.
[37] J. D. Frank, *Persuasion and Healing: A Comparative Study of Psychotherapy* (Baltimore: Johns Hopkins Press, 1961).

As the method evolved it came to require a great deal of time. The physician's part was a relatively passive one. The patient was allowed to bring forth the essential memories and feelings at his own slow pace, while the physician limited his activity to pointing out resistances and indicating possible connections among remembered events. Freud's belief that neurosis had its roots in early childhood added to the length of treatment. Recall of the initial pathological events seemed to happen only when a long chain of recovered memories led the way to them. Even with five appointments a week a thorough psychoanalysis was likely to require as much as three years, sometimes even more. To be psychoanalyzed represented an enormous commitment of time and money, but Freud was convinced that no other method could cure a neurosis in a lasting way.

From 1925 to 1955 psychoanalysis rose to a position of high respect. It became the standard of thoroughness against which all other methods were compared. But its popularity began to sag as interest grew in community mental health. The goal of making psychological treatment available to all who needed it could not be served by a method so long and expensive; the needs of society could be met only by devising more rapid ways of working. On scientific grounds, too, there was increasing criticism. The proposition was challenged that lengthy exploration into the patient's past history was necessary for effective treatment. Could not psychotherapy be reduced to economical dimensions without going back to naive forms of suggestion and persuasion?

Search for Shorter Methods

One way of dealing with this dilemma was a compromise in which the therapist took a more active role in treatment while preserving the essence of Freud's method. Many workers, deeply impressed by the psychodynamic view and unwilling to go forward without it, came to call their procedures *psychoanalytically oriented therapy,* under which heading they experimented with shortcuts and reductions of full-length psychoanalysis. This necessarily entailed spending less time on the recovery of past experience. Often it meant resorting to homely devices like advice, persuasion, encouragement, or a change of environment, though therapists felt that they could do these things more wisely because of their understanding of wish, anxiety, and defense. Strictly speaking, treatment is not psychoanalytic if it departs from the purpose of making unconscious urges conscious and therapy liberating them from irrational anxieties. But many workers were reluctant to give up the title of a method which had greatly enriched their understanding of human behavior.

Much more radical was the innovation introduced by Carl Rogers in 1942, in what came to be known as *client-centered therapy.*[38] Rogers dis-

---

[38] C. R. Rogers, *Counseling and Psychotherapy* (Boston: Houghton Mifflin Co., 1942); *Client-Centered Therapy* (Houghton Mifflin, 1951).

pensed altogether with the recovery of past experience; he did not even start with a detailed case history. He put the emphasis squarely on current feelings, and by responding to the feeling aspect of everything that was said he encouraged clients to recognize how they really felt. Rogers tried to avoid overt direction, suggestion, or persuasion; he limited his goal to helping people discover their true feelings. The method resembles psychoanalysis only to the extent that it clarifies feelings of which the client is not fully aware and thus frees them to guide behavior. If Freud's theory was correct that the important feelings were repressed and could emerge only after protracted resistance, there was much that client-centered therapy left unchanged. Rogers and his co-workers nevertheless reported that good results could often be obtained in a dozen or so interviews. Many puzzled young people were helped by this method to find themselves. Whether or not it is effective with severe neuroses has not been clearly established.

Behavior Modification

Late in the 1950's began a different approach to psychological treatment that rapidly achieved wide use and popularity. This approach became known as *behavior therapy* or *behavior modification*, and the emphasis on behavior rather than wish or feeling is highly characteristic. The methods used in behavior modification are partly new, partly old; as we shall see in a later chapter, persuasion, suggestion, even hypnotism often reappear in a new guise. What gives the various methods their unity is the application of experimentally tested laws of learning in order to change the abnormal behavior of which patients complain. Ideally, each step that is taken represents a deliberate use of some established principle of learning or unlearning, and the task is interpreted as changing in a beneficent way the behavior that is troublesome to the patient.

It may be cause for surprise that this conception emerged so late in the history of abnormal psychology. Mesmer, Charcot, Janet, Dubois, and Freud certainly believed themselves to be applying scientific principles for changing behavior, but they had to discover their principles through work with patients; there was no independent source of information to which they could turn. Those who began to practice behavior modification held that such a source was now in existence. Fourscore years of work in the experimental psychology of learning, even though much of it was done with animals, provided certain basic principles of behavior that could properly be applied to the treatment of neurosis, not to mention other disorders. The time had arrived for turning psychological treatment into a more strictly applied science.

Further cause for surprise may be found in the fact that behavior modification, the major innovation of the 1960's, goes back to Pavlov, who was older than Freud, and to Watson's behaviorism, which flourished vigorously as early as the 1920's. An experiment often cited in the literature of behavior modification was reported in 1924, only to lie fallow, with almost no attempt at further application, for the next thirty years—the very years during which psychoanalysis rose to its predominant position. This now famous experiment involved a direct application of Pavlov's conditioning principles in treating an irrational fear.[39] Three-year-old Peter had a strong fear of furry animals and furry objects that seemed to center on rabbits. This was clearly a conditioned fear response, and it was eliminated by a program of counter-conditioning. A pet rabbit was gradually introduced to Peter's presence, at first in a cage at a distance, when he was enjoying a pleasant meal or had the company of fearless playmates. On successive occasions the cage could be brought nearer without frightening Peter; then the rabbit could be released into the room; finally the boy touched and played with the rabbit in normal childlike fashion. Through a new conditioning process the once-feared animal had come to be associated with pleasant circumstances, and the phobia had vanished. But this heartening report had only a small effect on psychological treatment during the ensuing generation. The contrast between this lack of interest and the brilliant career of psychoanalysis offers a challenging problem to students of intellectual history. Perhaps part of the answer lies in the nature of behaviorism, a product of experimental psychology rather than medicine, and a movement which for many years prided itself more on its scientific status than on its practical application. Having arrived at last, however, behavior modification is a strong influence in present psychological treatment.

Family Psychotherapy

The conceptions of psychological treatment thus far described are historically rooted in what has come to be called the "one-to-one" situation, in which one therapist deals with one patient whose behavior and feelings stand in need of change. This situation, appropriate for many branches of medical practice, has come under criticism in recent years because of its implications about the nature of disordered personal behavior. In the social sciences, which have grown phenomenally during the last thirty years, human behavior is described as *interactions* among individuals rather than *reactions* of single individuals. Seen in this way, disordered personal behavior means disordered interactions with other people, and one is forced to ask what part the other people play in the disorder. The problem was first sharply realized when psychoanalytic methods began to be used with children. Attempts to produce beneficent changes in children proved to be of small avail if the parents were not prepared to change. If a child's feelings of inferiority were being maintained by parental attitudes of belittlement, efforts by the therapist to increase confidence and raise self-respect

[39] M. C. Jones, "A Laboratory Study of Fear: The Case of Peter," *Journal of Genetic Psychology*, XXXI (1924), pp. 308–15.

were almost certain to be nullified at home. Fairly soon in work with children a "two-to-two" procedure came into use: one therapist dealing with the child, another with the mother. The object was not to change two people separately but to change their interactions with one another, and this was best accomplished when the two therapists could cooperate effectively in carrying out their common task.

Presently it became apparent that the "two-to-two" situation was only a step toward a truly interactive conception of psychological treatment. The mother's interactions with her child cannot be wholly abstrated from her relations with other members of the family, who likewise play some part in the child's behavior. The whole family constitutes a social system, sometimes a fairly complex one in which there are alliances, rivalries, and subgroup formations; events in one part of the system have effects that spread throughout the whole. The suspicion arose that the family member who was sent for treatment might not necessarily be the most disordered one. A child referred for disruptive tantrums might prove to be responding in the only available way to chronic unfairness by parents or favored siblings, who were asking the therapist to quiet their victims so that they could continue their arrogant ways. Notice was taken that improvement by the "patient" sometimes caused other members of the family to become upset. To many workers it seemed that the family was the proper unit of treatment—the family was the "patient"—and that therapeutic efforts should be directed at changing what was disordered in the system as a whole.

Today there is widespread interest in family psychotherapy and a considerable attempt to put it in practice. Naturally there are practical difficulties such as persuading all members to participate and finding times when all can meet. It is not necessary, of course, for everything to be done with all members at once, but the group purpose is best emphasized by at least occasional joint sessions. Easing of tension may result simply from the members' realizing what is happening during family interactions—from becoming aware of one's own behavior, its effect on others, and the effects of others' behavior on oneself. Some benefit may thus be expected from insight, but this does not guarantee the changing of attitudes that are deeply habituated and strongly motivated. In practice, group sessions may be interspersed with "one-to-one" meetings, but the purpose is still to change interactions and bring about a less damaging operation of the family system as a whole.

Group Psychotherapy

The original impetus to group psychotherapy was a purely practical one. Psychiatrists in mental hospitals and large clinics, confronted by an impossible amount of work, could help a substantial number of their patients only if they invented some radical device for saving time. Here and there, starting about sixty years ago, workers began to experiment with the possibility of treating patients in groups. In the beginning these groups were considered to be classes; the group leader served as a teacher and sometimes even as a sort of preacher who used persuasive and inspirational methods. As the technique developed, it became customary for the leader to open each meeting with a talk about some psychological topic, such as defense mechanisms or emotions and their bodily accompaniments. Simple diagrams or drawings on the blackboard were used whenever possible, not only to clarify what was being said but also to serve as an anchorage point for subsequent discussion. Sooner or later the group members would be doing most of the talking, and it sometimes happened that they were able to bring up personal problems, discuss the problems of others, and free themselves from considerable burdens of guilt and anxiety. It was helpful and reassuring for patients to learn in this vivid way that disordered behavior was understandable and that their own guilty secrets and contemptible weaknesses were not unlike those of other people.

As experience with group psychotherapy increased, the didactic methods of the earlier classes gave place to an atmosphere more truly psychotherapeutic. Especially when the work was extended to less disturbed patients it became apparent that meetings might be conducted without prepared topics, in a client-centered fashion, the course of conversation being determined by the spontaneous offerings of group members. The part played by the group leader became less like that of a teacher, more like that of a psychotherapist using only such tools as the recognition of feelings and the interpretation of behavior. Group therapy can be conducted in different ways, ranging from directive tactics and active interpretation to a passivity and permissiveness, a virtual refusal of the leader's role, that almost forces the patients to take initiative.

Group psychotherapy, like family therapy, rests upon an interactive conception of human behavior. The locus of disorder is not the patient's behavior taken alone; it is his ways of interacting with other people. In individual treatment these interactions are largely left to the patient. New behavior may be explicitly encouraged, but it is not observed by the therapist and can be interpreted only in whatever form it is reported by the patient. Group psychotherapy brings this important step directly into the clinic. The therapist is in a position to interpret what is really happening in the patient's social relationships. Furthermore, the responses of other group members, growing more and more candid as the sessions progress, provide the patient with an insistent schooling in observing not only his own feelings but the effect he has upon others. He becomes fully alerted to the relation between his own behavior and the responses of others. The patient emerges from the work with a new and generally constructive social experience behind him. This bridges the gap that is often present in individual treatment between the patient's progress in his relationship with the therapist and his progress with the relationships of everyday life. In this respect group therapy is a more real experience than individual therapy. For some purposes this can be a substantial asset.

Group psychotherapy is currently in wide use both in mental hospitals and in community mental health centers. From it have sprung in recent years a variety of experiments in which group meetings are used not so much to treat disorders as to forward social sensitivity, personal growth, and a search for new kinds of experience. Training groups and encounter groups aim to bring about a sharper perception of human interactive behavior, a greater awareness of the accompanying feelings, and an enlarged freedom and naturalness in social living. These purposes differ little from those usually stated for group psychotherapy. The similarity serves to remind us that psychological treatment often does not fit the medical analogy of treating a disease. The goals are more aptly described as encouraging new learning, reducing blocks to development, and opening the way for new steps in personal growth.

PRESENT OUTLOOK

One of the strongest impressions to emerge from this historical introduction is that the study of abnormal psychology cannot be a simple matter. The range of happenings to be studied extends all the way from brain injuries through major psychoses, neuroses, and other serious troubles, to the more transient disorders of personal behavior that most people experience at some time in meeting the exigencies of life. Increasing one's knowledge means not just storing new facts; there must be a growth of sensitivity, an increase of perceptiveness, that makes it possible to reach intimate terms with the subject under study. This puts upon the student of abnormal psychology a special burden. He must become sympathetically perceptive in several different directions. Because the field includes disorders that are somatogenic, in whole or in part, he must open his mind to complex matters of brain injury and cerebral physiology, learning to perceive these problems with the eye of a biologist. Because it includes a wide range of psychogenic phenomena, in which learning plays the chief part, he must become acquainted with scientific behavior theory, viewing things with the eye of an experimental psychologist, while not neglecting the human complications of suppressed wish, defense, resistance, and confused feeling which can be apprehended only by the ear of a clinician. Because disordered personal behavior occurs in a social setting and is much affected by it, he must be able to assume the outlook of a sociologist. He must also accustom himself to deal with complex relations among all things. Abnormal psychology is no field for simplistic, doctrinaire modes of thought. Perhaps it is no field at all in the usual sense, yet it is unified by the fact of disordered personal behavior and consequent suffering. We cannot expect the understanding of this to be simple.

SUGGESTIONS FOR FURTHER READING

The history of psychiatry and abnormal psychology is surveyed in detail by G. Zilboorg and G. W. Henry, *A History of Medical Psychology* (New York, W. W. Norton & Co., Inc., 1941). This thorough history begins with the earliest known ideas about medical psychology; the topics covered in the foregoing chapter are discussed in Chs. 8–11, 13, 14. A less scholarly but informative and entertaining account is given by W. Bromberg, *The Mind of Man: The Story of Man's Conquest of Mental Illness* (New York, Harper & Row, 1937), especially Chs. 6–14. Students who wish to examine the care and treatment of disordered persons as an aspect of American social history will find profit in an older book by A. Deutsch, *The Mentally Ill in America* (Garden City, N. Y., Doubleday & Co., Inc., 1937), and in a new work by J. S. Bockoven, *Moral Treatment in Community Mental Health* (New York, Springer Publishing Co., Inc., 1972). Clifford Beers' autobiography, *A Mind That Found Itself* (Longmans, Green & Co., 1908; now published by Doubleday & Co., Inc.) still retains its value and fascination not only as the fountainhead of the mental health movement but also as a description of the mental state of a temporarily insane person.

The work of Mesmer, Janet, Freud, and Adler is briefly set forth by Clifford Allen, *Modern Discoveries in Medical Psychology* (2nd ed., London, Macmillan & Co., 1949), Chs. 1, 2, 4–6. No one has ever equaled Janet in the art of clinical description: *The Major Symptoms of Hysteria* (2nd ed., New York, The Macmillan Co., 1920), while in several respects out of date, conjures up the excitement that originally surrounded the study of this neurosis when it was an outstanding medical mystery and leaves the reader's mind full of memorable cases. Freud's own introduction to his work is still the most satisfactory: *A General Introduction to Psychoanalysis* (1919) and *New Introductory Lectures on Psychoanalysis* (1933), both available now as paperbacks. A systematic presentation of Adler's work, mainly in selections from his writing, is to be found in H. L. and R. R. Ansbacher's *The Individual Psychology of Alfred Adler* (New York, Basic Books, Inc., 1956).

A broad survey of psychological methods of treatment is provided by J. D. Frank in *Persuasion and Healing: A Comparative Study of Psychotherapy* (Baltimore, Johns Hopkins Press, 1961). An interesting essay on different ways of approaching the history of psychiatry, its place in the larger scene of human history, and who is best qualified to write it, is by O. M. Marx, "What Is the History of Psychiatry?" in *American Journal of Orthopsychiatry*, Vol. 40 (1970), pp. 593–605.

2

Clinical Introduction: Examples of Disordered Personalities

INTRODUCTION TO THE CASES

In the first chapter the field of abnormal psychology was described as the study of disordered personal reactions to life and its circumstances. We shall now pursue this study by examining some representative examples of disorder. What does it mean to be psychologically disordered? How does it feel, and how does it express itself in behavior? What are the symptoms? What sense can be made out of a disorder, and how can its causes be untangled? The answers to these questions are complicated, the more so because here, as in every matter pertaining to personality, it is necessary to allow for a very wide range of individual differences. But for this very reason we shall get a fairer impression of the problems if we start with case histories rather than with lists of symptoms or theoretical formulations. Disordered reactions occur in people. It is important to look at them first in their natural habitat. Case histories, moreover, are the chief element in the foundation of fact upon which abnormal psychology has historically been built.

The reader should be forewarned that the five cases described here will be frequently referred to in later chapters of the book. They display many of the problems and principles that will occupy us when we undertake to build up a systematic account of abnormal psychology. It will be assumed that the cases given in this chapter are well remembered, and with this in mind the reader should not only go through them but study and compare them carefully.

Main Varieties of Disorder

To gather up the matters discussed in the last chapter, and to provide a framework for everything that follows, we shall begin by giving a rough classification of the main varieties of disorder.

Psychoses. The distinguishing mark of psychosis is a substantial loss of contact with the surrounding world. Behavior is peculiar, speech is irrational, and the patient seems to make little effort at conformity with the world and people around him. *Psychosis* is roughly equivalent to *insanity*. The psychotic person gives scarcely any evidence of realizing that he is sick. However strange his world appears to others, it is reality to him. Naturally, psychotic patients often cannot manage their lives in a way satisfactory to others, and they constitute the great majority of the inmates of mental hospitals.

It was once customary to subdivide the psychoses into *organic* and *functional*. Organic psychoses were those having a known physical or organic basis, as was found to be true in the case of general paresis. Functional psychoses were those in which the disorder appeared to be the culmination of severe personal problems or of lifelong poor strategies of adaptation. This distinction is the familiar one between a *somatogenic* and a *psychogenic* disorder. It is useful in thinking about the psychoses provided we avoid the assumption that every disorder must be a pure case of one or the other. Especially with the two major psychoses described by Kraepelin—schizophrenia and manic-depressive disorder—there appear to be important interacting contributions from both sources, and no good can come of trying to force them into exclusive somatogenic and psychogenic categories.

Neuroses. In a neurotic disorder there is no fundamental break with reality. The person lives in the same world as the rest of us, but he lives there uneasily and unhappily. His troubles show themselves in anxiety, unjustified fears, obsessions and compulsions, and hysterical symptoms, the phenomena which, as we saw in the last chapter, Janet undertook to place under the two broad headings of psychasthenia and hysteria. Although allowance must be made for possible innate vulnerabilities, the neuroses have been most successfully conceptualized as *psychogenic,* hence largely as consequences of the personal history of learning. Faulty patterns of behavior in which anxiety and defense play too great a part culminate in some symptom or combination of symptoms that has a seriously crippling effect on the person's life.

Delinquent Disorders. In some instances delinquent and criminal behavior seems such a straightforward response to adverse social conditions that we hesitate to call it disordered. More commonly, however, there are irrational and self-defeating elements in delinquency that justify calling it a form of disorder. The trouble may show itself in active violation of social and legal codes, or more passively by leading a disorganized, irresponsible life. Habitual criminals and habitual ne'er-do-wells most clearly represent these possibilities, but disorders like chronic alcoholism, drug addiction, and certain forms of sexual deviance are often placed in this category. It should be borne in mind that becoming delinquent—failing to respond to socialization pressures—may occur for a large variety of reasons. Historically this category was defined by the fact of getting into trouble with legal and social agencies, an outcome that can rest upon widely different learning histories.

Psychosomatic Disorders. The fourth category contains those disorders in which the person suffers from a genuine bodily ailment of some kind but in which the ailment was originally provoked, in part, at least, by chronic conflict or emotional disturbance. The victim lives with sufficient emotional stress so that his bodily economy becomes deranged and breaks down at some point. Chronic digestive disorders, ulcers, certain kinds of high blood pressure, asthma, arthritis, and skin diseases seem to have at times a substantial psychogenic component. The conflicts and anxieties are usually concealed from awareness; typically, the sick person feels that he would be all right if the doctor could fix up his ailing body.

Lesser Maladjustments. There are many forms of maladjustment that are less serious and less far-reaching than the four varieties of disorder just described. In order to have a place for these milder disorders, the study of which is just as profitable as that of the more serious varieties, we introduce a fifth category rather indefinitely called *lesser maladjustments*. When we speak of disorders as less serious we imply both that their effects are less crippling and that recovery is less difficult. Mild maladjustment may be a chronic condition: sometimes unsolved problems are carried along throughout life. More commonly it is a temporary state rather closely related to difficult situations, and it is often resolved by the person's own effort and insight with little or no help from outside. In general we shall reserve the expression *lesser maladjustments* for those unhappy, uneasy, poorly adapted states which yet do not involve loss of contact with reality, an array of neurotic or psychosomatic symptoms, or an habitually delinquent or disorganized way of living.

This handful of broad categories will provide sufficient guidance for our present purposes. It barely suggests the difficulties inherent in capturing disordered behaviors in an exacting, rational diagnostic scheme. The problem of classification is a field of research in itself.[1] As lately as 1968 the American Psychiatric Association produced a revised set of diagnostic categories, in number, which has been more praised for its convenience than its logic.[2] At the same time voices have been raised against the possible misuse of diagnostic labels. Szasz in particular has argued that hanging the label of an alleged disease on someone may cut short the effort at understanding and may lead to unwarranted steps, such as commitment to a mental hospital, the long-range consequences of which are harmful.[3] As we shall see in our clinical examples, the attachment of diagnostic labels does not always play a helpful part in discovering what is the matter.

The Student's Attitudes Toward Abnormality

Many students feel a certain uneasiness when they first take up the study of abnormal psychology. Sometimes they have been told that the subject is upsetting. Perhaps they anticipate that descriptions of mental disorders and emotional conflicts will disturb and even alarm them. This uneasiness is not really justified, but the reader who feels it need offer no apology. Throughout history the behavior disorders, especially the various forms of insanity, have been viewed with suspicion and dread. This attitude lies deeply embedded in our cultural tradition, and few are wholly exempt from its subtle impress.

If seen in the proper perspective, abnormal psychology is not in the least upsetting. But it is important to keep the proper perspective. The best way to do this is to have clearly in mind, at the outset, *two important facts*, easily overlooked if one plunges heedlessly into the midst of the subject matter: (1) that abnormal psychology deals rather largely with phenomena which are simply exaggerations of normal processes, familiar to everyone in everyday life; and (2) that it puts a one-sided emphasis on breakdown and disorder in personality.

It is naturally disconcerting to read a case history, to recognize in it many experiences that are exactly like one's own, and then to remember suddenly that one is reading about an insane person. Yet strangely enough, it is exactly this sort of experience that the student ought to have if he is to understand the nature of disordered personal reactions. These can be understood because they are made up of the common stuff of human nature; they represent the outcome, under peculiar and trying conditions, of the person's struggle to live and satisfy his deepest needs. It is to be expected,

[1] See, for example, the review of recent work by L. Phillips and J. G. Draguns, "Classification of the Behavior Disorders," *Annual Review of Psychology*, XXII (1971), pp. 447–82.

[2] The scheme is given in W. S. Sahakian, ed., *Psychopathology Today: Experimentation, Theory, and Research* (Itasca, Ill.: F. E. Peacock Publishers, Inc., 1970), pp. 15–29.

[3] T. S. Szasz, "The Psychiatric Classification of Behavior: A Strategy of Personal Constraint," in L. D. Eron, ed., *The Classification of Behavior Disorders* (Chicago: Aldine Publishing Co., 1966), pp. 123–70.

therefore, that readers whose psychological health is flawless will find much in case histories that is familiar in their own experience. Like the patients, they are struggling to live and satisfy their deepest needs. The difference is in the outcome.

There is an experience reported so often by medical students that we might facetiously refer to it as "medical students' disease." This consists of feeling vividly in themselves all the symptoms they are studying in their textbooks: distinct palpitations when they are studying disorders of the heart, ticklings of the throat and labored breathing when they read about respiratory diseases, curious pains in the abdomen when they examine pictures of gastro-intestinal ailments. The student of abnormal psychology should not be alarmed if he, too, has numerous attacks of "medical students' disease" while reading about disordered behavior. Every type of disorder has much about it that can be duplicated in the experience of perfectly healthy people, though it occurs in healthy people with less prominence and disproportion. As a matter of fact, it is most unsatisfactory to be immune to "medical students' disease." A touch of the ailment is a sign that the reader is really opening himself to his subject, trying to grasp it and feel it rather than just reading about it.

While suffering this affliction, the student should not forget the comforting thought that abnormal psychology deals predominantly with inferior and unsuccessful forms of adaptive behavior. It thus tends to draw a picture which exaggerates failure and helplessness at the expense of successful self-direction. Most people are not helpless. Constructive activities are possible for them whereby they overcome at least some of the difficulties in their path. A course in abnormal psychology may start a person assessing his liabilities. Reading about anxieties, defenses, symptoms, moods, and other liabilities, he will find plenty of them in himself. The course does not offer a parallel opportunity for assessing assets. There is no classification of the chief varieties of heroism, fortitude, and persistence in the face of obstacles; there are no case histories of magnificent behavior under severe stress in shipwrecks and fires, on dangerous missions, on flights to the moon. It is our purpose in this book to compare the disordered with the ordered, wherever possible, but the material upon which we draw is necessarily weighted on the side of breakdown and failure.

1. AN ADOLESCENT MALADJUSTMENT:
WALTER LILLY

Our first example is a high school boy of 15 bearing the fictitious name of Walter Lilly.[4] The boy had caused alarm at school by walking out of his physical education class in an acutely disturbed state. The school's social

4 This case is taken from D. R. Peterson, *The Clinical Study of Social Behavior* (New York: Appleton-Century-Crofts, 1968), pp. 144–83.

worker described him as "hysterical and shaking all over," "incoherent and rambling in his talk," "agitated, depressed," and admitting to "ruminations about suicide," all of which suggested that he might be on the verge of a serious breakdown. Some months earlier Walter had several times left the physical education class to appear in the principal's office weeping copiously, and talks with the social worker had been instituted, but Walter's mother had requested that these talks be stopped. Seriously alarmed by the new turn of events, the school authorities now decided that Walter should see a clinical psychologist and told the parents that their son would be suspended if they did not agree. The situation confronting the clinical psychologist thus consisted of a badly disturbed adolescent boy, a resistive father and mother, and school authorities who had in effect forced the family to seek psychological treatment. Although far from ideal, this tangle of human relations is typical of clinical problems. Inevitably the person designated as the patient is part of a social system.

The clinical psychologist, meeting his new client in the waiting room, sees before him a large, plump youngster who immediately begins to shake with sobs. The father, who has brought him, urges him to stop crying, but his tears are still flowing when he reaches the psychologist's office. The following dialogue ensues.

E (Examiner). Walter, what's wrong?
C (Client). I'm scared I'm going to die.
E Afraid you're going to die.
C I think my heart's not right.
E It isn't working right?
C (Sniffs.) I'm scared to go anywhere.
E Mm hm.
C (Sniffs.) I want to get better like I used to be. (Cries continuously.) Last month I was so good.
E You were feeling better then.
C I wasn't scared. My heart was beating all right. I went and did things. . . .
E Yes . . .
C Now I'm scared. . . . I'm scared I'm going to die, and I don't want to die (sobs) because I . . . want to grow up and get a job (sobs). . . .
E And have a reasonably happy life. Sure you do. Of course you do. . . . What sorts of things happen to your heart that make you think it isn't right?
C It beats slow. And I'm scared to go to bed at night because I'm afraid I won't get up in the morning.
E Afraid you won't be able to wake up at all.
C (Sniffs, sobs.) Oh God . . . I've been this way all this month.
E Have you?
C Scared (cries) . . . get all light feeling in my head, a funny feeling like I'm going to fall over when I get nervous.
E Just dizzy . . . and you think you just might not be able to stand up at all.

C And I want to get better and have fun.

E Sure you do.

C (Sobs.) Everybody's been so good to me . . .

E Everybody's good to you, but you're still just as scared as you ever were, aren't you?

C (Sniffs.)

E What sorts of things go through your mind that frighten you so? What sorts of things are you thinking of?

C (Sniffs.) That I'll have a heart attack or something. You think you see people they go uptown and they fall over on the street you know . . . and things.

E You read about it or you hear about it. . . .

C Yes. . . .

E You think this might happen to you.

C I don't want to die.

E Of course you don't want to die.

On first reading, the psychologist's contribution to this dialogue may seem less than brilliant, but it is well adapted to the circumstances. Repeating what the subject has said is a way of recognizing his feelings and giving him assurance that he is understood, which at the outset is the most important thing to accomplish. Walter is not reproached for crying; his fear of heart failure is not ridiculed; he is given no reassurances which at this point would sound false; he is simply encouraged to tell his story. From what Walter says it is evident that anxiety—being scared—is the focus of his difficulty, and that his dread is capable of mounting to panic. To be afraid of going out and doing things, of sleeping at night, and of the physical education class clearly qualifies as disordered personal behavior rather than response to actual danger. But this is something for the examiner to notice, not for the client to be told.

As the interview continues, Walter describes his fear of the neighbors, two old people for whom he sometimes does chores. These neighbors, he is sure, look at him "like I'm no good," in spite of his efforts to please them. He goes on to tell, with renewed tears, of the death two years before of the grandmother who had lived in adjoining quarters. "Ever since my grandma died I've been no good," he sobs; "she'd help me, and she'd be right there when I needed her." At school he has one rather colorless friend, shy like himself, with whom he feels comfortable, but the rest of the children fill him with fear. He reports that they make fun of him, spread stories about him, laugh at his awkwardness in physical education, play practical jokes on him, and sometimes demand money which he does not dare refuse them. Evidently he is treated as a "goat" and cannot think of any way to improve his position. These remarks indicate that the feeling of being no good has become pervasive for Walter, especially since the death of the one person who was able to assuage it. He is helpless and hopeless. Asked much later in the interview what he would wish for if he had three wishes, he says, with renewed tears: "To have some friends, and to be myself again, the way I was, and to have a grandma that cares for me."

Are we dealing here with a disease or with accumulated difficulties of living? There is, of course, a "symptom" in the form of heart trouble, and it would be irresponsible not to have a physical examination. The results are negative; the functioning of Walter's heart proves to be entirely normal. This permits the interpretation that heart disease is simply an idea upon which the boy has seized in order to account for his dreadful feelings of acute anxiety and impending disaster. Shall we then call anxiety his "symptom"? If so, it is not a symptom in the same sense as chronic anxiety arising, for instance, from overactivity of the thyroid gland. Walter is anxious because he feels no good, because nobody respects him, nobody accepts him, nobody any longer gives him a kind look. This is not a disease. It arises from difficulties in living, and it takes an acute form when acquired patterns of behavior become wholly unworkable. The reader should ponder how he would feel if he construed his personal world to be as hostile and belittling as the one described by Walter. The anxiety appears less inappropriate in the light of Walter's belief that he has lost all possibility of being loved and valued.

But we have not yet considered the parents. Walter himself makes a remark late in the first interview that suggests a different pattern of interactions at home.

> C At home I get real mad. I have a bad mouth. I mean I get . . . angry and I scream off and say bad words. I know I shouldn't do that. . . . I get too many things in my head and I have to scream off. And at school I don't say a word to anybody. I just let them pick on me.

That he often behaved this way at home was confirmed by his father, who came for an interview a few days later directly from his job as a construction worker. Mr. Lilly said that he never hit Walter—"he's just too pitiful" —but that he sometimes got mad with the boy, especially when he "kept the whole family up half the night a-crying and a-moaning." What happened, the examiner asked, when Walter took to screaming off? With a nervous laugh, the father said, "Well, to tell you the truth, I guess we always give in . . . so's we won't bother the neighbors. They're sort of old, and I don't think they appreciate the noise."

Mr. Lilly was also asked about Walter's reaction to his grandmother, to which he replied that "she spoiled him rotten." This subject was amplified in an interview that was requested with Mrs. Lilly.

> E So then, how did she and Walter get along? I mean, how did she treat Walter that made her such a special person to him?
> C I don't know how to tell you this.
> E Well, do the best you can.
> C Well, as we know, and as you have said, he was spoiled. We'd correct

him, and Grandma, she . . . she'd say it wasn't the right thing to do, and she'd almost cry, so. . . .

E Would she?

C Yes. . . . Oh, I've seen the time where, well, we did, we had to have her in our home after she broke her hip . . . and when I tried to correct Walter, she'd cry. I'll tell you. . . .

E It must have been a very. . . .

C It was rough, I'll tell you, it's been a rough life. I don't advise anyone to do it.

E It must have been difficult for you. You were caught right between, weren't you?

C Well, yes. . . .

E Suppose Walter should do something that you thought he ought to be corrected about, and you tried to do it, and then, if I understand it, Walter would go running to Grandma. . . .

C Right, that's right.

E And she would protect him . . . and cry.

C Yes. . . .

E And say, "There, Walter, everything will be fine."

C Yes. . . .

E And don't you touch him. . . .

C Yes. . . .

E And would you correct him or wouldn't you? How would that turn out? Who won, Grandma or you?

C Well, I imagine Grandma did . . . just to keep the peace, I think, Grandma did.

E So Walter really wouldn't get corrected.

C Right.

The psychologist next visited the school, hoping not only to secure information but also to enlist cooperation in whatever program of treatment he decided to adopt. He learned that Walter had scored below average on a standard intelligence test and was doing barely passing schoolwork; there was no reason to hope that academic excellence could become a compensatory source of self-esteem. The physical education teacher confirmed the picture of the boy as physically awkward and as the butt of jeers and pranks by his schoolmates. It came out that Walter had cried and asked to be excused from a shop class in which the boys got a little rough, and had been allowed to take an art course instead. The teachers agreed that he never showed anger at school and seemed to be afraid of almost everything.

With this much information the psychologist felt able to take a first step toward treatment. Whatever the historical origins and full meaning of Walter's behavior might be, his crying at school had the effect of getting him excused from unpleasant situations, and his lamentations and screaming off at home yielded him both parental attention and his own way in matters of dispute. This gave the psychologist a chance to apply elementary learning principles and try to extinguish the behavior by removing its reinforcements. To do so required the cooperation of the school authorities, who were asked to pay no attention to Walter's crying and to excuse him from nothing on account of it. The psychologist himself in his meetings with Walter looked out the window whenever there was sniffing and sobbing, offering attention and response only when these accompaniments were absent. The parents likewise took part, attempting to carry out the following instruction:

> Don't scold him, don't argue with him, don't do a blooming thing when he cries. Just go on about your business. Pay no attention to him at all. But if he does anything else—nearly anything at all that a fifteen-year-old boy should do or talk about—then you talk to him. Show him you're interested in that.

Appealingly simple as this procedure sounds, we must not forget that Walter was suffering from acute anxiety. His behavior was not just a tactic to obtain results, and exitinguishing it would be unlikely to remove his real distress. The psychologist therefore began at the same time a program designed to reduce the intensity of the anxiety attacks. This program, called "desensitization," will be described more fully in a later chapter. In essence it involves developing a state of deep physical relaxation and calmness, then encouraging the client to imagine a series of scenes leading up to those that have previously set off anxiety. The procedure is analogous to the reduction of the child Peter's fear of rabbits, described in the first chapter; anxiety is reduced by introducing the feared stimulus in a safely controlled way (extinction) and by connecting it with a pleasant state (counter-conditioning). Once he is sufficiently trained in this procedure a person can sometimes be allowed to practice it by himself between visits to the therapist. Eight meetings and a certain amount of practice between times were devoted to this device for modifying behavior.

These two different lines of attack on Walter's problems brought results that were modestly favorable. From school it was reported that he had not cried for several weeks, certainly a real gain, but that he continued to play a passive and ineffectual part both in class and with the other children. At home he had stopped moaning and had taken some enjoyable trips with his parents, but his father reported an increase in angry behavior: "He may be an angel in school, but he's getting to be a hellion around home." In his sessions with the psychologist crying had disappeared, and his fear that he was going to die was substantially reduced. "Once in a while I still feel like something might be wrong with my heart," he said, "but I don't really believe that any more and it don't bother me like it used to." He no longer thought that the neighbors considered him no good, and his reply was more forward-looking when he was again asked to think of three wishes: "a car, good grades, and to be happier." Walter was definitely better; he had successfully emerged from the acute crisis. If contacts with the client had ceased at this point, the psychologist would have been justified in listing the case as improved.

We must not, however, be too quick to congratulate ourselves about a result of this kind. Walter had been relatively well until the last month before his acute attack at school. Has he simply been returned to that state, without substantial change in his difficulties in living? It is a gain, possibly lasting, that his immediate environment has stopped rewarding his childish tactics of crying and screaming, but this does not guarantee that he will adopt more mature strategies and discover new grounds for self-esteem. So long as he remains passive at school and angrily demanding at home there is still a risk that he will feel no good to the point of once more becoming acutely scared. How far to go in treating a case is always a difficult decision. One can never hope to forestall all possible problems. The best course is to weigh on the one hand the likelihood of being able to produce specific beneficent changes, and on the other the costs of doing so, reckoned in terms of the time, effort, patience, and insight of all concerned.

In Walter's case it was decided to attempt two further changes, one in his interactions with his father, the other in his behavior toward other adolescents. To expedite the first change, son and father were seen together for an hour each week. Talking things over among themselves, the three were gradually able to discern a pattern in those exchanges that caused friction and angry outbursts. The trouble would begin when Walter made a demand, like going to look for a second-hand car, that Mr. Lilly felt obliged to refuse. Walter would then increase his insistence, become irritatingly nagging, and finally shout, curse, and scream off at his father, who in turn became angry, occasionally to the point of striking his son. But then the father would feel guilty about his outburst and "make it up" to Walter by doing what had been demanded in the first place. Once this pattern was clearly perceived, somewhat to the surprise of both participants who did not realize what they had been doing, a program could be planned that was more compatible with self-respect on both sides. The psychologist proposed that when Walter made an insistent demand Mr. Lilly should decide at once whether or not he could meet it. If he could not, his decision would stand and he would pay no attention to Walter's nagging and tantrums, never changing his mind on their account. For his part, Walter should accept such decisions quietly and try to refrain from nagging. Needless to say, neither party found it easy to carry out these proposals. Arguments continued to arise, emotions to boil, and tempers to explode. But there was an encouraging reduction in the frequency of angry exchanges until at last a whole month went by without them. Son and father were learning how to keep out of a trap that was painful to them both.

When two people are involved in unsatisfactory interactions it is sometimes useful, as in this case, to see them together. This was impossible, however, with respect to Walter's peers, on whose time the psychologist had no claim. The most that could be expected in dealing with this problem was that Walter might change his behavior sufficiently to elicit a different kind of response from the other children. Attention was first paid to his giving money when it was demanded. The psychologist made use of dramatic dialogue to encourage Walter to take a stronger line with the juvenile thieves.

E What would you do? Suppose I come up and say, "Hey, Lilly, how much money you got?" What would you do?
C Probably give you a quarter (laughs).
E Oh, come on now, what would you say instead? Suppose I come up and say, "Hey, Lilly, how much money you got?"
C I haven't got any.
E What would he say then?
C He'd probably say, "You're a liar," and then I have to show him what I've got in my pockets, and then he'll go away if I really don't have any, but first I got to show him. If I don't do it, one time he ripped my pocket off. He did it once.
E Did he?
C Yes, I should have smacked him down, should have hit him real hard (laughs).
E Yes, or at least do something or say something besides just letting him have the money. Let's try it. "Hey, Lilly, how much money you got?"
C Nothing. I haven't got any money.
E You're lying. Show me.
C (Laughs.) Yes, I'll show you.
E That's what you do, isn't it. You just go ahead and show him. Try something else. "Go ahead, show me."
C (Laughs.) Get lost (very weakly, laughs).
E There you go. Fine. But put some feeling in it this time. GET LOST!
C Get lost!
E That's a little better. What would he do then? What is it you said that. . . .
C He'd probably walk off, like he did with the other kids. Maybe not.
E But the chances of his walking off are at least as good as if you just let him have the money. Let's try it again. "Listen, you're lying, you got some money. Show me. . . ."
C *Get lost!*
E That's better. Still not too convincing, but that's better.

The psychologist here uses *persuasion,* which as we saw in the last chapter has a considerable history as a method of psychological treatment. As used in this case, persuasion is directed toward changing a specific kind of behavior, and coaching is supplied by the psychologist who provides models of more assertive replies. It is to be anticipated, of course, that Walter will have great difficulty behaving this way in real situations, but the chances of success are at least a little raised by his having seen the possibility of greater assertion, rehearsed it, and presumably felt some desire to be able to report at a future interview that he had carried it out.

The extent to which Walter had been intimidated by his peers is revealed in a conversation that took place after he had taken a job as a stockboy at a grocery store.

C There's one guy at work that makes me awful nervous. I don't know. He's kind of quiet . . . something about him.

E You feel uncomfortable when he's around.

C Mm hm. Of course, maybe I should talk to him. . . . I don't know.

E Tell me some more about that.

C Well, he talks to everybody but me, and I figure, well, if you're going to be like that I can be snobby . . . I can stick my head up in the air and not talk. I don't know why he's that way.

E You feel he's sort of. . . .

C Independent. . . .

E Leaving you out deliberately?

C Yes. And you hate to see that. When he talks to somebody else and there you are and he won't say a word to you. But I do my job . . . I don't worry about him.

E What would happen . . . suppose . . . what would happen if you just came in and said Hi! and just started talking about something. What do you think he'd do?

C I don't know. Who would talk first, me or him?

E You.

C Oh. . . .

E What would happen?

C He'd probably talk. I don't know. . . . I don't know if I could do that. . . .

E Well, I know this would be hard for you, but suppose you talked to him anyway. What's the worst thing that could happen?

C Nothing. I can't really think of anything bad that could happen.

The psychologist guessed that Walter, in spite of his expressed doubts, would be able to take this small step, and therefore assigned it as "homework for next week." Walter took the necessary initiative and discovered that the other boy was willing to talk. This boy's silence, it came out later, was a response to Walter's apparent aloofness and suspicion—a good example on both sides of the self-defeating tactics created by social anxiety. Walter's small victory at the grocery store did not, unfortunately, lead to large triumphs in social confidence. Progress in this direction was slow; problems remained in his affectional relationships with others and in his evaluation of himself. He has a better chance to grow than he had before —this is all one can say, but it is enough to justify the effort put into psychological treatment.

Our first clinical example illustrates a number of points. Walter's problems exemplify what Alfred Adler described as an *inferiority complex:*

the client thinks of himself as in all respects no good and can find no grounds for self-esteem. The psychologist in conducting the interviews makes use of Carl Rogers' ideas about the recognition of feelings. He also employs techniques of behavior modification based on applying basic principles of learning: extinction, counter-conditioning, and control of reinforcement contingencies. In addition, he draws upon the historic method of persuasion, in which the subject's positive feeling toward the therapist inspires greater initiative in undertaking new kinds of behavior. But he does not confine himself to a one-to-one relation. The parents are drawn in and attempts made to modify their behavior, sometimes simply by giving advice, sometimes in joint meetings that exemplify family psychotherapy. A portion of the wider community becomes involved through enlisting the aid of the school authorities. These extensions of the program of treatment are typical of contemporary practice in community mental health centers. In Walter's case the choice of procedures is not doctrinaire. Each step is taken because it seems likely to produce a specific beneficent change. The results show the value of this practical eclecticism.

Walter's trouble is clearly psychogenic, not somatogenic. It represents a failure to outgrow childish demandingness at home and timid submissiveness at school, which together create as he grows older an increasingly unworkable pattern of living, painfully deficient in securing acceptance and building self-esteem. The steps taken to help Walter have little resemblance to medical treatment. The are more aptly described as re-educative, and their goal is a resumption of blocked personal growth.

2. AN ADOLESCENT MENTAL BREAKDOWN: KATHI HERMANN

Our next example is a German girl who entered a mental hospital at the age of 18. From this circumstance alone one might assume that Kathi Hermann suffered from a definite disease and that her troubles would have little resemblance to Walter Lilly's. We shall soon see, however, that Kathi was deeply involved in adolescent difficulties of living. If disease is present it must be deduced from her ways of handling these problems, not looked for as a thing apart. When Walter Lilly had the acute attack of anxiety that brought him to psychological treatment, there was the possibility that he would become disorganized to a degree that could be called "breakdown," but this did not happen. Events took a different course for Kathi, and our main task is to try to discover why they did so.

Childhood History

Kathi was an illegitimate child whose mother elected to have her, keep her, and bring her up. She was a lively, breast-fed baby, "normally defiant" during the second and third years, described at two-and-a-half by a family friend as "already a real personality." It was an unpropitious circumstance that the household consisted only of mother and child: when the mother was sick, as happened more than once, the child had to be bundled off to a home. Furthermore, from the age of five Kathi had an orthopedic difficulty that kept her in bed at a hospital for prolonged periods. These bouts continued after she entered school, but presently the trouble was corrected without residual handicap.

The picture of Kathi as a schoolgirl, given by her mother and herself, suggests vitality and forcefulness. From the start she got along well. Teachers' reports described her as a leader of her class to whom the other children paid heed. "Because I was respected by my classmates," Kathi said, "probably because I had the biggest mouth, I quickly found my way back into the school rut after the hospital stays." For a while she preferred boys as companions, finding it more fun to climb trees than to play with dolls. Her studies went well, and her artistic interests, stressed by the school, were strong, having gotten a good start during her periods as an invalid. Her mother recounted that she began painting early, played the main part in a children's movie, and sang a lot on the radio. One looks in vain for evidence of abnormality in Kathi's reported history from 7 to 13. That she was a bit of a tomboy is not unusual, and on the whole she sounds active, talented, socially competent, in good contact with her surroundings.

Beginning of Adolescent Rebellion

Trouble began, however, after puberty when she encountered the two common problems of sex and independence. To understand her difficulties with these problems we have to be better acquainted with her mother, who was so much the central feature of her childhood existence. When the mother brought Kathi to the mental hospital, she impressed the examiner unfavorably. "She gave the history in somewhat long-winded and gossipy fashion, and repeatedly referred to her numerous connections with people of high standing such as professors, doctors, well-known conductors and pianists." The mother's membership in such circles proved to be more a matter of aspiration than of fact. Starting from a strict middle-class upbringing, she had made for herself by creditable hard work a position in the administrative department of a professional organization, where she had frequent contact with professional people without being one of them. According to her daughter she was much wrapped up in this work and talked about it constantly, but not in a way that showed much empathy for its human aspects. Her attitude toward her child appeared to be a combination of spoiling, protectiveness, intrusive dominance, and a need for close companionship. Kathi said that her mother had often interfered with her friendships, driving away those companions who were not the "kind of people" she wanted around her daughter. When the hospital interviewer asked the mother about the sources of her information about her daughter, she replied that "of course" she always read Kathi's letters and diaries.

Establishing independence from such a parent, especially without such help as might have been afforded by a father and siblings, was bound to be more than commonly difficult. The evolution began for Kathi when at 14 she was sent for a few months to France. This exile was necessitated by the mother's entrance into a mental hospital following the break-up of an eight-year affair she had been having with an engineering inspector. Arrangements were made for Kathi to live with a French family and go to a private school with a curriculum much like the one she attended at home. Her substitute mother in the French family, she later told her doctor, turned out to be "peculiar": allegedly a lesbian, she had a large number of male friends. At all events, Madame undertook to loosen the hold of Kathi's mother. She encouraged the girl to abandon her neat and clean ways in favor of sloppy dress, and she indignantly declared that mothers had no right to burden their children with their own love affairs and business problems. Kathi cried a good deal over her mother's illness and their separation, but Madame's influence was timely and set in motion a cool new look at the mother–daughter relation. At school she simultaneously confronted the problem of sex. She saw girls being pushed into a corner and half undressed by boys, but she was careful not to get involved in such scenes.

Forces of rebellion had been mobilized, and conflicts with her mother grew more and more frequent after her return to Germany. Her need for companions of her own age became greater, but now, she told her doctor, her efforts were blocked by the presence at school of a strong exclusive clique which she understood to be engaged in drug orgies and other activities bordering on the criminal. In her loneliness she attached herself to a boy friend with whom she held agreeable philosophical discussions and who told her a great deal about the clique. The boy's heart was elsewhere, however, and when they parted she took an overdose of pills. In retrospect she said that she had not really meant to kill herself, but to see what it is like to be near death, part of her desire to get to know and experience everything. For months after this she suffered from a succession of physical, very likely psychosomatic, ailments, and her schoolwork went to pieces. A male teacher took an interest, tried to help her, sought like Madame to loosen the mother–daughter tie, and exchanged affectionate caresses with her. Later she found out, so she claimed, that this teacher was really a homosexual and had had relations with her former boy friend.

At this point the reader will have noticed what seems to be an excessive preoccupation with the theme of homosexuality. Bearing in mind that the history was given retrospectively when Kathi was in the mental hospital, we do not know just when she arrived at those interpretations, but they seem always to say that an observed heterosexual activity is not real, the actor being in truth homosexually inclined. But in describing her relation to the unfriendly clique she seemed to be recounting what she had experienced at the time. She felt that the clique was actively persecuting her. A former member who had been dropped warned her that this would happen. She even received anonymous telephone calls saying that she was likely to be kidnapped. Her mother became so alarmed by these calls that she notified the police. One day Kathi could not find anyone to give her a ride home from school. At last she asked a girl she did not know, and as she sat down in the car she noticed that the cars of other classmates and clique-members, standing behind them, were making strange, inexplicable movements. Retrospectively she wondered whether or not this persecution had originated with the girl for whom her boy friend had deserted her.

The idea of being persecuted—the paranoid theme—is so common in the psychoses that its appearance in an adolescent's ruminations always causes alarm. But persecution, like homosexuality, is a real fact in the world, and one must not jump too quickly to diagnostic conclusions. What Kathi reports on these subjects is not impossible, though it may seem improbable; further evidence would be needed before deciding that her testing of reality had broken down. In a way the most disquieting element in her story is her apparent misperception of the cars standing behind her. When the perceptual process itself is disturbed, there is added reason to fear that a schizophrenic breakdown is in the making.

A Beatnik Chapter

Perhaps to get her away from the apparently unfriendly atmosphere at school, Kathi, now almost 16, was sent for a term to a fashionable boarding school in Holland. At first she thought the other girls too prim, but soon she found a friend in Hanneke, who introduced her to quite a different world. Following her friend's example she began stealing at school, and soon she was taken to the country home where Hanneke's alcoholic and promiscuous mother maintained a gambling establishment. Here she became attached to a young man with a prison record, had sexual relations with him, and kept up a correspondence for some time after her return to Germany. Her mother was horrified to find her daughter turned into "an unkempt beatnik," "terribly fat, addicted, smoking," running around in skirts and sweaters that were far too tight and announcing that she found them sexy. Quarrels immediately began about going out alone at night. Further friction arose because of Kathi's new role at school as a fountain of sexual cnlightenment. Fearing a scandal, the mother took her out of school and shipped her off to a German boarding school. Kathi described herself as being at this point "sick of everything" and as having "lost all respect."

Kathi was disappointed in the boarding school, where she did not find avenues to adventure of the sort provided by Hanneke. The girls, she decided, were all promiscuous and the older teachers were lesbians. Studies no longer interested her and she soon had to repeat a grade. But the struggle to disengage from mother continued, transferred to the medium of letters. In the mother's view, the letters she received wre "sassy" and always demanded money. In the daughter's view, the letters she received were "nasty" and full of insults to her Dutch boy friend. At home for Christmas during the year in which she was 16, Kathi talked in a way that friends described as "disconnected and contradictory." One evening, becoming furious, she seized a bread knife and threatened to kill her mother; then, because mother would not stop screaming, beat her black and blue. Thereafter Kathi had the upper hand in quarrels. Her mother learned to "keep her mouth shut in order to have peace." But the victory was oddly marred. "I consider it weakness that she is not able to handle me," said Kathi, as if, much as she wanted to rebel, she had not counted on there being no one to help her control her impulses.

A Paradoxical Half Year

Kathi's career at boarding school ended abruptly when she was heard saying publicly that one of the teachers was a lesbian. As other girls had said the same thing, the mother angrily demanded of the school that they, too, should be dismissed. Possibly this maternal support was helpful to Kathi, who now returned home to enter a public school. During the next three months she appeared to her mother normal and calm, and by hard study she completed the requirements for the German equivalent of a high school diploma. She immediately entered a women's technical school where she felt "very much at home," and "finally found a nice group" to which she attached herself "without any misgivings." Taking just these facts we might hopefully conclude that the crisis of adolescent rebellion had passed. She had subdued her mother without losing a kind of basic backing, had found the support of congenial friends, and could once more organize her life in effective patterns. Unfortunately this prognosis is too optimistic. Four months after starting technical school, still just short of her 18th birthday, she entered the mental hospital.

Apparently the struggle for independence was only in abeyance. Kathi wrote in her diary that she was beginning to feel restless again. She had a transient sexual affair with a medical student which may not have been without its problems. At all events there were fresh outbursts against mother, in one of which she threw a cup of tea in her mother's face. During a visit they both made to a relative, Kathi became extremely excited, broke a lot of things in the kitchen, called her mother a whore and used similarly degrading language about her when talking to family friends. She was so violent that a physician was consulted and sedatives prescribed. On the morning before hospitalization Kathi again went into uncontrollable rage, accusing her mother of ruining her life. The mother, well aware of her daughter's capacity for violence, may have been in fear of her own life when she sought the services of the hospital.

Behavior and Treatment at the Hospital

Kathi slipped easily into the role of a patient under observation. Making lively talk with other patients on the ward and dramatically recounting her adventures, she even converted it into a star role. The history she gave to the psychiatrist was animated and vivid, and she laughed off those episodes that had caused disquiet as if they had been merely gags. This behavior can be viewed as an attempt to treat lightly a threatening situation and not be overwhelmed, but it was carried to extremes. The interviewer was impressed by a lack of correspondence between the flippant, giggling, excited narration and the emotions that must have accompanied the original events; the affect being shown was inappropriate to the content being described. Furthermore, the disconnected and wandering fashion in which the story was told suggested serious disorganization. It was judged that Kathi first needed calming down, and this was successfully accomplished by means of tranquilizing drugs. A tentative diagnosis of schizophrenia was entered in the books, but with the note that much more observation would be required to make it firm. Arrangements were then made for Kathi to be discharged not to go home to her mother but to live in the family of a professor of psychiatry near the technical school which she would continue to attend. In view of the repeated deadlocks in the mother–daughter relation, separation was deemed the safest and most practical step. How the plan worked out is for the future to tell.

On the Nature of the Disorder

Although Kathi Hermann and Walter Lilly are decidedly different people, there are certain similarities in their adolescent difficulties. Both have trouble in separating themselves sufficiently from parental influence and establishing successful relations with other young people. It is not hard to empathize with Kathi's struggles. In large part they are the universal ones of adolescence, and she is in tune with her times in wanting sexual freedom, in seeking to broaden and deepen the range of experience, even in choosing Hesse as her favorite author. She seems to have more than ordinary difficulty with sexual identity, as shown in her preoccupation with homosexuality; this would expectably add to the other burdens of adolescence. But her main themes—rebellious aggression and loneliness— are central problems for this phase of life. Kathi occasionally wrote poetry and stories. Her verses describing a screaming rage could come only from personal experience, as could her account, originally written in the first person, of a rebel who turns on his foe. This character, unable to "stand the pain any more," attacked his self-righteous torturers "in hellish joy" —"to see them tremble before him in cold, panicky fear, in terrible horror, gratified every drop of blood in his boiling veins." Doubtless she also knew the aftermath of this eruption, when her character "for a long time fell mute, twisted in endless pain." Her verses on loneliness sound equally poignant and personal. Wherever she goes she is doomed to loneliness, "alone in the currents of this world." In vain she tries to communicate and find her way back to a lost feeling of familiarity and belonging.

> I am a stranger in my own world,
> And nobody understands
> that I want to come back again.
> Nobody understands my words.

Because her feelings are so vivid and easily grasped, it is tempting to give Kathi's disorder a purely psychodynamic explanation. She is unable to escape from the trap of a dominant, intrusive mother who has also been her sole source of security. This engenders enormous rage, so great that it spills over into her relations with contemporaries, making her suspicious and accusatory and thus further obstructing her ways of escape from mother. Finally the rage breaks through in acts of violence, freedom is sought impulsively in ways and with companions ill-chosen, and judgment itself is shattered by the force of passion. According to this interpretation it is not necessary to speak of a disease. Rather than being schizophrenic, Kathi is a victim of unusual adolescent stress and is temporarily disorganized by it. Perhaps she is no more seriously disturbed than Walter Lilly, who had fits of crying and screaming and who was mistrustful of other adolescents, except that she is more of a fighter and therefore dangerous to her mother.

This explanation is appealingly simple, but we must not pass lightly over the question of disorganization. Are we to consider Kathi's stress sufficient cause to make any adolescent go temporarily berserk, or must we assume a vulnerability to disorganization which causes her to go to pieces where a steadier person would have found a more workable solution? Her disconnected talk, inappropriate affect, shrill giggling, and silliness at the hospital, taken together with the apparent perceptual distortion in the incident of the cars, suggested the kind of disorganization that is characteristic of severe schizophrenics. It is possible, therefore, that Kathi was born vulnerable to schizophrenic breakdown under stress.

To decide between these two interpretations is formidably difficult. Even with much more information—with extended observation and refined tests—it would be hard to come to a firm decision. The problem lies in what we might call the interwoven nature of personality: constitutional proclivities, acquired habits, and the stresses of events are in continual interaction, making it extraordinarily difficult to unravel the separate strands. In their uncertainty the hospital staff was probably wise to make allowance for both possibilities. Separation from the mother might be expected to reduce aggression; continuing in school might provide the chance to feel at home with contemporaries; maintenance doses of tranquilizers might control the tendency to excited disorganization; and living under a watchful professional eye might result in timely changes of program if these proved to be desirable.

3. CHRONIC MULTIPLE DISORDERS:
BENTON CHILD

As a contrast to the relatively young cases thus far described, we take next the example of a 40-year-old man who has been in and out of a mental hospital four times during the last seven years. He seems not to have profited greatly from these visits, although his condition has slightly improved. The case of Benton Child is not unusual. Hospital records abound with similar stories of people burdened by chronic complaints who reach bad moments that bring them in for shelter and treatment, who improve enough to be discharged, but who then cannot make a go of their lives outside and presently reappear at the hospital. In such cases the problem of diagnosis can be baffling. What is really wrong with the patient? Do the complaints arise from unusual difficulties in living? Do they point to habitual adaptive strategies that are proving unworkable in the face of current problems? Or are the patient's problems compounded by real handicaps or by distorted perceptions suggestive of mental disorders? It is no simple matter, as we shall see, to intervene beneficially in the lives of such chronically troubled people.

Benton Child was the sole offspring of an oddly matched couple. His mother's family, the Bentons, lived in a small community where they owned and operated a manufacturing business. The mother, graduate of a teacher's college and a two-year business course, served as secretary in the family business and largely directed it after her father's death. The father, Roy Child, a high school graduate, was factory manager at the time he married the boss's daughter. With respect to personal qualities the two seem to have been far apart. The father showed little interest in management, which he left more and more to his wife; at the age of 50 he stopped working altogether, and spent most of his time at home watching his health with great care. The mother not only continued to run the business but also held numerous offices in community organizations. So slight was the father's part in the family business that after his wife's death some of the Benton relatives criticized him for making a will in favor of his son instead of returning the Benton money to those who made it.

When Benton Child was born, both parents were in their thirties. This circumstance, his wife later told the doctor, was important for his development: his parents were too old to give him love and companionship, though generous in meeting his material needs. As regards material needs he could, as the hospital history records it, "get anything he wanted; he just went to his mother and asked for it and she would give it to him." Such indulgence does not necessarily signify love. It may be the easiest way for a busy mother to keep a child from being a bother. But the mother was also inclined to be overprotective. When Benton had trouble adapting to school she declared that he was "too good to play with the other children." It is probably not by chance that the father makes no appearance in these recollections. His influence at home may have been as small as his influence at work.

Benton does not remember disliking school when he first entered at the age of 6, but a little later he was sometimes "beaten up by other kids" and came to fear them. By the time he reached high school, where he was an "average" student, things were going better; he recalls that he "enjoyed dramatics and was a good singer." After graduation he attended a nearby small college for a year, where he "didn't flunk out, but didn't do well and dropped out." This ended his educational career, and at 19 he went into the family business, where he was carried on the payroll even when he chose to take somewhat liberal time off from work.

At about this time he met his future wife Deborah, and they were married two years later when both were 21. For several years the marriage appeared to be stable and satisfactory. The couple lived in a company-owned house with utilities provided. Benton's job was secure, and income was increased by Deborah's holding a job of her own in a nearby village. Although sexual relations had begun before marriage, there were no children for five years. But this relatively easy existence presently came to an end. During the next eight years two sons and two daughters were born. According to his wife's report, Benton was pleased to have her pregnant, but after the birth of each child he felt resentment at the inevitable loss of her attention. In the midst of this period of rapid family growth the Benton factory was seriously damaged by fire, and it was decided to wind up the business rather than attempt rebuilding. Benton was thus suddenly thrown on the job market and obliged to maintain his own home. After trying another line which proved uncongenial he was taken on by the company for which Deborah worked. His work was fairly mechanical, but it called for attention and care, and he set a high standard of perfection in performing it. These several circumstances made his life more difficult, and he met the stress by increasing his once moderate use of alcohol to the point where he was often losing time from work. Describing their home life later to the hospital social worker, Deborah allowed that between her job and her children she had little time to be a good housewife or an attentive wife. In order to reduce her own worries and responsibilities she had shifted from secretarial work to running a machine; "the doctor says it's the best medicine for me—at the end of the day I leave it."

Mounting difficulties of living form part of the picture thus far drawn, but these cannot be considered unusual. Raising four children in economic circumstances that require both parents to work is bound to be stressful, but most couples accomplish it without requiring the services of a mental hospital. In Benton's case, to be sure, we can assume an established expectation that things will be easy. As a child his demands on his mother were quickly met, and for a time in early adulthood he was spared the full responsibilities of worker, father, and householder. A person with such a history may experience average demands as excessively burdensome. The history taken at the hospital suggests, however, another possible contribution to Benton's difficulties. The record shows a series of ailments starting long before the period of stress. As a child Benton reportedly had low blood pressure and spells of weakness and dizziness. At 14 there was a curious episode when for ten days he was unable to walk; one is reminded of the hysterical paralyses described by Charcot and Janet. At 17 he suffered from "spells" of some kind which were diagnosed as mild epileptic attacks; as a consequence he took anticonvulsant medicine for several years until finally a more specific diagnostic test, an electroencephalogram, proved normal and discredited the original diagnosis. Physical complaints continued during the more stressful years. At 28 he complained of nervousness for which his doctor prescribed a tranquilizing drug. This prescription continued next year when he asked for treatment for "an icy burning feeling in his arm," and he has been on one or another tranquilizer ever since. When he was 32 he complained of "sinking spells," periods of weakness and vagueness which might occur even when he was sitting in a chair. Three years later he consulted a doctor again, this time because of nervousness, depression, and irritable rages; he was given a different tranquilizer. It is easy to write off those chronic complaints as reflections of tension and anxiety, but there is also the possibility of a constitutional burden. The theme of "low spells" is sufficiently recurrent to suggest a trait of low energy which might well encourage the passive dependent style permitted by his early surroundings.

Trouble in the Child family was deepened when Benton began to accuse his wife of unfaithfulness. This started after the birth of the second child, a year before his favored position in the family business came to an end. One of the evidences he used was the five-year interval before the first child was born. Being of Roman Catholic faith, the couple had not used contraceptives; Benton reasoned that he must be infertile, hence none of the children could be his own. That he chose this dubious interpretation reflects rather seriously on his judgment, but he became increasingly obsessed by the subject and used it to generate quarrels. Deborah denied the accusations. At first, they were not true, she later told the hospital authorities, but after three years of Benton's pestering she decided that she might as well have the pleasure for which she was being blamed, and began an affair. This was easily managed because husband and wife worked on different shifts, but eventually Deborah and her friend were involved in a minor boating accident under circumstances that confirmed Benton's suspicions. He began at once to go around with a 19-year-old girl whom he often brought to the house, and he complained in public about his wife's wretched cooking and housekeeping as well as her infidelity. During drinking bouts he became increasingly argumentative, quarrelsome, and hard to handle.

It was in consequence of one of his alcoholic episodes, occurring when he was 35, that Benton arrived at the state hospital. One evening he lay on the floor drunk, complaining of difficulty in breathing, but occasionally sitting up and cursing wildly. Deborah called a neighbor to help get him up, but he fought off the neighbor. She then called a doctor who after trying in vain to get him to take a sedative signed an emergency commitment form and called the police to take him to the hospital. The reader may feel that the specific incident hardly warrants commitment to a mental hospital. But there were four children in the house, and with the husband's behavior irrational and tending toward violence, something had to be done. In a community with limited mental health resources the hospital and the jail are the only alternatives.

The first commitment was of short duration. Nervous and shaky for two days, Benton quickly calmed down; by the third day he was talking rationally with other patients and asking to leave. He was allowed to visit home the first weekend, then to stay a week, and was finally discharged after 17 days, with advice to attend aftercare clinics provided by the hospital. The diagnosis entered in the hospital record was *"psychoneurosis, anxiety neurosis."* Tranquilizing drugs were the only recorded attempt at treatment.

More than two years elapsed before the second admission to the state hospital. In the meantime the relation between Benton and Deborah steadily deteriorated. In addition to periods of heavy drinking, Benton was now having mood cycles varying from tense and anxious to low and depressed. When tense he talked a great deal, exhausting his wife with an increasing flow of accusations. When low he seemed inaccessible and despairing, so that Deborah began to wonder about a risk of suicide. He stopped working and was at home all the time. Deborah found his behavior increasingly intolerable, began threatening to leave him, and finally had him evicted from the house. He retired to his parents' house, where he soon made himself unwelcome and wanted to return home, but Deborah agreed to this only on condition that he consult a psychiatrist. She said afterwards that at this point she no longer felt any affection for Benton, who had become "just an object" to her, a highly problematical object. To the psychiatrist Benton presented a picture of weakness. He complained that his legs were weak, and that he sometimes felt dizzy while driving; he had been trying to build himself up by exercises and inspirational books. When a physical examination disclosed no grounds for the complaints the psychiatrist, agreeing to see him every two weeks, recorded the diagnosis of *"personality trait disturbance, passive–aggressive, inadequate, immature."*

Before the new treatment could start, Benton's behavior at home became acutely alarming to his wife and upsetting to the children. At times silently withdrawn, he would at other times yell, scream, and throw himself on the floor. So a friend was prevailed upon to take him to the state hospital on a voluntary admission, a procedure with which this time he readily complied. His recovery on this occasion did not proceed as rapidly as before. He was full of complaints, some of them physical, like cold hands and feet, some of them centered on restlessness and worry, but the admitting physician noted a basic mood of depression and indifference that continued without change for at least 10 days. This time he was given antidepressant medication which did not, however, produce much improvement in his mood, and he was started in group psychotherapy, where it was noticed that he sought the most comfortable chair, smoked continuously, and took no part in the conversations. Deborah made it clear that she did not want him at home until "he's all well," and she urged him to "open up and talk to the doctors about the 'real you.'" As a voluntary patient, however, Benton had the right to request release, and he did so after two months, announcing his intention to live with his parents and return to his job. This time the recorded diagnosis was *"psychoneurosis, anxiety neurosis, with alcoholism, multiple somatic complaints, bizarre behavioral reactions, and depression."*

The events of the next three years can be briefly summarized. A month after discharge Benton again entered the hospital, having intentionally taken an overdose of his current medication. In explanation of this act he said, "I just can't seem to function out there." He had felt weak, he failed to find a job, and then his mother had become seriously ill. His third stay at the hospital lasted three months, during the course of which his mother died. He continued to feel inadequate and depressed, but the staff judged him to be "using the hospital as a shelter" and benefiting little from it, so his request was granted to leave and to live with his father. This proved to be a disaster. Two days later he was back, "afraid of everything, can't make decisions, can't get along with father, can't sleep." This time Benton remained in the hospital for nine months. He improved slowly, became calmer, took more interest in other patients, and worked regularly in the hospital bakery. He was presently allowed to go home to his wife for weekends. Difficult at first, these visits progressively got better; he began repainting the interior of the house and made himself so welcome that Deborah agreed to take him back. The hospital diagnosis at discharge, as if to leave no stone unturned, was *"schizophrenia, latent type."*

Information obtained from his visits to the aftercare clinics shows that for the next two years, to the present, he is doing all right. He returned to his job at his former place of employment, where Deborah was presently laid off, making him the sole breadwinner. His use of alcohol has stayed within bounds, his tranquilizer keeps him comfortable, and he and Deborah are getting along much better. It is too soon to conclude that his troubles are over or that his improvement will be permanent, but his condition at last report represents a distinct gain over the behavior and states of mind that caused him to become a hospital patient.

The reader, after receiving this much information, may still be left wondering what went wrong with Benton Child and why he made at least a partial improvement. The official diagnoses are cast as far as possible in the traditional language of disease, although the range—psychoneurosis, alcoholism, depression, schizophrenia—is too broad to be of much help. But the physicians include also a variety of terms that refer to learned traits and adaptive strategies, terms such as passive–aggressive, inadequate, and immature. The case presents a confusion of physical complaints, difficulties in living, and peculiarities of judgment—a situation that is not uncommon in the study of abnormal behavior. How much sense can we hope to make of it?

We can start with Deborah's account of her husband's personality. She sees him as immature and inadequate, and she blames this on spoiling by his mother. "Even today," she said at one point, "if he wants a new car or new clothes he merely asks his mother and she gets them for him." This dependence is carried over into the marriage relation. "His trouble is that he thinks I'm his mother. I have to make all the decisions. He leans on me. He never has made a decision in all his life." Deborah admits that her own personality is somewhat complementary: "I'm too domineering, everything has to go my way." One can imagine those two people drawn together at 19 because of this fit between their patterns of dominance and submission and because Benton perceived in Deborah a wife who would take care of him as had his mother. Unfortunately, this expectation prevented Benton from advancing to the point of being able to take care of anyone else, either his wife or his children. "He thinks he loves his children," said Deborah, "but he doesn't want them around." When he comes home "he wants the children to eat and be put to bed. He has never cuddled or loved them when they were small." Benton's dependence leads inevitably to resentment when his wife gives attention to the children instead of taking care of him. It leads him to respond like a child to a frustrating mother, with tantrums and depression rather than modulated attempts at compromise. During his fourth hospital stay Benton expressed agreement with this picture of himself: "I've never really grown up." His subsequent improvement can be attributed in part to his recognition that he had come to a dead end. Bereft of his mother, unable to get along with his father, too anxious and helpless to live alone, his only chance of leaving the hospital was to patch things up with Deborah and commend himself by such helpful actions as repainting the house. It remains to be seen whether this motive is strong enough to maintain a workable marriage relation.

There is a marked similarity between the pattern of Benton's marriage and that of his parents. His mother was the dominant member of the household, and his father, retiring early and fussing over his health, set a poor example of effectiveness. The hypothesis suggests itself that Benton's feeble enactment of the masculine role was copied from his father, a simple consequence of identification with the most available model. This explanation, however, cannot stand alone. Identification is not an automatic process that requires sons to copy fathers. There are plentiful instances in which the son of an ineffective father has rejected the model, taken pleasure in being the better man, and identified with some strong figure such as a maternal grandfather who, like Benson's, was successful in life. The likeness between father and son in this case could equally suggest that Benton had inherited his father's genetic make-up and was living with a handicap of low energy, lack of zest, and frequent fatigue. With our present knowledge it is difficult to disentangle the contributions made by constitution and by learning to any given pattern of life; unwise, however, to assume that all the influence comes from one source.

Benton's conviction of inadequacy was of long standing and included doubts about his sexual prowess. Going over his history with a doctor during his fourth hospitalization, he expressed the feeling that he was "not much of a man." He had "always felt" that his penis was unusually small. We can speculate that the first comparison might have been made with his father, but what he actually recollected was verification of this smallness by his schoolmates. He had had homosexual experiences in boyhood and again more recently. It was for these reasons that he believed his children were not his own, and in fact he became temporarily impotent after the fourth child was born. His reasoning exemplifies the pervasiveness of self-doubt. Instead of taking his wife's pregnancies as welcome proof of his manhood, he assumed that Deborah must have become unsatisfied and unfaithful. A deeply rooted conviction of inferiority can play havoc with the testing of reality.

What was happening meanwhile to the children in this troubled family? How did they fare in an atmosphere of parental friction and paternal instability? Shortly before Benton's first hospitalization Deborah became acutely worried about the two older children, young Benton and Milly, 12 and 10 years old. Both were given to uncontrollable outbursts of temper, and the boy especially alarmed his mother by throwing himself on the floor and screaming, a pattern the origin of which is not far to seek. Deborah was also afraid that the children's schoolwork was suffering, so on the advice of her doctor she arranged to have them visit a child guidance clinic. The children were seen at the clinic, their abilities were tested, and communication was opened with the school about young Benton's learning difficulties, which were judged to be minor and easily manageable. According to subsequent reports both children were doing well in spite of the troubles at home. Milly tended to be her mother's lieutenant in the family and began to show something of Deborah's manipulative dominance, thus coping successfully with social life at school. Young Benton did well in basketball, found in the teacher–coach a person to admire and emulate, and entered high school with firm plans to become a teacher of physical education and athletic coach. In this new framework of his existence there was no room for screaming fits on the floor. Nothing could better illustrate the point just made that sons do not have to copy their fathers. Young Benton was fortunate to find a worthy identification figure away from home, but it was not just luck. Copying an athlete occurs most readily in someone who has started to become an athlete. Recalling the father's early low blood pressure, his dizziness, his being beaten up by kids at school, and his episode of apparent paralysis at 14, it seems likely that the son is physically more vigorous and can therefore use a model who would have had no meaning for the father.

At the age of 40 Benton Child has had a great deal of private and public health care. He has been to many doctors for many complaints, and he has spent more than a year of his life at a state mental hospital. What has all this accomplished for him? The most consistent theme in his treatment seems to be to give him drugs. He has had anticonvulsant medication for non-existent epilepsy, antidepressant drugs which failed to elevate his mood, and continuous prescriptions of tranquilizers which may in fact have lessened his anxiety and tension. He and Deborah have spent many hours giving his history to the hospital staff, and there is a notation at one point that he talks about his problems without getting benefit from it. Group psychotherapy has been tried without observable effect, and the hospital has provided occupations which gave him some sense of usefulness. But all of this, representing a good deal of professional effort, seems to have left him just about where he was before, and his improved attitude at home can be attributed more to his having no other way out than to insights and new behavior generated by his treatment.

In contrast to the case of Walter Lilly, there seems to have been no direct and concentrated attack on Benton's life problems. No intensive effort was made to change the behaviors, such as demandingness, tantrums, accusations, and avoidance of decisions, that led to trouble, or to build up in specific ways the confidence that might enable him to take realistic initiative and raise his sense of competence. In all probability such efforts would have taken longer than they did with a youth like Walter Lilly, and they might not have worked at all. Benton's behavior had become deeply rooted, his sense of defeat more pervasive; and he had built alcoholic escape into his life pattern in a way that might have defeated all therapeutic intervention. Nevertheless, the reader will surely feel that a more concentrated attempt should have been made to deal directly with Benton's problematical behavior and feelings. Why did everyone skate around the edges, rely on drugs, use only group therapy, and avoid the central issue of disordered personal behavior? Should we not expect them to do better?

Undoubtedly we should, but it is only fair to ask: Who are "they?" These events took place not in a favored community with large medical resources but in the far more typical surroundings in which doctors are in short supply and overworked, in which community mental health facilities hardly exist, and in which the state hospital, the chief resource, is chronically understaffed. Walter Lilly was a lucky boy to have the large amount of time and personal attention that helped him to resume his growth. There was no one in the state mental hospital who had this amount of time to give to Benton Child. Even if the staff were larger so that intensive work could be done with selected cases, would Benton be a likely choice? Limited resources must be directed to the most promising cases, and it is doubtful that Benton, at his age, with his passivity and depressed affect, his lack of sparkle and low initiative, and his history with respect to alcohol, would have appeared in this light. Should the staff then be further enlarged so that there is time for all? The obstacle to such a plan is the taxpayers. Mental health care is exceedingly expensive, and a sudden doubling of the state hospital budget would require a substantial increase in the tax rate. If the reader is a taxpayer or expects soon to become one he will see that the problem is not simple. But when we say that "they" did not do very well in the case of Benton Child we should refer not only to the professional staff, which perhaps did all it had time for, but also to the taxpayers, who allowed the patient only such limited care as they thought they could afford.

4. A PROGRESSIVE BRAIN DISEASE:
MARTHA OTTENBY

For our fourth example, we take up the case of a woman, fifty-six years old, who suffers from a degenerative disease of the brain.[5] Martha Ottenby led a contented though rather uneventful life up to the age of fifty-four. At that point her husband and friends began to notice peculiar changes in her behavior, changes which steadily increased until it became necessary to send her to a mental hospital. She was found to have a rare brain disease for which no cure is known, and which is almost certain to bring about her death within a few years. In the meantime, however, she lives pleasantly enough in the hospital, unaware that her mind is disordered and that her recovery is impossible. To the student of abnormal psychology such cases offer an unusual opportunity to learn about the functions of the brain. By examining the evolution of symptoms, and by noticing the results of mental tests, we can construct a picture of the functions performed by those areas of the brain that have been injured by disease.

Nature of the Organic Disorder

It will be easier to understand this case if we first consider the nature of the patient's brain disorder. Martha Ottenby is diagnosed as having

[5] This case is taken from K. Goldstein and S. Katz, "The Psychopathology of Pick's Disease," *Archives of Neurology and Psychiatry*, XXXVIII (1937), pp. 473–90.

Pick's disease, a quite rare degenerative disorder which has nevertheless been of especial interest to neurologists because it acts selectively on the frontal lobes of the cortex and spreads only later to other areas. The cause of this condition is as yet unknown. There is some evidence that it runs in families, but in many cases, including the present one, a search of the family history reveals no other victims. Evidence for an infectious origin is altogether lacking. The time of onset is almost always in later middle life, suggesting that Pick's disease may be connected with aging and may be considered a premature aging of certain parts of the cerebral cortex. At all events, when a post-mortem examination of the brain is made, there is found to be a marked atrophy of the cortex, especially of the frontal lobes. In the affected areas the gray and white matter appears shrunken and of an abnormal color. Microscopic examination reveals that many nerve cells have disappeared, while those that remain show characteristic alterations of a degenerative type. The cortex seems to be undergoing a process of decay.

While it is doubtless proper to conceive of Pick's disease in this way, we must remember that the decay goes well beyond what is normal, even in very old people. We must also remember its highly localized character, confined to the cerebral cortex and in most cases still further limited, at least in the earlier stages, to the frontal lobes. Except for her brain disorder, Martha Ottenby is anything but decayed; she is not even old for her years. Her hair is gray, but she is a plump, ruddy woman with a strong healthy pulse, satisfactory blood pressure, normal reflexes, and every indication of sound physical health. Only one physical examination gives conclusive evidence of abnormality. This is a procedure known as the air encephalogram. It is performed by introducing air under slight pressure into the brain cavity, then taking X-ray pictures to show how the air has distributed itself among the tissues. Martha Ottenby's air encephalogram revealed a great deal of air congregated over the frontal lobes, especially at the frontal poles, indicating that the cortical tissue was considerably shrunken in these areas. This is as decisive evidence for Pick's disease as can be obtained prior to post-mortem examination.

It is like telling a story backwards to give the final diagnosis before relating the history of the case. In the present instance, we are justified by the extra profit to be derived from studying the history and the earliest symptoms when we know the nature of the underlying brain disorder. We shall now return to chronological order and see what can be gleaned from the patient's past life.

Personal History

Martha Ottenby was born in Sweden, where she grew up a jolly, sociable, active child of average intelligence. So far as could be ascertained, none of her grandparents, neither of her parents, and none of her five brothers and sisters, ever showed signs of mental disorder. Martha became a dressmaker at the age of twenty, and soon earned the reputation of a skillful worker. When thirty-two she came to the United States; at the late age of forty she married. This last event was not entirely happy, inasmuch as the husband shortly lost his money and ran into debt; moreover, in his discouragement he occasionally resorted to alcohol and came home badly intoxicated. To keep the household going, Martha continued her work as a dressmaker. It was hard to earn enough in this way, so that she was constantly worried about the precarious financial situation. But in spite of these difficulties Martha's life was not without its satisfactions. Except when marred by alcoholic episodes the marriage was happy and the atmosphere of the home pleasant. Martha was a neat housekeeper. She enjoyed her home and this made her able to be patient with her husband's difficulties and her own.

Earliest Symptoms

The earliest symptom of Martha's disorder was an apparently trifling matter: on several occasions she allowed food to burn on the stove. Her husband, having been married to her for fourteen years, was astonished at these lapses from her usual domestic efficiency. It seemed as if she were growing a little forgetful, so that when she momentarily turned away from her cooking it slipped out of her mind. Before long it became apparent that in several other ways her behavior was changing. She felt tired a good deal of the time, and had to lie down often during the day. Sometimes she was bothered by mild headache. Her interest in dressmaking began to diminish; she sat at home and spent most of her time reading weekly magazines. Presently her husband noticed another curious sign of forgetfulness: Martha read the same stories over and over without any loss of interest, apparently not realizing that she had read them several times before. Her standards of physical appearance declined; the neat, trimly dressed Martha began to look "sloppy" and untidy. If her attention was called to some carelessness in her personal appearance, she would become very angry. On the whole her mood was a little sad, in noticeable contrast to her previous cheerful disposition.

At about this point in her illness her brother died. Her reaction to this loss revealed clearly that her mind was becoming disordered. She kept imagining that she saw her brother outside and would run into the street to talk with him, sometimes forgetting that she was not fully dressed. If questioned, she knew that her brother was dead, but a short time later she would again be convinced that she saw him. She told of long conversations with the brother during his last illness, all of which the husband knew could not have occurred. At times she even launched into an actual conversation just as if her brother were making a call.

Her mental confusion became increasingly obvious and difficult. She herself began to feel "all mixed up," and she was confused about the

identity of people around her, though continuing to recognize her husband, her sister, and her dog. Bizarre thoughts came to her mind. Faulty
perceptions occurred: she saw a strange cat across the street with legs all
over its body, and she imagined that it would progress by rolling rather
than by walking. At this point it was decided to take her to the hospital.

Behavior at the Hospital

Upon arrival at the hospital, Martha's sadness increased to a point of
real distress. She fancied that a cat had come along with her, had died,
and now lay behind her bed. Her brother was still much on her mind.
She believed that he had been in the ward and had made a disturbance
there; at other times she saw him in the street and cried because he was
being sent away hungry. These unhappy imaginings soon gave place to
a more cheerful mood. She occupied herself with reading and without the
least trace of self-consciousness would sing loudly as she read.

In the course of time she settled down to a cheerful, quiet, orderly way
of life. She was generally to be found sitting on a bench, arms folded, a
smiling expression on her face, attentive to what was going on around her.
Visitors were greeted with smiles and friendly gestures, but no further
conversation would follow unless it were prompted by the other person.
She was cordial to the doctors and nurses, although unable to remember
their names. When engaged in conversation she showed animated interest.
The form and structure of her speech was not in the least impaired, the
only difficulty being a tendency to slip into Swedish, her mother-tongue,
and it seemed impossible to make her understand that the hospital staff
was not familiar with this language. She spent a good deal of time knitting
in the workroom, performing her work with interest and skill.

When called upon for an interview, or when given tests, Martha became uneasy. She gave quick, brief answers, waiting anxiously to see whether
they met the requirements. Suitable questioning revealed various defects
in her mental processes. She continued to report strange ideas, hallucinations, and delusions, chiefly centered around her brother. She was badly
mixed up about her age, her recent history, when she was married, when
she came to the United States, how long she had been at the hospital. She
could not give her home address correctly, and stated that she lived with
her children whose names she gave; these proved, however, to be the
names of her brothers and sisters, for Martha had no children of her own.
Along with these striking defects of memory there could be observed a
marked lack of initiative. Though friendly, Martha started no conversations. She never asked for things nor began enterprises on her own account.
It did not occur to her to wash herself, although she did so willingly
enough if the nurse took her to the washroom. When she grew sleepy in
the evening, she lay down fully dressed unless told to undress herself.

At first glance it is hard to make sense out of these mental changes. At one moment we seem to see a person hopelessly confused about the most elementary matters: her age, her address, her brother's recent death. The next moment we observe someone behaving in alert, friendly fashion, helping in the ward, knitting in the workroom, able to perform simple arithmetic problems. Just what is wrong in such a case? Is it possible to describe the mental changes in such a way as to make them intelligible?

Comparison with Previous Cases

In the three cases already discussed we attempted to understand disordered behavior by thinking of it as mainly misdirected adaptive behavior. In each case the person had encountered serious difficulties in living and had not developed successful ways of meeting the problems. There was no reason to suppose that the brain was, so to speak, out of order. Unskillful patterns of living can be acquired by intact brains as easily as skillful ones if favored by the conditions under which learning takes place. Walter Lilly might be accused of not using his head when he fails to speak to a fellow worker and concludes that the other boy does not like him, but it is anxiety that produces this result, not an inability to grasp the point once it is shown him. In Martha Ottenby's case it is possible to discern personal problems. The delusion that she lived with her children suggests the fulfillment of a wish denied in her actual life. The centering of her thoughts around her dead brother points to an unusual dependence on this brother and need for his supporting presence. Presumably her husband was a problem to her at least part of the time. But although these difficulties are discernible, we do not get the least impression that Martha became ill on their account or that her illness represents a strategy designed to solve them. Her trouble has no consistent personal meaning and serves no personal purpose. The disorder began in the brain tissues, not in the strategy of adaptation which the brain learns to carry out.

These examples serve to sharpen the distinction made in the first chapter between somatogenic and psychogenic explanations. The somatogenic hypothesis, as it might have been employed by Kraepelin, applies well to the case of Martha Ottenby, whose condition is the result of a disease. The examination of behavior and the analysis of mental changes has in her case the purpose of guiding the investigator to a correct diagnosis of conditions in her brain tissues. If a method of curing or preventing Pick's disease is found, it will undoubtedly have to do with chemical or metabolic conditions in the brain. The investigator can afford to overlook Martha's problems about children and about her brother except in so far as the expression of these problems displays mental deterioration. The somatogenic hypothesis applied in the wrong place leads to diagnostic blunders which keep people from receiving psychological help that may be much needed. Equal folly results from misplaced application of the psychogenic hypothesis. The investigator hunts relentlessly for personal conflicts and fails to see the evidence for a brain condition or other bodily ailment that could be arrested or cured. The really good psychiatrist must be equally alert to the signs of bodily disorder and the indications of emotional disorder, no matter how obscure and elusive these signs may be.

Reduction of Behavior to the Immediate and Concrete

In Martha's case, we want to make intelligible the behavior and mental changes brought about by her illness. What has the destruction of frontal lobe tissue done to her? As a first attempt at analyzing the changes one is apt to inspect the record and find out what mental functions seem to be impaired. Language is undisturbed, but grave weakness is found in the sphere of memory. Loss of interest and initiative played a prominent part in the description, and there were also changes of mood with evidence of a lowered capacity to control emotional expression. Such an analysis forms a natural starting point, but we must be very careful not to treat these various mental functions as if they were separate faculties of the mind. Are we right in saying that memory, as a whole, is weakened, and that interest and initiative have declined? Let us look again at the patient's behavior, this time with a careful eye for those small details which best serve to clarify a case.

One day the patient was asked to lead the way to the workroom, situated on an upper floor of the hospital. She went directly to the door of the ward and turned to the nurse to unlock it. Given the key she opened the door, locked it behind her, returned the key to the nurse, rang for the elevator and entered it upon its arrival. When let out at the proper floor she went straight to the workroom and sat down at her usual place, asking the supervisor for her knitting. Thus far she behaved without hesitation, even with vivacity. When asked almost at once to put away her work and accompany the doctor, she became bewildered and obeyed only after much urging. At this point an experiment was made. The patient was stopped a short distance from the elevator and led a little way along a corridor. The ground plan of the various floors being identical, this corridor corresponded to the one the patient would take on her own floor to reach her sleeping room. She now walked straight along the corridor and turned into the room corresponding to her sleeping room. Naturally she was perplexed to find herself in a strange room, but the most curious outcome of the experiment was that even after being told she was on the wrong floor she could not understand how the mistake had come about and was quite unable to find her way to the proper floor.

This sample of behavior deserves our most careful attention. It is not correct to say that the patient has lost the use of her memory. She remembers the way to the workroom, remembers that the ward door is locked and that it must be locked again behind her, remembers her place in the workroom and the knitting on which she was engaged. Memory images arise appropriately when they are necessary to carry out a definite task. Similarly, once a specific task has been instituted she show no impairment of interest and initiative. Yet the patient would never have started for the workroom of her own accord, and when interrupted in the course of her return she became completely disoriented as to the different floors. In practice she could follow the complicated route perfectly well, but when asked to describe it—to think of it in the abstract—she became altogether confused. She seems to fail when it is necessary to deal with experience abstractly, in her mind, without immediate perceptual promptings.

The hint that we get by examining this piece of behavior can be strengthened by looking at some other samples. Martha is asked about the season of the year, but she cannot tell what season it is. When the form of inquiry is changed to whether it is warm or cold, she answers that it is warm, referring, however, to the temperature of the room. Only when she looks out the window and sees snow does she decide that it is a cold season and agrees that it must be winter. She is given a test performed in the following manner: the experimenter makes a little design by laying small sticks on the table, then breaks it up and asks her to reproduce the design. Martha succeeds or fails in this test, not according to the complexity of the pattern or the number of sticks used, but according to the possibility of perceiving the design as a concrete and familiar object. Thus she succeeds in reproducing designs that remind her of a flag, a roof, a window, and even a letter of the alphabet, but she fails with quite simple designs when they do not resemble an object.

When we consider the various peculiarities of Martha Ottenby's behavior, it appears that she performs with relative success in concrete situations or when dealing with immediate impressions. Her trouble seems to come in dealing with any kind of abstraction. She is unable to stand apart from the immediate properties of the situation or to resist the behavior which it invites. She reproduces designs when they remind her of concrete objects, but not when they seem like abstract figures. She reacts correctly to the temperature of the room and to the sight of snow outside, but has a struggle to relate these facts to the relatively abstract idea of winter. She finds her way successfully, but cannot tell anyone how she did it and is hopelessly lost if the sequence of her actions is interrupted. What strikes us most about Martha's behavior is *immediacy* and *specificity*. It is governed by concrete impressions and present circumstances, by sight of corridor and snow, by the impression that somebody walking on the street is her brother. These immediate impressions exert such a powerful force on the patient that she cannot resist them or detach herself from their influence. It can be shown, by questioning, that she knows her brother is dead: she has not forgotten this fact. Yet when she sees someone who resembles him she surrenders so fully to this impression that for the moment she does forget not only that he is dead but that she herself is not properly dressed to run out on the street. This is what is meant by saying that her behavior is reduced to an immediate and concrete level. She has not lost memory, interest, initiative, or imagination as such; she has lost the power to use these processes in other than wholly concrete situations.

We thus learn a great deal from Martha Ottenby, even though it is impossible to cure her. As students of the brain we learn that there is probably an intimate relation between the frontal lobes and the capacity to transcend the immediate and the concrete. As students of mental processes, we obtain an enriched picture of what is meant by such transcendence. Even in commonplace acts it is necessary to detach oneself from immediate experiences, whether they arise from outside or from one's own thoughts. When we see a person who reminds us vividly of a former friend, we detach ourselves from the immediate force of this impression long enough to remember whether the friend is alive or dead, where we were accustomed to see him, whether it is at all likely that he might now be here. It is also often necessary to give an account of one's actions "in the abstract," that is, while not actually performing them. We can tell someone how to get from one place to another, without ourselves actually traversing the route. We can return to an interrupted task, picture it as a whole, and continue from where we left off, without having to go back to the beginning. These accomplishments seem commonplace enough, but Martha Ottenby's plight serves to remind us of their importance. Transcendence of the immediate and concrete seems to depend upon an intact cerebral cortex.

5. A PERSISTENT BUT UNSUCCESSFUL CRIMINAL CAREER: BERT WHIPLEY

The man who will serve as our final example differs in certain respects from the previous cases. As a youth he rebelled against authority and for a dozen years conducted a losing battle with the forces of law and order. Economic circumstances played a part in shaping his criminal career, but as we look into his history we find many instances of misguided, self-defeating behavior, making him a singularly ineffective criminal, and subsequent events confirmed his liability to serious mental disorder.

Example of a Bungled Crime

Our subject, whom we shall call Bert Whipley, comes to professional attention because of a remarkable series of events that occurred one weekend during the summer when he was twenty-three. Early one Saturday morning, having completed his sentence on several charges involving larceny of cars and burglary, he was given his release from the State Reformatory. His sister was waiting to take him home. On the way they stopped to call on a young married woman with whom they were both well acquainted. Before his imprisonment Bert and this young woman had spent considerable time together, with a rather one-sided result; she fell in love with him, but his emotions remained somewhat confused. During his stay at the Reformatory she expressed her devotion by visits and frequent letters. On this particular Saturday she declared herself eager to leave her husband and suggested that she and Bert go together to a distant part of the country where they might both find jobs and start a new life. Bert's replies were evasive and noncommittal. After the call he and his sister drove home to join their parents and several brothers and sisters, the Whipleys being a very large family. The rest of the day was spent contentedly enough, but by evening Bert felt restless and tired of talk, so he made a solitary round of several bars. Next day, a hot summer Sunday, the whole family went to a lake to swim and did not return until late afternoon. Toward dusk Bert wandered off by himself, found a car parked with the keys in it, and drove away on a main road leading out of the city.

He had gone about seven miles when he became aware of a car overtaking him and heard the challenging sound of its horn. Terrified, he put on all possible speed and swung out to pass the car ahead. He was approaching a curve around which another car suddenly burst into view. To avoid a collision Bert swerved off the road, coming to a jolting stop in a potato field. The pursuing car turned in after him and he immediately gave himself up to the men who stepped out. Almost at once he discovered that these men were not police officers, as he had supposed; they were the owners of the potato field returning to their farmhouse. But it was too late to escape. In the first breath he had admitted stealing the car, and he was turned over to the police.

This time Bert Whipley was sentenced to State Prison, but while awaiting transfer he managed to escape from the county jail, located downtown in his home city. To avoid detection before darkness fell, he slipped into a nearby moving picture theater where he sat trembling and shaking every time someone came down the aisle. Driven out by his own restlessness before dark, he made his way along the main street of the city hoping to reach a safe place where he could telephone to a friend to bring him a different suit of clothes. Caution demanded that he go by side streets and back alleys, but he wandered for half a mile along the central thoroughfare until he was picked up by the police. He received an addition to his sentence and landed in State Prison with four to six years staring him in the face.

What is the explanation of this curiously self-defeating behavior? When we consider all the circumstances it is not surprising that he turned again to crime. There was very little to induce him to "go straight." His previous experience with job hunting consisted mainly of having doors slammed in his face, and now, stigmatized as a convict, his chances were even poorer. His home was crowded and noisy; we can already judge from his behavior on that first evening that he found it disagreeable and irritating. It was much easier, skilled as he was in burglary, to fill his pockets quickly and go far away with his devoted girl friend. Burglary was his purpose when he stole the car and began the ill-fated drive that ended in a potato field.

That he preferred such a course to the miserable prospect of job hunting is easily understood, but what are we to make of his failure to carry out his criminal program? Judging from the criminal's point of view he could hardly have made a worse mess of it. Quite without justification he assumed that a car behind him on the road was in pursuit; he lost his nerve, wrecked the stolen car, and surrendered himself to civilians who had not the slightest intention of punishing him. Later he escaped from jail but concealed his whereabouts so poorly that it was an easy matter for the police to find him. He wants to be a criminal but he virtually brings about his own punishment, an inconsistency that points to severe difficulty of some kind.

Examination of the Patient in Prison

Suppose we visit the prison and look first at the prisoner's record. He made his first appearance in court at the age of seven, charged with "malicious mischief"—breaking windows in a school building. At fourteen he was arrested on various charges of stealing and was sentenced to the State Reform School. When he left reform school he went to another state where he was soon in its reformatory on charges of burglary and larceny. After serving his sentence there he returned to his native state, resumed burglary and larceny, and earned himself a long sentence in the State Reformatory. During nine years, up to the age of twenty-three, he was at liberty in the community for only twenty-two months. No self-respecting criminal would have any patience with such a record. Bert Whipley must have bungled many an enterprise before the episode with which we are familiar.

When we turn to the prisoner himself we find a mild-mannered young man of rather slight build and a somewhat anxious but intelligent expression. His general intelligence, as measured by various tests, is equal to that of the average college student. Serious literary interests appear in his conversation: besides good current literature he is reading Montaigne's *Essays,* and he tells us that his favorite book is Dostoievsky's *Crime and Punishment.* We discover that he has served as librarian at the Reformatory and that he is remarkably skilled in certain lines of craftsmanship. At any sign of interest in his work, however, he becomes self-critical and pronounces his efforts entirely worthless. This attitude of self-contempt proves to be pervasive. If we ask him about himself he quotes the opinions of the prison authorities to the effect that he is lazy, stubborn, disinclined to take courses and improve himself, unwilling even to learn a trade; and he does not seem to entertain any different opinion of his own. He tells somewhat guardedly about his various crimes, admitting that he has often been careless, thus contributing to his own capture. When he plans a burglary it never occurs to him that he might fail, but he becomes tremendously excited when carrying out his carelessly laid plans and is not unlikely to leave some telltale clue. Further study of Bert Whipley shows that in spite of his criminal behavior he has an unusual familiarity with feelings of guilt, in tests of imagination he produces two odd but pertinent stories. In one of these the principal character, having just completed a long prison sentence, gazes contentedly from a window which has no bars, but then in some inexplicable manner falls out the window to his death. In the other story the hero cheats on a school examination, but suffers untold torment and agony until he confesses to the authorities. When we compare these themes with Dostoievsky's *Crime and Punishment,* which describes a guilty conscience with such extraordinary detail and which culminates in a similar voluntary confession, we can hardly doubt that our subject is no stranger to the experience of guilt.

The Pattern of Contributing Causes

How are we to understand the personality and the self-defeating existence of this young man potentially so gifted? Like anyone else he has been exposed to cultural pressures designed to encourage stable, persistent, socially acceptable behavior. In spite of this he has become an habitual criminal with a propensity for getting caught. Our inquiry resolves itself into two questions: (1) how did the criminal tendencies, the persistent stealing, become fixated at the expense of stable socialized living; and (2) why does he fail in his criminal enterprises, losing his cunning at the critical moment so that he practically exposes himself to capture and punishment?

As might be expected, the answers are not simple. Several factors make their contribution. Some part is played by chronic environmental stress: poverty, unemployment, poor neighborhood influences, tempestuous scenes in the home. But the crucial influences are those attributable to modes of personal adjustment acquired during childhood and adolescence. In order to understand our subject's contemptuous attitude toward society, and his equally contemptuous attitude toward himself, we have to examine the history of the learning process whereby these attitudes were established.

The Whipley family circle contains many examples of psychological disorder. Bert's father has recently been committed to the State Hospital on account of chronic alcoholism and some suspicion of mental disorder. His uncle has been in mental hospitals several times, being finally committed for life to an institution for the criminally insane. An older brother has a record of delinquency and drunkenness. Two sisters have had severe breakdowns, requiring psychiatric treatment. In the past this loading of the family history with psychological disorders would have been assumed to indicate hereditary instability. More aware today of the importance of learning, we jump less quickly to such a conclusion, bearing in mind that the presence of even one disordered person in the household can create an unusual environmental pressure for the other members. While it is possible that Bert's alcoholic father transmitted some weakness through the channels of heredity, it is certain, as we shall see, that he influenced his offspring directly and powerfully through the avenues of learning. Much can be explained by examining the atmosphere in which Bert grew up and noticing the patterns of reward and punishment he received. This at all events is the proper starting point, even if in the end there are grounds for assuming innate vulnerability.

Attitudes Encouraged by the Parents. Bert's father was in a respected line of skilled work, not only practising but teaching his skill. Rather suddenly the demand for this type of work ceased. Thwarted and angry, the father was at home a great deal, used alcohol excessively, and literally terrified the household by his outbursts of furious rage. He tried to teach Bert, but lost his temper on the spot if there was any hitch in the learning. Gradually Bert became his scapegoat, receiving torrents of sarcasm, criticism, and abuse. Everything the son tried to do was made a subject of ridicule by the father. The mother, an easygoing housewife, tried to soften the quarrels, but her influence was small. She was indulgent to Bert when his father was not around. If he balked at household chores, she did them herself rather than make her son's lot harder. Sometimes when the parents had noisy and violent scenes, the neighbors would advise Mrs. Whipley to separate from her husband, but when he returned sober, tearfully apologizing, she always took him back. Bert grew up with a rankling sense of injustice. In front of callers, Mr. Whipley posed as the ideal loving parent, but the door would hardly be closed before he turned on his family to heap them with abuse. He posed as a religious man but slandered the church in private. He was brutal to his wife but was always taken back. So far as his father was concerned, Bert could see no justice in the family world.

Throughout his childhood and early adolescence, therefore, Bert's self-respect was steadily battered down by his father's ridicule and criticism. Neither parent offered real encouragement to stable and responsible behavior. Bert was in a state of chronic suppressed anger, nursing a sense of injustice, filled with contempt for law, order and good behavior, as hypocritically preached by his father. His parents unwittingly trained him into a pattern of domestic behavior that consisted of criticizing his father whenever possible, dodging the father's anger, and coming around for a hand-out from his mother.

Attitudes Encouraged by Neighborhood Companions. Meanwhile poverty brought the family into a neighborhood where Bert found many of his companions occupied with petty larceny. There were "good" boys and "bad" boys in the neighborhood, but it was among the latter that Bert began to find life most rewarding. Among these new friends he discovered a way of proving himself a "big guy" and commanding respect. He assisted two older fellows in stealing a car, in return for which he was allowed to go on a joyride which included pursuit by a police car and successful escape. He soon became an expert, organizing his own joyrides. The experience held a peculiar fascination for him because he found esteem and a sense of triumph, while at the same time hurling defiance and contempt at the symbols of law and order. He became a great fellow in a delinquent gang and his criminal career was fast established. In reform schools and jails he later met many unrepentant criminals who taught him that people who work for a living are "suckers," and who instructed him in the techniques of an easier way to get along. At the same time he began to find a curious satisfaction with prison life. When released, he experienced distinct uneasiness and anxiety.

The facts thus far discussed explain the strength of Bert Whipley's criminal tendencies. To put the whole matter in a nutshell: he was exposed to a system of rewards and punishments which discouraged every attempt at stable, socialized behavior and which generated an unusually strong satisfaction in criminal enterprises. What is not yet explained is the failure of Bert's crimes, his frequent capture and long imprisonments, together with the self-contempt and feelings of guilt which we found prominent in his personality. If it were merely a question of frequent capture, we might suppose that, being not very stable, he went to pieces under stress and lost his cunning because of excitement. This explanation, however, would ignore his guilt feelings, his careless planning, and the almost gratuitous exposure of himself to arrest. It appears that crime and punishment have a highly personal meaning to Bert Whipley, the understanding of which takes us again into his history.

An Early Experience of Guilt. When Bert was four years old he was jealous of his baby brother. This situation is a peculiarly difficult one for a small child to handle. He feels anger toward his new rival and resentment against his faithless parents, but if he shows any of this hostility he only makes matters worse by antagonizing his parents. At all events Bert was sick with a contagious disease, and his parents warned him to keep away from the smaller child. While his parents were out he lured the baby into his room and played with him for some time. Soon the brother was sick, and Bert's position deteriorated: the parents paid more attention than ever to the baby. His resentment rising, Bert's next act was unequivocally hostile. When no one was looking he slipped into the baby's room and set fire to the curtains so that the room filled with smoke and the baby began to cough. Fortunately the flames did not spread, but a few days later the baby's condition grew worse and he died. Bert received no punishment for his hostile action, but he was well aware of his parents' grief. Believing that he had killed the brother, he was left with a heavy load of guilt. For months afterwards he was haunted by a voice which seemed to ring in his ears saying "Put it out, put it out," and he would run to his mother screaming with terror. Ten years later he still sometimes heard the voice and experienced the rising panic. Nineteen years later he related the unforgotten incident with distinct signs of distress.

Presumably a single event must be of catastrophic proportions to leave an indelible mark on personality. The tendency of this particular experience would be to make Bert liable to guilt feelings—to considering himself evil and deserving of punishment. Such feelings would expectably creep up on him precisely at those moments when he was engaged in criminal activity. We do not know whether or not the effects of this incident were reinforced by other early guilt-producing situations, but the whole problem was kept alive during later childhood because of his stormy family life, the constant battering of his self-respect, his burning resentment, and the wonderful satisfaction he presently discovered in delinquent behavior. Successful crime had once caused him untold misery and terror, the terror that comes to a child who believes that his parents can never love him again. However strong his present motives toward delinquency, each criminal act had the power to call up some part of that misery and terror. His criminal accomplishments were thus repeatedly undermined by ancient feelings of guilt.

The Attraction of Prison

It might seem that dread of imprisonment would have had more effect than it did in curbing Bert's antisocial urges. Being in prison, however, was in many ways an adaptive solution for his difficulties in living. The restrictions and indignities of prison life served as a chronic punishment, kept guilt feelings in abeyance, and permitted him the satisfaction of griping about his unfair lot. His impaired sense of initiative was small handicap in an environment that allowed little initiative, and his sense of worthlessness was lulled by the postponement of real life tests. Prison afforded provision—food, shelter, rest, a chance to read—such as his mother had tried to provide for him in the stormy home. Life within prison walls was too congruent with many of his needs to act as an effective deterrent to criminal behavior. Of course it was not wholly satisfactory; when inside, he yearned for freedom, for the companionship of women, and for the chance to do what he pleased. But was there a danger that if he stepped forth to freedom he would, like the character in his story, fall unaccountably to his death?

Subsequent Events

That this was no idle symbol soon became apparent. After serving three years of his sentence Bert was released from State Prison on parole. It was a time when jobs were readily obtainable; furthermore, his parole officer was relatively sympathetic, and arrangements were made for Bert to receive psychological help. Conditions seemed as favorable as they would ever be for life outside. Almost at once things began to go wrong. Bert found it impossible to keep jobs; fatigue, illness, or mistrust of the employers put a quick end to each attempt. He found it impossible to observe the conditions of his parole, especially as regards the frequenting of bars. He began to be quarrelsome and created disturbances, becoming increasingly convinced that the people around him were evil and dangerous. Two months after his release from prison he became seriously confused and disoriented as to the time of day. While in this state he was arrested for picking a senseless quarrel. He was committed to a mental hospital where he remained for the next seven months.

This disastrous outcome casts additional light on his difficulties. The speed with which he passed into a confused and agitated state suggests an unusual weakness in organization. When studied in prison he had described anxiety at the time of previous releases, when he had to decide what to do and where to go instead of following an imposed routine. At the time of discharge he had shown uncommon uneasiness about directions for reaching offices to which he was supposed to report. He did not feel equal to the jobs he undertook or to the human relations they entailed. Apparently he faced life outside with a deep conviction that he could not cope with it, and he showed little capacity to endure even ordinary frustrations. These characteristics unfortunately did not change. More than twenty years later his history was still repeating itself. Once more we find him looking for casual employment, drinking heavily, creating a disturbance, showing signs of deep confusion, and being again committed to a mental hospital.

Classification of the Disorder

The case of Benton Child has prepared us for difficulties in classifying disordered behavior. Bert Whipley does nothing to clarify the problem. Part of his behavior belongs under the heading of *delinquency,* and the official diagnosis at the prison was *psychopathic personality.* The latter label is generally applied when the following characteristics are present: habitual delinquent behavior, a marked lack of moral scruples, insensitivity to the rights of others, and a generally erratic and purposeless way of living. This state of affairs differs from *neurosis* in that the underlying difficulties, whatever they may be, display themselves in overt behavior directed against society. Instead of being felt as internal, in the form of unhappiness and symptoms of various kinds, the troublesome tendencies are turned into overt action of a delinquent or criminal sort. Whipley corresponds in several respects to the typical *psychopathic personality,* but on one point the prison diagnosis must be considered wrong. It is highly characteristic of the psychopath that he feels no guilt or remorse. In respect to the rights of others—the victims of his stealing, for example—Whipley is quite free from self-reproach, but as we have seen he is heavily weighted with a much less appropriate feeling of guilt which originated in his early childhood. In this one respect, then, his condition resembles *neurosis* rather than *psychopathic personality.* It seems proper to say that he started with an early childhood neurosis and that his later experiences then turned him forcibly toward delinquency without entirely obliterating the effects of the earlier condition.

More has to be added, however, to cover the breakdowns that led Whipley into the mental hospital. The confused, disoriented, agitated state that preceded his commitments is typical neither of neurosis nor of psychopathic personality; it gives ground for a diagnosis of *psychosis.* Taking into account the mistrustful attitude toward others, a good first guess would be *schizophrenia, paranoid type,* but further evidence, including a marked progression from an excited to a depressed mood, led the hospital staffs to settle on the diagnosis of *manic-depressive psychosis.* In either case there is reason to assume some genetic contribution to his difficulties, though this would hardly be more than a relatively nonspecific vulnerability to disorganization and extreme moods. The picture that forms itself is of a person of less than average capability to hold together under stress having the misfortune of a turbulent history containing more than average amounts of stress. The strategies arrived at to deal with this imbalance—crime and capture, prison life, alcohol—provided no training in the direction of a normal way of life.

Thus when we ask what is wrong with Bert Whipley we find ourselves trying to untwist a tangled skein of influences that resulted in a lot of things being wrong. This makes him a good "textbook case," more typical of disordered personalities than an example who neatly fits one diagnostic category or has one sharply circumscribed problem. But what are the implications for treatment? The attempts made to help him with problems of everyday living when he was on parole were a failure. In the mental hospital his acute symptoms were brought under control but his way of living remained unchanged. Where else and how else would it be possible to intervene usefully, bearing in mind the possible genetic tendency to mood swings, the powerful allure of alcohol, the restless impatience that blocks holding a job, the negative value attached to work? By the time Bert Whipley was twenty-six the discouragements to stable living had come to outweigh any encouragements likely to be within the power of professional helpers. It would be better to meet such a case much earlier in life, when competition with destructive influences would have had more chance of success. But such timely meetings rarely take place unless the community's mental health services are unusually well developed.

CONCLUSION

In this clinical survey we have examined five representative examples of disordered behavior. We have seen five very different personalities, and we have looked at a wide range of burdens and difficulties in living. Is there any order in this diversity? Can we do more than explain single cases? Can we find out how the difficulties of life make one person maladjusted, another neurotic, another delinquent, another psychotic, while another passes through comparable vicissitudes without impairment to his psychological health? That is the task of abnormal psychology: to bring order, system, and understanding into facts as diverse as those described in this chapter. Obviously, the possibility of curing disorders, still more of preventing them, depends upon our being able to perceive them as expressions of general lawful processes. This requires that they be seen in relation to normal development, which forms the essential background for any systematic study of disordered behavior.

SUGGESTIONS FOR FURTHER READING

Two collections of case studies illustrating all the main varieties of disordered behavior have been published by A. Burton and R. E. Harris, *Case Histories in Clinical and Abnormal Psychology* (New York, Harper & Row, 1947) and *Clinical Studies of Personality* (New York, Harper & Row, 1955). Another two-volume work is *Case Studies in Childhood Emotional Disabilities,* edited by George E. Gardner (New York, American Orthopsychiatric Association, Vol. I, 1953, Vol. II, 1956). A case study that has become a classic is that of a delinquent by C. R. Shaw, *The Jack Roller* (Chicago, University of Chicago Press, 1930).

Of special value to the student who wants to try his own hand at interpreting case materials is a book by H. Weinberg and A. W. Hire, *A Case Book in Abnormal Psychology* (New York, Alfred A. Knopf, Inc., 1956), which consists of detailed clinical case reports with practically no interpretative comments.

Valuable for understanding is the study of the experience of disordered people as reported by themselves. An illuminating collection of first-hand accounts has been made by B. Kaplan, *The Inner World of Mental Illness* (New York, Harper & Row, 1963), which includes the autobiography of a deluded schizophrenic patient, L. Percy King. Further material of this kind is to be found in C. Landis and F. A. Mettler, *Varieties of Psychopathological Experience* (New York, Holt, Rinehart & Winston, Inc., 1964), and in V. W. Grant, *This is Mental Illness* (Boston, Beacon Press, Inc., (1963).

Case studies of people more or less normal or but slightly maladjusted are to be found in R. W. White's *Lives in Progress* (2nd ed., New York, Holt, Rinehart & Winston, Inc., 1966); in H. E. Jones's *Development in Adolescence* (New York, Appleton-Century-Crofts, 1943); and in Lois B. Murphy's *Personality in Young Children* (New York, Basic Books, Inc., 1956), Vol. II.

3

The Adaptive Process

Through history and through clinical examples we have seen that abnormal psychology covers a diverse subject matter. Some forms of disordered personal behavior lend themselves to interpretation as diseases, fitting the mode of thinking that prevails in medical practice. Other forms are better described as consequences of experience, as misdirected attempts to meet the difficulties of living. Many cases, of course, represent a combination of the two, but the underlying causes are so different as to require separate study. In this book we shall take up first the problems historically called psychogenic. They are of psychological origin, by which we shall mean that they arise out of the adaptive process whereby from childhood onward we learn how to deal with and live with our surroundings.

More is at stake in studying the adaptive process than finding out how to treat a neurosis or modify a piece of undesirable behavior. Psychological treatment, as we have seen, may not require uncovering the whole history of learnings that led up to the present complaint. Much better than treatment, however, is prevention, and progress toward prevention depends upon understanding how adaptive behavior can go astray at any level of development. In guiding one's own behavior, in bringing up children, in giving counsel to younger people, in working for conditions in the community and in the large society that will be conducive to fuller personal development, it is essential to have a background of knowledge about the growth of personality. This means knowledge of normal as well as abnormal outcomes, workable as well as unworkable patterns, and it implies recognizing the special hazards that go with different stages of growth.

MEANING OF ADAPTATION

Like other words in everyday use, *adaptation* is often warped by unwarranted implications. All too commonly it is considered a one-way process instead of an interaction between a person and his environment. It is then made to imply that all change must take place within the person so that he will conform to the expectations of others and to the prevailing demands of the social order. This view ignores the part played by people in changing their material and social surroundings so as to make the environment more hospitable to human needs. Sometimes the misunderstanding is innocent, but it easily lends itself to political use by those who want to force conformity upon others.

Another common misunderstanding is that of defining adaptation not as a process but as an end-state such as happiness, contentment, or peace of mind. The well-adjusted person, according to this view, is a happy, confident, buoyant person unburdened by problems. Unwittingly this notion ignores the tragic aspects of human experience and implies that all problems can be happily solved. There is nothing in the concept of adaptation that warrants blithe illusions about reality. In some circumstances the best possible outcome may still entail discouragement, sorrow, and enduring frustration.

Still another implication that on closer scrutiny proves illegitimate is the linking of adaptation exclusively with change. It is true, of course, that change is constantly occurring. Every step in development calls for something new; change must go on from day to day and from period to period throughout a person's life. In many situations, however, the adaptive problem is to resist distractions that would provide a welcome change, in order to stick to the task at hand. This can be a large problem for people whose livelihood depends upon uninteresting, monotonous work. It is present also to those who love their work but must put in long hours of reading, study, research, practice, or rehearsal in order to do it well. Children find the requirement of persistence a hard one, as we can see when it is lifted during recess periods or after school. What is needed for successful adaptation is a happy combination of flexibility to change and strength to persist.

The adaptive process represents the struggle of a person to come to terms with his environment. It implies a constant interaction between the person and his surroundings, each making demands on the other. Sometimes a mutually satisfactory bargain can be struck between these demands, or at least a bargain that is not unbearable for either side. It is when the striking of such a bargain is difficult that we can most clearly discern the hampering part played by disordered personal reactions.

MAIN FEATURES OF ADAPTIVE STRATEGY

Dealing with the problems of living requires attending to several things at the same time. Confronted by a crisis, we need to understand it, we need to keep from being too bady upset by it, and we need to do something about it. These three aspects of adaptive strategy can be stated more formally as follows: What we do is likely to be successful to the extent that (1) *adequate relevant information* can be brought to bear, (2) *affect* can be kept *supportive* rather than disorganizing, and (3) *competent action* can be discerned and attempted.[1] These have to be managed all at once, though with differences of emphasis depending upon the character of the problem. Putting the aspects of adaptive behavior into words may suggest that they are more conscious and calculated than is actually the case. The strategies implicit in behavior may be almost wholly unwitting, but we can understand them better with this analysis in mind.

Adequate Relevant Information

Much as we may admire forthright action in the face of difficulties, this can be a disastrous strategy if there is a shortage of relevant information. Taking plenty of time to size up a situation is common in both animal and human behavior. If we decide to put out food for hungry winter birds we may be disappointed at first by their hesitant acceptance of our hospitality, forgetting that they know nothing of our kindness and survive only through constant alertness to possible danger. Similarly, when children are placed in a new situation it is good strategy for them to look things over carefully before committing themselves to action. This is illustrated in studies of preschool children made by Lois Murphy in Topeka.[2] The children were observed in such novel situations as coming to the research center for the first time to take psychological tests, or attending an outdoor party at the psychologist's home. A few of the children blundered right ahead as if confident that everything would be all right; another few clung to their mothers and tried to turn their backs on the novel scene. The rest, staying cautiously close to their mothers at first, inspected the situation intently, and did not venture forth until they had completed their survey. Preschool children are usually too inexperienced to understand in advance what is involved in situations of this kind. It is therefore adaptive to begin by trying to build up relevant information.

In a study of adult behavior under stress, Hamburg and Adams were impressed by the prominence of seeking and using information.[3] The point is well illustrated by parents whose sick child receives the diagnosis of leukemia with short life expectancy. Enduring this painful crisis is helped by collecting relevant information. The parents, feeling that they may have been at fault, are relieved to learn that earlier reporting of the illness would not have changed the prognosis. Their bewilderment is re-

[1] R. W. White, *The Enterprise of Living: Growth and Organization in Personality* (New York: Holt, Rinehart & Winston, Inc., 1972), chap. 15.

[2] L. B. Murphy, *The Widening World of Childhood* (New York: Basic Books, Inc., 1962).

[3] D. A. Hamburg and J. E. Adams, "A Perspective on Coping Behavior: Seeking and Utilizing Information in Major Transitions," *Archives of General Psychiatry*, XVII (1967), pp. 277–84.

duced by collecting information on how they should behave toward the child during the time that remains. Sometimes an educated parent will zealously search the current medical literature looking for hints of new treatment that may have escaped the doctor's attention. The doctor himself, struggling to keep up with reports of medical research, also illustrates the adaptive importance of securing adequate relevant information.

Affect Supportive Rather Than Disruptive

A second main aspect of adaptive strategy is the avoidance or control of feelings likely to disrupt behavior and the strengthening of those that support it. We are subject to a variety of emotions that are capable of getting out of hand in the sense that they can disrupt or paralyze organized behavior. There are situations in which fear, anger, despair, grief, and excitement are clearly appropriate, but if they reach too great intensity they may interfere seriously with adaptive efforts. This possibility is recognized in everyday speech by common phrases such as wildly excited, too angry to speak, paralyzed by fright, consumed by grief, and crushed by despair. The preschool children in the Topeka study were indeed sometimes paralyzed by fright. This caused them to be speechless, immovable, and so rejective of proffered objects and social overtures that they could neither increase their information nor discover possible lines of action.

Grief has been the object of considerable study since the publication of a paper by Lindemann in 1944.[4] Bereavement is likely to involve extensive changes in the survivor's pattern of life. As Lindemann puts it, the bereaved person "is surprised to find how large a part of his customary activity was done in some meaningful relationship to the deceased and has now lost its significance." The crisis can ultimately be met only by developing new directions of interest and action, but acute grief, with its apathy, indecision, and burdensome physical accompaniments, tends to obstruct this development. Time is required to recover from bereavement. Time also plays an important part in recovery from accidents or illness that leaves a person with substantial permanent handicap. Studying a group of hospital patients in this situation, Hamburg and Adams noticed a number of instances in which the patients were at first relatively cheerful but disinclined to talk about or think about the future. Later they began to consider seriously the restricted lives they would have to live, and at that point their mood changed to one of depression. The adaptive process of seeking relevant information could go forward only at the speed at which the patient could tolerate the despair aroused by thinking about his diminished future.[5]

[4] E. Lindemann, "Symptomatology and Management of Acute Grief," *American Journal of Psychiatry*, CI (1944), pp. 141–48. See also J. R. Averill, "Grief: Its Nature and Significance," *Psychological Bulletin*, LCC (1968), pp. 721–48.
[5] Hamburg and Adams, *op. cit.*

Possibilities for Competent Action

Situations are stressful when we are unable to produce relevant and expectably effective actions. Even a situation as dangerous as space flight does not overwhelm the well-trained astronaut who knows what to do in almost any emergency. When someone seeks advice on a personal problem it is because he does not know what to do next; he has exhausted his available repertory without finding an acceptable solution. For the Topeka children, the discovery of a channel for competent action was often a turning point in the adaptive process. When they saw among the proffered materials something they knew how to handle, like beads to string or blocks with which to build, they could leave their mothers' sides and become immersed in action. This step did not always lead further: one child spent the whole time at the party building with blocks in a corner of the garage. But action tends to allay anxiety, increase a sense of competence, and thus lead on to less constricted behavior.

The discovery that something can be done played a significant part in the recent revolution of public attitudes toward mental health. Parents of mentally retarded children, for example, used to feel that their burden simply had to be borne as patiently as possible. Today they are likely to be members of associations for the mentally retarded, engaged in providing kindergartens for younger children, pressing for special classes for those of school age, and developing sheltered workshops for retarded adults. Taking action in this way is beneficial not only to the mentally retarded, whose prospects for maximal development have been greatly improved, but also to the parents, who need no longer suffer in silence and who get the support of other parents having the same problem.

Analysis of Two Examples

Understanding can be increased by making a closer analysis of specific adaptive tasks. To this end we select two familiar problems which are often met successfully but which sometimes become the occasion for disordered personal reactions.

Transition from School to College. The problems of the first year of college will serve as a first example. When a freshman arrives on the campus he is in many ways prepared by past experience to fit comfortably into his new life, but he will rarely be able to make the transition without distinct efforts toward adaptation. In several respects he qualifies as maladjusted until he can accomplish certain new steps in growth. For one thing he is quite likely to be a stranger in the material environment. He has to learn a new local geography so that he can find his way around. He must also learn new routines and schedules, and it is often true that he must take suddenly increased responsibility for managing his life. Perhaps for the first time he must do his own shopping, handle his own money, watch over his own health, and plan his work to meet deadlines a week or even a month ahead. Many study problems turn out to be difficulties in reaching this higher level of self-management. Similarly the freshman must learn to interact with new people whose backgrounds may differ widely from his own, whose histories he has not shared, whose interests he must discover. Often there are feelings of loneliness and isolation until progress can be made in the new social field. The strength of such feelings is attested by the joy that is experienced upon finding someone who comes from one's own county or who shares a favorite hobby. Part of a freshman's problems, then, can be summarized by saying that he has lost his habituated familiarity with the objects and people of his home environment and has to develop relevant information as to what is expected and what can be done in the college community.

Not always easy in making the transition is the control of disruptive emotions. Many freshmen are assailed by sadness at being separated from home and familiar surroundings. They may feel a little like crying and they may suffer at times from acute homesickness. Another not uncommon feeling is a certain anxiety over one's prospects of making the grade in the new enterprise. This anxiety may be experienced as a diffuse but lasting discomfort or it may become focalized upon social activity or upon scholastic exercises, particularly examinations. To the extent that sadness and anxiety obtrude themselves disruptively they are likely to have a further poor effect: these are feelings which one has been taught to suppress as much as possible, and their reappearance seems like a childish weakness. The emotions thus add insult to injury. But perhaps the most troublesome emotion is that of anger, usually experienced in the more subdued form of an indiscriminate dislike for the new surroundings and the new people. It is the college community that is making one feel frustrated; what more natural than to feel resentment toward the source of frustration? Yet this feeling, too, is not wholly acceptable. Presumably it conflicts with a desire to like the place and do well there; certainly it creates an obstacle to wholehearted attempts at adaptation.

Difficulty may also be experienced in mobilizing supportive feelings such as interest and enthusiasm. The freshman must arrive at what we may call a new economy of happiness. In his previous life he has probably worked out some kind of balance between joys and sorrows, satisfactions and frustrations; a balance sufficiently favorable so that his life has seemed worthwhile and valuable. To some extent he will have found his lines of excellence, maintained a basis of security, made some kind of rewarding place in his society. This balance is now temporarily upset, and it can be restored only in the course of time. Freshmen often experience a sharp and painful drop in prestige. As seniors in high school they may have attained local eminence as athletes, debaters, editors, actors, and officers of organizations. At college they are jolted down again to the youngest level of society. It may be that a freshman will learn to interact smoothly enough with his new environment but will nevertheless feel discontented, unable to find a living wage of happiness in a life so lacking in personal distinction. Sometimes a visit to his old school—a return to the scene of his former triumphs—will give his spirits a sudden boost, but he can reach a permanent new equilibrium only by finding sources of satisfaction, prestigeful or of other kinds, appropriate to his life of the present and future. Many students eventually find college life far more satisfying than anything they have known before, but they can mostly report that it took them time to make this discovery, to "find themselves." Building an economy of happiness in a new situation takes energy and patience.

Obviously the situation calls for new competent actions, but these may not be instantly discovered. When conditions are difficult, there is a tendency toward regression; that is, a tendency to fall back on forms of behavior that were satisfying earlier in life but have since been outgrown. A high school debating hero, for example, may come to college realizing that his new companions will not want to hear about his former triumphs, but if he meets hard sledding in his attempts to find common grounds of new interest he may discover, to his own consternation, that he is proudly telling about the three-state cup won by his debating team, that he is talking in his platform voice, or that he has reverted to a juvenile self-confidence in pronouncing judgments. His awareness of what is needed may not prevent him from slipping back a few steps to earlier modes of adjustment. Sometimes regression reaches further into the past. Bewilderment in the new scene may reinstate a dependent attitude in a person lately quite competent; he expects someone to take care of everything for him, or he asks for guidance in matters he could clearly work out for himself. Loss of one's most recent adjustive habits tends to throw one back on earlier ways of behaving just at the moment when new behavior is most needed. There is competition between the new and the old, and sometimes the old displays a disconcerting tenacity.

The transition from school to college is not a crisis that occurs suddenly. When challenges to adaptation can be anticipated, strategies can be set in motion beforehand. This is illustrated in a study by Silber and others of high school students getting ready to enter college in the fall.[6] The subjects were chosen because they showed a high level of competence in the important aspects of adolescent life and could be expected to face with confidence the important step before them. They proved to be not immune to anxiety, but they tried as best they could to deal with the transition in advance. Increased information about college life was sought by writing to their college, visiting the campus, and talking with college students and graduates among their acquaintances. Anxiety was controlled by reflecting that worry is normal, that nearly everyone entering college feels uneasy,

[6] E. Silber, D. A. Hamburg, G. V. Coelho, E. B. Murphy, M. Rosenberg, and L. D. Pearlin, "Adaptive Behavior in Competent Adolsecents: Coping with the Anticipation of College," *Archives of General Psychiatry*, V (1961), pp. 354–65.

that one need not aspire to overwhelming success right away; and by re-calling success in previous transitions such as the one from junior to senior high schools. With respect to competent action, many of the students sought practice in advance, a sort of rehearsal for college life. They began to read books which they considered to be at the college level. They worked unusually hard at term papers, anticipating that this type of work would be of great importance in college courses. They became interested in buying their own clothes and in budgeting their own time. Looking for summer jobs, they tended to reject those usually occupied by high school kids, like baby-sitting and mowing lawns; they preferred work identified with adult status and sought competition with adults on equal terms. These anticipatory actions helped reduce the changes actually re-quired when college opened in the fall.

It is easy to imagine the opposite of these competent strategies: anxiety and apathy, trying not to think about college, clinging to already familiar forms of satisfaction. Implicit in the study are useful hints for counselors. Telling an anxious student not to worry—trying to influence his total atti-tude—may be less effective than pointing out some of the specific anticipa-tory actions, not in themselves unduly awesome, that tend to reduce the magnitude of the step to be taken.

Staying in College: Sophomore Slump.　Our second example will illus-trate the problem of adaptation when the main requirement is not for change but for persistive endurance. The freshman, let us say, makes a successful transition to college, so that everyone who cares about him is pleased with his progress. But a time may come when the excitement of novelty dies down, when studying is felt as an increasingly wearisome grind, when efficiency breaks down and time seems to be more wasted than used. The student may feel anxious and guilty about this slump in his per-formance, but even stronger are feelings of boredom and restlessness that make it impossible to reverse the trend. Troubles of this kind may happen at any time, but they occur often enough during the second year to be nicknamed "sophomore slump." Not everyone has this experience, though a good many are aware of it in mild degree. But for some students there is a real crisis: habits of work collapse; social life loses its savor; feelings of worthlessness and boredom become disturbing; and the trouble may end by flunking out, leaving school, or (in extreme but not frequent instances) by a real mental breakdown. The student feels unable to secure adequate relevant information about what is happening to him, his affects are pre-dominantly disruptive and his economy of happiness destroyed, and his attempts at competent action have the character of restless blind stabs in the dark.

Although it is always necessary to allow for wide ranges of individual difference, we can perhaps recognize a common central theme in the loss of happiness. The glow of early success loses its warming power. The

student has proved to himself that he is equal to college studies and that
he can keep afloat in college life. He has proved to his parents and his
teachers back at school that he can fulfill their expectations for him. But
these motives are not enough to sustain him in those repeated acts of
initiative, planning, and self-discipline that are necessary for success at the
college level. Schoolboy motives of pleasing parents and teachers and
proving that you can get high marks have to be superseded by something
that is more in accord with mature adulthood. The student's education
must become meaningful for his own life. This may come about easily
if he finds college studies intrinsically interesting and knows that he will
always want to have some part in intellectual activities. It may come about
naturally if his studies have a clear relevance to a vocation he knows he
wants to enter. When actions are subordinated to strong interests and
cherished personal goals, we are able to resist distractions and endure
frustrations in order to perform them. Very likely, however, he will not
yet know what he wants to do with his life and may not feel that studies
have much bearing on his future. There are no rewards in a struggle that
seems pointless.

We must be careful at this point to avoid assuming that everyone ought
to adjust to college. The student in sophomore slump, wasting his time
and seemingly going to pieces, may be trying to carry out a sort of rebellion
against a kind of life that is not at the moment valuable for his personal
growth. It may be more important for him to take a job or to try something highly adventurous, proving his worth and finding his interests in
action rather than in studies. Students are sometimes well advised to drop
out of college for a while, deciding later whether or not they want to return. This may be the most effective way to quiet disruptive affects, permit the student to secure more adequate information about himself, and
open new channels for competent action that may restore the economy of
happiness to an acceptable balance.[7]

RELEVANT PRINCIPLES OF LEARNING

Up to this point we have discussed the adaptive process in everyday
language, using familiar human examples. The behavior shown in these
examples is not unusually complex as compared, for instance, with the
clinical cases considered in the last chapter. Adequate description, however, required the use of ideas such as self-esteem, the economy of happiness, interest, imagination, and planning—concepts that are familiar in
human experience but not easy to capture in a scientific system.

To reach a more fundamental conceptualization it is necessary to look
at the adaptive process from a different angle. For many years, since

[7] S. J. Hirsch and K. Keniston, "Psychological Issues in Talented College Dropouts,"
Psychiatry, XXXIII (1970), pp. 1–20.

Pavlov's momentous work on conditional responses, experimental psychologists have been investigating learning and trying to establish its basic principles. In the interests of scientific control, much of this work was done with animal subjects or with relatively simple human learning situations. Partly on this account the resulting principles did not at first seem useful in understanding clinical problems. During the 1960's, however, the chasm between laboratory and clinic was spanned by a rapidly growing demonstration that neurotic behavior, in particular, could be understood and treated through a deliberate application of basic laws of learning derived originally from animal experiments. These behavioral principles are clearly relevant to abnormal human behavior and therefore deserve careful consideration.

Conditioned Responses

The conditioned response was discovered in the early years of the twentieth century by the Russian physiologist Ivan Pavlov. The basic experiment, in which a hungry dog is fed just after the sounding of a bell and gradually comes to salivate upon this signal alone, is described in every textbook of psychology. It may be hard today to recapture the excitement originally created by this now familiar experiment. The association of ideas had long occupied a position of prominence as a theory of human mental life, and the demonstration that something similar went on in animal behavior—the association of the bell with food—strengthened a belief that the essence of the learning process had at last been discovered. To the early behaviorists conditioning became the key to learning and thus to most of the secrets of behavior. The central idea, of course, was not new. Pavlov's contribution lay in developing a laboratory situation in which the critical variable, the response to a stimulus, could be isolated and accurately measured. On this basis was built a whole program of experiments to study the characteristics of conditioned responses.[8]

Pavlov's basic experiment demonstrated that an originally unconnected stimulus could acquire the power to set off a response simply by being present along with the natural stimulus to that response, in this case food in the mouth. The sound of a bell or buzzer, the ticking of a metronome, a flash of light could serve equally well, and other responses, such as withdrawal from pain, could be conditioned to a wide range of stimuli. If we think of learning as the picking up of signals as to what is going to happen, the conditioned response experiments provide an appropriate paradigm. When one stimulus occurs repeatedly with another, it is likely that they are connected in the real world. The dog salivating at the sound of the bell was responding appropriately to the reality created by the experiments in which bell and feeding were made to happen together. But

---

8 T. A. Ban, *Conditioning and Psychiatry* (Chicago: Aldine Publishing Co., 1964), chaps. 1, 2.

the mechanism is not foolproof; it does not preclude the occasional formation of a conditioned response to a stimulus that is not actually relevant.

This possibility becomes greater when conditioned responses are formed quickly. It has been shown that when pain or danger are the unconditioned stimuli, evoking an anxiety response, it takes only a small number of occurrences to establish conditioned responses. The conditioned stimuli that thus gain the power to elicit anxiety may be almost anything that is present at the time of fright, regardless of relevance. Learning under conditions of fright tends to be global and indiscriminate, especially in early childhood. The conditioning of anxiety responses thus provides a believable origin for the irrational fears that sometimes plague people even in adult life. If a young child is terrified by witnessing an accident, let us say, he may afterwards display anxiety connected with the scene itself, with the neighborhood, with streets, with ambulance sirens, with red lights on top of cars, or with white coats as seen on the medical corpsmen who stepped out of the ambulance. Under certain circumstances conditioned responses of this type may persist into adult life, their origins forgotten, so that an otherwise composed person may experience extremely unpleasant anxiety at the sight of waiters in white coats or a school band in white uniforms. It is doubtless oversimplifying the matter to say that all seemingly irrational fears are handed straight down from early childhood frights with no intervening development, but the conditioning experiments certainly suggest how some of these fears got started.

Generalization

Adaptive imperfection may result also from the process of generalization. In one of his experiments Pavlov used a metronome beat of a certain frequency to establish a conditioned salivary response. He then noticed that salivation followed the sound of the metronome set at entirely different frequencies. Generalization of the conditioned stimulus can be said to have occurred when stimuli bearing some resemblance to the original one are shown to have picked up the power to elicit the response.

The point was illustrated in an often cited experiment by Watson and Rayner on the conditioning of fear reactions.[9] A year-old child called Albert, who reached out and played with everything that was put before him, including a pet white rat, was experimentally conditioned to fear the rat. This was accomplished by pairing the showing of the rat with a natural fear stimulus, the loud unpleasant sound made by striking a steel bar. Five combined presentations were enough to establish a strong fear response to the rat alone. Tests were then made with other objects put in front of Albert. Fear responses occurred to a rabbit, a dog, and a light-colored fur coat; a milder response was made to some partly wrapped cotton

[9] J. B. Watson and R. Rayner, "Conditioned Emotional Reactions," *Journal of Experimental Psychology,* III (1920), pp. 1–14.

wool; no uneasiness was aroused by the boy's blocks, with which he played with his customary vigor. He also played as usual with the experimenters' hair, oblivious of the dirty trick they had played on him in striking the steel bar in the first place. The generalization of the fear reaction was apparently determined by visual similarity to the furry white rat.

Another route for generalization was demonstrated by Diven in an experiment with adult human subjects.[10] After somewhat awesome preparations with attachment of wires to various parts of the subject's body and mention of electrical circuits, the experiment proceeded with a form of word association test. The subject was instructed to give a series of associations to each word in the list, continuing until asked to stop. The stop signal was called at twelve seconds. In the word list there was a repeating element: six times the word *red* occurred, followed by the word *barn*. When the subject had associated to *barn* for twelve seconds, he was given a startling and somewhat painful electric shock through electrodes on his ankle. Upon completion of the word list, a time interval was introduced, after which the whole procedure was repeated except that no electric shocks were given.

Anxiety was measured by means of the galvanic skin response (*GSR*) which roughly speaking indicates the amount of sweat produced on the palm of the hand. Toward the end of the first session and throughout the second, the largest *GSR*'s occurred on the word *barn*—the actual signal for the shock—but significantly above-average responses accompanied three other classes of words. These were (1) the word *red* which always preceded *barn*, (2) the word, whatever it might be, that followed *barn*, and (3) all words in the list having a distinctly rural association, such as "hay," "plow," "pasture," "sheep," in contrast to urban words like "pavement," "subway," "streetcar." The anxiety reaction spread thus to other signals related to the original signal either by *contiguity in time* (preceding or following it), or by *meaning* (belonging in the same area of experience, in this case the country). One subject, a foreigner, showed attachment of *GSR*'s to the preceding and following words but none to the rural words. It was found afterwards that because of his imperfect knowledge of English he had failed to catch the meaning of the word *barn*. In the great majority of the other subjects the meaningful associations of this word were utilized as channels of generalization.

Even more surprising than this result was the finding that the same generalization occurred when the subjects failed to realize consciously that *barn* was the actual signal. Of the fifty-two subjects who took part in the experiment, twenty-one were unable to say what word preceded the shock. This seems less remarkable when we remember that the shock was separated from *barn* by twelve seconds during which the subject gave a chain of word associations. It appeared, however, that failure to recognize *barn*

[10] K. Diven, "Certain Determinants in the Conditioning of Anxiety Reactions," *Journal of Psychology*, III (1937), pp. 291–308.

consciously did not in any way prevent the attachment of anxiety to the rural words. This feature of the experiment illustrates *unconscious perception:* the signal character of *barn* is somehow apprehended, but the subject is not aware of this fact and cannot report it. In a later repetition of Diven's experiment, it appeared that generalization spread more widely, on the average, when the connection between signal word and shock was not consciously perceived.[11]

Extinction

Of special importance for the understanding of abnormal behavior is the manner in which conditioned responses are unlearned. We are not doomed to repeat forever the responses we first learn, nor are we permanently enslaved to irrelevant stimuli picked up through contiguity or generalization. Experimental extinction was demonstrated by Pavlov simply by failing to reinforce the conditioned response. When the sound of the bell was no longer followed by food in the mouth, the salivary response eventually disappeared. Time was required to produce this result, and traces of the conditioned response were retained even when it appeared to have faded out. Sometimes it reappeared briefly after an interval of time, and it could be quickly brought back to full strength by a much smaller number of reinforcements than were needed for the original learning. But to all intents and purposes conditioned responses dropped out of the behavioral repertory when the conditioned stimulus was no longer followed by the unconditioned one.

Among its numerous services, extinction contributes to the making of finer discriminations and thus helps to undo the effects of generalization and of irrelevant cues. Pavlov's dogs first learned to salivate to any frequency of metronome sounds, but when only one frequency was followed by food the conditioned response to all other frequencies was extinguished and the dogs became accurate in discriminating the critical frequency. In like fashion a child starting with a generalized fear of white coats might discover that they sometimes occur in benign circumstances without frightening results, and he might presently come to discriminate between benign white coats and those worn by the shot-giving pediatrician and mouth-probing dentist, in whose presence a certain anxiety may continue to be reinforced.

Described in this way, extinction sounds like a perfect mechanism for ridding us of all responses that do not correspond to current actualities. Let Albert have a few exposures to the white rat without sound from the

---

11 J. R. Lacey, R. L. Smith, and A. Green, "Use of Conditioned Autonomic Responses in the Study of Anxiety," *Psychosomatic Medicine,* XVII (1955), pp. 208–27. A systematic analysis of generalization was undertaken by N. E. Miller, "Theory and Experiment Relating Psychoanalytic Displacement to Stimulus Response Generalization," *Journal of Abnormal and Social Psychology,* XLIII (1948), pp. 155–78.

steel bar and he will soon rejoice once more in the rat's company. Unfortunately, conditioned fear reactions are more quickly formed than they are extinguished. Albert's fear was learned in five repetitions; many more would probably be required to extinguish it. In the somewhat analogous case of Peter, the boy described in the first chapter who was afraid of rabbits, extinction had to be managed with the greatest care. Putting a rabbit too near would have caused panic and strengthened rather than weakened the fear response. To meet this difficulty the rabbit was first shown caged at a safe distance and only gradually, on subsequent days, moved closer and let out of the cage. Furthermore, this was done at meal times, so that extinction could be assisted by counter-conditioning—forming a new connection between sight of the rabbit and the satisfaction of eating. Here again, moving too fast would have been disastrous, causing panic to inhibit eating rather than the opposite. Simple as it sounds, the extinction of emotional responses calls for the most skillful management.[12]

The conditioned response in Pavlov's sense applies most directly to abnormal behavior having to do with emotional reactions. Irrational fears, guilt, angers, and jealousies play a considerable part in disordered personal behavior, and the concept of extinction is needed to understand how they can be unlearned.

Operant Conditioning

There is another kind of conditioning, important in both animal and human learning, which leads not to the picking up of signals but to the gradual shaping of responses. It is illustrated by Thorndike's historic experiments in which hungry cats were placed in cages and left to find out how to unlatch the door that stood between them and the food dish on the outside. As the cats could not fathom the mechanical principles used by the designer of the doors, they went through a variety of poorly directed clawings and bitings some one of which eventually caused the door to swing open. The principle was established that those random responses that opened the door and allowed the cat to reach the food were more likely to occur on a second trial, still more likely on a third, and so on until the cat used the correct action at once and escaped without delay. Thorndike formulated what happened as the *law of effect*, according to which the pleasure or satisfaction of eating the food strengthened the responses that had just preceded attainment of this goal. In language more technical and impersonal, the selective reinforcement of certain responses resulted from their having just preceded a reduction in the tension of the hunger drive. Reinforcement through drive reduction is a formula that has great explanatory power in understanding how animals and chil-

12 See above, p. 40; the reference is M. C. Jones, "A Laboratory Study of Fear: The Case of Peter," *Journal of Genetic Psychology*, XXXI (1924), pp. 308–15.

dren pick up sequences of behavior that are instrumental in securing what they want and avoiding what they fear.[13]

This way of learning is to be distinguished from the conditioned responses of Pavlov's experiments. It is not a question of attaching signals to a strong unconditioned response which itself remains unchanged. What is involved is the strengthening of a response that already exists in the animal's repertory but is not strong enough to emerge early in the effort to escape from the cage. Skinner uses the term *operant* to describe classes of behavior that exist in an animal's repertory; "the term emphasizes the fact that the behavior operates upon the environment to generate consequences." [14] "In the Pavlovian experiment," he continues, "a reinforcer is paired with a stimulus; whereas in operant behavior it is contingent on a response. Operant reinforcement is therefore a separate process and requires a separate analysis." He refers to the law of effect as *operant conditioning* and to the learning shown in Thorndike's experiments as an increase through reinforcement of the probability that a certain class of operants will occur.

In animal experiments Skinner has shown that by means of operant conditioning it is possible to shape behavior into forms that seem remote from the original repertory. The experimenter, of course, has to start from things the animal already tends to do, but by supplying a reward such as food at precisely the right moment he can gradually reinforce a chosen response, and by taking advantage of the natural variability of behavior he can selectively reinforce those versions of the chosen response that are closest to the new pattern he wants to produce. This is illustrated in teaching a pigeon to peck at a particular spot on the wall of the experimental box. When the learning is complete the pigeon pecks the spot and thus secures the food reward as quickly and expertly as a human being buying candy from a slot machine. But this result is produced by successively reinforcing bits of behavior that merely tend in the direction of the final performance. Skinner describes the procedure as follows:

We first give the bird food when it turns slightly in the direction of the spot from any part of the cage. This increases the frequency of such behavior. We then withhold reinforcements until a slight movement is made toward the spot. This again alters the general distribution of behavior without producing a new unit. We continue by reinforcing positions successively closer to the spot, then by reinforcing only when the head is moved slightly forward, and finally only when the beak actually makes contact with the spot. We may reach this final response in a remarkably short time. A hungry bird, well adapted to the situation and to the food tray, can usually be brought to respond in this way in two or three minutes. . . .

---

[13] The relation between this concept of learning and the growth of personality is summarized by Calvin S. Hall and Gardner Lindzey, *Theories of Personality* (2nd ed.; New York: John Wiley & Sons, 1968), chap. 11.

[14] B. F. Skinner, *Science and Human Behavior* (New York: The Macmillan Co., 1953), p. 65.

Operant conditioning shapes behavior as a sculptor shapes a lump of clay. Although at some point the sculptor seems to have produced an entirely novel object, we can always follow the process back to the original undifferentiated lump.[15]

This is all very well for pigeons, one may protest, but does it really apply to human behavior? And there is likely to be vehemence in the protest because no one likes to think of himself as a lump of clay which can be shaped according to a sculptor's whim. Visions come to mind of a brutal totalitarian state using an educational program based on operant conditioning to reduce its citizens to subservience, though this is at odds with Skinner's own vision as represented in his novel, *Walden Two,* which has its setting in a utopian enclave benignly conditioned toward humanitarian and cultural goals.[16] But we should hesitate to reject our kinship with pigeons, cats, and dogs, even though our larger brains and linguistic capacities introduce much that these creatures do not have. The following experiment by Ayllon and Haughton shows that under certain circumstances human behavior is influenced in the same literal way by immediate rewards and lack of rewards.[17] Two women who had been in a mental hospital for more than three years spent most of their time talking about their somatic complaints—their shot nerves, sleeplessness, aches, pains, and chronic ailments. It was decided to extinguish this talk by paying no attention to it, turning a deaf ear, while showing attentive interest to whatever more appropriate conversation the patients initiated. Under this regime, extended over many days, the frequency of talk about somatic complaints was greatly reduced. To complete the demonstration that the reinforcement program was responsible, the procedure was reversed and the patients were rewarded with attentive interest to their somatic talk, with the result that it soon increased threefold. Then the conditions were changed again, and over another stretch of time the two patients responded to the staff's lack of interest by almost never mentioning their bodily condition. It is not inappropriate to say that their conversation had been shaped by operant conditioning.

Skinner points out that the concept of operant conditioning helps to understand not only the acquisition of behavior but also its maintenance. On this subject he writes as follows:

Operant conditioning continues to be effective even when there is no further change which can be spoken of as acquisition or even as improvement in skill. Behavior continues to have consequences and these continue to be important. If consequences are not forthcoming, extinction occurs. When we come to consider the behavior of the organism in all the complexity of its everyday life, we need to be constantly alert to the prevailing reinforcements which maintain its behavior. We may, indeed, have little interest in how that behavior was first

---

[15] *Ibid.,* pp. 91–92.

[16] B. F. Skinner, *Walden Two* (New York: The Macmillan Co., 1952).

[17] T. Ayllon and E. Haughton, "Modification of Symptomatic Verbal Behaviour of Mental Patients," *Behaviour Research and Therapy,* II (1964), pp. 87–97.

acquired. Our concern is only with its present probability of occurrence, which can be understood only through an examination of current contingencies of reinforcement. This is an aspect of reinforcement which is scarcely ever dealt with in classical treatments of learning.[18]

This idea is clearly relevant to our behavior in everyday life. Certain regularities in our living, like doing our work each day or seeking familiar sources of amusement, would come to a stop if they did not yield their customary security and satisfactions. With little difficulty we give up our habit of going to the art cinema if the films cease to entertain us. When the same idea is applied to understanding clinical problems, it invites a search not into the patient's past but into the current circumstances that may be serving to reinforce and thus maintain the abnormal behavior. In making a diagnosis the therapist, according to Peterson, should ask himself the following questions:

What, in specific detail, is the nature of the problem behavior? What is the person doing, overtly or covertly, which he or someone else defines as problematic and hence changeworthy behavior? What are the antecedents, both internal and external, of the problem behavior and what conditions are in effect at the time the behavior occurs? What are the consequences of the problem behavior? In particular, what reinforcing events, immediate as well as distant, appear to perpetuate the behavior under study? What changes might be made in the antecedents, concomitants, or consequences of behavior to effect desired changes? [19]

It will be recalled that in the case of Walter Lilly, described in the previous chapter, both the school authorities and the parents were so worried by the boy's symptoms that they fussed over him, excused him from unpleasant requirements, and allowed him to stay at home, thus rewarding him for complaining about his fears. These reinforcement contingencies were gradually changed, and although there was much more to be done to complete the boy's treatment, this literal application of operant conditioning was valuable in getting things started.[20]

It will be noticed that in human instances of operant conditioning the reinforcement does not have to take the form of basic drive reduction. Children's behavior can be strengthened by rewards of food, but they are responsive also to reinforcements of a more social character such as attentive interest, approval, and evidences of esteem. These social rewards first acquire their power in early childhood, when the child's satisfactions and sense of security are largely mediated by adult caretakers. In the relative helplessness of infancy, attracting attentive interest becomes a necessary condition for most forms of drive reduction. This provides a believable origin for the value of social rewards, but in accord with Skinner's view

---

[18] Skinner, *Science and Human Behavior*, op. cit., p. 98.

[19] D. E. Peterson, *The Clinical Study of Social Behavior* (New York: Appleton-Century-Crofts, 1968), p. 57.

[20] *Ibid.*, pp. 144–83.

of the maintenance of behavior this value would be extinguished if it were merely historical. Attentive interest, for instance, must have strictly contemporary meaning, apart from its earlier connection with drive reduction, if it is to serve as a reinforcement in shaping and maintaining current behavior. Human behavior is capable of being reinforced by a wide range of social consequences. Although strict behaviorists sometimes shy away from the concept of motivation because of certain past misuses, it is legitimate to say that human beings have a wide range of motives beyond those usually conceptualized as drive reductions.

Social rewards differ from physical ones in that they cannot be paid out in standard coins, like pellets of food. We do not value the attentive interest and esteem of all people alike. The fallacy is obvious in the joking proposal that we should each carry in our pockets a little machine which, when the button is pushed, delivers into our ears a recorded stream of praise and expressions of high esteem. The reinforcing property of such verbalizations depends upon who says them, whether or not they come from a person whom we value and believe to be sincere. Teachers have sometimes been disappointed to find their words of commendation worthless with disaffected students who like neither schools nor teachers. Social workers have been grieved to have their friendship rejected by delinquents who fear and hate them. In psychological treatment the therapist can be a reinforcing agent only to the extent that he has secured the patient's confidence and respect. This gives added importance to Peterson's recommendation of the questions to be asked in making a diagnosis of problem behavior. Not only the reinforcing events that perpetuate the behavior must be discovered, but also the particular people who provide that reinforcement. One must try to judge what kinds of people the patient is most likely to care about, using this judgment as a guide in making recommendations for beneficent change.

Cognitive Organization

The principles of learning thus far discussed are clearly of great importance in understanding human behavior, both normal and abnormal. Their service in grasping disordered personal behavior and producing desired modifications cannot be doubted. But human beings are complex creatures whose behavior becomes elaborately patterned and whose transactions with their surroundings involve more than is commonly implied by stimulus and response. This complexity is recognized in the concept of cognitive organization. The stimulating conditions immediately present lead in many instances to a response only after a substantial amount of information processing in which prior experience plays a part. We are aware of this activity when we reflect on experience, think out problems and weigh different courses of action, but cognitive organization must be postulated for a wider range of processes than those of which we are aware.

The idea of cognitive fields helps bridge the gap that may have been felt between simple learning concepts and the naturalistic descriptions of the adaptive process used earlier in the chapter.

Even the behavior of animals sometimes requires the concept of cognitive organization. In his memorable studies of chimpanzees made during the second decade of this century, Köhler found it necessary to assume processes which in human experience we would call insight—a sudden new perception of a problem that shows us how it works. Chimpanzees do not pronounce the syllables "Ah-ha!" or shout "Eureka, I have found it!" but they sometimes act in a way to which these vocalizations would be appropriate. The animals were able to discover, for instance, that the gap between the floor and a high suspended banana could be closed by building a three-story tower of empty boxes. They were able to solve the problem of reaching a distant banana by fitting one stick into the hollow end of another to make a long pole. Particularly striking about these learnings was their suddenness: immobility and sullen staring gave place abruptly to coordinated actions which carried out the animal's new plan with relative efficiency.[21] It is hard to make sense of this without speaking of a cognitive field in which there can be both organization and reorganization, a field which is relevant to needs and which controls the pattern in which behavior will unfold. Of similar import were the researches of Tolman with rats. Even these relatively lowly animals could be seen in conflict situations hesitating, wavering, looking from left to right, exhibiting "vicarious trial-and-error" prior to action. If an animal looks before it leaps we can hardly avoid attributing a function to the looking, a process that yields information about the feasibility of the leap. Tolman spoke of a *cognitive map:* incoming impressions, as he put it, are "worked over and elaborated into a tentative map indicating routes and paths and environmental relationships." [22] Human beings need much more complicated cognitive maps, helping them to steer not only in physical but also in social space.

In recent years there has been a strong growth of research on cognitive development in children. A monumental figure in this tradition is the Swiss philosopher–psychologist Jean Piaget, who has taken infinite pains to find out how children come to understand the world around them. This learning is not a matter of passive registration; it is accomplished by an active process of investigation. Piaget emphasizes the inherent activity by referring constantly to the child's "construction" of reality.[23] He shows that even an idea like the permanent existence of objects, which seems to

21 W. Köhler, *The Mentality of Apes* (New York: Harcourt Brace Jovanovich, Inc., 1925).

22 E. C. Tolman, *Purposive Behavior in Animals and Men* (New York: Appleton-Century-Crofts, 1932); "Cognitive Maps in Rats and Men," *Psychological Review,* LV (1948), pp. 189–208.

23 J. Piaget, *The Construction of Reality by the Child,* trans. by M. Cook (New York: Basic Books, Inc., 1954). For an overview of Piaget's work see J. Piaget and B. Inhelder, *The Psychology of the Child* (New York: Basic Books, Inc., 1969) and J. H. Flavell, *The Developmental Psychology of Jean Piaget* (Princeton, N. J.: Van Nostrand Reinhold Co., 1963).

adults so central to all thought, is constructed by children through exploratory play. Piaget's subjects, even when less than a year old, did not let a novel object just sit there, but within the limits of their repertory of behavior explored it, tested it out, and discovered what it could be made to do. The child's understanding of the family circle and of human relations in general is likewise a process of construction out of his own experience.

Part of this construction can be accomplished simply by observing the interactions of other people and by listening to what they say. Ordinary conversation around the dinner table provides a child with a fund of impressions about human nature, all the more so if the adults are given to gossip. There is also the television, and there are also books. But the listener, the watcher, and the reader can be considered passive only in the sense that they are sitting still. Information input contributes to cognitive organization only when it is met by mental activity—when it is received with interested attention, construed in the light of previous experience, and thus effectively worked into the body of knowledge that guides future behavior.

Learning by observation is difficult to explain without reference to internal organization. Commenting on a series of laboratory experiments on imitation, Bandura and Walters point out that "when a model is provided, patterns of behavior are typically acquired in large segments or in their entirety rather than through a slow, gradual process based on differential reinforcement."[24] A child is capable of copying an admired adult's gait, tone of voice, expressive movements, and specific acts all at once, without being reinforced, like Skinner's pigeon, for a long series of approximations. Furthermore, a number of experiments have shown that reinforcement can be vicarious rather than actual. The degree to which nursery school children copy aggressive behavior shown in a film is influenced by the aggressive character's fate, by whether his behavior yields him rewards or punishments.[25] Observed behavior can be grasped as a whole, not only in its form but in its consequences, a feat of cognitive organization that spares us pain and speeds the growth of social behavior.

The scope of the cognitive field is enormously enlarged by human powers of abstraction and symbolic representation. An immense extension of the horizon results from the capacity to talk about and think about things that are not immediately present. Solomon Asch describes this in the following words:

Men live in a field that extends into a distant past and into a far future; the past and the future are to them present realities to which they must constantly orient themselves; they think in terms of days, seasons, and epochs, of good and bad

24 A. Bandura and R. H. Walters, *Social Learning and Personality Development* (New York: Holt, Rinehart & Winston, Inc., 1963), p. 106.

25 *Ibid.*, chap. 2; A. Bandura, D. Ross, and S. A. Ross, "Vicarious Reinforcement and Imitative Learning," *Journal of Abnormal and Social Psychology*, LXVII (1963), pp. 601–7.

times. . . . Because they can look forward and backward and perceive casual relations, because they can anticipate the consequences of their actions in the future and view their relation to the past, their immediate needs exist in a field of other needs, present and future. Because they consciously relate the past with the future, they are capable of representing their goals to themselves, to aspire to fulfill them, to test them in imagination, and to plan their steps with a purpose.

An integral part of man's extended horizon is the kind of object he becomes to himself. In the same way that he apprehends differentiated objects and their properties he becomes aware of himself as an individual with a specific character and fate; he becomes *self*-conscious. . . . Because he is conscious of himself and capable of reflecting on his experiences, he also takes up an attitude to himself and takes measures to control his own actions and tendencies. The consequence of having a self is that he takes his stand in the world as a person.[26]

To understand behavior in this expanded world of experience it is necessary to employ concepts capable of representing orientation toward the future. The term *proaction,* in contrast to *reaction,* has been proposed by Henry Murray to signify behavior that is steered by the anticipation of future goals and satisfactions. Under the heading of proactive behavior Murray puts such processes as the making of plans, the imagining of future possibilities, and the execution of serial steps that lead to distant goals—steps that are not necessarily rewarding in themselves.[27] But even if we consider much shorter segments of behavior there is reason to give prominence to the future-oriented concept of *plan.* This concept is made central in a theoretical discussion of learning by Miller, Galanter, and Pribram, who show that even so simple an act as hammering a nail into place can be understood only in terms of a plan. The action is initiated and its course guided by a plan to produce a certain result; it ends when that result is attained.[28] In short range or in long range, a great deal of our adaptive behavior is intelligible only as the consequence of flexible and at times elaborate cognitive organization.

This aspect of learning was conspicuous in the examples of the adaptive process used earlier in the chapter. It was especially exemplified in the search for adequate information when trying to deal with stressful situations, and in the planning and rehearsal of competent actions in advance of their critical use. In the diagnosis of disordered behavior it is pertinent to discover, through questioning, the nature of the cognitive field in which the patient is operating. There may be discrepancies between the way the patient sees things and the way the therapist supposes him to see them, and it is the patient's cognitive field that governs his behavior. Psycho-

26 S. E. Asch, *Social Psychology* (Englewood Cliffs, N. J.: Prentice-Hall, Inc., 1952), pp. 120–22.

27 H. A. Murray, "A Conception of Personality," in C. Kluckhohn, H. A. Murray, and D. Schneider, eds., *Personality in Nature, Society, and Culture* (2nd ed.; New York: Alfred Knopf, 1953), chap. 1.

28 G. A. Miller, E. Galanter, and K. H. Pribram, *Plans and the Structure of Behavior* (New York: Holt, Rinehart & Winston, 1960).

logical treatment can be assisted by steps that directly change the cognitive field: information on matters about which the patient is ignorant, advice on how to deal differently with a problem spouse or a problem child, even a certain amount of interpretation of the way the patient has been behaving. Therapeutic change, however, is far from simple. Before seeking treatment, patients may have been deluged with good advice and interpretations of their behavior which have had no effect in alleviating their complaints. They still need help because of inflexibilities built into the adaptive process that produce behavior and feelings highly resistant to change. The nature of these inflexibilities we shall now examine.

RECOVERY FROM FRIGHTENING EXPERIENCES

If human beings were perfectly designed to lead their lives under the civilized conditions they have invented, there would be no occasion for them to study abnormal psychology. Unfortunately we are not perfectly designed, certainly not for these conditions; we are here through having passed the acid test of survival in crude surroundings with only small beginnings of control over our environment. That we are at times so quarrelsome, at times so frightened, at times so unreasonably assertive and self-interested, at times so automatically conformist, suggests emotional endowments appropriate in the distant past but now likely to interfere with the most effective working of the adaptive process. As creatures go, we are remarkably reasonable, but we have obviously not yet proved reasonable enough to get along properly with our fellowmen or to make foresightful use of the earth's resources. Both the course of history and the daily news give us occasion for headshaking.

One of the endowments that can get us into trouble is a powerful response to danger, consisting of the impulse to flight and the emotion of fear. It is not surprising that this life-saving tendency should be prepotent over other forms of activity; once fear is aroused, we can think of nothing else until some sense of security is restored. As we saw in the first chapter, fear eventually came to occupy a central place in the understanding of neurosis. We are prone to neurotic behavior because of characteristic of the fear reaction that tend to freeze the adaptive process and make it in certain respects inflexible. To the extent that psychological treatment deals with changing these inflexibilities, its central task is the reduction of anxieties that are no longer appropriate to real dangers.

Nothing is gained at this point by making a systematic distinction between *anxiety* and *fear*. Many distinctions have been proposed.[29] Roughly speaking, it is customary to use *fear* when the object of danger is clearly perceived, *anxiety* when the object is unknown or vaguely discerned. Such

[29] K. Goldstein, *The Organism* (New York: American Book Co., 1939), pp. 291–307; P. M. Symonds, *The Dynamics of Human Adjustment* (New York: Appleton-Century-Crofts, 1946), pp. 136–38.

distinctions are more linguistic than psychological. Whatever the status of the arousing object, the basic emotional reaction is the same. In the literature on neurosis, *anxiety* is the term most often encountered, but it is used in a sense that includes all degrees of the fear reaction.

The Experience of Panic

Everyone knows what fear feels like when experienced in slight or moderate intensities. Few people, however, can remember the full force of their childhood panics, and fewer still, even of those who have been in great danger, can report the contents of acute anxiety in adult life. If we are to appreciate the role of anxiety in neurosis, we must realize the overwhelming nature of the experience of panic. The following excerpts describe a severe attack in a 36-year-old writer and teacher, William Ellery Leonard. Leonard was standing on a bluff looking out over a quiet lake, having left his walking companion in the woods behind. Painful recent events, the suicide of his wife for which most of the community held him to blame, had been causing mounting apprehension and waves of anxiety. As a small child he had narrowly escaped being run down by a locomotive, and it was this that gave special significance to a train which passed along the opposite shore of the lake and brought the panic to its climax.[30]

I stand looking out over the silent and vacant water, in the blue midday. I feel a sinking loneliness, an uneasy, a weird isolation. I take off my hat; I mop my head; I fan my face. Sinking . . . isolation . . . diffused premonitions of horror. "Charlie" . . . no answer. The minutes pass. "Charlie, Charlie" . . . louder . . . and no answer. I am alone, alone, in the universe. Oh, to be home . . . home. "Charlie." Then on the tracks from behind Eagle Heights and the woods across the lake comes a freight-train, blowing its whistle. Instantaneously diffused premonitions become acute panic. The cabin of that locomotive *feels* right over my head, as if about to engulf me. I am obsessed with a *feeling* as of a big circle, hogshead, cistern-hole, or what not, in air just in front of me. The train *feels* as if it were about to rush over me. In reality it chugs on. I race back and forth on the embankment. I say to myself (and aloud): "It is half a mile across the lake—it can't touch you, it can't; it can't run you down—half a mile across the lake." —And I keep looking to *make sure,* so intensely in contradiction to what the eye sees is the testimony of the *feeling* of that cabin over my head, of that strange huge circle hovering at me. . . .

Meanwhile the freight chugs on toward Middleton. I rush back and forth on the bluffs. "My God, won't that train go; my God, won't that train go away!" I smash a wooden box to pieces, board by board, against my knee to occupy myself against panic. I am intermittently still shrieking, "Charlie, Charlie." I am all the while mad with the terror and despair of being so far from home and parents. I am running around and around in a circle shrieking, when Charlie emerges from the woods.

[30] W. E. Leonard, *The Locomotive God* (New York: Appleton-Century-Crofts, 1927), pp. 304–7.

It should be added that this experience of panic was so intense and un-bearable that it was almost immediately forgotten. Leonard remembered only that he had had some sort of attack on the bluff. The full memory was gradually recovered more than ten years later during states of re-laxation induced to promote recall.

Relearning After Fright

The inflexibilities to which fear gives rise can best be understood by ex-amining what is involved in recovering from frightening experiences. Following a fright, the overwhelming impulse is simply to avoid the whole frightening situation. Perhaps the danger is so great that no other re-sponse is possible. Very often, however, the danger was only momentary (like a motor accident) or is such that, given a second chance, the person could really cope with it perfectly well. Furthermore, many dangers are incurred in the pursuit of vital interests which the person cannot sacrifice. The pilot whose plane crashes cannot afford to give up his livelihood. The active child does not want to surrender his explorations and adventures because on one occasion he has been frightened. Pride may be involved: the person is ashamed to continue being afraid. One has to come to terms with the circumstance of having been frightened. It means *renewed con-tact* with the threat, a new *appraisal* of its threatening character, and *new actions* to cope with it. It means, in short, new learning in the face of a strong motive to avoid new learning.

Obviously this is a precarious learning situation. It can easily happen that the dictates of safety will prevail, in which case avoidance will con-tinue, the appraisal of danger will not be altered, and extinction cannot take place. Several investigators of animal behavior have reported great difficulty in extinguishing responses that were first made to avoid shock or some other fearsome stimulus. In one experiment, for example, rats badly frustrated and punished in a discrimination problem continued indefinitely to make a fixed response, thus never discovering that punish-ment could be avoided by a more varied repertory.[31] In another study, dogs learned in a few trials how to avoid a severely painful electric shock, then continued to make the avoidance response through as many as 650 trials unreinforced by further shocks.[32] These observations give the im-pression that avoidance responses have been built into the animals' be-havior with a firmness that defies the usual modification by new experience. Precisely the same impression is conveyed by human neurotic behavior. William Ellery Leonard, frightened as a child by a locomotive, years later experiences an overwhelming urge to flee from a locomotive that is half

[31] N. R. F. Maier, *Frustration: The Study of Behavior Without a Goal* (New York: McGraw-Hill Book Co., 1949).

[32] R. L. Solomon and L. C. Wynne, "Traumatic Avoidance Learning: The Principles of Anxiety Conservation and Partial Irreversibility," *Psychological Review*, LXI (1954), pp. 353–85.

a mile away across a lake, and becomes panic-stricken when he cannot do so. Bert Whipley as an adult continues to punish himself for the fancied childhood crime of killing his baby brother. Behavior learned in the service of avoiding anxiety seems endowed with peculiar and often quite damaging persistence. Mowrer refers to this as the *neurotic paradox,* "the paradox of behavior which is at one and the same time self-perpetuating and self-defeating."

Common sense holds that a normal, sensible man, or even a beast to the limits of his intelligence, will weigh and balance the consequences of his acts: if the net effect is favorable, the action producing it will be perpetuated; and if the net effect is unfavorable, the action producing it will be inhibited, abandoned. In neurosis, however, one sees actions which have predominantly unfavorable consequences; yet they persist over a period of months, years, or a lifetime. Small wonder, then, that common sense has abjured responsibility in such matters and has assigned them to the realm of the miraculous. . . .[33]

Animal Experiments

The persistence of neurotic behavior seems less miraculous in the light of the unfavorable learning situation created by fright. Safety is involved: it is nip and tuck whether there will be new learning or a renewed attack of anxiety which will make future new learning all the more difficult. The whole problem is beautifully illustrated in Masserman's studies of experimental neurosis in cats, studies that include the process of recovery. We give a few examples.[34]

Masserman's cats were trained to depress a switch that first set off a bell or light signal and then dropped a pellet of food into a food box. When this habit was well learned, the cat was subjected to a sudden air blast at the moment of feeding, this being repeated on several occasions until avoidant behavior became well established. Various procedures were then adopted to study the process of recovery. Three of these are of particular interest here.

1. Solution of the conflict between fear and hunger was *forced* by placing the hungry cat in the cage and slowly pushing it toward the food box by means of a movable partition. All animals reached a state bordering on panic as they approached the scene of former air blasts. Some, upon seeing the food in the box, dove at it desperately and managed to eat; this put them on the way to recovery. Others became wildly panic-stricken, ate nothing, and left the situation in a state far worse than before.

2. Another method, called *retraining,* consisted of petting, stroking, and feeding the cat by hand when it was replaced in the experimental cage. Under this treatment the cat gradually calmed down and by slow degrees

[33] O. H. Mowrer, *Learning Theory and Personality Dynamics* (New York: The Ronald Press Co., 1950), p. 487.

[34] J. H. Masserman, *Principles of Dynamic Psychiatry* (Philadelphia: W. B. Saunders Co., 1946), pp. 135–42.

recovered the possibility of feeding from the box and depressing the switch. It even learned to tolerate the air blast and eat in spite of it. But if the process were rushed and the signals and air blast reintroduced too soon, the cat was thrown back into its anxious condition and further efforts at retraining were less effective. This procedure represents a combination of extinction and counter-conditioning—connecting the cage with pleasurable, relaxing stimulation to counteract the fear response. It is analogous to the treatment of Peter's fear of rabbits, described above.

3. The third method, *spontaneous working-through,* called for putting the hungry cat in the cage and leaving it entirely to its own devices. This procedure illustrates particularly well the fine balance between fear and the hunger driven urge to overcome fear. At first the animal ignored the switch, even refusing to eat a pellet of food placed upon it. As hours went by, however, the cat became increasingly restive and would approach the switch, touching it very gently. The first time the switch was depressed sufficiently to set off the bell or light signal, the cat would hastily retreat and make no effort to secure the pellet in the food box. After a while, growing bolder, it would depress the switch freely and feed without signs of alarm. Reintroduction of the air blast somewhat renewed the avoidant behavior, but in time the animal could learn that even this was harmless. Spontaneous working-through represents what might be called the normal method of getting over a fright—at least the unassisted method—but it can easily go astray if anxiety is too strong, in which case the situation remains permanently frightening.

A Human Example

With respect to relearning after fright, cats and young children are not as far apart as might be supposed. This can be illustrated by the example of a 2½-year-old girl who developed a powerful fear of using the toilet. The fear proved to be specific to the act of defecation; the little girl could urinate freely on the toilet, but in order to avoid having to defecate there she would steal away to some private spot and move her bowels in her pants. It is evident that this fear had not been created by an experimental blast of air, nor could the parents recall any incident in the course of their attempts at training that seemed capable of producing such a result. One of the findings that emerged from the work of Freud and his followers, however, was that young children have fantasies surrounding their excretory processes, and that these fantasies, primitive but powerful, may sometimes be alarming. The toilet is a place where things are washed down and disappear. Very young children have been known to be afraid that they would be flushed down if they sat on the toilet, or to believe that the feces which disappear are a valuable part of themselves. Thus it is possible to believe that this little girl's phobia came into existence not because of an externally initiated fright but because of an imagined danger.

If a fear of this kind appeared in a slightly older child, the first helpful step would be to try to dispel it by information: the toilet is not wide enough to flush down a child, the feces are not precious and we are always making more of them. Many a fear has been abated simply by setting the actualities straight. But it can easily happen that the parents' reassuring explanation has no effect on the avoidant behavior, as if it did not communicate with the child's own conception, which indeed may well be the case when the child's cognitive development is not far advanced. If the parents cannot reorganize the child's cognition so radically that defecating in the toilet becomes a different and safe stimulus, their options in dealing with the phobia become similar to those of Masserman in dealing with the cats. The first or *forced* solution would consist of placing the child forcibly on the toilet and awaiting the desired result. This tended to produce panic in the cats and would predictably make the problem worse. The third solution, *spontaneous working-through,* would call for doing nothing, in the hope that the child would eventually prefer to use the toilet in normal fashion, like her parents and siblings, and overcome her anxiety at her own pace. This entails the risk that nothing will happen, leaving the fear more fixed than ever, and in any event it might take an extremely long time. The second alternative, *retraining,* was therefore the one actually chosen by the parents in this case.

The retraining followed the principle of operant conditioning whereby new behavior is shaped by a program of rewards. To assist the desired result, fruit and liquids were made prominent in the child's dinner menu. Immediately after dinner, before she could go elsewhere, her father instituted daily 20-minute training sessions: while she sat on the toilet he sat next to her, entertaining her and telling her stories. Periodically she was urged to push hard and make gas in the toilet, and whenever she succeeded in making gas she received a small M & M candy and a lot of praise. This first step proved easy, so that after a few sessions she was regularly winning several M & M's each evening. However, she soon reached a critical point when the urge to defecate was so strong that she could no longer make gas without also having a movement. This frightened her and she held it in, often with great effort, all her father's exhortations and other tactics notwithstanding. Finally, he spanked her once, crisply but not very painfully, which resulted in an immediate bowel movement. This triumph earned her four large M & M's, abundant praise and affection, and the summoning of the rest of the family to share in the celebration. The procedure was repeated the next two times the urge was obviously strong, the surprise of the spank serving to relax the taut sphincter. Thereafter no spanking was necessary, resistance to pushing diminished, and she began to look forward to the evening sessions.

Soon she hit upon the idea of naming her feces as they arrived. Depending on size, they were first called Papa Bear, Mama Bear, and Baby Bear, but the idea of naming suggested wider possibilities. Before long, usually in an expansive mood, she began announcing in advance the characters to be produced, so that in the end all the local pet animals, all her relatives, and most of the neighbors had the honor of being on her guest list.

Overcoming the phobia took a long time. Treating anxiety is not a place to look for quick victories. Nearly a month of regular sessions occurred before the child went directly to the bathroom without hesitation. Only after eight weeks had her movements become so regular as to eliminate accidents. At this point candy rewards could be discontinued; social recognition sufficed to maintain the new behavior. Even so, there was a brief setback at ten weeks, with an unexplained accident in her pants and obvious renewed fear of the toilet. This time, however, three evening sessions with candy and guest lists were enough to subdue the anxiety, and thereafter the little girl had no further trouble.

Defensive Obstacles to Relearning

The difficulty of relearning after fright, as we have seen, comes from the circumstance that avoiding a dangerous situation is incompatible with finding out that it may not really have been dangerous. The cats in Masserman's experiment were capable of tolerating a blast of air while feeding, but their response to the first few experiences of the bizarre event prevented their finding this out. As long as they cowered at the far end of the cage there were no more blasts and no fresh appraisal of consequences. These cats, of course, were captive. Denied to them were the usual feline options of running away, climbing a tree, and permanently looking elsewhere for their food. The little girl was also in a sense captive. She was not allowed to use her chosen avoidant response, which was to move her bowels in her pants and thus make the toilet unnecessary. When fright is experienced and an avoidant response works it is a sound principle of survival, likewise a sound principle of learning, to keep on using that response on future occasions of danger. Pressure is required—the cats boxed in and made hungry, the child pushed toward socialized behavior—in order to counteract the seemingly sensible plan of keeping away from what scares you.

The plan is not as sensible as it seems. Our evolutionary heritage has equipped us to frighten too easily. Fear is an extremely unpleasant tension, and behavior that reduces it is likely to be powerfully reinforced. This is all very well in a dangerous world, but for a child in a family it often happens that events are not as dangerous as they seem. Toilets will not swallow you up, parental anger will not lead to injury and death, scolding does not imply abandonment, belittlement does not signify being forever cast out. Avoidant responses can be learned to any of these things, but it is evident that the child's development will be seriously crippled if he tries for total avoidance of parental anger, scoldings, and belittlements.

Apace with cognitive growth, these human stimuli require discrimination, an increasing knowledge of the extent of their effects under different circumstances, so that responses can be modulated and made more appropriate. But this implies continual reappraisal, and it is just this step that cannot be taken if avoidance has the right of way. Mowrer's expression, the *neurotic paradox,* refers to just such an outcome. The patient does not do what is good for him; for instance, he fails to stand up for his rights and allows himself to be pushed into a disadvantageous position. This can happen when self-assertion has remained indiscriminately associated with anxiety, so that the patient's need for anxiety-reduction overcomes his desire for his rights.

The adaptive process is thus capable of being crippled and made inflexible when the avoidance of anxiety demands too much of it. The result can be visible in the behavior of animals and young children, but in the human cognitive field there are counterparts of avoidance that manifest themselves less obviously in overt behavior—what might be called mental maneuvers for controlling anxiety. The yield from Freud's painstaking investigations of the recollections and free associations of neurotic patients included much information about this form of defensiveness, conceptualized as defense mechanisms.

DEFENSE MECHANISMS

The concept of defense was introduced by Freud in some of his earliest writings. Before long he substituted repression, which became for a while one of the keystones of his thinking. Later he reversed his position to the extent of reinstating defense as the general concept, with repression standing as one of the defense mechanisms alongside of projection, reaction formation. regression, turning against the self, and some four or five others. Anna Freud, in her book on defense mechanisms, takes the same general position, but recognizes that repression is entitled to a somewhat special status. She points out, for instance, that other defenses are very often combined with repression, and she entertains the possibility that "other methods have only to complete what repression has left undone." Repression, in her view, is entitled to a unique position because of the amount it seems capable of accomplishing and because of its damaging consequences.[35] Following this line of thought, we shall classify repression as a *primary* defensive process. Other defense mechanisms will take their place as secondary adjustments serving to fortify the primary defense.

Repression

Freud arrived at the concept of repression, as we have seen, in his early work with hysterical patients, when stubborn resistances to free association

[35] A. Freud, *The Ego and the Mechanisms of Defence* (London: Hogarth Press, Ltd., 1937), pp. 52–55.

gave way and events of great emotional importance were restored to awareness. It seemed evident that the resistance was not simply to talking about the events; the patient was truly unable to recall them until a deeper resistance had been overcome. This suggested that the original forgetting of the incidents was of an unusual character. Rather than fading out because they were unimportant, the memories had been pushed out because they were especially important but also acutely painful. In one of his definitions Freud said that "the essence of repression lies simply in turning something away, and keeping it at a distance, from the conscious." [36] In a later work, when he had given anxiety a central position in his theory of neurosis, he described repression in more clearly defensive language: memories, images, and impulses were excluded from consciousness when they tended to arouse unmanageable anxiety.[37] It was not Freud's idea that this sort of thing occurred all the time. He did not imply a general law that we tend to forget the unpleasant. A whole series of laboratory experiments designed to test the concept of repression, but perforce using relatively innocuous situations, did not at all come to grips with the problem.[38] Repression occurred only in situations that involved grave anxiety; moreover, it occurred most frequently and importantly in early childhood, when cognitive development was still at a primitive level. In addition, Freud showed by his usage that the most likely candidates for repression were wishes arising from instinctual urges which if expressed would lead to disastrous consequences. Not just specific situations, but all images connected with sexual or aggressive urges might have to be kept at a distance from consciousness if linked to anxiety.

Repression can thus be described as a primitive mental maneuver for avoiding anxiety. Danger-inviting impulses are excluded from awareness and thus also from overt behavior. This form of avoidance shares the shortcoming of overt avoidant behavior: it makes no provision for renewed encounters with danger and thus blocks the process of extinction. The dangers of early childhood are not simply isolated happenings, like witnessing an accident or nearly being run down by a locomotive. Whether we emphasize parental behavior or, like Freud, the impulses in the child that evoke parental behavior, the typical dangers are recurrent. The parents will again be punishing or rejective, the child will again have impulses toward naughtiness and self-assertion. It is vital for development that the alleged dangers in these interactions be reappraised and discovered to be to some extent manageable. Repression prevents this from happening. This

36 S. Freud, "Repression" (1915), in *Standard Edition of Freud's Works* (London: Hogarth Press, 1957), XIV, p. 147.

37 S. Freud, "Inhibition, Symptom, and Anxiety" (1926), in *Standard Edition of Freud's Works* (London: Hogarth Press, 1959), XX. For a scholarly analysis of Freud's not always consistent usage, see P. Madison, *Freud's Concept of Repression and Defense* (Minneapolis: University of Minnesota Press, 1961), especially chap. 1.

38 A critical survey of this experimental work is given by D. W. MacKinnon and W. F. Dukes, "Repression," in L. Postman, ed., *Psychology in the Making: Histories of Selected Research Problems* (New York: Alfred A. Knopf, 1962), chap. 11.

makes it, in Anna Freud's words, "the most dangerous mechanism. . . . The withdrawal of consciousness from whole tracts of instinctual and affective life may destroy the integrity of the personality for good and all." [39]

Repression of erotic impulses in childhood was judged by Freud to have especially long-lasting consequences. In his treatment of neurotic patients in the late nineteenth century, he repeatedly discovered great resistance to recalling any episodes, past or present, in which the patients had experienced sexual inclinations and fantasies. Childhood erotic tendencies, which in those days were often visited by violent disapproval, had been repressed only too well, so that in adult life even the most legitimate sexual feelings evoked anxiety sufficient to keep them out of awareness. But the sexual urge, of course, was not thereby eliminated, and the result was a state of tension in which its energies sought indirect outlets in dreams, disguised fantasies, and other symbolic manifestations. Later in the history of psychoanalysis, childhood aggression received similar emphasis: patients resisted the recall of anything that meant they had been angry, but their associations were filled with symbolic evidences of destructiveness. Repression was historically an essential aspect of the concept of unconscious motivation which has had such a large influence on contemporary thought.

Projection

Close inspection of other defense mechanisms shows that they regularly presuppose an element of repression. In other words, they consist of a defensive inhibition followed by secondary adjustments that serve to make the inhibition more secure. These secondary adjustments are part of the repertory of normal behavior. They become defense mechanisms only through their linkage with repression, which causes them to have the characteristics of excess and rigidity.

Projection is usually defined in some such way as the attribution of one's own thoughts, feelings, and impulses to other persons or objects in the outside world. Its basis lies in the fact that our own feelings tend to influence our perception of the world. Murray performed an experiment in which children were given two opportunities to judge the emotions being expressed in a series of photographs. Between the first and second judging, the children played a scary game of "murder," with the result that they found the faces markedly more malicious when seen the second time.[40] Sears used a method in which subjects rated themselves and each other on various personality traits. When subjects lacked insight into their own traits, they tended to give unduly high ratings on these traits to their acquaintances.[41] It is out of such raw materials—such motivationally colored

[39] A. Freud, *op. cit.*, p. 54.

[40] H. A. Murray, "The Effect of Fear upon Estimates of the Maliciousness of Other Personalities," *Journal of Social Psychology,* IV (1933), pp. 310–29.

[41] R. R. Sears, "Experimental Studies of Projection: I. Attribution of Traits," *Journal of Social Psychology,* VII (1936), pp. 151–63. This and Murray's study are reprinted in S. S. Tomkins, ed., *Contemporary Psychopathology* (Cambridge: Harvard University Press, 1943), chaps. 41 and 42.

perceptions—that the projective process is constructed. It becomes a defense when the recognition of one's own feeling entails anxiety and evokes protective inhibition. Projection then has so much work to do in maintaining the defense that it may reach the pathological proportions of a loss of reality testing.

Other Mechanisms

Projection can serve as a model for all the secondary defensive adjustments. We shall briefly mention some of the more important ones. Among these is the mechanism of *reaction formation*. This means the development of tendencies or traits that are the very opposite of tendencies we do not like in ourselves. To take a simple example, suppose a man comes to realize that he is very dependent and, feeling a bit ashamed of this discovery, resolves to be scrupulously self-sufficient in all respects. He may carry his independence somewhat to a fault, but it does not reach the proportions of desperate defense. Normal development often proceeds in just this way. Suppose, however, that his reaction formation had occurred in childhood, and had resulted from acute shock, say a sudden belittling rejection by the people on whom he depended, so that he repressed his own dependent impulses. Now the reaction formation serves the purpose of a daily denial of a threat still felt to be intolerable. He has to be self-sufficient in order to avoid fear, and his reaction formation will probably be extremely rigid. He will be one of those people who cannot even ask for a match.

Two further defensive processes are shown in the case of a young woman briefly described by Anna Freud.[42] The central problem was a jealous hatred of her mother, which, however, she dared not express lest she lose her mother's love. The first protective maneuver was a *displacement* of the negative feelings onto another woman. "Her mother continued to be a love-object, but from that time on there was always in the girl's life a second important person whom she hated violently." This hatred entailed less anxiety than hating her mother, but it still caused her suffering. Next she *turned inward* the aggression that was felt toward others. "The child tortured herself with self-accusations and feelings of inferiority, and did everything she could to put herself at a disadvantage and injure her interests, always surrendering her own wishes to the demands made on her by others." That this could be a solution shows the force of her anxiety lest her mother desert her, but after a while it too became unbearable. To relieve herself of such a burden of guilt, she resorted to projection and began to imagine herself the innocent victim of hate and persecution by others.

One further group of secondary defensive adjustments deserves mention because of its central importance in obsessional neurosis. To the group as a whole we can give the name *intellectualization,* referring to the tendency to take emotional conflicts into the sphere of intellect, divest

[42] A. Freud, *op. cit.,* pp. 47–50.

them of affective and personal meanings, and work on them as problems
in metaphysics, religion, political theory, etc. The word *rationalization*
has been applied to this type of defense, though usually not in its original
meaning of "making rational" but in the debased sense of "making excuses." Special forms of intellectualization have been called *isolation* and
undoing. The details of these processes can best be left to the later chapter
in which we study obsessional neurosis. At this point it is sufficient to
notice again that we are dealing with a normal adjustive process which
becomes a rigid mechanism only by association with a primary defensive
inhibition. The whole attempt to understand the world means capturing
it in the realm of intellect and making allowance for possible distortions
that spring from emotions and personal meanings. Only when intellectualization is preceded by the repression of threatening personal tendencies
and is prostituted in the service of concealing such tendencies can we call
it a pathological mechanism.

PROTECTIVELY BURDENED PERSONALITIES

What happens to the development of personality when strong conditioned avoidance responses are not extinguished? What happens when
"whole tracts of instinctual and affective life" are repressed and their
alleged dangers not properly reappraised? Obviously these unchanged
residues of childhood anxiety will be handicaps, but not enough so to
prevent growth from going forward. Their effect can best be described
as imposing a pattern of restrictions on development: nothing must be
done, no situations must be entered, that tend to arouse the original
anxiety. Growth can take place so long as it meets this limiting condition.

The effect can be clarified by taking the simpler example of a physical
handicap. Suppose that a child is afflicted with infantile paralysis and
recovers with substantial loss of locomotion. His whole development must
now take place in such a way as to allow for his limitation. In building
up competence and seeking the esteem of others, he will be unable to
use athletic achievement. Social adjustment must be accomplished without
his being able to dance or to drive a car. Some interests will be closed to
him because they demand prolonged standing. This particular defect does
not preclude a well-rounded and even distinguished career, but it nevertheless illustrates with simple clarity the effect of a limitation on the
process of development.

When there are important unresolved childhood anxieties, development
must similarly proceed so as to take account of a limitation. The defense
of warding off all memories of childhood danger situations, and all impulses that might recreate those dangers, may serve well enough at the
time, but it leaves the person in a vulnerable position. New situations
may forcibly remind him of the danger. His aggressive, sexual, or other
tendencies are bound to be aroused, and he has to build up his life in such

a way as to forestall the arousal of what is repressed. Taking as an example a child who senses real danger of losing parental affection, we can say that this child has got to develop in such a way that he will never, so far as possible, offend his parents. The surest way to do this is to subordinate his own wishes to those of his parents. As his world expands outside the family circle, his fear of rejection may be so generalized that he becomes vulnerable to additional threats. Rejection by his teachers, by his playmates and friends, later by his wife and employers and business associates, has the power to call up severe anxiety. He has to please them all. Any coolness, inconsideration, or belittlement becomes a thing to be avoided at all costs. His whole pattern of traits and tendencies is colored by this necessity. It sounds like a bad pun, but we might truly say that an infantile paralysis grips any tendencies in himself that might get him into a situation strongly reminiscent of the danger experiences in childhood. One can see the far-reaching limitation that affects his human relationships. He must never offend others, and they must always treat him well. The many traits and tendencies that he develops in order to bring about this result constitute in the end a sort of protective organization.

Every person grows up amidst limitations that tend to restrict the full flowering of personality. Many of these limiting conditions are actual and contemporary; we are today more sharply aware than ever before of the crippling effects of poverty and cultural deprivation. Our concern here, however, is with the special kind of limitation imposed by unresolved anxieties dating from early life that no longer correspond to actual dangers but that nevertheless impose themselves on adaptive behavior. Development can be seriously handicapped by obsolete conceptions of what is dangerous. We shall refer to the result as a *protectively burdened personality*—a pattern of personality that is burdened by having to maintain excessive protection against obsolete dangers.

In the literature, as indeed in earlier editions of this book, the protectively burdened pattern was described as the "neurotic" personality. This expression is still in common use, just as the adjective "neurotic" is still in wide use to describe an indiscriminate array of human peculiarities. But the term *neurosis* is needed for a more technical purpose, to designate a specific category of disordered personal behavior characterized by symptoms of certain kinds: the hysterical disorders, the phobias, and the obsessional disorders described in the historical introduction. There is nothing about so-called "neurotic" personalities that is not better indicated by calling them protectively burdened. Furthermore, the "neurotic" label suggests a closer and more inevitable relation that we have a right to presuppose between protectively burdened personalities and symptom neuroses. Fussing about terms may seem trivial, but in this case a careless use of "neurotic" is likely to obscure, as it has done in the past, the far from simple relation between a protectively burdened pattern of life and the outbreak of a symptom neurosis.

It is convenient to distinguish two kinds of constituents that make up the neurotic protective organization. In the first place there is usually evidence of *overdriven strivings:* certain goals in life and certain types of relationship with other people are pursued with a relentless intensity that betrays underlying anxiety. In the second place there are evidences of *protective traits* which serve to prevent the person from being stimulated in ways that would arouse his particular anxieties. If we conceive that both of these constituents have the purpose of making the person feel safe, the overdriven strivings accomplish this goal by an active seeking of symbols of security, whereas the protective traits achieve it by resistive exclusion of symbols of threat. The distinction does not imply, of course, that the two methods are mutually exclusive. We would expect to find them both at work in any well-developed protective organization.

Overdriven Striving

An overdriven striving should not be conceived of as wholly different in character from a normal or healthy striving. It is rather an exaggeration and rigidifying of an ordinary way of behaving. Nowhere is it more important than here to bear in mind the continuity between healthy and disordered behavior, and nowhere in our study is one more likely to have attacks of the "medical students' disease" described in the last chapter. Overdriven strivings are exaggerations of certain tendencies that are wellnigh universal in human behavior. They become exaggerated in the service of defense against anxiety.

These points can be made clearer by examining Karen Horney's broad classification of overdriven strivings, which she called "neurotic trends." [43] Believing that the more important anxieties have to do with relationships with people, she proposed that overdriven strivings should be grouped under the three headings: moving toward people, moving against people, and moving away from people. Moving toward people, also called a compliant trend, implies that the person feels a certain helplessness and tries to win the affection and esteem of others so that he can lean on them for support. Moving against people, also called an aggressive trend, means that the individual strives to surpass and defeat others, making himself strong enough to disregard their possible hostility. Moving away from people, detaching oneself from others and building up a more or less independent existence, has the effect of avoiding whatever threats may be contained in human relationships. Clearly these purposes are not in themselves abnormal. There are times when each one of the three is fully appropriate and highly desirable. Overdriven strivings are thus not brand new ways of behaving toward other people. They are exaggerated and rigidified versions of strivings that appear in everyone.

Normal people differ a great deal in the balance they establish among

[43] K. Horney, *Our Inner Conflicts: A Constructive Theory of Neurosis* (New York: W. W. Norton & Co., Inc., 1945), chaps. 2–5.

moving toward, moving against, and moving away from others. We would expect different patterns to result from different kinds of parental encouragement and from the social opportunities afforded by the neighborhood and the available groups. We would expect differences of temperament and ability to be influential. A considerable overemphasis on one or another trend is not inconsistent with good adjustment. We cannot call one of these strivings overdriven, then, unless in addition to having been favored by temperamental and environmental influences it is being seriously overworked in the interests of defense.

Criteria for Judging a Striving To Be Overdriven

There are three criteria by which defensive overworking can be recognized. (1) The first is indiscriminateness: a given attitude is assumed not only when appropriate but even in the most unsuitable circumstances. A person who craves affection and approval, for instance, must have it from everyone, even from bus drivers and store clerks who are of no real importance in his life. He may even require it from his children and pet animals. The trend has a compulsive intensity that does not permit it to be adapted to circumstances. (2) Another attribute of overdriven strivings is their insatiable character. The person seems never satisfied; he does not reach repose, but always needs a little more of the same kind of satisfaction. The man who moves toward people wishes that even a very congenial evening had been a little more congenial. The man who seeks triumphs wishes that even a signal success had been a little more glorious. The man who manages to separate himself from all close ties wishes that he could also be free from minor personal contacts. (3) The blocking of overdriven strivings creates disproportionate frustration, probably with signs of anxiety. If aggressive competitiveness, for instance, is serving a protective purpose, to be beaten in some competitive enterprise will throw the person into a state of desperation. For him the defeat means vital threat.

Need for Affection

That a striving to obtain affection could be overdriven was early recognized by Freud and his followers. The overdriven need for affection has been best described by Horney.[44] To have affection is certainly a good thing in itself. Such a striving, therefore, qualifies as overdriven only when it meets the three criteria just described: it is indiscriminately compulsive, it is insatiable, and when frustrated it gives rise to disproportionate despair if not outright anxiety. This intensity comes from the fact that the striving for affection is also serving as a striving for security. The person must have affection not only because it is good in itself but also in order to feel safe.

44 K. Horney, *The Neurotic Personality of Our Time* (New York: W. W. Norton & Co., Inc., 1937), chaps. 6–8.

Horney pointed out that the individual who seeks his security in this particular trend keeps working himself unwittingly into situations of conflict. He is in great need of love from others, but he is more or less incapable of giving anything in return. The original difficulty contained a repression of hostility in the interest of retaining parental affection. Lurking within him, but kept very firmly out of his awareness, is a resentful distrust of other people. Emergence of this hostility into consciousness would constitute a basic threat, calling up the original danger situations in which anger had to be repressed lest it offend the parents. But in every relationship from which he seeks to gain affection, this dangerous hostility is stimulated. He needs too much affection; he cannot tolerate the other person's being interested in some third person, and he cannot bear to be the object of any demands or criticisms. In other words, he expects a degree of blind devotion that he is highly unlikely to obtain from anyone, and he is therefore continually frustrated. He continues, however, to think of himself as loving the other person. Unable to become aware of the mixture of hostility in his feelings, he can never allow for them, outgrow them, perceive his deficiencies as a giver of love, and achieve in his relationships a reasonable balance of give and take. "In short," says Horney, "for a person who is driven by his basic anxiety and consequently, as a means of protection, reaches out for affection, the chances of getting this so-much-desired affection are anything but favorable. The very situation that creates the need interferes with its gratification." [45]

Because rejection was originally a danger signal, the protectively burdened person is highly sensitized to it. As a result he overacts in indiscriminate fashion to anything that may be considered a rebuff. If an appointment has to be changed, or if he is kept waiting a few minutes, his equilibrium will be badly upset. Going further, he may anticipate rejection wherever there is the least possibility of receiving it. "A person may, for example, ask a question angrily, because in his mind he has already anticipated a refusal." [46] It will be hard for him to take the initiative in seeking affection because he is so acutely sensitive to the possibility of being rejected. This is typical of the self-defeating conflicts that arise out of overdriven strivings. He must have affection, but at the same time he hardly dares seek it. If he is lucky enough to find an affectionate relationship, he will almost inevitably wreck it by his sensitiveness, demandingness, and failure to give anything in return. Under these circumstances it is obvious that the whole development of personality will be badly impoverished. The vital problems of friendship and love can never be made to come out right.[47]

45 *Ibid.,* p. 114.
46 *Ibid.,* p. 136.
47 The subtle ramifications of a neurotic overdriven striving can be fully appreciated only by reading a detailed individual case. In her book, *Self-Analysis* (New York: W. W. Norton & Co., Inc., 1942), Horney gives such a case, centering around a young woman's "morbid dependency" on a man. See pp. 47–52, 75–88, 190–246.

Needs for Superiority and Power

Both Adler and Horney were shrewd observers of overdriven strivings for power. In a culture which places a high value upon competitive success the goals of power and prestige are attractive to many people. Striving for these goals might be described as already culturally overdriven in many sectors of American society. This makes it easy for power and prestige to become symbols of security and to be chosen as the objects of overdriven strivings on the part of people whose basic anxieties have to do with inferiority and humiliation. When the need for power is overdriven by childhood anxieties it soon exhibits the familiar qualities of indiscriminateness and insatiability. There is a constant search for new worlds to conquer. The person is an autocrat in his office, takes a commanding part in business conferences, tells his wife and children how things are to be done at home, tries to raise the biggest dahlias of anyone in town, dominates the discussions at the parent–teacher association, and can be heard as the loudest and most frequent speaker even in casual gatherings. At the same time he is tremendously vulnerable to any obstruction of his need for power and prestige. It is then that anxiety creeps up on him, perhaps even to the extent that he looks for psychiatric rescue.

Implicit in the overdriven striving for power is the belief that everyone is hostile. Life is a competitive struggle, and the only way to avoid going under is to be on top. Along with the desire to have control over others there is usually an interest in recognition, in having one's power affirmed and acclaimed by others as an additional guarantee that they will not dare to be openly hostile. The intense concentration on the relationship of power, and the distrust of others which it both implies and engenders, crowds out other relationships and thus impoverishes the person's life in other dimensions. It will be hard for a husband, for instance, to think of his wife in any other way than as a person to be dominated to satisfy his own needs or as a person who will enhance his social position and economic prospects.

Protective Traits

In the course of growth a person builds up an array of traits which facilitate his adaptation to the world around him. He develops characteristic and relatively fixed ways of doing things. Gestures, for example, may be typically bold and sweeping in one person, small and hesitant in another; speech may be loud or soft, fast or slow; desks may be kept tidy or messy; work habits may be regular and persistent or spasmodic but intense. Such traits, like strivings, can be lured into the service of defense against anxiety. In addition to their convenience in general adjustment they can participate in a protective action against possible arousals of extinguished childhood threats. A well-developed series of protective traits can serve as a police patrol against the outbreak of anxiety.

This possibility is unusually well illustrated in the speech and surface traits of a psychoanalytic patient described by Reich, who introduced the striking expression *character armor* to describe protective behavior of this kind.[48] When first seen, the patient created an immediate impression of refined arrogance. His facial expression was haughty, his speech quiet and measured, his gait slow and restrained. He lay down on the couch in a composed fashion, his legs neatly crossed. Even when discussing painful recollections he maintained his evenness and dignity; in fact, these traits became more conspicuous when he approached topics presumably of high emotional importance. "One day tears came and his voice began to choke; nevertheless, the manner in which he put the handkerchief to his eyes was composed and dignified." [49] This patient was suffering from severe neurotic difficulties, and he knew that his cure depended upon a free expression of his feelings during his hours with the psychoanalyst; yet he was so strongly armored with habitual protective traits that for many weeks it was impossible for him to do anything but resist his own cure.

The services performed by protective traits become clearer when, as in the course of psychoanalytic treatment, they can be slowly broken down. When this occurred in Reich's patient, a second layer of character armor came to light. Beneath the courtly surface his attitude toward other people, including the physician, was highly critical, hostile, and derisive. He took delight in the misfortunes of others and was constantly on the alert for their shortcomings. Yet this, too, was in the nature of a defense, for it concealed very sharp and painful feelings of inferiority. A person who carries a burden of inferiority feelings can ease his load somewhat by discovering equal or greater weaknesses in others, but to express such disparagement openly would invite dangerous reprisals and counter-criticisms. By his dignified protective traits the patient managed to look politely contemptuous while at the same time preventing any real arousal of his own disturbing feelings of hostility and inferiority.

Protecting the Self-Picture

Traits do not usually stand as separate items in a person's repertory of behavior. They form an organized pattern, and to some extent they participate in the image or picture that each person has of himself. Most people are inclined to cherish and defend a favorable self-picture. To do so is by no means an abnormal phenomenon. Gardner Murphy describes as follows the human tendency to paint the self-picture in the best possible colors.[50]

Both perception and valuation of the self are complicated processes that take a long time to crystallize. But the result of all these developments is that like the

[48] W. Reich, *Character-Analysis*, trans. T. P. Wolfe (3rd ed.; New York: Orgone Institute Press, 1949), especially chaps. 4 and 9.

[49] *Ibid.*, p. 181.

[50] G. Murphy, *Personality: A Biosocial Approach to Origins and Structure* (New York: Harper & Row, 1947), pp. 529–30.

childhood rag doll, the self, scarred and tattered as it is, becomes a deeply treasured possession; for most of humanity, at least in competitive cultures, it is probably the central value of existence. However poor, confused, and inconsistent it is, it is central, and it must be defended not only against outer attacks but against a clear perception of its unloveliness.

When there is a heavy burden of anxiety, the self-picture becomes involved in the protective organization. Its defense becomes an acute issue. The patient cannot tolerate any blemish on this outermost layer of his armor, even in matters that seem remote from his central anxieties. Like other processes captured for defensive ends, the self-picture becomes rigid and cannot be modified in the light of new experiences. It also becomes, as Horney has shown, much more a creation of fantasy designed to put overdriven strivings and protective traits in a noble and glorious light.[51] Reich's patient provides a perfect illustration. One day the analyst, commenting on his aristocratic surface, called his behavior "lordly," and this led to the discovery that he cherished a very real image of himself as an English lord. This fantasy was based on a mere rumor that his grandmother had had an affair with an English lord and that his mother was half English; it included the notion that he was not the true son of his father, a small Jewish merchant in the German town where they lived. These fantasies had been elaborated consciously during the patient's childhood, and at puberty he had been able to translate them into actual protective behavior by imitating a very lordly and immaculate school teacher. The necessity of defense against obsolete dangers caused the patient to preserve and act upon this juvenile self-picture well into adult life.

The Costs of Protective Organization

The protectively burdened personality operates at a cost. To keep the unextinguished anxieties of childhood from being aroused with disruptive force, it may be necessary to maintain an unusually exacting self-picture, to restrict one's behavior by means of rigid protective traits, and to overdrive certain natural strivings that have become entangled in the web of defense. These ways of behaving have all been unduly strengthened because they have reduced anxiety and increased a feeling of security. But they tend to impair the flexibility of the adaptive process. They restrict the degrees of freedom available to the person in dealing with problems both of change and of persistence. Finding the right vocation, for instance, may be hampered by a pretentious self-picture that demands nothing less than top status, by protective traits that make for coldness and lack of involvement, or by an overdriven striving that necessitates pleasing everyone by one's choice. When protective burdens are heavy, a disproportionate part of a person's choices is dictated by defense and a disproportionate part of his energies is devoted to security. When the problem is seen in this way it

---

51 Horney, *Our Inner Conflicts, op. cit.*, chap. 6.

becomes legitimate to speak of certain consequences or costs of the protective organization. Most common among these are disturbing tensions and chronic dissatisfaction.

Disturbing Tensions

Even a generally successful protective organization is not likely to be uniformly effective. The situations that arouse anxiety cannot always be avoided, and the urges that are felt to be dangerous cannot be entirely held in check. The result may be restless tension or spells of irritation and frustration that do not seem sensibly related to existing circumstances. Furthermore, overt anxieties of a diffuse kind may from time to time disturb the protectively burdened person. Without really reaching panic, he may find himself bothered by fears of accident, fears of death, fears of going insane. The fear of going insane bears no relation to any real likelihood of doing so; it expresses in a symbolic way the person's dread of the confusion and anxiety that would overwhelm him if the protective organization were to break down. Tensions of this kind are likely to disturb sleep and may produce dreams that are full of trouble and foreboding. Sound sleep requires true relaxation, and protective organization cannot always work so effectively as to produce this boon.

Another source of unease is the tendency of overdriven strivings to create conflict. Because of their compulsive intensity they block and exclude other tendencies and even conflict with one another. As Horney pointed out in her discussion of moving toward, against, and away from people, if any one of these attitudes is lifted to compulsive intensity it more or less wrecks the chances of using the other two. Yet because the other two represent more or less universal human needs, it is not really possible to subordinate them completely. A person whose anxiety in human relationships can be held in check only by an overdriven striving for seclusive withdrawal does not thereby obliterate his wishes for affection, esteem, and glory. These wishes needle him from time to time; he cannot feel satisfied with the limitations imposed by his chief defense. If a second trend is also reinforced in the interests of defense, the situation is still more difficult. He feels anxious if he cannot have seclusion and he feels anxious if he cannot have competitive success. The very intensity and indiscriminateness of overdriven strivings make it almost impossible to harmonize them with each other and with the rest of the person's tendencies. The resulting conflict tends to be chronic because one at least of the parties is an insatiable overdriven striving that forms part of the whole protective system.

Chronic Dissatisfaction

Protective burdens tend to wax and wane, depending on the extent to which the obsolete anxieties are stimulated by external circumstances. But running through these ups and downs there is apt to be a thread of chronic dissatisfaction and hopelessness. Overdriven strivings tend to be insatiable, so that even when circumstances permit them a large amount of gratification they do not lead to enjoyment and repose. Because they are serving in the cause of defense as well as enjoyment, and because the childhood dangers remain unextinguished, the goal of satisfaction can never quite be reached. Furthermore, it is possible that natural desires, perhaps even imperious bodily cravings, become blocked by overdriven strivings. The original fear might have nothing to do with sex, for example, but adequate sexual satisfaction would be blocked if an overdriven tendency toward seclusive withdrawal became dominant in the person's life.

The eternally unsatisfied need for security and the other needs that may become blocked in protective organization are capable of creating a feeling that life is not rewarding or fully satisfactory. If the situation does not improve in the course of time, the person may become increasingly discouraged. He may change his job, move to another place, get married or divorced, but these alterations may well fail to relieve him of the costs of protective organization. Even if he reaches the conclusion that the obstacles to happiness are within himself, he may still see no way to change or remove these obstacles. Thus it can happen that a person seeks psychological treatment not because of symptoms, not because he has a disease, but because he wants to find a way out of the discouragement and futility that result from his protectively burdened pattern of life.

Comparison with Normal Organization

Before leaving this topic, it is well to remind ourselves of the continuity between normal and abnormal behavior. Tension and dissatisfaction are part of the human lot; no one can go through life without considerable visitations by these unpleasant states. Obviously one cannot always be contented, buoyant, and optimistic, especially in a time like the present when we are beset by formidable real problems. It is hard to draw any line between disturbing tensions or chronic dissatisfactions that are suitable responses to a real situation and those that result from the exactions of a protective organization. Such a judgment has to rest on some criterion of appropriateness. Responses that are being made to the obsolete dangers of childhood would be expected to show less appropriateness to the current reality, more rigidity, more compulsiveness, more occurrence both in season and out of season. Ideally, we should be able to respond in an appropriate way to each situation as it arises, perceiving both what is old and what is new about it and adapting our behavior accordingly. No one ever reaches such a standard—probably no one ever gets through childhood without residues of defense against its anxieties—hence the concept of the protectively burdened personality is a relative rather than an absolute one. It is most applicable when the pattern of living is clearly restricted by overdriven strivings and protective traits and when there are clear costs in the form of disturbing tension and chronic dissatisfaction, these being not appropriate to the actual circumstances and therefore presumably referable to childhood anxieties and defenses.

VARIETIES OF UNADAPTIVE OUTCOME

It should not be deduced from the foregoing account that the adaptive process produces a disordered result only because of obsolete anxieties and the protections against them. This is one way in which human lives can become miserable and ineffective, but it is not the only way. It is possible to imagine a person whose protective burdens are so light as to make little difference but who nevertheless struggles painfully with feelings of rootlessness, alienation from family, disappointment, lack of sustained interests—feelings of being adrift without sense of direction. Or it may be that childhood experience will have led a person, without conspicuous repression, into a path of delinquency that results in constantly increasing conflict with society and its law-enforcing agents. It is not always necessary to assume early anxieties and primitive defenses behind the two common disorders of middle childhood seen in community mental health centers, the child who is disturbingly aggressive and inconsiderate, and the child who does not live up to expectations in schoolwork. The protectively burdened personality has been stressed in this chapter because it has been carefully studied, especially by those using the protracted psychoanalytic method, and because anxiety is widely recognized as a common and important ingredient of disordered personal behavior. But there are other ways in which the course of experience produces unworkable patterns of living. In order to understand these problems better, we shall now turn to a more detailed account of the growth and integration of personality.

SUGGESTIONS FOR FURTHER READING

In Lois Murphy's *The Widening World of Childhood* (New York, Basic Books, Inc., 1962) will be found a mine of information about children's powers and methods of coping with the environment. Strategies of adaptation are discussed by R. W. White in *The Enterprise of Living: Growth and Organization in Personality* (New York, Holt, Rinehart & Winston, Inc., 1972), Ch. 15.

Principles of learning are staple fare in most elementary textbooks of psychology. The original classic on operant conditioning is B. F. Skinner's *Science and Human Behavior* (New York, The Macmillan Co., 1953). Imitation and vicarious learning are added to simpler pictures of conditioning by A. Bandura and R. H. Walters in *Social Learning and Personality Development* (New York, Holt, Rinehart & Winston, Inc., 1963). The relation of learning theory to personality is well summarized in Ch. 11 of C. S. Hall and G. Lindzey's *Theories of Personality* (2nd ed., New York, John Wiley & Sons, Inc., 1968). Its value in clinical work is discerningly set forth by D. E. Peterson, *The Clinical Study of Social Behavior* (New York, Appleton-Century-Crofts, 1968).

A small book by W. E. Fischer, *Theories of Anxiety* (New York, Harper & Row, 1970) gives a broad survey of historical and contemporary views of anxiety. The classic work on defense mechanisms is Anna Freud's *The Ego and the Mechanisms of Defence* (London, Hogarth Press, Ltd., 1937). Two works by Karen Horney, *The Neurotic Personality of Our Time* (1937) and *Our Inner Conflicts: A Constructive Theory of Neurosis* (1945) retain their value as expositions of the protectively burdened personality; both were published by W. W. Norton & Co., Inc. There is considerable similarity between Horney and Alfred Adler, who described the equivalent of "neurotic trends" under the heading of "character traits" and whose concept of "style of life" is close to that of protective organization. Adler's *Understanding Human Nature* (Philadelphia, Chilton Co., 1927) satisfactorily describes his outlook. Of all students of personality Gardner Murphy has been most explicit in relating human defensive tactics to the protection and enhancement of the self-picture; see his *Personality: A Biosocial Approach to Organization and Structure* (New York, Harper & Row, 1947).

4

Development of

Personality:

Early Childhood

The growth of personality is a continuous process. It does not pass through sharply separated steps, divide itself into neat chapters, and move toward maturity one aspect at a time. But we cannot describe it lucidly by talking about everything at once, and there is justification for the idea that the most important problems have their critical periods at different times of life. In this and the following chapter we shall therefore follow a rough chronology of significant developmental problems, considering them as phases of growth that are normally traversed without mishap but that sometimes give rise to lasting difficulties of living.

Development is theoretically reducible to basic laws of learning and motivation, but it would be misleading to base our thinking on the analogy of simple learning situations or of problem solving when all the elements are clearly in view. The main problems endure for long periods; they are also somewhat subtle and pervasive in their impact. The child learns slowly, by successive attempts, to deal with his environment. He learns unwittingly, with but little cognitive grasp of the true nature and scope of the problems. He learns with the limited understanding and experience that is appropriate to his age, which means that he may apprehend situations in a way that differs greatly from an adult view. We often speak metaphorically of the child's "first collisions" with the major problems of growth, but we must remember that his early patterns of behavior are wrought over weeks and months, not produced once and for all in well-defined critical situations.

Response to the major problems of development in childhood may be highly successful, but it may fall short of success in various ways. The solutions achieved in the early years, good or bad, exert an influence over the subsequent course of development. According to some workers they determine basic traits of character which stay with us throughout life. For our present purpose a more limited claim is sufficient: when poorly adjustive solutions are reached in childhood there will be difficulty in meeting similar situations in later years. It is worth noticing, furthermore, that the concept of regression implies a reanimation of earlier ways of behaving. When later obstacles bring out regression, the importance of childhood patterns of behavior is likely to be much increased. These points will become clearer as we examine the main growth problems in detail.

DEPENDENCE AND DEPRIVATION

Childhood Dependence

The child begins life in a state of virtually complete helplessness. Discomforts are removed and gratifications provided almost entirely through the actions of those who are taking care of him. Outside of restless activity and the very important act of crying there is not much that the small baby can do about his troubles. For the first six months or more it is fair to say that his world revolves around hunger and its satisfaction. In a healthy baby hunger is the outstanding pain and its relief the outstanding satisfaction. The lips, mouth, and tongue are among the most sensitive regions of his body. Around the act of feeding cluster a great many secondary sources of pleasure: stimulation of the mouth; the pleasurable act of sucking and swallowing; being picked up and rocked and cuddled.

The child's earliest experiences of want and of gratification thus take place in connection with feeding. They also take place in connection with the mother, or whoever is regularly taking care of the child. The mother becomes the first important human object in the baby's world. Her behavior toward him has a lot to do with establishing a feeling of security. Depending on her attitude, the baby's world can become a place where you get what you need within a comfortingly short time and in good measure, or at the other extreme a place where you have to cry yourself black in the face for niggardly rewards.

Different cultures vary greatly in their attitudes toward the infant and his needs. In some parts of the world there is great leniency and indulgence at this stage; in others it is believed that early deprivations harden the infant for the difficulties that lie ahead. Our own society has undergone a decided change of attitude during the last sixty years. In 1914 the United States Children's Bureau first published a bulletin called *Infant Care.* Since then there have been frequent revised editions which tell a remarkable story of changing fashion in expert opinion.[1] As regards the first year of life the trend is clearly in the direction of greater indulgence. In the earlier editions the baby was to be efficiently fed according to a regular schedule, regardless of his own indications of hunger, and weaning was to be accomplished with firmness and decision. Today it is recommended that babies be fed when they cry ("self-demand schedule"), that they be held and cuddled and played with, and that they be weaned gradually so that the feeling of deprivation will never become unbearable. Behind this recommendation lies the idea that dependence, ultimately a liability to be outgrown, is at first a thing to be encouraged and strengthened. Helplessness is the natural condition of the infant; he should be made happy in it and given gratification.

Naturally one wonders whether or not this attitude toward infancy is just another turn of the wheel of fashion. Probably not; the present outlook is based upon considerably better observation than has ever before been available. In a long series of studies at a children's hospital Ribble has collected evidence that infants prosper better when they are given plentiful "mothering"; that is, when they are held, cuddled, patted, rocked, and given a surplus of loving attention beyond the strict necessities of daily care. "Mothering" has a favorable effect even on physical development: it promotes stronger respiration, firmer sucking and swallowing, better digestion. One might almost suppose that the infant's nervous system needed the extra priming that comes from the stimulation involved in "mothering." However this may be, Ribble's observations include cases of severe disorder, physical and emotional, when "mothering" was for some reason interrupted without provision of a substitute who could act and feel much like the real mother.[2] These observations have been sustained by other workers, particularly by Spitz, who made a comparative study of children reared in a foundling home and children reared in the nursery of a penal institution. At the foundling home one adult took care of each group of seven or more children, obviously with little time to spare. The nursery children, in contrast, were in the care of their own mothers, who, being inmates of the institution, had plenty of time to spare. The differences between the less "mothered" and the more "mothered" children were striking. Rate of mortality and susceptibility to illness were much higher in the foundling home; motor and language development were much retarded: signs of distress, such as screaming and odd repetitive behavior, were much more

1 Martha Wolfenstein, "Trends in Infant Care," *American Journal of Orthopsychiatry,* XXIII (1953), pp. 120–30.

2 Margaret A. Ribble, *The Rights of Infants* (New York: Columbia University Press, 1943); "Disorganizing Factors of Infant Personality," *American Journal of Psychiatry,* XCVIII (1941), pp. 459–63.

common. Spitz gives the name "hospitalism" to the pattern of defects observed so frequently among the foundling children, and he points out the many ways in which close interchange between mother and child fosters the growth of security and confidence.[3] In another study Spitz has shown that children of six months or so who are abruptly separated from their mothers sometimes develop a depressed and lethargic condition that is difficult to cure.[4]

Experimental Studies of Deprivation

At first these finding were greeted with a certain amount of skepticism. Critics thought they detected a note of unscientific sentimentality in the emphasis on mothering. Yet it is a matter of common knowledge that cats mother their kittens and dogs their puppies with ministrations such as licking that go far beyond the mere provision of nourishment. Experiments were begun with various species of animals to test the consequences of early deprivations. Puppies were reared in an artificial environment that restricted both sensory input and motor activity.[5] Chickens were separated from the flock and raised in social isolation.[6] Chimpanzees were deprived of visual experience by being kept in darkness for the first three months of life.[7] These and many other experiments, summaries of which are available,[8] showed that an insufficient exercise of natural capacities at the beginning of life would often injure the later use of these capacities. In some cases it was even shown that portions of the nervous system did not develop properly when no demands were made upon them in the form of stimulation.[9]

Particularly pertinent are the experiments made by Harlow in which baby monkeys were provided with mechanical mother surrogates.[10] The artificial mothers, made of cloth or of wire, provided abundant milk through a conveniently placed nipple, emitted bodily warmth, and were set in positions suitable for clinging; in all these respects, they were designed to be good mothers. Harlow was able to show, in the first place, that cling-

---

[3] R. A. Spitz, "Hospitalism: An Inquiry into the Genesis of Psychiatric Conditions in Early Childhood," *Psychoanalytic Study of the Child*, I (1945), pp. 53–74.

[4] R. A. Spitz, "Anaclitic Depression," *Psychoanalytic Study of the Child*, II (1946), pp. 313–42.

[5] W. R. Thompson and W. Heron, "The Effect of Early Restriction on Activity in Dogs," *Journal of Comparative and Physiological Psychology*, XLVII (1954), pp. 77–82.

[6] A. Baron, G. B. Kish, and J. J. Antonitis, "Effects of Early and Late Social Isolation on Aggregative Behavior in the Domestic Chicken," *Journal of Genetic Psychology*, C (1962), pp. 355–60.

[7] A. H. Riesen, "Arrested Vision," *Scientific American*, CLXXXIII (1960), pp. 16–19.

[8] D. W. Fiske and S. R. Maddi, *The Functions of Varied Experience* (Homewood, Ill.: The Dorsey Press, Inc., 1961), chaps. 3, 4.

[9] A. H. Riesen, "Effects of Stimulus Deprivation on the Development and Atrophy of the Visual Sensory System," *American Journal of Orthopsychiatry*, XXX (1960), pp. 23–36.

[10] H. F. Harlow, "The Nature of Love," *American Psychologist*, XIII (1958), pp. 673–85.

ing and contact are of great importance for satisfaction and security. To a baby monkey a cloth mother is far more acceptable than one made of wire. In the second place, observing the animals' development into adulthood, he showed that the mechanically reared monkeys remained almost comletely unresponsive to other monkeys, so much so that very few of the females produced offspring and only one was observed to try to nurse her young. The central deprivation to which they had been exposed, that of interaction with a living member of the species, resulted in a permanent incapacity for social response.[11] But in further experiments it was possible to show that the mother was not the sole source of this social development. Motherless infants raised in groups of four, or raised in separate cages but allowed a daily period of play together, showed normal social and sexual development, permitting the conclusion that "opportunity for infant–infant interaction may compensate for lack of mothering."[12] Some form of early warm and friendly contact seems essential to keep the monkey from developing into a surly, suspicious adult.

Adaptive and Maladaptive Possibilities

The animal experiments and the observations of Ribble and Spitz have to do with deprivations very early in life. In the human case this means the first year or so, when the most serious deprivations are likely to be bound up with the quality of maternal care. In a study by Provence and Lipton a comparison was made between 75 family-raised infants and 75 infants reared in an institution, two groups that were observably different in the amount of maternal care and stimulation they received.[13] The largest differences were in relations with people. During the first year of life the institutional infants developed a bland amiability toward adults but little sign of strong feeling; "the tenuousness of emotional ties was striking," and there were "no signs of increasing attachment to a particular person." Interactive games such as "pat-a-cake" and "peek-a-boo" were developed hardly at all, and language growth was retarded. There was even some lag in motor and postural development and in the zestfulness of exploratory play with inanimate objects. In a follow-up study of 14 of the institutional children who were later adopted, the authors noticed "dramatic gains" in development after a year or two of family life. But they detected "residual impairments of mild to severe degree in capacity for forming emotional relationships" and in certain other aspects of growth, including impulse control and imaginative play. Residual effects of this kind can

11 H. F. Harlow and M. K. Harlow, "A Study of Animal Affection," *Journal of the American Museum of Natural History,* LXX (1961), No. 10.

12 H. F. Harlow and M. K. Harlow, "Social Deprivation in Monkeys," *Scientific American,* CCVII (1962), pp. 2–10.

13 S. Provence and R. C. Lipton, *Infants in Institutions* (New York: International Universities Press, 1962).

be detected much later, according to a study by Goldfarb.[14] Fifteen children brought up in institutions to the age of 3 were carefully matched with fifteen whose early years had been spent in the more favorable climate of foster homes. The children were examined and tested at about 12 years of age, by which time it might be supposed that the consequences of their early upbringing would be obliterated. The two groups proved to be significantly different in several respects: the institutional children were behind on various tests of intellectual ability, their speech was less well developed, they were rated lower on friendly contact with the examining adults, and in an experimental game they more often broke the rules without signs of guilt.

These and similar findings support the idea that an insufficiency of maternal care is detrimental to development during the early years. The effects can be partially compensated if later conditions are more favorable, but at least in some cases there is enduring weakness especially in human attachments if these tendencies have not been stimulated early in life. According to Erikson the words "trust" and "mistrust" are best suited to express what infants learn at this stage of life.

For the first component of a healthy personality I nominate a sense of *basic trust,* which I think is an attitude toward oneself and the world derived from the experience of the first year of life. By "trust" I mean what is commonly implied in reasonable trustfulness as far as others are concerned and a simple sense of trustworthiness as far as oneself is concerned. . . . The firm establishment of enduring patterns for the balance of basic trust over basic mistrust is the first task of budding personality and therefore first of all a task for maternal care.[15]

Development of a sense of trust is an adaptive outcome, forming a basis for later affectionate relations and for self-respect. When the outcome is mistrust, children appear unapproachable and unresponsive to adult helpfulness. Familiar to workers with delinquents is the young person who cannot accept their warm and well-meant interest, rejects help, and tries to be totally self-sufficient, beholden to no one.[16] Yet it is at least sometimes true that behind this surliness, with its feeling of isolation, there is a lingering hunger for the provision of one's wants by others. This outcome was illustrated in the case of Bert Whipley, who could organize delinquent joyrides and execute solitary feats of burglary but who felt himself an outcast and secretly yearned for the provided life of a prison inmate. The independence that follows from basic mistrust is of a different quality from self-reliance founded on trust.

14 W. Goldfarb, "Emotional and Intellectual Consequences of Psychologic Deprivation in Infancy: A Revaluation," in P. H. Hoch and J. Zubin, *Psychopathology of Childhood* (New York: Grune & Stratton, Inc., 1955), pp. 105–19.

15 E. H. Erikson, "Identity and the Life Cycle," *Psychological Issues,* I (1959), No. 1, pp. 55–56.

16 A. Bandura and R. H. Walters, *Adolescent Aggression* (New York: The Ronald Press Co., 1959).

There is thus a good deal of reason to believe that infants should be encouraged in their dependence. The value of mothering, considered as the provision of nourishment, care, stimulation, and the comforts of bodily contact, has more than a sentimental basis. At the same time nobody can doubt that infantile dependence carried over into later life is a severe handicap to adaptation. The case of Benton Child, who expected everyone to take care of him, illustrates the destructive effect of too liberal provision of one's wants. But indulgence should not be regarded as a major hazard during the first year of life. The behavior to which we attach the word "spoiled" is not likely to be a simple consequence of early excessive gratification. If in every child there are dependent inclinations, there are also urges, coming to full force a little later, that make for independence. These urges lead to a good balance between dependence and self-reliance if they are not blunted by continuing parental indulgence or overprotection. Benton Child's adult dependence probably results less from early gratifications than from a combination of his own low energy and a continuing parental policy of spoiling that undercut the experience of self-initiated achievement.

EARLY GROWTH OF COMPETENCE

Exploratory Play

Careful observation shows that even from the beginning there is another side to the infant besides passive dependence. Very early there are signs of spontaneous activity, taking forms such as following and fixating with the eyes or exploring and experimenting with the hands. The nature of this activity becomes clearer toward the middle of the first year, when manipulation becomes an absorbing occupation. By the time he is a year old, the child may be spending as much as five or six hours of his waking day in exploratory play which is not related to the hungers, pains, and anxieties that still require the mother's ministrations. He develops his repertory of actions by manipulating all objects within reach; he tests in playful babbling his power to make various kinds of sounds; and he learns about the properties of his own body by successive attempts to sit up, crawl, and take steps in an upright position. This kind of activity appears to be self-rewarding, and its biological function seems to lie in learning about the properties of things and what can be done with them—in other words, in becoming competent to deal with the environment.[17]

The zest for active exploration presently invades the sphere of the mother's ministrations. It is discovered that water can be dribbled from the wet washcloth onto the floor, that milk will spread in an interesting

[17] R. W. White, "Motivation Reconsidered: The Concept of Competence," *Psychological Review*, LXVI (1959), pp. 297–333.

way over a flat surface, that utensils produce a gratifying series of sounds when banged or thrown from the high chair. David Levy selects what he calls "the battle of the spoon" to illustrate the nature of such actions and their relation to being mothered.[18] One day the child seizes the spoon and undertakes to load it and steer it into his mouth. As the spoon is likely at first to miss its target and to reach some other part of the face upside down, the maneuver is far from resulting in a more efficient intake of food; but the child may continue it insistently, resisting his mother's attempts to recapture her maternal role. Levy points out that the behavior cannot be classed as aggressive; it is not done to annoy the mother, however surely it may produce this result when she thinks about cleaning up. It is part of an urge to do things autonomously, to control the environment as much as possible through one's own initiative.

It is important to notice that this movement on the child's part toward competent independence will often conflict with his mother's desire to minister to his wants. The most important reward for the child lies in the feeling of efficacy that comes from producing an intended result through his own expended effort. This is not something the mother can bestow. The point is made clear in an intensive observational study of mothers and their babies.[19] Certain mothers were happiest during the infant's first six or eight months, when his helplessness called forth and deeply gratified their desires to provide. The emergence of autonomous activity frustrated them and irritated them, as in the following example.

It was both reported by Mrs. A. and observed that Billy was more difficult to dress. He did not "cooperate" in this as he had before and it looked as if his mother's usual ways of restraining him by distraction or touch could no longer control his drive to activity. When his mother tried to hold him on her lap, he tried to get down. He was reaching out and scratching at her neck or face in a provocative way and she was scolding him with a new sharpness in her tone. He also was making persistent grabs for the spoon during feeding and she found this annoying.

In contrast, other mothers felt themselves somewhat imprisoned during the early months and joyfully welcomed the signs of autonomy, seeing in them both proof of the child's normality and a harbinger of greater freedom for themselves.

During the second and third years of life the child emerges rapidly from his early condition of helplessness. One of the major advances is learning to walk. This makes it possible to explore the house and yard, to venture into the street, and sometimes to escape from parental supervision. Particularly important is the increased mastery of speech, permitting the child to name objects, form concepts, issue commands, grasp more fully the

18 D. M. Levy, "Oppositional Syndromes and Oppositional Behavior," in Hoch and Zubin, *op. cit.*, pp. 204–26.

19 R. W. Coleman, E. Kris, and S. Provence, "The Study of Variations of Early Parental Attitudes," *Psychoanalytic Study of the Child*, VIII (1953), pp. 20–47.

things that are said to him. In due course he discovers the powerful properties of the word "no" and begins to test the extent to which he can resist and control the human part of his environment. These experiments on his part usher in a time that has often been called the period of two-year-old negativism. When the child begins to issue or resist commands, there is a direct confrontation of wills, a clear-cut problem of who is going to prevail. The child, as Stern expressed it, now "realizes himself as a living entity, a one complete center of power; he wishes to affirm himself, his existence, his importance, and to increase it." [20] The parents, too, have something to affirm, partly in the child's interest, partly in the service of their own pride. Today we regard as harsh the old-fashioned advice that at this point in life it is necessary to "break the child's will" and "show him who is boss," but no experienced parent will suppose it possible to give the child's urges toward competence a totally free rein.

Competence and Self-Esteem

Acts such as reaching and grasping, pulling and crawling, standing up and walking without support are done intentionally and, to the extent that they are successful, they yield a feeling of efficacy. The baby trying to pick up a ball finds himself either competent or incompetent to do so. The child trying to walk a few feet from one support to another knows whether he succeeds or fails. In his attempts to walk the child is apt to have an appreciative audience which gives him a large social reward, but he does not require approval in order to know that he has succeeded. Mind and muscles have been pitted against an unknown but unmistakable force that tries to pull him to the floor, and they have proved competent to triumph over this force.

The importance of such experiences for a child can easily be imagined by thinking of the value we attach to analogous happenings in adult life. A sharp difference of feeling is evident between the fisherman's accounts of the one he caught and the one that got away. Similarly contrasting experiences visit the woodsman who fells one tree exactly where he intended it to fall but sends another a little wrong so that it crushes valuable young growth. Backing a car into a parking space with one deft swoop is a different matter from attaining the same end after several awkward attempts. When an act comes out as intended, the person not only achieves a specific goal but senses himself as having been able or *competent* to achieve it. He has been efficacious in carrying out his plan, and this contributes to his *sense of competence*, which is an important ingredient of *self-esteem*.

There can be no doubt that self-esteem is tremendously affected by the income of esteem that is received from others. There can also be no doubt that a good many kinds of excellence have to be socially defined before the

[20] W. Stern, *Psychology of Early Childhood* (New York: Holt, Rinehart & Winston, Inc., 1930), p. 492.

child can have any way of judging success or failure. It is a mistake, never-theless, to suppose that self-esteem is wholly a matter of esteem income—that no coin can ever be minted within. The esteem we feel for another person is not whimsically bestowed; it is related to what he has actually done. He, too, can often judge what he has actually done. In addition, he can ap-preciate the full discrepancy, if such there be, between what he did and what he intended to do. The experience of efficacy, based on the effective-ness of one's own activity in dealing with the environment, is a vital root of self-esteem. Silverberg puts the matter strongly:

> Throughout life self-esteem has these two sources: an inner source, the degree of effectiveness of one's own activity; and an external source, the opinions of others about oneself. Both are important, but the former is the steadier and more de-pendable one. Unhappy and insecure is the man who, lacking an adequate inner source for self-esteem, must depend for this almost wholly upon external sources. It is the condition seen by the psychotherapist almost universally among his patients.[21]

The contribution of competence to self-esteem can be seen most clearly when mind and muscles are pitted directly against inanimate obstacles. The issue is unmistakable in such problems as whether one can climb a cliff, drive a tractor so as to plough a field, fix up an ancient jalopy so that it will again speed over the road. It is equally proper, however, to speak of *social competence*, even though the many purposes and subtle nature of human interactions tend to obscure one's discernment of effective activity. Our intentions as regards other people are not always clearly conscious, and the approval or disapproval we encounter often seems to supply the only criterion of success. It is true, nevertheless, that there are tremendous in-dividual differences in social competence, ranging from the person who feels unable to influence others at all to the person in whom a habit of command has become second nature. Feelings of social competence are presumably built up out of experiences in which one has found it possible to produce intended effects in other people: to make them respond to you, help you, serve you, love you, accept your love, learn from you. Com-petence has the same meaning, if not the same ease of observation, in social interaction as it has in dealing with natural forces.[22]

The Inferiority Complex

The most common deviation from the satisfactory growth of competence and self-esteem is a pattern of behavior and feeling historically called an

[21] W. V. Silverberg, *Childhood Experience and Personal Destiny* (New York: Springer Publishing Co., Inc., 1952), p. 29. "Activity" has been substituted for the author's word "aggression," a procedure which he sanctions (p. 18, footnote).

[22] For a comparative case study of two people differing in social competence, see R. W. White, *The Enterprise of Living: Growth and Organization in Personality* (New York: Holt, Rinehart & Winston, Inc., 1972), chap. 2.

inferiority complex. For the sake of a rounded picture we should include the opposite deviation, the development of a boundless overconfidence and conceit, which presumably might result from a combination of high natural abilities, opportunities, and exceptional social rewards. Possibly some such people are successfully absorbed in occupations that make a virtue of overconfidence, but more commonly they cannot escape being trimmed down by circumstances and by other people, often with a painful loss of zest and with real suffering to themselves. Extreme conceit persisting in adult life is usually to be regarded not as a simple overconfidence but as a compensatory tendency or reaction formation against dangerous feelings of worthlessness. It acts more like an overdriven striving than an overrewarded one.

As we saw in the first chapter, the concept of the *inferiority complex* was introduced by Alfred Adler, who made it central in his theory of neurosis if not in development as a whole. Adler's concept is so valuable that we should not ruin it by indiscriminate use. Everyone is inferior in a great many ways. Most people do not mind this in the least. Their self-esteem is dependent on only a small range of excellencies. Failure in many areas may mean little if it is compensated by success in just one area. As Allport observes, "Only in terms of ego-psychology can we account for such fluid compensation. Mental health and happiness . . . depends upon the *person* finding some area of success *somewhere*. The *ego* must be satisfied." [23] Much the same point was made by William James with memorable illustrations.

I, who for the time have staked my all on being a psychologist, am mortified if others know much more psychology than I. But I am content to wallow in the grossest ignorance of Greek. My deficiencies there give me no sense of personal humiliation at all. Had I "pretensions" to be a linguist, it would have been just the reverse. So we have the paradox of a man shamed to death because he is only the second pugilist or the second oarsman in the world. That he is able to beat the whole population of the globe minus one is nothing; he has "pitted" himself to beat that one; and as long as he doesn't do that nothing else counts. He is to his own regard as if he were not, indeed he *is* not.

Yonder puny fellow, however, whom everyone can beat, suffers no chagrin about it, for he has long ago abandoned the attempt to "carry that line," as the merchants say, of self at all. With no attempt, there can be no failure; with no failure, no humiliation. So our self-feeling in this world depends entirely on what we *back* ourselves to be and do.[24]

In a relatively integrated personality, which enjoys reasonable esteem somewhere, feelings of inferiority will be absent or transient and of small importance. It is justifiable to speak of an inferiority *complex* only when

23 G. W. Allport, "The Ego in Contemporary Psychology," *Psychological Review*, L (1943), pp. 451–78.

24 W. James, *The Principles of Psychology* (New York: Holt, Rinehart & Winston, Inc., 1890), Vol. I, p. 310.

the person continually makes unfavorable comparisons between himself and others, covering far more lines of excellence than any one individual could hope to carry. If such a person hears someone tell a story well, he wishes he might possess this excellence and laments his inferiority as a storyteller. The next moment someone else entertains with a song, and he feels miserable that he cannot do likewise. Then card playing starts, and he has a chance to deplore his mediocrity at cards. A single evening will provide him with an opportunity to feel inferior in a dozen ways. But it is not these dozen inferiorities that trouble him. It is rather the overall fact that he does not have sufficient competence anywhere to form a nucleus of self-esteem and satisfy the self as a whole. If he could find some real excellence of his own, he would be willing to forego distinction in storytelling, singing, and cards.

In our clinical introduction we studied two cases in which feelings of inferiority were close to the heart of the problem. Walter Lilly at 15 exhibited an extreme degree of social incompetence, as shown in his inability to resist demands for money, his anxiety at speaking to a fellow worker who did not speak first, and his unmodulated tactics of screaming for what he wanted at home. His social incompetence—his feeling that initiative was impossible and other people simply could not be influenced—was not compensated by satisfactions elsewhere, such as might have been provided by good academic achievement or special interests and skills. As a result he felt worthless to a degree that on occasion caused him severe anxiety. Benton Child at 40 likewise exhibited a lack of social initiative and of compensating excellence in other spheres. His consequent low self-esteem invaded his sexual life, interfered with his potency, and led him to the curious hypothesis that his children were not his own. An additional example of pervasive inferiority feelings is provided by Bert Whipley's deprecation of the commendable products of his craftsmanship.

Adler traced the origin of the inferiority complex to early family life and to belittlement of the small child's attempts to be efficacious. Too strenuous a put-down program by parents or by older siblings make it difficult for a child to feel that his desires can have appreciable influence. Yet the sense of competence can also be blunted, as we have seen, by too quick provision for every need and too complete protection from every difficulty. During the second and third years, when we urge toward competence begins to blossom, a child most needs an environment in which his initiatives toward physical and social objects produce real effects and in which his legitimate accomplishments command respect. Growth of a sense of competence would seem to be best supported when a child's initiatives are allowed to go forward as far as may be practicable and safe, when he is coached in doing things he wants to learn to do, and when whatever he does well is appreciated and admired. Respect requires a generous spirit, free from envy, competitiveness, and hostility—a spirit not easy to maintain through the wear and tear of dealing with children. Other circumstances contribute to inferiority feelings: low energy, handicaps, poor health, limited capacity, prejudice, a deprived environment. But their deleterious effects can be at least somewhat mitigated if the home atmosphere makes it possible for the child's initiatives sometimes to prevail and be respected.

DISCIPLINE AND SELF-CONTROL

During the second and third years the child increasingly runs afoul of the law. At this stage of life the law is represented by parental expectations and discipline. The child discovers that there are many restrictions upon his freedom. He must not order his parents around or be rude to visitors. There are also things that he is supposed to do, such as sharing his toys with other children, finishing up the food on his plate, putting away the playthings that a busy day has scattered all over the house and yard. The world proves to be full of strange moral hazards, and one must learn how to accommodate one's desires to the often mysterious requirements of the social order.

One of the fields of battle is toilet training. The parents demand a change in what must seem like the eminently satisfactory plan of relieving the bowels whenever one feels so inclined. Dollard and Miller, analyzing the requisite learning in stimulus–response terms, point out the inherent difficulty in the problem that is set for the child. The naturally strong connection between pressure in the bowel and the response of evacuation must be weakened so that a whole series of new responses can be inserted: at first, calling parents; later, going to the bathroom, unbuttoning, sitting on the toilet. This learning must be accomplished, moreover, at a time when the child is still far from adept at the use of verbal cues and can have little understanding of the purpose of the training.[25] The parents, if trained in their own childhoods to feel disgust toward evacuation and its products, may find it hard to conduct the educative program with patient tolerance. It is not surprising, therefore, that strong emotions are often aroused on both sides and that the adjustive solution reached upon this issue sometimes sets a precedent for later responses to discipline and authority.

The problem of discipline should not be seen simply as a struggle between the child's desires and the parents' restrictions. What the parents require is not a complete suppression of the child's impulses; they ask rather that he guide his impulses into socially acceptable channels. As Murray has pointed out, cultural and parental prescriptions can usually be described as "time-place-mode-object formulas which are allowed or insisted upon for the expression of individual needs."

25 J. Dollard and N. E. Miller, *Personality and Psychotherapy* (New York: McGraw-Hill Book Co., 1950), pp. 136–38.

A child is allowed to play during the day but not at night (time). He may defecate in the toilet but not on the floor (place). He may push other children but not hit them with a mallet (mode). He may ask his father but not a stranger in the street for money (object). No need has to be inhibited permanently. If an individual is of the right age and chooses the permitted time, the permitted place, the permitted mode and the permitted object, he can objectify any one of his needs.[26]

The child is being asked to pattern his behavior in ways which may seem at first difficult and frustrating, but the culture does not require the complete surrender of fundamental desires. In the end it is no hardship to use the toilet if one is available or to give up playing in the street if there are other places to play.

These considerations are necessary in order to grasp the true nature of the growth problem when discipline and control are the issues. There is almost always something for the child to do if he can become able and willing to do it. The crucial point here is his willingness: can he learn to pattern his behavior in expected ways without damage to his sense of competence and hence to self-esteem? Erikson points out that meeting a parental requirement can be a matter not of surrender but of pride in accomplishment.[27] But such an outcome is not easy when the child is a mere toddler and the source of constraint is the very adults upon whom his security depends. At first, the two most available responses are helpless yielding or angry resistance. Neither of these responses leads to feelings of pride. Anxious surrender to discipline means the simultaneous sacrifice of one's desires and one's self-direction. Impassioned resistance salvages pride only for a moment and cannot long be maintained against the force of parental disapproval. A sense of competence can be built only upon willing acceptance of what is required.

Adaptive and Maladaptive Possibilities

To this solution of the problem the child brings definite assets. He may seem resistant to constraint, but on the whole he would like to grow up. There can be very substantial rewards in becoming able to meet adult requirements. Self-esteem is increased when obedience to regulations carries with it a feeling of achievement. Becoming socialized entails sacrifices, but it is not entirely a bad bargain. Parents can make the bargain more favorable by permitting the child's initiative to have a part in the learning, and by greeting his achievements with expressions of true respect. The first point is partly a question of timing. It is obviously foolish to expect successful bowel training before the neuromuscular system is sufficiently mature to control the sphincters, or to expect the child to be quiet before he is

[26] H. A. Murray, *Explorations in Personality* (Fair Lawn, N. J.: Oxford University Press, 1938), p. 136.
[27] Erikson, *op. cit.*, pp. 198–99.

capable of sustained inhibition. The timely moment for a piece of training is one at which the child himself initiates appropriate acts. In a recent study of child development, made in a situation where many of the parents believed in a maximum of permissiveness, it was observed that the children often insisted upon feeding themselves, dressing themselves, and using the toilet in adult fashion before the parents had taken steps toward training.[28] The second point is a question of the parents' attitude. It goes without saying that they do better when they are patient and allow for relapses and slowness in the learning process. But the crucial feature would again seem to be respect: the possibility of taking generous pleasure in the child's accomplishments and giving expression to affectionate esteem.

Maladjustive solutions occur when the learning process deviates too widely from the course just described. Departures can occur in two directions. There can be spoiling, in this case generally called *indulgence,* when the parents make too few serious demands—when they do not have the firmness to require that the child pick up his toys or inhibit his aggressiveness, for example. Permissiveness can be carried to the point at which adult friends hate to call at the house, knowing that the atmosphere will be too child-centered for serious conversation. There are even instances in which a family has found it difficult to rent living quarters, so disastrous has been the effect of childhood self-expression on real estate previously occupied. The effect of this laxity is to delay the growth of control: the child is given too little incentive to master impulses, and remains longer their victim. The problem of meeting discipline is thus postponed, leaving it to teachers and playmates who can hardly be expected to deal with it patiently. Probably the more serious maladjustments spring from the opposite course, which here takes the form of *coercion.* When discipline is brought about by coercive methods the results are not apt to be satisfactory. Whether the child is tricked into obedience by clever parental devices, ridiculed and made to feel shame, or threatened with painful and terrifying punishments, he will have a sense of being forced and there will be little willingness in his response. He is left with no middle ground between a hopeless fight and unconditional surrender.

The effects of coercive discipline can be conveniently grouped into two patterns. One solution can best be described as *anxious conformity.* Desires and resentments are suppressed, and the person becomes a model of cleanliness, goodness, sharing, and all-around propriety. If these traits persist into later life they may create an outwardly good adjustment to society and its requirements, but behavior will lack spontaneity and confidence, and the person will be ill-prepared when the environment begins to make conflicting demands upon him. The other solution is an enduring

28 S. Chess, A. Thomas, and H. Birch, "Characteristics of the Individual Child's Behavioral Responses to the Environment," *American Journal of Orthopsychiatry,* XXIX (1959), pp. 791–802.

resentment against demands, an essentially negative attitude even when overt resistance is impossible. In extreme cases the person might become a professional nonconformist, doing everything in a way that obviously differs from social expectations. More commonly he might conform in outward behavior but not with any sense of willingness or warmth; his latent rebellion is then apt to leak out in irritating ways like missing appointments or keeping everyone waiting. This guerrilla warfare against demands, often unwitting and compulsive, has little resemblance to nonconformity and criticism of the social order arrived at later through mature judgment. Indeed, it may interfere with such purposes: the person cannot brook the demands made upon him to participate in organized political action.

Guilt and the Concept of Superego

Freud originally developed the concept of the superego to explain the irrational guilt feelings and self-punishments observed in the free associations of neurotic patients. He noticed that the patients felt forced by norms which were not consistent with their current values. Irrational guilt feelings often occur in normal people. A student from a strict background may decide to adopt the standards of more liberal college companions, only to discover that when he does so he feels as if he were committing crimes and deserving punishment. In neurotic patients such feelings can be of crippling severity. The moral compulsions and scruples seem completely autonomous or *ego-alien:* "The individual seems to have no say in the matter of the self-imposed rules; whether he likes them, whether he believes in their value, enters as little in the picture as his capacity to apply them with discrimination." [29]

The reason for the power and irrationality of guilt feelings lies in the circumstances of their origin. They go back to infancy; Freud said to the fourth and fifth years, but later workers with children trace them to the earliest parental restrictions. Conscience, Freud observed, is not present from the very beginning.

Small children are notoriously amoral. They have no internal inhibitions against their pleasure-seeking impulses. The role which the superego undertakes later in life is at first played by an external power, by parental authority. The influence of the parents dominates the child by granting proofs of affection and by threats of punishment which to the child mean loss of love and which must also be feared on their own account. . . . It is only later that the secondary situation arises, which we are far too ready to regard as the normal state of affairs; the external restrictions are introjected, so that the superego takes the place of the parental function, and thenceforward observes, guides, and threatens the ego in just the same way as the parents acted to the child before.[30]

[29] Karen Horney, *New Ways in Psychoanalysis* (New York: W. W. Norton & Co., Inc., 1939), p. 208.

[30] S. Freud, *New Introductory Lectures in Psychoanalysis* (New York: W. W. Norton & Co., Inc., 1933), p. 89.

Freud's picturesque way of conceptualizing his observations should not be taken to imply processes of a different order from general principles of learning. The childhood superego can be considered a group of learned responses perhaps not as well organized in a system as Freud implied. The "introjection" of parental restrictions can be expressed as a simple learning process: the child acts on some impulse, the behavior is punished (or punishment threatened), and this linkage with punishment causes the action to be internally inhibited thereafter. Allowance must be made also for positive ideals such as cleanliness, self-reliance, perfection; here the cognitive aspect of the learning is a little more complicated, but the ideals may persist with irrational force in later life. All the attitudes and valuations that are taken over wholesale from the parents during the early years of childhood are included in Freud's concept of superego, which might therefore be described as the childhood version of conscience.

It is not surprising that the childhood version should fall far short of the discrimination and judgment that are implicit in adult ethical standards. Learned at a time of great cognitive immaturity, superego valuations have an absolute, uncompromising, black-and-white quality that is at odds with a mature outlook. According to Piaget's influential studies, young children do not grasp even the central principle of morality, its relation to social living; they interpret rules in an absolute sense, as if rules existed like physical laws and were never subject to change.[31] If primitive valuations and primitive guilt feelings become entrenched and isolated from progressive modification, they can become disturbing forces in personality. The person may be subjected to an unbearable burden of guilt if his childhood conscience continues to pass archaic moral judgments on his behavior. This was dramatically illustrated in the case of Bert Whipley, who as an adult could still be made acutely uncomfortable by reminders of his baby brother's death, and who failed in his career as a criminal because of a compulsion to get himself punished. The results may be no better if a person remains allied with his superego and becomes a literal embodiment of its virtues. This sacrifice is likely to make him envious of anyone who dares violate a single rule, so he attacks such people with the cruel venom of the self-righteous. What we might call a fixated superego can be a serious obstacle to mature behavior.

In general, the superego becomes fixated when the child feels that he is loved, yet when there is also a certain anxiety about retaining this love. Research has shown that disciplinary methods which involve a denial of love produce the strongest evidences of guilt and the most strenuous introjection of parental standards.[32] Of course the child must have something to lose by disobedience; if he does not feel loved in the first place he will

[31] J. Piaget, The Moral Judgment of the Child (New York: Harcourt Brace Jovanovich, Inc., 1932).
[32] R. R. Sears, E. E. Maccoby, and H. Levin, Patterns of Child Rearing (New York: Harper & Row, 1957).

not be much affected by the idea that his parents cannot love him when he is naughty. There must be love, but there must also be a sense of danger that love can be lost. Under the circumstances the child does not dare to question parental norms or to behave in any way that may imperil the tenuous relation. He is scared. This blocks the growth of sympathy and insight, the outflow of feeling toward other children who might help him gain new perspectives. It prevents the use of his own experience and judgment. So much is at stake in being perfect as the parents mean it that he cannot give up or modify those patterns of behavior. Fixation of the superego is encouraged by society's timidity in allowing the individual to think for himself, especially on moral matters. It is easier and safer to keep people in line. Under these circumstances the outgrowing of an initial fixation is doubly difficult.

AGGRESSION AND ITS MANAGEMENT

In this book we use the word *aggression* to refer to tendencies that aim at injury and destruction. Such tendencies are accompanied, when fully conscious, by feelings of anger and hate. In everyday speech and even in the psychological literature one frequently finds aggression confused with self-assertive behavior such as competition or dominance. While it is true that aggression can easily become fused with assertive tendencies, we shall stick closer to facts if we distinguish the two and reserve aggression specifically for man's angry, destructive, and hateful inclinations.

Nature of Aggression

In the infant's earliest responses to discomforts such as hunger, sleepiness, and unpleasant external stimulation, it is impossible to distinguish between rage and anxiety. The pattern of rage presently emerges as a general struggling and vigorous flailing of the arms and legs. The situations that most clearly evoke this response involve interference with activities and a restriction of movement, as in dressing or changing the diapers; and the child's movements, although not yet directed at an object, are of some service in getting rid of the restriction. In the second half of the first year, the child's manipulative activities, in themselves exploratory rather than aggressive, may lead at times to frustration and pain. An animal too roughly explored, for instance, may act in self-defense; and the child, perhaps after being consoled, may try rather insistently to repeat the rough treatment. During the second year of life, there is clear emergence of acts with an aggressive intent. Striking and kicking may be "carried out with a mischievous facial expression and with clear signs of enjoyment. . . . Finally the child clearly realizes that what he does *hurts*. The child has experienced pain and discomfort from aggression directed toward him, and he now connects his inner experience with his own overt activity.

This usually takes place during the third year of life." [33] It is now possible to speak of truly aggressive, hostile behavior.

It is valuable to compare these facts, found by direct observation of young children, with what has been learned through psychoanalysis about the conscious and unconscious workings of hostility later in life. Here it appears that aggression has some of the characteristics of a drive like sex, although it is not based on a somatic state that urges toward periodic satisfaction. The same words apply to aggression that Fenichel applied to sex: aggressive urges, "if they cannot find gratification in their original form, have the capacity to change, to alter their objects or aims, or to submit to repression by the ego and then to make themselves apparent again in various ways and in different disguises." [34] Suppose that a man's ire is aroused at work when his boss unjustly criticizes him. He says nothing, but when he gets home he kicks open the front door, yells at the dog, criticizes his wife's cooking, remembers to pay his union dues, decides to attend a political rally which is aiming to throw the incumbent party out of power, goes to bed and dreams that he knocked a heavier opponent out of the ring. The postponements and ramifications of aggression are many and subtle. Nursery school teachers know the sight of angry and distressed children throwing things around, breaking toys, hitting other children, not because of anything that happened in school but because of chronic frustration at home. Adults sometimes harbor resentments and grudges for years, finally taking them out through channels far removed from the original circumstances. Aggression can wait and can transform itself in innumerable ways.

These facts about aggression have led to two rather different conceptualizations. According to one view, advanced by Freud, aggression is the product of a pool of instinctual energy, the "death instinct," which is bound to overflow even without unusual provocation.[35] Freud's idea fits the age-old conviction that there is an evil streak in human nature; but his equating of this with instinctual drive energy has evoked much criticism, especially from those who do research on the physiology of instinctual behavior. According to the other view, aggression is always a response to frustration.[36] It is instigated by outside events: events which prevent the attainment of some needed gratification, which restrict or interfere with free activity, or which constitute a painful injury either to the body or to self-esteem. Without frustration there would be no aggression. If this sounds simpler and more flattering to our nature than Freud's grim idea, it does not in the end much soften the picture of human de-

[33] B. Mittlelmann, "Motility in Infants, Children, and Adults," *Psychoanalytic Study of the Child,* IX (1954), pp. 161–62.

[34] O. Fenichel, *The Psychoanalytic Theory of Neurosis* (New York: W. W. Norton & Co., Inc., 1945), p. 56.

[35] S. Freud, *Beyond the Pleasure Principle* (London: Hogarth Press, Ltd., 1922).

[36] J. Dollard, L. W. Doob, N. E. Miller, O. H. Mowrer, and R. R. Sears, *Frustration and Aggression* (New Haven: Yale University Press, 1939).

structiveness. Frustration is an inevitable consequence of the socialization process and of the objective conditions under which life takes place. If we take into account the nature of our mental processes, our capacity to remember, to imagine, and thus to brood upon unfairness or insults to our pride—and even to do so unconsciously—there is no real incompatibility between the frustration hypothesis and the simmering rages and lasting resentments that suggest pools of aggressive energy.

Problem of Channeling Aggression

In childhood, aggression manifests itself in relatively crude forms such as angry outbursts and tantrums. The tantrum is a forceful method of securing what one wants, but it meets with decreasing success as the months go by and the child grows more capable. The restrictive force comes from the mother, who discovers that if she does not curb tantrums in her child she will have to curb them in herself. This illustrates the difficulty of the educative process, but children are entitled to help in controlling their explosive outbursts. No child enjoys being in a temper. The violent force of the urge may even arouse his anxiety. What he wants is not to be angry but to remove the cause of frustration. In the course of time he will be able to learn that frustrations can be better removed if anger is controlled sufficiently to permit coherent and perceptive action. One learns, for instance, that losing one's temper in an argument makes one both ridiculous and ineffective. The young child is ready enough to express his aggression, but he is also soon able to realize that he gets better results by controlling it. On this his parents and teachers can build.

It soon happens, however, that aggression is caught up in more complex patterns, and these create far greater adjustive difficulties. The child's daily social experiences, taking place mostly within the family circle, occur with people upon whom he is dependent, whom he loves, but who make demands on him which arouse aggressive feelings. His parents meet his needs and give him affection but also move him along the road toward socialization. One of the things that complicates human relationships even in the earliest years is the alternation of love and hate that we call *ambivalence*. The objects of love and aggression are the same; at times they call out these conflicting feelings practically at the same moment. The child soon discovers that there can be no easy solution to this problem. If anger, complaints, and criticism are expressed too freely they are likely to invite return expressions of hostility and to imperil future harmony. Frustration begets aggression but aggression may bring about a disastrous loss of security and esteem. Thus aggression is always potentially present in the family circle as an added complication to the other problems of emotional growth.

In a most general sense there are three possible types of reaction to any problem involving frustration and aroused aggression. Following the scheme originally proposed by Rosenzweig, there can be named the *extra-punitive, intropunitive,* and *impunitive* types of reaction.[37] The extrapunitive reaction implies that hostility is directed outward: objects or people other than oneself are indignantly perceived as to blame for the experienced frustration. The intropunitive reaction represents a directing of blame and anger against oneself: it is my fault that I did not act more wisely or that I provoked anger in others. The impunitive reaction seeks to minimize or condone the aggressive elements in whatever has transpired: the episode should be forgotten or not taken seriously. Each of these general ways of dealing with aggressive impulses is appropriate and realistic under certain circumstances. The child, however, is hardly in a good position to know what is appropriate and realistic, especially when he is dealing with obscurely perceived ambivalences in himself and in those around him. Under these circumstances it is easier for him to take his cue from the general attitudes of his parents, a matter in which families greatly differ. Studies with young adult subjects indicate that some people are quite consistently extrapunitive, others consistently intropunitive, in their response to frustrations both in daily life and in laboratory tests. There is evidence to suggest that these preferences are established in childhood and are influenced by the attitudes prevailing in the family circle.[38]

Aggression and Competence

The problem of adjusting loves and hates within the family circle is well illustrated in the example of sibling rivalry. With the birth of a new sibling, the older child has to accept a reduction in parental attention. He witnesses the baby enjoying privileges of dependence that he himself is in the process of outgrowing. Inevitably he feels jealousy and expresses hostility, but extrapunitive behavior does not remove the frustration nor win back the parents' love. The birth of a younger sibling sometimes upsets a child badly, perhaps precisely because for a while there seems to be no avenue for competent action. It takes time to discover possible rewards in the role of the bigger child who perhaps helps with the baby's care but in any event is esteemed for virtues of his own.

There is a reciprocal relation between aggression and competence. A situation with which one is competent to deal need not be more than momentarily frustrating. Much has been written about the desirability of expressing aggression rather than bottling it up in continuously simmering resentment. There may be a certain relief in so doing, but more valuable than blowing off a head of emotional steam is to produce some real change in the frustrating circumstances. Clinical workers often encounter situations, like that described in the second chapter between

[37] S. Rosenzweig, "Types of Reaction to Frustration," *Journal of Abnormal and Social Psychology,* XXIX (1934), pp. 298–300.
[38] D. H. Funkenstein, S. H. King, and M. E. Drolette, *Mastery of Stress* (Cambridge: Harvard University Press, 1957).

Walter Lilly and his father, in which a parent and child repeatedly arrive at an angry impasse that neither of them really wants. Many a client thus troubled has been encouraged to ventilate his aggression and get it out of his system. Perhaps he then feels less tense and guilty, but what really gets the aggression out of his system is learning a more competent way of dealing with the situation, so that the impasse is avoided and the anger is not constantly refueled. Sometimes an angry mother, given a wise tip on how better to handle her infuriating child, comes to her next appointment with a report of success, a restored sense of competence, and not a trace of remaining anger.

In the residential treatment of emotionally disturbed children, in whom aggression is often a stubborn problem, it has been found valuable to stress not just self-control but the discovery of more competent ways of dealing with frustrations. More effective, according to Trieschman, than trying to stop a piece of aggressive behavior is to propose alternative behavior that to some degree expresses the child's feelings but in a way is less disruptive and self-defeating. A child can be taught, for instance, "a way to ask to join in a game instead of stealing the ball." Trieschman has made a study of tantrums, showing how at each stage the child even in his fury tries to maintain some effect upon his environment and accomplish some kind of purpose. The angry child's wild alternatives, such as "either fix it or I'll smash it," can be countered with a more reasonable proposal to try to fix it or else replace it. Naturally such maneuvers do not work on every occasion, but in the course of time the steady pressure to find more modulated, more effective ways of dealing with frustration is heeded, and the need to blow one's top is thereby reduced.[39]

Maladaptive Possibilities

Successful management of aggression implies a flexible system of controls and outlets. Crude manifestations, like crude perceptions, give place to discerning ways of dealing with frustration, and it is an especially happy outcome when anger is channeled toward social evils about which something constructive can be accomplished. A flexible system of controls and outlets is most easily attained when the child begins his development in an atmosphere that is tolerant but firm on the subject of aggression. Maladjustive possibilities lie in too wide a divergence in either direction: when little attempt is made to curb aggression, or when the attempt is so strenuous that no outlets are left for reducing the tension.

The first may appear on the surface to be the lesser of the two evils. Adults who, when angry, smash the furniture or punch somebody in the face are scarcely conducive to socialized living, but their behavior does not necessarily imply enduring malice or calculated hate. There are, how-

[39] A. E. Trieschman, J. K. Whittaker, and L. K. Brendtro, *The Other 23 Hours* (Chicago: Aldine Publishing Co., 1969), especially chaps. 1 and 7.

ever, more complex patterns of childhood influence in which the inadequate curbing of aggressive tendencies leads to very serious consequences. One can take as an example the case of Johnny Rocco, published by Evans.[40] A boy is brought up in a large family in desperate financial straits. He is given rough treatment by older siblings, receives scant affection from his harassed mother, is early turned out into the streets of a badly disorganized neighborhood. The family has a bad reputation with the police, and he is treated roughly in that quarter. He thus grows up in an environment where aggression is curbed only by other aggressions, where the obvious avenue to security lies in being more toughly aggressive than the other fellow, where at the same time serious frustrations constantly mobilize his hostility to a maximum. In situations of this kind, which appear frequently in the history of delinquents and criminals, poor control of aggression is by no means the only problem. It is true, nevertheless, that when other frustrations are severe the failure of family and neighborhood control over aggression leaves wide open an outlet that can have serious maladjustive consequences for both the individual and society. On slum streets, according to those who have lived there, aggression in the form of fighting is given active social encouragement rather than control.[41]

When aggressive impulses are met with too strenuous a campaign of suppression, several possible consequences may follow. The most obvious pattern is that of a person who can never openly express aggression nor even become aware of hostile feelings in himself. Such people show serious blocks in asserting themselves even in the most legitimate fashion. They must avoid aggression by such a wide margin, so to speak, that they cannot express any desires with which it might be remotely connected. We can scarcely assume that hostility is dead in these people; we must therefore suppose that it is aroused but somehow spends itself internally. Perhaps the intropunitive reaction brings about a kind of self-hate and feeling of unworthiness, or perhaps the anger is bottled up with no outlet except a chronic raising of the blood pressure or some other somatic effect. Neither consequence is compatible with good adjustment or good health. Horney describes the "vicious circle" that is likely to operate when aggression is too heavily suppressed.[42] A child who has to stifle his hostility finds himself placed all too often in a weak position. He cannot defend himself or demand justice. An unfair punishment has to be accepted, favoritism toward a sibling has to be overlooked or even taken as a true sign of one's inferiority and worthlessness. Thus the child must simply put up with it when others encroach upon his rights and wishes, and this allows them

[40] Jean Evans, *Three Men: An Experiment in the Biography of Emotion* (New York: Alfred A. Knopf, Inc., 1954), pp. 3–87.

[41] O. Lewis, *The Children of Sanchez: Autobiography of a Mexican Family* (New York: Random House, Inc., 1961); C. Brown, *Manchild in the Promised Land* (New York: The Macmillan Co., 1965).

[42] K. Horney, *The Neurotic Personality of Our Time* (New York: W. W. Norton & Co., Inc., 1937), chap. 4.

to do so more and more. Furthermore, in order to maintain the repression of his own hostility, he can hardly prevent the adjustive mechanism of projection from coming into play. He perceives his own hostility as an attribute of other people, but this only makes him feel still weaker, a helpless person in a hostile world.

In many cases the suppression of hostility is less complete. Sometimes the rejected aggression creeps back in the form of a general ambivalence: the person has difficulty liking what he wants to like or loving the people he wants to love. There is always something a little wrong with everything, a little deserving of criticism. In other cases aggression displays itself only in particular channels, generally with somewhat remote objects, but displays itself here with peculiar force and irrationality. To take one example, Frenkel-Brunswick and Sanford found that anti-Semitic sentiments are strongest in individuals whose outward behavior conforms to rigid standards of propriety. The outstanding feature of a group of strongly anti-Semitic American college women studied by them was a "restricted, narrow personality" with a strict conventional upbringing "to which there is complete surrender. Basic impulses, which are conceived as low, destructive, and dangerous, have to be kept repressed and can find only devious expressions, as for instance in projections and 'moral indignation.' " [43] When aggression is too forcibly driven underground it is capable either of wrecking individual adaptation or of being channeled outward in dangerous and irrational ways. The latter possibility is unfortunately assisted by a variety of societal devices that tend to legitimatize violence, most spectacularly in the case of military action.[44]

THE FAMILY AS ENVIRONMENT FOR GROWTH

Throughout our study of the problems that offer special adaptive difficulties, we have had before us the picture of young children in interaction with their parents. In the earliest learnings, in fact throughout childhood, the behavior of the parents is a highly significant feature of the child's environment. As we sketched the normal course of development, we kept thinking of the parental attitudes likely to encourage it. These attitudes are not the only determinants of psychological development, nor are the experiences of childhood the only ones that shape personality. But the effect of parental attitudes is sufficiently important so that we should examine some research on the topic.

We have just passed through a period in the history of abnormal psychology during which the problems of parent–child relations ·   · seriously

[43] E. Frenkel-Brunswick and N. Sanford, "Some Personality Factors in Anti-Semitism," *Journal of Psychology*, XX (1945), pp. 271–91. The complete description of this research is to be found in T. W. Adorno *et al., The Authoritarian Personality* (New York: Harper & Row, 1950).

[44] N. Sanford and C. Comstock, eds., *Sanctions for Evil* (San Francisco: Jossey-Bass, 1971).

oversimplified. The relation between mother and child, for instance, was not described interactively but was seen as a one-way sequence of cause and effect: the mother's behavior and feelings were the cause; the child's behavior and feelings were the effect. Perhaps we should excuse this as a legitimate attempt to simplify a difficult scientific problem, and it certainly led to some valuable research; but unfortunately it also led to making the mother the scapegoat for whatever was wrong with the child. The mother was pictured as the whole cause of the child's illness, and the therapist perceived his task as the hard one of undoing her evil influence. Clinical descriptions of twentieth-century mothers were at times more than faintly reminiscent of seventeenth-century accounts of witches.

We have seen, and we shall continue to see, that maternal attitudes are of great importance in the child's life. But we must get beyond the idea that they are causes in a simple cause–effect relation. Thinking interactively, we must allow that the child brings something to the relation. He is more than formless clay; each child is born with a certain individuality which from the very start exercises an influence upon the mother. We must also allow that before very long the other members of the family begin to have some importance for the young child, who becomes a member of a domestic social system with ramifying interactions. The attitudes of father and siblings begin to be felt, and one can interpret their effects only in the light of the positions and interactions of each member of the family constellation. These two changes in the image or model of what we are studying do not make the problem of parent–child relations simpler, but they keep us more faithful to the facts.

We begin with some studies done largely under the older outlook, after which we shall consider individual differences in young children and the family as a social system.

Studies of Parental Attitudes

Acceptance–Rejection. Acceptance implies that the child is loved and receives kind and thoughtful treatment. Rejection means that the child is felt to be frustrating and a nuisance, or that the parents have no time for loving care and consideration. The importance of the acceptance–rejection variable is widely recognized. Horney made rejection her central theme in explaining neurotic anxiety.

A child can stand a great deal of what is often regarded as traumatic—such as sudden weaning, occasional beating, sex experiences—as long as inwardly he feels wanted and loved. Needless to say, a child feels keenly whether love is genuine, and cannot be fooled by any faked demonstrations. . . . More frequently than not, in my experience, the essential lack of warmth is camouflaged, and the parents claim to have in mind the child's best interest. Educational theories, oversolicitude, or the self-sacrificing attitude of an "ideal" mother are the basic factors contributing to an atmosphere that more than anything else lays the cornerstone for future feelings of immense insecurity.[45]

Baldwin and his collaborators reach the conclusion that "acceptance–rejection is the fundamental dynamic; it is the amount of acceptance which determines and delimits the other aspects of parental behavior."[46] This team of investigators observed a population which included among others a group of farm families and a group of college teachers and professional people whose status and background were equivalent to those of an upper-middle-class urban group. As a group, the latter parents showed a fairly high degree of acceptance. In contrast, the farm parents tended toward an attitude described as "casual." "Children on a farm," these investigators comment, "are, as a rule, neither warmly and affectionately accepted nor coldly rejected and resented. Instead they are accepted in a matter of fact way, given sufficient attention to take care of their needs, but left on their own a good deal of the time."[47] This study brings out the close relation between parental attitudes and sociocultural background. In the small middle-class urban and suburban family of today, which has lost most of its economic and educational functions, the meaning of home to the child becomes largely a matter of relations with parents. Acceptance or rejection, in particular, become the overwhelmingly important feature of home life. In recent years abundant studies of social class and ethnic background have shown the far-reaching relations among social position, future expectations, and attitudes toward children.[48]

There have been numerous studies on the effects of acceptance and rejection. Accepted children are found to be more confident, stable, and friendly. They may be calm and deliberate or lively and enthusiastic, but in either case their interest in their surroundings tends to be alert and unimpeded. In contrast, rejected children are more apt to be unstable and confused, perhaps restless and rebellious, perhaps apathetic or indifferent. But these consequences have to be considered in relation to a second dimension of parental attitudes.

High and Low Control. When children are strongly dominated, the effects are likely to show in their attitude toward authority and their power of initiative. Much depends, of course, on whether the domination is fused with acceptance or with rejection—on whether discipline is kindly or cold. As Baldwin points out, socialization requires a certain amount of control

[45] Horney, *The Neurotic Personality of Our Time, op. cit.,* p. 80.
[46] A. L. Baldwin, J. Kalhorn, and F. H. Breese, "Patterns of Parent Behavior," *Psychological Monographs,* LVIII (1945), No. 3, p. 53.
[47] *Ibid.,* p. 58.
[48] U. Bronfenbrenner, "Socialization and Social Class through Time and Space," in *Readings in Social Psychology,* E. Maccoby, T. Newcomb, and E. Hartley, eds. (3rd ed.; New York: Holt, Rinehart & Winston, Inc., 1958), pp. 400–25; M. M. Tumin, *Social Stratification: The Forms and Functions of Inequality* (Englewood Cliffs, N. J.: Prentice-Hall, Inc., 1967).

and restriction, but if the pressure is too strong the child's conformity is secured "at the expense of personal freedom in areas which are not intended to be restricted. Conformity to cultural demands is not easily obtained without robbing the child of that personal integrity which gives him a mind of his own and which supports him in his attempts to satisfy his curiosity and to carry out his ideas and phantasies in dealing with the real world." [49] Studies of strongly dominated children bear out this contention. Such children are apt to be obedient, well-behaved, and in good control of quarrelsome and other disruptive tendencies, but the control seems to spread to unintended areas such as affection, curiosity, and fanciful invention; as a consequence the children feel shy, perhaps inferior, and they are easily bewildered in dealing with other children or with novel and imaginative schoolwork. Low control seems favorable to resourcefulness and independence, but along with these go tendencies toward overconfident conceit and an impatient rebelliousness that interferes with continuous application and sustained endeavor.[50] It can be inferred that when parental attitudes deviate either toward very high or very low control the children are likely to run into adaptive difficulties.

Maternal Overprotection. Some of the relationships discussed thus far emerge with striking clearness in a study of maternal overprotection by Levy.[51] This investigator studied in great detail twenty cases of extreme maternal overprotection. The mother's behavior was characterized by (1) excessive contact (mother being the child's sole and constant companion even up to ages such as 12 and 16), (2) infantilization (dressing child of 8 and accompanying him to school, shining shoes for boy of 15), (3) prevention of independent behavior (helping with homework, excusing from chores, preventing the formation of friendships). Levy points out that such a situation almost constitutes a controlled experiment in parent–child relationships: the effect of maternal overprotection is to minimize other influences acting upon the child, even the influence of his father. The twenty cases were selected in such a way that they all represent a marked degree of *acceptance*. But the cases break down into two sharply differentiated groups on the dimension of high and low control. Some of the mothers were very much bent on trimming the child to a desired shape. Their offspring were docile, clean, neat, obedient, polite, diligent in schoolwork, but so timid and submissive on the playground that their companions called them sissies and fools and their teachers considered them problems in social adjustment. In the rest of the cases the maternal attitude was so indulgent as to give what Levy calls "a luxuriant growth to

[49] A. L. Baldwin, "Socialization and the Parent-Child Relationship," *Child Development,* XIX (1948), pp. 127–36.

[50] W. C. Becker, "Consequences of Different Kinds of Parental Discipline," in M. L. Hoffman and L. W. Hoffman (eds.), *Review of Child Development Research,* Vol. I (New York: Russell Sage Foundation, 1964).

[51] D. M. Levy, *Maternal Overprotection* (New York: Columbia University Press, 1943).

infantile tendencies" with no barriers to the expression of aggression. At home these children would often break loose with slapping, kicking, throwing food on the floor, impudence, and a general high-handed tyranny. With other children they were cocky and bossy, inclined to show off, very poor at friendship and cooperation.

The twenty children were all patients at a guidance clinic, and Levy reports that efforts at therapy were rather ineffective, inasmuch as neither mother nor child really desired to change. Nevertheless in a follow-up study several years later it was found that only four were seriously maladjusted and several were doing very well. In spite of their early handicap of either excessive domination or excessive indulgence, they had at least enjoyed the advantage of being accepted—the assurance that they were loved and esteemed by the most important person in their world.

Individual Differences in Children

We turn now to the child as an active participant in family interactions. As Erikson puts it, "a baby's presence exerts a consistent and persistent domination over the outer and inner lives of every member of a household." [52] If such be the case we must certainly begin to consider the *effects of the child's attitudes on the parents.* Do overprotective mothers choose dominative or indulgent roles out of their own preference, or does the child's docility or activity force these roles upon them? Do infants show from the start persistent differences in level of activity and in responsiveness to the mother's ministrations?

On the question of activity level, the extensive observations of Margaret Fries are of great interest.[53] During the first ten days of life, infants can be readily classified as quiet, moderately active, or active. The differences are stable and can still be observed five years later. Everything the child does is influenced by his activity level. Extreme passivity, showing itself in a small amount of curiosity and exploratory play, delays the growth of reality testing and competence in dealing with the environment. Extreme activity may result in an impulsiveness so great that the child achieves little stable mastery of his surroundings. From the very start activity level affects the character of interactions with the mother. A quiet baby sucks less avidly and may even fall asleep during nursing, causing the mother to feel rejected. Active babies, on the other hand, sleep less well and cry more often; later, their adventurous zeal may put the mother's patience under great strain and cause her to feel excessively dominated. Those

[52] E. H. Erikson, "Growth and Crises of the 'Healthy Personality,'" in C. Kluckhohn, H. A. Murray, and D. M. Schneider, *Personality in Nature, Society, and Culture* (2nd ed.; New York: Alfred A. Knopf, Inc., 1953), p. 189.

[53] Margaret E. Fries, "Psychosomatic Relationships Between Mother and Infant," *Psychosomatic Medicine*, VI (1944), pp. 159–62; Fries and P. J. Woolf, "Some Hypotheses on the Role of the Congenital Activity Type in Personality Development," *Psychoanalytic Study of the Child*, VIII (1953), pp. 48–62.

babies who are reported to be "good" and "easy" presumably manage to avoid rejecting or over-controlling their mothers, and thus prevent a deterioration of the maternal attitude. Activity level has been thoroughly studied in young children by Escalona, who like Fries shows it to be a relatively stable characteristic over time.[54] The way in which this trait affects growth and interaction is brought out in detail by Brazelton, who describes three very different babies—active, average, quiet—all of whom, however, developed normally at their own rate and in their own style.[55]

Without doubt there are other important dimensions to the individuality that shows itself so early in the child's behavior. Recent reports from a growth study of normal children suggest possible value in a scheme of no less than nine variables, though some of these may prove to overlap.[56] The authors of these studies use distractibility as a variable separate from activity level; they speak also of positive and negative mood, high vs. low response thresholds, intense vs. mild reactions, approaching vs. withdrawing, and the degree of regularity in behavior. The studies seem to indicate that quite a variety of child-rearing regimes can lead to excellent results, especially with children who do not have extreme scores on these variables. The drastic bad effects of certain parental attitudes perhaps occur only (1) when the attitude is fairly extreme and (2) when the child is fairly vulnerable because he tends, for example, toward low response threshold, intense reaction, and negative mood. The child's response immediately influences the behavior of the parents, who may thus be pushed to more rejective or more protective attitudes than they had in the beginning. If we think in these interactive terms, it is much easier to understand the fact that in most families with an emotionally maladjusted child there are other children who fare much better. Parental attitudes are not complete fixtures; they develop in interaction with each particular child.

The Family as a Social System

Remembering that each person in a family interacts with every other person, we can understand that in the end each family must be interpreted as a social system. As Henry and Warson point out, "We must attempt to understand child development in terms of household—or even broader —configurations." [57] Increasingly the eyes of research are being focused on the *family constellation*. Henry and Warson describe such a constellation in the case of a certain little girl by saying that she lives in five

[54] S. K. Escalona, *The Roots of Individuality: Normal Patterns of Development in Infancy* (Chicago: Aldine Publishing Co., 1968).

[55] T. B. Brazelton, *Infants and Mothers: Differences in Development* (New York: Delacorte Press, 1970).

[56] A. Thomas, S. Chess, H. G. Birch, M. E. Hertzig, and S. Korn, *Behavioral Individuality in Early Childhood* (New York: New York University Press, 1963).

[57] J. Henry and S. Warson, "Family Structure and Psychic Development," *American Journal of Orthopsychiatry*, XXI (1951), pp. 59–73.

families: one including her grandmother and her sister, one including her parents and her sister, and so forth. These five families represent somewhat different systems of interactions among the actual people present in the household. To speak of five families is somewhat metaphorical, but it conveys a vivid impression of the range of significant influences in family life.

The case of Bert Whipley has already provided an example of the way a child's interaction with two parents is affected by their interaction with each other. The father, frustrated in his occupation, vented his anger on both wife and son. The son became critical and resentful of the father, respecting his authority. From the kindly mother he received some consolation; but because of her submissive, indulgent relation to the father, she could give him no sense of support and security. If in fancy we leave unchanged the attitudes of the two parents toward Bert but alter their relation to each other, conferring on the mother the strength to control her husband and thus to protect and fortify her son, it is easy to see that the atmosphere of the household would have been entirely different. The pattern of interaction that actually prevailed among these three members of the Whipley family was recognized some time ago by Aichhorn, in his studies of delinquency, as peculiarly fatal for socialized development.[58] Support for this contention is provided by Bandura and Walters in an investigation of aggressive adolescent boys.[59]

Considered as a social system, the family has characteristics that go beyond the sum of individual interactions. Ackerman has identified and described several different types of family adaptation.[60] This lead has been pursued by Hess and Handel in an intensive study of "nonclinical" families.[61] These workers point out that families differ in the relative emphasis they place upon being an individual and being a family member. They differ also in the strength of boundaries that separate them from the community. Couples enter marriage with different conceptions of what family life means, based on their own prior experience. Even allowing for disagreement in this respect between the parents, it is possible to discern that one family, for instance, sees itself as a haven of security in a hostile world, attaching great importance to internal harmony and doing things together; another emphasizes unselfishness both at home and abroad, encouraging participation in serious community activities; while a third puts the main stress on individual achievement, each member in his own way. Three such families plainly constitute different environments for the growth of children. Families differ also in their strategies for meeting internal stress. Disharmony can be denied, played down, quietly tolerated,

[58] A. Aichhorn, *Wayward Youth* (New York: The Viking Press, Inc., 1935), chap. 4.
[59] A. Bandura and R. H. Walters, *Adolescent Aggression, op. cit.*, p. 312.
[60] N. W. Ackerman, *The Psychodynamics of Family Life* (New York: Basic Books, Inc., 1958).
[61] R. D. Hess and G. Handel, *Family Worlds: A Psychosocial Approach to Family Life* (Chicago: University of Chicago Press, 1959).

seriously worked upon, or noisily expressed and shared with the neighborhood.

The idea of the family as a system of interactions underlies a paper by Vogel and Bell on the emotionally disturbed child as a family scapegoat.[62] When the relationship between the parents is full of unresolved conflicts which threaten to disrupt it, tension may be relieved by deflecting hostility and blame to one of the children. The victim is unconsciously selected because he most readily symbolizes the parents' conflict. When the mother, let us say, is fiercely ambitious and the father lazily unsuccessful, the conflict is most easily visited on the child who makes a poor start in school. Becoming a bone of contention, the child is exposed to the confusing crossfire of maternal nagging criticism and paternal defense with implicit support of failure. The family stays together but at the cost of a hard time for one of its younger members.

Sibling relations, which often play a conspicuous part in clinical studies, require the concept of the family as a social system. Brothers and sisters play a variety of parts in each other's lives: models, allies, friends, playmates, nuisances, rivals, enemies. Because the number and sex distribution of siblings is so variable, the subject has offered obstacles to systematic research. Birth order, however, has been considerably studied, and there is virtual agreement that first-born children differ in certain respects from second-born. Alfred Adler was responsible for the idea that an eldest child is likely to become the parents' foreman who directs the younger children. This notion is supported in a research covering three generations by McArthur, who describes first children as more commonly adult-oriented, sensitive, and serious, second children as more commonly peer-oriented, friendly, and easygoing.[63] Other studies tend to confirm these differences and show in addition that first-born children are more likely than later ones to do well in school, attend college, enter professional training, and achieve later eminence.[64] These are average differences, however, which by no means preclude the opposite outcome in which the second child is the parents' foreman and the first child a black sheep. Here the concept of role in a social system becomes helpful.[65] The role of parents' ally and agent is readily available to the first-born child, who is there first and is more mature, but he may not seize it, especially if there is much hostility in relation to the parents. This role is available to the second child only if the first has left it open; otherwise, the alliance of parents and eldest child encourages the second-born to edge out of the family circle and seek

62 E. F. Vogel and N. W. Bell, "The Emotionally Disturbed Child as a Family Scapegoat," *Psychoanalysis and the Psychoanalytic Review*, XLVII (1960), pp. 21–42.

63 C. C. McArthur, "Personalities of First and Second Children," *Psychiatry*, XIX (1956), pp. 47–54.

64 W. D. Altus, "Birth Order and Its Sequelae," *International Journal of Psychiatry*, III (1967), pp. 23–32; J. R. Warren, "Birth Order and Social Behavior," *Psychological Bulletin*, LXV (1966), pp. 38–49.

65 R. W. White, *The Enterprise of Living, op. cit.*, pp. 103–111.

a position for himself among friends. Many other roles, of course, are available to children in a family. Some of these may prove to be unworkable and frustrating in the course of time. The family "brain" may come to yearn for something besides good grades; the epitome of virtue may feel the need to experience vice; the jester may aspire to be taken seriously; the indulged favorite may want to be respected. As the individual grows, roles also should grow, but sometimes they prove to be stubbornly overlearned.

To summarize this section it will be useful to recall the case of Benton Child. Benton's mother qualifies as overprotective and as indulgently low on control. His father, preoccupied with his own health, gives the impression of being mildly rejective, but the mother was the stronger of the two and her attitude had the greater impact. As an only child Benton had no cause to elect the role of parents' foreman and was free to continue in that of parents' baby without the danger that he would be surpassed and humiliated. None of these influences would have prevented his becoming a lively and colorful, if somewhat spoiled, young man, but this outcome was precluded by a marked passivity that appears to have been rooted in constitution. Benton Child's case thus illustrates the necessity to take account of a variety of influences converging to produce any given pattern of personality and personal problems.

SUGGESTIONS FOR FURTHER READING

The topics taken up in this chapter are discussed more fully in R. W. White, *The Enterprise of Living: Growth and Organization in Personality* (New York, Holt, Rinehart & Winston, Inc., 1972), which contains chapters on dependence, the early growth of competence, conscience, aggression, parental attitudes, biological individuality as seen in constitution and temperament, and the family as a social system, including the influence of brothers and sisters (Chs. 3–11). The general problems of development are painted on a wide canvas by Erik H. Erikson in *Childhood and Society* (2nd ed., New York, W. W. Norton & Co., Inc., 1963). Based more on "representative description rather than theoretical argument," this book draws on case histories, anthropological field studies, folk literature, and biography to set individual development in the full perspective of social organization. More technical in purpose is J. Dollard and N. E. Miller's *Personality and Psychotherapy: An Analysis in Term of Learning, Thinking, and Culture* (New York, McGraw-Hill Book Co., 1950), which analyzes the processes of development, neurosis, and therapy in the concepts of a particular learning theory—reinforcement theory. For the student who wishes to pursue Freudian theory in detail, there is Otto Fenichel's complete and scholarly work, *The Psychoanalytic Theory of Neurosis* (New York, W. W. Norton & Co., Inc., 1945), of which the first six chapters present developmental psychology.

The name of John Bowlby occupies a prominent place in current thinking about dependence and attachment in young children. See especially J. Bowlby, *Maternal Care and Mental Health*, Monograph Series No. 2 (Geneva, World Health Organization, 1951); M. D. Ainsworth *et al., Deprivation of Maternal Care: A Reassessment of Its Effects,* Public Health Papers (Geneva, World Health Organization, 1966); both published in one volume (New York, Schocken Books, 1966). The psychoanalytic view of dependence and its place in development is discussed in detail by H. Parens and L. J. Saul, *Dependence in Man: A Psychoanalytic Study* (New York, International Universities Press, 1971).

Arguments for the importance in development of an urge toward competence are given by R. S. Woodworth, *Dynamics of Behavior* (New York, Holt, Rinehart & Winston, Inc., 1958), Chs. 4, 5; and by R. W. White, "Motivation Reconsidered: The Concept of Competence," *Psychological Review,* LXVI (1959), pp. 297–333. Alfred Adler's ideas, including the inferiority complex, can be gathered most readily from the survey of his works, with extensive excerpts, by H. L. Ansbacher and R. R. Ansbacher, *The Individual Psychology of Alfred Adler* (New York, Basic Books, Inc., 1956).

Freud's views on the superego are to be found in his *New Introductory Lectures on Psychoanalysis* (New York, W. W. Norton & Co., Inc., 1933), Ch. 4. A behavioristic analysis of the development of self-control is given by A. Bandura and R. H. Walters, *Social Learning and Personality Development* (New York, Holt, Rinehart & Winston, Inc., 1963), Ch. 4.

An historically important work on aggression is *Frustration and Aggression* by J. Dollard, L. W. Doob, N. E. Miller, O. H. Mowrer, and R. R. Sears (New Haven, Yale University Press, 1939). The same topic is discussed in the light of extensive experimental work by A. H. Buss, *The Psychology of Aggression* (New York, John Wiley & Sons, Inc., 1961).

In *The Changing American Parent* by D. R. Miller and G. E. Swanson (New York, John Wiley & Sons, Inc., 1958) will be found a valuable review of American child training as well as a new research study of families in and around Detroit. A good descriptive as well as systematic account of the effects of various child training practices is contained in *Patterns of Child Rearing* by R. R. Sears, E. E. Maccoby, and H. Levin (New York, Harper & Row, 1957). A fine exposition of parental attitudes and their effects on development is given by A. L. Baldwin, *Behavior and Development in Childhood* (New York, The Dryden Press, 1955), Chs. 20, 21. For the study of families as social systems, see R. D. Hess and G. Handel, *Family Worlds: A Psychosocial Approach to Family Life* (Chicago, University of Chicago Press, 1959).

5

Development of Personality: Later Childhood and Adolescence

The statement that development is a continuous process extending through the whole life span does not seem calculated to arouse controversy. But if one goes on to ask which segments of the span are most influential in shaping adult personality, argument springs into being. At one extreme it is contended that the earliest learnings all but dictate the future; the tree grows as the twig is bent. Freud aligned himself with this theory in his conviction that the main outlines of personality were firmly set by the age of five, subject thereafter to no more than superficial alteration. In similar vein Adler believed that the style of life, the personal strategy for meeting difficulties, was laid down in the family circle during the earliest years and became a lasting characteristic. But others have taken the view that personality is more flexible and contemporary, changing as situations change, sustained no more by past than by current stimulus patterns and current reinforcement contingencies. The twig may be bent, but the ultimate shape of the tree depends more on subsequent conditions of growth.

The problem of sameness and change in human development can be solved only by breaking it down analytically and trying to discover what aspects, under what circumstances, tend to be resistant to change. It is pertinent to point out, however, that if observation is largely confined to people seeking help for difficulties of living, repetition is bound to be more conspicuous than change. One of the causes of difficulty is inability to adapt one's behavior to new circumstances. The cases studied in our clinical introduction provide abundant illustration. Benton Child, for instance, treats his wife as if she were his mother, continuing to lean on her support and initiative instead of assuming new roles of husband and father. His case is far from unique, but plenty of men manage to grow up in like situations, responsive to the new demands of adulthood. Bert Whipley fails to learn that more precaution is necessary to avoid capture by the police, repeating his blunders as if impervious to experience. Successful criminals must surely have been more adept at modifying their methods. Even if we take the simplest phobia as an example, it is evident that the patient is somehow stuck with a fear which in another person would have undergone a process of extinction. Understanding disordered behavior means in many cases discovering the conditions that make behavior repetitive rather than adaptive.

The assumption that underlies this chapter is that the new experiences of later childhood and adolescence provide opportunities to learn new behavior and unlearn inappropriate old behavior. In the spirit of ideas advanced by Sullivan, we picture the child's enlarging social world as offering a chance to correct such residues of family training as may have been harmful.[1] Being at school and mingling with other children bring new kinds of experience: studying, competition, group memberships, cooperation, close friendships, presently interest in the other sex, then becoming part of the world of adulthood. These enlarging situations do not necessarily make for a corresponding enlargement of personality, but they give this a chance to happen. We shall continue in this chapter to look for both the adaptive and the maladaptive possibilities inherent in each aspect of development.

MENTAL DEVELOPMENT AND EDUCATION

Competence During the School Years

A child's sense of competence and self-esteem is strongly affected by his experience in the family circle. Occasionally it is so blasted by criticism and ridicule that the child can no longer trust his own experience of competence. Usually the balance between encouragement and discouragement is more favorable to self-esteem so that the child is better able to utilize his own sense of competence. In any event an important chapter in estab-

[1] H. S. Sullivan, *The Interpersonal Theory of Psychiatry* (New York: W. W. Norton & Co., Inc., 1953).

lishing self-esteem has already been written before the child leaves the bosom of the family.

Nevertheless it is fair to say that a whole new arena opens when the child ventures outside, particularly when he goes to school. In the worlds of school and playground he find an opportunity for a new deal as regards the estimation of competence. In the schoolroom there are new tasks, new challenges to competence, and he soon comes to realize that these tasks have ultimate significance in the grown-up world, which gives him, as Erikson expresses it, "a token sense of participation in the world of adults." [2] Perhaps this participation can be sensed most easily in learning to master tools and produce useful objects, but the "three R's," if at first a little abstract, can soon be appreciated as part of the equipment needed to take part in adult affairs. At its best the school serves to develop and maintain in the child what Erikson calls *a sense of industry* and a positive identification with those who *know* things and know how to *do* things." [3] This opens a prospect upon new kinds of excellence which put pressure especially on mental competence or intelligence. Being good at school-work, finding oneself comfortably effective in the operations required by one's lessons, becomes a bastion of self-esteem for part of the pupils, while for others the wearisome daily grind produces a general sense of inadequacy in this sphere.

There is also the playground, where the experience of competence depends upon a different repertory of effective actions. Strength, agility, and good coordination are important foundations of self-esteem in this sphere, with qualities more socially colored, such as assertiveness and humor, coming in as important adjuncts. In direct comparison with others of the same age, the child must prove himself worthy of respect because he handles himself well in the games and banter of the group. It is a sharp strain for many children when they pass from the atmosphere of a child-centered home into the competitive realities of even a friendly play group. They must now show what they have in the way of physical prowess, courage, manipulative skill, outgoing friendliness, all in direct comparison with other children of their age. The penalties for failure are humiliation, ridicule, rejection from the group. Even the last is probably a less basic threat than rejection from parental love, but it is none the less an acute threat.

As the child grows he meets an increasing array of situations which put his competence to the test. His experiences of competence and incompetence become differentiated with respect to different spheres of activity. A boy proves particularly competent, let us say, in walking and running, not as good in building with blocks or handling small objects, decidedly

[2] E. H. Erikson, "Growth and Crises of the 'Healthy Personality,'" in C. Kluckhohn, H. A. Murray, and D. M. Schneider, *Personality in Nature, Society, and Culture* (2nd ed.: New York: Alfred A. Knopf, Inc., 1953), p. 212.

[3] *Ibid.,* p. 214.

poor in drawing, writing, and other fine coordinations. The ratio of success and failure is different in each sphere, and if the experiences of competence continue in a fairly consistent fashion there will eventually be differences in the confidence with which each sphere is approached. The boy of our illustration, entering a new school, will run buoyantly to the playground, confident that he can deal with whatever he may encounter, but he will enter the crafts room somewhat dubiously and will take up penmanship with a weary feeling that he is never any good at this kind of stuff. Children show decided differences in over-all level of confidence, but they also typically differentiate their competence in different spheres, and this tendency increases with age. In the normal course of growth self-esteem is nourished more and more from one's better spheres of competence, injured less and less by one's poorer spheres.

School Phobia

The child's long educational journey starts with a single step, that of getting to school. For many children this step awakens anxiety. It means exchanging the familiar satisfactions of home for a place full of other children and of adults whose friendliness and ability to keep things in order are unknown. To the child's eyes there are real dangers, and some degree of uneasiness is appropriate. Time is required to discover that the new environment can be endured, possibly even enjoyed.

Occasionally the anxiety released by the prospect of school is too great to be managed. The child becomes unable to remain at school without the mother's constant presence, or he wakes up in the morning with pain and nausea that expresses his dread of going at all. Often the parents and the school authorities, fearing the consequences of panic, agree to postpone school attendance for the time being; but the results are no better when the attempt is resumed.

This is the phenomenon now widely known as *school phobia*. The fear may be simply of going to school, but it may become attached in phobic fashion to "the teacher, the other children, the janitor, eating in the lunchroom, or almost any detail of school life. . . . When we trace the anxiety to its source, it is invariably found to originate in the child's fear of being separated from his mother." [4] This fear is transparently present when the child will go only if the mother accompanies him and stays in sight throughout the school day. We are led at once to the expectation that school phobia will occur when the child is already highly dependent on the mother and has built up little faith in his own competence. Clinical investigation shows that this is often the case; but it shows also, in accord with an interactive interpretation of parent–child relations, that the dependence is not

---

[4] S. Waldfogel, J. C. Coolidge, and P. B. Hahn, "The Development, Meaning and Management of School Phobia," *American Journal of Orthopsychiatry*, XXVII (1957), pp. 754–80.

wholly on the child's side. On the basis of a strong affection coupled with a good deal of doubt about her maternal competence, the mother identifies with her offspring, tends to be overprotective, and makes herself unnecessarily subservient to the child's needs and whims. The child comes to have a certain power over the mother, but his "parasitic clinging is resented by the mother as it impinges on her own freedom of movement. . . . The child responds as well to the rejection he can sense as to the indulgence in which he luxuriates." [5]

In this entangling relationship, separation is felt to be dangerous by the mother as well as the child. The situation is complicated by the mother's unwitting communication of her anxiety. Her verbal reassurances may be given in a quavering voice, accompanied by tremulous gestures. The child may readily pick up these cues and, just as unwittingly, exploit the mother's dread to escape from his own. School phobia can thus be understood only by recognizing "the unequivocal importance of the child–family unit," for it is true that "although the child suffers, the parents appear to suffer more and to be at the mercy of their youngster." [6] To think of school phobia as a disease or as a disorder located in the child is clearly inappropriate.

in mother too

Overachievement and Underachievement

All teachers are aware that some of their pupils do not perform at the level of their capabilities. There is the child, obviously bright if one assesses the quality of his mischief or of his competence on the playground, who seems never to direct appreciable energy to a school lesson; there is also the child who slaves at every assigned task and at great cost produces a good performance. For research purposes, potential is measured by intelligence tests and achievement by school grades. Underachievement is thus defined as school grades well below intelligence scores, and overachievement as school grades well above. The latter possibility is not paradoxical when we bear in mind that intelligence tests do not really measure a fixed innate potential.[7] At most they suggest current capacity to do schoolwork, but this is enough for the present purpose. We deduce that both overachievement and underachievement have to do with motivation, perhaps also with expectations that emanate from the parents.

In the beginning, children presumably do not have an intrinsic interest in their education. Schooling is presented to them first as an adult requirement. Much of the art of teaching consists of awakening an intrinsic interest in the work, but this is never uniformly successful, and in any event there are constraints and irksome requirements at school, so that the open-

[5] L. Eisenberg, "School Phobia: A Study in the Communication of Anxiety," *American Journal of Psychiatry*, CXIV (1958), pp. 712–18.

[6] S. S. Rodin, "Psychodynamic Aspects of School Phobia," *Comprehensive Psychiatry*, VIII (1967), pp. 119–28.

[7] J. McV. Hunt, *Intelligence and Experience* (New York: The Ronald Press Co., 1961).

ing of a new term is rarely felt to be an occasion for rejoicing or the final session a day of mourning. In many families college and even graduate school have become passionate family requirements, so that higher education may continue to be felt as something that is done to please the adult world. This relation between schooling and adult requirements provides an important clue to the motivational aspects of both overachievement and underachievement.

One possibility for understanding academic underachievement came to light in a study by Kimball, who found subjects among boys clearly from advantageous backgrounds attending a prominent private college preparatory school.[8] Evidence was obtained through tests and interviews that the conspicuously underachieving boys were severely at odds with their fathers, not in the sense of open strife and quarrels, but in the form of hostile feelings coupled with anxiety and difficulty in expressing the feelings. The father was typically demanding with respect to educational attainment; the son, unable to fight back in any other way, failed to put effort into studying and thus sabotaged the father's expectations by a poor academic performance. But there are other possible patterns. In a study of boys with at least average ability but stubborn educational handicaps, the investigators discovered a different set of family interactions.[9] The fathers combined an unusual dependence on their wives, which made them see the sons as rivals, with a conviction of their own limited capacities. Consciously wanting the sons to succeed, they unwittingly anticipated failure for them and hoped for it, lest they be surpassed; it was noticed that when they tried to help their sons with schoolwork they soon became impatient and belittling. The mothers were not of much help, for they seemed to share with the fathers an image of competitive success as aggressive and destructive, hence not a quality they would be glad to see in their sons. One is reminded here of the use of a child as a scapegoat in maintaining the expectations and fictitious beliefs necessary for the harmony of troubled parents.

Overachievement expectably results from a family situation in which academic excellence is held to be of supreme importance. It implies also a willingness on the part of the child to fulfill this expectation, indeed a zeal to do so in order to stand high in parental favor. The parents may be overdriven by wanting to compensate for their own lack of education; the child may be overdriven by wanting to stand first among sibling rivals. Even so, the achievement regime may be successful if the child's capacities are equal to the strain. But working at or beyond the limit of capacities means vast and continuous application. Other aspects of development may

8 B. Kimball, "The Sentence-Completion Technique in a Study of Scholastic Underachievement," *Journal of Consulting Psychology*, XVI (1952), pp. 353–58; "Case Studies in Educational Failure During Adolescence," *American Journal of Orthopsychiatry*, XXIII (1953), pp. 406–15.

9 M. G. Grunebaum, I. Hurwitz, N. M. Prentice, and B. M. Sperry, "Fathers of Sons with Primary Neurotic Learning Inhibitions," *American Journal of Orthopsychiatry*, XXXII (1962), pp. 462–72.

lag behind, and eventually there may be a surge of rebellion against the Spartan straight-A regime, or there may be deep inferiority feelings over not quite equalling the parental aspirations. Often enough the phenomenon of sophomore slump, discussed in Chapter 3, occurs in erstwhile over-achievers who have come to wonder if the effort is really worthwhile.

Dropping Out of School

At the present time about a quarter of the students in American high schools drop out without receiving a diploma. In comparison with earlier times this is a small proportion. Dropping out used to be considered a sensible move on the part of a person who found no interest in high school studies. It meant assuming adult responsibilities more promptly, and it did not preclude later vocational success. Recently, however, because of changed attitudes in the job market, dropping out has come to be considered a serious problem. Technological changes have reduced the proportion of jobs requiring little thought or skill, and a high school diploma has come to be regarded as the minimum requirement for all but the lowest grades of occupation. Dropping out of high school now puts a person in a vocational trap: the range of jobs for which he can ever qualify is severely limited. It is significant that many current dropouts say that they plan to get a diploma later by night classes or correspondence courses.

On the basis of several studies Schreiber has drawn a composite portrait intended to portray the average high school dropout.[10] Two factors are typically involved: a negative attitude toward studies and a lack of social involvement at school. Limited aptitude for school work as shown in below-average scores on intelligence tests plays some part, but is usually not in itself the decisive factor. Performance has been poor and attitude apathetic for some time, so that schoolwork yields nothing better than feelings of incompetence and inferiority. There is little participation in extracurricular activities and little sense of belonging in high school society; most of the dropout's friends are already out of school. Presumably such a student has not made a favorable impression on the teachers and may be known chiefly as a disciplinary problem. To the dropout school is both boring and unfriendly, hardly an environment in which one wants to stay. Unfortunately the decision made at 16 may be much regretted in later years, when applications for jobs are turned down because they are not supported by the magical diploma.

Ability and Interest

In contrast to these several maladaptive possibilities, life at school may prove to be conducive to strong growth. This is especially likely when

10 D. Schreiber, ed., *Profile of the School Dropout* (New York: Alfred A. Knopf, Inc., Vintage Books, 1968), p. 6.

ability can be well utilized and interest aroused. There is certainly a difference between the sense of competence that comes from doing something well and the experience of interest that makes one want to engage in certain kinds of activity for their own sake. A child who is simply proud of mastering difficult lessons on electronics has a different experience from one who finds electronics utterly fascinating and wants to learn more and more. But these two experiences—of competence and of intrinsic interest —often go together, and they have somewhat the same effect on development. Whether the inclination is for sports, for craftsmanship, for school studies, for music, for art, for managing others, it can serve as a point of integration in personality.

The integrative action can be pictured as follows. The person now has a reliable line along which he can function with growing mastery and pleasure. In the sphere of his excellence he repeatedly enjoys the experience of competence and thus provides his self-esteem with a strong inner source. His ability is fairly likely to bring social as well as intrinsic rewards, and his development can then be guided by an efficient selective principle. Confident of esteem in one area, he can begin to discard the skills and roles that offer less promise. Moreover, he can begin to select the groups and companions whose esteem he will seek and value. He no longer has to care about every "bunch" in his high school, or even about the "leading crowd"; he needs only the shared interest and esteem of the hi-fi nuts, the drama crowd, or the budding nuclear physicists. If he goes to college he will probably know what subjects he most wants to study, and he may shortly discover a group of like-minded companions who will become his chief social circle. Even his vocational problems will be solved in advance so long as there are opportunities in the line dictated by his central cluster of competence and interest. The contrast is obvious between this outcome and the vocational indecisions of a person who has never been engrossed in this way, who knows neither what he is especially good for nor what especially turns him on. Vocational guidance in such a case is directed toward trying to clarify both points.

SOCIAL DEVELOPMENT: RELATIONS WITH GROUPS

Effects of Membership on the Individual

When an individual becomes a member of a group, his life is in many respects enriched and expanded. His strength is increased: the group can accomplish many things and resist many pressures where he alone would be helpless. His courage is increased by the sense of shared responsibility and group support. His purposes become solidified and his feelings of personal worth become established in the framework of group purposes and group values. He receives an income of friendliness, approval, recognition, and he gladly expends these things upon other members of the group. In time of stress he has the double satisfaction of helping others and receiving help from them.

On the other hand, membership in a group entails certain restrictions. The individual can no longer do just what he pleases. His initiative may be submerged because the group decides to do something some other way. He may want to play third base, but the group puts him in right field. The group defines for him a number of possible *roles* and helps him to select those he is best fitted to play. It provides him with a set of *norms,* indicating by approval or disapproval the kinds of behavior considered within that group to be right or wrong, good or bad, loyal or disloyal. These roles and norms constitute a social structure or framework within which he finds his place as a member of the group. If membership yields him sufficient satisfaction and enrichment, he willingly accepts the restrictions of the social framework.

The action of groups and their effect on the individual can best be observed under relatively simple conditions. Urban street-corner delinquent gangs were chosen for observation in a historically important set of studies by Thrasher, Zorbaugh, Clifford Shaw, and W. F. Whyte.[11] Such gangs form spontaneously and build up their own internal organization with little influence from historical tradition or from the norms of the existing social order. In spite of their informal origins and lack of legal and conventional sanction, these gangs exert a tremendous effect on their individual members. Within his gang, the boy, often from a distressing home in a disorganized neighborhood, finds himself accepted, esteemed, taken seriously. In company with gang members he can perform deeds of recklessness and bravado that would be impossible alone. When sick or in trouble, he receives sympathy and assistance. The gang becomes a point of anchorage in the social ocean. He feels strong and happy with his group, lonely and depressed if he is separated from it. As Thrasher expresses it:

Any standing in the group is better than none, and there is always the possibility of improving one's status. Participation in gang activities means everything to the boy. It not only defines for him his position in the only society he is greatly concerned with, but it becomes the basis of his conception of himself.[12]

Within these gangs there is a definite hierarchical structure. There are leaders and followers, and there are all kinds of specialized roles based on particular talents. Social pressure in the form of applause and preferment, ridicule, scorn, and ostracism keeps the individual members in their places and enforces the norms of the gang. In delinquent gangs the most serious

---

[11] F. M. Thrasher, *The Gang* (1927); H. W. Zorbaugh, *The Gold Coast and the Slum* (1929); C. R. Shaw, *The Jack-Roller* (1930), *The Natural History of a Delinquent Career* (1931), *Brothers in Crime* (1938); W. F. White, *Street Corner Society* (1943). All published by the University of Chicago Press, Chicago. Of more recent vintage is E. Liebow, *Tally's Corner: A Study of Negro Street Corner Men* (Boston: Little, Brown & Co., 1967).

[12] Thrasher, *ibid.,* p. 332.

offense is "squealing," which sometimes receives even the death penalty. If a gang member is caught, he is expected to "take the rap" no matter how hard it may be. Living in a precarious relation to the police, the gang must always act as a loyal unit. There can be no fraternizing with outsiders or members of rival gangs. The individual member comes to occupy a clearly defined place both within the group and in relation to the rest of the social order.

The effects of group membership cannot be listed wholly on the side of developmental assets. As we saw in the last chapter, the family circle, itself a group, sometimes has a destructive effect on an individual member, especially when this member is rejected, intimidated, or given stifling discipline. Groups outside the home are fully as likely to have an injurious effect on some of their members. Groups at school, well run by an adult supervisor, may sometimes achieve an atmosphere that is highly favorable to growth, but spontaneous groups of children or adolescents, dedicated not at all to developmental goals, may work in quite the opposite fashion. They can be cruel in rejecting a member who is slow, clumsy, or not "on the ball" in group activities. They can seize upon handicaps, peculiarities of appearance, class status, religious and ethnic differences, and use them as grounds for psychological ostracism if not outright expulsion. They can intimidate those who object to the way things are done, buying conformity with the threat of ridicule or physical violence. When a few "strong men" are in control of a group they can stifle initiative with as much force as an authoritarian parent. It would doubtless be possible to spell out the good and bad effects of groups on development just as in the last chapter we weighed the consequences of various parental attitudes. Neither group memberships nor family memberships invariably favor healthy growth.

Formative Influence of Memberships at Different Ages

It is during the early school years that group activity begins to assume an important place in children's lives. The period that extends roughly from six to twelve has been called the *juvenile era* by Sullivan, who saw *competition* and *compromise* as its chief problems in social learning.[13] Sullivan pointed out that "juvenile society itself encourages competitive efforts of all kinds," and that "in addition, the authority figures encourage competition—that is, they do in any culture that values competition." [14] Compromise likewise is valued and enforced by juvenile society and favored by the school authorities. It is apparent that this stage of group life will be of great importance in developing a child's experience of social competence. What amount of influence will he have over others, in the sense

13 Sullivan, *op. cit.*, chap. 15.
14 *Ibid.*, p. 231.

of winning competitions, leading and persuading others, making suggestions, or at least being included in activities? In a study of cabin groups at a boys' summer camp each boy was questioned as to "who is able to get the others to do as he wants them to do." Within each cabin of eight boys there was substantial agreement, even quite early in the season, as to the degree of social influence exerted by each member; a clear hierarchy had already been established.[15] Groups during the juvenile era provide schooling in the give and take of social living in its less personal and intimate aspects. According to Sullivan, "the school years are a time when a degree of crudeness in interpersonal relations, very rarely paralleled in later life, is the rule. But, in spite of this, the opportunity which is laid before the young juvenile for catching on to how other people are looked upon by authority figures and by each other is an exceedingly important part of the educative process." [16] For some children this may be a hard chapter in social growth, but for others the juvenile era is a season of flowering in which certain unfortunate consequences of life in the family circle can be remedied.

During adolescence the functions of age-mate groups become more complex. The society of one's peers begins to take over the supporting role that has hitherto been maintained by the family. Blos points out that "belongingness to the group" to some extent "replaces family ties"; this is the secret of the adolescent's tremendous dependence on the esteem and approval of his peers.

The group of contemporaries is uncompromising in its demands that the adolescent conform to its standards of behavior and belief. It offers him in return a security in group belongingness and in collective responsibility at a time when he is abandoning childhood relationships and reorienting himself in terms of mature goals. In response to the pressures of peer culture, his family patterns of relationship, identification, and feeling life are gradually modified in the direction of group norms. . . . The great dependence on group support and belongingness is naturally at its height at a time when the adolescent leaves the family, its protection and support, and has not yet the capacity to function independently on a mature level.[17]

The height of dependence on the group comes at fourteen and fifteen years. Thereafter the young person becomes increasingly able to choose the groups with which he will become identified and to influence the roles he will assume. During adolescence, group memberships mediate the transition from family-member and child roles to roles as an independent maturing adult.

[15] R. Lippitt, N. Polansky, and S. Rosen, "The Dynamics of Power," *Human Relations,* V (1952), pp. 37–64.

[16] Sullivan, *op. cit.,* 230.

[17] P. Blos, *The Adolescent Personality* (New York: Appleton-Century-Crofts, 1941), pp. 250–54.

Maladaptive Possibilities

In a rough way we can distinguish two general maladaptive possibilities in the realm of group relations: (1) *social isolation,* in which the person does not sufficiently receive the educative benefits of membership in groups; and (2) *social enslavement,* in which the person has learned to respond so automatically to the expectations of everyone around him that he develops no stable sense of self, no real ego-identity of his own.

Social Isolation. Many forces may conspire to prevent a child from entering readily into groups. Fragile physique or unusual sensitiveness may handicap him from the start, predisposing him to shy, tense withdrawal from the normal bruisings of child society. Geographical isolation may get the child off to a poor start as regards social experience. A serious obstacle is offered by parental overprotection. Perhaps the parents apprehensively interfere with the child's social contacts or try to bind him by creating a too perfect environment at home. If he is accustomed to whine for his own way or to demand it aggressively, he will react badly to the give and take of the group and probably suffer rejection. On the other side of the picture, the difficulty may lie less with the individual than with the groups he is in a position to join. The first available group may be dominated by children with bullying tendencies who enjoy making the newcomer miserable. Or it may be that after an auspicious beginning the child discovers himself rejected because he belongs to a different class, race, nationality, or religion from the majority in the neighborhood. If he moves a great deal, he will experience a certain feeling of rejection merely because he is a newcomer who must be assimiliated to already existing groups.

When circumstances pile up to hinder satisfying membership in the more available groups, it sometimes happens that the difficulty is solved by searching out or even bringing together a small and special group with congenial interests. In such cases the child is not isolated from other human beings, though he may feel ill at ease in large and boisterous groups.

In the event that this avenue is not open, an attitude toward others develops which can best be described as evasive. The child is unable to satisfy needs for companionship, unable also to experience competence in having desired effects on others. This was well illustrated in our clinical introduction by Walter Lilly, who could not resist requests for money and who dared not speak to a taciturn, perhaps equally shy, fellow worker. Social interaction in such a case becomes an area of helpless incompetence in which the initiative always comes from others and one has to endure whatever they please to put forth. Opposition is foredoomed, argument is hopeless, even a friendly overture means doing what the other person wants. Under these circustances social interactions yield neither pleasure nor self-respect. Attempts will be made to avoid them, but as this is never possible, resentment builds up against other people, who are experienced as intrusive and annoying. This resentment still further blocks the desire for social contact.

When these circumstances prevail, the person tends to remain shy, re-tiring, homebound, limited in his interests to things that can be done by himself. He does not learn the give and take of group relations and re-mains a stranger to convivial good fellowship. He may compensate in fantasy for the lack of expanded selfhood that comes from human inter-actions at their best, but he will never feel quite certain of his actual posi-tion in the social organism. Certain developments will be harder for him, especially those which depend on separation from parental support. With-out the compensating support of his age-mates at adolescence, he will feel less confidence in separating himself from parental supervision and opinions and in carrying out a mature sexual adjustment. Unless he is in the mean-time developing exceptional talents that bring him back into relation with others, he is likely to feel progressively isolated and insignificant.

Sometimes this situation is met by a reaction-formation. Rather than realize that his social inclinations are frustrated and that he himself is rejected, the person develops the role of contemptuous independence. He rejects the very idea of membership in stupid, commonplace groups with their plebeian interests and petty politics. He tends to inflate himself into an important personage who can achieve great things if not hampered by the mob or by the interference of friends. He tries to pump up in him-self the feeling of strength and importance that actually comes most readily through social memberships. With exceptional talent such a person may accomplish something, but his usual fate is essential isolation, ineffective-ness, and bitter resentment.

Social Enslavement. Another path along which social development can go astray is excessive conformity to the expectations of others. The person who travels too far in this direction comes to guide his behavior entirely by what other people want of him or expect of him. He finds it impossible to make suggestions or express wishes of his own unless these are sure to please the people immediately around him. Depending heavily on group affiliation, he may make himself unusually skillful at playing the right role in the right place. People oriented in this way become expert in meeting the expectations of each company they happen to be in, and they never err by telling the sex joke, the Scotch joke, the joke on the President, the joke on the party out of power, to the wrong audience. This sensitivity to what will please others has the effect of pleasing others and is therefore judged by them to be evidence of remarkable social adjustment. Never troublesome to others, such a person may be regarded as something of a mouse, but he is not in danger of criticism or rejection. And these seem to be the dangers his behavior is intended to avoid.

Social enslavement is favored by various circumstances. To some extent it can be absorbed directly from parents: discrepancies between parents' well-mannered behavior toward other adults and the things they say about them in private must often strike the child as meaning that his parents are afraid of other people. When children are forced prematurely into group activities, when their social careers are pushed by their parents rather than by their own motives, interaction may become a chore best dealt with by falling in with what the other children want. If entrance into groups proves difficult, the child may undertake to buy his way by deference and docility. If the child's social hunger is particularly acute, as is sometimes the case when he has experienced rejection in the family circle and needs a new source of security, it will be difficult for him to run the slightest risk of not being accepted.

The maladjustment that underlies excessive conformity comes to light most clearly when the person is faced by conflicting expectations. This is particularly likely to happen in times like the present, when social standards and values are changing. There is inherent contradiction among some of our long-cherished values: for example, between brotherly love and competitive success. With such conflicting norms in the background, it is all the more likely that the groups available to any one person will uphold contradictory values. When a socially enslaved person is forced to decide which of two group values he will espouse as his own, he is likely to feel confused and bewildered. No stable inner pattern, no integrated self, can serve him as a point of reference. He must announce his true colors, but he is a chameleon. The core of his maladjustment lies in the fact that he has leaned on social judgments and has not brought his own desires, peculiarities, and sense of competence into his conception of himself. The self-picture is diffused and fails in its integrative function.

People whose social interactions have developed in this way are characterized by David Riesman as *other-directed:* their contemporaries are the source of direction," and they become adept at "paying close attention to the signals from others." [18] Another aspect of social enslavement is described by Erich Fromm under the title of *marketing orientation.*[19] Economic success is increasingly dependent upon getting along with other people in a large concern and commending oneself to the purchasing public; this invites the young person of today to consider himself and his personality in the light of a marketable commodity. To receive promotions or new jobs one must be salable and in fashion, fitting the current pattern of a personable young businessman or businesswoman. Self-esteem here depends upon conditions more or less beyond one's control, and there thus tends to develop a constant fear of setbacks, a relentless striving for success,

[18] D. Riesman, *The Lonely Crowd: A Study of the Changing American Character* (New Haven: Yale University Press, 1950), pp. 18–22.

[19] E. Fromm, *Man for Himself* (New York: Holt, Rinehart & Winston, Inc., 1947), pp. 67–82.

and a ceaseless need for confirmation by others. Success is so heavily defined as being what others want you to be, rather than as doing certain things with effective skill, that the opinions of others become almost the sole source of self-feeling and self-esteem. "The marketing personality," in Fromm's view, "must be free of all individuality." [20]

The later consequences of social enslavement were examined with particular care by the Swiss psychiatrist C. G. Jung.[21] They are seen most clearly in cases having the following pattern: the patient is a person in middle life who has been well adjusted and successful, but who feels an intolerable discontent, uneasiness, frustration, and sense that his life has become meaningless. To understand such cases Jung introduces the concept of the *persona*.

> The word "persona" is really a very suitable expression for it, since *persona* originally meant the mask worn by an actor to signify his role. . . . It is a compromise between the individual and society as to the kind of semblance to adopt, what a man should "appear to be." He takes a name, earns a title, represents an office, and belongs to this or that . . . Society expects, and indeed must expect, that every individual should play the role assigned to him as completely as possible. Accordingly, a man who is also a pastor, must not only carry out his professional functions objectively but at all times and seasons he must play the role of pastor in a flawless manner. Society demands this as a kind of security. . . . It is therefore not surprising that everyone who wants to be successful has to take these expectations into account.
>
> The construction of a collectively suitable persona means a very great concession to the outer world. It is a real self-sacrifice which directly forces the ego into an identification with the persona, so that there are people who actually believe themselves to be what they present to the public view. . . . These identifications with the social role are a very fruitful source of neuroses. A man cannot get rid of himself in favor of an artificial personality without punishment. The mere attempt to do so releases, in all the ordinary cases, unconscious reactions in the form of moods, affects, fears, compulsive ideas, feelings, vices, etc.[22]

When a person has made the mistake of identifying himself too completely with his social roles—with his persona—and is paying the price in irritability and discontent, he can restore his well-being only by striking a new bargain with the demands of society. He must remove the "false wrappings of the persona," as Jung put it, and regain contact with those aspects of himself that have been suppressed in the process of social adjustment. In his new bargain with society there will be room for the fulfillment of what is more or less peculiar to himself. Instead of a persona he will become, in today's popular phrase, a "real person."

20 *Ibid.*, p. 78.
21 C. G. Jung, *Two Essays on Analytical Psychology,* trans. H. G. and C. F. Baynes (New York: Dodd, Mead & Co., Inc., 1928), especially pp. 163–71 and 202–32.
22 *Ibid.*, pp. 164–65, 209–10.

SOCIAL DEVELOPMENT: INTIMATE RELATIONS

Interacting with others in groups is an important educative experience, but it does not offer a complete curriculum in social development. One of the attributes of maturity is to be capable of sustaining and enjoying intimate relations with one's spouse and closest friends. Behavior in groups, which is relatively public behavior, does not provide the conditions that are essential for the growth of intimacy. These conditions can be met only in what we may call a private relationship between two people, one in which confidences can be exchanged and secret aspirations shared. In later childhood most children seek a closer, more personal relationship with someone who can be considered a special friend or chum. Important new developments in social interaction get under way.

Because these developments are apt to appear at a time when puberty is not far away, and because later an intimate relationship is often also a sexual one, it is sometimes supposed that the friendships of the years from ten to thirteen can be attributed to the burgeoning sexual need. The full significance of these relationships is overlooked, however, if we think of them as solely erotic, especially if, because they typically start between children of the same sex, we regard them simply as a disturbance on the way to heterosexual adjustment. Close friendships between children play a highly constructive part in the growth and integration of personality. They strengthen the understanding of oneself and others, and they lay important foundations for appreciative, loving relationships in later life.

In their early stages close friendships may engage but a small part of the child's feelings. Helene Deutsch points out that girls between 10 and 12, as part of the process of breaking away from dependence upon parents, develop a strong need for secrecy. To surround her person with secrecy, the girl needs a partner, and she is apt to find one in another girl like herself in age and interests, "with whom she giggles and titters, with whom she locks herself up in her room, to whom she confides her secrets." Some of these secrets may have to do with the sexual facts of life, but Deutsch's studies indicate that "expression of intense tenderness between girls is not found at this time, and mutual masturbation almost never occurs under normal circumstances." The close relationship serves the purpose of ego development rather than erotic satisfaction. Guilt is lessened by sharing supposedly guilty secrets; support is obtained in the process of emancipation from adult control; above all, "identification with a similar being can strengthen the young girl's consciousness that she is an independent ego." "The positive aspects of such friendships are paramount," Deutsch concludes, "and lack of them is a serious loss in this period of life." [23]

A unique part is played by close friendships in discovering and defining the self. From the competitions and compromises that occupy juvenile

[23] Helene Deutsch, *The Psychology of Women: A Psychoanalytic Interpretation* (New York: Grune & Stratton, Inc., 1944), Vol. 1, pp. 13, 15, 27–28.

groups one may emerge with a fairly clear sense of one's social competence and reputation for prowess, but the more private aspects of experience can be defined and corrected only in an intimate relationship. Here it is possible to speak of things that one would not disclose to the world at large, to consider new dimensions of personal worth besides those that receive group approval. Here it is possible, for example, to speak of the fears one has endured and combatted in order to meet a group standard; great relief and strengthening may follow the discovery that the other person, too, has been fearful in situations where externally he performed well. Here also it is possible to mention one's hopes and aspirations for the future and thus to secure some social reflection on what has hitherto been private—but perhaps not wildly fantastic. When in adolescence the desire for intimacy shifts to a member of the opposite sex, the goal of self-definition still plays a prominent part. In Erikson's words, "to a considerable extent adolescent love is an attempt to arrive at a definition of one's identity by projecting one's diffused ego images on one another and by seeing them thus reflected and gradually clarified. This is why many a youth would rather converse, and settle matters of mutual identification, than embrace." [24]

In the course of time, very often before the shift of interest to a person of the opposite sex, youthful friendships become charged with strong emotional meanings, and it is through this that they perform their most important service for development. This topic has been most fully expounded by Sullivan, who attributed to the close friendships of preadolescence the power to correct various faults in the child's previous social growth. The friend takes on a new meaning: his interests and his happiness assume an importance equal to one's own. With his chum the child "begins to develop a real sensitivity to what matters to another person; and this is not in the sense of 'what should I do to get what I want,' but instead 'what should I do to contribute to the happiness or to support the prestige and feeling of worthwhileness of my chum.' " [25] This interest in the other person can properly be called love, even when no overt sexual element is discernible. It involves wanting to understand the other person, wanting to encourage and help him, wanting to share interests with him, all of which maximizes the chances that true mutuality will emerge. In friendships of this kind an injured self-respect, battered in the competitions of group life, can be brought back to health; a new sense of worth can be nourished by the friend's appreciative concern. Fortunate experiences of this sort pave the way for the mutual affectionate relationships of adult life.

Maladaptive Possibilities

It is as true of friendships as it is of groups that their effect on development is not always constructive. Sometimes one of the partners dominates

24 E. H. Erikson, *Childhood and Society* (2nd ed.; New York: W. W. Norton & Co., Inc., 1963), p. 228.

25 Sullivan, *op. cit.*, p. 245.

or exploits the other. Sometimes the overtures from one side are not answered by real interest or understanding. Perhaps the need for intimacy in one partner evokes only a need for erotic experience from the other. Rebuffs in forming intimate relationships may produce wariness, reserve, and a tendency to shut in one's private concerns. Sometimes, on the other hand, a friendship will prosper so warmly that jealousy is aroused when either of the partners takes an interest in someone else. The consequences may be painful and may discourage future attempts at closeness; in such cases, however, the person may well have experienced developmental benefits before the relation came to grief.

Even though the going is not always smooth, it is a mistake to keep children out of a major pathway toward maturity. Sometimes teachers and group workers make a policy of breaking up pairs of children so that they will mingle more widely in the group. Presumably in some cases the children continue their friendship in secret, thus learning the valuable lesson that adult ineptitude need not spoil their growth. Otherwise they can only assume that there is something wicked about intimacy, which will certainly hinder their progress toward emotional maturity. It is a common complaint among young people that they have lots of acquaintances but no real friends. On this account they feel lonely, but they also feel a little like strangers to themselves, for they have not had enough chances to find out, through intimate interaction, what they are really like.

SEXUAL DEVELOPMENT

Early Childhood Sexuality

One of Freud's most important contributions was the discovery that sexual needs are active throughout childhood. As we saw in the first chapter, Freud called attention to many aspects of child behavior that should clearly be called sexual, even when allowance is made for the fact that genital maturity and power of procreation have not been reached. The most indisputable example is masturbation, which is universally practiced by children of both sexes, generally with increasing interest during the fourth and fifth years. Growing directly out of this is curiosity about the sexual organs and the anatomical differences between the sexes. This may lead to experimentation with other children and a quest for information from adults. Sexual excitation is undoubtedly much less differentiated from other forms of pleasant bodily stimulation than it will be after puberty when the special excitability of the genital organs reaches full development. Nevertheless we would overlook crucial problems of development if we tried to deny the presence of sexual elements in childhood behavior.

For the child to bring his sexual activities into line with adult expectations is an early and difficult problem of adaptation. In the past our culture was generally hostile to childhood sexuality. Requests for sexual enlightenment were condemned as dirty and disgusting, and masturbation, widely believed to produce disastrous consequences, was suppressed by coercion and direful threats. These attitudes have been gradually replaced by a tolerant disregard of childhood sexuality, now regarded as harmless, and even by encouragement on the part of parents determined to avoid the warping consequences of repression. But in large segments of our society the young child, and later the adolescent, is still asked to constrain sexual impulses within a fairly rigid formula of time, place, mode, and object. The sexual impulse often does not take kindly to the expected constraints, and its control can become a source of severe conflict.

The Family Circle

Childhood sexual feelings are probably at first associated only with the parts of the body from which they are derived. Their attachment to outside objects results from learning. From his study of the free associations and memories of neurotic patients, Freud came to the conclusion that the child's sexual feelings become attached first to members of his own family. Freud brought the matter under more direct observation when in 1909 he published the detailed case of a five-year-old boy named Hans.[26] This boy not only played with his own penis but on occasion invited his mother to do so and frequently asked to be taken into her bed and cuddled. At the same time he was afraid of his father, and when the many suppressions and disguises of this fear were untangled it proved to be directly related to the anger he supposed his father was feeling on account of his cuddling with his mother. Since then it has become a commonplace to notice that children around four and five take what looks like an erotic interest in their mothers, fathers, and siblings. The display often includes demands for an exclusive relation, with jealousy and hostility toward those who claim to share it. Freud was particularly interested in the little boy's erotic attachment to his mother. He called this the Oedipus situation, naming it from the tragedy by Sophocles in which Oedipus unwittingly kills his father and marries his mother. Freud also described the little girl's interest in her father and jealousy of her mother, which has sometimes been called the Electra complex.

The importance of these erotic attachments has been vigorously debated. It can be pointed out that love and sex are not the same, that the child's love for his mother is deeply grounded in the satisfaction of his dependent needs, that the Oedipus complex reflects "the possessive attachment to a person upon whom the child depends for his gratifications and security, with jealousy and hostility against competitors." [27] Sometimes fear of re-

---

[26] S. Freud, "Analysis of a Phobia in a 5-Year-Old Child," reprinted in *Collected Papers* (New York: Basic Books, Inc., 1959), Vol. III, pp. 149–289.

[27] F. Alexander, "Educative Influence of Personality Factors in the Environment," in C. Kluckhohn, H. A. Murray, and D. M. Schneider, *Personality in Nature, Society, and Culture* (2nd ed.; New York: Alfred A. Knopf, Inc., 1953), pp. 421–35.

jection seems to be an important element: "Hanging on to a person out of sheer anxiety is easily confounded with love, and in the child's own mind seems like love." [28] Again, the Oedipus situation can be viewed as one in which the child, now increasingly aware of himself as a person and wanting to be treated like an adult, finds the desired esteem imperiled by his parents' interest in each other and in his siblings: "What hurts anyone, whether boy or girl, is to be pushed aside in favor of another—jealous dogs show the same mechanisms as children." [29] Seen from a sociological angle, the Oedipus situation can be treated as a problem of group structure. For the first time the child, hitherto secure in a two-person (dyadic) relationship with his mother, confronts a three-cornered (triadic) relationship. The human triangle is essentially unstable, tending to become a pair with the third person "relegated to an inferior rank; in other words, the triadic pattern has a tendency to exclude one of the three participants through pair combination." [30] It is not surprising that in his first brush with the "eternal triangle" the child should experience important adjustive difficulties.

Most problems of development can properly be viewed from several angles. It should be noticed that none of the views just described challenges the importance of affectionate relationships and jealousies within the family circle. On this point Freud is sustained; the challenge is directed rather at interpreting the main motives as sexual ones. For our present purpose we need claim only that erotic motives are likely to be included in the pattern. Sexual feeling is a natural accompaniment of affectionate relations, especially when they include caresses and other bodily contacts. The important point is that members of the family are the earliest available objects to which sexual feelings can become attached. However strong or weak it may be, the child's erotic interest rests at first within the family circle. This initial learning must all be unlearned at a later date when the sexual urge reaches maturity and the force of the culture's incest barrier is more clearly apprehended.

Sex Roles and Imitation

After about the third year of life, sexual behavior can no longer be adequately described in terms of drive and satisfactions. The child becomes aware of his or her sexual identity. One of the items in the Stanford–Binet Intelligence Test for age 3 is the question: "Are you a little boy or a little girl?" The majority of 3-year-olds answer correctly, and some of

[28] Karen Horney, *New Ways in Psychoanalysis* (New York: W. W. Norton & Co., Inc., 1939), p. 83.

[29] G. Murphy, *Personality: A Biosocial Approach to Origins and Structure* (New York: Harper & Row, 1947), p. 533.

[30] J. H. S. Bossard, *Parent and Child* (Philadelphia: University of Pennsylvania Press, 1953), p. 40.

the brighter ones are contemptuous of such a foolish question. Sexual identity is soon discovered to imply a good many aspects of behavior having hardly anything to do with anatomy or bodily pleasure. The child gradually learns a complete sex role. Being a girl means playing with dolls, being clean and pretty, helping mother around the house; being a boy means not playing with dolls, liking rough and tumble and outdoor adventure, and helping father with outside chores. These traditional sex role expectations are today under severe criticism. Their relation to biologically determined differences seems slight, and their social function of promoting an ultimate division of labor between the sexes appears to be badly overdone. Even so, the conception of masculine and feminine roles, including many aspects of behavior, is deeply rooted in our culture, and most children are unlikely to escape its impact.

In learning his or her sex role the child is likely to make use of the most available models, father and mother. Copying the behavior of models is the easiest way, especially in the beginning, of acquiring social roles and other patterns of social behavior. It can happen, however, that the appropriate model is in some way compromised, so that the parent of the same sex appears more worthy of imitation. The daughter of a steady, affectionate father and an irresponsible, alcoholic mother may reject the feminine role and prefer to take father as her model. The son of a steady, affectionate mother and an irresponsible, alcoholic father may see nothing worth emulating in the masculine role. These reversals in the copying of sex roles do not necessarily interfere with later sexual behavior, which is affected by many other influences. But they occur with what looks like more than chance frequency in clinical cases in which there is marked disturbance in sexual functioning.

The Relearning Required at Puberty

Puberty is marked by a fairly rapid series of physiological changes. Secretion of sex hormones is sharply increased, the sensitivity of the genitals is heightened, and the sex urge assumes its adult form as a powerful drive that demands periodic relief of some kind. This change in itself, coupled with the appearance of the secondary sex characteristics of the body and the attainment of adult stature, represents a formidable problem of adjustment. The management of a strengthened and unruly impulse precipitates new conflicts and calls for new learning. But this is not the whole difficulty. As we have seen, sexuality already has a history, and this history has provided training not altogether suitable for the steps now to be taken. Insofar as sexuality has connected itself with other people, these are likely to include parents, siblings, and friends of the same sex who now constitute inappropriate objects. On top of this, the young person may have acquired the attitude that sex is a reprehensible and dangerous urge, so that alarm is experienced over its no longer deniable presence in oneself. Even those children who have been taught to welcome the signs of sexual maturing may be surprised by all that they are welcoming.

There are strong forces on the side of growth. One of these is the sex urge itself, which activates fantasy and inquiry even when overt behavior is still blocked. Another is the customary pressure toward heterosexual interests, the expressed expectations that dating, for instance, will soon be in order. Among age-equals the adolescent finds strong support in channeling sexual urges toward young members of the opposite sex. From adults the encouragement is likely to be qualified and less enthusiastic. It may amount to active discouragement if parents are fearful of youthful impulsiveness and premature entanglement. On the whole, however, there are considerable forces on the side of the relearning required at puberty, and these help in loosening the now unsuitable object choices left over from childhood.

Maladaptive Possibilities

Sexual maladjustments can arise at any point in development. Disordered behavior in young children sometimes has its roots in misunderstanding about sex and in anxieties created by injudicious threats and punishments. Psychiatric work with young patients almost always includes explanation of the "facts of life," which enables the child not only to get the facts straight but also to realize that they can be talked about without shame. Childhood troubles in the sphere of sex can readily extend their influence by blocking the relearning that is required at puberty. Difficulties in adult life can be conceived as failures to accomplish this relearning. When sex has been treated with respect rather than disgust or fear, when it has been gently restrained without creating alarm, then its inappropriate childhood history can be readily outgrown during adolescence and the foundation laid for good adult adjustment. When stages of the childhood history become fixated, or when the relearning after puberty is directly blocked by hostile cultural attitudes, maladjustment is likely to ensue.

For the sake of a symmetrical theory we might list indulgence as one of the causes of fixation. Such evidence as we have, however, does not make a strong case for harmful consequences of indulgence. As we have seen, it is no longer supposed by the students of the subject that childhood masturbation either injures the child at the time or makes for difficulty in achieving later sexual adjustment. So effective is the incest taboo that parents rarely indulge the child to the point of permitting a riotous growth of erotic interests within the family circle. What happens with neighbor children behind bushes or in cellars is more apt to satisfy curiosity than to produce erotic overindulgence, and we might find in it at least the merit of taking sex interest out of the family. The Kinsey reports show that homosexual contacts of one kind or another are fairly common experiences in childhood and early adolescence; [31] it cannot be supposed that their mere occurrence creates a fatal obstacle to the growth of heterosexual interest. It is possible, of course, that unrestrained erotic indulgences before puberty may increase the difficulty of later relearning, but the frequency of sexual incidents in the candid story of almost anybody's childhood suggests that indulgence is not a weighty cause of maladjustment.

The outstanding cause of fixation and blocking of development is therefore the association of sex with feelings of inferiority, guilt, disgust, and especially fear. When sexual feeling is suppressed and denied because it implies something shameful and dirty, or when it is even more completely repressed because it awakens anxiety, the chances of its participating in new learning at puberty are sharply reduced. The consequence may be a general inhibition of sexual interest and behavior. In extreme cases the person never dares to venture into an erotic relationship and is thereby barred from marriage. More commonly the interference is less complete, but sex can be experienced only as something shameful and demeaning; its power to deepen love and happiness and to strengthen the marriage relationship is thus thrown away. Sometimes the inhibitions upon sex are opposed by a reaction-formation, much energy being thrown into demonstrations of sexual freedom, but the need to furnish constant proofs of liberty, potency, and seductive capacity usually interferes with the attainment of satisfying mutual relationships. Fully developed shared sexuality implies a freedom from anxieties, inferiority feelings, compensatory motives of conquest; and it is just these intruders that constantly spoil it when sexual development has taken place in an atmosphere of prudish intolerance.

The following excerpt from a case history illustrates some of these points. A college freshman found himself waking up in the night with terrible attacks of anxiety, the only content of which seemed to be the fear of going insane. It appeared that when he was 4 or 5 his mother tried to stop him from masturbating by telling him that he would go insane. This threat did not suffice, but it was sharply reinforced when the family happened to drive by a state hospital. The boy saw patients behind barred windows making frightening noises, while his mother explained that those people were insane, a condition worse than death. This was a real threat, being locked up and separated from your parents, and it precipitated a reaction-formation. Throughout childhood and even throughout his high school years the boy renounced sex in all its forms. He had many activities and many friends. A group of congenial boys and girls "tore around" together, but he was careful to emphasize the "wholesome cleanness" of their relations. Arriving at college he was shocked by dormitory

---

[31] A. C. Kinsey *et al.*, *Sexual Behavior in the Human Male* (Philadelphia: W. B. Saunders Co., 1948), pp. 168–71, 623–31; *Sexual Behavior in the Human Female* (Saunders, 1953), pp. 113–14.

conversation, still more shocked to notice that his eyes tended to linger on magazine pictures of pretty girls before he hastily turned the page. He did not permit himself to masturbate, and his sole sexual outlet consisted of wet dreams from which he awakened in acute anxiety. At 5 he had been so scared that at 17, confronted by the rising strength of the sex need, he could only repeat the desperate defense of complete suppression, a defense which he could maintain during the day but not at night. He was unable to avail himself of the encouragement toward heterosexual interest offered by his classmates or even to accept the permissive attitude of a college counselor whom he consulted. During his college years he fell in love several times, but he broke off each affair with the decision that full devotion to his lifework required celibacy. Only several years after graduation did he overcome his anxiety about sexual behavior, and even when this had ceased to be a problem he continued to have much more than average dread of anything suggestive of insanity.

It would seem from this account that an open, natural, untrammeled attitude toward sex would be the best protection against problems. As a generalization this may be true, but not all the problems of sexual development vanish so easily. College counselors find their services in demand by students who believe in and practice maximum sexual freedom. Even when sexual encounters are physically successful, which is not always to be expected when the partners are relatively inexperienced, they may not lead to the anticipated feelings of satisfaction. This is less paradoxical if we bear in mind that sexual behavior is for many people not just a way of reducing a drive but an expression of much more of themselves: their capacity for loving, for deep feeling, for mutuality. The relearning required at puberty calls for outgrowing childlike attitudes toward love objects—jealousy, dependence, demandingness, petulance—and sexual intercourse does not accomplish this by magic. Furthermore, sexual freedom, like any other doctrine, can degenerate into a rigid demand. Clinical reports are beginning to appear in which the patient undertook early intercourse out of a sense of duty to parents who extolled its virtues, or to save face with experienced peers. When sexuality is prompted by these external pressures rather than by inner need and readiness, it may fail altogether to contribute to personal growth.

SELF AND EGO IDENTITY

The Concept of Self

Taking a short historical perspective, it can be said that the self or ego has recently emerged and risen to prominence in psychology. Taking a longer perspective, the self has experienced a brief absence from the center of the psychological stage and has now returned to play the indispensable role allotted to it by serious thinkers throughout the ages. The self was placed in obscurity only for that brief period—perhaps from 1880 to 1930 —when psychology, fascinated by the methods and models of the physical sciences, devoted itself to experiments on elementary processes and postponed the attempt to understand the person as we know him in everyday life. From abnormal psychology, which of necessity continued to take people as its subject matter, this concept was never really absent. The self or ego is one of the most difficult concepts in the whole realm of thought. It would simplify things if we could do without it. But no one can write sensibly about people without using this concept or its equivalent. As Allport put it, "the existence of one's own self is the one fact of which every mortal person—every psychologist included—is perfectly convinced." [32]

The necessity of using the concept of the self does not confer the privilege of misusing it. As we use concepts in our thinking, they tend to get firmer and harder. Thought about fluid events tends to curdle and form solid clots. Before long we begin to think of the self as if it were a lump in the personality. It becomes an entity so sharply bounded that arguments begin as to whether a certain piece of behavior belongs in the self or out of it, proceeds across an ego boundary, or involves a collision between the ego and something else. In the end the self is standing like a solid boulder of granite in the midst of personality, and one's thinking about it is as flexible as granite. Yet perhaps a more serious danger lies in animating the boulder again in order to invest it with magic powers. "What is unnecessary and inadmissable," said Allport, "is a self that is said to perform acts, to solve problems, to steer conduct in a trans-psychological manner, inaccessible to psychological analysis." [33] If the self is reinstated as a little man in the head who directs behavior, one's thinking about it becomes as realistic as a children's television program or a cartoon comedy.

Need for a Unifying Concept

In spite of its dangers we need the concept of the self. Without it we have no point of anchorage for the personal pattern of tendencies that is characteristic of each individual. When we speak of a personal pattern our phrase carries several implications. It means, first, that the individual's tendencies form an *arrangement of related strivings,* rather than a list or chance conglomeration. It means, in the second place, that this pattern has no standard form, but *differs from one person to another* according to his nature and history. It must have still a third implication if we are going to talk about living people rather than inanimate systems. It must mean that the tendencies are patterned in order to accomplish the maintenance and expansion of a living unit. They function within an organism,

[32] G. W. Allport, "The Ego in Contemporary Psychology," *Psychological Review,* L (1943), pp. 451–78.

[33] G. W. Allport, *Becoming: Basic Considerations for a Psychology of Personality* (New Haven: Yale University Press, 1955), p. 55.

and they are *patterned to make that organism live and grow.* That is the principle that governs the patterning and makes it intelligible.

The concept of the self helps us to bear in mind the basic fact of the unity of the organism. If we forget this basic fact, we are apt to talk about urges and differentiated tendencies as if they were tenants in a boarding house, each leading an independent life and submitting to a pattern of rules and regulations only because the other tenants interfere so badly. In practice none of us regards either himself or anyone else as a boarding house full of independent tendencies. If I lose my temper and make a childish scene, I do not blame one of my tenants, the aggressive urge; I blame myself for letting this tenant get out of hand. If my neighbor starts an unpromising venture and makes a success of it, I do not congratulate his need for achievement; I congratulate the man. We think of ourselves and others not as conglomerations, not as a bundle of separate responses, not even just as patterns, but as units.

Most of us show our loyalty to the concept of a unitary self by our surprise when it is questioned. Stevenson's *Dr. Jekyll and Mr. Hyde* strikes us as a profoundly true yet extremely fantastic tale. Profound truth lies in its description of conflict between different tendencies within the person. But it seems like wild fantasy to suppose that such a conflict could divide the personality into two separate selves with separate identities and an imperfect awareness of each other. Stevenson himself, even with all the freedom of fiction at his disposal, felt it necessary to introduce a magic drug to accomplish the transformation. There are, of course, real cases of multiple personality in which two or more selves function within the same individual. That they are so rare, and that they strike us with such wonderment, testifies to the stubborn tendency of personality to become organized into a unitary self.

A unifying concept becomes particularly valuable when we want to take account of man's constructive and long-range behavior. The setting of distant goals, the discharging of obligations, the making and keeping of promises, the taking of initiative and persisting against obstacles, the struggle to live up to ideals, the whole forward movement whereby a person becomes an independent, effective, and at the same time reliable human being—all of this activity implies a very high degree of organization. It implies a hierarchy of tendencies so ordered that the ones affirmed to be of most importance are given right of way over the less important. To say that this hierarchy takes shape in the interests of the *self,* and that things are more important or less important to a *self,* seems at present the most satisfactory way to conceptualize the whole difficult subject.

Formation of the Self

There can be no doubt that the self, like everything else in an organism, develops and changes a great deal in the course of life. Its nucleus appears to be what is experienced as "I" and "me," as distinguished from every-thing else that is "not me." This distinction, whatever its primitive basis, is amplified and strengthened by learning: children find out by investiga-tion that the foot is part of "me" and the favorite toy is not. As time goes on, "myself" assumes a fuller and richer meaning. It is compounded of bodily sensations, feelings, the image of one's body, the sound of one's name, the continuity of one's memories, all leading to the experience of oneself as a unique and separate person having a continuous existence. Particularly important is the feeling of activity and initiative. One's self is experienced not only as an object but as an agent. This feeling of activity, whatever its nature, is a highly characteristic feature of the ego system. In experiments using hypnotism it is possible to divest behavior temporarily of the feeling of active participation. It is then experienced as occurring of its own accord, and the experience is indeed a curious one.

Around this enduring nucleus are presently gathered many accretions. Awareness of oneself and knowledge about oneself are heavily influenced by social interaction. A child builds up his sense of self out of the re-sponses made to him by other people; through their acts and attitudes he learns how they perceive him and is influenced to perceive himself in the same way.[34] This process can be observed in bald form when parents apply adjectives to children and children begin to apply them to each other. The child's knowledge that he is strong, naughty, smart, or silly becomes formulated to a considerable extent through the labels applied by others. Gardner Murphy describes the situation as follows:

> Children are forever classifying one another by the use of good and bad names, applying to one another the nouns and adjectives which they have heard used in such a tone as to make them appropriate for praising or damning. . . . Most of the trait names that are used represent general action tendencies; and as soon as they are applied to oneself, or as soon as one finds himself applying them to others, they stimulate a trait psychology in their user. . . . Generalities are evoked by means of labels; the child lives up to the terms employed. . . . The child forms general ideas about himself. *In short, the self becomes less and less a pure per-ceptual object, and more and more a conceptual trait system.*[35]

These accretions to the enduring nucleus of the self are subject to continuous change. The pattern is formed and reformed many times in the course of life. You may remember but little of what you were like as a child, though you do remember it as your childhood continuous with your life today. You may remember more clearly yourself as a high school sophomore, though only with a pleasant sense that you are not like that any more. A less sympathetic observer might point out more continuities than you would care to admit, but certainly you are not just the same from year to year. A particularly large reworking occurs at adolescence,

34 G. H. Mead, *Mind, Self and Society* (Chicago: University of Chicago Press, 1934).
35 Murphy, *op. cit.,* pp. 505–6.

when family membership weakens and social acceptability becomes a more vital attribute of self. In the course of time the pattern of selfhood becomes more stable. In this it is assisted by social pressure. "With age and greater responsibility, the individual organism is persuaded more and more to act like a unit, to phrase the multiplicity and incongruity of its wants in terms of the multiple expressions of a fixed self." [36] It is easier to live with others when they function as unified selves, and we encourage them to do so. The self is thus shaped into a unity from both directions at once. On the one hand it is attached to the enduring nucleus represented by one's sense of personal identity. On the other hand its various accretions are pressed toward unity by the requirements of social living.

Ego Identity

This shaping toward unity from both directions is captured by Erikson in the concept of *ego identity*. This expression signifies a sense of being a distinct individual in one's own right within a social framework. It includes one's self as a continuous, active personal being; and it also includes one's self as a meaningful part of the surrounding human group. As Erikson puts it:

It is this identity of something in the individual's core with an essential aspect of a group's inner coherence which is under consideration here: for the young individual must learn to be most like himself where he means most to others—those others, to be sure, who have come to mean most to him. The term identity expresses such a mutual relation in that it connotes both a persistent sameness within oneself (selfsameness) and a persistent sharing of some kind of essential character with others.[37]

The sense of identity is strengthened by the progressive mastery of useful actions such as walking, talking, reading, or carpentry. These are experienced as achievements by the child himself, and their value is further affirmed by consistent recognition on the part of adults. But their value for ego-identity depends upon their being relevant to adult reality; they open the way to a feeling of partnership in a larger world—to the feeling that one has a place and function in the world.

The process of identification plays an important part in this growth. "Ego identity," says Erikson, "develops out of a gradual integration of all identifications," patterned "in order to make a unique and a reasonably coherent whole." Identification refers to copying or imitating the behavior of others when this is done out of a feeling of wanting to be in some respect like the other person. Beginning with the family circle, the child imitates selected aspects of other people's behavior all along the way, adopt-

36 *Ibid.*, p. 489.

37 For the exposition of this concept, see Erikson, *Childhood and Society, op. cit.* especially pp. 207–18, 237–43; also "The Problem of Ego Identity," *Psychological Issues,* I (1959), No. 1, pp. 101–64.

ing those patterns that seem to suit him and dropping out the ones that prove unworkable. Erikson regards adolescence as the most decisive period in the growth of ego identity, when the time is first ripe for establishing a firm sense of oneself in adult perspective.

In a study of college students based on interviews, Marcia describes four types of what he calls *identity status*.[38] Students in the first category, *identity foreclosure,* seem never to have had doubts about who they are; the values of home and the opportunities ahead are sufficiently congenial to be accepted without struggle as a basis for living. In the next status, *identity diffusion,* are students who are relatively adrift and uncommitted but not especially worried about it; lack of a sense of identity does not create a feeling of crisis. Marcia calls the third status *moratorium:* the subjects are uncommitted with respect to values and life plans, but feel that they must discover themselves before the end of college and are working hard at it. The fourth status, *identity achievement,* represents arrival at firm commitments to occupations and values; unlike the first group, this commitment has been achieved after a period of diffusion, crisis, and struggle. In a rough way these descriptions represent a range of normally adaptive solutions to the problems of identity in late adolescence. They may even occur in sequence. A study by Perry shows a fairly regular progression during the college years. At the start, values and truth itself seem absolute; learning means discovering the right answers. Then comes recognition of the relativity of values, the wide range of what have been considered right and wrong answers in different times and circumstances. This can be disconcerting, suggesting that nothing is any better than anything else. If the student continues to grapple seriously with the problem, he finally recognizes the necessity for responsible personal choice and commitment, reaching decisions as to what is worth working for in his time and circumstances.[39]

Maladaptive Possibilities

Because the sense of self is actively present, starting early, throughout the course of development, many of the maladaptive possibilities discussed in these two chapters can be seen as having a deleterious effect on identity. This is conspicuously true of feelings of incompetence and inferiority, with their injurious consequences for self-respect. It is true also of social isolation, and notably true of social enslavement, in which responding to the expectations of other people largely swamps recognition of one's own preferences and powers of initiative. Perhaps the maladaptive possibilities connected with self and identity should consist of a summary of all that has gone before. But in the recent literature much attention has been paid

[38] J. E. Marcia, "Development and Validation of Ego Identity Status," *Journal of Personality and Social Psychology,* III (1966), pp. 551–59.

[39] W. G. Perry, Jr., *Forms of Intellectual and Ethical Development During the College Years* (New York: Holt, Rinehart & Winston, Inc., 1970).

to a phenomenon common in our time in which identity diffusion is the central complaint. "I don't know who I am" is the sentence often chosen to represent this condition, from which we learn that knowing "who I am" —having ego identity—is an essential aspect of an organized, purposeful, satisfying sense of living. The person who complains of not knowing who he is will probably amplify the description by saying that his life seems meaningless, that what he is doing is without point for the future, that nothing is really important or useful, and that existence is zestless and boring. There is more to this than a sense of personal inadequacy or a depressed mood. The person cannot see how he can fit into the world, so to speak, as the world that he knows about is now constituted; no valuable interaction can be discerned. "I don't know who I am" is expanded into "I don't know who I can be in the world as I have experienced it."

Erikson describes an acute form of identity crisis, as seen in so-called "borderline" patients. The patients in question originally received this odd title because they were considered to be on the edge of psychosis, at times schizophrenic or acutely depressed, at other times in good contact with reality. More recently the term has come to be used to signify a disorder in its own right, "a chronic form of personality organization with specific ego weaknesses." [40] The composite portrait of acute identity diffusion drawn by Erikson is based upon patients between the ages of sixteen and twenty-four, the time of life that typically demands "simultaneous commitment to physical intimacy, to decisive occupational choice, to energetic competition, and to psychosocial self-definition." Attempts at intimacy fail in the sense that even during lovemaking there is no feeling of closeness but only a sort of confusion and distance. Time perspective becomes diffused, so that along with "a sense of great urgency" there is a loss of the experience of time as producing orderly change. There is "an acute upset in the sense of workmanship, and this either in the form of an inability to concentrate on required or suggested tasks, or in a self-destructive preoccupation with some one-sided activities, i.e., excessive reading." And sometimes it happens that the patient adopts a *negative identity,* choosing some way of life of which the family violently disapproves, in a blind stab at finding some pattern of identity to replace the existing emptiness.[41]

Less severe manifestations of identity diffusion are apparent in a group of college dropouts studied by Hirsch and Keniston.[42] Subjects were chosen who were in good academic standing and financially unpressed, but who were dropping voluntarily out of Yale College. The decision to leave school was not hasty or impulsive; it involved much thought, pain,

[40] J. M. Collum, "Identity Diffusion and the Borderline Maneuver," *Comprehensive Psychiatry,* XIII (1972), pp. 179–84. See also R. R. Grinker, B. Werble, and R. C. Drye, *The Borderline Syndrome* (New York: Basic Books, Inc., 1968).

[41] E. H. Erikson, "Identity and the Life Cycle," *Psychological Issues,* 1 (1959), No. 1, especially pp. 122–32.

[42] S. J. Hirsch and K. Keniston, "Psychological Issues in Talented College Dropouts," *Psychiatry,* XXXIII (1970), pp. 1–20.

often self-reproach, and it was made only when staying became wholly unbearable. The authors regard dropping out not as a disorder or weakness but as a possibly wise adaptive step when the student's developmental necessities are not in phase with what is offered by the college environment. The students suffered from a work paralysis which had been going on for some time. Their time perspective had collapsed, especially as regards future orientation, so that they felt themselves living in a disconnected present. They described their existence as having become hollow, empty, meaningless; even social life seemed a bore; and the possibility of really living seemed to exist only away from the academic environment. Self-reproach assailed them for not going through college as so many others do; this entailed a changed conception of themselves and a search for a new self in a more congenial environment. Intensive interviews with these subjects disclosed acute difficulties, not usually overt, in relation to parents, especially to fathers. More than others, the dropouts had formed identifications with the fathers as strong and worthy models, had responded to college requirements as to those of their fathers, but had become belatedly disillusioned about their fathers, whose faults and weaknesses they had at last begun to understand. Identification with father played such a large part in their own identity that when it failed there was not enough left to prevent confusion. It is as if the student said, "If I cannot be my worthy father's worthy college son, because my father is not worthy, then who am I?" Search for a new self had become an urgent problem, and for the time being, at least, college could not be felt as the proper place for it.[43]

The results of this study are illuminating, but they must be taken to represent only one of several different ways in which ego identity can become problematically diffused. Another avenue to weak identity is offered by social enslavement, the other-directed attitude, and the marketing orientation already described. Furthermore, the finding of identity is made harder when occupations are seen as forbiddingly impersonal, perhaps even as morally compromised, and when the economy is subject to major criticism. Many young people today have trouble picturing a significant life in traditional occupational slots and do not want to make themselves part of a technological system with so many destructive consequences. Ego identity depends upon a successful relation between the individual and society. Its difficulties may lie on both sides.

GENERATIVITY

One of the most essential aspects of adult living is taking care of the people upon whom the continuing of human existence depends. This

---

[43] For further material on college dropouts see L. A. Pervin, "Identification, Identity, and the College Dropout," *Journal of the American College Health Association*, XIV (1966), pp. 158–64; L. A. Pervin, L. Reik, and W. Dalrymple, eds., *The College Dropout and the Utilization of Talent* (Princeton, N. J.: Princeton University Press, 1966).

means primarily the care of the young, the nurturing of those creatures now small and relatively helpless who will grow up to be the next generation of adults. Under civilized conditions this care includes an extended education and the provision of many facilities for well-rounded development. Caring thus extends to the institutions that contribute to youthful development and guidance. Allport described this aspect of maturity as *extension of the sense of self*. It is shown when the welfare of another person or of a valued cause becomes as important as one's own welfare; "better said, the welfare of another is *identical* with one's own." [44] Erikson proposes the word *generativity*, which is "primarily the concern in establishing and guiding the next generation." He adds that "mature man needs to be needed," emphasizing the mutuality that is inherent in caring and being the object of care.[45]

On the long path toward becoming a caring adult, boys are almost at once handicapped: they are discouraged from playing with dolls. If they learn an average version of the male sex role they may be still further crippled in developing their caretaking talents, understanding that such things belong in the province of women. But the care of animal pets is not prohibited, nor is the care of property. It is generally the boys who mow the lawn and help repair the house. The nurturing of younger siblings might seem to offer perfect training, but here the situation is so complicated by jealousy and rivalry that the caretaking spirit is easily smothered and the behavior, if it occurs at all, is only a wearisome duty. Cherishing the feelings and self-respect of others struggles forth again in the friendships of late childhood and early adolescence. Even these harbingers of adult caring do not receive unqualified social support, being often discouraged, as we saw, in favor of group activities.

Nurturant tendencies are thus likely to have a checkered history, more so for boys than for girls. They are not likely to show to best advantage during late adolescence, when personal growth and ego identity are understandably matters of great concern. They are more strongly called forth when there is commitment to an occupation and when there is a spouse and children standing in need of care. At this point, failure to mobilize generativity has a variety of maladaptive consequences.

Maladaptive Possibilities

Continuing dependent tendencies offers one of the gravest obstacles to becoming a caretaker. This was shrewdly described by a college girl whose roommate had suffered a devastating family tragedy. She responded warmly to her roommate's sorrow and bewilderment, trying her best to be a sympathetic and helpful listener. After a while, however, she became aware

---

[44] G. W. Allport, *Pattern and Growth in Personality* (New York: Holt, Rinehart & Winston, Inc., 1961), pp. 283–85.

[45] Erikson, *Childhood and Society, op. cit.*, pp. 266–67.

of an unwelcome resentment; why must she always hear the other girl's problems when she so much wanted help with her own? A frequent theme in clinical histories, especially those involving marital difficulties, is continuing childlike dependence of husband on wife, wife on husband, sometimes even of parents on children. Being inappropriate to the actual demands of adult life, these needs are constantly thwarted. The resulting anger and hostility effectively destroy the generous spirit of caring.

Enduring self-centeredness can also stand in the way of generativity. College students chronically complain that many of their teachers are not interested in teaching them or in knowing them as persons. Often the complaint is justified: the teacher, an expert immersed in some branch of knowledge, is in fact preoccupied with his research, his publications, and his intellectual career, and has not advanced to the point of wanting to help younger people share his interests. Under these circumstances he teaches only because it is required and hastens back to "his own" work. His interest in students is conditional upon their becoming disciples and helping him carry forward "his own" research.

It should be allowed, however, that the balance can tip too far in the opposite direction, so that caring for others swallows up the possibility of having any life of one's own. There are college teachers who devote themselves generously to their students, giving time, appreciative criticism, and encouragement in abundance, but producing no work of their own; perhaps in the end they become less stimulating mentors. The problem occurs most typically in women who become completely engrossed in caring for their children and making a home, only to discover a mounting resentful tension over abandoning their other interests and talents. It is also possible for nurturant tendencies to get out of hand in occupations centered on helping people. Psychotherapists and social workers are sometimes made painfully aware that their desire to be helpful has been exploited by their clients, and that they have failed to use the possibly less sympathetic techniques that would actually have been more effective.

LIFE PATTERNS: WORKABLE AND UNWORKABLE

In these two chapters we have passed in review a series of problems in development stretching from early infancy to young adulthood. In each case we have tried to indicate successful ways of dealing with the problem, but we have also considered the maladaptive consequences arising from a less successful handling. It is evident from this account that difficulties in living exist in great number and variety. The person who travels the whole pathway of growth without picking up a single maladaptive tendency appears an improbable fiction. But it is necessary to think of personality as an organization rather than an additive collection of traits, maladaptive or otherwise. It is also necessary to bear in mind the enormous variety of external conditions amidst which different people lead their lives. We cannot talk about maladaptive tendencies without considering the circumstances that make them maladaptive; what goes in one situation will not go in another. The most pertinent question to ask about the consequences of a given developmental history is whether or not the person has achieved a workable pattern for living the particular life that is open to him.

Take the question of dependence in an adult male: the example of Benton Child naturally springs to mind. Benton did not outgrow the dependent tendencies fostered by his protected and indulged childhood, but when he married Deborah, who was full of initiative and liked to dominate, it looked for a while as if a workable pattern had been achieved. There are plenty of instances of successful marriages based on a dominant-dependent relation between wife and husband. In the Childs' case, however, the pattern soon proved to be unworkable. The force of Benton's dependence, the immaturity of his petulant demandingnes, and his failure to assume minimum family responsibilities, made the burden of family life too one-sided for his wife to bear. No hopeful signs appeared of gains in self-confidence or of nascent generativity. Strife ensued, stress developed, alcohol was enlisted, and Benton's behavior became disordered to a degree that led to the mental hospital.

Earlier we noticed that abnormal psychology covers a broad subject matter: some forms of disordered behavior lend themselves to interpretation as diseases, others as misdirected attempts to meet difficulties of living. In the last three chapters we have been dealing with the second variety. But here the line between normal and abnormal, ordered and disordered, is anything but sharp. Overcoming residual dependence, struggling to attain a sense of competence in different spheres, trying to reach a modus vivendi with authority, working on the poisons of aggression and resentment, keeping up in school, getting along with groups, finding close friends, searching for love and sexual fulfillment, seeking to establish ego identity, advancing to generativity—all of these are difficult achievements, and there are plenty of people who attain them only slowly and with painful effort. Struggling with difficulties of living is not a disease. It is not, properly speaking, an illness to have an inferiority complex, to be socially isolated, to be an enslaved conformist, to be bewildered about identity. These difficulties can be so troublesome that a person seeks psychological help, but even this step does not turn them into diseases. To be sure, they can have a part in more specific forms of breakdown—the neuroses, psychosomatic disorders, psychoses, and other conditions historically classed as medical problems. But this part is contributory; it is not in itself a sufficient explanation of the more severe clinical disorders. Unworkable patterns of living build up stress. They generate disruptive emotions like anger, despair, or anxiety. They thus increase the chances that one of the long recognized clinical syndromes will make its appearance. What more is involved in such an outcome? We shall consider this question first in the class of psychological disorders called the neuroses.

SUGGESTIONS FOR FURTHER READING

The topics taken up in this chapter are discussed at greater length by R. W. White in *The Enterprise of Living: Growth and Organization in Personality* (New York, Holt, Rinehart & Winston, Inc., 1972). The relevant chapters are 12–14 and 16 on social competence and membership; intimacy, love, and sex; education and intellectual growth; and self and ego identity. Many of this chapter's topics are discussed also in Gardner Murphy's *Personality: A Biosocial Approach to Origins and Structure* (New York, Harper & Row, 1947). In Chs. 20–22 Murphy considers the origins, evolution, and enhancement of the self; in Chs. 32 and 34 and in Part Six as a whole the problems of group membership, social roles, and cultural determinism. Murphy's treatment is reflective and theoretical, not easy but eminently worthwhile.

Noteworthy contributions to the theory of social development were made by Harry Stack Sullivan, whose recorded lectures are available in book form [*The Interpersonal Theory of Psychiatry* (New York, W. W. Norton & Co., Inc., 1953), especially Chs. 12–18]. The manner in which individual behavior is shaped by memberships in groups is the subject of an informative chapter in T. M. Newcomb's *Social Psychology* (New York, The Dryden Press, 1950), Ch. 14.

The best account of the growth of the sense of self is G. W. Allport's chapter on the subject in *Pattern and Growth in Personality* (New York, Holt, Rinehart & Winston, Inc., 1961), Ch. 6. The concept of the self and the pitfalls in its use receive judicious treatment in the same author's *Becoming: Basic Considerations for a Psychology of Personality* (New Haven, Yale University Press, 1955), Chs. 10–13. Long a champion of the ego in psychology, Allport nevertheless fears that the concept may become hopelessly solidified; in its place he favors calling "all the regions of our life that we regard as peculiarly ours" the *proprium,* then attempting to build up an adequate description of the various propriate functions. Erik H. Erikson in *Childhood and Society* (2nd ed., New York, W. W. Norton & Co., Inc., 1963) develops the important idea of *ego identity,* which serves to relate the concept of self to the individual's place and function in society; see especially pp. 161–234. Erikson's conception of the self, like the one presented in this chapter, places emphasis on the experience of competence as well as the social responses evoked by one's behavior. See also his *Youth: Identity and Crisis* (New York, W. W. Norton & Co., Inc., 1968).

6
The Neuroses

The first task in a chapter on neurosis is to salvage the word itself from its current indiscriminate use. As a term, *neurosis* has a history that should long ago have led to its abandonment. Originally it was used to designate a group of less severe disorders presumed to represent a mild derangement of the nervous system. As knowledge advanced, these "nervous disorders" proved to be precisely the ones that defied explanation in neurological terms. Charcot exposed the neurological nonsense of hysterical symptoms like glove anaesthesia or like paralysis that could be removed by hypnotic suggestion. Freud elucidated the anxieties, defenses, and symbolic meanings that made it possible to think of neurosis as an outcome of misdirected adaptive effort. By the 1920's neurosis signified a disorder in which, however widely the learning process had gone astray, there was nothing wrong with the neurons. Unfortunately this failure of lucidity did not earn the term a decent burial. Instead, the adjective "neurotic" was picked up in both professional and popular speech and applied to almost any behavior suggestive of anxiety, inhibition, or indeed any quality that one did not happen to like. Gone thus riotously out of bounds, "neurotic" became a handy epithet for putting down rivals in arguments, and it was even applied to whole societies by their critics.

Introducing a new term might be conducive to clarity, but it is hardly practicable to drop a word like *neurosis* which occurs constantly throughout the technical literature of abnormal psychology. Our best course, therefore, is to restrict the term in the manner of its original use and reserve it for a particular class of psychological disorders. Historically a neurosis was recognized by fairly specific complaints or troublesome symptoms. The most common of these were anxiety atatcks, phobias, obsessions and compulsions, amnesias and dissociated states, and the whole gamut of hysterical symptoms.

It is perhaps not necessary to limit the concept literally to just these patterns, but care must be taken not to extend it as a blanket term to cover difficulties of living which do not come to a head in some relatively specific disabling symptom. The importance of this point will become clear in later chapters on psychological treatment. Treating a phobia is quite a different matter from trying to be of assistance in a struggle to achieve warm personal relations or in a puzzled search for identity.

This chapter will be occupied mainly by descriptions of the several varieties of neurosis. These descriptions, however, will point toward a final section where, with images of the disorders freshly in mind, we can take up important and controversial theoretical questions. These include the nature of the presenting symptoms, the part to be attributed to anxiety and defense, the relative weight of past history and present problems, and the relation of form of neurosis to constitutional vulnerability and acquired strategic style.

ANXIETY STATES

On first thought, it might seem that anxiety states constitute a refutation of the whole anxiety theory of neurosis. If a neurosis, with all its cost to the person, comes into existence to prevent anxiety, how can one of its symptoms be the very anxiety it is supposed to prevent? This apparent dilemma vanishes when we recollect that anxiety can break through in any form of neurosis under a particular set of circumstances. If a phobic patient suddenly encounters the object he has been avoiding, anxiety may break through in panic proportions. If a patient with a hand-washing compulsion is prevented from washing his hands, he will experience acute discomfort and dread. Furthermore, patients who complain only of anxiety states do not have them all the time; only on occasion do they find themselves bordering on panic. It is therefore still possible to think of anxiety attacks as representing the momentary failure of protections that usually keep the patient reasonably serene.

The diffuseness and indefiniteness of the danger are the most trying features of neurotic anxiety states. Nothing in the actual situation seems to warrant the eruption, hence no sensible steps can be imagined to avoid it. The cartoonist Steig represents this by drawing a little gesticulating demon on the end of a stick attached to the back of a person's head—whichever way the victim turns, the demon is out there behind him, never in sight.[1] The patient may feel that he is going insane, that he is trapped amidst dangerous forces, or merely that something indefinably dreadful is going to happen. All sorts of devices may be tried to keep control, like physical ac-

[1] W. Steig, *About People* (New York: Random House, Inc., 1939), drawing entitled "Anxiety," p. 105.

tivity or intense mental work, but often these are of no avail. The sensation of losing one's grip may add to the panic.

The psychotherapist who receives such a patient for treatment necessarily subscribes to the view that the seemingly causeless anxiety must have causes. Not much can be done until he can discover what the patient fears —what the stimulating conditions are that set off the anxiety attacks. This can be achieved only by a careful scrutiny of precipitating situations, as well as the patient is able to report them. Understanding current situations can sometimes be amplified by examining those that the patient recalls from earlier life. Certain common features may be apparent in the series of fright-provoking situations, thus establishing a pattern of immediate causes of which the patient had never been fully aware.

An Illustrative Case

This procedure is shown in the following classically clear case reported years ago by the British psychiatrist H. V. Dicks.[2] A man of forty came for treatment on account of severe anxiety attacks characterized particularly by fear of enclosed places, difficulty in breathing (especially at night), and a most unpleasant sense of impending disaster. He had always been contemptuous of psychology and sought the aid of a psychiatrist only as a desperate last resort. He had just resigned after a distinguished career in the Government service. Considering the Government's policy too liberal, he made his resignation a matter of principle. He was living at home and considering starting out as a novice in a new profession when the anxiety attacks began to overwhelm him.

Working back through his career it was discovered that he had had some earlier bouts with anxiety. The most recent occasion was at the time of demobilization following World War I, in which he served as battalion commander and was decorated at a very early age. This circumstance well illustrates the lack of relation betwen neurotic anxiety and real danger: it was when demobilized and safe that the patient had attacks of anxiety. Previous to these attacks he had had another round of trouble when he entered college as a freshman. For a while he could not sit in lectures; if he went at all he took a seat next to the door so that he could leave at any time. Before this there was one attack at the age of seven when he had to sit through a church service under dimly lighted Gothic arches. Various anxieties connected with the Oedipus situation were uncovered, but they showed few links with the contents of his anxiety attacks. Finally the chain of incidents was completed by the patient's recalling a scene that took place in infancy when he had an attack of bronchial pneumonia. He was lying in a cot, coughing and nearly suffocating, in acute panic but at the same time furiously angry with his mother, who stood by unable to relieve his

[2] H. V. Dicks, *Clinical Studies in Psychopathology* (Baltimore: Wm. Wood & Co., 1939), pp. 27–28.

distress. The images included a tent over his cot and various other details. From outside sources it was possible to verify that he had had bronchial pneumonia at the age of eighteen months, and that a tent over the bed was one of the measures used for treatment.

The form of the patient's anxiety attacks—the breathing difficulty and fear of enclosures—was apparently set by this initial panic. His attack in church would seem to have been stimulated by the heavy arches (reminding him of the tent) and the necessity to sit still (helpless restraint). But we can understand his later attacks, especially the ones that sent him for treatment, only if we know something about the development of his personality. The patient was the eldest son and also the eldest of his circle of cousins. His parents encouraged him strongly to take the role of a big boy. He successfully assumed this role, becoming proud and markedly independent. Identifying himself with authority and the moral code, he emerged as the leader and disciplinarian of his younger relatives. This pattern was continued in school, won again in college, given much scope when he served as an army officer, and carried on while he was in the Government service. He became an energetic and successful man with a strong need for superiority. One can discern, however, that his career had something of the overdriven quality that characterizes a protective organization. It was when activity, success, and superiority were blocked that he gave way to anxiety attacks: when he lost his school distinction and became a "nobody" at college; when he lost his military distinction and became a "nobody" at demobilization; when he lost his distinction as a Government official and became a "nobody" without a vocation.

This case illustrates the tenacious consequences of a single tremendously frightening experience. So strong was the conditioning that the child was lastingly burdened with a liability to respond with acute fright to certain types of situation. To a small extent the effective stimuli were physical: low roofs and enclosed places. More important, however, were features that revivified the feelings of helplessness, loss of power, and entrapment that had been in full force on the first occasion. As the patient's personality developed, it was encouraged to take a form that happened to serve admirably as a means of counteracting his liability. His pattern emphasized independence (rejecting the useless dependent longings), activity (preventing a passive state of helplessness), and power (the opposite of being unable to influence his mother). These strivings were effective, yielded gratification, and led to a constructive life. There was only one flaw: when they were all blocked, so that he was reduced to the status of a "nobody," he developed not just the frustration that anyone might feel under such circumstances, but more than that—acute anxiety attacks. The flaw was a small one. If circumstances had permitted him to advance steadily as a Government official, having his own way and directing others until he became at last a respected elder statesman, his attacks at demobilization might have been the last and he would have been counted a well-adjusted man.

Problem of the Choice of Symptoms

When it is possible to work out the history of a case with the fullness and coherence of the one just studied, one feels as if one had reached an explanation of the patient's neurosis. But the phenomenon has been explained only in a limited sense. Even granting that the reconstruction is flawless, which may be far from true, the patient's neurosis has been explained only in the sense that one event has been related to another in an intelligible sequence and that the whole thing has been envisaged as a compromise between the growing personality and its need for security. What have not been explained are the things that did not happen. Why did the patient develop no phobias to keep him from getting into the crucial situation of being a "nobody"? Why did he develop no delusions of grandeur to help him through such situations? One can easily think of various devices that seem to fit the circumstances well enough. These ways of dealing with his problems were not chosen by the patient. Phobias and delusions seem not to have been available to him. In order to have a full explanation of the case, we would need to be able to state why certain alternative solutions were not available.

The problem thus raised is generally referred to as the problem of the choice of neurosis. Let us admit from the start that expressions such as "choice of neurosis" and "choice of symptoms" are singularly unhappy, suggesting as they do a conscious and volitional process of choice. The production of neurotic symptoms is of course not in the least a conscious act. The central question still exists, however, and can be phrased as follows: how does it come about that the patient develops just this kind of neurotic symptoms rather than some other kind? Why hysteria rather than obsessional neurosis? Why anxiety attacks rather than hysteria? Then, pressing the question into a narrower focus, why hysteria in the form of blindness rather than in the form of deafness? A general discussion of this problem is more appropriate at the end of the chapter when our description of the common symptom syndromes is complete. The question is raised at this point simply to call attention to something that is easily overlooked in attempting to understand the lawfulness of neurotic symptom formation.

PHOBIAS

A phobia can be defined as an irrational dread of an object, act, or situation. The word "irrational" differentiates it from a normal fear, and is inserted to indicate that we speak of a phobia only when the thing that is greatly feared offers small actual danger. When a patient shows intense fear of something that is in fact harmless, we have to assume that the real threat lies somewhere else. The patient must be either repeating responses to childhood dangers no longer real or responding in oblique fashion to current sources of anxiety.

Phobias cannot readily be classified. They have sometimes been named according to the object or situation that is feared. At one time medical writers favored attaching Greek prefixes to indicate every possible object of morbid dread. A few of these fancy names, such as claustrophobia (morbid dread of closed or constricted spaces), have become harmlessly lodged in the scientific vocabulary. In older medical literature there were literally hundreds of them: for instance, melissophobia (morbid dread of bees), gephryophobia (morbid dread of crossing water), parthenophobia (morbid dread of virgins), homilophobia (morbid dread of sermons). The list becomes endless because there is really nothing that cannot be an object of morbid dread. Lest the reader become a victim of onomatophobia (morbid dread of names), he should be assured that this pretentious vocabulary is now largely obsolete.

Most people are familiar with fears which they know to be out of proportion to real danger. Many adults are more afraid of snakes or rats or mice than is warranted by harm likely to come from these creatures. Others experience irrational uneasiness on high places, in small enclosures, or in crowds. In an age when airplane travel has become common, not a few travelers have recognized a discrepancy between published statistics of risk and their own discomfort while in the air, and some have found it impossible to use this method of transportation. The prevalence of such fears in an average community has been studied by interviewing a representative sample of the population. Fear of snakes was reported by 39 per cent— this in a region with few poisonous snakes—while fear of heights was mentioned by 30 per cent. These fears have something in common with phobias, but they differ in seriousness of effects. In the same community the prevalence of mildly disabling phobias was 7.5 per cent and of severely disabling ones much less than 1 per cent (2.2 per thousand).[3] To fear snakes and high places may be annoying, perhaps also a small insult to pride, but one's life is not really disrupted by avoiding them. With a true phobia—a phobic neurosis—the disruption becomes grave. Perhaps the patient cannot leave the house unaccompanied, cannot go to work, cannot go shopping or cross streets or ride in cars, cannot take part in any social life. Avoidance of anxiety reaches proportions that interfere in critical ways with normal living.

Taken together with anxiety states, phobia can be considered the simplest form of neurosis. In our historical introduction we noticed a large convergence of opinion on the idea that the central problem of neurosis is anxiety and its management. On this fundamental proposition there is agreement between psychodynamic theorists, whose ideas can be traced back to Freud, and learning theorists, whose original inspiration was Pavlov. Whatever else may be involved, phobias must certainly be considered to originate in the conditioning of anxiety responses.

[3] S. Agras, D. Sylvester, and D. Oliveau, "The Epidemiology of Common Fears and Phobia," *Comprehensive Psychiatry*, X (1969), pp. 151–56.

Phobias as Conditioned Anxiety Responses

The excessive and inappropriate anxiety that characterizes a phobia suggests a conditioned anxiety response laid down in one or more situations
of unusually acute fright. This conception is developed by Eysenck and
Rachman, who postulate that "neutral stimuli which are of relevance in
the fear-producing situation" or which "make an impact on the person" are
likely to be included as conditioned stimuli for the anxiety response.[4] Especially in childhood, when perception is still relatively global and undifferentiated, a large cluster of stimuli may thus become dangerous, and the
range may be further extended by generalization to stimuli of a similar
nature. The process is illustrated, as we saw in Chapter 3, by the child
Albert, who was experimentally conditioned to fear a pet white rat and who
became afraid also of rabbits, a dog, light-colored furs, and cotton wool.[5]
Through these learning processes a basis is laid for later phobic fear of
objects slightly similar or associatively linked to the original cause of fright.

This conception, based on Pavlov's model of the conditioned response,
can be supplemented by explicit use of the concept of operant conditioning.
Ullmann and Krasner contend that operant conditioning "plays a major
role in both the development and maintenance of phobic behaviors." [6]
The behavior associated with phobic stimuli is avoidance, and this response
is reinforced by anxiety-reduction. Even incipient anxiety responses—faint
stirrings of uneasiness that might result simply from imagining the feared
stimulus—are sufficiently noxious so that whatever abates them becomes reinforced. Thus it can happen that phobic avoidance is maintained and
strengthened over time so that it competes successfully with behavior necessary for normal living. A patient unable to cross streets must greatly restrict his life, but all impulses to go out are overruled by the heavily
reinforced behavior of keeping out of streets. The avoidance response prevents new learning. Extinction cannot occur if the feared stimulus is so sedulously avoided that no new appraisal can be made of its danger.

Phobias in childhood can often be understood in these simple terms.
The historic case of Peter, who feared rabbits but who recovered from this
fear by gradual deconditioning, appears to require no additional concepts.[7]
Equally straightforward is an adult case of phobia, described in detail by
Wolpe, which seemed to be entirely the consequence of a recent motor accident.[8] The car in which the patient was riding was hit violently at a
crossing by another car moving against a red light. Physical injuries kept

[4] H. J. Eysenck and S. Rachman, *The Causes and Cures of Neurosis* (San Diego: Robert
Knapp, 1965), pp. 81–82.
[5] See above, pp. 100–1.
[6] L. P. Ullmann and L. Krasner, *A Psychological Approach to Abnormal Behavior* (Englewood Cliffs, N. J.: Prentice-Hall, Inc., 1969), pp. 293–98.
[7] See above, pp. 40 and 102–3.
[8] J. Wolpe, *The Practice of Behavior Therapy* (New York: Pergamon Press, 1969), pp.
236–55.

the patient at home for only a short time, but when she tried to go out again in the car she suffered unbearable anxiety. She also suffered, of course, almost unbearable boredom and frustration if she could never leave home. The treatment was difficult, requiring in the end 60 therapeutic hours, but it was all concentrated on deconditioning the various stimuli to fright—cars approaching from the side, cars crossing in front, and so forth. The plan of treatment used in this case made it possible for the patient to ride again in cars without discomfort.

Clinical studies suggest, however, that considerable complications may be involved in a fully developed phobia. These can be interpreted as complications of the basic principles of learning and motivation, but they have often been described in somewhat different language.

Phobias as Protective Displacements

Frequently it seems that the object of which a patient is afraid is only a fragment of any likely situation of fright. The phobia is of sirens, or of streets, or of sporting goods shops, or even of anything that involves the number 13. Such objects of dread may have had some part in the original constellation of fear stimuli, but they seem like peripheral items rather than central dangers. It is as if the boy Albert were thrown into panic only by cotton wool while no longer being upset by the pet white rat. To explain this characteristic, the proposal has been made that anxiety aroused by the central stimuli has been blocked and then displaced to peripheral stimuli which have the property of being more avoidable. Especially when anxiety is linked to recurrent impulses of one's own which are being contained by repression, a gain in security may result from concentrating fear upon an avoidable outside object. For a woman to have a phobia of being alone on the street may be a more comfortable solution than recognizing impulses to seek sexual contacts there. For a man to have a phobia of shops where firearms are displayed may give him less distress than becoming aware of his own urges toward violence. Repression of dangerous impulses is kept secure by this maneuver of externalization.

Displacement presumably occurs along associative channels, depending initially on stimulus generalization. We examined such a process in Chapter 3 when studying Diven's research.[9] In that experiment associative connections served as effective guides for generalization, even when the subject was unaware of the original stimulus, so that anxiety responses became linked to all rural words in a list as well as to the word "barn" which had been followed by electric shock. Using such channels, the phobic patient may be said to fasten upon associations that neatly substitute for his real source of threat. But there is more to it than is implied by stimulus generalization. Unlike Diven's normal subjects, who became uneasy about "barn" and everything rural, the phobic patient is terrified only by some

9 See above, pp. 101–2.

rural item such as "plough," and does not manifest anxiety about barns. This is the peculiarity that is accommodated by the concept of repression plus protective displacement. The central danger, linked to one's own impulses, is more successfully avoided by pushing the threat some distance away.

This conception of phobia as entailing a protective displacement of anxiety was first put forward by Freud in the historic case of the five-year-old boy Hans.[10] The child, Freud became convinced, was in the midst of the Oedipus conflict, and his central fear was of the angry punishment he anticipated from his father because of his possessive feelings and actions toward his mother. His fear did not present itself in this form, but rather in the form of a phobia of horses on the street. This was an avoidable threat, whereas the father could not be avoided. The connecting lines passed through all kinds of childhood scenes, fantasies, and ruminations. Hans played with his father, who pretended to be a horse; he saw a horse with a black muzzle that reminded him of his father's mustache; he played with other children, pretending that he was a horse, and fell down in the course of the play; he saw a horse fall down and struggle with its feet. All these and many other elements entered the associative tissue, until at last he was in panic at seeing horses on the street and hearing the sound of their feet. With the achievement of this symptom he was no longer afraid of his father.

Described in this highly condensed way, without the evidence given in some detail in the original paper, Freud's reconstruction of the associative chain sounds decidedly arbitrary. His report has often been criticized on this ground. An alternative explanation would be that Hans's phobia started from a bad fright when he saw a horse fall down, and that fear of the father was not a related motive. But this likewise may be too facile. The human capacity for associative elaboration and symbolization is enormous, even in childhood; it is not implausible that anxieties should be blurred and subject to reworking. Many workers who do not share Freud's preoccupation with the Oedipus theme have found the concept of protective displacement essential in understanding their patients' phobic symptoms. It is a possibility that should not be overlooked.

Phobic Vulnerability and Current Stress

Not uncommonly a phobia assumes neurotic proportions at some point in adult life after having been quiescent perhaps since early childhood. This requires the assumption that something has happened recently to increase the strength of the anxiety response so that it reaches a newly disruptive level. Such strengthening would seem improbable if the revived dangers were merely historical and had nothing to do with the patient's

---

[10] S. Freud, "Analysis of a Phobia in a Five-Year-Old Boy" (1909), reprinted in *Collected Papers* (New York: Basic Books, Inc., 1959), Vol. III, pp. 149–289.

current problems. The model of events that appears most applicable is the same one we used in studying anxiety states. Childhood panic occurs, and this creates a liability to experience panic again if the person encounters forcible enough reminders of the original dangers. But as the child grows up, perceives with more discrimination, and becomes capable of more competent action, situations of great helplessness are largely avoided and violent anxiety is not touched off. Then come problems in adult life that cause diffuse anxiety in their own right. This lowers the threshold for all responses to danger and thus calls up fairly soon those that were conditioned in the early situation of panic. The phobic symptom is a product of current anxiety utilizing responses that were first laid down under past stress.

This abstract statement can be made clearer by an example. No phobia has ever been as carefully studied as that of William Ellery Leonard, a poet, writer, and teacher who made his disability the central theme of a highly detailed autobiography.[11] At the age of 36, he had the extraordinary experience which we used in Chapter 3 to illustrate the subjective state of panic, an experience of overwhelming dread as he stood on a bluff overlooking a lake, along the other shore of which a freight train was moving.[12] From that day on, he suffered from a crippling phobia which kept him from going any distance away from home. By taking quarters across the street from the university he became able to resume his work as a teacher, but trips away from home, even not very long walks, would quickly be stopped by rising panic. Leonard receive some professional advice, but he was largely his own physician, using relaxation and so-called "auto-hypnosis" to increase recall of earlier frights and thus, he hoped, blunt their force. He eventually remembered what was probably the initial panic, when at age 2 he stood too near the track on a station platform and was almost run down by a thundering locomotive—the "locomotive-god" of his title. Another major fright occurred at age 9 when he was chased out of the schoolyard by a group of jeering children after disgracing himself by making a puddle on the floor under his desk. From then until 36 he had occasional mild attacks of seemingly senseless uneasiness, but he was not unusually fearful and his freedom of movement was unrestricted, even as regards traveling by train. He married the daughter of a family much respected in the community, a girl known to be highly sensitive and subject to depressions. A few weeks before his attack on the bluff she committed suicide. The community, which had come to regard Leonard as demanding and self-centered, almost unanimously blamed him for her death. His level of anxiety mounted uncomfortably, and the situation was similar enough to the scene in the schoolyard—disgrace and rejection—to touch off the long quiescent panic responses of early childhood. On the bluff he had apocalytic visions with details drawn from both early scenes. Then amnesia descended on

[11] W. E. Leonard, *The Locomotive-God* (New York: Appleton-Century-Crofts, 1927).
[12] See above, p. 112.

this horrible experience, but now he must never venture any distance from home.[13]

In the clinical literature it is sometimes reported that phobias tend to spread. The patient is at first afraid only of riding in elevators, but then small rooms become taboo, the subway must be given up, perhaps all public enclosed places must be avoided. In such cases the assumption seems warranted that there is rising anxiety about current problems, together with an early established phobic vulnerability with respect to enclosed places. When avoiding elevators provides insufficient relief, stimulus generalization begins to operate and more things are imbued with properties of danger. The process is understandable but misguided, so to speak, in that it controls current anxiety only by imposing increasing restrictions on everyday living.

Secondary Gain from Phobias

When a person suffers from a neurosis, this fact has certain effects on the environment. One of the most common results is that the patient enters the status of a sick person rather than a foolish or irritating or selfish one. This may produce gains in the form of sympathy, excuse from work, and providing of services by other members of the household. Adler was particularly fond of pointing out these gains from illness. Perhaps a need to dominate is served by the symptom: fear of going on the street forces some member of the family to accompany the patient at the latter's pleasure. Perhaps it is escape from hopeless competition that is served: nobody expects a sick person to be out winning victories and setting records. Leonard's phobia appears to have had certain punitive consequences related to guilt over his wife's death yet anger at being held to blame for it. Punishing to him was the narrow restriction of his life space and discomfort when he tried to extend it. But perhaps there was also an attempted punishing of the community, saying in effect, "Look what you have done to me by blaming me for my wife's death." The ultimate consequences of a phobia can be far-reaching.

Effects of this kind are often given the name of *secondary gain*. This usage follows a distinction originally made by Freud. *Primary gain*, he argued, lies in the control or better management of the anxiety that is the central problem of neurosis. This form of gain may be disadvantageous in every other respect, imposing crippling restrictions on the patient's life. *Secondary gain* consists of whatever advantages are found to accrue from the fact of having symptoms: gains from illness and other effects on the patient's environment. When we turn to the more complex forms of neurosis, especially hysteria, this distinction will be difficult to maintain. Sometimes a symptom seems to have been guided from the start by anticipation, however unwitting, of the effect it would have on the environment. This

---

[13] Excerpts from this case will be found in B. Kaplan, ed., *The Inner World of Mental Illness* (New York: Harper & Row, 1964), pp. 311–22.

is less characteristic of phobias, where secondary gains are really secondary and often not especially large. But when they occur they are certain to add to the difficulty of bringing about a favorable change in the patient.

The extent to which a phobia is complicated by protective displacement, involvement in current life problems, and secondary gain probably varies a great deal from one patient to another. The techniques of behavior modification, aimed straight at removing the symptom without searching for anything that might lie behind it in the past or present, have had their greatest success with phobias. The implications of this finding will be considered in detail in the following chapters on psychological treatment. In general, however, prospects have improved during the last fifteen years that a phobia will be successfully treated within a reasonably short length of time.

OBSESSIONAL NEUROSIS

There are two names for the symptom syndrome to which we now turn our attention. Some workers prefer the designation *obsessional neurosis,* others prefer *compulsion neurosis.* Sometimes it is proposed to subdivide the syndrome into conditions dominated by obsessional thoughts and conditions in which compulsive actions predominate. The underlying processes are probably too similar to justify the separation.

Characteristics of the Symptoms

An obsession is an idea or desire which forces itself persistently into the patient's mind in what he experiences as an irrational fashion. A compulsion is an act actually carried out, which similarly forces itself upon the patient. Obsessive ideas and compulsive acts are often closely linked: for instance, the obsession that there may be dangerous germs on one's hands leads to the compulsion of handwashing. Minor obsessions and compulsions are familiar in everyone's experience. We keep wondering whether we turned off the gas burner, or we knock on wood after mentioning our good fortune. These everyday phenomena resemble neurotic obsessions and compulsions to the extent that they are sensed as irrational. We know they are foolish, but they seem to have a little push of their own and it is easier to let them have their way. In neurotic obsessions and compulsions, this quality is greatly magnified. The ideas and acts are like foreign bodies, forcing themselves upon the patient yet experienced as no part of the self. Moreover, they often betray that they are working in the service of defense. If the patient tries to stop his obsessive ruminations or his compulsive rituals, he is plunged into an attack of anxiety.

Obsessional symptoms occur in great variety. The patient's mind may be full of thoughts about infection and disease, making it necessary for him to wash his hands a hundred times a day and to take precautions that would put a modern hospital to shame. He may have rituals in regard to dressing or going to bed which make these actions laborious and time-consuming. He may be troubled by intrusive blasphemous thoughts when he is trying to concentrate on his prayers. Orderliness may become the demon in his life, committing him to an endless task of straightening, arranging, recording, and filing. Particularly trying are obsessions concerning harmful and violent acts: the patient is invaded by ideas of burning the house down, cutting his wife's throat, strangling his children, throwing himself in front of a truck. The danger that such acts will be carried out is small to the vanishing point, but the patient has no feeling of control over them and constantly fears that he will turn them into realities. The lives of obsessional patients are easily reduced to ineffectiveness and misery. Their energies are tied up in symptoms, and they are filled with doubt, vacillation, uneasiness, and helplessness. Occasionally an attack of anxiety breaks through.

Close scrutiny of the contents of obsessive symptoms shows that they can be classified under two headings: (1) Part of the symptoms give expression to aggressive and sexual impulses. Murderous hostility, destructiveness, dirtiness, and sexual urges in a crude and violent form reveal themselves in the content of obsessional thoughts. It is as if the suppressed *antisocial impulses* returned to this guise to plague the patient. (2) The rest of the symptoms give expression to *self-corrective tendencies.* Orderliness, rituals, cleanliness, propitiatory acts, self-imposed duties, and punishments all testify to the patient's need to counteract and set right his antisocial tendencies. Guilt feelings are his almost constant companions. Perhaps he reads in the paper about a murder that was committed many miles away. So strong is his guilt that he becomes obsessed with the idea that he committed the murder and deserves terrible punishment. The division of the symptoms into these two classes, *antisocial impulses* and *self-corrective tendencies,* gives an immediate insight into the nature of the conflict. A childish conception of evil joins battle with a childish conception of righteousness and punishment.

Obsessional symptoms sometimes have a sudden onset, but very often they make their appearance gradually. When the symptoms develop gradually, it is almost always the self-corrective ones that make the first appearance. The symptom picture is first occupied by derivatives of the defensive process. Only later do signs of the anxiety-linked impulses creep into the scene.

Distinctive Features of Obsessional Neurosis

Although the obsessional syndrome frequently overlaps with others, especially with phobias, it has a number of characteristics which roughly differentiate it from the other patterns.

1. Elements of conflict are more fully represented in consciousness than is the case in any other neurotic syndrome. The antisocial tendencies and the self-punitive tendencies can be read in the patient's obsessions and compulsions. The representation in consciousness is of course somewhat peculiar, falling far short of a frank recognition of one's tendencies. There is much symbolizing and disguising, and in any event the patient does not experience the tendencies as a part of his ego. They have a peculiar status. The patient knows that his obsessions and compulsions are inside him; he does not use projection and attribute them to external forces. Yet they feel to him like foreign bodies, not part of the tissue of the self. They intrude themselves from unknown parts of his mind. Apparently the mechanism of repression plays a less drastic part in obsessional neurosis. Its place is taken by this semi-detachment of the impulses from the self.

2. The struggle between anxiety-linked impulses and defensive processes is carried on in the realm of intellect. In this realm it is possible to make an extensive use of displacement. The patient finds himself ruminating on the philosophical implications of the dichotomy between love and hate rather than perceiving that he has certain hateful impulses toward someone he loves. The treatment of obsessional patients is often badly delayed by this tendency. The patient raises theoretical objections to the physician's way of conducting the treatment and tries to get into a long argument on basic assumptions.

3. It seems generally agreed that aggressive impulses occupy an unusually large place in the obsessional patient's basic conflicts. Sexuality is by no means excluded, but hostility is so predominant that it may be considered the central issue.

4. Certain character traits appear to be particularly common among obsessional patients. These patients seem to favor a certain pattern of protections. Generally they show a great interest in orderliness and cleanliness, which they carry to extremes. They are also conscientious and idealistic; they want to be never angry, always kind and considerate of others. All of these traits are socially desirable if not carried to extreme lengths, but their force in the patients suggests a strong reaction formation against aggressive, destructive, messy tendencies. Two other traits often appear in the pattern: stubbornness and stinginess. For all their idealistic outlook the patients do not want to be hurried or directed, and they hate to have others make demands on them.

These distinctive features of obsessional neurosis imply a pattern of adaptation—a strategic style—that is different from what is seen in other neurotics. This style has been characterized in various ways. Salzman emphasizes the interest in absolute control, along with the feeling that any loss of control would constitute an unbearable public display of inadequacy and imperfection. This requires the guidance of one's life by conscious rules, principles, and conventions, and careful preparation in advance to meet all possible emergencies. Salzman mentions the example of a lawyer in court who had an anxiety attack when opposing counsel introduced an argument which he had not anticipated. Actually the argument was of no importance, but the mere fact of being surprised and caught unprepared was a sufficient stimulus to violent anxiety.[14] A different aspect of the adaptive style was emphasized by Angyal, who spoke of a *pattern of non-commitment* which he thought might arise from a childhood atmosphere conducive to "abiding confusion as to whether the world is basically friendly or inimical." [15] This pattern is especially clear when decisions have to be made; long delay, and a careful balancing of factors which always seem equal, show the person's reluctance to commit himself to a final course of action. Shapiro describes the obsessive-compulsive style as one of "tense deliberateness and effortfulness." "It is a mode of activity in which the individual exerts a more or less continuous pressure on himself, while at the same time living and working under the strain of that pressure." But the demands are not experienced as one's own; rather, they seem to arise from a job to be done, an expectation to be met, a duty to be performed—some inherent requirement outside the self. There is little room for zest and enthusiasm in a life thus structured, and there tends also to be some "loss of the experience of conviction." [16] The acute symptoms of obsessional neurosis exhibit many of these characteristics in exaggerated form.

Example of the Mechanisms of Isolation and Undoing

It is hard to convey the degree to which the obsessive patient's actions and thought processes become clogged unless we use an actual illustration.[17] A boy of seventeen had severe conflict over masturbation. His pastor gave a talk denouncing the practice, and advised that one should never associate with a boy who masturbated. The patient knew a boy who masturbated, and he now found it difficult to keep away from him. But when he passed him on the street he felt distinctly uneasy. The first symptom was a little ritual consisting of turning around and spitting whenever he passed the wicked boy. This is a perfect example of *undoing:* the patient cleansed himself and expressed rejection immediately after permitting the danger of contact. The symptom was insufficient, however, to deal with the anxiety generated by these threatened contacts, and the next defensive strategy was a phobia. The patient had a morbid dread of meeting the bad boy, avoiding the possibility as much as possible. The phobic system soon began to expand until it included the whole section of the

14 L. Salzman, "Obsessions and Phobias," *International Journal of Psychiatry,* VI (1968), pp. 451–76.
15 A. Angyal, *Neurosis and Treatment: A Holistic Theory,* E. Hanfmann and R. M. Jones, eds. (New York: John Wiley & Sons, Inc., 1965), chap. 11.
16 D. Shapiro, *Neurotic Styles* (New York: Basic Books, Inc., 1965), chap. 2.
17 O. Fenichel, *Outline of Clinical Psychoanalysis* (New York: W. W. Norton & Co., Inc., 1934), pp. 160–64.

city in which the other boy lived. The patient made a compulsive stipulation that no member of his own family should enter that section.

From this point the symptoms invaded his thinking more and more fully. A severe obsessional neurosis took the place of the phobias. The patient found himself thinking about the forbidden section of the city. Even this contact in thought had to be prevented. He developed an elaborate technique of *isolation:* he would stand still and fix upon an image of the forbidden region until the image was bereft of all meaningful connections and stood all alone in his mind. To effect one of these isolations took quite a while, often as much as an hour. Before long he was dividing the whole world into good and bad, which increased the scope of his isolations. Even language fell into the two categories, so that he had to choose carefully lest a good and bad word make contact by being in the same sentence. The whole thing became so laborious that he deliberately thought about the forbidden things in order to strengthen the images and make their isolation easier. Thus the anxiety-linked impulses crept stealthily back into the symptoms.

This excerpt from a case history has been given only to illustrate the mechanisms of undoing and isolation and the general blocking of normal thought processes that occur in obsessive patients. The reason for his extreme anxiety on the subject of masturbation must be assumed to lie somewhere in the boy's childhood history. We shall now examine a longer excerpt from another history in order to show the neurotic process in relation to the whole development of personality and to specific crises occurring in the course of life.

An Illustrative Case: Peter Oberman

Peter Oberman had the misfortune to lose his faith in both of his parents at about the same time. While small he enjoyed his mother's affectionate and watchful care and the weekend visits of his father, who was a traveling salesman. Growing independence soon taught him to regard his mother as an object of contempt. She was an extremely timid woman who felt the world to be a dangerous place in which one must be constantly on guard against sickness, injury, accidents, and kidnappers. She constantly restrained him with images of danger, and as he became an active boy of eleven he resented the resulting overprotection. With a boy across the street he began to study electricity and radio. His mother, who greatly feared electricity, expressed her apprehension, and this was the last straw for Peter. He saw the full absurdity of her timid ways and began to treat her as a fool.

At this juncture his father changed jobs and was at home a great deal. He interested himself in his son's affairs with which he seriously interfered. Very close with his money, he would occasionally buy expensive presents for which he would expect the deepest gratitude, but they were never the right presents. When Peter wanted a photography set, his father got him a pool table; when he wanted a bicycle, he was given a moving-picture outfit. His father deplored his taste in radio programs and forbade him to listen. If Peter came home a minute later than the expected time, he had to brace himself for a veritable tirade. He was terrified, and he could see that his mother also was terrified by his father's insistence and anger. Furious at the domestic dictatorship, he never quite dared to resist it. At length things came to a more severe crisis. He frequently saw his mother in tears, comforted by his grandfather. The father had fallen in love with another woman and was spending nights away from home. Peter's emotions were deeply involved in the tangle; he swore at his father and used obscene language about the other woman. The father, now harboring some guilt feelings of his own, would stalk away in silence.

Both of Peter's identification figures thus crumbled into the dust of his contempt. From neither could he expect esteem or really considerate love. He turned to his grandfather, lately a widower, who occupied the apart-ment upstairs. The lonely old man responded warmly, and soon there was an active sharing of interests. The grandfather, a scholarly man, was an ardent admirer of Marx and the doctrine of economic determinism. He and Peter followed political events with intense interest. The grand-father bestowed much affection and praise, and at the same time inspired the eleven-year-old boy with ideas about science and the social order which must have been somewhat beyond his understanding.

Since he had rejected his mother and his father, since the atmosphere at home was completely intolerable, it became for Peter Oberman an overwhelmingly important matter not to lose his grandfather. The old man had suddenly become his only source of reliable affection. The idea of losing him aroused a desperate anxiety. But he was old; like the grand-mother, he might die. Peter began to be visited by anxious thoughts which seemed to force themselves into his mind. He had images of the house catching fire; he was afraid it would be struck by lightning or shattered in a high wind. He thought of various ways in which harm might come to his grandfather, and then he began to develop symptoms which had the character of magical acts designed to prevent this catastro-phe. If the thought crossed his mind that the house might burn, he felt compelled to touch something in order to avert the danger. If he had such a thought while stepping on a crack, he had to step on the crack again to cancel the thought. Soon he needed to perform extra touchings for good measure, and sometimes he would spend nearly an hour going through one of these operations. When people began to notice his peculiar be-havior, he developed a technique for discharging all the unlucky thoughts of the day in the privacy of his bedroom at night. If he pointed four times (a lucky number) to the southwest (a lucky direction), he could counteract the danger. But he never felt satisfied. He had to point $4 \times 4 \times 4 \times 4$ times, 256 times, and this took half an hour. He invented short cuts like stamping his foot to stand for groups of numbers, but in the end no time was saved. If the ritual could not be completed, he felt absolutely miserable. He was at the mercy of *obsessive thoughts* and *compulsive actions,* all of which had the significance of *undoing* the harm contained in a destructive thought.

It may seem paradoxical that Peter should entertain destructive thoughts that included his grandfather, the very source of his remaining security. It becomes less strange when we consider the circumstances from the point of view of an eleven-year-old boy whose faith in his father and mother has lately been shattered. He well knew that his father could show loving affection, yet quickly withdraw it and let him down. He well knew that his grandfather represented in a sense a false security, because he was old and would presently die. The trouble was that he needed love so badly that he could not resist the grandfather's affectionate interest, yet it was a restraint, an unwelcome restraint, for an eleven-year-old boy to spend so much time with an old man and hear him talk endlessly about barely comprehensible subjects. Though for the most part he could not stand the thought of his grandfather's dying, there were times when part of him secretly desired this event.

When Peter was twelve his grandfather did die. The fatal ailment was attributed by relatives to distress over the father's love affair—a further proof of the father's power to destroy Peter's happiness. Peter's grief was uncontrollable. His tearfulness lasted for several months, and his digestion was badly upset. He wanted to preserve his grandfather's apartment just as it was, and when this proved impossible he photographed every room from every angle, not even omitting the toilet, keeping the negatives locked up where no harm could befall them. He began a diary in which was recorded every incident that in any way reminded him of his lost protector. But his feeling of weakness and helplessness was now so great that he required more far-reaching reassurance. His maturing intellectual powers seized upon ideas received from his grandfather and developed the notion of a universal determinism, the understanding of which would give him complete control over everything. He dedicated his life to the laws of the electron and the atom, which he conceived as universal laws applicable to society and man as well as nature; his grandfather had already schooled him in economic determinism. Then he began to draw up life plans for himself, listing his liabilities and assets, taking hours to get every detail in perfect order. At fourteen he read Einstein, believing that if he could understand this great man he could understand anything.

This turn of events represents the launching of an overdriven striving. To restore some measure of confidence in himself, he developed a compensatory striving for superiority in the special form of omniscience. Through understanding, through familiarity with the basic laws of nature, he was going to control everything, including his father and his own tempestuous emotions. That a boy with superior intellectual gifts should become interested in philosophy between twelve and fourteen and should be attracted by sweeping generalizations is not in itself extraordinary. In Peter's case, however, curiosity was a secondary motive; he was using philosophy to compensate himself for a feeling of weakness, to make himself feel masterful and omnipotent. His preoccupation with ideas and future plans was more than a natural unfolding of real powers; it was a desperate measure designed to avert anxiety. As a result he overdid it, set his goals too high, and spent fruitless hours struggling to work out an unchallengeable system of truth. It is this excess, this rigidity, that distinguished his overdriven striving from a straightforward expression of healthy impulses.

When Oberman reached college, his condition had considerably improved. At high school he had done well, achieved some social participation, and contrived to overcome his compulsive rituals. His overdriven striving gave sufficient security without wrecking his social adjustment. The new environment, however, revived several of his problems, and the threat of compulsory military service touched off many of his early childhood fears. His first course in philosophy challenged the naturalistic system he had worked out for himself. He spent so much time trying to revise his thinking and free it from contradictions that he neglected his regular studies, lost appetite, and, as he himself put it, "walked around in a daze all summer." When in the company of his classmates he found himself showing off, giving a "big line," trying to impress with his superior knowledge, even telling lies in his struggle to put himself foremost. Any little failure brought on protracted daydreams of omnipotence. One day he bungled a recitation in elementary German: for hours he daydreamed about a future invitation from the university to give a series of lectures in German. The overdriven striving was speeded up and stiffened to a point where it was again indistinguishable from obsessive symptoms.

Impending military service awakened a host of fears. He was afraid of being kicked around at training camp, and especially of physical injury. His relations with his father had not prepared him to react well to authority. Anxiety mounted steadily, so that after two months in training he arrived at complete neurotic breakdown. Separated from the service, he sought professional help for a thorough treatment of his neurosis. This took a long time, as is often the case with obsessional neurosis, but the results were good. He presently entered an exacting course of professional training and was in due time embarked on a successful career.

DISSOCIATED CONDITIONS

We turn now to a group of disorders generally classed with hysteria, but characterized by peculiarities especially in the realm of memory. Whether we are dealing with a brief amnesia, a more extended fugue, or a fully developed double or multiple personality, the central feature of the disorder is a forgetting of personal identity. The patient forgets who he is and where he lives. He loses the symbols of his identity and also the memories of his previous life that support a continuing sense of selfhood. The phenomenon is familiar through newspaper reports of cases of amnesia. Perhaps the patient is so confused by the loss of memory that he approaches a police officer to ask for help. In other cases—these are the ones technically called *fugues*—he may go on for quite a while functioning as an adequate new person, perhaps with a new name. There are reports of cases in which a patient has remained in a fugue state for months and even years. Conceivably, such a change might be permanent, but we would have no access to such cases.

It is a little unfortunate that the term *amnesia* has been captured by the press for just this particular type of memory disorder. Literally, *amnesia* means any kind of pathological forgetting, whether caused by drugs, brain injuries, old age, or psychogenic factors. The cases we are considering here represent a particular type of amnesia, the forgetting of personal identity. This particular pattern seems to be wholly psychogenic in character. The forgetting is somehow connected with anxious conflict and represents an attempt to do something about that conflict.

Amnesia for Personal Identity

The following example reported by McDougall is remarkable for its transparency.[18] A British color-sergeant in World War I was carrying a message, riding his motorcycle through a dangerous section of the front. All at once it was several hours later, and he was pushing his motorcycle along the streets of a coastal town nearly a hundred miles away. In utter bewilderment he gave himself up to the military police, but he could tell absolutely nothing of his long trip. The amnesia was ultimately broken by the use of hypnosis. The man then remembered that he was thrown down by a shell explosion, that he picked up himself and his machine, that he started straight for the coastal town, that he studied signs and asked for directions in order to reach this destination.

It is clear, in this case, that the amnesia entailed no loss of competence. The patient's actions were purposive, rational, and intelligent. The amnesia rested only on his sense of personal identity. The conflict was between fear, suddenly intensified by his narrow escape, and his duty to complete the dangerous mission. The forgetting of personal identity made it possible to give way to his impulse toward flight, now irresistible, without exposing himself to the almost equally unbearable anxiety associated with being a coward, failing his mission, and undergoing arrest as a deserter. When he achieved physical safety the two sides of the conflict resumed their normal proportions and his sense of personal identity suddenly returned.

---

[18] W. McDougall, *Outline of Abnormal Psychology* (New York: Charles Scribner's Sons, 1926), p. 258.

In wartime there are many cases of amnesia and fugue which, like the preceding one, originate under traumatic conditions. In civilian life the same phenomenon occurs under less violent circumstances, but generally in connection with what amounts to an emotional crisis in the patient's life. Abeles and Schilder in a study of sixty-three cases found that "some unpleasant social conflict, either financial or familial, was significant in the immediate cause of amnesia," although behind these immediate conflicts "deeper motives are found." [19] A more detailed report of five cases from the Menninger Clinic has the special advantage that the precipitating events and the content of the amnesic period were carefully recovered in all their personal meaning for the patient.[20] These studies support the idea that forgetting one's identity is a defense against intolerable anxiety when some powerful need or wish becomes uncontrollable. As is so often true, the wish is ordinarily suppressed because the patient is what he is, occupying a certain social position and having certain responsibilities and obligations. When the wish is strengthened, usually by some external crisis, so that it can no longer be suppressed, personal identity has to be blotted out, as if the patient said, "It can't be I who does such a thing."

Valuable information can thus be obtained by studying what patients recall about the situation in which a symptom came into being. A method has been developed by Luborsky for examining these situations the moment they occur. The technique, called the symptom-context method, requires the tape-recording of therapeutic interviews. It is then possible to examine the conversational context just preceding any symptom—pain, headache, fast heartbeat, anxiety—that the patient reports to have occurred. Among the symptoms studied in this way by Luborsky is momentary forgetting, as when the patient starts to say something and then cannot remember what he was going to say.[21] These are, of course, minor instances of amnesia with fairly prompt recovery of the lost thought, but there is almost always a clear connection between the memory failure and an uneasy or embarrassing topic. The forgettings of these patients, not unknown also to the rest of us, may be small models of what happens on a large scale in amnesia for personal identity.

Multiple Personalities

A psychiatrist may live out a long and active professional career without encountering a single case of multiple personality. Such cases are not at

19 M. Abeles and P. Schilder, "Psychogenic Loss of Personal Identity," *Archives of Neurology and Psychiatry*, XXXIV (1935), pp. 587–604.

20 E. R. Geleerd, F. J. Hacker, and D. Rapaport, "Contribution to the Study of Amnesia and Allied Conditions," *Psychoanalytic Quarterly*, XIV (1945), pp. 199–220.

21 L. Luborsky and A. H. Averbach, "The Symptom-Context Method: Quantitative Studies of Symptom Formation in Psychotherapy," *Journal of the American Psychoanalytic Association*, XVII (1969), pp. 68–99; L. Luborsky, "New Directions in Research on Neurotic and Psychosomatic Symptoms," *American Scientist*, LVIII (1970), pp. 661–68.

all common. Taylor and Martin combed most of the literature up to 1944, and found only seventy-six reported cases.[22] The total was still less than a hundred in 1972, according to Horton and Miller, who found "less than a dozen reported cases in the last fifty years." [23] Nevertheless, multiple personalities are worthy of mention because of the important problems they raise.

Multiple personalities can be considered as more extreme forms of what we saw in amnesias and fugues. In well-developed cases there is a loss of personal identity, but instead of the amnesic period being dominated by one imperious wish, it becomes an arena in which a whole new personality develops. The patient feels like a different person, and he gradually builds up the memory system of a different person. A second independent personality does not spring into existence all at once. The second sense of personal identity can be created only out of accumulated memories. But once the second system has begun to round itself into a separate self, the person may begin to function as two individuals. Today he is Mr. X, who has no memory of anything Mr. Y. has ever done. Tomorrow he may be Mr. Y, who has no recollection of anything Mr. X has ever done. One can imagine the hopeless confusion this creates not merely for Mr. X and Mr. Y but for everyone with whom Mr. XY comes in contact.

The study of multiple personalities in a way recapitulates the history of abnormal psychology. At first they were looked upon as queer nervous weaknesses. Later the emphasis was placed on dissociation. Cures were attempted by using hypnosis to reassociate the dissociated fragments. When Morton Prince wrote *The Dissociation of a Personality* in 1905, describing the celebrated Miss Beauchamp who had three main personalities, he emphasized the dramatic changes from self to self, the ensuing complications, and the problem of synthesizing the different selves by making them aware of each other's memory systems.[24] Fifteen years later he carefully reconsidered the case in the light of the newly developing dynamic psychology.[25] He showed that one of the personalities had "existed" for a long time as the rebellious and playful fantasy life of an otherwise very prim and proper child. This meant that when, in early adult life, the patient reached a severe neurotic breakdown, there already existed in her a long-standing semi-independent series of memories that served as the nucleus for one of her new selves. He also showed that each of Miss Beauchamp's three per-

[22] W. S. Taylor and M. F. Martin, "Multiple Personality," *Journal of Abnormal and Social Psychology,* XXXIX (1944), pp. 281–300.

[23] P. Horton and D. Miller, "The Etiology of Multiple Personality," *Comprehensive Psychiatry,* XIII (1972), pp. 151–59.

[24] M. Prince, *The Dissociation of a Personality* (London: Longmans, Green & Co., Ltd., 1905).

[25] M. Prince, "Miss Beauchamp: The Psychogenesis of Multiple Personality," *Journal of Abnormal Psychology,* XVI (1920), No. 1. Reprinted in Prince's *Clinical and Experimental Studies in Personality,* A. A. Roback, ed. (Cambridge: Sci-Art Publishers, 1939), pp. 185–268.

sonalities could be conceived as representing a group of strivings, with their associated attitudes and values, such as would offer a certain inherent contradiction even in the most healthy person. One personality embodied a series of saintly virtues, another a strong independent ambition, another an impish and playful quality. In short, Prince conceived that Miss Beauchamp developed separate personalities where a healthy person would simply have conflict of motives. Twenty years later the case was again reconsidered by McCurdy, who viewed the several personalities in the light of reactions to the physician.[26] Dr. Prince was the center of the patient's world during several years of treatment. In her saintly personality she was submissive and respectful toward him. Her impish self was slangy, saucy, teasingly affectionate. The ambitious and independent side of her represented rebellion against his dominance and made its first clear appearance at the time when there was conflict between patient and doctor. McCurdy suggests that these more contemporary motives lay behind the different personalities, and that the apparent separateness of the selves was encouraged by the constant use of hypnotism for treatment.

It is well to be skeptical about multiple personalities, especially when the opportunity has existed for them to be dramatized in hypnotic states. Undoubtedly a case of multiple personality can be played up or played down according to the physician's predilection. It is nevertheless probable that they are perfectly genuine phenomena which sometimes occur without any help from the doctor. This appears to be true of the case reported in 1972 by Horton and Miller, who had no prior expectation that multiple selves would appear and who took pains to offer no encouragement.[27] Their patient nevertheless disclosed three different selves, amnesic for one another, which had been in existence at various times during the four years since her father's death—these in addition to a fourth personality that included the memories of all but had great difficulty living with the highly conflicting tendencies of the others. These authors attach central importance to problems of identification. If during development the situation favors many unstable identifications rather than a few stable ones, the chances are increased that the resulting "selves" will be difficult to integrate. But it seems likely in addition that multiple personality reflects a pervasive self-dramatizing adaptive style. This trait has often been mentioned in connection with the more physical forms of hysteria.

CONVERSION HYSTERIA

Our discussion of conversion hysteria can be relatively brief. Because it was the first neurosis to attract persistent medical attention, our historical introduction (Chapter 1) has already made us familiar with many of its

---

[26] H. G. McCurdy, "A Note on the Dissociation of a Personality," *Character and Personality*, X (1941), pp. 33–41.

[27] Horton and Miller, *op. cit.*, pp. 151–59.

manifestations. Charcot's and Janet's studies of hysteria were milestones in modern thinking about neurosis. Freud's first work, in association with Breuer, dealt with a typical if extreme case of hysteria. Our present task will be to summarize the general facts insofar as they are known today.

Varieties of Conversion Symptoms

In addition to the amnesias, fugues, and multiple personalities considered in the last section, hysterical symptoms take a wide variety of bodily forms. On the motor side there are the *paralyses* which may include an arm, a leg, both legs, or one whole side of the body. These symptoms can be distinguished from true organic injuries by the fact that normal reflexes are retained in the paralyzed area, and that little or no muscular degeneration occurs. Sometimes the diagnosis is made still easier by the anatomical nonsense that characterizes the symptom: both hands, for instance, may be paralyzed, while the arms retain their motility, a state that could be produced organically only by a highly peculiar nerve injury in both wrists. Other motor symptoms are *mutism* (inability to speak), *aphonia* (inability to speak above a whisper to "voice" the speech), *tremor,* and *tics* (spasmodic jerking in a small coordinated group of muscles). On the sensory side there are the many varieties of *anaesthesia.* These may accompany the paralyses, but they sometimes occur alone. Within any one sense department the anaesthesia may take a number of forms. In vision, for instance, the possibilities include total blindness, blindness in one eye, contraction of the visual field to a small focal point, blindness in the left half or right half of both eyes, and many other curious fragmentations of the visual process. Another symptom is the *hysterical fit,* which in some respects resembles an epileptic seizure but can generally be distinguished from it. Finally, there are sometimes *hysterical twilight states* in which the patient is confused and distressed, experience having an unreal and dreamlike quality. The loss of contact with reality is less complete than would be the case in psychosis.

Symptoms of this sort have for some time been known as *conversion reactions.* The term is derived from an idea of Freud's that the energy of a repressed instinctual urge becomes diverted into sensory-motor channels in such a way as to block the functioning of some organ. Regarded even by its inventor as difficult to understand or to verify, this notion of converted energy is of no value today, but the name persists, and with it the fact that the seemingly bodily symptoms are not plausible consequences of physical impairment. Discarding the language of hypothetical energetics, we still have to explain what Charcot originally discerned as the oddly mental character of the bodily disabilities.

Psychological Basis of Conversion Reactions

Like other forms of neurosis, the conversion reaction can profitably be considered a defense against anxiety. "Its essential and distinctive feature," according to Fairbairn, "is the substitution of a bodily state for a personal problem; and this substitution enables the personal problem as such to be ignored." [28] Enlarging on this statement, Ziegler and Imboden propose that not just anxiety but any strong negative feeling—shame, disgust, loss of self-esteem—may be the reason for defense. They further emphasize the communicative aspect of the symptom. The patient with a conversion symptom they see as "enacting the role of a person with 'organic' illness, symbolically communicating his distress by means of somatic symptoms." The maneuver distracts both other people and the patient himself from recognizing the personal problem, whatever its nature, and in addition the fact of illness may be "useful as an instrument in negotiating interpersonal transactions." [29] In everyday life it is sometimes observed that a person with weighty emotional problems becomes relaxed and serene when afflicted with a real organic illness, which provides a blameless excuse for shelving the problems and accepting the invalid's role. The hysterical conversion reaction achieves much the same result without benefit of true organic illness.

There are thus two sides to conversion hysteria: the personal problems from which escape is sought, and the mechanism whereby symptoms are produced. Both points are illustrated in the following example.[30]

A married man of twenty-eight was in a motor accident. He sustained minor scratches and was otherwise apparently unhurt, but he emerged from the accident completely blind. The absence of any injury that could be responsible for loss of vision led to a diagnosis of hysteria. It was discovered that the accident occurred while he was driving to the maternity hospital to see his wife and first-born child. His first remark to the psychiatrist was that he could not tie his wife down to a blind man and would now divorce her.

This strange sequence of events becomes intelligible if we work out the patient's history and discover the personal meaning of the situation that so startlingly made him blind. First we discover a clearly *overdriven striving* in the patient's previous behavior, an exaggerated trend toward independent self-sufficiency. He early separated from his parents and established an independent life for himself, resolving at the same time that he would never marry. He was attracted to women, but kept all relationships at a purely sexual level and discontinued them at the first hint of deeper feeling and especially at the faintest threat of marriage. His history showed that the purpose of this overdriven striving was to hold in check all feelings

[28] W. R. D. Fairbairn, "Observations on the Nature of Hysterical States," *British Journal of Medical Psychology*, XXVII (1954), pp. 105–15.

[29] F. J. Ziegler and J. B. Imboden, "Contemporary Conversion Reactions: II. A Conceptual Model," *Archives of General Psychiatry*, VI (1962), pp. 279–87. Reprinted in L. Y. Rabkin and J. E. Carr, eds., *Sourcebook in Abnormal Psychology* (Boston: Houghton Mifflin Co., 1967), pp. 165–72.

[30] W. Malamud, "The Psychoneuroses," in J. McV. Hunt, ed., *Personality and the Behavior Disorders* (New York: The Ronald Press Co., 1944), Vol. II, chap. 28.

of dependence on women. The mother had been extremely domineering and the father weakly submissive. While we cannot precisely recover the earliest anxiety in this case, it evidently had something to do with the parental relationship. Dependent longings entailed unwilling submission to the mother's iron rule, a thing to be hated and feared because it made one resemble the weak and helpless father. Therefore dependent longings constituted a danger, and the trend toward self-sufficiency served to hold them in check.

The patient's overdriven striving was not allowed to prevent the satisfaction of his sexual needs; it functioned merely to prevent his relationships from satisfying anything besides sex. His safety lay in his freedom to walk out of any relationship. An equilibrium was established which worked well enough for several years. *Disturbance of the equilibrium* began when his sexual adventures brought him in contact with a woman who in certain respects reminded him of his mother and stimulated his dependent longings. This was so satisfactory that he permitted the relation to develop. He sought her advice and allowed her to make decisions. He grew increasingly uncomfortable—anxiety was evidently stirring—but he finally consented to marriage on the condition that they would never have children.

One can say at this point that he had suspended his overdriven striving in order to gratify dependent longings, but he kept the guarantee that he could escape at any time if this new equilibrium proved unbearable. His tension and discomfort show that it was only just bearable. Then suddenly his avenue of escape was blocked: his wife became pregnant. He demanded an abortion, but she refused. Throughout the pregnancy he was increasingly uneasy. He did not know why he felt this way, but in the course of later analytic treatment he recovered memories that showed how earnestly he had hoped the pregnancy would not mature and how tenaciously he clung to the notion that escape from the marriage would still be possible. When his wife went to the hospital his anxiety came into the open, taking the twisted form of terror lest something happen to the mother or child. Finally he learned that both were well, and that he could see them. He jumped into the car and drove toward the hospital. Then the accident happened, and he was unable to see them.

Knowing about the patient's past and his chief overdriven striving, we can understand that the successful birth of the child pushed him to the point of panic. But this does not account for the highly specific symptom of blindness. By what process was it possible for this symptom to come to his rescue? We know only that the patient apparently considered blindness an adequate ground for divorce, now that his wife had a child to support. If this idea was in his mind before the motor accident, it might have influenced the direction taken by defensive inhibition. One can easily speculate that the patient had hoped he would never live to see the proof of his permanent bondage, thus focalizing the danger on seeing, so that going blind became a way of preventing contact with the threat. But there is no direct evidence for such associative connections, and even if they were operative in the patient they would not fully explain the conversion symptom. There are many things in our lives that it is painful to see, but we see them none the less.

Placement of the Symptoms

The problem of the location and form of hysterical symptoms is still so poorly understood that we can do no more than suggest a number of possibilities.

1. An old study of hysterical tremor, made by Kretschmer during World War I, suggests a mechanism that can be described as unwitting reinforcement.[31] Tremor is part of any severe anxiety reaction, and it is often present in soldiers exposed to grave danger. Ordinarily it subsides when the danger is past, but in certain cases it was found to persist and become a lasting symptom. Kretschmer pointed out that reflexes can be reinforced by a voluntary diffuse tensing of the whole motor system. The knee jerk can be amplified by clenching the hands and slightly tensing all the musculature. This reflex cannot be increased by direct volition, which actually interferes with the automatic act and adds a secondary voluntary kick. Only a gentle diffuse hypertonicity of the muscles facilitates reflexes. This indirect reinforcement in no way changes the character of the reflex, which is still not in the least sensed as voluntary. The tremor patients, therefore, could be conceived of as involuntarily sustaining their reflex tremor by keeping up a slight hypertonicity of the musculature. The aid they were giving to the tremor would not enter consciousness or stir up guilt feelings. If this unwitting aid were continued for a short while so as to prevent the tremor from subsiding, the symptom would become established as an independent habit system that would continue indefinitely. Kretschmer considered that his hypothesis was to some extent verified by the fact that treatment consisting of prolonged muscular relaxation often stopped the symptom, especially in its early stages. Relaxation counteracted the unwitting trick whereby the patient sustained his tremor.

Strictly speaking, this hypothesis applies only to one type of symptom, hysterical tremor originating under the traumatic conditions of combat. It would be easy to generalize from this finding to all conversion symptom formation, but the clue remains a useful one.

2. A somewhat similar process occurs when the symptom starts with a true organic injury. Unwitting prolongation turns what should be a temporary disability into a permanent thing. There are various reflex responses which tend to immobilize an injured part. The muscles of a wounded leg, for instance, will stiffen to prevent further motion and pain.

[31] E. Kretschmer, *Hysteria*, Nervous and Mental Disease Monographs, No. 44 (New York: Nervous and Mental Disease Publishing Co., 1926).

If these immobilizing reflexes are prolonged by a mechanism akin to Kretsch-mer's, the wounded leg becomes an hysterically paralyzed leg.

In a recent study made at a Veterans' Hospital in Appalachia, conversion symptoms were found in something like a quarter of the patients, a far larger proportion than would be expected in a civilian institution. The investigators noticed that the symptom was commonly placed in some organ that was the site of previous injury or disability. They also advanced the opinion that the hysterical mechanism was more readily available in a population much given to overt expressions of aggression and to blaming its frustrations on external circumstances, including physical health.[32]

3. Symptom formation may be favored when some organ is in a special condition at a crucial moment of crisis. There was a good example of this in the historic Breuer case: [33] a paralysis of the right arm had its origin in the occasion when the patient, watching beside her father's sick bed, dozed and had a terrifying nightmare while her arm hung in an awkward position, "asleep" over the back of the chair. In neuroses of traumatic onset it sometimes appears that the symptom falls on an organ system that was highly active at the moment of acute crisis. If an explosion catches the soldier in the act of firing his rifle, the symptoms may place themselves in the form of paralyzed hands, bent neck, closed eye, etc.[34]

4. Direct connection between some organ system and serious conflict may serve to choose the location. This is particularly true in what are called *occupational* neuroses—for example, mutism or aphonia in a sales-man, paralysis of the fingers in a pianist, writer's cramp in a writer, or, to extend slightly the meaning of "occupation," sexual impotence in a Don Juan. In all such cases there are conflict and anxiety over carrying out the occupation successfully, and the symptom definitely prevents further ac-tivity. For example, a veteran—from Appalachia, as it happened—who worked as a railroad brakeman developed an hysterical weakness in his right hand which prevented him from exerting a sufficient grip on levers. A minor war injury to his right hand some years before suggested the site of the symptom, and since he received financial compensation because of it there was considerable secondary gain for being disabled.

5. Anticipated *secondary gain* seems to play an especially important part in hysterical symptom formation. The gain is not consciously anticipated nor the symptom voluntarily devised, but the symptom shows an unmis-takable relation to certain effects on the patient's environment. This is nicely illustrated in one of the cases of H. V. Dicks.[35] A middle-aged mar-ried woman had to nurse her mother-in-law, who was paralyzed in both legs. Her husband forced her to do this, and seemed to become concerned

---

[32] E. A. Weinstein, R. A. Eck, and O. G. Lyerly, "Conversion Hysteria in Appalachia," *Psychiatry*, XXXII (1969), pp. 334–41.

[33] See above, pp. 26–27.

[34] A. Kardiner, *The Traumatic Neuroses of War* (New York: Paul B. Hoeber, Inc., 1941).

[35] Dicks, *op. cit.*, p. 93.

only with his mother, forgetting his wife. One day the wife took a walk, feeling rebellious, but at the same time very anxious as she became dimly aware of angry wishes that the old lady would die. She felt faint and sat down on a park bench. A moment later she tried to rise, only to discover that both her legs were paralyzed and that she now needed as much of her husband's attention as did his mother.

6. In many cases, including the one just mentioned, the symptom is in part a product of imitation. This is shown, for instance, in a study of student naval aviators who developed conversion reactions that put them out of action during training. In 70 per cent of the cases the site of the symptom was an organ system in which one of the parents had had serious illness.[36] The assumption might be made that when a symptom is needed, so to speak, to avoid acute anxiety, patterns of illness are unwittingly adopted which in the patient's past experience have been seen to provide legitimate exemption from struggle. The role of illness is more easily copied than invented.

Various mistaken ideas about hysteria can be set straight by these and other recent studies. Hysteria is not, as was long supposed, a disorder peculiar to women, though its incidence is greater in women. It is not a disorder peculiar to the nineteenth century or to the populations studied by Charcot, Janet, Freud, and Prince; it still occurs, and if it seems less frequent today this may be the result of more refined methods of diagnosis. It is not a disorder peculiar to backward rural areas where education is limited and medical ideas crude. The naval aviators, all college graduates, at once put this conception to rout, but suggest an alternative interpretation. Naval aviators, the study showed, are recruited from highly achievement-oriented backgrounds, have typically done well in competitive sports, tend to accept no excuses for anxiety or failure, and thus see physical illness as the only legitimate ground for escaping unbearable strain. In this they are consistent with the extroverted, aggressive Appalachian veterans, and it is further consistent that conversion hysteria among men is currently common only in psychiatric facilities connected with military services.[37] Presumably the more tolerant a society becomes about accepting anxiety, nervousness, depressed feelings, and other subjective complaints as grounds for exemption from full participation, the less urgent is the need for a symptom that emulates a physical disease. In this connection it appears that medical knowledge has a real effect on hysterical symptom formation. The dramatic old-fashioned symptoms like the glove anaesthesia are no longer available to educated people, especially those trained as physicians, nurses, or medical secretaries. Cases are reported in which there is detailed simulation of a complex disease like multiple sclerosis, but it turns out that

36 T. F. Mucha and R. F. Reinhardt, "Conversion Reactions in Student Aviators," *American Journal of Psychiatry*, CXXVII (1970), pp. 493–97.

37 R. Rabkin, "Conversion Hysteria as Social Maladaptation," *Psychiatry*, XXVII (1964), pp. 349–63.

the patient has picked up the necessary details in the course of being examined for possible organic disorder. More often among relatively sophisticated patients the hysterical symptom takes the form of pain. The favorite conversion symptom, so to speak, in contemporary hysterias is pain in some part of the body believed by the patient to be organically diseased.[38]

PROBLEM OF THE CHOICE OF NEUROSIS

There is widespread agreement that neurosis has its roots in anxiety. It is one of the hazards of our being creatures with a powerful propensity toward fear and flight. There are good evolutionary reasons for this propensity, but it can sometimes get us into trouble rather than out of it. Whether neurotic symptoms are considered to be fairly direct products of the conditioning of anxiety responses, protected from extinction by learned avoidance reactions, or whether they are described as a more remote consequence of early childhood anxiety, protected from relearning by defense mechanisms and subject to substantial amounts of displacement and associative elaboration, the central theme is always anxiety. Conceivably this is too narrow; following Tomkins' sophisticated analysis of human affects we should seriously consider expanding the formula to include other negative feelings such as disgust and shame.[39] Even so, it is not likely that anxiety will be denied a major position in the theory of neurosis.

This basic agreement, however, covers only part of the ground. At one time it seemed reasonable to contend that neurotic symptoms flowered out of the conflict that lay behind them, representing some portion of the anxiety reaction itself (like tremor), some portion of the defensive processes (like a hand-washing compulsion), or some portion of the impulses that awaken anxiety (like sexual fantasies or obsessive ideas of violence). These ideas need not be entirely discarded—they are possibilities—but their generality is not established, and in any event they fall seriously short of explaining the large variety of neurotic phenomena described in this chapter. Why does one person have plain anxiety attacks, another a circumscribed phobia, a third a crippling set of obsessions and compulsions, a fourth an amnesia for personal identity, while a fifth blossoms forth with an hysterical paralysis of the lower limbs?

Historically this problem has been entitled the *choice of neurosis*. The expression will do provided we remember that "choice" is not being used in its common meaning of a conscious selection of alternatives. Presumably an imposter, a malingerer, or a gifted actor can voluntarily produce fairly convincing replicas of neurotic symptoms, but this is certainly not how it happens with real neuroses. As we saw in our historical introduction, Janet

[38] F. J. Ziegler, J. B. Imboden, and E. Meyer, "Contemporary Conversion Reactions: A Clinical Study," *American Journal of Psychiatry*, CXVI (1960), pp. 901–10.

[39] S. S. Tomkins, *Affect, Imagery, Consciousness,* Vol. II (New York: Springer Publishing Co., Inc., 1963).

made a start on the problem by postulating two different types of constitutional vulnerability. One type, the *hysteric,* suffered from a natural weakness in maintaining the organization of personality under conditions of stress. Such people were vulnerable to dissociation, hence to the whole range of conversion symptoms and dissociated states described in the last two sections of this chapter. The other type, which Janet called *psychasthenic,* was free from the liability to fall apart in this way, but was much given to rumination, doubt, inner debate, and similar subjective operations which became crippling under conditions of severe stress. Janet's conception of these matters may not have been wholly correct, but he was touching upon human differences familiar in everyday life. We all have acquaintances who might be described as habitually "cerebral" in the sense of thinking about their experience, turning things over in their minds, and rarely acting with impulsive abandon. Obsessive and compulsive symptoms appear to be consistent extensions of these qualities. We know other people who are more inclined to leap before they look, who immerse themselves in each experience, who seek excitement and a touch of drama in everything they do. It would surprise us if such a person, even under great stress, displayed the repetitive rituals and philosophical entanglements that ensnared the "cerebral" Peter Oberman. Hysterical symptoms seem to be a consistent extension of a dramatic, communicative style of living.

Current Research

There is now considerable research that bears in one way or another on individual differences of the kind just described. Commenting on this research, Korner postulates two regulatory principles for dealing with stimulation. One of these "will serve to sift, to diminish or to make manageable incoming stimuli" by means of analysis and reflection. The person will tend to avoid strong and novel excitations, and when dealing with anxiety will most easily employ defense mechanisms of intellectualization and isolation. The other principle favors "the management of strong stimulation through motor or affective discharge, through hypermotility, impulsivity, action rather than reflection," and it is characteristic that novelty and excitement are welcomed rather than avoided.[40] Korner's own research, done with infants 2 to 4 days old, indicates that differences in the management of stimulation already exist at birth, and other workers have found similar stable preferences during the first few years of life.[41] Especially relevant is the finding by Kagan and co-workers that as early as the age of two, and more clearly during the school years, children differ stably with

[40] A. F. Korner, "Individual Differences at Birth: Implications for Early Experience and Later Development," *American Journal of Orthopsychiatry,* XLI (1971), pp. 608–19.
[41] A. Thomas, S. Chess, H. G. Birch, M. E. Hertzig, and S. Korn, *Behavioral Individuality in Early Childhood* (New York: New York University Press, 1963); S. K. Escalona, *The Roots of Individuality: Normal Patterns of Development in Infancy* (Chicago: Aldine Publishing Co., 1968).

respect to speed of processing information. This was shown, for instance, in a test of problem solving involving selection of the best among several responses. School children having a "fast conceptual tempo" answered quickly with the first thing that struck them as appropriate, and made many errors. Other children, the "reflective" ones, delayed their response as if considering the alternatives, and made few errors.[42] The cognitive differences disclosed in this research have a good deal in common with the constitutional differences originally postulated by Janet.

The most thorough and persistent research on basic dimensions of personality has been done by Eysenck.[43] Using a large number of tests and relatively precise experimental measurements, and treating the results with sophisticated mathematical analysis, Eysenck has built up evidence for two stable independent dimensions along which people vary, one called *neuroticism,* the other called *extroversion–introversion.* The neuroticism dimension covers qualities with respect to which all varieties of neurotics tend to differ from the normal. "At the one end we have people whose emotions are labile, strong, and easily aroused; they are moody, touchy, anxious, restless, and so forth. At the other extreme we have the people whose emotions are stable, less easily aroused, people who are calm, even-tempered, carefree, and reliable." [44] The second dimension, extroversion–introversion, owes something to Jung's historic speculations about the outward or inward turning of interest, though some change of meaning inevitably results from translating Jung's shrewd impressions into practical measurements.[45] This is the dimension that bears on the choice of neurosis. Conversion hysteria and dissociated states are related to extroversion, while phobias and obsessive neuroses go with introversion. By giving the tests to criterion groups consisting of patients independently diagnosed as hysteric, obsessive, and phobic, these relationships have been satisfactorily confirmed.

In studying dimensions it is easiest to describe the ends, the extreme cases, but necessary to remember that the majority of people fall somewhere in the middle. Eysenck uses the following expressions, among others, to describe the extreme extrovert: "sociable, needs to have people to talk to, craves excitement, acts on the spur of the moment, likes change, prefers to keep moving and doing things; altogether his feelings are not kept under tight control." The extreme introvert, in contrast, is described as "quiet, retiring, introspective, reserved; he tends to plan ahead, does not like ex-

---

[42] J. Kagan, "Information Processing in the Child," in *Readings in Child Development and Personality,* P. H. Mussen, J. J. Conger, and J. Kagan, eds. (New York: Harper & Row, 1965), pp. 313–23; N. D. Repucci, "Individual Differences in the Consideration of Information Among Two-Year-Old Children," *Developmental Psychology,* II (1970), pp. 240–46.

[43] H. J. Eysenck, *The Structure of Human Personality* (3rd ed.; London: Methuen & Co., Ltd., 1970); in briefer form, Eysenck and Rachman, *The Causes and Cures of Neurosis, op. cit.,* chaps. 2–4.

[44] Eysenck and Rachman, *ibid.,* p. 20.

[45] C. G. Jung, *Psychological Types, or the Psychology of Individuation* (1920), trans. H. G. Baynes (New York: Harcourt Brace Jovanovich, Inc., 1924).

citement, likes a well-ordered mode of life, and keeps his feelings under close control."[46] Going further with his experimental analysis, Eysenck has found evidence for the hypothesis that extroversion–introversion depends on the relative strength of excitatory and inhibitory processes in the cortex, a conception that owes a good deal to Pavlov. It may seem paradoxical, in view of overt behavior, that predominant excitation is attributed to introverts and predominant inhibition to extroverts. But the introverted pattern certainly suggests cortical excitation and can be interpreted as a way of maintaining control, whereas the extreme extrovert, seeking novelty, change, and excitement, can be understood as trying to overcome the dulling effects of excessive cortical inhibition. The precise basis of this dimension needs clarification by future research, but the correlations seem well established between type of neurosis and the tests of extroversion–introversion.

Neurosis and Difficulties of Living

As we saw in the historical introduction, study of the neuroses began in connection with medical practice, and they were interpreted to be forms of disease. When the nervous disorders proved to have no sensible relation to disordered nerves, they were called psychogenic but still cast in the medical model. When it became clear that psychogenic disorders resulted from learning processes and responses to difficulties in living, and when in consequence their correction had to be defined in terms of relearning, the educative process was still described as one in which a doctor treated a patient for a disease. This bit of history offers a wry commentary on inertia in human thinking, but the medical model escaped challenge while most of the work remained in the hands of physicians. The appropriateness of this model becomes a sharp issue today because professional workers trained in other ways than medicine, especially psychologists, have been able to deal successfully with neurotic difficulties, and want to establish their right to use their skills in this way. It is the scientific problem, however, rather than the professional one, that concerns us at this point. With evidence now at hand, how can we best understand the phenomenon called neurosis?

Understanding seems to require that we keep in mind at least four considerations: (1) constitutional vulnerability, (2) vulnerability created by early anxieties, (3) adaptive style, and (4) current stress.

1. Eysenck's two dimensions of neuroticism and extroversion–introversion are most plausibly interpreted as evidences of constitutional differences. If a child is born with the innate organization that will cause him later to score high on the neuroticism scale—this might mean in the beginning mainly a low threshold for anxiety—he will have a greater likelihood of getting into trouble with his anxiety somewhere along the way. If he starts with a relatively extreme endowment of extroversion, he will be more likely

to meet later stress through hysterical symptoms. If strongly introverted by nature, he will be vulnerable to phobic or obsessive patterns when encountering severe difficulties of living. As with most constitutional qualities, these outcomes do not follow inevitably. They simply occur more easily when other necessary conditions are present.

2. Differences can be presumed in the extent to which different children are exposed to severe anxiety. If a single fright is very severe, or if, probably more typically, there are repeated situations of danger such as incurring parental anger or loss of love, a person becomes predisposed to strong anxiety in later circumstances which in some manner resemble the original ones. Such circumstances may never occur, but if they do they elicit anxiety that is much more intense than the current situation warrants. Being blamed for a wife's suicide would be stressful for anyone, but it precipitates a stubborn phobia only when childhood fright has created special vulnerability.

3. Extroversion and introversion are associated not only with different symptom patterns but also with different adaptive styles. Adaptation requires flexibility, and this will be restricted if one style is developed too strongly. People whose style is "cerebral," like Peter Oberman, may do well in occupations requiring reflective thought or detailed workmanship but experience difficulty when decisions have to be made or when strong feeling is appropriate. The success of a strongly preferred adaptive style thus depends on the circumstances of one's life. Preferred style may work well for a time, only to fail when circumstances change. Adaptive styles, of course, are not confined to the two that we have examined in connection with neurosis. In an account based on clinical studies, Shapiro describes, in addition to the hysterical and obsessive-compulsive, a paranoid style and an impulsive style, the latter associated with behavior tending toward delinquency.[47] A person's adaptive style determines the types of situation he is likely to find least manageable, hence most stressful. If the stress is sufficiently acute, neurotic symptoms develop which are congruent extensions of the preferred adaptive style.

4. Whatever the importance of past conditionings and vulnerabilities, current stress is an essential ingredient of neurosis. Peter Oberman's case is especially instructive: he was ridden by symptoms after his grandfather's death, when he first went to college, and when he was drafted for military service, but between these occasions he had periods of successful functioning. Current difficulties of living are most likely to precipitate a neurotic reaction when they have one or more of the following effects: first, they contain strong reminders of earlier dangers; second, they upset the preferred adaptive style, defensive traits, and overdriven strivings; third, they call out increased defensive processes that become crippling. To illustrate, let us

[47] Shapiro, *op. cit.* See also a chapter on strategies of adaptation in R. W. White, *The Enterprise of Living: Growth and Organization in Personality* (New York: Holt, Rinehart & Winston, Inc., 1972), chap. 15.

suppose that a man whose personality has developed along coolly intellectual lines becomes attracted to a warm, expressive woman. The situation is enough like his childhood relation to his mother to touch off anxiety connected with early dependence. It threatens his "cerebral" adaptive style and blocks his overdriven striving toward impersonal aloofness. It thus leads to a speeding up of these protective operations so that he becomes phobic of feminine companionship and obsessively entangled with inner debates about love, hate, dependence, and freedom.[48] Being attracted, falling in love, contemplating marriage can be regarded as intrinsically stressful but not, for most people, sufficiently so to elicit a neurotic reaction. In order to have such a drastic effect current stress must touch certain vulnerabilities, innate or acquired, and must threaten preferred security operations.

If these considerations are valid, neurosis is a phenomenon of learning and thus of ways of meeting the difficulties of living. The neuroses differ from other outcomes of this universal struggle in that they come to a focus on one or another of those crippling states, physical or mental, that historically have been described as symptoms. When we look closely at these symptoms, they become intelligible as products of conditioning and learning in circumstances in which avoidance of anxiety looms large. They do not fit a medical mood; they are not diseases in any accurate sense of that term. Their only true resemblance to medical problems is that their form seems to be influenced by certain constitutional vulnerabilities. Otherwise it must be counted an historical accident that neuroses were conceptualized as diseases. It is important to emphasize this point as we turn in the next two chapters to the subject of psychological treatment. The literature on this topic is still pervaded by the imagery of a doctor treating a patient. This familiar image must not be allowed to divert attention from what is actually involved in providing psychological help. The central problem is one not of healing but of relearning.

SUGGESTIONS FOR FURTHER READING

The older literature on the neuroses contains a wealth of description that is still valuable today. Pierre Janet's *Major Symptoms of Hysteria* (2nd ed., New York, The Macmillan Co., 1920) is unsurpassed for its clinical descriptions of dissociated states and hysterical symptoms. Readers familiar with French have access to the same author's classic account of phobias and obsessions: *Les Obsessions et la Psychasthenie* (Paris, Alcan, 1903). Morton Prince's *The Dissociation of a Personality* (2nd ed., London, Longmans, Green & Co., Ltd., 1913) is fascinating reading, though a little on the dramatic side. It should be followed by his more conservative paper, "Miss Beauchamp: The Psychogenesis of Multiple Personality," reprinted in *Clinical and Experimental Studies of Personality* (2nd ed., Cambridge, Sci-Art Publish-

[48] This summary of precipitating factors is adapted from O. Fenichel, *The Psychoanalytic Theory of Neurosis* (New York: W. W. Norton & Co., Inc., 1945), pp. 454–57.

ers, 1939), Ch. 7. An excellent discussion of the problems raised by multiple personalities, for both abnormal and general psychology, occurs in Ch. 18 of Gardner Murphy's *Personality: A Biosocial Approach to Origins and Structure* (New York, Harper & Row, 1947).

From the psychoanalytic standpoint the different forms of neurosis are briefly described in F. Alexander and H. Ross's *Dynamic Psychiatry* (Chicago, University of Chicago Press, 1952), Ch. 5. The subject is covered in scholarly detail by Otto Fenichel in *The Psychoanalytic Theory of Neurosis* (New York, W. W. Norton & Co., Inc., 1945), especially Chs. 11–14. An independent psychodynamic view is taken by Andras Angyal in a posthumous work edited by E. Hanfmann and R. M. Jones, *Neurosis and Treatment: A Holistic Theory* (New York, John Wiley & Sons, Inc., 1965); hysteria is described as based on a pattern of vicarious living, obsessional neurosis on a pattern of noncommitment. Adler's view of neurosis can best be obtained from H. L. Ansbacher and R. R. Ansbacher's edited and annotated selections from his writings, *The Individual Psychology of Alfred Adler* (New York, Basic Books, Inc., 1956), especially Chs. 9–11, 15. A strictly behavioristic interpretation of the neuroses is offered by H. J. Eysenck and S. Rachman, *The Causes and Cures of Neurosis* (San Diego, Robert Knapp, 1965). The authors make the subject sound as simple as Fenichel makes it sound complex. Less restricted in its conception of behaviorism is the discussion of how neuroses are learned in J. Dollard and N. R. Miller, *Personality and Psychotherapy* (New York, McGraw-Hill Book Co., 1950), Chs. 10–13. The relation between behavioristic theory and personality is summarized by C. S. Hall and G. Lindzey, *Theories of Personality* (2nd ed., New York, John Wiley & Sons, Inc., 1968), Ch. 11, and is the subject of an extended essay by D. E. Berlyne, "Behavior Theory as Personality Theory," in E. F. Borgatta and W. W. Lambert, eds., *Handbook of Personality Theory and Research* (Chicago, Rand McNally & Co., 1968), pp. 630–82.

Strongly recommended for its clinical acumen and stimulating ideas is David Shapiro's *Neurotic Styles* (New York, Basic Books, Inc., 1965).

7

Psychotherapy:
Individual Methods

Most of what we know about the neuroses was learned in the course of trying to treat them. If one sat down to devise a logical plan for understanding psychogenic disorders, one would probably start with a program for finding out the facts by observation and experiment, after which this knowledge could be applied to the practical art of therapy. Historically the process moved in the opposite direction. Practical art preceded science and became the means for accumulating a body of knowledge. More rigorous scientific methods have lately been applied where possible, but a great deal of what we know about psychogenic disorders still rests on the observations, the wisdom, and the blunders of people who tried to cure them.

Starting from the specific task of treating neuroses, psychotherapy has today expanded in many directions. As an activity it flourishes and is much in demand. Variations in method and theory are constantly appearing, sometimes in the belligerent form of new schools of thought. This burgeoning may well be a token of vitality, but it is not necessarily a sign of clear thinking. If the reader hopes to find that psychotherapy is perfectly understood, that everyone agrees on how it should be done, and that its results can be presented with the sharpness of surgical statistics, he must be prepared for disappointment on all three counts. In recent years there has been an admirable quickening of interest in research on both process and outcome, but the difficulties are formidable, as we shall see, and the results thus far seem small compared to what needs to be known.

This is the appropriate point in our study to take up psychotherapy. We have already covered its original sphere of operation, the neuroses, and its currently enlarged domain, difficulties of living and unworkable patterns of adaptation. Psychotherapists everywhere, including those on college campuses, are quite as likely to find themselves dealing with troublesome dependence, inferiority feelings, social ineptitude, and identity crises as with disorders that manifest themselves as phobias, hysterias, and obsessional states. Furthermore, psychotherapy has specific uses in connection with many of the disorders to be described in the rest of this book. Understanding these applications will be easier if we take up at once the difficult but intriguing problems of treatment by psychological means.

NATURE OF PSYCHOTHERAPY

In this book we shall use *psychotherapy* as an inclusive term to designate all forms of treatment designed to deal with psychogenic disorders. This is the traditional usage and the one we believe will prevail in the future. But the reader should be prepared to find considerable variations in current usage. Since the advent of new techniques of behavior modification, some workers have advocated a sharp distinction between psychotherapy and behavior therapy, reserving for the latter the special glory of being scientific. Others have wished to make psychoanalysis a separate category and psychotherapy a term for all procedures not directly inspired by Freud, reserving for the former the special glory of going to the real roots of the matter. Both of these divisions, it will be noticed, turn psychotherapy into a second-rate category, muddle-headed in the one case, superficial in the other. The polemical purpose is clear, but the logic of such separations is feeble. In a basic sense behavior therapy, psychoanalysis, and other forms of psychotherapy belong in the same boat. As we examine them in more detail, we shall observe that in spite of large differences in procedure they are all committed to the fundamental idea that disordered behavior is acquired through learning and can be changed by unlearning and relearning.

Promotion of Relearning

Calling a disorder psychogenic means thinking of it as a pattern of learning that is faulty in the sense of yielding unworkable results in current circumstances. One's conception of learning, as we saw especially in Chapter 3, may emphasize in different degrees such aspects as conditioning, insight, cognitive fields, emotion, and motivation, but there is no doubt that a phobia, for instance, is learned and that unlearning is the only cure. Seen in this light, all forms of psychotherapy involve attempts to create a situation that is favorable for relearning. In one-to-one treatment, on which we shall concentrate in this chapter, the favorable situation has to be created by means of conversation taking place in the therapist's office. Conversation in an office seems suitable for many kinds of professional activity, such as a lawyer counseling a client about his rights or a broker making suggestions about investments. But if the client needs to get over being afraid of crossing streets or meeting people, if he is troubled by sexual problems, if he needs to overcome inferiority feelings and build self-respect, it is not self-evident that talking in an office holds the key to the desired change.

There are more than ordinary obstacles, furthermore, to the kind of relearning that is necessary to ameliorate difficulties of living or to lift neurotic symptoms. We regard it as normal, though not necessarily easy, for our patterns of behavior to change if in new circumstances they turn out badly. When a person turns to psychotherapy it is because his behavior fails to change. He continues to repeat the same patterns even when the consequences are uncomfortable and self-defeating. The therapist in his office must try to bring about change in behavior and in feelings that have already shown themselves to be stubbornly resistant to change. Typical of this rigidity are forms of behavior that have been strongly overlearned during childhood, that serve as defenses against anxiety, or that satisfy some unwitting resentful or protective purpose in current life. The therapist is called upon to change what neither circumstances nor the client's own efforts have thus far been able to change.

Corrective Emotional Experience

It is, of course, a mistake to think of this relearning as an intellectual process. Although Freud described the goal of psychoanalysis as replacing what is unconscious by what is conscious, and although much has been written about increasing the patient's insight, it became a tenet of psychoanalytic theory that the curative forces do not lie in the realm of intellect. This is recognized in a formulation by Alexander, who wrote that the basic principle is "to re-expose the patient, under more favorable circumstances, to emotional situations which he could not handle in the past." The patient must "undergo a corrective emotional experience," and his "intellectual understanding of the genetics has only an accessory significance." [1] Other theorists have been equally explicit in locating the essential change in the realm of feeling, and there is widespread agreement, which includes behavior therapists, that the reduction of anxiety is one of the most central problems. It is useless to tell the phobic child that the rabbit is not dangerous. He must learn for himself, through controlled exposures that actually arouse some degree of anxiety but produce no painful consequences, that a rabbit is not a reason for panic. Similarly the adult neurotic patient must progressively feel the anxiety derived from his earlier history, and thus learn to respond to obsolete dangers at their true current value. Conditions must be created in which the patient will dare to reappraise his anxieties and relax his defenses.

1 F. Alexander, T. M. French, *et al.*, *Psychoanalytic Therapy* (New York: The Ronald Press Co., 1946), pp. 66–67.

Relearning of this kind requires something more than is ordinarily implied in a relation between doctor and patient. Once we conceive of psychotherapy as a relearning process, we can see that the learner needs strong continuing motivation to work at his problems and that his relation to the therapist is an evolving, integral part of the whole experience.

The Therapeutic Relation

At first thought it may seem that a psychotherapist commands only small forces for doing his job. His aim is to bring about a process of growth in his client, and this can only be encouraged, not hurried or pushed or performed by the therapist for the client. His resources seem tiny compared to the surgeon, who in a brief operation can remove an infected appendix and put his patient on a rapid road to recovery. They seem tiny when compared to injecting a drug that quickly subdues an infection or re-establishes a chemical balance. The psychotherapist cannot make the kind of radical intervention that is often possible with bodily processes. He has to promote relearning, and all he can do is provide favorable circumstances.

The forces at his command seem slight also when put alongside those that may have created the disorder and that still may be acting to sustain it. Perhaps for twenty years the parents of the client created conditions that built up maladaptive patterns of behavior; now the therapist comes in with the assignment of creating conditions to undo all that learning. Perhaps the client's current life is full of exasperating frustrations; the hour in which the therapist tries to assist growth has to compete with many hours during which a tyrannical boss keeps mobilizing anxieties old and new. There is nothing remarkable in the fact that psychotherapy can fail. The wonder is that it ever succeeds.

But the psychotherapist holds at least one strong card at the beginning of treatment. He is in a position to establish a unique relationship with the client, one that is in some respects unusually favorable for new learning. The client is unhappy and discouraged. Whatever steps he has taken to help himself have proved of no avail. Everyone is tired of hearing about his problems, tired even of his having problems. The relation with the therapist fills him with new hope. This time his listener is a person with scientific training who is uncommitted to any goal save health. This person is presumed to be wise in human suffering and experienced in setting it right. He listens to the story of fears, shames, and inhibitions, and without blaming the client for shortcomings he indicates that such matters interest him because they are the seat of the trouble and of its possible change. One looks in vain among the other relationships of life for just this combination of qualities. The pastor is too strongly identified with standards of right and wrong. The friend will not listen very long without giving nervous reassurance or talking about his own troubles.

The loved one may listen, but cannot be counted upon to give authoritative advice. No one hits the happy combination of interest, detachment, and knowledge that characterizes a skillful psychotherapist. It is this unique atmosphere that supports the client's growth.

In a recent systematic study of the various meanings attached to psychotherapy, Reisman takes this unusual combination into account. Arguing that psychotherapy should be defined by what the therapist does rather than the effects produced, he concludes that psychotherapy is "the communication of person-related understanding, respect, and a wish to be of help." [2] Person-related understanding represents the sphere of the therapist's expertness, respect stands for his attitude of valuing and not blaming the client, and the wish to be of help signifies his motivation to persist in promoting relearning as long as there are beneficial results.

Initial Steps

The therapeutic situation is initially established by what the therapist does in the first few meetings. Some of the things that happen are common to all schools of thought. Information must be exchanged: the therapist must learn about the client's life situation and about the complaints that prompt him to seek treatment; in return, he must give some idea of what is involved in his usual methods of treatment. Whatever else is done, there must be a certain minimum of interviewing, history-taking, and explanation. The manner in which these initial steps are carried out goes far toward defining the therapeutic relation.

In the nature of the case the therapist is cast in the role of an expert from whom help is sought. On the whole, however, psychotherapists have been inclined to play down the superior–inferior aspect of the relation in order to maximize those aspects that resemble friendship and represent sympathetic understanding. Much has been written about the importance of a display of warmth by the therapist, but this pleasant word, suggesting an emanation of heat from a radiator, does not carry us far toward understanding actual transactions. More definite is the therapist's attentive interest whereby he hears and grasps the import of what he is told. In a clinical report on work with combat troops who had undergone schizophrenic breakdown, Eissler noticed that the patients responded favorably to indications of interest on his part, even when what they were saying was relatively trivial. Eissler described himself as animated by a rescue fantasy; he wanted to save the young men, and this wish stimulated his interest and sharpened his attention. He remarks upon the "special joy" that is experienced when an attentive listener gives himself fully to what you have to say.[3] There is threefold value to a patient in feeling that he

---

[2] J. M. Reisman, *Toward the Integration of Psychotherapy* (New York: John Wiley & Sons, Inc., 1971), p. 123.

[3] K. R. Eissler, "Remarks on the Psychoanalysis of Schizophrenia," in E. B. Brody and F. C. Redlich, eds., *Psychotherapy with Schizophrenics* (New York: International Universities Press, 1952), pp. 130–67.

is being understood. He experiences a sense of competence at having put his messages across; he is reassured that the therapist's guidance will be appropriate; and he feels that the therapist takes him as a person of value. What is often described as routine history-taking can thus be much more than a routine. It can serve to vivify the therapist's role as one who understands, respects, and wishes to be of help.

When this happens, the client's motivation is favorably affected. He experiences trust and hope, both of which are vitally important at the start of a difficult task.[4] People come to psychotherapy often in desperation, sometimes with initial enthusiasm. Their motivation seems strong, but it is not yet channeled into what will actually be required of them. As treatment proceeds, the therapist "constantly faces the task of urging the patient to examine old fears and to experiment with new patterns of behavior."[5] This can be hard, often painful, and the motive of getting well may falter badly if not aided by more immediate wishes. If during the initial encounters the client comes to feel that he is the object of interest and value, he will in turn value and feel interest in the therapist, and he will be moved to please the therapist and maintain the latter's esteem. Becoming an important person to the client, the therapist can serve as a strong source of encouragement and influence.

Specific Techniques

What has been discussed thus far is common to all methods of psychotherapy. What more can the therapist do? After the initial steps he moves on to the specific techniques that he considers most likely to produce the unlearning of old and the learning of new adaptive patterns. In an older tradition he might rely entirely on suggestion, hypnosis, persuasion, or plain physical relaxation. In the psychoanalytic tradition he would instruct the patient in the none too easy art of free association. If direct methods of behavior modification are to be employed, he will teach the client the part he is to play in whatever procedure is chosen. It is from this point on that we enter the realm of controversy, of contending schools of thought, that is so conspicuous a feature of contemporary psychotherapy. Agreement on the basic principle that psychotherapy means relearning does not in the least guarantee agreement on how the relearning can best be accomplished. Being a successful psychotherapist clearly implies putting one's heart into one's work; this undoubtedly makes it harder to view the work with critical detachment. The student who becomes interested in reading more widely on this subject will find himself plunged into an atmosphere of strenuous polemics. The tone is set by reports of patients beautifully cured by one's favorite method after having been hopelessly

4 J. Frank, "The Role of Hope in Psychotherapy," *International Journal of Psychiatry*, V (1968), pp. 383–412.

5 D. R. Stieper and D. N. Wiener, *Dimensions of Psychotherapy: An Experimental and Clinical Approach* (Chicago: Aldine Publishing Co., 1965), p. 124.

bogged down, if not made worse, by somebody else's method. But the goal of our present survey must be to disclose the principles at work in different methods of treatment. At the risk of spoiling a lot of good fights we must try to see what actually happens during the use of specific techniques. We must even face the consequence, if it so appears, that schools of psychotherapeutic thought are not as different as they would like to be.

We begin with behavior therapy, which uses principles directly related to learning theory and which works with relatively simple conceptions of disordered behavior.

BEHAVIOR THERAPY

In earlier chapters we have already touched several times on behavior therapy. When looking into the history of abnormal psychology (Chapter 1) we noticed the curiously delayed arrival of this offshoot of American behaviorism, followed by spectacular growth and popularity during the 1960's. When examining the adaptive process (Chapter 3) we touched upon Pavlov's historic work on conditioned responses, including the processes of acquisition, generalization, and extinction. We also took note of Skinner's ideas about operant conditioning and reinforcement, illustrating with an experiment in which the content of mental patients' conversation was changed by the staff's paying attention to certain themes and paying no attention to others. When describing the neuroses (Chapter 6) we noticed the applicability of conditioning principles especially in understanding anxiety states and phobias. It is evident that certain long-recognized principles of learning have a direct bearing on disordered behavior.

What distinguishes behavior therapy from other forms of psychotherapy is the attempt to base all procedures on principles of learning already demonstrated by experimental work. In practice this usually implies principles of conditioning and deconditioning as originally demonstrated in experiments with animals, although some use can be made of the more complex learning processes studied in human beings. The goal is to make treatment an application of experimental psychology, and in the behavioristic tradition to conceive of it as a modification of behavior rather than as a change in subjective states like feeling, confidence, or self-respect.

An Early Example: The Treatment of Enuresis

Success along these lines was obtained some years ago by the Mowrers, who invented a technique to overcome bedwetting in children. An apparatus was devised whereby the first moisture on a pad placed in the bed set off a bell loud enough to wake up the child. In due course the stimuli preliminary to urination became connected with the response of waking, enabling the child to control himself long enough to reach the bathroom.[6] The method has had considerable use ever since. In a review covering twenty-five years, Lovibond reports that an initial arrest of bedwetting is obtained on the average in 90 per cent of the cases treated. This good news is somewhat marred, however, by figures showing a rather high rate of subsequent relapse. Weighing several relevant studies, Lovibond sets 34 per cent as a probable figure for relapse as shown by follow-ups one to three years later; "the main problem still appears to be the reduction of the relapse rate."[7] Evidently the conditioning method does not produce wholly stable results. But if two out of three cases are lastingly cured, conferring on the children a gratifying sense of mastery and on the parents a welcome relief from anxiety and the washing of sheets, the achievement is by no means negligible.

Systematic Desensitization

The deconditioning technique known as systematic desensitization was devised by Joseph Wolpe, who more than anyone else was responsible for bringing behavior therapy to life after thirty years of only sporadic interest. Reasoning from experiments with animals and children, Wolpe searched for a way to produce gradual deconditioning of anxiety responses in neurotic adults. This proved to be possible if the patients vividly imagined the objects of their dread, provided they were at the same time thoroughly relaxed and calm in the therapist's reassuring presence. Pains had to be taken to keep them from imagining so vividly as to precipitate an acute attack of anxiety. To this end, therapist and patient worked out beforehand a list or hierarchy of situations the patient feared, arranged from least to most provocative of anxiety. A hierarchy on fear of high places might start with looking up at one from below and proceed through graded steps to a climactic scene in which the patient stands on a precipice looking down. Treatment began with imagining the most innocuous scene several times over until it no longer aroused uneasiness; then the next scene would be imagined and deconditioned; and so on up the list until the patient in his fancy could stand on the dreaded spot looking serenely down into the depths below. Such a result could not, of course, be obtained quickly. Many repetitions and occasional setbacks usually stretched the work on a single list over 15 or 20 sessions, and if the patient had more than one focus of fear, so that several hierarchies had to be constructed, even more time might be required. On the average, however, systematic desensitization called for less time than did other methods of psychotherapy applied to similar disorders.

The reader may be surprised that just imagining the things of which

---

[6] O. H. Mowrer and W. M. Mowrer, "Enuresis: A Method for Its Study and Treatment," *American Journal of Orthopsychiatry*, VIII (1938), pp. 436–59.

[7] S. H. Lovibond, *Conditioning and Enuresis* (New York: The Macmillan Co., 1964), p. 142.

you are afraid should have so much power to reduce fear. And what happens when the patient gets up on the real precipice? It is therefore important to recognize the power of imagination, under just the right circumstances, to elicit strong affective responses. When therapist and patient are at work constructing the hierarchy, the patient can say that he is most terrified by high places without actually going straight into a panic; he can report what he knows without experiencing its full affect. In a dream of high places, however, the patient would indeed be panic-stricken, and a scene vividly imagined in a relaxed or drowsy state can have the affective properties of a dream. Wolpe's procedure involves training the patient to relax deeply; in some cases hypnotism is used to promote both physical relaxation and vivid imagery. Then the therapist proposes each scene and the patient imagines it, with the safeguard that if he gets too scared he will signal the therapist to call the scene off and encourage renewed relaxation. Real anxiety is unquestionably involved, and the deconditioning can be almost as effective as if the therapist accompanied the patient through a hierarchy of real events. Case reports show that, although it may be something of a jolt to pass from the imagined to the real precipice, the majority of patients can do it. This is, of course, more than they could have done prior to treatment.

Systematic desensitization can be interpreted as a simple process of extinction. Conditioned anxiety stimuli are given, no painful consequences follow, and the conditioned response thus becomes weakened to the vanishing point. Wolpe believes that a second principle is involved which he calls *reciprocal inhibition*. Extinction of the anxiety aroused during the treatment is assisted by activation of an antagonistic autonomic response, in this case calm relaxation. The theory depends upon the known antagonism between the sympathetic and parasympathetic divisions of the autonomic nervous system, which govern respectively preparation for emergencies and maintaining peaceful vegetative processes, and by the common sense thought that one cannot be anxious and calm at the same time. Wolpe attributes the manageability of the anxiety aroused during systematic desensitization to the damping effects of the induced relaxation. Not all behavior therapists agree that reciprocal inhibition is an important principle. Reverting to our discussion of the therapeutic situation, it is worth pointing out that the reassuring presence of the therapist may have a good deal to do with the patient's tolerance of anxiety. Desiring the therapist's esteem, reassured by his implicit promise to stop scenes that become unpleasant and to restore calm, the patient may well be emboldened to find out how much anxiety he can bear.[8]

---

[8] The highly influential first book on desensitization was J. Wolpe, *Psychotherapy by Reciprocal Inhibition* (Stanford, Calif.: Stanford University Press, 1958). For a more recent exposition see J. Wolpe, *The Practice of Behavior Therapy* (New York: Pergamon Press, 1969).

An Example of Systematic Desensitization

To make the therapeutic process clearer we shall take an example originally reported by Rachman.[9] The patient, Miss A. G., a 24-year-old teacher, suffered from a phobia of injections, dating back at least to the age of six or seven. When an injection could not be avoided she was panic-stricken and always fainted. She sought treatment when an impending trip that was important to her entailed a series of inoculations. This phobia was her central complaint, but she also had an intense fear of inserting internal sanitary pads, and she mentioned a sexual problem consisting of pain and anxiety during intercourse; in addition, her answers on a standard test gave evidence of general feelings of insecurity. The therapist chose systematic desensitization for the two focalized complaints and undertook "to relieve the feelings of insecurity by discussion and reassurance."

Two hierarchies were constructed, one on injections and one on sanitary pads. The first started with picturing a hospital in the distance and led up to receiving an injection in a doctor's office. The second began with an image of an unopened box of pads in a drugstore and proceeded to imagining the act of insertion, which in reality the patient was unable to perform. In the course of 22 sessions spread over several months, the desensitization procedure was carried out successfully through both hierarchies. At the end of this A.G. had no difficulty with sanitary pads, and she received her requisite injections somewhat nervously but without fainting or lasting upset. She was elated at this success and reported that she felt in general a lot better. Follow-up after five years showed that she had held her gains and that her symptoms had not recurred.

The elimination of the two phobic responses seems clearly related to the desensitization procedures, but Rachman's report suggests that reassuring discussion made more than a negligible contribution to the total result. At the fifth session A. G. talked about her protracted love affair and her doubts about it; "after some discussion, her feelings and motives became more lucid and she experienced some relief." To the twelfth session she came so depressed because of a setback in her love affair that desensitization was postponed in favor of "non-directive, cathartic discussion." At the fifteenth session she told of having to give up an attempt at sexual intercourse because of intense pain and anxiety; this made her wonder whether or not she had a physical defect. Questioning showed that there had been inadequate foreplay, so she was "given information and advice about love-play and was told to relax fully before lovemaking." At the eighteenth

9 S. Rachman, "The Treatment of Anxiety and Phobic Reactions by Systematic Desensitization Psychotherapy," *Journal of Abnormal and Social Psychology*, LVIII (1959), pp. 259–63. See also H. J. Eysenck and S. Rachman, *The Causes and Cures of Neurosis* (San Diego: Robert Knapp, 1965), pp. 68–78.

interview she told of having intercourse without "even the slightest pain," which greatly reassured her on the subject of sexual adequacy. Without detracting from the accomplishments of systematic desensitization, we have to allow that another problem area, sex and her love affair, was being simultaneously treated by techniques of advice, information, and sympathetic listening, evidently with satisfactory results. A literal-minded scientist might see in this an experiment spoiled: there is no way to determine the relative contribution of the different techniques to the total result, or to decide what interaction there might have been between the diminishing phobias and the improving sexual situation. But if we were to consult Miss A. G., she would almost certainly say that she had received good therapy.

The Phobic Element in Neurosis

Systematic desensitization is at its best when the patient complains of phobia—a circumscribed irrational fear of a specific object or clearly defined situation. Extinguishing an anxiety response can be straightforwardly accomplished if there is a known, restricted conditioned stimulus to which the patient can be systematically exposed. It has been remarked that behavior therapists seem to encounter more phobic patients than do the adherents of other schools of psychotherapeutic thought. This apparent difference may well be due to the method of diagnosis: behavior therapists take special pains to look for phobic elements in their patients' complaints, trying to pin down specific stimulus patterns that are most conducive to anxiety. Diagnosis, of course, is always influenced by the therapist's theoretical expectations and by his experience of his own effectiveness. A Freudian analyst, whose skill lies in promoting free association and in piecing together the subtle patterns of feeling generated by past experience, is attuned to perceive relations among the different things he is told by a new patient. Very likely he would interpret Miss A. G.'s case as a sexual disorder, with anxiety and resistance to sexual experience expressing itself as pain during the sexual act, as fear of inserting anything in the vagina, and symbolically as fright of the painful insertion involved in hypodermic injections. The behavior therapist achieved good results by viewing the trouble as three disorders, using systematic desensitization for the two phobias, instruction and encouragement for the sexual difficulty.

When we studied phobias in the last chapter, however, we met with evidence that an irrational fear might not be just itself, so to speak, but part of a more complex adaptive operation. Thus in one case, for instance, a phobia of leaving home, though related to childhood frights, broke forth only later in life under conditions of bereavement and social disgrace, and it played a part in dealing with this current situation. Lazarus, a behavior therapist who espouses a "broad-gauge" approach, cites the case of a man who developed a sudden crippling phobia of crossing bridges.

No earlier history involving bridges could be elicited, but it
the patient crossed a long bridge every day to get to work, t.
been offered a promotion, and that he had experienced heavy re.
to accept so much new responsibility. The bridge phobia is here p.
a larger pattern of threat to self-esteem; it could be considered a fa.
saving device. Its removal would be unfortunate if the therapist were not
prepared to deal also with the conflict between the patient's self-esteem
and his dread of responsibility. This further step might also be accomplished by principles of behavior therapy, but the more "broad-gauged" the
techniques become, the less different they seem from those practiced by
other schools of thought.[10]

Operant Conditioning Methods

Wolpe's work is founded on the model of Pavlov's conditioning experiments. He describes a large number of techniques based upon this model
and adapted to purposes other than desensitizing a phobia. Some of these
methods, however, involve principles of operant conditioning, and it is
often hard to draw the line within a given technique between these two
modes of influence. "Behavior therapies that apply the principles and
technology of the operant learning paradigm," say Kanfer and Phillips,
"are more widely used for a greater diversity of target symptoms, and
within more varied social contexts, than are any of the other behavior
therapy models." [11] What distinguishes operant conditioning, as we saw
in Chapter 3, is its emphasis on the consequences of behavior rather than
the stimulating conditions. Reinforcement is the key concept, and the
goal is to control the reinforcement contingencies in such a way as to
diminish the frequency of undesirable responses and increase the frequency
of desired ones. Operant conditioning thus provides a means of promoting
and shaping new behavior as well as suppressing pathological modes of
responding. The principle was illustrated in Chapter 2 in the case of
Walter Lilly, when parents, teachers, and therapist alike agreed to pay
no attention to the boy's crying, screaming, and fears of dying—especially
to excuse him from nothing and let no benefits accrue on account of this
behavior—but to show interest and engage in conversation when he talked
in a more mature way. This principle is effective, of course, only to the
extent that the therapist is in control of the reinforcement contingencies.
Not by accident, the most striking instances of behavior modification
through operant conditioning have occurred in institutions, where the staff
had extensive control over the environment.

Operant conditioning can be carried in a great many different ways.
Among its virtues is flexibility: procedures can be devised that meet the

10 A. A. Lazarus, *Behavior Therapy and Beyond* (New York: McGraw-Hill Book Co.,
1971), pp. 33–36.
11. F. H. Kanfer and J. S. Phillips, *Learning Foundations of Behavior Therapy* (New
York: John Wiley & Sons, Inc., 1970), p. 317.

peculiar conditions present in each case, and workers with the method have shown great ingenuity in this respect. In one-to-one treatment with adults, the therapist's approval or disapproval is probably a critical reinforcing agency. The client's motive of wanting his troubles alleviated gains significant support to the extent that he comes to care about the therapist's interest and esteem. With children the rewards can be more primitive—child therapists are large purchasers of candy—but generally with the intention later to replace food reinforcements with social ones. When a client's behavior is marked by deficiencies, as is usually the case —poor social initiative, lack of assertiveness, sexual timidity, feeble power of concentration—programs of reinforcement, often coupled with those intended to reduce anxiety, can bring about beneficial change within a reasonably short time.

If positive reinforcement can shape desirable new behavior, can negative reinforcement be used to suppress undesirable responses? This raises the much discussed question of punishment as a method of control. The therapeutic version of this larger problem is known as *aversion therapy*. It consists of connecting pathological behavior with an immediate aversive stimulus powerful enough to suppress it. If a client's problem is alcohol, he can be given a drink along with a drug that quickly induces violent nausea and vomiting. If homosexual interest is bothering him, he can be placed in an experimental situation where looking at same-sex nude pictures brings on painful electric shock which is relieved by looking at opposite-sex pictures. Aversion therapy is certainly capable of suppressing an undesirable response rather quickly, but it is, as Lazarus remarks, "usually a harrowing experience" which tends to "hurt people or rob them of their human dignity." [12] This can be somewhat mitigated by combining aversive therapy with positive training, and perhaps altogether avoided in a method advocated by Cautela in which aversive imagery takes the place of overt punishing events.[13] In a thorough review, Kanfer and Phillips note that "misgivings about possible undesirable side effects" have held back both research and application, but they conclude that these are unnecessary "when the procedures are properly constructed and applied to suit the individual circumstances." [14]

Operant conditioning has been used with a variety of problems not hitherto considered to be within the scope of psychotherapy. A collection of fifty case studies edited by Ullmann and Krasner shows the wide range of these endeavors.[15] As mentioned earlier, Ayllon and others have modified the behavior of severely disturbed mental patients by combinations of food and social rewards so that the patients became more comfortable,

12 Lazarus, *op. cit.*, p. 235.
13 J. R. Cautela, "Covert Sensitization," *Psychological Record*, XX (1967), pp. 459–68.
14 Kanfer and Phillips, *op. cit.*, chap. 7.
15 L. P. Ullmann and L. Krasner, eds., *Case Studies in Behavior Modification* (New York: Holt, Rinehart & Winston, Inc., 1965).

manageable, and socially responsive. Mute schizophrenics and autistic children have been induced to speak, patients with bizarre and inconvenient habits have given them up, and occasionally there has been sufficient progress to justify discharge from the hospital. Mentally retarded children have also benefited from operant methods, becoming trained in ways that make institutional or home care much easier and that facilitate maximum use of capacity.[16] The human value of such work should not escape our notice even if it seems more natural to call it training than psychotherapy.

In order to make the principles plain we have undoubtedly made behavior modification, especially operant conditioning, sound easy. Reinforcement is a seductive term. Vanity may prompt us to believe that simply by conferring our smiling approval, communicating our frowning displeasure, or withholding our interest, we can omnipotently shape the behavior of everyone around us. What undercuts this happy conceit is the recollection that others are simultaneously engaged in shaping us. But in any event disordered behavior is the kind least likely to change in response to superficial reinforcement; otherwise it would have changed long ago. To be an effective therapeutic reinforcer requires training, skill, and sensitivity. It requires a therapeutic relation in which the client trusts and respects the therapist and comes to care a great deal about meeting his expectations. It requires also a detailed knowledge on the therapist's part of such technical problems as what schedules of reinforcement are more appropriate in different circumstances and how to manage transitions from one type of reward to another. Before concluding that behavior therapy is easy, one should read the solid 600-page book by Kanfer and Phillips, who describe in detail the now abundant research and clinical observations that constitute the necessary learning foundations for practical work in this field.[17]

Assertive Training

The method of behavior modification known as assertive training was included by Wolpe in his first book and has become part of the technical equipment of most behavior therapists.[18]

Assertive training, generally speaking, is required for patients who in interpersonal contexts have unadaptive anxiety responses that prevent them from saying or doing what is reasonable and right. . . . The patient may be constantly placating other people because he fears to offend them, or because he feels a moral obligation to place the interests of others before his own. He may allow people to maneuver

16 B. L. Baker and M. H. Ward, "Reinforcement Therapy for Behavior Problems in Severely Retarded Children," *American Journal of Orthopsychiatry*, XLI (1971), pp. 124–35.
17 Kanfer and Phillips, *op. cit.*
18 Wolpe, *Psychotherapy by Reciprocal Inhibition, op. cit.*, pp. 114–30. Wolpe mentions earlier advocacy of this method by A. Salter, *Conditioned Reflex Therapy* (New York: Creative Age Press, 1949).

him into situations he does not desire. He may be unable to express his legitimate wishes. . . . Assertiveness usually involves more or less aggressive behavior, but it may express friendly, affectionate, and other non-anxious feelings.[19]

Assertive training represents a head-on attack on social inhibition, on what in Chapter 5 we called social enslavement. This is different from dealing with a phobia. Social anxiety is diffuse and can be aroused by a large variety of stimulating conditions. True to his theories, however, Wolpe tries to focalize the problem and deal with it by reciprocal inhibition and extinction. He seizes upon the particular relation in which the patient's lack of assertion has its most damaging consequences—perhaps the relation with spouse or employer—and works for a modification of behavior at just this one point. If this proves successful, the consequences may be broader: daring to assert oneself in one situation may generalize to other situations.

If reciprocal inhibition is to be enlisted as well as extinction, an emotion must be mobilized that is antagonistic to anxiety and will therefore dampen it. To this end Wolpe tries most commonly to arouse anger. He may tell the patient that he should be ashamed to let others bully him and rob him of his rights. In addition he may propose assertive remarks for the patient to make and engage in a rehearsal of scenes, as was done in the case of Walter Lilly. The patient is then urged to attempt some degree of assertion when he is next in the actual situation. To one patient Wolpe reports using these words: "It is in the social sphere that your behavior is deficient and it is there that I want to see you make a start. . . . What I expect of you is to stand up for your legitimate human rights, to express your views as clearly and as forcefully as possible no matter how critical of you other people appear to be. Stop being on the defensive, and stop apologizing for yourself."[20]

Social anxiety is very common. A certain amount of it can be considered the average result of human socialization. Countless people have become aware of this in themselves, have been angry at themselves for such submissiveness, and have resolved to be more assertive next time. Undoubtedly this self-treatment sometimes works, but it is a common experience to realize after the next time that one has been as submissive as ever, held back by a powerful reluctance. What is there about assertive training that makes it any better than self-help? In successful instances Wolpe interprets the sequence as follows: the patient grows angry, the anger inhibits anxiety (reciprocal inhibition), assertive behavior takes place, and the consequences are not harmful (extinction). But is it true in fact that the patient must get angry to initiate the sequence? Remembering the therapeutic situation and the therapist's expectations so clearly communicaed, it seems more likely that the patient faces simply a conflict of

[19] Wolpe, *The Practice of Behavior Therapy, op. cit.,* pp. 61–63.
[20] Wolpe, *Psychotherapy by Reciprocal Inhibition, op. cit.,* pp. 123–24.

anxieties. He dreads being assertive, but he also dreads reporting back to the therapist that he has not been assertive and does not deserve esteem. Inhibition of anxiety by anger may be a superfluous concept in assertive training, giving this method a spurious look of novelty. For this form of therapy is essentially an application of the time-honored method of persuasion. It depends upon the patient's having developed a strong respect for the therapist and a powerful need to live up to his expectations.

Assertive training is easy to grasp in principle, but the practice is anything but a simple matter. Neither therapist nor client has control over the third party toward whom assertiveness is to be directed. Wolpe cautions: "Never instigate an assertive act that is likely to have seriously punishing consequences for the patient." [21] But one cannot expect that the target person, accustomed to a dominant relation with the patient, will simply subside and take it when the worm suddenly turns. The extinction process will thus rarely proceed smoothly; part of the consequences of the patient's new assertiveness will be felt as painful and may increase rather than extinguish the anxiety. The therapist may thus be kept busy for many sessions with further persuasion and encouragement. Procuring even the first bit of assertive behavior may prove to be a long job. Being assertive, being angry, talking back, arguing may be so foreign to the patient that anxiety blocks them from the start. It is here that coaching with possible things to say and rehearsal by means of role playing in the therapist's office can be especially useful.

Evaluative Comments

We shall postpone to the end of this chapter the extraordinarily difficult problem of assessing therapeutic results. Suffice it to say here that the first reports by behavior therapists claimed rates of cure as high as 90 per cent, and that subsequent reports, sliding down to more moderate figures such as 65 per cent, still give ground for confidence that behavior therapy is effective. Furthermore, the reports show that the time necessary for successful behavior modification is likely to be less than with other methods, and a great deal less than with standard psychoanalysis. This means a large practical saving, and it makes a start toward spreading psychotherapy to clients of lesser means. For these reasons alone, behavior therapy justifies its claim to an important place in psychological treatment.

Looked at historically, this movement came as a fresh breeze at a time when psychoanalysis was passing its peak and when Freud's theoretical scheme was beginning to look like an obstacle to further progress. There is an appealing directness about the analysis of disordered behavior into the specific situations that most upset the client and the circumstances that keep rewarding maladaptive responses so that they are not unlearned. There is a refreshing air of common sense about going straight to the task

21 Wolpe, *The Practice of Behavior Therapy, op. cit.*, p. 67.

of reducing anxiety and encouraging new behavior, and applying for these purposes the most elementary principles of learning. Readers of the literature are likely to feel that behavior modification is a no-nonsense approach, working for definite goals by definite means, dispelling a lot of theoretical clouds, and using concepts that lend themselves to being tested.

Yet it is the very simplicity of behavior therapy that has provided ground for serious criticism. Sloane points out the tendency to explain changes in mechanical terms—extinction, reinforcement, reciprocal inhibition—without giving proper credit to the therapeutic relation, although this relation lends itself to a naturalistic explanation in terms of learning and motivation.[22] This is a tendency we noticed when describing systematic desensitization and assertive training, and it has been severely criticized in reviews by both Wilkins and Locke.[23] That the learning principles invoked are often much too simple is the burden of an article by Breger and McGaugh, who in effect ask that a larger place be made for cognitive learning and the more complex meanings characteristic of human experience, as contrasted with animals.[24] When studying the neuroses in the last chapter we took note of the value of behavior modification in connection with anxiety states and phobias, but its applicability in the hysterias and obsessional disorders was far less evident, and such adaptive problems as finding ego identity, which have extensive intellectual content, seem even less likely to find solutions through concepts derived from Pavlov's dogs. The strength of behavior therapy lies in using simple methods with simple problems; its weakness, in using simple methods with complex problems.

The task for the future is thus to find out what range of difficulties is best handled by behavior modification. The following words by the "broad-gauge" behavior therapist Arnold Lazarus make the point clearly.

The achievement of profound insights will frequently fail to eliminate tics, phobias, compulsions, or perversions, whereas operant conditioning, desensitization, or even straightforward hypnotic suggestion may often quell these "symptoms" with neither relapse nor substitution. Should we then abandon the quest for self-knowledge in favor of conditioning techniques? Indeed, if one's goal is to overcome enuresis, or to teach an autistic child to speak, or to instigate prosocial behaviors among schizophrenic inmates, the clinical and research evidence suggests that it would be foolhardy to bypass direct behavioral approaches. While even here, more attention to the patient's interpersonal relationships may well enhance the effects of

22 R. B. Sloane, "The Converging Paths of Behavior Therapy and Psychotherapy," *International Journal of Psychiatry*, VII (1969), pp. 493–503.

23 W. Wilkins, "Desensitization: Social and Cognitive Factors Underlying the Effectiveness of Wolpe's Procedure," *Psychological Bulletin*, LXXVI (1971), pp. 311–17; E. A. Locke, "Is 'Behavior Therapy' Behavioristic? (An Analysis of Wolpe's Psychotherapeutic Methods)," *ibid.*, pp. 318–27.

24 L. Breger and J. L. McGaugh, "Critique and Reformulation of 'Learning-Theory' Approaches to Psychotherapy and Neurosis," *Psychological Bulletin*, LXIII (1965), pp. 338–58.

specific reconditioning, it is obvious that instruction or training in a specific area will probably lead to improved performance in that area. Stutterers will usually find fluency exercises more helpful than introspection for their speech; phobic patients will usually respond better to desensitization than to psychoanalysis; social skills are more readily acquired through behavior rehearsal (modeling and role playing) than through advice or nondirective interviews. Since it is not always easy to determine when limited problems of function or dysfunction become entangled with far-reaching problems of meaning, therapists should try to determine what they are dealing with before plunging ahead with deconditioning or reconditioning techniques. . . . To desensitize a phobic patient, for instance, without first establishing whether his phobia is a straightforward avoidance reaction, or a psychotic mani-festation, or a symbolic retreat, or a face-saving or attention-seeking device, or a weapon in family or marital strife violates the cardinal rule—"diagnosis before therapy." [25]

And if the phobia proves to be not a straightforward avoidance reaction, then the methods appropriate for dealing with it will be more like those that have been developed by other schools of thought.

PSYCHOANALYSIS

It is not strictly correct to speak of any one procedure as standard psy-choanalysis. Each worker who uses the method originally devised by Freud adapts it somewhat to his own personality and to the very different prob-lems offered by his patients. Freud once likened psychoanalysis to chess, in which only the opening moves and a few typical concluding situations can be taught. With allowance for all the variation that must necessarily exist, however, we shall still be justified in referring to those forms of psychoanalysis as standard which have these characteristics: (1) the system-atic use of free association, interpretation, and transference neurosis, and (2) the goal of uncovering and resolving the major emotional problems of the patient's childhood. By standard psychoanalysis, then, we really refer to the *full-length* variety, much as it was originally set forth by Freud.

Standard psychoanalysis takes a very long time. Treatment is usually scheduled for one hour a day, five days a week. In spite of this rigorous schedule, it is rare for a psychoanalysis to be completed in less than one year; it is common for the treatment to last two or three years, and in some cases improvement is reached only after periods of five or more years. These figures become startling when we realize one of their implications—that a busy psychoanalyst who used only the standard technique would have time in his whole professional career to treat barely more than a hundred cases. In practice, even those psychoanalysts who consider the full-length method ideal are likely to spend a good deal of their time in shorter procedures, psychoanalytically oriented but using shortcuts and accepting more limited goals.

[25] Lazarus, *op. cit.*, pp. 218–19.

Free Association

Psychoanalysis is distinguished in the first place by its use of the specific technical tool of free association. The use of this tool is intended to promote the recognition of feelings by both patient and physician. It may even be considered a radical device for achieving this goal. Insofar as the patient is successful in giving free associations, everything he says is governed by an emotional logic rather than a conscious and critical logic.

The early sessions of psychoanalysis are devoted to the taking of a case history. When this is accomplished, the patient is instructed in the technique of free association. Alexander summarized what is communicated to the patient in the following words: [26]

> The patient is requested to report everything that occurs to him in the analytic session. He is asked to verbalize everything that occurs to him in the original sequence and form without any modification or omission. He is asked to assume a passive attitude toward his own trains of thought; in other words, to eliminate all conscious control over his mental processes to which he gives free rein and merely report them.

This technique tends to heighten the activity of feeling, including feeling that is usually suppressed. As Alexander put it, "Once the patient abandons the conscious control and direction of his ideas, the train of free spontaneous associations is guided more by the repressed material than by conscious motives."

The most interesting fact about free association is the obstacles it encounters. It was through a study of these obstacles—the silences, blockings, embarrassments, and anxieties of the patient which came to be called resistance—that Freud built up his concept of repression. It is worthwhile to point out and expressly reject a common misunderstanding about free association, the idea that it opens a highway over which repressed memories and fantasies roll smoothly into consciousness. No such miracle takes place, and the maximum effect that can possibly be attributed to the free association technique is a small reduction in the efficacy of habitual defenses, a weakening of the top layer of conscious control. Small as this change may be when thought of in terms of behavior dynamics, it is just enough to upset the delicate balance of personality organization in favor of hidden feelings. If repressed material starts to ooze upward, there is now an appreciable interval before it is met by the customary defenses, a precious moment during which the physician, if not the patient himself, can catch a glimpse of both parties to the conflict.

An Example of Free Association and Resistance

Free association and the resulting resistances play such a central part in psychoanalysis that we may profitably stop to examine a brief example.

[26] F. Alexander, *The Medical Value of Psychoanalysis* (New York: W. W. Norton & Co., Inc., 1937), pp. 40–41.

The following excerpt gives the opening remarks of a college student during his first hour of free association. After hearing the instructions from the examiner (E) the subject (S) proceeded as follows:

S: The thing uppermost in my mind at present is the hour exam I just had. Rather easy exam. I wasn't feeling particularly brilliant this morning. I don't know whether I made any mistakes or not. Quite a bit hinges on this exam because I want to get a scholarship for the second semester. If I get it, I will be able to carry through my work to my Master's degree. If I don't, I don't believe I'll be able to make it. It's hard to borrow money these days. I would like to keep on at college though because with the kind of work I get here I will get the kind of job I want. I am particularly interested in research work and this course that I am taking fits me for that.

E: I am afraid you are telling me a story rather than telling me what is coming into your mind. (After the first few sentences E has been giving a reasoned statement of his financial position. This is contrary to instruction and hence constitutes the first manifestation of resistance.)

S: I have an experiment this afternoon and I'm darned if I know what it is about. (This remark may contain a double meaning: S is wondering what the present session is about, as well as the afternoon's experiment. But he has abandoned his first form of resistance, the next topic being a good example of free associations.)

S: I wonder how my Dad is getting along. He is on his last legs, so to speak. Dad and I never got along very well. I remember one time when I was a youngster I was supposed to be watching some cows that were grazing near an orchard. I got so interested in reading that I forgot about the cows and they entered the orchard and ate some of the fruit off the trees. Dad was angry as the devil. He came around the corner and made a bee-line for me and I ran and he, being the old backwoods type, took a healthy swing at me with his foot as I went by and he slipped and nearly broke his arm on the wet grass. (At this point S turned around on the couch to look at E.)

E: What did you think when you turned around?

S: The reason I turned around was to look directly at you.

E: Why did you want to look directly at me?

S: If you are trying to put over a point and look directly at the person it is generally better. In sales work, for instance . . . (Again S has departed completely from free association to the idea of making a point and selling an argument. This is another form of resistance, similar to the first. At the same time he has dramatized his feeling toward E. Doubtless annoyed because E corrected him on account of his first lapse from the fundamental rule, he thinks of an earlier incident in which he lapsed from duty but eluded his father's wrath, and indeed turned the tables by being the cause of his father's hurting himself. This line of thought, however, awakens so much anxiety that he has to turn around to make sure that E is not getting angry. At this point E again reminds S of the fundamental rule.)

S: (Long pause.) I am to report what comes into my mind and nothing seems to come in. I don't care much for your paintings that you have, or whatever they are.

E: What don't you like about them?

S: I have disagreeable memories of paintings of that type. The framed diploma is a plain-looking thing to have on the wall. Is that yours, by the way?

E: Tell me what comes into your mind about it.

S: I thought it might be yours, but when I look at the inscription, it says "M.D.," so I guess that can't be yours. (For a moment S appears to free associate, but he has chosen another method of resistance, that of describing objects in the room. Almost at once his feelings betray themselves: he criticizes the objects, and leads up to a very neat indirect way of saying to E, "You are no doctor.") [27]

The subject, in this case, was not a patient but a participant in a study of personality. He was therefore treated less gently than would be advisable in the first session with a troubled neurotic individual. The excerpt nonetheless illustrates the difficulty of abandoning one's conscious vigilance. It shows the resistance and even anxieties that creep into the free associative process as soon as it is instituted.

Interpretation

Free association is the first distinguishing mark of psychoanalysis. The second point that distinguishes it from other methods is the systematic use of interpretation. It is true that interpretation enters to some extent into many therapeutic procedures, although it is scrupulously avoided in behavior therapy and in client-centered counseling. In psychoanalysis, however, it is the outstanding means used to bring about corrective emotional experience. As Hendrick put it, "The analyst has become essentially a technician in reducing unconscious resistance. The chief implement in his technique is interpretation." [28] Hendrick makes it plain that interpretation is not used to instruct the patient, but rather to bring about a new feeling on his part. "The role of the analyst as interpreter," he continues, "is not to paraphrase what the patient reports, but to indicate at appropriate moments what he is *not* reporting." The psychoanalyst deliberately tries to point out to the patient that he is using a defense, that he is shifting away from a topic that has occurred to him, or that he is apparently trying to conceal something. This is the specific implement that psychoanalysis uses against the patient's defenses. Free association is designed to heighten the prominence of these defenses; interpretation is designed to show them to the patient and slowly wear them down.

[27] This case is fully described in H. A. Murray, *Explorations in Personality* (Fair Lawn, N. J.: Oxford University Press, 1938), chap. 7. See especially pp. 639–40.

[28] I. Hendrick, *Facts and Theories of Psychoanalysis* (2nd ed.; New York: Alfred A. Knopf, Inc., 1939), p. 215.

It is obvious that the timing of interpretations is a matter of crucial importance. They must be given precisely at the moment when the patient is able to take them, and no sooner. If the patient cannot take them—if they awaken too much anxiety—he is forced to apply defenses against the interpretations and the analyst, and this delays the progress of treatment, in some cases even causing it to be broken off. An interpretation is rightly timed when the patient is able to perceive his defense, experience the impulse against which it is a defense, realize that he need not be afraid of this particular impulse, and thus achieve a relaxing of the defense. There is a gain of insight in this process, but its chief value lies in the corrective emotional experience. The essential thing is that the patient has stopped being afraid of some impulse in himself. Usually the feeling that results is one of relief and relaxation with a renewed outpouring of free associations.

At first the interpretations are directed at relatively superficial defense. They may have reference to "character armor" such as mannerisms, tricks of speech, or minor acts that pass as conventional. Perhaps it is noticed that the patient repeatedly follows a sequence which consists of making a critical remark but denying that it is his own view of the matter. One day he says that an interior decorator might consider the therapist's wallpaper too dark, though he himself likes it. Another day he observes that a person with sinus trouble would not care for so much tobacco smoke in the consulting room, though he himself is happily free from that trouble. If the analyst calls his attention to this sequence, the patient is likely to be surprised; he has never noticed it himself. But if the interpretation has been correctly timed the patient will realize both his defense and the hostile impulse that necessitates the defense. He will be able to feel his own real annoyance and to relax his defense at least to the extent of expressing distaste for dark wallpapers and smoke as his own feelings rather than someone else's. That interpretations have different effects from noninterpretive comments has been shown experimentally by Garduk and Haggard, using a large number of measurable variables like reaction time, silence, expressed affect, and the content of subsequent associations.[29]

Comparing these initial tactics with those of behavior therapy, it is evident that they signify a different conception of the nature of neurosis. On one basic point, to be sure, there is no difference: relaxing a defense and desensitization both signify the extinction of anxiety. But the behavior therapist assumes that in the early interviews he can isolate the really important anxiety situations and concentrate on reducing these specific fears. The psychoanalyst, in contrast, assumes that he cannot arrive at the primal dreads except by helping the patient to work his way inward and backward, so to speak, through layers of defensive traits, overdriven strivings, the whole protective organization that has been built up over the years

[29] E. L. Garduk and E. A. Haggard, "Immediate Effects on Patients of Psychoanalytic Interpretations," *Psychological Issues,* VII (1972), No. 4.

against possible repetitions of childhood panic. The analyst's approach to the problem is necessarily time-consuming. Extinction requires repetition, so that each interpretation has to be repeated a good many times. But anxiety keeps cropping up in different guises, defenses are manifold, and a whole series of corrective emotional experiences has to take place. Only after a slow progress through peripheral defenses can one reach the original anxieties, the avoidance of which has so long been crippling development.

Transference Neurosis

One of Freud's most important concepts was that of *transference*. He arrived at it gradually after noticing that patients, instead of attending strictly to their own conflicts, manifested a variety of personal feelings toward the physician. These feelings might be positive, consisting of an interest in the doctor's affairs, cordiality, expressions of gratitude, and eagerness to accept every interpretation. They might be of an opposite character, hostile and angry, displaying themselves in a multitude of criticisms and in a stubborn intensification of resistances. These feelings appeared so regularly and forcefully during analytic treatment as to convince Freud that they were more than responses to the actual situation or to the behavior of the therapist. He judged that they were *transferred* from the patient's past, that the relation to the analyst had reanimated attitudes of a primitive sort dating from early childhood. Justification for this view lay in the sharp disparity between the patient's often stormy passions and the professional attitude of the analyst. Furthermore, the childhood origins revealed themselves in such telltale signs as the whining voice of a demanding child or the terrified guilt of a child that has offended its parents. Freud adopted the bold idea that transference need not be an impediment in treatment. It could be drawn into the service of cure.

Transference neurosis refers to an acute development that occurs fairly regularly in full-length psychoanalysis and that is considered essential for a complete cure. The relation to the analyst is intensified to a point where it becomes more important to the patient than does his own recovery. He seems to be engaged in a struggle with the analyst, trying to win various kinds of emotional satisfaction from him. In this stage it becomes abundantly clear that the patient's attitudes have little relation to the actual situation; they are "transferred from earlier ones, especially from childhood conflicts with the parents." Freud referred to this development as a "new edition" of the old neurosis. The following paragraph from Hendrick deserves careful attention.[30]

Because this occurs with such consistency in every analysis, we can understand that the transference has developed to a point where the transference emotions are more important to the patient than the permanent health he is seeking. This is the

---

[30] Hendrick, *op. cit.*, p. 208.

point where the major unresolved, unconscious problems of childhood begin to dominate. They are now reproduced in the transference with all their pent-up emotion. The patient is unconsciously striving for what he failed to gain or to do without in actual childhood. Only those who have observed it will appreciate how fully much of the reaction to the analyst at this period is like a child's. Petulance, irritability, defiance, even a childishness in tone of voice are frequent, even in people who are otherwise quite mature.

The transference neurosis occurs with little direct provocation from the analyst. But it is fair to say that the whole analytic situation encourages this particular development. The psychoanalyst typically makes himself a shadowy figure, a blank screen on which the patient can project whatever fantasies lie close to his heart. The analytic patient lies on a couch, relaxing in the interests of free association. The therapist sits out of sight and does not have much to say. As a matter of policy, most analysts rule out any social contacts with patients outside the office. While always present as a source of reassurance and strength if necessary, the therapist does not become as clearly differentiated a figure as those one meets in daily life. Peck described his role as follows: "He loans himself, as it were, for the subject to react upon in a sort of test experience, and, instead of being drawn into that experience, his part is to reveal to the patient what is going on." [31] By restricting himself to this part he makes it easier for the patient to use him as father, mother, authority figure, rival, or whatever person is needed to re-enact the essential childhood drama.

The working through of the transference neurosis is accomplished by the familiar implements: free association and interpretation. Interpretation operates with its greatest effectiveness at just this point. If a patient has been expressing fury at the analyst for not showing the loving attention of a father, and if he then experiences sharp anxiety lest the father punish or desert him, it becomes peculiarly easy for him to appreciate the archaic character of his feelings. The discrepancy between the actual therapeutic situation and his childlike demands and fears is dramatic and inescapable He relives the early anxieties, but there is no punishment or other aversive consequence. The situation is perfect for the extinction of anxiety.

Dream Analysis

The analysis of dreams plays a prominent part in standard psychoanalysis. We have not discussed it up to this point because in spite of its prominence it introduces no new therapeutic principles. Dreams may be regarded as spontaneous free associations. They are used in psychoanalytic treatment as a starting point for further free associations, and sometimes as objects for interpretation. They are of service to the extent that they allow feelings and attitudes to leak into awareness faster than might other-

[31] M. Peck, *The Meaning of Psychoanalysis* (New York: Alfred A. Knopf, Inc., 1931), p. 188.

wise be the case. What they bring forward, however, is utilized no differently from other material.

When a patient is undergoing psychotherapy his sleep is likely to be
disturbed by a great many tensions set up during the treatment and left
unresolved at bedtime. Psychotherapy is a disturbing business. It stirs up
feelings and problems that one would prefer to avoid. The dreams that
occur concurrently with treatment are therefore likely to be numerous and
heavily loaded with matters pertaining to the illness. Among other things
they often portray with crystal clearness the state of the transference relationship. Direct expression of transference emotions, whether affectionate
or hostile, is for most patients not easy. Even free association does not always suffice to bring such material into verbal expression. Here the patient's dreams will often take the lead, expressing this feeling in disguised
but dramatic form and thus opening a road for less roundabout expressions.[32] Dreams thus help to keep the treatment in motion and sometimes
pull it out of doldrums when everything seems blocked. Occasionally a
dream marks a dramatic and significant change, becoming the means of
sudden forward progress. An example of this kind is seen in the following
case.

An Illustrative Case

A method of treatment that tends to be as long as psychoanalysis can
be illustrated only by choosing certain critical points. In the following
case, briefer than most, it proved possible through fortunate circumstances
to develop the transference neurosis quickly.[33]

A businessman of forty-two years had suffered for a long time from an
uncontrollable jerking of his arms. On three occasions he had had brief
periods of unconsciousness. Neurological examination failed to disclose
any sign of brain injury which might account for these attacks or for the
jerking. The patient had a long history of irritability and a domineering
attitude which injured his human relationships. At one point his wife
divorced him on account of these intolerable traits, but later they were
remarried. The immediate occasion for seeking medical help was the fact
that his wife was again considering separation. In addition, for a number
of weeks he had suffered a complete loss of sexual potency.

The patient's troubles were discerned to have their origins in his relation to his father. The father had been a self-made man with huge self-
confidence and a violent temper. He was a tyrant both at home and in his
business. He never tired of making the son feel inferior, and though at
times there was sharp conflict between them, the son always gave in. Among

32 An illuminating analysis of a series of dreams dealing with progressive changes in
the transference relationship is given by T. M. French, *The Integration of Behavior,
I. Basic Postulates* (Chicago: University of Chicago Press, 1952), especially chaps. 17, 18, and
33–35.
33 Alexander, French, *et al., op. cit.,* pp. 55–65.

other things the father had intimidated the patient in the matter of sexual expression. To meet all this pressure and somehow preserve self-respect, the patient had built up his own assertive and domineering attitude. He was ruled by a vast compensatory need to appear important and strong. When the father died, the patient took over the family glassware works and with great energy expanded it well beyond what his father had been able to accomplish. He felt impelled to surpass his father, yet along with all his competition and rebellion there was a great deal of admiring devotion.

From the very start the patient reproduced in the therapeutic situation his combined attitudes toward his father. He wanted rules to be made for him, and scrupulously obeyed one or two that had to be suggested. But his conversation was otherwise designed to impress the analyst with his importance, and whenever the analyst explained anything he quickly began to explain something about which he himself was expert: business or sports. He literally tried to force the doctor to become tyrannical so that he could rebel and compete with him. This attitude was so clear that the analyst undertook to create a corrective emotional experience by behaving in just the opposite fashion. He let the patient take the lead, avoided statements that could be thought arbitrary, admitted the limitations of psychiatry, expressed admiration for the patient's good qualities, took an interest in his business and social activities. Under this treatment the patient became distinctly confused. He plainly thrived in the permissive, encouraging atmosphere, but he was unable to check his competitive feelings and still tried to fight battles with the analyst. This offered the perfect opportunity for crucial interpretations. The patient could not help seeing that his aggression was completely out of relation to the analyst's behavior. His chief overdriven striving was exposed and he became able to enter a more genuine relationship with the doctor.

The change in his attitude toward the therapist was soon reflected at home. He became less domineering and was able to assume a more appropriately benevolent and helpful role toward his son. But his need to make a tyrant out of the analyst finally yielded only after a particularly vivid dream and its aftermath. The patient dreamed that he had manufactured some glassware and that the analyst angrily broke it all to pieces. The dream reminded him of an occasion when his father smashed a set of glassware because he did not like the design. During the hour which began with the reporting of this dream, the analyst asked the patient to tell more about his work. The patient eagerly embarked on a condescending lecture. The corrective emotional experience occasioned by thus assuming authority over the therapist was so great that the patient thereafter recovered his sexual potency. His old role of the now-rebelling, now-submitting son could be outgrown as he found it possible to have a relation of friendly give and take with an authoritative person. As he achieved this new learning on the social plane he outgrew his sexual intimidation.

The remaining hours of treatment were devoted to fuller discussion of the transference relationship. In childhood the patient had often been obliged to accept help from his father, but the father had always made him feel inferior on such occasions. This led him to react with a compensatory striving to prove that he was really the better man. Accepting help from the analyst had thus reanimated from the start the very core of the neurotic problem. The analyst's radical assumption of exactly the opposite role, giving help along with interest, permissiveness, and a complete lack of the father's dogmatic self-confidence, led to an unusually rapid corrective emotional experience. At the end of treatment the patient's arms no longer jerked, which may be taken as presumptive evidence that the jerking originated from the tension of suppressed rage. His emotional and sexual relations with his wife were better than ever before, talk of separation had ended, and his irritable and domineering tendencies had greatly diminished. The patient was at least much improved, if not fully cured.

Comparison with Behavior Therapy

It is possible to make a convincing case that the whole psychoanalytic procedure rests upon the same learning principles that are used in behavior modification. Several workers, including Dollard and Miller and Bandura, have attempted to make this translation in a systematic way.[34] We have been following this tradition in our account thus far, assuming that any theory of behavior, even one like Freud's that is expressed in its own psychodynamic vocabulary, must be basically a theory about learning and motivation. Although behavior therapy and psychoanalysis have often been pictured as poles apart, they have in common such fundamental principles as conditioning, extinction, counter-conditioning, and reinforcement. The psychoanalytic vocabulary is a good deal richer than the sparse language of learning theory in describing developmental and clinical observations. It has words for such phenomena as defense mechanisms, "character armor," overdriven strivings, and the protectively burdened personality— words, that is, to represent the more complex and cumulative patterns seen in disordered behavior. But any theory of human behavior must make allowance for human cognitive versatility and for the extensive powers of symbolization that are characteristic of the human species. These are not violations of basic learning principles; they are enlargements of them.

Seen in this light, the tactics of behavior therapy entail the assumption that a neurotic complaint is a relatively isolated thing, not heavily entangled with other aspects of personality. It can be understood in simple learning

---

34 J. Dollard and N. E. Miller, *Personality and Psychotherapy* (New York: McGraw-Hill Book Co., 1950), chaps. 14–20; A Bandura, "Psychotherapy as a Learning Process," *Psychological Bulletin*, LVIII (1961), pp. 143–59. See also E. Wolf, "Learning Theory and Psychoanalysis," *International Journal of Psychiatry*, VII (1969), pp. 525–61.

terms and undone with simple conditioning procedures. The only concession made to a more systemic conception of behavior is in reports sometimes given that when the client's complaint is eliminated he feels better also in other respects. The trouble may have begun early in childhood, but it has persisted without widely invading other aspects of life. The tactics of psychoanalysis can be represented as proceeding on the assumption of maximum entanglement. The frights of childhood have indeed invaded other aspects of life, perhaps a great many of them, leading to an organization of personality that is widely restricted in the interests of protection. A person's defense against anger, for instance, originating in terrifying scenes with a domineering father, is represented now not just in a phobia of authoritative males but in a cool, polite demeanor designed to forestall aggression from anyone. Perhaps it has also had a part in the person's becoming interested in international law and the cool, polite settlement of world tensions through the action of a world court. The psychoanalytic patient is perceived as having dozens of anxiety situations, any of which upset him if the defenses do not work, and these, as well as the core fears from childhood, must all be the object of treatment. If this is not done, the patient remains a seriously crippled, defensively burdened person even if it should happen that the core anxiety was deconditioned. Putting it in terms of behavior therapy, the patient as seen by his psychoanalyst needs to be desensitized on dozens of lists and given assertive training in dozens of situations. Behavior therapy covering so much ground might have to go on for three years. It would then consist not just of removing the complaint but of remaking the personality, as psychoanalysis claims to do.

Naturally one wonders who is right, but the question is not legitimate. Unless one assumes that the whole history of psychoanalysis over three-quarters of a century is a vast system of illusions foisted on innocent patients, or that the briefer but now extensive history of behavior modification is simply a tale of ignorant blundering, the conclusion must take account of both methods' legitimate findings. There seems to be no theoretical reason for doubting that neurotic complaints can vary widely in extent of embeddedness in other aspects of personality. There seems also to be no reason to question the desirability of "remaking the personality" when it is so protectively burdened that life has become a chronic misery. Error starts with the assumption that one method of treatment is good for all.

A modest statement by Peck, who was an analyst, sets the tone for a reasonable view of the topic. "Psychoanalysis," wrote Peck, "is the major surgery of psychotherapy. Like major surgery, analysis does not help everything, nor is it usually the first method to be thought of in trouble. It should be reserved for those problems which less radical procedure does not reach." [35] It should be reserved, to paraphrase, for those cases in which re-

35 Peck, op. cit., pp. 159–60.

moval of the complaint brings other complaints to the surface. One of the earlier tenets of psychoanalytic doctrine, to the effect that removal of a "symptom" would lead to the appearance of another "symptom" if the underlying forces were left unaltered, has been effectively challenged by behavior therapists whose follow-ups show that in most cases no substitute symptom appears. But there are other cases in which a person who has learned, let us say, to endure closed spaces and to assert himself better, still suffers the costs of protective organization—disturbing tensions and chronic dissatisfaction—and is still bothered by depression, loneliness, emptiness, a conviction that life is not being well spent. These are the suitable candidates for psychotherapeutic "major surgery."

Because psychoanalysis and behavior therapy both came into existence as methods of treating neurosis, it is fair to compare their accomplishments in reaching this goal. Psychoanalysis, however, fairly early came to have additional meaning. Freud toward the end of his life became pessimistic about the value of his method considered simply as a treatment of neurosis. He remained unshaken, however, that he had invented a unique method for exploring the true nature of human development and finding the real internal determinants of human behavior. A sweeping claim, surely, but not wholly an idle one, as the cultural acceptance of his ideas widely testifies. Psychoanalysis thus provides a way of answering the human need for self-understanding, with its expected dividend of becoming able to make one's life richer and wiser. Many are the people who simply want to know about their defensive tactics, their "character armor," their hang-ups, perhaps partly out of curiosity but mainly so that they can attain more straightforward, warm, rich living. Freud's way of fostering these ventures in self-exploration is so long and expensive that it remains a luxury of the rich; the ordinary citizen must rely on the old-fashioned method of reflecting on his experience or on more economical devices presently to be described. But the boon of self-understanding conferred by psychoanalysis is much esteemed by those who have received it. They are likely to evaluate their treatment in these terms more than by neurotic complaints removed.

OTHER FORMS OF PSYCHOTHERAPY

We have now described the two most prominent schools of thought about psychotherapy. Behavior modification, with its historical roots in Pavlov and behavioristic psychology, and psychoanalysis, with its background of medical practice and of Freud's discoveries, represent two distinctly different ways of going about treatment, even though they have a presumed common basis in learning and motivation. To describe schools of thought with their differences, however, is easier than giving a realistic picture of the actual practice of psychotherapy. In the therapeutic situation flexibility is more likely to be a virtue than theoretical purity. We have described a behavior therapist pausing in his schedule of systematic desensitization to hear about a patient's love affair and give needed sexual instruction. A strict psychoanalyst is as likely to stop listening to free associations and give sexual instruction or other practical advice that he perceives to be urgently needed. Many psychotherapists prize flexibility above theory and deliberately aim for an eclectic use of techniques. Research in which therapeutic sessions have been recorded and then evaluated by independent judges shows that therapists of different theoretical allegiances behave less differently than their theories would lead one to suppose.[36] Being fundamentally a human interaction, psychotherapy must be seen as a process in which both parties, responsive to one another, feel their way toward a desired goal.

The picture of the complete therapist who can use whatever method is needed is appealing, but it perhaps appeals to one's fantasies of omnipotence more than to one's common sense. Everyone likes and does some things better than others. Being able to devise ingenious applications of learning theory may not go with empathic listening to free associations. Like all people, psychotherapists must be allowed scope to "do their own thing" and not try to be superbeings. Further difficulty lies in the fact that different methods of treatment are not always compatible. A patient cannot be set for systematic desensitization and at the same time taught to embark upon free associations. There is thus an enduring problem of finding the right therapist for the right patient, and this is something we cannot expect will always be done perfectly.

Psychoanalytically Oriented Therapy

Psychoanalysis has been practiced long enough to have developed a number of distinctive offshoots. The early defectors from Freud's group, Adler and Jung, developed under the headings respectively of *individual psychology* and *analytical psychology* distinctly different therapeutic techniques of their own.[37] Somewhat later a number of psychoanalysts who came to be called *neo-Freudian*, represented by Horney, Sullivan, and Fromm-Reichmann, made additional variations in the full-length standard technique.[38] Proposals for shortening the time without abandoning the basic psycho-

36 F. E. Fiedler, "A Comparison of Therapeutic Relationships in Psychoanalytic, Nondirective and Adlerian Psychotherapy," *Journal of Consulting Psychology*, XIV (1950), pp. 436–45.

37 H. L. Ansbacher and R. R. Ansbacher, eds., *The Individual Psychology of Alfred Adler* (New York: Basic Books, Inc., 1956), chaps. 13, 16; C. J. Jung, *Modern Man in Search of a Soul* (New York: Harcourt Brace Jovanovich, Inc., 1933), chaps. 2, 3.

38 K. Horney, *New Ways in Psychoanalysis* (New York: W. W. Norton & Co., Inc., 1939); H. S. Sullivan, *The Psychiatric Interview* (New York: W. W. Norton & Co., Inc., 1954); E. Fromm-Reichmann, *Principles of Intensive Psychotherapy* (Chicago: University of Chicago Press, 1950). A searching and detailed comparative study of Freud and his offshoots is R. Munroe, *Schools of Psychoanalytic Thought* (New York: Holt, Rinehart & Winston, Inc., 1955).

analytic conception were made in 1946 by Alexander and French.[39] Many workers originally trained in psychoanalysis have gone further and practice what they refer to as *psychoanalytically oriented psychotherapy*. This expression implies that the therapist is familiar with psychoanalytic principles; that he acknowledges the importance of unconscious motivation and the defense mechanisms; and that he attempts to use these insights in understanding his patients and planning their treatment. It does not imply using the standard technique. There may be considerable departures dictated by circumstance and limitations of time, and the goal of resolving all major emotional problems may be replaced by an attempt to resolve only those problems that are most acute and most ripe for resolution. Even if contact with a patient has to be limited to a few brief sessions, these workers believe that their psychoanalytic insights help them to act wisely.

Client-Centered Therapy

Differing widely from psychoanalysis, yet equally far from behavior modification, is a method of psychotherapy introduced in 1942 by Carl Rogers. This widely used method will repay careful examination.

Rogers first gave his method the title of non-directive counseling.[40] This reflected his belief that the client should always take the lead in the therapeutic process. As described by Rogers, the counselor does not intervene by asking questions, by giving information or advice, or even by directing the course of the conversation. His goal is to help the client grow in the client's own directions, and his role is confined to encouraging and ratifying this growth. To this end, he employs a single therapeutic tool called the acceptance, recognition, and clarification of feeling. He simply re-states what the client has just said, but he re-states the feeling side of it rather than the content. This is not as easy as it sounds. All our habits of conversation are built on the idea of responding to content. If someone says, "I didn't have a good time at X," a very natural social response would be, "Oh, didn't you? I thought it was a fine place when I was there." To borrow one of Rogers' examples, if a student says that his study habits are wrong and that he is not really so stupid as his grades indicate, it is natural to ask him what his grades are. In both cases the response is made to content, not to feeling. The respondent talks about the objective characteristics of X or the objective grades on the student's report card. It is quite another matter to respond to the feeling that was expressed: the first person's dislike of X, the second person's disappointment with his grades and concern lest they be taken as the true measure of his ability. The special quality that makes a conversation therapeutic, as Rogers first stated it, lies in responding to feeling.

39 Alexander, French, *et al., op. cit.*
40 C. R. Rogers, *Counseling and Psychotherapy* (Boston: Houghton Mifflin Co., 1942).

In a later publication Rogers changed the title of his method to *client-centered therapy*.[41] He now amended his account in order to avoid the elusiveness of the word "feeling." The counselor must learn to perceive things as the client perceives them, to enter as fully as possible into the client's "internal frame of reference," and to "indicate to the client the extent to which he is seeing through the client's eyes." [42] This description change does greater justice to the cognitive aspect of what is to be recognized: not just loose feelings, so to speak, but matters of deep concern to the client, such as the extent of his academic ability and its meaning for his future prospects and sense of worth. Still later, Gendlin arrived at a further refinement. "Feelings are really 'felt meanings,' " he wrote; "implicitly complex experiencing of situations. . . . Not to distract or digress from the experiential process of the client's concretely felt meanings, but to point to them, help him wrestle with them, carry them forward by our personal and exact response to them or inquiry concerning them—that is the principle." [43]

Difficulty in finding the right words to convey just what the client-centered therapist accepts, recognizes, and clarifies should not be taken to mean that it is unimportant. We shall not go far wrong if we think of it as the client's deepest personal concerns, whatever they may be at a particular time. When the therapist is successful in his recognitions, the client finds himself in a unique situation. The way he feels, the way things look to him, the things that really matter to him, are constantly appreciated and are clearly the things in which the counselor, too, is interested. Successful recognition of the internal frame of reference thus leads to the expression of more and more feelings. The client has probably never before had a listener who paid so much attention to his personal concerns. As a result, it often happens that within a single hour he talks about many things he has never told anyone else.

The consistent use of this single therapeutic tool distinguishes client-centered therapy from other forms of treatment in which advice, information, interpretation, conditioning procedures, and practical assistance may be intermingled. The Rogers technique deserves its original title of "nondirective." The client is simply given his head. At times the therapist is almost amusingly evasive. He replies to anxious queries by acknowledging that the client feels anxious or he parries a request for advice by recognizing that the client would like someone to settle the question for him. But he sticks to his principle of responding to the experiential process as it is disclosed to him, and the client soon learns that he himself must take the initiative.

41 C. R. Rogers, *Client-Centered Therapy* (Boston: Houghton Mifflin Co., 1951).
42 *Ibid.*, p. 34.
43 E. T. Gendlin, in J. T. Hart and T. M. Tomlinson, eds., *New Directions in Client-Centered Therapy* (Boston: Houghton Mifflin Co., 1970), chap. 29, pp. 546–47.

Changes Occurring Through Client-Centered Therapy

Success is of course not universal, but this method is clearly capable of producing significant changes. A substantial number of research studies based upon many series of recorded interviews tends to confirm a fairly regular course of events.[44] Time is spent at first in defining or *structuring* the situation. More than likely the client will want direction and will accept with difficulty the idea that the hour belongs to him. As he gets used to this, the client at first uses the opportunity to pour out *negatvie feelings:* doubts, guilts, inferiorities, anxieties, and hostilities. This is followed by "one of the most certain and predictable aspects of the whole process," the faint and tentative expression of *positive impulses.* Social feelings, love, self-respect, the desire to be mature make their appearance in the client's conversation. When these are duly clarified there begin to be distinct signs of the *achievement of insight.* Having expressed so many feelings on both sides of the ledger, the client begins to see himself in a new light. He begins to talk about possible decisions and courses of action. Before long one witnesses the *initiation of positive actions,* possibly minute but generally significant. The timid high school boy takes the step of going to a dance; the formerly frantic and resentful mother devises a way of showing affection and respect for her child; the prim and prudish young girl comes to the decision of styling her hair as the other girls have done. The first positive actions may be hardly more than symbolic. They may be initiated only after a series of attempts to persuade the counselor to sanction or advise them. But in any event they are important because they represent just the kind of step the client has been unable to take before. They constitute the first short but crucial steps in the journey toward greater self-confidence and greater self-insight that characterize clients successfully treated.

In spite of the gentle character of the influence brought to bear in client-centered therapy, it is capable of producing a corrective emotional experience. By reflecting back upon them the feeling implications of each thing they have said, by showing that he understands and sympathizes with their personal struggles, the therapist gives clients the chance to find out for themselves at least some of the things that are the matter with them and to discover their next constructive steps. Change occurs, and it occurs in a fairly short time. We must put the question, therefore, whether the change is profound, whether it is enduring, whether the accompanying insights have a lasting effect on future development.

To look first on the bright side, we take one of Rogers' most successful examples, the case of sixteen-year-old Barbara.[45] During her junior year

---

[44] Rogers, *Client-Centered Therapy, op. cit.,* chap. 4; C. R. Rogers and R. F. Dymond, *Psychotherapy and Personality Change* (Chicago: University of Chicago Press, 1954). See also Hart and Tomlinson, *op. cit.,* chaps. 8–14.

[45] Rogers, *Counseling and Psychotherapy, op. cit.,* pp. 185–94, 211–13, 223–28, 250–51.

in high school this girl had what was described as a "nervous breakdown," characterized by "fears and sensations of an overwhelming sort which were very troubling." Her case appears to qualify as at least a mild neurosis. The root of her difficulty was discerned to be in an overstrict religious background and in a too strong identification with her scholarly father. Sixteen sessions of client-centered therapy brought about the following changes in her insight, accompanied by appropriate positive actions. (1) She passed from rather fantastic intellectual ambitions and an intense desire for perfection to a more realistic acknowledgment of what any one person, and herself in particular, would be able to achieve. This progress did not end in a sad sense of limitation but rather in a cheerful acceptance of things as they are. (2) She changed from an "ultra-saintly person, afraid of any social instincts, to a person who wanted to get along with and enjoy other young people." Her social interests were very greatly expanded. (3) She had always "hated sweetheart stuff," but as the interviews progressed she was first able to acknowledge a distinctly affectionate interest in a certain boy friend, then later to appreciate the "puppy-love" character of this infatuation, recognizing its shallowness compared to what she really wanted. (4) Starting from the position that she wanted to be a man and greatly disliked children, she gradually came to feel that the role of woman and wife would not be objectionable. Her dislike of children began to evaporate.

If these changes sound bland and conformist, we must remember that her earlier positions had not worked; they led to breakdown. Considering her youth and her apparent capacity for change, there is little reason to doubt that the benefit would be permanent. Unfortunately the amount of change does not always seem to be so large as it is in this example. When one studies the case of Herbert Bryan, for instance, a neurotic in his late twenties, whose eight interviews are printed verbatim in Rogers' earlier book,[46] there is room for considerable doubt as to whether the improvement was more than transient. Many problems clearly touched upon in the client's conversation were as unsolved at the end as at the beginning, and it is hard to feel confident that the brief spurt of self-assurance shown in the last two interviews would carry him through future difficulties. In contrast to Barbara, the course of whose life appears to have been set right by client-centered therapy, Herbert Bryan, older and with a more stubborn neurosis, sounds as if he left treatment very much as he came to it.

Evaluation of Client-Centered Therapy

The method developed by Rogers has been widely adopted, especially by non-medical counselors. It is appreciated for its clarity, its consistency, and the fact that it is unlikely to do the client any harm. It is all too easy during a therapeutic interview to mix up the principles one is employing

[46] *Ibid.*, pp. 261–437.

and thus to destroy the efficacy of any of them. Thus an inexperienced or careless therapist may proceed for a while non-directively, thus affirming his respect for the client's ego, then be tempted into an interpretation which says in effect that he does not quite trust the client's ego, then hope to go back to the non-directive atmosphere just as if he had not wounded the client's ego. Rogers has shown how this kind of confusion can be avoided. He has shown how to proceed consistently on the basis of respecting the client's ego and letting him take all the initiative. Whatever else it accomplishes, this work should have a profoundly clarifying effect on the training of future therapists, who should hereafter be able to realize much more clearly what they are doing at each moment, even if they decide to use other therapeutic tools besides the recognition of feelings.

But this desirable effect of Rogers' work should not overshadow the real limitations that soon began to be apparent in client-centered psychotherapy. Considerable criticism was evoked by his arrogation of the terms "non-directive" and "client-centered," with its implicit suggestion that all departures from this method must be autocratically directive and centered elsewhere than in the client. Perry and Estes took issue with the idea that counseling ceases to be client-centered the moment the counselor does anything except recognize feelings. "Any counselor-participation," they said, "which is assimilated by the client to a set in which he perceives himself as ultimately responsible for initiative and evaluation is properly described as client-centered." [47] Once the client has adopted this set the counselor will not break it merely by using his knowledge at appropriate places to give advice and make suggestions. Other workers expressed disapproval of the rigid use of a single therapeutic process regardless of circumstances. Beier, for example, called attention to the large number of "involuntary clients" many counselors must deal with: delinquents, prisoners, employees, persons referred by the courts. The principles enunciated by Rogers appear to imply that these unmotivated people cannot be helped, yet it often happens that a little preliminary work consisting of advice, information, and persuasion turns them into motivated clients who profit from counseling.[48] Saslow pointed out that in the psychosomatic disorders the patient is often initially concerned only to be free from his physical symptom. Through proper guidance during the medical study such patients often come to see the need for psychological treatment. In cases of this common kind "a determined refusal to expand the client-centered orientation probably implies refusal to benefit a great many clients." [49]

The sharpest and most systematic criticism of client-centered therapy

47 W. G. Perry, Jr., and S. G. Estes, "The Collaboration of Client and Counselor," in O. H. Mowrer, ed., *Psychotherapy: Theory and Research* (New York: The Ronald Press Co., 1953), p. 105.

48 E. G. Beier, "Client-Centered Therapy and the Involuntary Client," *Journal of Consulting Psychology*, XIV (1952), pp. 332–37.

49 G. Saslow, "Psychotherapy," in *Annual Review of Psychology*, V (Stanford: Annual Reviews, Inc., 1954), p. 315 .

came from Thorne, who considered it "definitely not the complete answer to all therapeutic problems, even in mild personality disorders." [50] Thorne laments the failure to obtain any kind of history, pointing out that the counselor cannot be sure he has really uncovered the major problems if he does not permit himself to ask questions about the patient's past life. Furthermore, what facts the patient elects to reveal are not checked by corroborative evidence from other sources. As a result it is to be questioned whether a "comprehensive evaluation of the dynamic mechanisms operant in the total personality" has been made. Not enough is done to prevent the treatment from concentrating on one small and secondary portion of the patient's difficulties. Some of the published reports justify Thorne's remark that the patient "browsed along the edges of his problem, coming to grips with it only in terms of a few partial insights." It is the duty of the counselor to prevent this kind of evasion from taking place, unless he judges that greater insight would be seriously disturbing. It is his duty to use whatever methods are appropriate on a given occasion, including reassurance, support, and direct advice. Above all, in Thorne's view, it is the counselor's duty to use his knowledge to formulate in his own mind what is wrong with the client and to develop the best possible plan of treatment.

These criticisms say, in effect, that client-centered therapy cannot be used for all problems. Like behavior modification and like psychoanalysis, it is no panacea. The perfect clients for it would seem to be intelligent, reflective, puzzled young people, struggling with difficulties of living and having no more than mild neurotic complications. Client-centered therapy has been extended in various directions, including work by Gendlin with hospitalized schizophrenics,[51] but usually with concessions to other modes of working. In a sense the method captures the essence of therapeutic interviewing, and it continues to be valuable whenever interviewing is part of a treatment program, even if other techniques are also included.

Existential Psychotherapy

The emphasis placed by Rogers and his followers on the client's experiential process and internal frame of reference puts them close to another school of thought very different in background. Existential psychoanalysis originated in Europe out of an attempt to modify Freud's scientific outlook with the view of man arising from existential philosophy. Giving philosophical debts to Kierkegaard, Husserl, and Heidegger, it has been especially developed by two Swiss psychiatrists, Ludwig Binswanger and Medard

50 F. C. Thorne, "A Critique of Non-Directive Methods of Psychotherapy," *Journal of Abnormal and Social Psychology*, XXXIX (1944), pp. 459–70; "Directive and Eclectic Personality Counseling," in J. L. McCary and D. E. Sheer, eds., *Six Approaches to Psychotherapy* (New York: The Dryden Press, 1955), chap. 5.

51 E. T. Gendlin, "Research in Psychotherapy with Schizophrenic Patients and the Nature of That 'Illness,'" *American Journal of Psychotherapy*, XX (1966), pp. 4–16; reprinted as chap. 15 in Hart and Tomlinson, *op. cit.*

Boss.[52] Existentialism raises questions about the scientific understanding of human behavior; as Binswanger put it, "man is no longer understood in terms of some theory—be it a mechanistic, a biologic or a psychological one." The emphasis is shifted to *being*, to personal experiencing in the present. Psychotherapists, according to Rollo May, must ask themselves: "Can we be sure that we are seeing the patient as he really is, knowing him in his own reality; or are we seeing merely a projection of our own theories *about* him?" They must further ask themselves: "How can we know whether we are seeing the patient in his real world, the world in which he 'lives and moves and has his being,' and which is for him unique, concrete, and different from our general theories of culture? In all probability we have never participated in his world and do not know it directly; yet we must know it and to some extent must be able to exist in it if we are to have any chance of knowing him."[53] Existential therapy differs from other forms in calling not for new techniques but for an uncommonly high standard of knowing another person as he really is.

Existential therapy has had wide popularity in Europe and is a significant movement in the United States. Many have felt that it addressed itself more directly than other methods to the deeper contemporary concerns of mankind. Ford and Urban give existential therapists good marks on a number of points.

> They share with others, such as Adler and Rogers, an emphasis on the importance of subjectively observable responses; attention and awareness are fundamental, not only as they affect a person's present behavior but also as they determine what he will learn and how he will change in the future. These writers share with Adler the notion that how a person represents future events to himself (goals and objectives) has much to do with the way he can behave in the present. They have not missed the critical purpose of psychotherapy, and they stress the importance of the patient actually performing new and constructive responses in the everyday world; these concrete patterns of interaction become the ultimate test of the success of psychotherapy. . . . They point to a pattern of difficulties frequent in present-day patients, isolation and loneliness, which they interpret to result from the person's learned avoidance of significant interactions with people. They emphasize a person's identity, or awareness of himself, as a basic antecedent to human behavior.[54]

Further Variations

For our present purposes it is unnecessary to go further in describing the many varieties of contemporary psychotherapy. In the main, each va-

[52] L. Binswanger, "Existential Analysis and Psychotherapy," in F. Fromm-Reichmann and J. L. Moreno, eds., *Progress in Psychotherapy* (New York: Grune & Stratton, Inc., 1956), pp. 144–48; M. Boss, *Daseinsanalyse and Psychoanalysis* (New York: Basic Books, Inc., 1963).

[53] R. May, E. Angel, and H. F. Ellenberger, eds., *Existence: A New Dimension in Psychiatry and Psychology* (New York: Basic Books, Inc., 1958), pp. 3, 4.

[54] D. H. Ford and H. B. Urban, *Systems of Psychotherapy: A Comparative Study* (New York: John Wiley & Sons, Inc., 1963), p. 474.

riety is characterized by laying special stress on some one aspect of the therapeutic process. Thus we find Laing giving the central place to "the relation *between persons; psychotherapy must remain an obstinate attempt of two people to recover the wholeness of being human through the relationship between them.*" [55] A school of thought started by Frederick Perls known as *Gestalt therapy* puts the emphasis on the organizational processes revealed by the client during the treatment hour; "the therapist can see the individual experiencing certain needs, trying to fulfill them but failing because the process is interrupted somehow or is cluttered up." [56] In a different vein Glasser speaks of *reality therapy*, maintaining that clients can attain relatedness, respect, and self-respect only by outgrowing their tendency to deny the realities around them and learn to fulfill themselves within a realistic framework.[57] These and other variations entail different degrees of anxiety-reduction, insight-seeking, and persuasion, some tending to be tough and direct, others gentle and highly sensitive. In a human process as involved as psychotherapy there is certainly room to emphasize different aspects and to take a variety of attitudes. That there should be a babel of voices is thus understandable, but the student's task would be easier if the voices were more inclined to restrict their claims and sound less like fresh revelations.

The current proliferation of techniques and schools of thought makes one wonder whether we are moving toward greater clarity or greater confusion. Perhaps it is not too gross an oversimplification to set up psychoanalysis and behavior modification as outside stakes marking the extremes of the field. Psychoanalysis represents an extreme not only in time required but especially in thoroughness of probing and recovering relevant memories of the patient's past life. Common to all other methods is a greater emphasis on the present—on present behavior, present reinforcement contingencies, present feelings as expressed in conversation, defensive and adaptive processes observable during the therapeutic hour, unwitting motives deducible from current behavior. Behavior modification represents an extreme in limiting the field of observation to objective behavior and rejecting the relevance of subjective experience. All other methods, including "broad-gauge" behavior therapy, make a larger place for human cognitive versatility and for the personal meanings that surround each patient's complaint, assuming that something can be gained if the patient comes to see things differently. The two trends move in the same direction. They presage possible future agreement on the "belief that an objective examination of troublesome problems in living, undertaken in the context of a professional relationship over time, can clarify them and increase one's autonomy and mastery of feelings, impulses, and patterns of

55 R. D. Laing, *The Politics of Experience* (New York: Ballantine Books, Inc., 1967), pp. 50, 53.

56 R. Wallen, in J. Fagan and I. L. Shepherd, eds., *Gestalt Therapy Now* (New York: Science and Behavior Books, Inc., 1970), p. 10.

57 W. Glasser, *Reality Therapy: A New Approach to Psychiatry* (New York: Harper & Row, 1965).

behavior." [58] Prediction is hazardous, but there would seem to be enough underlying convergence to justify the hope of a post-Freudian post-behavioristic conception of psychotherapy that has outgrown its controversial origins. In this respect practice may already be ahead of theory, and it will be gratifying when theory catches up.

CHOICE OF PATIENTS FOR PSYCHOTHERAPY

Although corrective emotional experience and subsequent relearning do not seem to imply any special kind of talent, psychotherapists have the obligation to try to estimate a client's chances of developing and profiting by such experiences. Is the prospective client likely to progress well in treatment, or will there be a stubborn battle with minimal results? Will the candidate stick to his task in spite of anxieties, angers, and frustrations, or will he break off in the middle, possibly the worse for his experience? To these strictly psychological considerations is added the practical one of time. Psychotherapists, being usually in short supply relative to the demands made for their services, tend to choose the most promising candidates from among those they might reasonably expect to help. The population that receives psychotherapy is thus not a representative sample of neurotics, of people struggling with difficulties, or indeed of any other category of disordered behavior. It has been chosen for its promise.

Any process of selection opens the way to all kinds of personal preference. Even though everyone recognized this possibility, it came as a rude shock to discover that the chances of a patient being selected for treatment were significantly correlated with social class position. Hollingshead and Redlich, in a noteworthy analysis of the prevalence and treatment of disorders in a whole community, were responsible for bringing this disturbing fact to light.[59] Taking only the publicly supported clinics, where the therapists are on salary and the patient's financial arrangements, if any, are made with someone else, they showed that senior psychiatrists prefer to work with patients high on the social ladder, turning over those of lower class to internes and medical students. Class position proved to be very definitely related to both the amount and the expertness of treatment received. These findings were a painful blow to the staff members of the clinics, who did not have the slightest intention of practicing class discrimination. But the authors were able to show that all the psychiatrists in the community belonged to the top social classes, some having arrived there quite recently.

The findings deserve careful scrutiny, for it is not likely that they represent pure snobbishness on the part of the psychotherapists. Two factors seem to be responsible for the pattern of selection: one of intelligence and

58 H. H. Strupp, R. E. Fox, and K. Lessler, *Patients View Their Psychotherapy* (Baltimore: The Johns Hopkins Press, 1969), pp. 9, 10.

59 A. B. Hollingshead and F. C. Redlich, *Social Class and Mental Illness: A Community Study* (New York: John Wiley & Sons, Inc., 1958).

the other of general outlook. Research on social stratification uses number of years of schooling as one of its criteria for placing people in the class structure. This suggests that the psychotherapists were choosing partly on the basis of effective intelligence as shown in the first interviews; they preferred the better educated, intellectually livelier candidates. The research also showed great differences in outlook between higher and lower class positions. Patients with relatively little schooling, whose outlook is narrow and who tend to consider their fate to be largely in other people's hands, tend also to think of emotional disorders as analogous to physical disease. As causes they think most naturally of infections or bumps on the head, and they expect to be cured, if at all, by a pill or an injection. The idea of achieving a richer and healthier life through understanding one's own behavior is foreign to most people with limited educational background. To get well just by talking seems absurd. They expect the doctor to do something, and what a patient expects, as Frank has shown in various researches, has an important influence on outcome.[60]

Hollingshead and Redlich's study was made at a time and in a community in which psychotherapy was largely dominated by psychoanalytic thought. Even when shorter methods were used, they were best adapted to patients accustomed to living hopefully, reflectively, and at least with a fair amount of intellectual control. The report reminds us of the importance of a kind of compatibility between therapist and patient. Summarizing a considerable body of research since this report appeared, Hans Strupp characterizes as follows the attributes of a good patient as seen by therapists.

Patients considered good prognostic risks are described as young, attractive, well-educated, members of the upper middle class, possessing a high degree of ego-strength, some anxiety which impels them to seek help, no seriously disabling neurotic symptoms, relative absence of deep characterological distortions and strong secondary gains, a willingness to talk about their difficulties, an ability to communicate well, some skill in the social-vocational area, and a value system relatively congruent with that of the therapist. Such patients also tend to remain in therapy, profit from it, and evoke the therapist's best efforts. By superficial criteria, such patients may not appear very sick; however, neither our culture nor our psychological tests are very sensitive to unhappiness, silent suffering, and despair.[61]

Strupp makes the further point that "only a relatively restricted band of the population meets these criteria, which, incidentally, are not very different from the ones originally postulated by Freud." When we think back to the crude hypnotic tactics of Mesmer and to the only slightly more sophisticated suggestive methods of Charcot, we are perhaps justified in saying that Freud started psychotherapy on a kind of social ascent, paying little

60 J. D. Frank, "The Influence of Patients' and Therapists' Expectations on the Outcome of Psychotherapy," *British Journal of Medical Psychology*, XLI (1968), pp. 349–56.
61 H. H. Strupp, "Psychotherapy," in *Annual Review of Psychology*, XIII (1962), pp. 470–71.

attention to the needs of average clinical patients and turning it into a refined method of self-development with aims far beyond the removal of symptoms and the relief of immediate suffering.

Behavior modification, however, seems better designed to appeal to a broader band of the population. The behavior therapist is a person who does something, whose talk is preliminary to the use of some clear-cut technique which the patient can hold responsible for his betterment. Behavior modification may thus be the method of choice not only when the complaint seems circumscribed, like a phobia, but also when the patient has difficulty thinking of a complaint in any other light. This does not imply that behavior therapy cannot be used with intellectually sophisticated clients, though some of these have been known to express disappointment at not learning more about themselves. But it does suggest the necessity of specifying the types of population when making comparative studies of outcome.

RESULTS OF PSYCHOTHERAPY

One might suppose that the results of psychotherapy would long ago have been measured and put on an objective basis. If the whole enterprise were new we might think it legitimate to proceed experimentally without being sure of the results, but the assessment of outcomes should certainly be given high priority; otherwise there is a risk of continuing to offer treatment that does no good and may even be harmful. By now, surely, outcome research has spoken in clear tones, giving psychotherapists a fairly precise idea as to what they are likely to accomplish. This seemingly sensible expectation, however, dissolves as soon as one starts to think about the problem of measurement. What do we mean by a successful or unsuccessful outcome, how do we assess it, who is to make the judgment, and how are the findings to be steered around the statistical pitfalls that lie in the path of such investigations? If research has moved slowly, it is not because of failure to recognize the importance of knowing the results of psychotherapy. It is because of the almost insurmountable difficulty of making the necessary measurements.[62]

Reported Results

A survey of more than 50 reports, including some 15,000 patients, was made in 1960 by Eysenck.[63] Results are generally expressed in terms of

[62] The problems were well described by M. Zax and A. Klein, "Measurement of Personality and Behavior Changes Following Psychotherapy," *Psychological Bulletin*, LVII (1960), pp. 435–48. See also H. H. Strupp and A. E. Bergin, "Some Empirical and Conceptual Bases for Coordinated Research in Psychotherapy: A Critical Review of Issues, Trends, and Evidence," *International Journal of Psychiatry*, VII (1969), pp. 18–90. Discussion of this article by nine experts in the field follows in the same journal, pp. 116–68.

[63] H. J. Eysenck, *Handbook of Abnormal Psychology: An Experimental Approach* (New York: Basic Books, Inc., 1961), pp. 712–15.

several degrees of improvement; but if we gather into one group such headings as "cured," "much improved," and "improved," calling these successful outcomes, and interpret "slightly improved" and "not improved" as unsuccessful outcomes, the findings show a reassuring consistency. With adult patients the proportion of successes hovers around two thirds. With children, results at termination of treatment show almost exactly this same proportion of successes, while results estimated from later follow-up studies carry the figure above 70 per cent. Taking these figures at face value, we can see that being able to help two thirds of one's patients would be ground for considerable satisfaction.

It is noteworthy in the figures for adults that long-term psychoanalysis did not show better results than briefer forms of treatment; if anything, the outcomes were poorer. How to interpret the meaning of this difference introduces us at once to the difficulties of research. On the face of it, the results could mean that standard psychoanalysis is an inefficient method of treatment. But two considerations prevent this from being an unqualified conclusion. In the first place, as a method of last resort psychoanalysis may be undertaken mainly by patients with whom shorter methods have failed. If the psychoanalyst's patients are drawn to an appreciable extent from other people's failures, the results cannot be directly compared with those of other workers and do not necessarily reflect on the method. In the second place, by aiming to liquidate the original anxieties and to change all aspects of personality distorted thereby, psychoanalysts have set themselves exceedingly high standards of improvement. The removal of a specific complaint such as a phobia would not be counted a success in the absence of more extensive changes deemed essential for a true cure. But this brings into view another difficulty about measurement. Evaluation of personality change, especially the extensive kind demanded by psychoanalytic theory, is an extremely difficult undertaking. The judgments made by the therapist and the patient will do as a rough first approximation, but scientific objectivity requires that the evaluation be made by a team of independent experts. Furthermore, the evaluation ought to be repeated after a substantial interval of time in order to assess the enduring quality of the change. The resources and cooperation needed for such a massive enterprise are not easily enlisted. If there is today a fairly widespread reaction against psychoanalysis as a method of treatment, it is based more on dislike of the time, cost, and restriction to a small number of favored patients than on acceptable research findings about outcomes.

When Eysenck's survey was made there was as yet little information about the results of behavior therapy. However, Wolpe had already reported 90 per cent success with an unselected series of 210 neurotic patients; [64] and Lazarus a few years later, reporting on 408 patients, gave 78 per cent for the whole group and 62 per cent for the patients whose neu-

---

[64] Wolpe, *Psychotherapy by Reciprocal Inhibition, op. cit.*

roses were most severe.[65] On the face of it, these figures could mean that behavior modification is the most effective method of psychotherapy. But again the conclusion cannot be unqualified. If in the localities where this work was done behavior therapy tends to be the first form that is sought, then "easy" cases as well as "difficult" ones will be included in the sample. Furthermore, behavior therapists, aiming simply to remove the complaints or symptoms, probably set themselves the least exacting standard for considering a case successful. At all events, Eysenck and Rachman pronounce the evidence afforded by these and other studies "suggestive but not conclusive," and say that "a definitive conclusion must await carefully controlled studies in which careful selection procedures, methods of assessment, follow-up studies, and control subjects are used."[66] And Lazarus himself states that "there are still no acceptable data which would entitle anyone to make claims for the overall superiority of behavior therapy."[67]

When definitive conclusions are finally reached they will almost certainly be in the form of statements about what methods are best for what purposes and for what types of clients. Much to the point is the observation by Strupp and Bergin "that psychotherapy as currently practiced is not a unitary process and is not applied to a unitary problem."[68]

Spontaneous Remission

There is, of course, a logical flaw in all reports of change that do not include a control group. For a strict statistical demonstration of the effects of psychotherapy, there should be a control group of similarly disordered people who receive no treatment and whose change over an equivalent period of time can be satisfactorily measured. This research design allows for the possibility of spontaneous remission. Success with two cases out of three can be attributed wholly to psychotherapy only on the assumption that untreated clients do not improve. This is not a safe assumption. Untreated disorders may get worse, but they may get better, and the rate of spontaneous remission may exceed that of spontaneous intensification. The only protection against this possibility is a design that incorporates a control group. Attempts to use this design have thus far been badly hampered by difficulties of measurement and by doubt that any available group really constitutes a true control. Patients received for treatment but then not given treatment—mainly because of staff shortages and long waiting lists—probably come nearest to meeting the requirements of a control group, and there is some evidence of a tendency toward spontaneous remission in such groups.

Some years ago Eysenck startled the psychological world by asserting

[65] A. Lazarus, "The Results of Behavior Therapy in 126 Cases of Severe Neurosis," *Behavior Research and Therapy*, I (1963), pp. 65–78.
[66] Eysenck and Rachman, *The Causes and Cures of Neurosis, op. cit.*, p. 248.
[67] Lazarus, *Behavior Therapy and Beyond, op. cit.*, p. 16.
[68] Strupp and Bergin, *op. cit.*, p. 19.

that there was no proof that psychotherapy of any kind did any good.[69] He claimed that the widely reported average rate of success, 2 out of 3 or 67 per cent, did not exceed the rate of spontaneous remission over comparable periods of time. If this were so, neurotic patients could be expected to get well as often and as quickly without treatment as with it, and there would be no excuse for wasting effort on psychotherapy. As a forensic exercise challenging psychotherapists to furnish proof of their worth, Eysenck's paper may well have had a temporary good effect, but his statistical reasoning did not bear up under scrutiny. The two studies on which he based his estimated high rate of spontaneous remission were unsuitable for comparison with results of psychotherapy. One of these studies, by Denker, was a survey of five hundred patients who were receiving disability payments from an insurance company because of neurotic disturbances severe enough to keep them from work. The patients were under the care of general practitioners untrained in psychotherapy. A two-year follow-up showed that 72 per cent had been able to resume work and had not felt a need to seek medical help again.[70] People with neurotic complaints who apply for disability benefits cannot be considered comparable to people who seek individual psychotherapy. Moreover, the criterion of returning to work and asking no further help is hardly the same as what a therapist means by improved; it could signify boredom at having nothing to do and disgust with the doctor for failing to bring about a cure. The second study, by Landis, showed that two thirds of patients in mental hospitals diagnosed as psychoneurotic were discharged within a year as recovered or improved, without having received specific psychotherapy.[71] Again it is evident that people hospitalized for neurosis and people who seek individual psychotherapy are not comparable groups, and in any event the criterion of discharge depends on numerous practical considerations as well as the patient's psychological condition. The controversy raised by Eysenck has been critically reviewed after twenty years by Subotnik, who finds studies like Denker's and Landis's "quite useless as a basis for comparison with results of psychotherapy." [72] There is still no numerical base rate for spontaneous remission.

Whatever their rate, we know that spontaneous remissions sometimes occur. In the chapter on neuroses we saw that current stress generally makes a contribution to the outbreak of neurotic symptoms, even if these also have origins in earlier life. Present situations may heighten the reminders

---

[69] H. J. Eysenck, "The Effects of Psychotherapy: An Evaluation," *Journal of Consulting Psychology*, XVI (1952), pp. 319–38.

[70] P. G. Denker, "Results of Treatment of Psychoneurosis by the General Practitioner: A Follow-up Study of 500 Cases," *New York State Journal of Medicine*, XLVI (1946), pp. 2164–66.

[71] C. Landis, "Statistical Evaluation of Psychotherapeutic Methods," in L. E. Hinsie, ed., *Concepts and Problems of Psychotherapy* (New York: Columbia University Press, 1937).

[72] L. Subotnik, "Spontaneous Remission: Fact or Artifact?" *Psychological Bulletin*, LXXVII (1972), pp. 32–48.

of early childhood dangers, obstruct the use of habituated defensive measures, or call out defenses so strong that they disrupt behavior. But circumstances can also move in the opposite direction so that they weaken reminders of childhood anxiety or strengthen defenses without making them too burdensome. A person who experienced childhood panic about rejection, for instance, may come into a congenial group which gives constant evidences of acceptance, or a person who has all but crippled his endeavors by excessive caution and meticulous attention to detail enters an occupation where these qualities are of great importance and are hailed as rare excellencies. Furthermore, an untreated neurosis may eventually build up so much desperation that the person, feeling that he cannot go on like this any longer, will at last take active steps to lead a more rewarding life and will tolerate the increased anxiety which this at first entails. There is thus good reason for recognizing the phenomenon of spontaneous remission and of spontaneous fluctuation in neurotic disorders. Experienced clinicians judge it highly improbable that two thirds of the people who come for psychotherapy would pull out of their troubles without help. Most of these clients have already tried to do so without success. But spontaneous remission is certainly not an impossibility.

The Client's View

Readers are bound to be dissatisfied with the grievous shortage of sound information about the results of psychotherapy. It is indeed hard to *prove* anything in this intricate realm of research. But the fact remains that a great many people seek psychotherapy and that in two cases out of three both therapist and client believe that substantial benefit results. Both therapist and client, furthermore, attribute this change to the treatment and would probably laugh at the suggestion that the client was just getting well spontaneously. A study by Strupp and associates puts emphasis on what clients think of their treatment, and clients are certainly entitled to a hearing.[73]

The Strupp research was conducted by sending an extensive questionnaire to former patients of a group of therapists who agreed to this procedure. The therapists in the sample were mostly psychoanalytically oriented, and the patients had been seen for a minimum of 25 interviews, the average number being 70. The success rate of these relatively long-term treatments fell close to the usual 67 per cent. The majority of patients considered their therapy "exceedingly beneficial," enabling them to "deal more effectively with the vicissitudes of a decidedly imperfect society." The answers tended to confirm the importance of the therapeutic relation, apart from the specific techniques employed.

Irrespective of variations in the form of therapy and other considerations, the emergence of a "warmth" factor was particularly noteworthy. It permeated all rat-

73 Strupp, Fox, and Lessler, *op. cit.*

ings and assessments—those of patients as well as therapists. We concluded that a sense of mutual trust was unquestionably a *sine qua non* for successful psychotherapy; in its absence, little of positive value was accomplished. There was additional evidence that overshadowing this attitudinal-emotional factor was the patient's conviction that he had the therapist's respect. This faith in the integrity of the therapist as a person may be called the capstone of a successful therapeutic relationship under which all other characteristics are subsumed. When it existed, both patient and therapist were articulate about its presence.[74]

To the clients it was an asset to feel that the therapist was keenly attentive, natural, unstudied, reassuring, and careful not to injure self-respect. More common when the outcome was unsuccessful were comments that the therapist made the client feel like "just another patient," that he appeared neutral and passive, that he missed some of the client's real feelings, that he talked in abstract language, and that he caused or allowed the client to be angry with him. Undoubtedly the clients wanted more attention and friendship than was compatible with a professional relation. Some of them mentioned as a sign of progress their acceptance of being in fact "just another patient" rather than the therapist's sole concern.

The chief changes in themselves described by the clients are listed under these headings: better interpersonal relations; increase in self-esteem; greater interest, energy, and satisfaction in living; and a greater sense of mastery. Following are some of the actual words used:

I like being around people, which I did not before. . . . Many times I put myself in the position of a "therapist" and listen—and try to understand other people's problems as they relate to them rather than to myself.

Another big change was one of really listening or involving myself; now I find I see people in a different light.

I think the greatest change has been getting my confidence back.

I'm sure I'm a different person in attitude. I feel so much more relaxed—more confident, sure of myself, more attractive, and above all, my husband and my daughter enjoy me more.

I now feel capable of accomplishing certain goals which I formerly regarded as desirable but unattainable. I rarely need tranquilizers (or beer) to cope with tension.

I'm able to find satisfaction and happiness in small ways that I had overlooked before, probably because I was too busy worrying about myself.

Most importantly, I am able to feel joy and pain, which even with the latter is good, because *I'm* living, and not just something parasitic. I can trust another person enough to care, and to risk the consequences of the caring.

Much better able to lead my life as I please and better able to cope with life as it comes day to day. Feel freer to tell others what I think and where to get off! Better able to live with fussy and "disturbed" parents.[75]

74 *Ibid.,* pp. 17–18.
75 *Ibid.,* pp. 67–71.

Excerpts of this kind make it clear that psychotherapy can be experienced as producing important and desirable changes. These changes, furthermore, are consistent with the general idea that the task of psychotherapy is to create conditions favorable for corrective relearning that involves strong feelings. The lowering of anxiety and guilt, the relaxing of defensive inhibitions, and the learning of more rewarding patterns of behavior are all represented in the descriptions. The fundamental principles of psychotherapy need not be regarded as hopelessly complex. They all have to do with removing blocks in the learning process and promoting new growth. The processes are partly understood and wholly understandable.

SUGGESTIONS FOR FURTHER READING

The literature on psychotherapy has become voluminous in the last few years. A fine initial orientation, with historical sweep, can be obtained from Jerome D. Frank's *Persuasion and Healing: A Comparative Study of Psychotherapy* (Baltimore, Johns Hopkins Press, 1961). A collection of case studies representing a large variety of therapeutic methods has been assembled and edited by A. Burton, *Case Studies in Counseling and Psychotherapy* (Englewood Cliffs, N.J., Prentice-Hall, Inc., 1959). For an excellent brief survey, lucid and non-partisan, see R. W. Heine, *Psychotherapy* (Englewood Cliffs, N.J., Prentice-Hall, Inc., 1971).

The therapeutic relation is searchingly examined in Frieda Fromm-Reichmann's *Principles of Intensive Psychotherapy* (Chicago, University of Chicago Press, 1950), Ch. 1, and by Carl Rogers, "The Characteristics of a Helping Relationship," in M. I. Stein, ed., *Contemporary Psychotherapies* (New York, The Free Press of Glencoe, 1961), pp. 95–112.

Prominent in the short history of behavior therapy is Joseph Wolpe's first publication, *Psychotherapy by Reciprocal Inhibition* (Stanford, Calif., Stanford University Press, 1958). Wolpe's book, *The Practice of Behavior Therapy* (New York, Pergamon Press, 1969), covers much the same ground. The "broad-gauge" view of behavior modification is given by Arnold Lazarus in *Behavior Therapy and Beyond* (New York, McGraw-Hill Book Co., 1971). A work of impressive scholarship, reflecting the large amount of research already done, is F. H. Kanfer and J. S. Phillips, *Learning Foundations of Behavior Therapy* (New York, John Wiley & Sons, Inc., 1970).

Freud's *General Introduction to Psychoanalysis* (New York, Liveright Publishing Corp., 1920) gives a good introduction to his view on treatment in Chs. 27 and 28. I. Hendrick devotes Part III of his *Facts and Theories of Psychoanalysis* (2nd ed., New York, Alfred A. Knopf, Inc., 1939) to the same topic. A more detailed and technical account of psychoanalytic technique, departing somewhat from the classical formulations to take account of recent advances in ego psychology, is L. J. Saul's *Technique and Practice of Psychotherapy* (Philadelphia, J. B. Lippincott Co., 1958). A searching study of the effects of interpretation has been given by J. Strachey, "The Nature of the Therapeutic Action of Psychoanalysis," *International Journal of Psychoanalysis,* 1934, Vol. 15, pp. 127–59. The topic of transference is the subject of a detailed discussion by B. Wolstein: *Transference, Its Meaning and Function in Psychoanalytic Therapy* (New York, Grune & Stratton, Inc., 1955). The problem of relating psychoanalysis to learning theory was dealt with systematically by J. Dollard and N. E. Miller, *Personality and Psychotherapy* (New York, McGraw-Hill Book Co., 1950).

For client-centered psychotherapy the sources are two books by Carl R. Rogers, *Counseling and Psychotherapy* (1942) and *Client-Centered Therapy* (1951). Both are published by Houghton Mifflin Co., Boston. These should now be supplemented by a book edited by J. T. Hart and T. M. Tomlinson, *New Directions in Client-Centered Therapy* (Boston, Houghton Mifflin Co., 1970), containing numerous research and theoretical papers and a verbatim interview, "Looking Back and Ahead," with Rogers. The most instructive work in English on existential psychotherapy is R. May, E. Angel, and H. F. Ellenberger, eds., *Existence: A New Dimension in Psychiatry and Psychology* (New York, Basic Books, Inc., 1958), which includes translated case histories by Binswanger. Descriptions and comparisons of ten different "systems" appear in a book by D. H. Ford and H. B. Urban, *Systems of Psychotherapy: A Comparative Study* (New York, John Wiley & Sons, Inc., 1965).

Various attempts have been made recently to analyze the central processes in psychotherapy, those that might be supposed common to all methods. Ford and Urban undertake this in their final chapter. It is also the subject of a thoughtful volume by Erwin Singer, *Key Concepts in Psychotherapy* (New York, Random House, Inc., 1965) and an essay by John M. Reisman, *Toward the Integration of Psychotherapy* (New York, John Wiley & Sons, Inc., 1971).

8

Psychotherapy:
Group Methods

Compared to individual psychotherapy, the treatment of people in groups has a short history. As we saw in the historical introduction, group psychotherapy began some sixty years ago as a time-saving device in dealing with patients in mental hospitals, and its larger potentialities were only gradually perceived. It came into its own after World War II and is now widely used, either as an adjunct or alone, for many varieties of disordered behavior. Reflecting on all that was said in the preceding chapter, we can easily understand the misgivings aroused by the proposal to treat people in groups. Individual psychotherapy is a difficult, delicate, and highly personal proceeding; would not the presence of other people simply create interference and nullify the possible good effects? Group methods, however, are congruent with important trends in the understanding of human behavior, trends away from an individualistic toward a social or interactive conception. The client who is seen alone in the therapist's office is in fact a member of a family and of other social groups. His complaints often center on his interactions with these other people, and their behavior may have a good deal to do with what is wrong. Treating people in groups is thus in a sense more realistic than the "one-to-one" relation; getting along better with other people is facilitated by having some of them there. But we should not conclude from this that group methods are necessarily superior. Our task is to discover what they accomplish under what conditions, and what they presumably cannot be expected to accomplish.

FAMILY THERAPY

The idea that psychotherapy should not be confined to one person designated as the patient emerged gradually from experience with the traditional "one-to-one" method of treatment. Psychoanalysis as practiced by Freud involved a minimum of contact with people in the patient's social orbit. Change was expected to occur through transference relations with the therapist, the patient being responsible for carrying over his gains to his own social environment. When psychoanalysis was extended to children, however, the plan of isolating the treatment was clearly out of place. One could hardly suppose that change in a child's behavior would long survive if there were no answering change on the part of the parents. A similar shortcoming of individual psychotherapy came to light in connection with marriage counseling. It takes two to make a marital fight, and if peace can be restored this must be through a change of feeling in both contending parties.

Origins in Child Guidance: Treatment of Child and Mother

The first step toward family psychotherapy was the practice of drawing the mother into a simultaneous therapeutic relation. This soon became the standard practice in child guidance. The mother is usually the one who brings the child to the office and who is most upset by his condition. For practical rather than theoretical reasons the father was almost never included. He could always escape on the plea that he had to earn money to pay for the treatment. The more recent capture of the elusive clinical father in family psychotherapy has revealed the bias that resulted from the earlier concentration on the clinical mother. Strong emphasis on the mother–child relation is legitimate up to a point, but the father's part in the child's trouble is usually far from negligible.

Before the advent of family psychotherapy the treatment of child and mother was generally done on a "two-to-two" basis. While the child was in one therapist's office, the mother gave her version of the difficulty to another therapist, receiving client-centered counseling, advice, encouragement, and support as might be needed. In an early account of work based upon this plan, Allen pointed out that since mother and child are likely to have a deeply entangled relation, their separation at the clinic provides a good setting for the work of untangling.[1] The child experiences the novelty of being able to behave without maternal supervision and criticism. By slow degrees he makes his own relation with the therapist and assumes responsibility for his own actions. Children often try to make the doctor assume responsibility; they want him to treat them the way their mothers do. The significant step of doing things because they want to, rather than

---

[1] F. H. Allen, *Psychotherapy with Children* (New York: W. W. Norton & Co., Inc., 1942).

to please the doctor or resist him, comes later and with difficulty. The mothers meanwhile change in much the same direction. Frequently the mother has been as much enslaved to the child as the child has been to the mother. Both parties need to be disentangled so that they can become individuals in their own right.

The procedure is illustrated in the case of Solomon, a ten-year-old boy suffering from tics and general nervousness.[2] Whatever their origin, the symptoms served the purpose of enslaving an already devoted mother who fussed anxiously over Solomon's difficulties. The child soon discovered that the therapist was not going to fuss anxiously over his symptoms, and these were rarely manifested at the office. At the third interview Solomon stated that his mother thought he was better. At almost the same moment the mother was telling the social worker that the symptoms were very much worse; then she suddenly blurted out, "What will I have left when the children are grown?" Her own difficulty in letting Solomon, her youngest child, grow up was clearly a contributing cause of his illness. Solomon, meanwhile, began to learn the satisfactions of growing up, though he resisted them stoutly for a time. There were several scenes in which he debated whether he should bravely go to bed alone rather than having his mother take him upstairs at night. He tried to cajole the therapist into ordering this new behavior, and his feelings were hurt when the therapist said that the act should not be done simply to please him. Finally, however, Solomon began to do things on his own initiative. He expressed an interest in growing up and being like his older brothers. The change in both child and mother was neatly symbolized at the close of the last interview. For the first time Solomon struggled uncomplainingly to put on his heavy coat with its awkward collar, working until he succeeded, and for the first time his mother did not offer to help him.

It seems likely in this case that work with Solomon alone would have gone to waste. He readily gave up his symptoms at the office, but would he ever have been able to discontinue them at home if his mother solicitously fussed over him and thus rewarded the symptoms? Treatment of the mother alone would also have gone rather slowly. Would insights gained at the office survive the primitive appeal of her child's tearful trembling at the prospect of going to bed alone? Each party could make rapid and substantial progress only when the other party also changed.

Treating the Family as a System

The bold step of trying to influence the whole family is certainly in accord with present theories about the nature of social systems. In practice, however, it is no small feat to secure the cooperation of all the members of a family. Ackerman, a strong advocate of family psychotherapy, favors interviewing the whole family at the very beginning, and points out that

---

[2] *Ibid.*, chap. 6.

the first interview can provide useful cues.[3] Much can be deduced from the way the members enter the room, offer greetings, and distribute themselves among the available chairs. Conflict, confusion, the dominance hierarchy, and preferred modes of acting as a family may reveal themselves sharply in the problem of seating. Significant family alignments, alliances, exclusions, and scapegoating may come to light early in the proceedings. The therapist meanwhile tries to create an atmosphere of rapport that will favor a reduction of concealments and defenses. To achieve a therapeutic result "he must permit himself to be drawn into the center of the family disturbance," but he must also preserve objectivity and freedom so that he can serve as umpire and even as controlling authority if things threaten to get out of hand.[4] Family psychotherapy is obviously no job for a novice. To improvise appropriate action in what can easily become a whirlpool of passions requires rare gifts of alertness and a seasoned skill in grasping the meaning of behavior.

It is not easy to shift one's focus from individual to family therapy. Haley brings out the difficulties in a paper in which he contrasts the outlook of the beginning family therapist with that of the experienced worker.[5] Trouble begins with the word "patient." When family problems are brought for treatment, one member is considered the patient by the other members of the family. The beginning therapist, out of habit, may fall in with this nomination and perceive his task as curing the patient with the help of the rest of the family. As Haley puts it, "the experienced family therapist . . . struggles to find a better term than 'patient' for the family member chosen to be it." The trouble is not inside one person; it lies in the entire family system, in the whole set of relations prevailing among all the members, and it will not be resolved without changes in the system. The beginning therapist, again, true to his previous experience, may start by taking a lengthy history and trying to establish a diagnosis of the problem. But any family arriving for help is likely to be in a state of crisis. The experienced therapist tries to intervene almost at once to reduce acute tension and otherwise to show that something useful can happen. The beginning therapist may be tempted to make interpretations and point out to the family members how much, for instance, they hate one another. This can go to the point of "torturing a family by forcing them to concede their unsavory feelings about each other." The experienced therapist avoids this useless exercise and tries in a more positive way to resolve the difficulties that are creating the hostility. The differences between individual and family therapy outweigh the similarities, and this must show in the therapist's behavior.

[3] N. W. Ackerman, *The Psychodynamics of Family Life* (New York: Basic Books, Inc., 1958).

[4] N. W. Ackerman, "Further Comments on Family Psychotherapy," in M. I. Stein, ed., *Contemporary Psychotherapies* (New York: The Free Press of Glencoe, 1961), pp. 245–55.

[5] J. Haley, "Family Therapy," *International Journal of Psychiatry*, IX (1970–71), chap. 6.

In a paper reflecting on more than fifteen years of experience with family treatment, Ackerman describes the method as "therapeutic intervention on the emotional processes of a natural living unit, the family entity, viewed as an integrated behavior system." [6] The interview unit consists ideally of the whole family, although at certain points some members may be excused in order to concentrate on a particular pair, possibly the husband and wife or a child and a parent. The goal can be described as producing a more healthful, satisfying family life. This implies easing the anxieties, competitions, and resentments that spoil the positive aspects of interaction. The therapist's task is to provide a timely challenge to the rationalizations and defensive disguises whereby the members conceal from themselves the destructive aspects of their relationship. This is mainly accomplished by a device which Ackerman calls "tickling the defenses."

This is essentially a technique of confrontation which points especially to contradictions between conscious attitudes and patterns of action, to discrepancies between verbal utterances and nonverbal communication, as reflected in facial expression, movement, mood, posture, and gesture. Especially important here is the exposure of unreal and impossible demands, the challenge of fruitless blaming and vindictive encroachment on other family members, and the undermining and challenging of hypocritical self-justifications.

Obviously the therapist must be expert in tickling the right defenses at the right time. He must be skillful in maintaining a sense of justice and impartiality, distributing his challenges fairly among the members. His whole usefulness depends upon being trusted as a person who has the sympathy to understand but the wisdom to stand apart from the family conflicts. Family treatment is taxing alike for the family and the therapist. Beall has called attention to instances of getting off on the wrong foot because the therapist too quickly becomes allied with certain family members and accepts their myths. By the simple act of accepting one member as "the patient," for example, the therapist may implicitly make a "corrupt contract" with the others to exempt them from any share in the trouble.[7]

Family therapy can be of great value. It is capable not only of relieving the suffering of the person designated as patient but of improving the conditions of family life for everyone involved. But it is not a panacea and cannot be expected to work in all circumstances. Ackerman points out that "for some families, realistically speaking, it may be too late to reverse the forces of fragmentation." There must be hope and desire for an improved life together. Success is sometimes blocked when the family contains in one member "a concentrated focus of malignant destructive motivation," perhaps because of a paranoid psychosis or an habituated criminal

[6] N. W. Ackerman, "Family Psychotherapy Today: Some Areas of Controversy," *Comprehensive Psychiatry*, VII (1966), pp. 375–88.

[7] L. Beall, "The Corrupt Contract: Problems in Conjoint Therapy with Parents and Children," *American Journal of Orthopsychiatry*, XLII (1972), pp. 77–81.

bent. A member so disposed cannot accept any "tickling of defenses" and will react destructively to any improvement by others. The therapist, we must remember, does not have unlimited resources for bringing about a favorable change. Ferreira points out that a family self-image or "myth" may be so ingrained that no member can tolerate its being challenged. He describes, as an instance, a family in which the father was a happy man, always smiling, bothered by nothing, setting a tone for all the other members. Everyone had symptoms of some kind, and disturbed family life was easy to infer, but the family sat with fixed grins, "as if saying in a sort of nonverbal chorus, 'See how happy we are.'" The therapist finally challenged the father's happiness, saying that he appeared profoundly unhappy behind his cheerful mask. The shot struck home: the father's smile disappeared and he looked serious and sad. But first one, then another member came to the rescue, pronouncing the therapist wrong and the father unfailingly happy, until the father's smile returned in full force. Challenge to the myth of happiness was more than this family could bear.[8]

In recent writing about family psychotherapy there is a strong tendency to speak of the critical events in terms of communication theory. This is valuable provided one keeps in mind that strong feelings and motives are present; family disorders do not consist just of defects in communication. But poor communication tends to increase misunderstanding, especially when words of appreciation remain unspoken and annoyances are allowed to mount into chronic resentments. Thus when a family is basically motivated to stay together but disturbed by conflicts, much of the therapeutic work takes the form of opening channels of communication so that the forces of solidarity can prevail over those of disruption.

What Happens in Family Therapy

These general statements may leave the reader mystified as to what actually goes on in family psychotherapy. Helpful in making the proceedings vivid is a book by Virginia Satir, *Conjoint Family Therapy*, which includes a variety of sample conversations.[9] Several of these involve a family consisting of Joe and Mary and their children, Johnny (10) and Patty (7); Johnny's poor work and unmanageable behavior at school is the avowed reason for undertaking family therapy. In an early conversation the therapist asks the children what ideas they had about coming.

Patty: Mother said we were going to talk about family problems.
Therapist: What about Dad? Did he tell you the same thing?
P: No.

[8] A. J. Ferreira, "Family Myth and Homeostatis," *Archives of General Psychiatry*, IX (1963), pp. 457–63. Reprinted in J. G. Howells, *Theory and Practice of Family Psychiatry* (New York: Brunner/Mazel, 1971), chap. 14.

[9] V. Satir, *Conjoint Family Therapy: A Guide to Theory and Technique* (rev. ed.; Palo Alto, Calif.: Science and Behavior Books, Inc., 1967), especially chaps. 10–14.

Th: What did Dad say?

P: He said we were going for a ride.

Th: I see. So you got some information from Mother and some from Dad. What about you, Johnny? Where did you get your information?

Johnny: I don't remember.

Th: You don't remember who told you?

Mother: I don't think I said anything to him, come to think of it. He wasn't around at the time, I guess.

Th: How about you, Dad? Did you say anything to Johnny?

Father: No, I thought Mary had told him.

Th: (To Johnny) Well, then, how *could* you remember if nothing was said?

J: Patty said we were going to see a lady about the family.

Th: I see. So you got your information from your sister, whereas Patty got a clear message from both Mother and Dad. . . . (To Mother) Were you and Dad able to work this out together—what you would tell the children?

M: Well, you know, I think this is one of our problems. He does one thing with them and I do another.

F: I think this is a pretty unimportant thing to worry about.

Th: Of course it is, in one sense. But then we can use it, you know, to see how messages get across in the family.

This incident illustrates the practice of bringing each member of the family into the conversation, letting each person speak for himself. When members try to speak for each other, the therapist may stop them and insist that even the children must speak for themselves. Parents may thus for the first time hear themselves described by their children. The excerpt also brings to light the parents' unwitting preconception that Johnny, as "the patient," need not be given the courtesy of an explanation, whereas Patty, the well child, was told where they were going. The failure of communication with Johnny is further shown in the following excerpts:

M: (About Johnny) His pleasure is in doing things he knows will get me up in the air. Every minute he's in the house, constantly.

Th: There's no pleasure to that, my dear.

M: Well, there is to him.

Th: No. You can't see his thoughts. You can't get inside his skin. All you can talk about is what you see and hear. You can say it *looks* as though it's for pleasure.

M: All right. Well, it looks as though, and that's just what it looks like constantly.

Th: He could be trying to keep your attention, you know. It is very important to Johnny what Mother thinks.

Here the therapist tries to introduce an alternative explanation of the child's behavior that is less negative. In the following conversation with the father, this enlightenment is produced by hearing directly from the child.

F: I mean, he never wanted me to stay and watch him play baseball.

Th: Tell me, how did you explain this to yourself? Why do you think he didn't want you to watch?

F: Well, that's the trouble, I never have been able to figure it out.

Th: Well, one way to find out is to *ask*. Let's ask Johnny. He can tell you. Maybe he is uneasy when Dad is around.

J: I'd just get embarrassed, sometimes.

Th: You'd get embarrassed.

J: Uh huh. Cause he had Patty with him and Patty is always making a fuss. The other guys would laugh.

Even these few exchanges suggest a situation in which Johnny has become a focus of parental anger and Patty is preferred to him. Johnny's "symptoms"—his school difficulties—are part of a problem in family interaction and are not likely to abate until the whole system of interactions has changed. The therapist thus becomes concerned with all the relationships, including the marital one, which is approached in the following conversation beginning with the children.

Th: Of course everybody disagrees every once in a while. Let's see now, if I were in your house and Mother and Dad were mad at each other, what would I see?

J: Mother goes to her room.

P: Mother cries.

Th: Mother would be in her room crying. And where would Dad be?

J: Dad usually beats it.

Th: Dad tries to solve things by leaving the house?

P: Daddy gets mad when Mother cries.

J: Daddy gets mad when Mother cries.

Th: How do you decide this? That Dad is mad because Mother cries?

P: He slams the door. . . .

Th: How about that, Dad? Do tears make you angry? Or are you already mad at Mary for something and then Mary cries?

F: Somehow, I don't know, somehow she has this way of making me feel that it's me—that I am the one who . . . .

Th: Mary's tears make you feel you have been the one who is wrong, is that it? You feel at fault?

F: Exactly. She won't listen when I try to explain.

Th: What about you, Mary? How do you know when Joe is displeased?

M: He turns on the TV so loud you can hear it in the laundry room.

Th: So then he shows his anger by shutting you out, is that it? And she shows her anger by shutting you out with her tears. And either way you can't find a way to get close enough to work things out.

(The therapist then asks how the disagreement is finally solved.)

F: I give in. That's what I do.

M: That's what you think. You're as stubborn as they come.

F: How? How am I more stubborn than you?

M: *Many's* the time I've come around to you.

Th: I think that . . . .

J: Daddy, when are we going to the beach? You promised we could go, and we never do.

F: As soon as it's warmer we'll go. It's too cold to go to the beach.

M: Of course we did promise them . . . .

Th: I think we should . . . .

P: You said we could go a couple of weeks ago.

Th: I think both children get upset when their mother and father disagree. Maybe they think someone will get hurt. But I don't see any dead bodies around, do you? Mother looks in one piece. Dad looks in one piece.

M: They do get upset. We try not to argue in front of the kids.

Th: But of course they know when their parents have pain. The important thing is that ways can be found to work on this. That's why we are here, to find ways to work on this.[10]

The insights that occur through conversations of this sort do not produce immediate miraculous changes in behavior. Joe and Mary may soon quarrel again in front of the children, Johnny may continue to be exasperating, and favor may again be shown to Patty. But the automatic character of these interactions may well have been broken, so that the members of the family can begin to imagine avoiding an impasse, behaving in alternative ways, getting around the customary blocks in communication. The next occasion of conflict may catch them unawares, but afterwards they will see more clearly what could have been done to avoid useless embattlement. Over time considerable change can take place, so that all members experience family life as more harmonious and rewarding.

Marital Counseling

After this introduction to family psychotherapy the value of joint treatment for marital problems seems obvious. Time was required, however, to unseat the preference even here for individual psychotherapy. Kohl describes numerous cases in which the more troubled member of a discordant pair sought individual treatment and began to improve, whereupon the other member became increasingly troubled and was obliged to seek help.[11] Nothing could demonstrate more clearly the interactive

[10] The excerpts are from Satir, *op. cit.*, pp. 143–44, 148–50, 151–52.

[11] R. N. Kohl, "Pathological Reactions of Marital Partners to Improvement of Patients," *American Journal of Psychiatry*, CXVIII (1962), pp. 1036–41; reprinted in Howells, *op. cit.*, chap. 50.

nature of marital disorders. Discordant partners were sometimes assigned to two individual therapists who every so often consulted together. Occasionally a person passing the door when one of these consultations was in progress would be amused to hear the voices of the two therapists raised in an angry quarrel as each defended his client's point of view. Marital counseling is best performed by bringing the contending parties together in the presence of one counselor who can point out the failures of communication at the very moment when they occur.

Describing marital tensions as seen in a psychological clinic, Dicks calls attention to the important part played by role expectations.[12] Frequently, he points out, we project upon the person we love and marry a set of expectations derived from previous experience with parents, or even from fantasy. The role of spouse is thus overlaid with personal meanings, and disappointment may be felt if the actual spouse enacts the role in some different fashion. The son of a mother who waits on her husband by inches and the daughter of a father who waits on his wife by inches will do well not to marry one another; each will be expecting what the other least expects to give. Discrepancies of expectation with regard to dominance, submission, and initiative can also create frustration and resentment. The case of Benton Child, described above in Chapter 2, illustrates an initial harmony between a passive-dependent husband and a dominant wife, followed by discord after the birth of children, when the husband proved unequal to paternal responsibilities and the wife needed help in caring for the family. Benton's expectations were derived from his mother's indulgent spoiling, which applied both to his father and to himself. A somewhat similar example of marital discord is described by Main, who notes the complicating presence of a mutual projection upon the partner of unacceptable tendencies in the self. The husband, who greatly feared his own assertiveness and hostility, magnified these qualities in his wife and was himself docile and sexually impotent. The wife, who was anxious about her lack of education and social training, magnified these faults in her husband and badgered him to the point that he seemed more stupid than he actually was.[13] Each party thus behaved in a way that exaggerated the faults of the other, but in the end it proved possible to abate these trends and put the marriage on a workable basis.

More is involved in marital discord than a failure of communication. The closeness of marriage stirs up deep feelings not only of love but of anxiety and hostility. Improvement of communication, however, may well be the most effective point to intervene in order to set in motion a process of change.

---

[12] H. V. Dicks, "Experiences with Marital Tensions Seen in the Psychological Clinic," *British Journal of Medical Psychology*, XXVI (1953), pp. 181–96; reprinted in Howells, *op. cit.*, chap. 9.

[13] T. F. Main, "Mutual Projection in a Marriage," *Comprehensive Psychiatry*, VII (1966), pp. 432–49.

PSYCHODRAMA

Another form of psychotherapy using people in groups is the *psychodrama* originated by J. L. Moreno.[14] The essential principle of psychodrama is to stimulate the expression of feelings through unrehearsed, spontaneous play-acting. Other patients take part in the action, and still other patients and observers make up the audience. Moreno himself has surrounded the procedure with an array of grandiose concepts, but the central ideas seem to be quite simple. Drama stands as a midway point between fantasy and reality. It is real in the sense that there is a stage with lights, a group of spectators, and other actors toward whom one is behaving. It is unreal in the sense that the whole thing is only a play. Unrehearsed drama has a certain similarity to free association. Giving free associations is real in the sense that a therapist is listening and that relief from a neurosis is being sought. It is unreal in the sense that what one says is illogical and fantastic, quite unsuitable for communication in everyday life. Proponents of psychodrama maintain that it is better than free association as a means of securing expression. Although at first it may be hard for patients to act with freedom, they can be slowly induced into an atmosphere in which they learn to express themselves with great spontaneity and often with great enjoyment.

The following case report by Sarbin will make the procedure clearer.[15] A seventeen-year-old high school boy semed quite incapable of social relationships. Listless and shy, he stayed by himself most of the time, but from interviews and tests it was clear that he fantasied himself as a popular high school boy. He was first asked to participate as a spectator while other patients acted their psychodramas. Then he was asked to prepare a short scene of his own for a subsequent session. He chose the role of a radio commentator and gave a simple scene that required no supporting characters—altogether a safe and undemanding performance. At the next meeting he was requested to serve as a minor character in a drama being enacted by other patients. He was the buddy of a soldier who received abusive treatment from a tough sergeant. He was able to imitate freely the actions of his buddy and even develop them in his own way. For his next assignment he prepared an original scene calling for several supporting characters. For the first time he was able to act without self-consciousness, genuinely absorbed in the drama. Next he took the part of father in another young patient's drama. This role proved highly congenial; he "stole the show" as he acted out what were unmistakably his own father's attitudes toward him. Only after this success was he requested to enact what corresponded to his own most cherished fantasy. He was asked to depict a

14 J. L. Moreno, *Psychodrama* (Beacon, N.Y.: Beacon House, Inc., 1946), especially Sections 1, 2, and 6.
15 T. R. Sarbin, "The Concept of Role-Taking," *Sociometry*, VI (1943), pp. 273–85.

day in the life of a high school boy. Choosing various characters to represent his parents and his fellow students, he put on a spontaneous drama remarkable for its animation and conversational freedom as well as its revelation of his emotional difficulties at home.

There were various other sessions, but what concerns us more is the patient's off-stage progress. Instead of sitting alone he began to come into the center of the group. Instead of retiring between scenes he began to use these intervals for conversation with others. Listless shyness gave place to more alert participation. The parents were surprised at the rapid increase of interest in people and events and at his spontaneous seeking for companionship. The patient even gained weight while these improvements were going on. In the realm of psychodrama he had become able to behave in a way that corresponded to his ego-ideal and that gave him self-esteem. The change carried over into new behavior in everyday life.

Psychodrama would seem to be an excellent technique for people with a certain degree of generalized inhibition and difficulty in expressing themselves. It supplies just the right lift and social support for overcoming inhibitions that are not too deeply rooted. New behavior can be rehearsed under fictional conditions before being attempted in real life. Moreno has used psychodrama for marriage problems and even for matrimonial triangles.[16] Here it is sometimes successful in liberating the deeper feelings that discolor and clog the relationships. A scene can be started from whatever clues the parties offer in their preliminary interviews. Although these clues may have to do with superficial or side issues, "it is a reliable psychodramatic experience," according to Moreno, "that, once the subjects are working on the therapeutic stage, they are carried by the momentum of psychodramatic dynamics from the surface to the deeper level of their relationship." [17]

Psychodrama has had a less spectacular rise than family psychotherapy. According to Polansky and Harkins, it "has not had the widespread application its potentialities warrant." [18] They regret this because, in their view, "it is a mode of treatment which can be helpful to a substantial portion of patients a large proportion of the time—which is about all one can say about any of the psychotherapies." They recognize that not all therapists find it congenial to participate so actively, exhibiting the "interpersonal energy, moment-to-moment inventiveness, and occasional controlled flamboyance" that make the method effective. They recognize also that there are risks in a situation that sometimes mobilizes so much feeling in several patients at once. But they report favorably on a program of psychodrama in a private psychiatric hospital, where as an adjunct to individual treatment it has sometimes "brought to life" a listless or withdrawn patient

16 *Ibid.*, pp. 233–45, 328–49.

17 *Ibid.*, p. 329.

18 N. A. Polansky and E. B. Harkins, "Psychodrama as an Element in Hospital Treatment," *Psychiatry*, XXXII (1969), pp. 74–87.

who otherwise was not making progress. The addition of videotape play-back reportedly increases the effectiveness of the method with hospital patients.[19]

GROUP PSYCHOTHERAPY

If we were to be fussy about language we would say that this section needed a more exact title. Family therapy and psychodrama certainly qualify as group psychotherapy, but in practice this more general term has come to imply groups of a particular kind. Typical of group psychotherapy as currently practiced is a meeting of a therapist and perhaps eight adult or adolescent patients who at the outset are unacquainted. In the course of a series of sessions the members of the group will become well acquainted, and sometimes lasting friendships are formed. In essence, however, group psychotherapy involves work with a group of strangers, and one of its strengths may well lie in the circumstance that the members are bound by no formal ties after the work is completed. Social learning in the group can thus be a trial run or dress rehearsal, so to speak, with people toward whom one has no future commitments. In this respect it differs sharply from family treatment.

Within this definition there is room for great variety. Early workers with group therapy, experienced in individual treatment, enacted their new roles with as litle change as possible from their old ones. Before long there was much the same range of opinions about group therapy as existed with respect to individual treatment. Some workers advocated a strictly "group-centered" procedure that copied the permissiveness and non-directiveness of Rogers' client-centered psychotherapy.[20] Some adhered as closely as possible to Freudian psychoanalysis and concentrated on interpreting the transference reactions that occur during the meetings.[21] Others favored a principle of flexibility, using different degrees and kinds of activity according to the nature and circumstances of the group.[22] Still others, chiefly those working with more seriously disturbed patients, found it advisable to use tactics of a more directive character.[23] Similarly, there was a range of opinion about the length of time required to secure good results. Twenty to forty weekly sessions represent an average duration in many

19 J. Y. Gonen, "The Use of Psychodrama Combined with Videotape Playback on an Inpatient Floor," *Psychiatry*, XXXIV (1971), pp. 198–213.

20 N. Hobbs, in C. R. Rogers, *Client-Centered Therapy* (Boston: Houghton Mifflin Co., 1951), chap. 7.

21 H. Ezriel, "A Psychoanalytic Approach to Group Treatment," *British Journal of Medical Psychology*, XXIII (1950), pp. 59–74; J. D. Sutherland, "Notes on Psychoanalytic Group Therapy: I. Therapy and Training," *Psychiatry*, XV (1952), pp. 111–17.

22 S. R. Slavson, "Group Psychotherapies," in J. L. McCary and D. E. Sheer, *Six Approaches to Psychotherapy* (New York: The Dryden Press, 1955), chap. 3.

23 J. W. Klapman, *Group Psychotherapy: Theory and Practice* (New York: Grune & Stratton, Inc., 1946).

clinics and outpatient services, but one worker, George Bach, who argued strongly that group therapy should be intensive, considered a group still new when it had met only fifty times and stated that "intensive group psychotherapy certainly does not represent a short-cut in terms of therapy hours, although it is economically easier for most patients." [24] Already in 1955 group psychotherapy was being offered in a variety of shapes and sizes.

The Course of Group Therapy

It will be clear from the variations just described that we cannot give a standard account of the course of group therapy. Yet in order to convey some idea of what happens we must select certain features, even if they are not universal. In work with neurotic patients the group is likely to number about eight. Meetings are held once or twice a week, with leader and group members sitting informally around a table. At first the members direct all their remarks toward the leader, and it is evident that they expect him to answer questions, give advice, and generally function in an authoritative manner. The leader meets this by a method described by Foulkes as "leadership by default"; he simply says, "Let me hear what *you* think about this question." [25] As in individual therapy, patients at first find this non-directiveness quite frustrating, but the leader's "defaulting" eventually forces them out of their initial attitude of dependence. It can now be observed that patients begin to talk to each other rather than to the therapist; they may even begin to favor each other with therapeutic suggestions. From this point on, the leader serves chiefly as an alert interpreter, though occasionally he will have to steer things more actively to protect a member from being overwhelmed by advice or diagnosis on the part of other members. Presently the leader begins to raise questions about the motives behind what is being said. He wonders what prompted A to give the advice he just gave to B. This examining of motives is gradually taken up by the group members, who start to become aware of their own motives and the consistent kind of impact they have on others. C discovers, for example, that his remarks are always directed toward the less assertive patients, and he thus learns that he tends to be fearful of reprisal. D discovers that he always intervenes when there is tension between two other patients, and he thus realizes the force of his own fear of hostility. Much of this discovery is made spontaneously or with the help of other group members. The leader is no longer the only source of interpretations.

What is talked about in these meetings? The patients discuss their symptoms and other things that are troubling them. They air the exasperations of their current life. The talk about the process of therapy and

24 G. R. Bach, *Intensive Group Psychotherapy* (New York: The Ronald Press Co., 1954), p. 213.

25 S. H. Foulkes, "Concerning Leadership in Group-Analytic Psychotherapy," *International Journal of Group Psychotherapy*, I (1951), p. 319.

speculate on what is involved in getting well. A good deal of time may be spent in narrating important episodes in their past lives. As time goes on, the conversation turns more and more to what is happening in the group: how the patients feel about the leader, how they are affected by the behavior of other members of the group, how they themselves seem to affect others. This bringing to expression of feelings and counter-feelings, so different from what happens in ordinary social life, constitutes a unique experience in human relations and may well prove to be the central advantage of group psychotherapy over individual treatment.

A technique that adheres more literally to psychoanalytic principles has been developed by a group of workers, notably Bion, Ezriel, and Sutherland, at the Tavistock Clinic in London. The distinguishing feature of their method is the early and consistent use of interpretation. Although the interpretations include behavior of patients toward one another, there is a major emphasis on the relationship with the therapist. If a patient displays a certain attitude in the therapist's presence, it may be that he thereby conceals an attitude toward the therapist which is laden with anxiety. Thus, as Nevitt Sanford expresses it, "Interpretations regularly take the form: you express this relationship, e.g., solicitude for other members of the group, because you must avoid this relationship, e.g., hostile jealousy of their supposed better standing with the therapist, because you fear this calamitous result, e.g., total and irrevocable rejection." [26] These interpretations are believed to have much the same effect as transference interpretations in individual psychoanalysis. The clear discrepancy between the patient's unconscious fear, for instance, of rejection, and the actual attitudes of the therapist serves to dramatize for the patient the irrational element in his own behavior and provides him with an opportunity to reappraise the obsolete danger.

An Illustrative Episode

The following episode, taken from a book by Berne, illustrates several aspects of group psychotherapy, including the fairly uncommon one of humor used to increase insight.[27]

Sophia was always ready to complain about how things were at the office, and each week she said she could not make up her mind whether to continue in the group or go to Europe. When the other members of the group said that she was really trying to make her mind up whether to get better or to look for a magical solution to her troubles in Europe, she evaded the issue for a long time. On this particular day, she asked them again if she should stay in the group or travel. They

---

[26] N. Sanford, "Clinical Methods: Psychotherapy," in *Annual Review of Psychology*, IV (Stanford: Annual Reviews, Inc., 1953), p. 318. For a discussion of Bion's influential thinking on group psychology, see M. J. Rioch, "The Work of Wilfred Bion on Groups," *Psychiatry*, XXXIII (1970), pp. 56–66.

[27] E. Berne, *Principles of Group Treatment* (New York: Oxford University Press, 1966), p. 254–56.

replied rather effectively, wondering again how they were supposed to deal with a question like that, and politely asked her to explain its purpose. But Dr. Q thought from the way she broached the question on this occasion that she was perhaps ready for a showdown, so he decided it was best to interrupt them and go to the heart of the matter. She had previously been asked several times why she did not want to get better, and had pretended not to understand the question. On the hypothesis that she was now ready to answer, Dr. Q therefore asked:

"Why don't you want to get better?"

She replied, laughing nervously, "Because getting better would mean doing the things my parents always wanted me to do, and I have to spite them."

"That reminds me of a story," said Dr. Q. "One night in the middle of winter a policeman found a drunk sitting on a doorstep, shivering and shaking and freezing, and he asked him what he was doing there. The drunk said, 'I live here,' so the policeman said, 'Then why don't you go in?' The drunk said, 'Because the door's locked,' so the policeman said, 'Why don't you ring the bell?' The drunk said, 'I did, but they didn't answer,' so the policeman said, 'Then why don't you ring again? You'll freeze to death out here.' And the drunk said, 'Oh, let them wait.'"

Almost everybody in the group laughed. Two nodded, and Jim said, "That's me, all right." Sophia also laughed. Then Dr. Q added:

"Unforunately, parents sometimes say things that are right. Are you planning to spend the rest of your life getting back at your parents, or do you think some day you'll get better?"

"Well," replied Sophia, "maybe some day I'll get better."

"Well, if you're going to die eventually, why not do it now, and save all that time and grief?"

"I'll think about it," answered Sophia, whereupon Dr. Q immediately turned his attention to someone else.

Even in so short an episode it is possible to observe the alertness, skill, and sensitivity that is needed for the conduct of group psychotherapy. The therapist picks up through some clue—manner, tone of voice, choice of words—that the patient may now be ready to consider more seriously her repetitive question. It would have been easy to think, "There she goes again," and pass on to more promising topics. When the answer comes, representing a significant gain in the patient's insight, the therapist at once tells a story that illustrates humorously the patient's plight—the self-destrutive character of spite. This procedure is hazardous: had the story not been perfectly appropriate, or had the mood of the group been slightly different, the patient might have felt that she was being ridiculed. Happily, another member says, "That's me," and everyone is able to laugh together. The therapist then clinches the interpretation in a challenging statement and attempts to persuade the patient to act soon. Why does he so quickly give this up and turn away? It would have been easy to insist a little triumphantly upon the correctness of the insight and the changed behavior that might well follow. But the patient's reply—"I'll think about it"—is not negative or resistant. She accepts her insight and the therapist's enlargement of it, but she asks for time to get used to its difficult implications. The therapist recognizes that she should have this time, and by changing the subject he protects her from possible further comments by other members of the group. It would have been easy indeed to bungle some step in this brief transaction and thus throw away the chance to help the patient.

The Group as Environment for Change

Appreciation of the value of group psychotherapy has increased steadily over the past thirty years. At first considered superficial, recommended chiefly for patients who could afford nothing better, it is now accepted as a method having properties of its own that make it for many purposes superior to individual treatment. One of its best services is a quick decrease in the sense of isolation. The patients become vividly aware that other people have problems like theirs and that these problems need not be cause for shame. At first a patient may feel strange and inhibited in the group, but there is a good chance that feelings of group solidarity will presently prove helpful in bringing about a beneficent change.

Another valuable property of group treatment is that the therapist has the patient's social behavior under direct observation. In individual treatment he can witness such behavior only in relation to himself; he learns about other social interactions through the patient's biassed report. The group method allows the therapist to see what really happens in the patient's relations with others. He can observe what tactics are employed, what games are played, what defenses prevail, and what distortions there may be in social perception. At appropriate times he can point these out, and the group members are likely to assist by telling the patient how they feel about his behavior. The patient may be unpleasantly surprised to learn that his tone of voice is condescending, that his apologies are irritating, that his wisecracks are a bore, or that his superficial chatter keeps everyone at arm's length; pleasantly surprised if his stumbling attempts to express appreciation and understanding meet with a warmly encouraging response. The therapeutic group provides an unusually favorable opportunity for change in interactive behavior.

In a thoughtful paper Guttmacher and Birk point out several additional advantages of group psychotherapy.[28] The group therapist, they believe, offers a more realistic identification figure. He is seen in action, so to speak, participating in a social group, unlike the individual therapist who serves as permissive audience for one patient. Furthermore, the patient must from the start share the therapist with other group members; the role of favorite child is closed and intimations of sibling rivalry are constantly present. On this account, the authors believe, group treatment is especially appropriate when passive and manipulative dependence are important problems. They cite the instance of a patient who was stuck in

---

[28] J. A. Guttmacher and L. Birk, "Group Therapy: What Specific Therapeutic Advantages?" *Comprehensive Psychiatry*, XXI (1971), pp. 546–56.

the gratification provided by an individual therapeutic relation and who made progress only after being transferred to a group which dealt forthrightly with her exorbitant demands. They advocate group treatment also for patients, variously categorized as "acting-out," delinquent, or "character-disordered," who locate the source of their trouble exclusively in the outside world. At the start these clients are serenely unware of their own part in their destructive and self-destructive behavior. "In individual therapy," the authors say, "such problems may be extremely difficult to confront because the patient does not come with anxiety about his behavior and a wish to change it. However, in the group setting his behavior can be faced more squarely. The patient cannot be so evasive because his actions are directly observed and his distorted view of them can be challenged." They cite the case of a young woman who was fearful of men because, as she told it, starting with her father they had always treated her so badly. Presently she began to form a relation with a young man in the group, and soon everyone could see the force of her resentment and the active way she provoked hostile responses from her would-be friend. For the first time she realized her own part in her persecutions and was motivated to change her behavior.

Group psychotherapy is currently in wide use with many kinds of clients. It has an accepted place in mental hospitals with psychotic patients. It is frequently used either alone or as an adjunct in treating the neuroses. With suitable adaptations it is appropriate for other disorders and for a great variety of problems in living. But individual treatment has advantages of its own; it is unlikely to be displaced by group methods. Encouraging as the group may be, it cannot provide quite the security of the individual session, nor can it permit the long-continued probing and struggle that may be necessary to change defensive habits dating from early childhood. Not all kinds of desirable change require a group environment; not all kinds would be facilitated by the presence of other patients. In clinical practice the recommendation is often made, when manpower is available, that a patient receive both individual and group psychotherapy. This reflects the belief that each has its virtues and that both together will maximize the possibility of change.

An Application to Children: Activity Groups

Among the many variations of group treatment that have been tried with children and adolescents we choose a single historical example that is still highly instructive. Experiments with activity groups were worked out by Slavson and tested in New York City under the sponsorship of the Jewish Board of Guardians.[29] Small "clubs" were formed for children in the age range from eight to thirteen, providing them with the opportunity to meet, play, practice handicrafts, and occasionally take trips, under the

---

[29] S. R. Slavson, *An Introduction to Group Therapy* (New York: Commonwealth Fund, 1943).

guidance of a carefully trained leader. Outwardly resembling the numerous clubs already in existence in most communities, these activity groups actually had a psychotherapeutic purpose. Children were chosen who needed practice in social adjustment, either because they were shy, submissive, and isolated, or because they were aggressive, self-willed, and unaccustomed to sharing. They were chosen, one might say, from a middle zone of social ineptitude: on the one hand, not too badly maladjusted to preclude participation in a group; on the other hand, not capable of going directly into an ordinary group organized without therapeutic intent. Slavson's activity groups are analogous to group pspchotherapy as practiced with adults, except that no attempt is made to instruct or to point out feelings. The corrective experience comes from simply being in the group under the conditions about to be described. If the child is in need of more radical treatment, this is accomplished by simultaneous individual therapy carried out by someone other than the group leader.

The therapeutic character of the groups is maintained by the behavior and attitude of the leader. His behavior is designed to create maximally favorable conditions for social learning. At the outset his attitude is almost completely permissive. He busies himself with handicrafts, takes little notice of aggressive and destructive behavior, allows the group to blow off steam and then bring itself to some kind of order. He is friendly and gentle but not too personal; he carefully avoids establishing relations that will lead to feelings of favoritism and "sibling rivalry" within the group. Keeping to this half-impersonal role, he nevertheless makes it a business to give recognition and praise whenever a child does something well. This sets a fashion which eventually is copied by the children. Group recognition as well as the leader's recognition becomes available for all good performances.

Under these circumstances social development takes place with gratifying speed. The group is given the chance to try mischief, roughhouse, disorganized fooling around, and to discover for itself the greater satisfactions of orderly cooperative behavior. These satisfactions are strengthened by the leader's reward in the form of recognition, but the leader does not take the initiative in producing the orderly behavior. Spontaneously a sense of responsibility develops in the group, so that the chores connected with having the meetings and serving refreshments are more and more taken over by the children. At the end of six or eight months of weekly meetings most of the children have progressed sufficiently with their social adjustments and social skills so that they can transfer to ordinary clubs and neighborhood groups.

ENCOUNTER GROUPS

In recent years there has been a fast proliferation of experiments with meetings designed to promote better human relations. Perhaps the widely used word *encounter* will serve as a heading for the many variations that have developed. These meetings have a good deal in common with group psychotherapy, but their intent is different. The purpose is training rather than treatment. The earliest training groups (T-groups) were developed shortly after World War II, when world-wide destructiveness had again emphasized the dire need for a better understanding of human relations. In 1946 the first Human Relations Conference was held at Bethel, Maine. Here a group of generally successful people discovered how much they could learn about social interaction simply by interacting and focusing their attention on how they did it. In a research done much later with problem-solving groups, Moment and Zalesznik called attention to two dimensions of competence, the technical and the interpersonal.[30] The "technical specialists" contributed good ideas about the objective features of the problem to be solved, but they were obtuse to the feelings of others and engaged in constant put-downs. The "social specialists," less fertile with solutions to the problem, listened to others, expressed appreciation and respect, suggested compromises, and thus maintained a harmonious atmosphere for work. Some, of course, could do both, and some neither, but the two kinds of "specialists" dramatize the dual nature of cooperative work. The original purpose of T-groups was to increase sensitivity to the human relations aspect of joint endeavors. T-groups were designed, according to Argyris, "to provide maximum possible opportunity for the individuals to expose their behavior, give and receive feedback, experiment with new behaviors, and develop awareness and acceptance of self and others." [31] Usually present was the additional goal of understanding the conditions that make group work productive and efficient.

The reported success of training groups presently suggested purposes of a more general kind. Could not the group method be used to increase human contact, to melt defenses and promote direct, warm, untrammeled interactions? Would it not be possible in a group of similarly disposed strangers to drop the conventional images, role enactments, and protective strategies that guide everyday living and thus at last to experience authentic human encounters? There followed a rapid spread of sensitivity training groups, encounter groups, marathon groups, and other groups designed to stimulate powerful emotional experience. Although some of these groups have a regular schedule of meetings, there is a strong trend toward making them short and intense. Marathon groups, for instance, meet continuously for two days, with time out only for a night's sleep. Institutes such as Esalen at Big Sur in California, dedicated to the enrichment of experience and release of potentials, offer weekend programs as well as more lasting group meetings. Along with this trend goes a multiplying of what might

[30] D. Moment and A. Zalesznik, *Role Development and Interpersonal Competence* (Boston: Harvard Business School, Division of Research, 1963).
[31] C. Argyris, *Interpersonal Competence and Organizational Effectiveness* (Homewood, Ill.: The Dorsey Press, 1962).

be called "shock" methods: free use of the sense of touch, nude bathing, emotional catharsis, and the development of dramatic scenes that elicit direct expressions of support and love. Such experiences are seen, for instance by Schutz, as opening the way for "the fulfillment of one's potential." [32] An institute called Orizon in Washington, D. C., provides participants with "the opportunity to take a sufficient leave from your daily self" in order to open "the potentialities for deeper experiencing of life" that are "within each of us." [33] Not just those whose personal behavior is disordered, but "each of us" is seen as a suitable client.

Compared to the purposes of group psychotherapy these goals seem extravagant. Compared to the methods of traditional group treatment, which entail a gradual learning process extended over time, the one-shot weekend seems an improbable shortcut. On the face of it there is little reason to suppose that marathon weekends are likely to displace either group or individual psychotherapy in the treatment of people with well-rooted disorders of behavior. But the argument is made by Ruitenbeek that brief intense encounters have appeal and possible value to people, increasingly numerous in our time, who are seriously alienated from their own feelings.[34] This complaint can be a side-effect of neurotic inhibition or of psychotic withdrawal, but there is reason to regard it as often a problem in its own right. Many contemporary clients, according to Ruitenbeek, are vague in their complaints but discontented with life. "Their childhood memories are not necessarily traumatic or even very bad, but there is not too much they feel good about." They function well but somewhat mechanically in everyday life, but "they lack the touch of intimacy and warmth, which are the ingredients for plain happiness and satisfaction." They tend to be "other-directed" and passive in their relations with people. "It is somewhat amazing," Ruitenbeek comments, "to find out in talking to these patients that the idea of confrontation and decision-making in their personal lives is something which is alien to them." [35] For this particular malady an important gain may come from a concentrated attempt to mobilize strong unaccustomed feelings.

As yet there is no sound information on the results of encounter groups. Some participants report that they felt reborn and go home with a much improved feeling about family and friends. Others have a wonderful time but return or go elsewhere for other sessions, as if the encounter were an exhilarating intoxication that did not carry over to sober everyday life. There are reports in medical journals of occasional neurotic or psychotic breakdown following an encounter experience. Much controversy surrounds the training of leaders and the selection of participants. With

[32] W. D. Schutz, *Joy: Expanding Human Awareness* (New York: Grove Press, 1967).
[33] Quoted by C. Goldberg, "Group Sensitivity Training," *International Journal of Psychiatry*, IX (1970–71), pp. 165–92.
[34] H. M. Ruitenbeek, *The New Group Therapies* (New York: Avon Books, 1970).
[35] *Ibid.*, pp. 28–29; see also pp. 215–22.

groups that are at least partially open to the public it is impossible to do more than a superficial screening of candidates. Furthermore, the skill required for screening, especially for recognizing candidates likely to be more disturbed than helped, implies extensive experience with mental patients, but group leaders are not necessarily drawn from professional mental health workers, whose training has certainly not encouraged the use of methods so informal, so improvised, and at times so theatrical. Many leaders of encounter groups have fallen into the work because it felt congenial and they found themselves good at it. Speaking especially of training groups, Gottschalk and Pattison lament the lack of professional standards and training programs for leaders as well as the shortage of research on outcomes.[36] But organization of this kind is always a later development; even psychoanalysis in its earliest years was practiced largely by gifted amateurs. The encounter movement is in an early stage. The risks of such a stage must not be ignored, but it is too soon to have a sound balance sheet of results.

THE THERAPEUTIC MILIEU

Turning back to more institutionalized forms of therapeutic activity, we close this chapter with brief notice of a changed approach in mental hospitals and correctional institutions. The older concept of an asylum, where the mentally sick could be removed from society, and kept out of harm's way—symbolized by building mental hospitals on remote hillsides far from the crossroads of life—is steadily giving place to the idea of the hospital as a therapeutic milieu in which everything is arranged to be conducive to recovery. An early step in this direction was the introduction of occupational therapy, through which in the reassuring setting of work with inanimate objects the patients might recover their interest in the environment, perhaps even in the social part of it. Another step was the self-service cafeteria, offering the patients the opportunity, whether they took it or not, to make mealtime social contacts of their own choosing. Exercises, games, dances, and other recreations followed in all hospitals that tried to keep abreast of the times. The goal is to make the whole experience in the mental hospital a therapeutic one. There is now a large literature on the theme that the mental hospital or the correctional institution, considered as an elaborate social system, can be so organized that all inmates have a chance to benefit from their membership in it.[37]

36 L. A. Gottschalk and E. M. Pattison, "Psychiatric Perspectives on T-Groups and the Laboratory Movement: An Overview," *American Journal of Psychiatry*, CXXVI (1969), pp. 823–29.

37 For instance, Maxwell Jones, *The Therapeutic Community* (New York: Basic Books, Inc., 1953); A. H. Stanton and M. S. Schwartz, *The Mental Hospital* (New York: Basic Books, Inc., 1954); M. Greenblatt, D. J. Levinson, and R. H. Williams, eds., *The Patient and the Mental Hospital* (New York: The Free Press of Glencoe, 1957).

In practice it usually does not work that way. Quite apart from possible administrative and financial difficulties, the shift from custodial to therapeutic practices involves a profound change in the attitudes of the hospital staff. This means a change in the outlook not only of doctors but also of nurses, attendants, and other workers who are in contact with the patients most of the time. One is reminded of the old joke about librarians who consider it their duty to keep books clean and intact rather than to have them read; if the job is perceived and valued in this way, it is quite a wrench to change to a less orderly but more educational conception. In like fashion, the nurse who has prided herself on keeping the patients in her ward clean and tidy or the attendant who has measured his success in terms of keeping the ward quiet and controlling aggressive outbursts cannot easily sacrifice their established virtues as custodians for the unknown possibilities of a therapeutic role.[38] Nor should we suppose that the new view is always easy for doctors, who have to manage the hospital community and who are aware that there is, after all, a custodial element in the whole operation, failure in which will bring down the wrath of relatives and civic authorities.

The transformation of custodial wards into therapeutic ones has been well described by von Mering and King.[39] They point out the great force of what they call the "legend of chronicity," the assumption that the patients are there to stay and cannot be expected to get better. The unfortunate thing about this legend is that it guarantees exactly what it predicts: the attitudes of those who believe it creates an atmosphere in which the patients will indeed not get better. The staff acts to get the day's work done with the least fuss, and the patients are allowed to sink ever more deeply into their own preoccupations. Quite different is the situation when someone becomes convinced that the ward can be run on a therapeutic basis. When the patients are given generous attention with the implication that things can be better, even severely regressed schizophrenics, who no longer keep clothes on and are incontinent, can recover their lost habits, respond a little to the staff, show an interest in the activities of the ward, and even make a few awkward steps toward helping one another. Less disorganized patients can accomplish much more: they may take over many of the routine jobs, working in groups as dormitory or linen closet helpers; they may arrange birthday parties and other festivities; and they may work out a program of improving and redecorating the ward. Such projects generate pride in the living quarters and reawaken pleasure in social interaction.

While sitting around the tables making things to improve the appearance of their ward, the women began to talk to each other as they had never done before. It was as if a group of apartment dwellers, who formerly had only nodded to each

---

[38] A tragic and hilarious caricature of one such nurse is given by K. Kesey, *One Flew Over the Cuckoo's Nest* (New York: Viking Press, 1962).

[39] O. von Mering and S. H. King, *Remotivating the Mental Patient* (New York: Russell Sage Foundation, 1957).

other in passing, were suddenly thrown together in close association, and for the first time began to find out what their neighbors were like.[40]

Yet all of this is accomplished with a minimum of prodding by the staff. It represents the salutary influence of a warm interest that also implies confidence and respect.

Administrative resistance to experiments of this kind is often overcome by the discovery that the financial cost of a "remotivated" ward is less than it was before. The human profit is decidedly encouraging. Some patients advance to making home visits and perhaps to ultimate discharge, while those who remain as permanent residents have the benefit of more alert and rewarding lives. When the "legend of chronicity" is replaced by a "legend of recovery" the results are, to be sure, submiraculous; but there is a distinct change, and it is almost always in the direction of better lives for everyone concerned.

When we say it is better for everyone concerned, we include the staff along with the patients. As Greenblatt has pointed out, there are in American mental hospitals about twenty attendants or aides to every nurse and every doctor, a large corps of people in constant contact with patients but untrained to be more than watchdogs. Often these workers have no feeling of participation in the therapeutic process.[41] One of the most promising moves away from the custodial concept is the training of attendants to realize their importance to the patients, to treat them with friendly respect, and thus to exert a true therapeutic influence. Increasingly attendants and nurses are being used as therapeutic agents in behavior modification programs aimed at fostering independence and self-care, shaping positive social behavior, and reinforcing self-assertion.

Another plan that has proved successful in some places is to establish a form of patient government. This allows the patients to take major responsibility for recreational and social life, raise money to purchase supplies and equipment, supervise housekeeping and the serving of food, and help to orient new patients to hospital life.[42] Participation with management in running the hospital makes it distinctly their concern, and serves as a useful vehicle for effective reality testing.

Only a beginning has been made with turning the mental hospital into a therapeutic community. Enough has been done, however, to show that betterment is possible in the lives of even severely ill schizophrenic patients. The deteriorated hospital patient was partly a product of crude custodial treatment, representing retreat from a social environment that offered no inducement to stay in contact.[43] Although we cannot suppose that all mental patients will be able to resume a normal life, the new conception

40 *Ibid.*, p. 123.
41 M. Greenblatt, in *The Patient and the Mental Hospital, op. cit.*, chap. 36.
42 *Ibid.*, p. 617.
43 R. E. Kantor and W. G. Herron, in *Reactive and Process Schizophrenia* (Palo Alto: Science and Behavior Books, Inc., 1966), pp. 139–46, give an excellent summary of identity-stripping and similar aspects of custodial incarceration that contribute to dyssocialization and regression.

of treatment can give to many what we might call a normal hospital life and can lead others back to the outside world which for a time they found too difficult.

SUGGESTIONS FOR FURTHER READING

On the subject of family psychotherapy a good starting point is Virginia Satir's *Conjoint Family Therapy* (rev. ed., Palo Alto, Calif., Science and Behavior Books, 1967), a straightforward presentation with numerous excerpts. A large and thorough work, containing both the author's conceptualization of family treatment and relevant papers written by other workers, is J. G. Howells, *Theory and Practice of Family Psychiatry* (New York, Brunner/Mazel, 1971). Recommended also is N. W. Ackerman's *Treating the Troubled Family* (New York, Basic Books, Inc., 1966).

On marriage counseling Bernard Greene's *A Clinical Approach to Marital Problems: Evaluation and Management* (Springfield, Ill., Charles C Thomas, 1971) will be found both comprehensive and practical. A special issue of the journal *Comprehensive Psychiatry* (Vol. 7, October, 1966) contains a series of diverse papers on both family treatment and marriage counseling.

The inescapable classic on psychodrama is J. L. Moreno's *Psychodrama*, Vol. 1 (Beacon, N. Y., Beacon House, 1946), which most readers will find exceedingly difficult. An easier acquaintance with this method can be made through an essay by L. Yablonsky and J. M. Enneis, "Psychodrama Theory and Practice," in *Progress in Psychotherapy*, Vol. 1, edited by F. Fromm-Reichmann and J. L. Moreno (New York, Grune & Stratton, Inc., 1956).

There are now many works on group psychotherapy. Among them, I. D. Yalom's *The Theory and Practice of Group Psychotherapy* (New York, Basic Books, Inc., 1970) is especially recommended. Valuable also is Eric Berne's *Principles of Group Treatment* (New York, Oxford University Press, 1966), which is intended as a manual of instruction for future practitioners. J. A. Johnson, Jr., in *Group Psychotherapy: A Practical Approach* (New York, Blakiston Division, McGraw-Hill Book Co., 1963) devotes 214 pages to reporting and analyzing the actual events in an outpatient group; the illustration is of great value in making group treatment come alive for readers.

An informative book on encounter groups, containing a large number of contributions, has been put together by Arthur Burton as editor—*Encounter: Theory and Practice of Encounter Groups* (San Francisco, Jossey-Bass, 1969). For a readable and thought-provoking survey of the newer encounter methods, sympathetic yet critical, there is H. M. Ruitenbeek's little book, *The New Group Therapies* (New York, Avon Books, 1970). Marathon groups are described and evaluated by Elizabeth E. Mintz in *Marathon Groups: Reality and Symbol* (New York, Appleton-Century-Crofts, 1971). That serious efforts to evaluate the effects of training groups are now well under way is shown in a book edited by C. L. Cooper and I. L. Mangham, *T-Groups: A Survey of Research* (New York, John Wiley & Sons, Inc., 1971).

In *The Therapeutic Community*, edited by J. J. Rossi and W. J. Filstead (New York, Behavioral Publications, 1972) will be found a collection of key articles on this timely topic. A lively paper by B. B. Zeithin, "The Therapeutic Community—Fact or Fantasy?" together with three rejoinders appeared in *International Journal of Psychiatry*, Vol. 7, April, 1969, raising a number of critical issues.

9

Delinquency and
Criminal Behavior

The psychological origins of disordered personal behavior were discovered in the course of treating neurotic patients. The neuroses and psychotherapy, to which we have devoted the last three chapters, can thus be regarded as the classical themes in modern dynamic psychology. Upon their study was founded the *psychogenic hypothesis,* in accordance with which we have learned to look for causes of disordered behavior in such realms as attitudes learned in the family circle, critical problems in childhood emotional development, the personal meaning of events, and above all the effects of anxiety and the defensive operations used to hold it in check. The illumination provided by this way of thinking is not confined to the neuroses and lesser maladjustments. In this chapter and the next three we shall extend our survey to several more varieties of disordered behavior in which psychological factors play a significant part. The neurotic person typically conforms in outward ways to social expectations, taking out his inner conflicts and frustrations upon himself in the form of symptoms, suffering, fatigue, and chronic dissatisfaction. In contrast, the people to be studied here can be described as *acting out* some part of their problems at the expense of others, taking advantage of society by violating codes and conventions for personal gain and sometimes doing harm to their victims. The superego in neurotics is strong and all too effective in suppressing unsocialized impulses. It is for this reason that psychotherapy puts such emphasis on the expression of imprisoned feelings. In this chapter we shall be dealing with people in whom conscience either is feeble or can be circumvented to permit leakage of antisocial conduct at certain points.

Delinquency and criminal behavior are defined by society and the law rather than by psychology and medicine. A young person is designated delinquent, an older person criminal, when his behavior violates the rules and standards of society. The child who runs away from home, the truant from school, the gang member who breaks windows and steals from fruit stands, the professional thief, the racketeer, the embezzler, and the first-degree murderer all qualify for membership in the social outgroup with which we shall be concerned in this chapter. It is obvious that we are not dealing here with a single type of disorder. We can assume in advance that among the people classed as delinquent or criminal there will be many varieties of personality and many kinds of contributing cause. Our problem is to consider the numerous ways in which a person comes into opposition to the standards of society. Delinquent and criminal behavior bear a significant relation to surrounding social and economic conditions. The whole problem forms a chapter in social pathology as well as a chapter in abnormal psychology.

PROFESSIONAL CRIME

White Collar Crime

Exhaustive classification of criminals is not possible because half to three quarters of all crimes are never reported, but if it *were* possible, almost everyone would be included. A national survey found that 91 per cent of the sample interviewed had committed violations for which they might have received jail or prison sentences.[1] It is almost equally impractical to document the extent of the most common form of crime in our society: white collar crime. This includes embezzlement, fee-splitting, illegal financial manipulations, tax evasion, price-rigging, bribery, patent infringements, false and misleading advertising, and unfair labor practices. Most of these crimes are never discovered; they get lost in the complications and convolutions of business procedures. Little heed is paid to them because, as a rule, they do not present a direct, recognizable threat to personal safety, and the victims are usually collective society rather than specifiable individuals or groups. The total cost of such crime is inestimable, but reportable income that goes unreported for income tax has been estimated to range from $25 billion to $40 billion each year. It is likely that this total cost is substantially greater than the economic cost of "ordinary" crime.[2] Sutherland has shown that corporate crime is pervasive.[3] He investi-

---

[1] *The Challenge of Crime in a Free Society,* Report of the President's Commission on Law Enforcement and Administration of Justice (New York: E. P. Dutton and Co., 1968), p. 38.

[2] R. W. Winslow, ed., *Crime in a Free Society.* Selections from the President's Commission on Law Enforcement and Administration of Justice (Belmont, Calif.: Dickenson Publishing Co., 1968), p. 178.

[3] E. H. Sutherland, *White Collar Crime* (New York: Holt, Rinehart & Winston, 1961).

gated 70 of our largest corporations and found that *every one of them* had been found guilty by a court or regulatory commission for violation of antitrust, false advertising, patent, copyright, or labor laws. The average number of violations was 14. Probably the most celebrated example of corporate crime is the conspiracy of 29 electrical equipment companies to fix prices illegally, which resulted in prison sentences for seven high ranking executives in such corporations as General Electric and Westinghouse.[4] The offenders in this case were quite aware that their activities violated the law, and they took elaborate precautions to prevent detection. All of these men were affluent and otherwise law-abiding and scrupulous; their criminal behavior cannot be explained by poverty, defective socialization, or personal pathology. Basing his analysis on the study of embezzlers, Cressey argues that white collar criminals must rationalize their behavior in such a way that a violation of trust or law does not appear *wrong*.[5] It may even be construed as appropriate, under the circumstances. In the testimony of the electric company executives a typical justification was that price fixing is commonly accepted practice.

Obviously, white collar crime is extremely difficult to detect or prevent, and some might argue that it is not worth the effort and cost to do so. However, in one sense it is the most threatening of all forms of crime because of its corrosive effect on the moral standards of our society. Fraudulent business practices, blatant income tax evasion, and devious financial transactions promote cynicism toward society and disrespect for the law. Effective control of white collar crime would necessitate substantial restriction of what is now felt to be personal liberty, a price we are reluctant to pay.

Organized Crime

Organized crime refers mainly to a vast business empire called the Mafia, the Syndicate, or more recently La Cosa Nostra, which controls illegal gambling, loan sharking, and narcotics. Most of its income derives from gambling, which grosses between $9 billion and $20 billion a year, all of course tax-free.[6] The Mafia is, in fact, a federation of coordinated racketeer "families" whose criminal activities are governed by a council of about a dozen overseers. Some of their "business dealings" utilize strong-arm tactics and blatantly illegitimate methods: extortion, terrorism, monopolization, bribery, fraud, and the like. However, the core of their activity consists of covertly supplying illegal goods and services, which is enormously profitable because there is a huge market for them despite the laws against them. Much of their profits are in turn invested in legitimate business enterprises

---

4 J. Herling, *The Great Price Conspiracy* (New York: Van Rees Press, 1962).
5 D. R. Cressey, "The Respectable Criminal," in J. F. Short, ed., *Modern Criminals* (Chicago: Aldine Publishing Co., 1970), pp. 111–14.
6 *The Challenge of Crime in a Free Society, op. cit.,* p. 29.

with which the Mafiosi identify themselves publicly. The leaders own grocery stores, bars, restaurants, automobile agencies, race tracks, and are highly placed in the garment industry, the coin-operated machine industry, the olive oil and cheese business, construction, trucking, and many others.[7]

The motivation for organized crime bears some similarity to that for white collar crime. Racketeers consider themselves as businessmen who take advantage of lucrative opportunities for profit, and they probably feel justified in their criminal activities much as do corporate executives who conspire to rig retail prices. However, the Mafia is in most respects a deviant subculture like the street gangs we shall discuss next, with a distinctive organizational structure and an explicit code of conduct and values at odds with those of society at large. The code has been so successful and the "business" so profitable that it is easy to see how people in some segments of society are recruited and assimilated in that subculture. Thus we are dealing here with a group which is socialized to an alien system of moral standards. The economic advantages and social solidarity of the subculture are powerful inducements to adhere to its moral code, so "treatment" consists mostly of enforcing the law, and rehabilitation is, understandably, extremely difficult.

JUVENILE DELINQUENCY

"Law and order" has been a major political issue in the 1960's and 1970's. If you ask the average citizen what forms of crime he is most concerned about, he would list first the violent crimes against persons, like murder, rape, armed robbery, and physical assault. Next would come crimes against property, like burglary, larceny and theft, which constitute more than four fifths of the total in the Uniform Crime Report of the FBI, the popular image in the communications media notwithstanding.[8] Of least concern are the so-called "victimless" crimes like drunkenness, disorderly conduct, gambling, prostitution, and vagrancy, which are by far the most common crimes committed, but present little threat to personal safety or the social order. In this chapter we shall consider primarily the first two kinds of criminal behavior, which share the psychological distinction of bringing direct, and usually deliberate, harm to the welfare of others.

"Studies made of the careers of adult offenders regularly show the importance of juvenile delinquency as a forerunner of adult crime."[9] The earlier a juvenile is arrested or brought to court for an offense, the more

[7] *Ibid.,* p. 443.
[8] L. E. Ohlin, "The Effect of Social Change on Crime and Law Enforcement," in H. S. Ruth *et al., The Challenge of Crime in a Free Society: Perspectives on the Report of the President's Commission on Law Enforcement and the Administration of Justice* (New York: Da Capo Press, 1971), p. 25. The Uniform Crime Index includes seven common *predatory* crimes: murder, forcible rape, robbery, aggravated assault, burglary, larceny over $50, and auto theft. No victimless crimes are included.
[9] *The Challenge of Crime in a Free Society, op. cit.,* p. 152.

likely he is to carry on criminal activity in adult life. And the more serious the first offense, the more likely he is to commit serious crimes later. Therefore an understanding of criminal behavior must begin with the study of juvenile delinquency. We shall center upon three kinds of delinquents: subcultural delinquents, neurotic delinquents, and psychopaths. These correspond roughly to three syndromes of personality found by Jenkins in delinquent children and guidance clinic referrals, labeled the *socialized delinquency, overanxious,* and *unsocialized aggressive* syndromes, respectively.[10]

Cultural Deviance

Behavior that is called delinquent sometimes results from an entirely normal process of psychological development. If a boy is brought up in a clan of pirates, he will develop a superego that tells him never to work for something when it is possible to steal it. Identifying with his father, he will build an ego-ideal of bigger and better piracy. In such a case the process of socialization is accepted. The person is called a criminal by the major society, but within the minor society of pirates he is simply growing up to be a solid and respected citizen. Before concluding that a given case of delinquency represents a failure to accept prescribed standards of conduct, it is necessary to ascertain what standards of conduct prevail in the family and in the immediate neighborhood. Merrill reports the case of the three Maguire brothers who during late childhood and early adolescence ran up a collective total of twenty-four court appearances.[11] The mother was always in court to defend them, and the father saw no objection to their eking out the slender family income derived from his business as a peddler. The Maguires were a well-knit, affectionate family, free from conflicts and emotional disorders, handicapped only by somewhat limited intelligence which made it difficult to earn a living. Every social agency knows cases of this kind in which the whole family pattern is one of delinquency.

In cases of this kind the individual is not delinquent from that segment of society which is closest to him. He is better described as a *cultural deviant:* "a product of a particular subculture which sanctions activities that are considered antisocial or inadequate by the larger society." [12] He

10 R. L. Jenkins, "Psychiatric Syndromes in Children and Their Relation to Family Background," *American Journal of Orthopsychiatry,* XXXVI (1966), pp. 450–57. Associated with *socialized delinquency* were bad companions, gang activities, cooperative stealing, habitual truancy from school and home, and being out late at night. The *overanxious* syndrome included mostly neurotic traits like shyness, apathy, sensitiveness, and submissiveness, but lacked the impulsive and aggressive tendencies found in many neurotic delinquents. The *unsocialized aggressive* syndrome included assaultive tendencies, starting fights, cruelty, defiance of authority, malicious mischief, inadequate guilt feelings.

11 M. A. Merrill, *Problems of Child Delinquency* (Boston: Houghton Mifflin Co., 1947), pp. 284–89.

12 S. K. Weinberg, *Society and Personality Disorders* (Englewood Cliffs, N. J.: Prentice-Hall, Inc., 1952), p. 288.

may be a loyal and conforming member of his subculture, identified with others, capable of feeling guilt if he violates their standards, free from guilt when he acts in sanctioned opposition to the alien larger society. The situation can be dramatized by an item from a case history: a mother expected her children to provide food for the family by stealing it from neighboring vegetable gardens and roadside stands, and the children were punished if they returned from their missions empty-handed. There may be nothing capricious about the discipline or vague about the standards in a deviant subculture. It is only to the larger society that the cultural deviant presents a problem.

Deprivation and Social Disorganization

Most crime is committed in the slums of large cities, where predominantly minority groups reside, schools are inferior, and social disorganization is extreme. People move constantly. The neighbor of today is gone tomorrow, and his place is very likely taken by a family of different national origin and different language. Diverse cultural standards flourish side by side with little interaction and little community solidarity. Under these circumstances it is difficult for parents to maintain control over their children, even though the majority try to do so. The parents have to work single-handed without reinforcement from the neighbors. In a stable community each family is known and each child is known in the neighborhood. Reputations have to be maintained, and behavior is governed by neighbors and acquaintances as well as by members of the family. It is this extended reinforcement of standards that is lacking in a disorganized area. In its place are the street corner gangs and the opportunity to become an apprentice in an adult criminal group.

Prison populations reflect the same factors. The majority are young, single men who are poor, undereducated, and come from disorganized families. They typically have had limited access to educational and occupational opportunities.[13] Often the first step in the rehabilitation of criminals is to teach them how to read and write. Naturally, being reared in circumstances of extreme relative deprivation breeds envy and hostility toward the privileged people who enjoy easy access to the desirable rewards of affluent life. For an ignorant black hoodlum, mugging a rich banker in Central Park represents not only a unique economic gain but also a small retribution for being frustrated and deprived of those same rewards for no understandable reason.

Immaturity

Many criminal actions are simply immature solutions to difficulties in life. As can be seen in the accompanying table, police arrests indicate that the majority of all crimes covered by the FBI Crime Index are committed

---

[13] *The Challenge of Crime in a Free Society, op. cit.,* p. 151.

Total Arrests by Age*

	Age When Offense Charged					
	10–19	20–29	30–39	40–49	50–59	Over 59
Percentage of distribution	35.0%	27.1%	14.0%	12.7%	7.6%	3.4%

* Uniform Crime Reports, 1970; see footnote 14.

under 30 years of age, and the frequency of arrests declines steadily with age.[14] This is consistent with the interpretation that with increasing maturity criminals abandon the life of crime and, presumably, find alternative ways to achieve their goals legitimately.

Further evidence for the hypothesis of immaturity is the fact that more than half of all homicides, aggravated assaults, and forcible rapes are committed against family members and personal acquaintances.[15] Domestic disputes account for as much as 50 per cent of a patrol officer's calls in a high crime area, many involving violence.[16] Crimes that occur in these circumstances are seldom deliberately planned, but erupt impulsively in the heat of anger or sudden temptation. Such crimes occur less frequently as domestic life becomes more stabilized, or alternatively as resignation and acquiescence increase. Auto theft and forcible rape occur less frequently as the adventurousness and passions of youth dwindle and legitimate access to cars and women improves. Crimes against property probably diminish with age because perpetrating them is both strenuous and hazardous. And we may even hope that some criminals give up the life of crime because they get caught or "see the light" and find better ways to achieve their goals in life.

A formal diagnostic system has been developed that classifies juvenile offenders according to interpersonal maturity, with seven levels from lowest to highest.[17] Youths at the lowest levels are considered the least psychologically mature, by which is meant that they have no feeling of control over their destiny, are cognitively simple and concrete, have no internalized values or standards, are impulsive and cannot delay gratification, and are "time-bound" to the present, with little appreciation for future or past events. Youths at higher levels have achieved varying degrees of progress toward maturity in these respects. Treatment at youth correctional institutions is calibrated to each youth's particular level of maturity, with specific procedures designed to help him acquire the psychological skills he needs and can learn.

[14] U. S. Department of Justice, *Uniform Crime Reports for the United States—1970* (Washington, D. C.: Government Printing Office, 1970, pp. 126–27.
[15] *The Challenge of Crime in a Free Society*, op. cit., pp. 138–39.
[16] F. J. Remington, "The Limits and Possibilities of the Criminal Law," in Ruth *et al.*, op. cit., p. 55.
[17] C. E. Sullivan, M. Q. Grant, and J. D. Grant, "The Development of Interpersonal Maturity: Applications to Delinquency," *Psychiatry*, XX (1957), pp. 373–85; D. R. Miller, *A Construct Validity Study of the Interpersonal Maturity Level Classification System*, unpublished doctoral dissertation, University of Massachusetts, 1972.

Failure to Introject Parental Standards

Socialization can be regarded as the outcome of a bargain that is struck between parents and child. The child's part of the bargain is to give up the privileges and unrestraint of a small child in favor of the responsibilities of a larger one. The parents' part of the bargain is to set models of considerate and socialized behavior and to make it worth the child's while, in the coin of affection and praise, to undertake the required sacrifices. The parents, who are in the position to manage the bargain, must steer a middle course and maintain a workable balance. The demands they make must be neither too small nor too great in proportion to the rewards they give. Conversely, the rewards they give must be neither too small nor too great in proportion to the demands they make.

One pattern is for the parents to make no demands and set no standards. The child is simply "spoiled," allowed to do everything he pleases with no loss of rewards. This gives him no motive to take the uphill road toward socialization. He expects everything to come easily, as his just due, and it is easy for him to slip over into the attitude that he might as well take what he wants. This kind of training produces indifference, perhaps mild contempt, toward the restraints and ideals of society. Often enough, however, the result is merely a passive, dependent, irresponsible attitude rather than a career of crime. Indulgent overprotection may, but probably does not regularly, predispose to enduring delinquency.

A contrasting pattern is that in which demands are made but rewards of love are more or less completely withheld. The parents are severe and unloving; they require that socialization shall take place, but they give the child no praise or affection when he succeeds, only punishments when he fails. The child's sacrifices are thus made unpleasant, and nothing is offered to cancel the aggression that he feels in submitting to such a bargain. As a result he submits to it less and less until he becomes an avowed rebel against the constraints of society. He is not only indifferent to social standards; he is actively hostile toward them.

In the 1930's the Cambridge–Somerville Youth Study was launched to determine some of the causes of juvenile delinquency and what could be done to prevent it. Extensive material, including the family background, was gathered on more than 500 boys who were believed to have a high risk for delinquency. Years later, when it was known which boys had actually become delinquent, the family backgrounds of the delinquent and non-delinquent groups were compared.[18] One of the most important influences proved to be the cohesiveness of the family and the consistency of discipline. Much higher rates of subsequent delinquency were associated with families described as quarrelsome, neglectful, and lax in discipline. Particularly conducive to a criminal career was a regime of punitive but erratic disci-

18 W. McCord, J. McCord, and I. K. Zola, *Origins of Crime* (New York: Columbia University Press, 1959).

pline; whereas consistent discipline, even when severe, led to better sociali- zation. With respect to parental behavior the investigators found that love on the part of the mothers, even when they were anxiously overprotective, and warmth and a relative passivity on the part of the fathers were associ- ated with fewer delinquent outcomes. When fathers were cruel, neglectful, or absent, and when mothers were cruel, neglectful, or passively helpless, the rates of ultimate delinquency were high.

In a study of aggressive adolescent boys by Bandura and Walters, the findings are related more closely to theory.[19] Serious delinquency turns not only on failure to absorb parental standards but on an active, hostile oppo- sition to them. This opposition depends upon the possibility of hating the parents, at least the one most closely associated with standards. If the child clings to a hope of getting love from the parents, his hostility will be re- pressed and he will be in a fair way to start a nuclear neurotic process. Bandura and Walters therefore attach importance to the vicissitudes of dependence and to the hostility growing out of shortages and deprivations of love. Once the scales are tipped toward hostility, the boy embarks on a course characterized by active aggression and self-sufficiency. When es- tablished, this course tends to be self-perpetuating: dependence is feared, signs of love and esteem are mistrusted, and friendly relations are thwarted by a quick display of aggression. One of the findings made by Bandura and Walters was that aggressive adolescents fared less well with everyone, even with their contemporaries, than did the control group. The investi- gation also showed the importance of relations between fathers and sons. "The fathers of aggressive boys were typically hostile to, and rejecting of, their sons, expressed little warmth for them, and had spent little time in affectionate interaction with them during the boys' childhood." [20] Anti- social aggression was especially likely to be the outcome when the mothers, rather than mitigating this state of affairs, added to it by discouraging de- pendence and perhaps subtly rewarding the steps toward self-sufficiency.

It is clear that the causes of delinquency are numerous and that their influence is often reciprocal. A secure relation with the mother can counter- balance a hostile one with the father, but if the security is insufficient the two relations may become a joint influence toward delinquency. Erratic punitive discipline and a disorganized neighborhood may combine to pro- duce a result that neither would often produce by itself.

Children Who Hate

Redl and Wineman studied intensively a small group of highly aggres- sive boys, ranging in age from 8 to 11, who were selected for treatment at Pioneer House in Detroit.[21] They considered that these boys fitted the

[19] A. Bandura and R. H. Walters, *Adolescent Aggression* (New York: The Ronald Press Co., 1959).

[20] *Ibid.*, p. 354.

[21] F. Redl and D. Wineman, *Children Who Hate: The Disorganization and Breakdown of Behavior Controls* (New York: The Free Press of Glencoe, 1951).

theoretical notion of low ego strength. Small frustrations, like a momentarily stuck door or having to wait for a traffic light, threw them into violent temper tantrums. Mayhem prevailed most of the time. A large phonograph was used at first mainly for climbing and jumping down, while the records went sailing through the air at the walls or at other children. Personal possessions, even those most treasured, were almost immediately lost or broken. Signs of guilt feeling were rare, and when confronted with their misdeeds the boys seemed unable to recognize their own part in them, blaming everyone else for what happened. Enforcement of rules was hazardous for the staff and quiet could be obtained at meals and at bedtime only by force of superior numbers.

The picture of impulsivity and destructiveness could hardly be more complete, yet from a different perspective the children's behavior showed effective organization. It was clear that they were not simply *showing* impulse gratification; they were bent on *defending* it at all costs. In this endeavor the boys displayed many evidences of ego strength. They shrewdly appraised that part of reality that might endanger their impulsive exploits, and effectively manipulated people and events to protect their delinquent fun. The boys found excuses for their misconduct with amazing deftness, and showed great intuitive skill in picking companions who would fit in with their plans and support their escapades. Equally sharp was their appraisal of staff members, who obviously constituted a threat to their delinquent ways. Sensing the "battle-relevant areas," they soon learned what type of argument would appease or divert or fool the staff most readily, and what cajoling or affection-seeking behavior was most effective to protect their right to be impulsive and aggressive.

Conscience in these boys was heavily submerged but not absent. Every so often there would emerge some piece of considerate behavior, some act of kindness, that represented a "value island" retained from the past. Tough as the boys had learned to be, they showed traces of dependent love and of identification with non-delinquent values. Their histories were full of neglect, rejection, broken homes, disorganized neighborhoods, and a lack of stable identification figures. Yet occasional glimpses of attachment showed through the seemingly impenetrable wall of human coldness and disinterest. The boys were not total strangers to supporting love, though they must have been badly disappointed in it. They consequently had taken the pathway of self-indulgence, hating the adult world that tried to stop them. One of their defensive measures was to keep out of affectionate relationships lest they be tempted and disappointed again.

Membership in Delinquent Groups

In an earlier chapter we studied the importance of group memberships in the development of personality.[22] We saw that in early adolescence

22 See above, pp. 174–77.

group membership rose to a peak of importance in the individual's life, taking over to a considerable extent the functions of emotional support hitherto concentrated in the family. Many delinquents are unhappy at home. Long before puberty they welcome and need whatever support and recognition can be obtained from group memberships. The group may early become the boy's or girl's only home in an emotional sense. Groups outside the home generally mean more in the lives of delinquents than they do in the lives of other children.[23]

Of itself, however, this fact does not explain the superior attraction of *delinquent* groups over those that stay out of conflict with law and order. Even in an area that suffers from maximum social disorganization there is a choice of groups. The peculiar attraction of the delinquent group arises from the exciting and lawless character of its activities. Delinquent groups are often in a state of crisis. The excitement is highly advantageous to one who wants to drown the memory of a distressing home life. Even more important is the lawlessness. The individual who needs support in his rebellion against parental standards finds this support in good measure in a group that rebels against all of society's standards.

Walter Miller has studied street gangs intensively for many years and he considers them a stable part of urban lower-class life that complements the family in socializing the adolescent, albeit sometimes in unfortunate directions.[24] Through participation in a gang a youngster acquires vital knowledge of lower-class culture, training in individual competence, the uses and abuses of authority, the reasonable limits of law-violating behavior, and the skills of interpersonal relations. In contrast to the extreme disorganization of his neighborhood and family, the gang may be his most reliable and rewarding form of human association. Gangs are oriented primarily around recreation and crime, so their leaders are usually selected for their athletic prowess, crime skills, and fighting ability. One leader, for example, had especially wide authority because he was a hard drinker, an able street fighter, a skilled football strategist and team leader, an accomplished dancer and smooth ladies' man, and one of the most criminal of the older gang members, being among the relatively few who had "done time." [25] Since criminal activity is a prime source of prestige, aspiring leaders step up their criminal involvement in order to assume or solidify their leadership positions. This is dangerous, of course, because it increases the risk of apprehension. The social structure of the gang is quite flexible, however, and when a leader gets caught, other stand-by leaders are ready to take his place.

There is an obvious hierarchy within the gang. Younger and less capa-

[23] A. K. Cohen, *Delinquent Boys: The Culture of the Gang* (New York: The Free Press of Glencoe, 1955); J. F. Short and F. L. Strodtbeck, *Group Process and Gang Delinquency* (Chicago: University of Chicago Press, 1965).
[24] W. B. Miller, "White Gangs," in Short, *op. cit.*, p. 82.
[25] *Ibid.*, p. 79.

ble members have inferior status, while older, more experienced members serve as surrogate parents for their protegées, with the responsibility for showing them the ropes. Identification processes normally found within the family are transferred to the gang, so that the reputation of the gang and the gang leaders take on tremendous psychological significance. Most of the fabled gang fights result from some form of threat, real or imagined, to someone's reputation as a man.[26] And, of course, within the delinquent subculture successful crime is one of the principal symbols that adulthood has been achieved.

The Neurotic Delinquent

The subcultural delinquents discussed to this point may become *socially* deviant without necessarily being *psychologically* deviant. The neurotic delinquent, while sharing the impulsive and aggressive tendencies of most delinquents, also has psychological conflicts that cause tension, guilt, remorse, depression, and discouragement.[27] This syndrome is also referred to as *neurotic psychopathy* or *acting-out neurosis,* which is high in guilt.[28] All of the elements are illustrated in the case of Bert Whipley. He consciously chose delinquent companions when others were available, and he went joyriding in stolen cars because it was great fun. He found welcome esteem from older boys when he successfully stole some number plates for them. He greatly enjoyed the thrill of riding at high speed while a rain of police bullets spattered around the tires. Particularly important was the chance to defy, insult, and outwit the police. Joyriding in stolen cars is easier than might appear. Bert completed something like fifty such missions without being caught or hurt. It was a perfect means of demonstrating the powerlessness of all that his father espoused. However, combined with this audacious behavior was the paradoxical motive to seek punishment in order to alleviate an unconscious sense of guilt. Strictly speaking, it is a neurotic mechanism, showing that part of the parental standards had been fully introjected. Thus we can see that both the doing and undoing of Bert's antisocial behavior were neurotically motivated.[29]

Treatment of Juvenile Delinquency

As we have seen, juvenile delinquency is not a single syndrome. It is a way of behaving that is adopted by many different kinds of children for many different reasons. The prevention of juvenile delinquency is thus

26 J. F. Short and F. Strodtbeck, "Why Gangs Fight," *ibid.,* pp. 33–44.

27 D. R. Peterson, H. C. Quay, and T. L. Tiffany, "Personality Factors Related to Juvenile Delinquency," *Child Development,* XXXII (1961), pp. 355–72.

28 J. C. Finney, "Relations and Meaning of the New MMPI Scales," *Psychological Reports,* XVIII (1966), pp. 459–70.

29 For an interesting case study of this particular problem, see D. J. Levinson, "Criminality from a Sense of Guilt: A Case Study and Some Research Hypotheses," *Journal of Personality,* XX (1952), pp. 402–29.

an operation on many fronts. The obstacles presented by deviant sub-cultures and delinquency areas do not belong strictly in the psychologist's province, yet it may be that little can be done to change the family at-mospheres that contribute to delinquency until these central economic and social problems are brought nearer to solution. In the meantime, the at-tempt to bring favorable influences to bear on young people through social service and recreational agencies may show little outward result. Such is the conclusion of the ten-year Cambridge–Somerville Youth Study, which found little difference in the incidence of delinquency between a group of boys given abundant services of this kind and a group given no special services.[30] The forces disposing toward delinquency seem to outweigh those than can be mustered in later childhood by social agencies.

The alternative to prevention is treatment, and our interest here is in the possibility of using psychotherapy. In any attempt at treatment the therapist starts at a serious disadvantage. To the delinquent he is an enemy; he represents law and order and is presumed to be trying to con-vert his patient to the hated cause. Few delinquents come willingly to psychotherapy. The therapist has to convince them that it is worth their while. Recognizing the difficulty of engaging the individual in therapy, some programs of *guided group interaction* have been set up, which attempt to shape the attitudes and norms maintained by a group of delinquents, rather than the behavior and attitudes of any one of its members.[31] It is reasoned that, since the normative support for delinquency comes from the peer group, it is necessary to change the values of the whole system by working directly with the group as a unit. In such programs group mem-bers have a stake in the fate of all other members because they participate with the staff in solving any problems that come up.

In an ingenious departure from the conventions of psychotherapy, Slack has shown that chronic delinquent boys who are unreachable because of their contempt for professional help can be brought into a kind of treat-ment by the expedient of hiring them for pay.[32] They are engaged to assist the experimenter by telling their life stories to him and his tape recorder, and by taking a number of his psychological tests. The subject need not perceive for some time that any personal benefit is intended. During this time he has a chance to contemplate his own life, to establish confidence in the therapist, and to find out what psychotherapy would be like. Confidence will be felt more readily if the boy finds in the therapist someone who can

30 E. Powers and H. L. Witmer, *Experiments in the Prevention of Delinquency: The Cambridge–Somerville Youth Study* (New York: Columbia University Press, 1951).

31 S. Wheeler, L. S. Cottrell, Jr., and A. Romasco, "Juvenile Delinquency: Its Prevention and Control," *Task Force Report: Juvenile Delinquency and Youth Crime*, Report to the President's Commission on Law Enforcement and Administration of Justice (Washington, D. C.: Government Printing Office, 1967), p. 423.

32 C. W. Slack, "Experimenter-Subject Psychotherapy: A New Method of Introducing Intensive Office Treatment for Unreachable Cases," *Mental Hygiene*, XLIV (1960), pp. 238–56.

see things from his point of view and convey a sense of alliance, yet not be taken in by the bluff and big talk that is part of his usual stock in trade. Slack's highly unconventional method has shown promise of success where nothing else is likely to succeed.

In a residential setting a behavior therapy program has been used with some success, by systematically rewarding cooperative and prosocial behaviors, while punishing (by withholding positive reinforcers) lying, stealing, and cheating.[33] In a similar effort Schwitzgebel found that positive rewards brought about desired changes in the behavior of his delinquents, whereas punishments did not.[34]

Redl and Wineman emphasize the necessity of creating a therapeutic milieu which will subtly affect the child throughout his waking hours.[35] The highly aggressive children treated at Pioneer House represent a group that can neither be reached by the usual psychiatric interview nor reformed by the unsympathetic application of restraints. They must live in a therapeutic environment characterized by affection, good care, much tolerance and permissiveness, yet also a firm insistence on really essential rules and standards. They must be provided with programs of activities that will stimulate constructive interests and thus encourage controlled behavior. They do not need scheduled interviews, but the alert worker must exploit whatever opportunities are provided by events and spontaneous crises to have impromptu interviews, striking when the iron is hot. Under this regime it is possible to salvage children who otherwise seem destined for permanent antisocial careers. Unfortunately the method calls for such a large and well-trained staff that it usually requires a greater financial outlay than society is willing to make for its delinquent members. Pioneer House itself was run as an experiment for less than two years, then closed for lack of community support. The problem of resources, human and financial, looms even more darkly here than in the treatment of the neuroses.

PSYCHOPATHIC PERSONALITY

We turn now from the broader consideration of delinquency and criminal behavior to a problem more strictly psychiatric. It is evident that delinquents and criminals cannot be characterized in any simple way and that their difficulties with society have important roots in disordered social and economic conditions. The possibility remains, however, that *some* criminals suffer *primarily* from true psychological disorder which interferes with the process of socialization. While neurotic delinquents like Bert Whipley have secondary psychological conflicts, the psychopathology

[33] J. Burchard, "Systematic Socialization: A Programmed Environment for the Habilitation of Antisocial Retardates," *Psychological Record,* XVII (1967), pp. 461-76.

[34] R. Schwitzgebel, "Short-term Operant Conditioning of Adolescent Offenders on Socially Relevant Variables," *Journal of Abnormal Psychology,* LXXII (1967), pp. 134-42.

[35] F. Redl and D. Wineman, *Controls from Within: Techniques for the Treatment of the Aggressive Child* (New York: The Free Press of Glencoe, 1952).

in these cases must be quite fundamental to explain their persistent and callous antisocial behavior.

A Problem in Psychiatric Classification

Psychopathic personality originated as a diagnostic concept with an English psychiatrist, Prichard, who in 1835 described a "form of mental derangement" in which intellect seemed unimpaired but moral principles were "perverted or depraved," the "power of self-government" was lost or diminished, and the individual was incapable of "conducting himself with decency and propriety in the business of life." [36] It was generally believed that they suffered from some hereditary weakness of the nervous system; hence the term *constitutional psychopathic inferiority* was commonly used. These two ideas—a defect in the realm of socialized behavior and an innate weakness lying behind it—have continued to dominate most thinking about psychopathic personality. It has proved impossible, however, to reach general agreement as to what should be included under this heading. Kraepelin distinguished seven subtypes: the Excitable, the Unstable, the Impulsive, the Eccentric, Liars and Swindlers, the Antisocial, and the Quarrelsome. Some current textbooks add sexual deviations to the list, and others include addiction to alcohol and drugs. Such liberality tends to defeat the purposes of psychological understanding.

More recent diagnostic formulations, offering various labels (*character disorder, sociopathic personality, psychopathic personality*), have consistently attempted to narrow the category and define it in more positive terms.[37] The people now diagnosed as psychopaths have developed in such a way that parental and social standards have never been introjected; they have failed to respond adequately to the process of socialization. Cleckley rules out those cases in which social standards are rejected only in respect to some one particular kind of behavior, such as alcoholism or deviant sexual behavior in a person otherwise adapted to social demands. He also rules out cases in which crime is adopted as a positive way of life, the subcultural criminals who are enemies of society but loyal and stable members of culturally deviant groups. Besides the neurotic delinquents, who are sometimes considered *secondary psychopaths,* there remains a relatively homogeneous group of true or *primary psychopaths* who need not be diagnosed negatively, by exclusion of other possibilities, but have a characteristic pattern of symptoms.

Central Pattern of Traits

The psychopath makes an unusually pleasing impression in interviews: superficially charming, alert, well-informed, able to talk well. Intelligence

[36] J. C. Prichard, *Treatise on Insanity* (London: Gilbert and Piper, 1835), p. 15.

[37] *Diagnostic and Statistical Manual: Mental Disorders* (2nd ed.; Washington, D. C.: American Psychiatric Association, 1968); H. Cleckley, *The Mask of Sanity* (4th ed.; St. Louis: The C. V. Mosby Co., 1964).

is good and does not deteriorate. Nervousness, neurotic signs, delusions, and irrational thinking are absent. One soon finds out that he is very unreliable, inclined to lie and deceive. He does not accept blame for his misconduct nor feel shame about it, but readily gives a plausible excuse for everything that has occurred. While he is able to reason satisfactorily, in some cases even brilliantly, he shows very poor judgment about his behavior. He gets into the same trouble over and over again, never learning from his experience. No life plan is followed consistently unless it be a plan to make life a failure. In his personal relations he is egocentric and incapable of real love or attachment. Strong, deep, and lasting feelings do not seem to exist. Although he talks a great deal about feelings, he gives the impression of merely using words without insight into the nature of real emotion. Cleckley has termed this tendency toward verbalizations devoid of emotional meaning *semantic dementia.* "The psychopath knows the words but not the music," so he is incapable of empathy or genuine concern for others.[38] Understandably, his sex life is usually impersonal, trivial, and poorly integrated. He manipulates and uses other people for his own ends, yet often manages to persuade them through glib explanations of his sincerity and good intentions. The psychopath is impulsive and unable to delay gratifying his needs, regardless of future consequences; although he understands the advantages of postponing gratification in an intellectual way, future events—whether good or bad—have no emotional significance for him. Though he may *simulate* emotional reactions, he actually experiences little anxiety or fear. Vanity is another common characteristic: an exaggerated concern with appearance, status, and reputation.

It is clear that we are dealing with a fairly serious disorder, with grave disturbances emotionally, in foresight, and in the control and organization of behavior. Cleckley considers the condition serious enough to be classed as a psychosis. Although the psychopath outwardly presents a "convincing mask of sanity" and a mimicry of human life, he has lost contact with the deeper emotional accompaniments of experience and with its purposiveness. To this extent he may be said to have an incomplete contact with reality, and it is certainly very hard to approach him and influence him therapeutically.[39]

A Sample Psychopath

A particularly good example is Richard Hickock, one of two men who slaughtered a family of four in a vain robbery attempt in their home.[40] He had a good home on a farm in Kansas. His parents were strict, reli-

38 J. H. Johns and H. C. Quay, "The Effect of Social Reward on Verbal Conditioning in Psychopathic and Neurotic Military Offenders," *Journal of Consulting Psychology,* XXVI (1962), pp. 217–20.

39 Cleckley, *op. cit.,* chap. 59.

40 T. Capote, *In Cold Blood* (New York: Random House, Inc., 1965).

gious, hard working, and loving. The children were hardly ever allowed to leave the yard and visit with playmates. They were always "semi-poor," not well off but with the necessities and a few luxuries provided for, like most Kansas farm families during the Depression and war years. Dick was not a bad pupil in school, and could have done better than average if he had applied to his studies only a fraction of the effort he gave to sports. He was a star athlete in basketball, baseball, track, and football. Two colleges offered him football scholarships, and he wanted to go to college to become an engineer, but his family had no money to afford the other college expenses, so upon graduating from high school he took a job as a railway trackman. Subsequently he worked periodically as an ambulance driver, car painter, and garage mechanic.

Through most of his childhood Dick was no trouble to anybody, a cheerful boy who got along well in school, was popular with his classmates and obedient to his parents. The first inkling of criminal tendencies came at 17, when he was arrested for breaking into a drugstore. The next year he suffered head injuries in an auto accident that left his handsome face slightly askew and, according to his father, changed his personality so he "just wasn't the same boy." [41] Now he became sulky and restless, ran around with older men, drank and gambled. Not everyone agreed with his father's testimony, which after all was given at his son's murder trial, where evidence for brain damage might have swayed the jury to recommend a milder sentence. A neighbor claimed that Dick would "steal the weights off a dead man's eyes"; he would have gone to jail "more times than you can count, except nobody around here ever wanted to prosecute. Out of respect for his folks." [42]

He was married and divorced twice, having three sons by his first wife, all in the short space of about six years. [43] He got deeply into debt from gambling and imprudent living shortly after his first marriage at 19. Though he was working, he began stealing things and writing fraudulent checks. Eventually he served seventeen months in prison for stealing a neighbor's hunting rifle, and the experience soured him, making him feel the whole world was against him. When he returned home he was contrite, promising his father he would never do anything more to hurt him because he had been a "pretty good old dad" to Dick, and he seemed to mean it sincerely. But this mood did not last.

Even as a hardened criminal Dick was personable, clean-cut, and affable, "a fellow any man might trust to shave him." [44] He was a likable extrovert with a wonderful smile that really worked, sane but not too bright (though his I.Q. was tested at 130). He was fastidiously attentive to personal hy-

41 *Ibid.,* p. 328.
42 *Ibid.,* p. 193.
43 Both his wives were only 16 years old. Dick was a *pedophile* who delighted in seducing pubescent girls, the only neurotic aspect of the case.
44 *Ibid.,* p. 108.

giene and the condition of his fingernails. His athletic body was covered with sexy, aggressive, and sentimental tattoos: bosomy nudes, dragons devouring human skulls, and bouquets dedicated to Mother and Dad. There was also a hard side of his personality. To Perry Smith, his partner in crime, Dick was authentically tough, pragmatic, invulnerable, "totally masculine." Less appealing were his lack of aesthetic appreciation and his callous insensitivity to the feeling of others. He felt no guilt about making empty promises of marriage to ensure the seduction of a teen-age Mexican girl, and it thrilled him to run over mongrel dogs on the highway. He was an expansive, dominant type who spent his money freely for vodka and women after a windfall from passing bad checks. Dick had a way with women and boasted conceitedly of his amorous conquests.

While in prison Dick learned from another inmate, Floyd Wells, of a prosperous farmer named Clutter who usually had about $10,000 in a wall safe, and an attractive 16-year-old daughter. Dick began to devise a "flawless" plan to steal that money and leave no witnesses, even if there should be a dozen people in the home that night. To this end he chose as his partner Perry Smith, a "cold blooded killer" who claimed to have beaten a "nigger" to death with a bicycle chain, just for the hell of it.[45] (In fact, he had never killed anyone.) Incredible as it sounds, Dick seems to have reckoned that he would be less vulnerable to prosecution in the event of capture if Perry did the killing, but there would be no capture if, as he insisted over and over again, they left no witnesses. At the scene of the crime Dick was brutal and sadistic to the victims; he obviously gloried in having them tied up at his mercy. It was Perry who put pillows under their heads to make them comfortable and reassured them that everything would be all right, and it was Perry who prohibited Dick from raping the girl.[46] Dick was angry that there proved to be no safe and no $10,000; they found less than $50 altogether. Yet despite all his bluster and threats, Dick only held the flashlight while Perry slit Mr. Clutter's throat and finished off all four helpless victims with shotgun blasts to the head.[47]

Much of Capote's book concerns the escapades of the pair after the killing: repeated sprees of check forgery in Kansas City and Florida; a brief sojourn living it up in Mexico; looking vainly for a motorist to rob, kill, and discard in the desert. It is hard to believe that a man as shrewd as Dick Hickock would think they could travel with impunity throughout the Southwest, even returning to his home territory to pass bad checks in Kansas City. He was planning to impersonate an Air Force officer, so he could pass "a bundle of confetti" (worthless checks) on the Strip at Las Vegas, when they were apprehended. Dick had concocted a fantastically convincing alibi for the night of the murder, which he delivered with disarming

[45] *Ibid.*, p. 69.
[46] *Ibid.*, p. 313.
[47] Perry had a seriously disordered personality structure diagnosed as "very nearly that of a paranoid schizophrenic." *Ibid.*, p. 334.

facility, but the two men were tried and convicted of first degree murder. They had taken precautions, but not enough, and they ultimately confessed to the crime. After more than five years of appeals, both men were hanged in 1965. In character to the last, Dick's last statement before the execution was: "I just want to say I hold no hard feelings. You people are sending me to a better world than this ever was." Then, as if to emphasize the point, he greeted with a handshake and a charming smile the four men who were mainly responsible for his capture and conviction.[48]

Psychogenic Aspects of the Disorder

The most important clue to a possible psychogenic factor in such cases would appear to lie in the weakness of feeling toward other people. The emotional blunting, the lack of affectional ties, the mimicry of love without evidence of real feeling all point to a possible disturbance in the child's early human relations. Parental rejection immediately comes to mind; but, as we have seen, this can also produce neurotic and delinquent outcomes. The neurotic craves human relations, the delinquent fights them, but the psychopath seems to be merely indifferent. We can make the hypothesis of a very early injury to affectionate relations, a serious deficit of gratifying love and care perhaps even in the first year. Lacking a strong initial attachment to the mother, the child as he grows up may learn to adapt shrewdly enough to the realities around him and may become socialized to the extent of presenting a pleasant front; but the real meaning of his life is still the direct gratification of impulse, and this childlike value is not importantly tempered by close affectional ties or by a feeling of involvement in the human community.

The concept of parental rejection does not seem to fit the childhood situation in the case just described, although several investigators consider it a primary etiological factor.[49] It has been found repeatedly that psychopaths have more than their share of parental loss through death or separation.[50] However this is also common for drug addicts, neurotics, alcoholics, and psychotics, so by itself it could not explain the psychopathic outcome distinctively. Robins argues that broken homes do not *cause* psychopathy, but rather reflect pathology in the parents, especially the father, which simultaneously contributes to psychopathic outcome in the child and marital discord between the parents.[51]

How might the child-rearing practices of the parents shape the traits characteristic of the psychopath? Clearly moral behavior is learned through

[48] *Ibid.*, p. 379.

[49] Jenkins, *op. cit.;* W. McCord and J. McCord, *The Psychopath: An Essay on the Criminal Mind* (Princeton, N. J.: Van Nostrand Reinhold Co., 1964) contains a survey of the literature.

[50] J. Oltman and S. Friedman, "Parental Deprivation in Psychiatric Conditions," *Diseases of the Nervous System,* XXVIII (1967), pp. 298–303; L. N. Robins, *Deviant Children Grown Up* (Baltimore: The Williams and Wilkins Co., 1966).

[51] Robins, *ibid.*, p. 179.

experience with rewards and punishments administered, usually, by the parents. Typically, bad behavior is penalized immediately and directly because parents, like research psychologists, have learned that delayed or indirect punishments do not effectively produce resistance to subsequent temptation.[52] However, Maher points out that "sometimes the punishment may be forestalled or at least reduced in severity by suitable expressions of repentance and promises not to repeat the behavior." [53] In learning theory terms, the child who can consistently avoid punishment in this way learns verbal repentance behavior while losing any fear of punishment for forbidden acts. Consider our sample psychopath in the light of this hypothesis. We were told that the Hickock parents were hard-working, conscientious and strict, yet loving. Capote's account makes clear that the father, the main disciplinarian, was also extremely loyal to his son and denied repeatedly any criminal intent in Dick's actions. If it were characteristic of Mr. Hickock to set stringent restrictions on Dick as a child but continually postpone punishments for violations when the boy gave evidence of repentance, he might well have molded a manipulative moral attitude and extinguished fear of punishment. It may seem a large leap from smooth-talking your father out of a spanking to getting away with murder, but with a lifetime of reinforcement behind it such developmental experience might be a significant determinant.

Another possible source of the psychopathic way of behavior is modeling. As we saw in Chapter 5, modeling plays a major role in the acquisition of conscience. How often it has been demonstrated that children do as their parents *do* rather than as they say! [54] Psychopathic tendencies may be acquired, in part, by imitating one's parents. Consistent with this is Robins' finding that many fathers of psychopaths are themselves antisocial or impulsive.[55] In the Hickock case, the evidence is insufficient, but it does not seem to point in this direction.

Still another possibility has to do with delay of gratification. Arieti hypothesizes that a child learns to postpone gratification through consistent training to expect substitute rewards at progressively longer intervals of time.[56] In place of an immediate reward a mother may offer love and praise and a promise of a future bonus if the child can inhibit the impulse or postpone the pay-off. Thus promises and hopes of future gratification retain a flavor or echo of mother's approval and tenderness, secondarily reinforcing the postponement. Now if we assume that a child

[52] R. L. Solomon, L. H. Turner, and M. S. Lessac, "Some Effects of Delay of Punishment on Resistance to Temptation in Dogs," *Journal of Personality and Social Psychology,* VIII (1968), pp. 233–38.

[53] B. A. Maher, *Principles of Psychopathology* (New York: McGraw-Hill Book Co., 1966), p. 216.

[54] J. Aronfreed, *Conduct and Conscience* (New York: Academic Press, 1968). Bandura and Walters, *op. cit.*

[55] Robins, *op. cit.*, p. 179.

[56] S. Arieti, *The Intrapsychic Self* (New York: Basic Books, Inc., 1967).

is reared in a broken home or has rejecting parents, forebearance may hold no such emotional compensations, so he will remain childlike in his attitude toward impulse gratification. In the Hickock case we do not have the necessary information about the mother, though difficulty in delaying gratification was certainly prominent in the son's behavior.

Somatogenic Aspects of the Disorder

During the second half of the nineteenth century there were repeated attempts to show that criminals were constitutionally inferior. This conception of the problem was a natural consequence of the somatogenic hypothesis which for a time completely dominated psychiatric thinking. The criminal behaved differently from other people, therefore something must be different about his constitution or his nervous system. The results of these investigations are not particularly impressive. Although voices are still raised for constitutional inferiority, there is no compelling evidence that requires a somatogenic hypothesis in this sweeping form.

Less easy to dismiss is the much more specific hypothesis that the particular disorder we are discussing here—psychopathic personality—is related to brain injury or brain inadequacy. Sometimes following a severe head injury, as happened with Dick Hickock, and sometimes following an attack of encephalitis (which is known to injure brain tissue), the behavior of a previously well-adjusted child will change in what might be called a delinquent direction. The child becomes overactive and aggressive; he has outbursts of emotion and irritation, and he is unable to concentrate or to accept the restraints of the schoolroom. He seems to have lost some of the regulating control that previously characterized his behavior. Under such circumstances it is harder for him to accept the restraints of socialization. The control of impulse and temper, the postponement of immediate satisfactions, the mere restraint of sitting still at table or at school become suddenly more difficult than they were before. In view of these facts it is at least a legitimate hypothesis that some subtle inadequacy of cerebral tissue might underlie the psychopath's inability to be governed by the standards and restraints of society.

There is impressive consistency in a multitude of studies showing that from 31 to 58 per cent of all psychopaths have abnormal electrical activity in the brain, as measured by electroencephalogram (EEG).[57] The ab-

[57] R. G. S. Arthurs and E. B. Cahoon, "A Clinical and Electroencephalographic Survey of Psychopathic Personality," *American Journal of Psychiatry*, CXX (1964), pp. 875–82; S. K. Ehrlich and R. P. Keogh, "The Psychopath in a Mental Institution," *Archives of Neurology and Psychiatry*, LXXVI (1956), pp. 286 95. Reviews of several studies involving hundreds of subjects are presented in R. J. Ellingson. "Incidence of EEG Abnormality Among Patients with Mental Disorders of Apparently Nonorganic Origin: A Criminal Review," *American Journal of Psychiatry*, CXI (1954), pp. 263–75, and in J. R. Knott, E. P. Platt, M. C. Ashby, and J. S. Gottlieb, "A Familial Evaluation of the Electroencephalogram of Patients with Primary Behavior Disorder and Psychopathic Personality," *EEG and Clinical Neurophysiology*, V (1953), pp. 363–70. Details of the EEG procedures are discussed in Chapter 15 of this book.

normalities are mainly of two kinds. Most commonly reported is an exceptionally high frequency of very slow waves, which are characteristic of normal infants and young children but diminish with increasing age.[58] Within the psychopathic groups the slow-wave pattern has been found to be associated with aggressiveness, impulsiveness, poor motor coordination, developmental retardation, and inadequate socialization. The second type of abnormality is a positive spike in the EEG recordings, found in as many as 40 per cent of highly impulsive and aggressive psychopaths.[59] This pattern appears mostly in cases with a history of overwhelming aggressive and destructive urges, often triggered by trivial provocations and resulting in severe damage to property and injury to others. These "attacks" are so violent and unrestrained as to suggest an epilepsy-like seizure, yet they often include actions requiring considerable skill and precision, and afterwards the person can discuss them with full awareness and no apparent feeling of guilt or anxiety.

An obvious hypothesis is that psychopathic behavior reflects cortical immaturity, especially in cases where slow waves are frequent. Many psychopathic traits are childlike: egocentricity, impulsiveness, inability to delay gratification. If the hypothesis of maturational retardation is correct, one might expect psychopathic behavior to decrease with age. Consistent with this is Robins' finding that a third of her diagnosed psychopaths became less grossly antisocial with age, usually between the ages of 30 and 40, and the finding by Gibbens et al. that psychopaths with EEG abnormalities have a better prognosis than those with normal EEGs, presumably because of outgrowing their cortical immaturity.[60] There are limitations, however, to the hypothesis. It does not explain how the EEG abnormalities come about. They might be acquired during childhood through infection or head injury; they might result from birth damage or injury during the fetal period; or they might be the product of hereditary influences. Furthermore, one should not exaggerate the parallels between childlike and psychopathic behavior, which may represent quite different processes. Finally, the hypothesis is a little shaken by the fact that 15 per cent of the general population exhibit EEG abnormalities and do not become psychopathic. On the other hand, it is certainly plausible that cortical immaturity *contributes* in some way to psychopathic behavior; for example, it may explain

[58] D. Hill, "EEG in Episodic Psychotic and Psychopathic Behavior: A Classification of Data," *EEG and Clinical Neurophysiology*, IV (1952), pp. 419–42. S. Bay-Rakal, "The Significance of EEG Abnormality in Behavior Problem Children," *Canadian Psychiatric Association Journal*, X (1965), pp. 387–91.

[59] J. R. Hughes, "A Review of the Positive Spike Phenomenon," in W. Wilson, ed., *Applications of Electroencephalography in Psychiatry* (Durham, N.C.: Duke University Press, 1965), pp. 54–101. H. D. Kurland, C. T. Yeager, and R. J. Arthur, "Psychophysiologic Aspects of Severe Behavior Disorders," *Archives of General Psychiatry*, VIII (1963), pp. 599–604.

[60] Robins, *op. cit.* T. C. N. Gibbens, O. Briscoe, and S. Dell, "Psychopathic and Neurotic Offenders in Mental Hospitals," in A. V. S. de Reuck and R. Porter, eds., *The Mentally Abnormal Offender* (London: J. and A. Churchill, 1968), pp. 143–49.

the psychopath's alleged inferior capacity for conditioning, especially of fear responses, and his consequent undersocialization.[61]

Another speculative formulation is summarized by Hare.[62] Many of the slow waves and positive spikes found in psychopaths' EEG records apparently emanate from the temporal lobes and the associated limbic system. Though poorly understood, the limbic system is believed to play a central role in sensory and memory processes and the central regulation of emotions. Specifically it has been implicated in the regulation of fear-motivated behavior, including learning to inhibit a response in order to avoid punishment.[63] Hare hypothesizes that the clinical observations of impulsivity and social insensitivity in psychopaths may be attributable to malfunction of inhibitory mechanisms in the limbic system.

Treatment

The treatment of the psychopath is anything but an inviting task. He brings no motivation to psychotherapy because he sees nothing wrong with his behavior. Most forms of therapy are ineffective because they presuppose a future orientation and substantial capacity for emotional relationship with the therapist, both of which are lacking in the psychopath. Under present laws governing commitment to mental hospitals, the psychopath cannot be kept long at an institution because he is not mentally deranged in the sense of intellectual confusion or disorientation. For the most part psychopaths move in and out of the portals of institutions as readily as they move in and out of jobs, spending a good part of their time at liberty where they are costly to society. Nevertheless there is promise in some recent therapeutic ventures, such as the therapeutic milieu constructed by Maxwell Jones in England.[64] The McCords reported a form of milieu treatment reasonably effective for 15 psychopathic children at the Wiltwyck School in New York, primarily due to four factors: "the rapport between children and counselors; the absence of punitive frustration; the subtle but powerful social control exerted not only by the adults but also by the boy leaders; and individual and group psychotherapy." [65] There was, unfortunately, no control group against which to compare their improvement. Similar programs in Denmark and Holland have also had some success.[66]

[61] H. J. Eysenck, *Crime and Personality* (London: Methuen & Co. Ltd, 1964).

[62] R. D. Hare, *Psychopathy: Theory and Research* (New York: John Wiley & Sons, Inc., 1970), pp. 33–34.

[63] R. A. McCleary, "Response-modulating Functions of the Limbic System: Initiation and Suppression," in E. Stellar and J. Sprague, ed., *Progress in Physiological Psychology*, Vol. 1 (New York: Academic Press, 1966), pp. 209–72.

[64] M. Jones *et al., The Therapeutic Community: A New Treatment Method in Psychiatry* (New York: Basic Books, Inc., 1953); "Society and the Sociopath," *American Journal of Psychiatry*, CXIX (1962), pp. 410–14. The therapeutic milieu concept is discussed in Chapter 8 of this book.

[65] McCord and McCord, *op. cit.*, p. 161.

[66] Hare, *op. cit.*, p. 114.

Thorne assumes that psychopathic behavior reflects a maladaptive *life style* that is maintained by reinforcement from family, friends, and associates.[67] For successful treatment he therefore recommends an extremely authoritarian approach, with the therapist controlling the psychopath's financial resources. Relatives and friends must agree not to rescue the psychopath from his difficulties, so he must face the consequences of his own behavior. The therapist insists on the psychopath's gradually exerting some limits and controls over his own behavior. The psychopath is denied protection from the legal and social consequences of his actions. The therapist makes it clear that he knows how to deal with psychopaths, and will be convinced of good intentions only through actions and not words. The psychopath must be shown repeatedly that his behavior is self-defeating. The therapist should search for leverage to force socially acceptable behavior, resorting to financial incentives, which he controls, as a last resort. Thorne candidly admits that the treatment may cost $15,000 per year for as long as ten years, so he hasn't won many legislators to his side.

Authoritarian programs may be useful for institutional treatment. A British study compared the effectiveness of two treatment regimes, one essentially self-governing, with tolerant staff members and intensive group therapy, the other more authoritarian, with a sympathetic but firm type of discipline and only superficial individual counseling.[68] After six to nine months of treatment, patients were permitted to take day jobs in the community, returning to the hospital each night. Neither group showed changes in personality or adjustment during the treatment, but the group treated under the authoritarian regime were convicted of significantly fewer offenses during the year after discharge. Thus work training in a friendly but disciplined residential setting may be more effective for treating psychopaths than the permissiveness that is usually recommended in the treatment of neuroses.

Many psychopaths give up their antisocial behavior in middle adulthood, attributing the change to fear of further punishment or loyalty to their spouses.[69] Rather than concentrating our efforts on extended hospitalization or psychotherapy, which have not proved very effective, Robins therefore recommends supporting the pressures toward conformity in the psychopath's social environment and trying to prevent his becoming isolated from family, friends, or neighbors. They may be able to do what highly trained professionals can not: limit his antisocial activities.

Behavior therapy is normally used to reduce anxiety or remove symp-

[67] F. C. Thorne, "The Etiology of Sociopathic Reactions," *American Journal of Psychotherapy*, XIII (1959), pp. 319–30.

[68] M. Crafts, G. Stephenson, and C. Granger, "A Controlled Trial of Authoritarian and Self-Governing Regimes with Adolescent Psychopaths," *American Journal of Orthopsychiatry*, XXXIV (1964), pp. 543–54.

[69] Robins, *op. cit.*, p. 236.

toms, and therefore has seldom been employed for treating psychopaths. Hare offers the intriguing suggestion that behavioral techniques be used for the opposite aim, namely, to increase fear and anxiety in order to augment their motivating influence.[70] It is problematic whether psychopaths would respond to such conditioning, but it is an experiment worth trying.

SOCIETY'S RESPONSE TO CRIME

A basic dilemma has evolved in modern jurisprudence over what response society should make to criminal behavior. In a cogent analysis of this dilemma Maher points out that selecting the right response has proven difficult because criminal punishment is intended by society to serve more than one purpose.[71] On the one hand punishment is considered a morally justified retribution for violating society's laws. This *revenge* motive is based on the premise that everyone is responsible for his own behavior, so when someone commits an offense against society he *deserves* to suffer for it. This is a remnant of the old principle: "an eye for an eye, and a tooth for a tooth. . . ." On the other hand punishment is intended by society to prevent the recurrence of crime either by directly detaining the criminal (incarceration) or by rehabilitating him or by deterring future violations with the threat of stiff penalties. Holding to both of these objectives has caused society to work at cross purposes with itself. The revenge motive calls for penalties against previous actions, with the severity of the penalties graduated, understandably, according to the seriousness of the crime. The prevention motive, however, calls for penalties gauged to probable future actions, which obviously requires assessment of the psychological motivation for the crime and may be quite unrelated to its magnitude.

Judges, lawyers, legislators, and clinicians have striven conscientiously to reconcile this melange of purposes so as to serve best the interests of society and still protect the rights of the offender. The effort has had only modest success. The McNaghten Rules provided the guidelines for many years to judge whether an offender was morally responsible for his alleged criminal actions, and hence subject to full retribution for the crime.[72] When a plea of insanity is entered, the question whether the defendant

[70] Hare, *op. cit.*, pp. 117–18.

[71] Maher, *op. cit.*, pp. 208–12.

[72] In 1843 Daniel McNaghten murdered a government clerk whom he mistook to be Sir Robert Peel, the Home Secretary for the British government. McNaghten said he was instructed to commit the murder "by the voice of God," and was acquitted by reason of insanity. A committee of judges was convened to recommend general criteria for "legal insanity." They concluded that a defendant is legally insane if he labored under such defect of reason from disease of the mind as not to know the nature and quality of the act in which he was engaged, or, if he *did* know it, that he did not know that what he was doing was wrong.

committed the crime is not contested; only whether he deserves to be punished for it. Traditionally, insanity has been ground for exoneration, when based either on the McNaghten Rules or on the ground that the crime was motivated by a pathological irresistible impulse. In practice, of course, the legal decision about responsibility has become simply a decision about treatment, with different dispositions reserved for those who are responsible and those who are not. When a psychiatrist or psychologist is asked to testify about a defendant's responsibility he is really being asked: "What should we do with him?" Much confusion and probably some injustice has arisen at this point in the judicial process because the courts have tried to satisfy simultaneously the public demand for retribution and the often contrary dictates of rehabilitation.

The dilemma is probably best illustrated in the case of murder. By far the most murders are committed by usually law-abiding citizens in the heat of extreme provocation against friends or relatives. At almost any other time they would not desire or be inclined to carry out the act, and once it has been done they typically feel great guilt and remorse over it. Follow-up of such murderers, once released after serving their sentences, shows that they seldom repeat the crime. Current laws call for severe penalties for murder because of the magnitude of the crime: death or imprisonment for life or a very long term. This serves mainly the purposes of retribution and deterrence. If the law were designed, however, to serve *only* the purposes of rehabilitation and the prevention of recurrence in this individual, many murderers of this type might receive light sentences or none at all. Obviously laws must seek some compromise between general deterrence and individual rehabilitation, but we may hope that the gradual abandonment of capital punishment and other recent flexibilities in applying the law indicate that modern society is outgrowing the archaic need for revenge.

Psychological Differentiation of Criminal Types

As society moves toward a judicial system more oriented to prevention and rehabilitation, the mental health professions can expect to be called on more and more to provide the knowledge to assess the criminal's prognosis and to enlighten society's response to criminal behavior. Of particular service in this regard is Brown's formulation of how moral behavior is acquired.[73] The critical aspects of moral behavior are knowledge, feelings, and conduct. Moral knowledge, or awareness of the rules of society, is acquired through concept formation and cognitive learning. Moral feelings, such as guilt, shame, and remorse, are learned by classical conditioning. Moral behavior is dependent on knowledge and feelings, and is governed by the principles of instrumental and imitative learning. From

[73] R. Brown, *Social Psychology* (New York: The Free Press of Glencoe, 1965), chap. 8.

this perspective it is obvious why the *psychopath* has the poorest prognosis of the four types of delinquents considered in this chapter. There is little question that he knows, on a cognitive level, what society considers to be right and wrong, but he behaves immorally because he is unable to experience moral feelings with sufficient intensity for awareness of the rules of society to have any impact on his behavior.[74] Treatment should therefore be concentrated on kindling some spark of moral feeling, as indicated in the last section, unless this proves impossible due to some constitutional inability to be conditioned. In either case, neither judicial leniency nor conventional psychotherapy seems indicated.

The *neurotic delinquent* knows the rules and has some capacity for moral feeling, but misbehaves presumably because of some distortion in the process of socialization, which allows antisocial behavior to serve neurotic ends. Psychotherapy and other conventional treatments for psychological disorder would seem to have the best prospect of helping in this case, though firmness and some attention to supporting moral feelings would probably not be amiss. Delinquents are delinquents, after all, because they break the rules.

The socialized or *subcultural delinquent* has good knowledge of the rules of his subculture, strong moral feelings, and good conduct by the standards of that subculture, but he follows the wrong rules. Society's response in this instance should be to expose continually the discrepancies between the two moral codes, and to reassert constantly that the deviant code cannot win. This may be accomplished to some extent by public education, but inevitably society must also set limits against individual violations by enforcing the law. Psychotherapy hardly has much to offer here, except as an adjunct to rehabilitation when the criminal is willing to "go straight."

The *white collar criminal* knows the right rules, has strong moral feelings and generally good conduct, but in circumscribed areas he distorts intellectually the interpretation or application of the rules in such a way as to evade moral culpability for his criminal conduct. In most cases of this sort the prognosis should be good, even with moderate penalties because the social censure of criminal conviction is a powerful instrument in the lives of affluent, otherwise respectable, citizens. There are, of course, some white collar criminals who violate the law with *conviction,* and these

---

74 Hare, *op. cit.,* pp. 106–7. This aspect of psychopathy has played havoc on the legal definition of insanity. It may be argued that a psychopath is no less insane because his knowledge of right and wrong is *emotionally* blocked from bearing on his conduct than is the schizophrenic whose knowledge of right and wrong is *intellectually* inaccessible. In the Hickock trial the prosecution realized that a full psychiatric diagnosis of "severe character disorder" could be used by the defense to mitigate the penalty for the murder, and therefore objected to the court-appointed psychiatrist giving any further testimony than to answer yes or no to the question whether the defendant knew right from wrong at the time he committed the crime. The objection was upheld. Thus limited by the McNaghten Rule and prohibited from elaborating, the psychiatrist was forced to answer in the affirmative, foreclosing any further consideration of insanity.

may be regarded and treated like subcultural criminals who adhere to a deviant code of ethics.

Making the state's reaction fit the offender's potential for reform is called *prescriptive penology*.[75] To make it work, Glaser accurately observes, will require that much more than the current portion of correctional expenditures (less than one per cent) will have to be spent on *research* to measure the effectiveness of alternative correctional practices.[76] Nevertheless, he is convinced we will see much more prescriptive penology as we pass through the 1970's, along with three specific trends. There will be continual redefinition of "crime" to limit offenses for which penalties are imposed to those which produce a definite victim. Punishment policies will be based increasingly upon controlled experiments to test the effectiveness of penalties as general deterrents, rather than upon a passion for revenge. And correctional measures for persistent offenders will become more diverse and flexible, calibrated to the life history of the criminal more than to the seriousness of a particular crime. Here the primary focus will be on facilitating success in legitimate alternatives to crime rather than merely on restraining offenders for some duration of confinement. This means more emphasis on training for legitimate employment and more liberal use of probation and work release programs that allow prisoners to work during the day in the community, returning to confinement at night. Prescriptive penology makes eminently good sense. Though it will not resolve every "challenge of crime in a free society," [77] it is a step in the right direction.

SUGGESTIONS FOR FURTHER READING

A good place to begin the study of criminal behavior, as obviously many others have done, is with E. H. Sutherland's and D. R. Cressey's authoritative textbook, *Criminology* (8th ed., Philadelphia, J. B. Lippincott Co., 1970). A systematic study of the influence of child-training practices and family relations in delinquency is made by A. Bandura and R. H. Walters in *Adolescent Aggression* (New York, The Ronald Press Co., 1959). *Children Who Hate,* by F. Redl and D. Wineman (New York, The Free Press of Glencoe, 1951) contains one of the most detailed descriptions of ego functions that has yet appeared. For a vivid account of the lives and thoughts of youth gang members, see L. Yablonsky, *The Violent Gang* (New York, The Macmillan Co., 1962).

The Report of the President's Commission on Law Enforcement and Administration of Justice, *The Challenge of Crime in a Free Society* (New York, E. P. Dutton Co., 1968) is an extremely informative and authoritative source of general information about crime and delinquency, which was written by the nation's leading experts in criminology. The Federal Bureau of Investigation publishes each year

[75] D. Glaser, *Adult Crime and Social Policy* (Englewood Cliffs, N. J.: Prentice-Hall, Inc., 1972), p. 105.

[76] *Ibid.,* pp. 109–10.

[77] This is the title chosen for the Report of the President's Commission, *op. cit.*

a compendium of valuable statistics on crime and law enforcement, *Crime in the United States: Uniform Crime Reports* (Washington, D. C., Government Printing Office, 1973). *Crime and Justice* (New York, Basic Books, Inc., 1971) is a useful collection of papers by leading authorities, edited by L. Radzinowicz and M. E. Wolfgang. *Modern Criminals* (Chicago, Aldine Publishing Co., 1970), edited by J. F. Short, Jr., presents a selection of papers with a sociological slant on various types of criminals; the papers were previously published in *Trans*-action magazine. Daniel Glaser's *Adult Crime and Social Policy* (Englewood Cliffs, N. J., Prentice-Hall, Inc., 1972) is an extremely erudite and provocative analysis of crime as a social problem.

H. Cleckley's *The Mask of Sanity* (4th ed., St. Louis, C. V. Mosby Co., 1964) is a thorough study of the psychopathic personality, liberally illustrated with interesting histories. The whole subject is well reviewed, with a study on treatment, by W. and J. McCord, *The Psychopath: An Essay on the Criminal Mind* (Princeton, N. J.: Van Nostrand Reinhold, 1964). R. D. Hare's *Psychopathology: Theory and Research* (New York, John Wiley & Sons, Inc., 1970) is a brief, well written volume on the same subject, with emphasis on the somatic basis of the disorder. *In Cold Blood* (New York: Random House Inc., 1965), though written by a literary figure, Truman Capote, is an extremely compelling psychological study of two extraordinary criminals that is well worth reading.

10

Drug Dependence

What do tobacco, alcohol, and narcotics have in common? Obviously, they all contain chemicals that affect the central nervous system in a way experienced as pleasurable but are hazardous to health if taken in immoderate amounts. More importantly, from a clinical viewpoint, their intoxicating effects may acquire a compulsive allure that is so powerful as to defy rational control. There is probably no sphere of psychopathology where the demarcation from normal behavior is so difficult to draw. Unfortunately, there is no mistaking the damage done by excessive drug use; that is easily measured in rates of disease, mortality, traffic accidents, divorce, suicide, and crime.

Each of these forms of drug dependence has a long history reaching back many centuries, but they have become a much more serious clinical and social problem in recent years as the availability of drugs has increased. Drug dependence may be regarded as a disorder of modern technological society because drugs serve as auxiliaries for coping with the recurrent psychological stresses of modern living. Useful auxiliaries should refresh and sustain a person under stress, as lunch breaks, energetic physical exercise, and favorite hobbies do. But drugs generate needs that seem to expand as stress increases, and these can become insatiable and immune to reasoned moderation. These needs are often not so much physical as social and psychological. Recurrent themes are that the drugs stimulate or "turn on," soothe or relax, create a friendly mood, bolster self-confidence, facilitate sexual performance, yield insight, or help you to forget. Examined closely, these reports suggest that people who use drugs are bored, tense, alienated, insecure, sexually inhibited, confused and worried—not just "hooked" on chemicals. Considering how widespread the use of drugs has become, it seems that drug dependence reflects disorder in our way of life, as well as

pathology in the individuals themselves. Our primary business is to understand the individuals, though we should not lose sight of the larger social
issues.

We shall begin with smoking, the most common and least psychologically
crippling form of drug dependence, then proceed to the more severe forms.

SMOKING

The facts about tobacco are rather simple, not nearly as ambiguous to
the impartial observer as the great controversy surrounding it would lead
one to believe. Annual per-capita cigarette consumption in the United
States increased from less than 50 at the turn of the century to about 4,200
in 1968.[1] At the same time consumption of other forms of tobacco—pipe
and chewing tobacco and cigars—has declined substantially. The rapid increase in cigarette smoking reached a plateau in the early 1960's, probably
because of the growing suspicion that it might endanger physical health.[2]
From 1957 on there were various public statements by Surgeons General of
the United States reporting with increasing confidence the causal connection
between smoking and various lung and heart diseases, most notably cancer of
the lung. In 1964 the Advisory Committee on Smoking and Health published its report documenting the hazards. They assembled evidence from
animal experiments, clinical and autopsy studies, and population studies, all
of which were consistent with the conclusion that cigarette smoking causes
cancer and other diseases of the respiratory system and contributes to a
variety of other diseases of the heart, circulatory system, and abdomen.
The most compelling evidence came from prospective studies that kept
track of 1,123,000 men starting in 1951 and included 37,400 who died
before 1964. The investigators compared the death rates of smokers and
non-smokers from various diseases.[3] Among smokers there were almost
eleven times as many deaths from lung cancer. The mortality ratios were
less, but still overwhelmingly impressive, for bronchitis and emphysema
(6.1), cancer of the larynx (5.4), oral cancer (4.1), cancer of the esophagus
(3.4), peptic ulcer (2.8), and other circulatory diseases (2.6). Overall, 68
per cent more smokers than non-smokers died from all causes. Moreover,
the death rates were highly correlated with the number of cigarettes smoked
each day and the duration of the smoking habit.

It was predictable that cigarete consumption would decline, and it did

---

[1] U. S. Public Health Service, *Smoking and Health,* Report of the Advisory Committee
to the Surgeon General of the Public Health Service (Washington, D. C.: U. S. Department of Health, Education and Welfare, 1964), Public Health Service Publication No.
1103, p. 26; B. Mausner and E. S. Platt, *Smoking: A Behavioral Analysis* (New York: Pergamon Press, 1971), p. 1.

[2] W. I. Skinner, *Tobacco and Health: The Other Side of the Coin* (New York: Vantage
Press, 1970), p. 60.

[3] U. S. Public Health Service, *op. cit.,* p. 29.

in 1964 by 2 per cent.[4] But anyone familiar with habitual smoking could also predict that it would rise in 1965 to about the same level as in 1963. What this and a multitude of experimental studies showed is that new information about health hazards may change attitudes about the danger and *temporarily* reduce smoking, but over the long term it has little effect on smoking behavior.[5] In 1966 a law was passed that required every cigarette package sold in this country to display prominently the following warning: "Caution: Cigarette Smoking May be Hazardous to Your Health." Much more stringent measures were proposed in Congress, but they failed. Tobacco is a $10 billion industry that spends over $250 million annually on advertising, and 21 of the 50 states derive a substantial portion of their income from tobacco production.[6]

Subsequent reports from the Public Health Service confirmed and strengthened the conclusions of the first report.[7] They showed that some of the initial conclusions were too conservative; for example, it was found that the mortality ratios for smokers of more than a pack a day are as high as 30.[8] As the evidence mounted, pressure on government agencies increased until all cigarette advertising was finally banned from radio and television in 1971.

A Gallup poll in 1969 indicated that the message was not only getting through—that had already happened in 1964—but also having some effect. The survey showed that 40 per cent of a national sample of adults smoked cigarettes, as contrasted with 45 per cent of those polled in 1958. A third of the non-smokers had previously smoked but given it up, and 41 per cent of the smokers reported that they had cut down on cigarettes. The wonder is that *any* rational person would continue smoking when he knew and understood the facts. Continued smoking by so many people suggests formidable use of the defense mechanism of *denial*. Despite lip service to the proposition that smoking is harmful to health, many people deny their own personal vulnerability in order to continue servicing their lips with cigarettes. To understand such a strange compulsion we need to know what makes smoking so gratifying.

---

[4] Skinner, *op. cit.*, p. 27.

[5] Mausner and Platt, *op. cit.*, p. 105; J. W. Swinehart, "Changes Over Time in Student Reactions to the Surgeon General's Report on Smoking and Health," *American Journal of Public Health*, LVI (1966), pp. 2023–27.

[6] W. G. Meserve, "Congressional Action on Smoking and Health," in E. F. Borgatta and R. R. Evans, ed., *Smoking, Health and Behavior* (Chicago: Aldine Publishing Co., 1968), p. 259.

[7] U.S. Public Health Service, *Use of Tobacco: Practices, Attitudes, Knowledge, and Beliefs—Fall 1964 and Spring 1966* (U.S. Department of Health, Education and Welfare, Public Health Service, National Clearinghouse for Smoking and Health, 1969); U.S. Public Health Service, *The Health Consequences of Smoking: A Public Health Service Review— 1967 and 1968 Supplement* (Washington, D.C.: U.S. Department of Health, Education and Welfare, 1967 and 1968), Public Health Service Publication No. 1696.

[8] D. Horn, "The Health Consequences of Smoking, in Borgatta and Evans, *op. cit.*, p. 74.

The Tobacco Habit [9]

Most people begin smoking before they are 20 because it is symbolically associated with adult status, independence, adventure, and attractiveness. The smoking habit is both acquired and maintained for social reasons. Initially, the group pressures for social conformity are great and smoking, once initiated, becomes a powerful cue symbolizing affiliation, group cohesion, and the sharing of pleasure. It is easy to observe that when one person "lights up" after a meal or at a party, other smokers in the group find it difficult not to follow suit. The rewards most often cited for smoking are that it relaxes and reduces tension.

Nicotine is a mild stimulant that is not especially toxic. Tars are the principal cancer-causing component of cigarette smoke, but the stimulating properties of nicotine may play a significant etiological role in cardiovascular diseases. Smoking is best characterized as an *habituation* rather than an *addiction* because there is no physical "abstinence syndrome" upon quitting. Discontinuation is hard, as with any habit, but breaking the chemical dependence is less difficult than interrupting the psychogenic urges. "Nicotine fits" are mild signs of emotional disturbance more attributable to being deprived of a desired object than to physiological need for nicotine. For this reason treatments aimed at counteracting the chemical or sensory needs established by smoking have been generally unfruitful, whereas those aimed at breaking the psychogenic urges have been more successful.

The World Health Organization offers four distinctions between drug addiction and drug habituation.[10] In contrast to an addict, an habituated person desires to continue taking the drug but does not have an overwhelming compulsion to get it at all costs; shows little or no tendency to increase the dose; manifests some degree of psychic dependence on the effect of the drug but no physical dependence and hence no abstinence syndrome; and does not carry his behavior to a point that is detrimental to society. Being an habituation, smoking is not presumed to reflect serious personality defects from underlying psychological disorders that might become manifest in other ways if the drug is removed.

In summary, the habitual use of tobacco is related primarily to psychological and social drives. It improves the self-image, fosters feelings of social affiliation, and relaxes tension. The habit is reinforced and perpetuated by the chemical actions of nicotine on the central nervous system, which explains why nicotine-free tobacco and other substitutes do not yield satisfaction. There is some evidence that smokers are more neurotic than average and more extroverted, but the latter might be an *effect* of

---

9 This review is based primarily on U. S. Public Health Service, 1964, *op. cit.*, pp. 32–34 and 349–79, and on Mausner and Platt, *op. cit.*, pp. 6–15.

10 World Health Organization, *Seventh Report by the Expert Committee on Addiction-Producing Drugs* (Technical Report Series No. 116, 1957).

greater exposure to social stimuli and social influence rather than a cause for smoking. There is no question that smoking increases under temporary stress, so it evidently serves a tranquilizing function.

The Will To Break the Habit

The first step in breaking the smoking habit is a firm decision to stop. Mark Twain was a devoted pipe and cigar smoker often quoted as saying he could quit with the greatest of ease and had in fact done so "hundreds of times." He would point out that life is nothing more than one calculated risk after another and "nobody ever comes out of it alive." Obviously treatment stands little chance of success in a happy recidivist like Mark Twain. However, even firm resolve is often not sufficient to ensure success. It is remarkable that two renowned psychologists as committed to rationality as Gordon Allport and Sigmund Freud should die of cancer because they could not stop smoking. Allport smoked cigarettes until he learned that he had terminal lung cancer, less than a year before his death in 1967 at the age of 70. Freud's lifelong war with tobacco is an epic with such poignancy that it merits recounting in some detail.[11]

Freud suffered an attack of influenza in 1894, at the age of 38, which left him with an irregular heartbeat. His best friend and closest associate at the time, Dr. Wilhelm Fliess, informed Freud that this was due to smoking cigars, and ordered him to stop. He tried to stop or cut down his ration, but failed. Later he did stop but his subsequent depression and psychosomatic symptoms proved unbearable and within seven weeks he was smoking heavily again. Fliess persisted in ordering Freud to stop and once more he did—for 14 very long months. He suffered throughout this period and then resumed because the torture was "beyond human power to bear." On another occasion he decided to stop again, since his pulse was very bad and he couldn't keep to a ration of four cigars a day; this time he was smoking again within a month. Freud continued smoking 20 cigars a day, and struggling against the habit, until he developed cancerous lesions of the right palate and jaw in 1923, when he was 67. A successful operation was performed, the first of thirty-three he would have to bear before he died. He was free of cancer for eight years although other places in his mouth began to go through the familiar series of precancerous stages. He was repeatedly warned by eminent specialists whose judgment he trusted that smoking was the cause. Occasionally he tried very hard to stop and thought he had succeeded, but each time he resumed because, so he insisted, it helped him to think. By now Freud was having recognizable attacks of "tobacco angina" whenever he smoked; even partially denicotinized cigars producted cardiac discomfort. In 1930, at 73, Freud was hos-

---

[11] Based on an article by R. Brecher *et al.*, "Report on Smoking and the Public Interest," *Consumers' Union Report* (1963), and on J. I. Rodale, *If You Must Smoke* (Emmaus, Pa.: Rodale Books, Inc., 1970), pp. 253–54.

pitalized for his heart condition. He recovered almost overnight simply by giving up cigars. But after twenty-three days he started smoking a cigar a day. Then two. Then three or four, and soon twenty again. In 1936, at the age of 79, and in the midst of his endless series of mouth and jaw operations for cancer, there was more heart trouble, which was again relieved as soon as he stopped smoking. Freud was, of course, a peculiarly interested analyst of compulsive habits and he was thoroughly disgusted by his own inability to break the smoking habit. By now his jaw had been entirely removed and an artificial jaw substituted; he was almost constantly in pain; often he could not speak or eat or swallow. Still he smoked an endless series of cigars until he died of cancer in 1939, at the age of 83, after many years of intense suffering.

Many might feel that Freud's case was so extreme that he was in fact *physiologically* dependent on cigars, but it is clear that he was not. The crucial test was during abstinence: at no time that he quit, cold turkey, did he have withdrawal symptoms (e.g., fever, chills, nausea, delirium) such as are found in alcoholics or heroin addicts. Quite the contrary, his physical health improved because of relief from nicotine stimulation. That he suffered so abominably demonstrates that *psychological* dependence is not to be dismissed lightly. Freud's sensory and emotional needs had become so structured around smoking that the courageous will to stop, which he amply demonstrated, was outweighed by the attendant costs to his whole emotional economy. Let us therefore not underestimate the power or tenacity of psychological habituation.

Influencing Smoking Behavior

Three kinds of measures have been used to limit smoking: educational and public information campaigns; restrictions on the sale, advertising, and use of tobacco; and various forms of treatment for the smoking habit. Early reports have shown little success in any of them. Public information has quite effectively persuaded most people of the health hazards in smoking, but regular smokers lag behind ex-smokers and non-smokers in accepting this conclusion.[12] To prevent the development of habitual smoking, several educational experiments have been attempted in public schools. These also have succeeded in making the children's attitudes toward smoking more negative without influencing their action very much.[13] The legislative actions to raise taxes on tobacco, require the warning on every cigarette package, and restrict advertising in the media have been too recent to judge their impact. While tobacco consumption shows signs of slight decline, the impact has by no means been substantial.

12 J. Wakefield, ed., *Influencing Smoking Behavior*, Report of the Committee for Research in Smoking Habits to the Norwegian Cancer Society (Geneva: International Union Against Cancer, 1969), Technical Report Series, Vol. 3, pp. 23–28.
13 H. Leventhal, "Experimental Studies of Anti-Smoking Communications," in Borgatta and Evans, *op. cit.*, pp. 96–98.

Various treatments for the smoking habit have been tried, including nicotine substitutes like *lobelin,* placebo therapy, psychotherapy, group therapy, aversive conditioning, and tranquilizing drugs. One ingenious procedure was derived from an operant conditioning rationale. The premise was that smoking behavior is usually maintained by a regular pattern of social cues in the daily rituals: mealtimes, social gatherings, coffee breaks, stress periods, and so on. Therefore, smokers were equipped with an electric timing mechanism programmed to ring a bell at random times throughout the day as a signal to smoke. Then and only then they were to light up. In this way the smoking habit would be dissociated from the powerful social cues and attached instead to various *irregular* places and times of the day, so it would later be easier to give up smoking altogether. Most treatments for the smoking habit have had results like those reported at the Norwegian "weaning clinics": dramatic success immediately followed by many relapses, especially in the first few months after treatment.[14] Follow-up studies showed that 85 per cent stopped smoking by the end of treatment, irrespective of method, but the number of "cures" dropped to 30 per cent after six months and to 16 per cent after eighteen months. The latter figure is possibly no larger than the number who would have given up smoking without treatment.

William Thackeray, the nineteenth-century novelist, wrote: "I vow and believe that it [smoking] has been one of the greatest creature-comforts of my life—a kind companion, a gentle stimulant, an amiable anodyne [pain killer], a cementer of friendship." [15] Apparently a lot of people agree, both before and after treatment. If it just didn't do such unfortunate things to the lungs and heart. . . .

PSYCHOACTIVE DRUG DEPENDENCE

Because the "drug problem" has forced itself rather dramatically into public awareness in recent years, it comes as a surprise to many people that dependence on psychoactive drugs has a history reaching back thousands of years. In some cultures drug addiction is as common and as widely condoned as alcohol abuse is in the United States today. There is good reason, however, to argue that the magnitude of the drug problem has changed. Partly this is because the number of drug abusers has increased substantially. More important is the sudden upswing in detrimental effects upon society at large. It has been estimated that $3 billion in thefts each year and more than half of all crimes against property in New York City are committed to maintain heroin habits. Drug overdose and drug-related crimes of violence are now the leading cause of death

14 Wakefield, *op. cit.,* p. 67.
15 Skinner, *op. cit.,* p. 97.

between ages 15 and 35 in New York and other metropolitan cities.[16] Probably the greatest cause of concern is the growing proportion of addicts among younger age groups and minority races, where it can be expected that the users take to drugs because of immaturity or their disadvantaged status in society.[17] Whereas previously drug dependence was concentrated among whites and distributed throughout the adult age range, now most users are minority group members in their twenties or teens.

The psychological reasons for taking psychoactive drugs are not much different from those for smoking tobacco or drinking alcohol: pleasure, stimulation, relaxation, social facilitation, and so on. But the effects can be much more distinctive and emphatic, which probably explains in large part how easily they can induce dependency. There are, of course, wide differences in the effects of various psychoactive drugs. The simplest way to classify them is according to their pharmacological effects, as stimulants ("uppers") or depressants ("downers"). However, we shall consider them in five groupings that conform to the distinctive ways in which they are used, in each case focusing on one particular drug for illustration.

Marihuana [18]

Marihuana is obtained from the dried or crushed leaves and flowering tops of cannabis, an Indian hemp plant which grows wild in many parts of the world, including the United States. Typically, the small crushed fragments are rolled into thin homemade cigarettes, called joints, that are smoked for an intoxicating effect. Although illegal in many countries, marihuana continues to be used by millions, especially in Asia and Africa, just as it has been for several thousand years. The use of "pot" has shown the sharpest increase of all the psychoactive drugs in this country, especially on college campuses. Health authorities believe that eight to twelve million Americans have used the drug at least once in their lives, though estimates run as high as twenty-five million.[19] Perhaps a million of these are "pot-heads" who make chronic marihuana intoxication a way of life. Marihuana does not cause physical dependence, as do heroin, barbiturates, and some tranquilizers, but the most recent evidence shows that the body *can* develop some tolerance to the drug at sufficiently high dose levels, making

16 P. Whitten and I. Robertson, "A Way to Control Heroin Addiction," *Boston Sunday Globe,* May 21, 1972, pp. 38–42.

17 H. F. Fraser, "Patterns of Abuse of Narcotics: An Historical Review," in C. J. D. Zarafonetis, ed., *Drug Abuse: Proceedings of the International Conference* (Philadelphia: Lea and Febiger, 1972), p. 146.

18 This review is based on a U. S. Public Health Service brochure, *Marihuana: Some Questions and Answers* (Washington, D.C.: U. S. Department of Health, Education and Welfare, 1970), Public Health Service Publication No. 1829.

19 U. S. Public Health Service, *Marihuana and Health,* Second Annual Report to Congress from the Secretary of Health, Education and Welfare (Washington, D. C.: Government Printing Office, 1972), p. 38a.

increasingly larger doses necessary to get the same effects.[20] Many scientists believe that it can produce psychological dependence if taken regularly.

Hashish is the potent dark brown resin from the tops of high quality cannabis. Because of the high concentration of resin, it is often five or six times stronger than marihuana, although the principal drug ingredient, *tetrahydrocannibol* (THC), is the same. Therefore, the physical and psychological effects are quite similar, differing only in intensity. The main effects of cannabis are stimulative, although in very large doses this shifts toward depressant effects. The subjective experience depends greatly on the user's expectations, the circumstances, and the strength and quantity of the drug used. Typically time is distorted and seems much extended; five minutes may seem like an hour. Space may seem enlarged or otherwise distorted. Sounds and colors are intensified. Thought becomes dream-like, and it is not unusual to believe that one is thinking better. Sensory illusions are common, but hallucinations or delusions are rare, except with heavy doses. Frequently the user withdraws passively and just savors his "high." Occasionally uncontrollable laughter or crying may occur. Sometimes the effects are quite frightening or very unpleasant, giving rise to unfounded suspiciousness or marked anxiety. In a few cases, especially among emotionally vulnerable youths, such reactions may border on panic or lead to a paranoid state or a temporary break with reality.

From a clinical viewpoint, it is known that marihuana interferes with thinking, speech, and recent memory. It can impair judgment and logical thinking while at the same time causing the user to believe that his mental functioning is as good as ever or even enhanced by the drug. Performing any complex task that requires good reflexes and clear thinking may be impaired, making such tasks as driving particularly dangerous.

The federal laws against possessing, selling, or giving away marihuana were moderated in 1970, classifying such offenses as misdemeanors rather than felonies, but the potential penalties still remain large: up to one year's imprisonment and/or a $5,000 maximum fine. The penalties are even more severe for second and subsequent offenses, especially for providing it to minors under 18 years of age. The laws are severe because for many years marihuana was considered to be like a narcotic, and there has been

---

[20] This may startle some readers who have experimented with pot occasionally and found that it took less to get "high" each successive time they smoked. This "reverse tolerance" or sensitization effect is attributable more to psychological factors than to the physiological action of the drug. The facts are these. In two recent double-blind studies, experienced marihuana smokers were unable to distinguish between the intoxicating effects of active marihuana cigarettes and placebo "joints" with the active drug (THC) removed. On the other hand, rats and pigeons have developed *profound* tolerance to THC. Moreover, older studies in the 1940's showed that chronic marihuana smokers develop minimal but definite tolerance from smoking daily for one month. Therefore, there is little doubt that tolerance can develop to the active ingredients of cannabis if the amounts taken are large enough. The opposite effect noted by occasional users is very much dependent upon one's personal expectations of marihuana smoking. E. F. Domino, "Panel Discussion: Hallucinogens and Marihuana," in Zarafonetis, *op. cit.*, pp. 354–55.

strong resistance to relaxing the legal restrictions against it because it is well known that about 80 per cent of narcotic addicts have used marihuana previously. Therefore it is believed by some that smoking pot leads to (causes) the abuse of other, more dangerous drugs like heroin. In fact, very few of the millions who use marihuana go on to use narcotics, so no causal connection has been established. It is probably true that some persons who are predisposed to abuse a drug may be more likely to abuse other, stronger drugs, especially if they are very young and emotionally unstable. It is not yet known how much easy access to marihuana may influence such people to try narcotics. The opinion of experts on drug abuse seems now to be shifting clearly toward reducing the legal penalties against marihuana use.[21] In discussion of this issue reference is frequently made to Prohibition, the "noble experiment" that failed to shut off the flow of alcohol, which is a more costly menace to society than marihuana. If 25,000,000 Americans have used pot and a third of them still do it regularly, then enforcement of laws against using it becomes ludicrous. Recent trends in law and public opinion seem to be coming around to the view that marihuana use and abuse should be treated as a social and medical problem rather than a legal one. We will have more to say later about "decriminalizing" drug abuse. However, we should not allow impassioned disputations of how innocuous marihuana is to obscure an indisputable fact: like *all* in*toxic*ants, marihuana is toxic or poisonous to the body and especially to the brain. There is no doubt that it is physically harmful; the only questions are *how* harmful it is, physically and socially, and how much damage individuals and society are willing to accept from its use. These are the issues that require further empirical investigation.

Hallucinogens

The best known and most fully researched hallucinogenic or psycho-tomimetic drug is lysergic acid diethylamide. Since most people can't pronounce the last word, under the influence of the drug or otherwise, it is usually referred to as LSD or acid.[22] Other less known but powerful hallucinogens include peyote, mescaline, psilocybin, CMT, and STP. LSD is a man-made chemical obtained from a fungus that grows as a rust on rye grain. It is so powerful that one ounce of LSD provides 300,000 average doses. An average dose amounts to a tiny speck of colorless, tasteless, ordorless material that is usually taken in pill or capsule form, although the amount of active material is so small it can be placed in a cube of sugar or almost any other food. Its effects usually last from eight to twelve hours.

21 L. Grinspoon, *Marihuana Reconsidered* (Cambridge, Mass.: Harvard University Press, 1971); J. H. Brenner, "Drugs and Society," in Zarafonetis, *op. cit.*, pp. 115–24.

22 This review is drawn mainly from a U. S. Public Health Service brochure, *LSD: Some Questions and Answers* (Washington, D. C.: U. S. Department of Health, Education and Welfare, 1970), Public Health Service Publication No. 1828.

The physical effects are like those of most stimulants: enlarged pupils, flushed face, chilliness, perhaps a rise in temperature and heartbeat, and a slight increase in blood pressure. The psychological effects can be quite dramatic. Marked changes in sensation, especially vision, are typical. Unusual patterns are seen and the meaning of what is seen is transformed. *Synesthesias* occur in which one experience is translated or merged into another so that, for example, smells may be felt or sounds may be seen. Illusions and hallucinations can occur and delusional thoughts are sometimes expressed. The sense of time and of self are strangely altered. Emotional variations are marked, ranging from bliss to horror, sometimes within a single experience. One of the most confusing, yet common, experiences is to feel two strong but opposing feelings at the same time: happy and sad, or depressed and elated, or relaxed and tense. Arms and legs may feel simultaneously heavy and light. The normal feeling of boundaries between one's body and space may be lost. Memory and logical thinking remain intact, up to a point, but they become impaired with larger doses, giving way to feelings of great understanding, new insights, a sense of rebirth. Nearly always these "enlightenments" turn out to be fleeting or spurious. Many experts believe that chronic or continued use of LSD distorts judgment and impairs the ability to concentrate and think rationally. Christopher Mayhew, a member of the British House of Commons, captured the sublime ambiguity of the "psychedelic experience" in a letter to the London Times describing his own experiment with an LSD-type hallucinogenic drug. "I experienced the beatific vision, eternal life, heaven. It was all there as the saints had described it—ecstasy, timelessness, illumination and unity, or if you prefer it, depersonalization, time disturbances, light hallucinations and the disintegration of the ego." Some users believe that LSD fosters creativity because it heightens sense impressions, but objective studies show conclusively that paintings, writings, and other works created under the influence of the drug are noticeably poorer than otherwise. The enhancements claimed are entirely subjective and not consensually valid.

The overwhelming majority of people take LSD for the "high"—to feel better. This may be because they are unable to deal with life's frustrations, or feel alienated. Other reasons given are: curiosity, because friends do it, "kicks," self-understanding, or a search for religious or philosophical insights. Unhappily, not all "trips" produce euphoria, pleasant sensations, and gratifying imagery. Sometimes the trip is a bad one or "bummer" in which the images are terrifying and the emotional state is full of dread and horror. Because of the distorted time sense—a few minutes may drag on like hours—this may seem like a terrible nightmare that will never end. In extreme cases this may lead to panic, as the user grows more and more frightened because he cannot "turn off" the drug's action. He may forget that a drug has changed his thinking and feeling, and fear that he is losing his mind. *Flashbacks,* or recurrences of some of the features of the LSD trip days or months after the last dose, may occur without apparent cause, leading the user to believe that he is becoming psychotic. In some individuals this concern has caused anxiety and depression leading to suicide. Even good trips have led to accidental death. Cases have been reported, for example, where LSD users felt they were invulnerable or could fly and consequently walked in front of moving cars or attempted to fly from high windows, with disastrous results.

An LSD Trip with Extra Mileage

There is some question whether LSD in itself can cause mental illness in an emotionally stable individual, but there is little doubt that the drug can precipitate acute and sometimes long-lasting disorders in susceptible persons. Often those who are most vulnerable emotionally are the most attracted to LSD, in the hope that it will solve their problems or provide "instant insight." A professional psychologist found out about this danger the hard way. He was a clinical researcher and very much interested in the mind-altering potential of the hallucinogens. Early in the 1960's he was corresponding with Professor Timothy Leary, who was experimenting with all sorts of drugs. At one point Leary wrote that he had acquired incredible insights from taking LSD. Among other things he had come to understand that there is but *one mind*. In the fall of 1960 his correspondent also began some experiments with the drug, using volunteers and himself as subjects. Usually he administered small doses, but one time he himself took 2,000 micrograms, a very large dose. A few days after that he delivered an enthusiastic lecture about LSD at a Veterans' hospital. Several clinicians in the audience were struck by a subtle but unmistakable looseness in his thinking. His lecture was slightly grandiose, rather disjointed, and contained several large leaps of inference. No one mentioned a clinical diagnosis of manic psychosis, but there was general consensus among those who attended that this was a very eccentric psychologist. He became increasingly agitated in succeeding weeks, reportedly without taking any more drugs, until he was hospitalized about two months later in such bad shape that he had to be transported to the hospital in a straitjacket. There followed a deep psychotic depression that lasted several months, despite the very best treatment available in an exclusive private hospital. Within weeks after his release and about seven months after the first talk, he delivered another lecture to a professional audience. This time he carefully analyzed the subjective enthusiasm which LSD had created in him initially and then gave a sober account of his long psychotic episode. From this presentation one got the impression that the awesome power of LSD has both enhancing and destructive aspects.

It is not yet known how LSD works in the body, but it seems to affect the levels of certain brain chemicals like serotonin and norepinephrine, and to produce changes in the brain's electrical activity. Animal experiments suggest that the brain's normal filtering and screening processes become blocked, causing it to be flooded with unselected sights and sounds. Chronic LSD users continue to be overloaded with sensory stimulation, which may explain their inability to think clearly and to concentrate on a task or goal. Considering the potent impact of LSD it is not surprising that many studies indicate that it may cause chromosomal damage in the user and offspring.[23] Two cases of acute leukemia have also been attributed to LSD.[24] However, other studies have found contrary results and it is still too soon to conclude that there is a direct link between LSD and chromosomal damage or birth defects. The evidence is sufficiently strong so that women of child-bearing age are particularly urged not to use the drug. The federal penalties for possessing, producing, selling, or giving away LSD illegally are quite severe, and there is not much public sentiment to change them because of the general consensus that it is a dangerous drug.

Stimulants [25]

Cocaine is probably the oldest and most widely used stimulant in the world. For centuries it has been the practice of natives in the Andes Mountains of South America to chew coca leaves, and it is estimated that six million still do so regularly in Bolivia and Peru.[26] The most commonly used stimulants in this country are amphetamine (Benzedrine), dextroamphetamine (Dexedrine), and methamphetamine (Methedrine). Slang terms for these drugs are "pep pills," "bennies," and "speed." They stimulate the central nervous system and are best known for their ability to counteract fatigue and sleepiness. Drivers take them to stay awake on long trips; students take them while cramming for exams; and athletes take them to get "hyped up" for competition, although sporting associations have banned their use.[27] The Japanese used them to reduce aviator and industrial-worker fatigue during World War II, being unaware of their

---

[23] W. W. Nichols, "Genetic Hazards of Drugs of Abuse," in Zarafonetis, *op. cit.*, p. 99; D. B. Louria, "Medical Complications of Illicit Drug Use," *ibid.*, pp. 590–93.

[24] S. Cohen, "Information and Misinformation about Drugs," in J. R. Wittenborn, J. P. Smith, and S. A. Wittenborn, eds., *Communication and Drug Abuse* (Springfield, Ill.: Charles C Thomas, 1970), p. 288.

[25] This section and the two following on sedatives and narcotics are based largely on the U. S. Public Health Service reprint, *Students and Drug Abuse* (Washington, D. C.: Government Printing Office, 1969), pp. 8–10 and 15–16, which was originally published in the NEA journal, *Today's Medicine*, March, 1969. The descriptions of "speeding," "crashing," and violence are taken from J. C. Kramer, "Some Observations On and a Review of the Effect of High-Dose Use of Amphetamines," and R. C. Smith, "Speed and Violence: Compulsive Methamphetamine Abuse and Criminality in the Haight-Asbury District," both in Zarafonetis, *op. cit.*, pp. 253–61 and 435–48.

[26] D. C. Cameron, "The Many Faces of Deviant Drug Use," in Zarafonetis, *op. cit.*, p. 20.

[27] A gold medal for first place in a swimming contest at the 1972 Olympics was revoked when tests after the race showed traces of a stimulant in the winner's urine. For many years the athlete had been taking the drug for an asthmatic condition (see Chapter 12), and he had failed to obtain the necessary clearance to take the drug while competing.

abuse potential.[28] Civilian use in Japan began in 1945 and it was estimated in 1954 that two million Japanese used amphetamines intravenously, with 600,000 believed to be chronic users. Placing the drug on prescription was inadequate to halt the epidemic, so the government passed very stringent laws against its use and initiated a massive educational campaign which finally brought the problem under control by 1958.

Amphetamines stimulate the release of norepinephrine (a substance stored in nerve endings) and concentrate it in the higher centers of the brain. This speeds up the action of the heart and the metabolic processes for converting food into the chemicals the body needs. Besides increasing the heart rate, they are capable of raising the blood pressure, cause heart throbbing and rapid breathing, dilate the pupils, and cause dry mouth, sweating, headache, diarrhea, and pallor. And they depress the appetite. For some of these effects they have been prescribed by physicians to treat overwhelming sleepiness, depression, obesity, and even colds (they shrink the nasal membranes and relieve "stuffy" heads).

Psychologically, amphetamines (in moderate doses) produce feelings of alertness, self-confidence, and well-being. These last for some hours, but eventually they give place to a letdown with mildly depressed feelings. Heavier doses cause jitteriness, irritability, unclear speech, and tension. On very large doses people appear withdrawn, with their emotions dulled and unable to organize their thinking. Speed can drive a person to do things beyond his physical endurance that leave him exhausted. Long-term heavy users are usually irritable and unstable and, like other drug abusers, they show varying degrees of social, intellectual, and emotional breakdown. The most extreme form of breakdown is a toxic paranoid psychosis, usually accompanied by auditory and visual hallucinations, which may require hospitalization. It was previously believed that such effects signified the release of underlying psychotic trends, but scientists and users alike agree now that almost everyone will experience paranoia under sufficiently high and prolonged doses. Abruptly withdrawing the drug from a chronic user can result in a deep and suicidal depression.

Stimulants do not produce physical dependence as do the narcotics, but the body does develop a tolerance so that larger and larger doses are required to feel the effects. Serious abuse stems from extreme psychological dependence on the mental and emotional effects. Often the critical step comes when drugs, which are usually swallowed as pills, are taken instead in liquid form by injection into a vein. This is known as "speeding" or "shooting up." The experience goes far beyond the general well-being that results from moderate doses. The first intravenous injection produces almost immediately an ecstatic experience called a "rush" or "flash" that has been likened to a full body orgasm.[29] Indeed some individuals claim

28 M. H. Seevers, "Drug Dependence and Drug Abuse: A World Problem," *The Phar-macologist*, XII (1970), pp. 172–81.

29 Smith, *op. cit.*, p. 438.

to have reached sexual climax shortly after injection. Before long the
drug is likely to be taken in a spree over a day or two, and gradually the
sprees become longer, the doses larger, and the injections more frequent,
in order to get the same level of "flash" and perpetuate the high. After a
period of several months the user is a "speed freak" who injects the drug
many times a day in large doses, and remains awake continuously for three
to six days, becoming increasingly tense, shaky, and paranoid as the "run"
progresses. The runs are interrupted by bouts of profound sleep, called
"crashing," which last a day or two before another run begins. The severity
of the crash is related to the length of the run, the amount and quality
of the drug taken, and the physical and psychological condition of the user.
For the novice after a short run it is mildly unpleasant, with fatigue, mild
depression, and ravenous hunger. As the length of the run is extended
and the condition of the user deteriorates, the crash includes deep depression, hallucinations, and extreme fatigue, which are so unbearable that
experienced speed freaks try to blot it out by taking a depressant drug such
as a barbiturate or heroin to induce sleep immediately. Alternating the
drugs or taking speed and heroin simultaneously (the "San Francisco Speed-
ball") often leads to narcotic addiction. It is not surprising that most of
the young white heroin addicts in the Haight-Asbury district had previously used speed compulsively.

The pattern of serious drug abuse is fairly regular.[30] Stronger forms of
a drug tend to displace weaker ones. More rapid techniques of acquisition
become preferred to slower forms of absorption. Speed may be taken first
as a pill, then "snorted" for more immediate effect and ultimately injected.
This should come as no surprise to psychologists because immediate reinforcements are the most powerful ones, and a needle in a vein provides
the quickest delivery of a drug to the brain. Experimentally arranged
intravenous self-injection of amphetamines in rats is just as strongly reinforcing, and is characterized by periods of intake and abstinence entirely
analogous to the patterns seen in human speed freaks.[31] Finally, more
dangerous (and expensive) drugs displace less dangerous ones. *Once a person is assimilated in the drug culture,* the steps of progression are predictable: from pot to LSD, from LSD to speed, and from intravenous anything
to intravenous heroin.

The Violence Associated with the Speed Culture

The life style of speed freaks is so frantic that most people not on speed
can't stand to be around them, so they congregate together, talk and
fantasize and bicker endlessly, and share their plans and dreams for the

30 S. Cohen, "Patterns of Drug Abuse—1970," in Zarafonetis, *op. cit.,* p. 337.
31 R. Pickens, R. Weisch, and L. E. McGuire, "Methamphetamine Reinforcement in
Rats," *Psychonomic Science,* VIII (1967), pp. 361–72; R. Pickens and W. C. Harris, "Self-
administration of D-Amphetamine by Rats," *Psychopharmacologia,* XII (1968), pp. 158–63.

future. A lot of attention is naturally given to maintaining their supply of drugs. Occasionally there are sudden outbursts of violence, especially if the group has been "running" for a long time on large doses of speed. On long runs their activity becomes very frantic and irrational. Roger Smith cites as an example the torture-rape of a teen-age girl who was a heavy user of speed and barbiturates. She was accused by another girl in a large group of stealing a barbiturate pill. The girl denied the theft, but the accuser began to assault her. This focused the attention of the entire group on the victim, and they proceeded to "train" or gang-rape her. When a member of the group was later asked why he didn't try to stop it, he explained that this would put him on her side, in the minority, which is a very dangerous place. "You have to imagine how heavy those people were into that; if you go against them you best come out shooting."

Because the law prohibits (albeit ineffectively) the nonmedical use of stimulants, the speed scene is a criminal subculture in which most users lead a marginal existence. In order to maintain that existence and provide a steady supply of drugs, it is common to resort to prostitution, robbery, or one of several "hustles" involving the distribution of drugs to other users. The primary cause of violence is related to the practice of "burning," or selling highly adulterated drugs. A street hustler usually deals in small quantities, hoping to realize enough profit to pay for the cost of his own drugs. But in the euphoria and expansiveness created by an injection he may shoot all the speed he had purchased for resale and then have no money to buy additional drugs. Then he may package any substance that looks like speed and attempt to sell it on the streets. He may be lucky for a while, but veterans in the speed culture consider "burning" an offense which cannot go unpunished. After all, there is no police force to ensure the quality of the drugs they buy. Punishment may take the form of a large money payment or a beating. Some "burn artists" are knifed or shot. Many of the overdose deaths in the drug culture are not accidental, but are deliberately executed sentences. In one instance, a burn artist was given the choice of being shot or taking a massive dose of LSD (ten 500-mcg. capsules). He chose the latter and was discovered by the police days later, wandering the streets naked and totally incoherent.

The medical complications of chronic stimulant abuse or an overdose are severe hypertension, cerebral hemorrhage, hepatitis (from poor hygienic techniques during injection), convulsions, coma, and sudden death.[32] Angrist and Gershon reported the case of a 24-year-old man who had taken amphetamine heavily for two years, shooting a "spoon" at a time several times a day.[33] He came to a hospital after injecting a "spoon" of street speed because he began to feel influenced by electric waves and forces possibly emanating from a machine operated by "people in the back-

[32] Louria, *op. cit.*, p. 589.
[33] B. Angrist and S. Gershon, "Possible Dose-Response Relationships in Amphetamine Psychosis," in Zarafonetis, *op. cit.*, pp. 264–65.

ground," and became convinced that a police raid was imminent. To avoid prosecution, he had swallowed the remaining three "spoons" in his possession and then jumped from a second-story fire escape to elude his persecutors. In the hospital he showed auditory hallucinations which cleared after two days, and ideas of influence that diminished gradually over two weeks. The diagnostic impression after clearing was chronic paranoid schizophrenia with superimposed intoxication. About a year later he was caught in an actual police raid and swallowed what is estimated at 10 to 15 grams of amphetamine to destroy the evidence. (Even one gram is a very large dose.) Three hours later he was a raving maniac, throwing his arms up in the air and rolling his head around, so far gone that he didn't realize what was going on. He was taken to a hospital in shock and assisted by a respirator, but he died less than fifteen hours after taking the overdose.

The graffito sometimes written on the wall of a drug clinic reads: "Just give me Librium or give me Meth." [34] It reflects an attitude of many young drug users who come to the clinic because they just took the "wrong drug" or too much of the "right" one, but do not question the life style of drug involvement. In the case just reviewed, one could claim that the young man's premature death was due to an overdose caused by the criminalization of drug dependence. That is partly true but an additional cause of death was a whole life style gone wrong. Speed kills.

Sedatives

These are a large group of drugs made for medical purposes to relax the central nervous system. The best known are the barbiturates, made from barbituric acid, which was first manufactured in 1846. There are long-acting, slow-starting forms like phenobarbital (Luminal) and amobarbital (Amytal). The most commonly abused forms are short-acting, but with immediate effect, like phenobarbital sodium (Nembutal) and secobarbital sodium (Seconal). Slang terms for these are "barbs" and "goof balls."

In normal doses barbiturates mildly depress the action of the nerves, skeletal muscles, and heart. They slow down the heart rate and breathing, and lower the blood pressure. For these effects they are beneficial for diagnosing and treating mental illness, relaxing patients before and during surgery, and treating tension disorders like ulcers, high blood pressure, epilepsy, and insomnia. In higher doses the effects resemble drunkenness, with confusion, slurred speech, and staggering. There is impairment of the ability to think, to concentrate, or to work, and emotional control is weakened. Users may become irritable, angry, and combative, and then finally fall into deep sleep.

[34] D. E. Smith, "A Physician's View of the Adolescent Drug Scene," in Zarafonetis, *op. cit.*, p. 273.

Barbiturates distort sense perception and slow down motor reactions, so they are an important cause of automobile accidents, especially when combined with alcohol abuse. Barbiturates tend to heighten the effects of alcohol, which explains in part why one study found more than half of the psychiatric patients who abused sedatives had also abused alcohol at some time.[35] Reactions to the drug are stronger at some times than others and users become confused about how many pills they have taken, which leads to accidental overdose and sometimes death. Barbiturates are a leading cause of accidental poison deaths in the United States and one of the most common means for committing suicide.

Almost all sedatives produce physical as well as psychological dependence. Barbiturate addiction is considered by some experts more difficult to cure than narcotic addiction. The body requires increasingly larger doses to feel their effects. Abrupt withdrawal of the drug produces an abstinence syndrome with cramps, nausea, delirium, convulsions, and in some cases sudden death. Therefore withdrawal should take place under medical supervision in a hospital with gradually reduced dosages over a period of several weeks. Several months are required for the body to return to normal.

The sale of sedatives, like that of stimulants, is closely regulated by federal agencies. All sales to the public must be obtained by prescription. The penalties for illicit dealing in the drugs include heavy fines and imprisonment. However, one in four of all the prescriptions doctors write for mood-affecting drugs is for a barbiturate, and probably an equally large supply is obtained illegally, without prescription. A large number of the people who abuse sedatives are mature adults, businessmen, housewives, and professionals, who lead productive lives and use the drugs to relax tension, blow off steam, and forget their worries. Because of their respectability, barbiturate addiction was not regarded as a very serious social problem until it found its way recently into the urban youth culture, where in combination with speed and heroin it contributed to crime and decadence and the inexorable corruption of younger and younger lives. Then the magnitude of the problem and the dangers of these drugs became clear. This evolution of social consciousness may seem self-serving and unfair to young dissidents who believe in their right to use the drugs as they choose, but behind it lies a sound, if vaguely articulated, principle. There is tolerance for individuals to abuse drugs to the extent of damaging or even destroying their own lives, but society sets limits when such abuse reaches epidemic proportions and especially when the individual's abuse impinges substantially on the lives of others. Hopefully, following the Japanese example, individuals will set their own limits when the dangers of the drugs are publicized widely enough.

35 W. E. Bakewell and A. Wikler, "Symposium: Non-narcotic Addiction. Incidence in a University Hospital Psychiatric Ward," *Journal of the American Medical Association,* CXCVI (1966), pp. 710–13.

Narcotics

The principal narcotics are opium and pain-killing drugs derived from opium, which is obtained from the juice of the poppy fruit. The derivatives include heroin, the most widely used by far, morphine, paregoric, and codeine. The opiates can be taken orally or inhaled, but they are most often injected intravenously. Heroin depresses the central nervous system and reduces hunger, thirst, and the sex drive. For this reason many heroin addicts lose tremendous amounts of weight and suffer from malnutrition. Emotionally, heroin reduces tension, relieves fears and worries, and creates a glowing sense of euphoria. Its effectiveness in killing pain accounts for its principal medical use. The "high" makes a person feel very sure of himself, and this is followed by a period of inactivity bordering on stupor. It is well known that heroin leads to addiction, both physically and psychologically. Once the habit is started, the body develops a tolerance for the drug. Because it is outlawed for non-medical use, heroin is expensive on the street. As the habit gets bigger and more expensive—some habits cost hundreds of dollars a day—the addict is usually forced into a life of crime to pay for his drugs. Like the speed freaks described earlier, most narcotic addicts pay their way through drug dealing, prostitution, and a variety of street "hustles." Even more of the serious crimes of burglary, armed robbery, and forgery are associated with narcotics. Once crime and degradation have become a way of life, the emotional dependence on heroin is locked in as a way to escape facing life. The abstinence syndrome upon withdrawal can be quite severe, as with barbiturates, but the symptoms may be alleviated under medical treatment. Fear of the withdrawal keeps many addicts "hooked."

The health of an addict is often bad. He may be sick one day from the effects of withdrawal and sick the next from an overdose. He can never be sure of the purity of the heroin he buys on the street and this leads to accidental overdoses. His life span is drastically shortened. The medical complications of chronic narcotic abuse are heart infection, tetanus and hepatitis (both from unhygienic use of needles), and various respiratory and circulatory difficulties.[36]

According to a conservative estimate there are 108,000 narcotic addicts in the United States.[37] Other estimates have run higher, and one reached a total of 700,000.[38] Among black addicts, who are in the majority, drug use often starts around 16 or 17 years of age; the users are likely to be already socially deviant, coming from broken homes, being school dropouts, marital failures, and chronically unemployed.[39] They are usually in trouble with their families and almost always in trouble with the law.

[36] Louria, *op. cit.*, p. 585.
[37] Ball and Chambers, *op. cit.*, p. 5.
[38] Whitten and Robertson, *op. cit.*, p. 38.
[39] Ball and Chambers, *op. cit.*, pp. 8 and 200.

Immaturity and alienation permeate the descriptions of most addicts. Perhaps the most uncharitable characterization is made by Chuck Dederich, a former alcoholic and the founder of Synanon, which will be discussed shortly: "Dope fiends shoot dope. As long as they are dope fiends, they are not much good; they are slobs and thieves, with the temperaments of nasty little children. When they stop using dope, they're something else again. They need self-respect and then general respect more than they do sympathy." [40]

A Case History

The life of Charlie Hamer demonstrates that narcotic addiction signifies much more than habitual dependence on a chemical.[41] He was born in 1903 in Henryetta, Oklahoma, the youngest of five children. He was fatherless at the age of one. His mother reared the children with little supervision, for which she had neither the time nor the ability. He was arrested at ten for stealing coal and domestic fowls and at 17 for drunkenness, disturbing the peace, and fighting. At 19 a local Chinese family introduced him to opium, which he smoked for three years. His first hypodermic injection took place at 22 with the residue from an opium pipe. One year later he began using morphine intravenously. This drug was obtained in the pure form from unethical doctors, pharmaceutical houses, and peddlers. He built up a larger tolerance and used 15–25 grains per day, obtaining money for the drugs by theft, robbery, confidence games, and the like. Then he began alternating with cocaine and was introduced to heroin at 30. When he was 34 he migrated to California and was free of drugs for six years but used alcohol to excess. Then he began to use opium again, both orally and by injection, shipped out with the Merchant Marine and for two years used many drugs throughout the world: heroin, cocaine, hashish, morphine, the works. When he returned he used heroin constantly until joining Synanon when he was 56 years old. He was married and divorced three times between the ages of 22 and 44. He was arrested dozens of times for forgery, theft, robbery, vagrancy, suspicion of robbery, possession of narcotics, addiction, and forgery of narcotic prescriptions. Almost half of his adult life was spent in county jails, state penitentiaries, and federal hospitals for addicts.

Psychological Aspects of Drug Abuse

Bearing in mind the different effects of the drugs we have been describing, one might suppose that each user would have his favorite drug and would become addicted only to the one that best fitted his needs. Especially should this be true for "downers" and "uppers"; it seems paradoxical

---

[40] L. Yablonsky, *The Tunnel Back: Synanon* (New York: The Macmillan Co., 1965), p. 379.

[41] *Ibid.*, pp. 16–25.

to crave both unless they have been worked into a complementary temporal pattern. We would guess from everyday experience that there are people who, perhaps as a matter of innate constitution, feel slightly "down" a good deal of the time: quiet types who tire easily, often feel a little sleepy, and never refuse a cup of coffee. Before amphetamine was placed under legal restriction, a small daily dose was sometimes prescribed for people of this type, who reported themselves to be more alert and lively as a result. But for these same people a daily dose of a tranquilizer would be harmful, lowering their energy still further, whereas maintenance doses of a tranquilizing drug are often felt to be indispensable by people who otherwise would suffer all day from tension and jumpy nerves. Eysenck has shown experimentally that extroverts and introverts, as defined by his measuring instruments, respond to different drugs in ways that are reliably different.[42] Are we not therefore entitled to suppose that "speed" abuse will take hold in people who have difficulty getting up speed, that narcotics will get their grip on those who crave a dreamy escape from trouble and pain, and that LSD will seduce people whose habitual boredom is drowned in the excitement of novel, unearthly experiences?

It is not improbable that preferences of this kind exist and influence the course of drug abuse. But there is the case of Charlie Hamer who tried them all, and his case is not unusual. Widespread today is a pattern of drug abuse that includes everything; the use of drugs is accepted as a way of life. The implicit expectation seems to be that one's whole feeling experience, up or down alike, is to be produced and guided by chemical means. The underlying rationale is a caricature of push-button technology. There is a switch, a pill, a drug for every need, including how one feels. The appeal of drugs is that they can switch on all kinds of feelings, soothing, exciting, mystical, even blasting, and one wants to be sure to experience them all. We can infer that the main psychological need satisfied by drugs as a way of life is the need to overcome what might be called an affective anaesthesia. There is a marked parallel here to what we noticed in Chapter 8 when studying encounter groups; there, too, much importance is attached to securing a strong, even violent, expression of feeling. Probably those who crave emotional encounters and those who crave drugs come from overlapping groups, sharing an emptiness of feeling that seems to be common in our time. Another feature of contemporary alienation that adds to the attraction of drugs as a way of life is a deep-seated passivity. As we saw, Ruitenbeek described this quality, often encountered in contemporary young patients, as a seeming unfamiliarity with the expending of personal effort and the making of personal decisions.[43] If one does not have command over one's actions and associated feelings, the temptation may soon become overwhelming to let drugs do it all.

42 H. J. Eysenck, *The Structure of Human Personality* (3rd ed.; London: Methuen & Co., Ltd., 1970).
43 See above, Chapter 8, p. 306.

To the extent that alienation of this sort lies behind drug abuse it is difficult to mobilize the motivation necessary for successful treatment. Many who lead the drug way of life come from grievously depressed backgrounds; one cannot honestly picture for them a glowing future if they kick their habit. Others come from affluent homes, but have rejected the "establishment" in such wholesale terms that no glow is possible in their own picture of the future. The situation illustrates once more the close relation between personal pathology and social conditions. Sometimes anxiety becomes enlisted on the side of treatment: the drug abuser becomes panic-stricken about medical consequences. A more valuable ally, however, is the need for self-respect, and sometimes this need can be rekindled from the ruins that would be considered, objectively, a human wreck.

Treatment for Drug Dependence

Synanon was founded in 1958 and staffed with drug addicts. It was originally housed on the beach in Santa Monica, California, but now has several chapters scattered through the country. Much of the impressive success of this organization in curing addiction comes from recognizing at the start that treatment only works if the addict genuinely wants it to work. Often the crucial test is his initial willingness to undergo the agony of withdrawal by kicking the habit "cold turkey." The two cardinal rules of living at Synanon House are: no drugs and no physical violence. One of the most controversial aspects of the treatment is the verbal-attack therapy employed in the "synanon sessions." This is a form of encounter group experience in which each member takes a turn being challenged, grilled, and criticized for his faults, emotional weaknesses, suspect motives, and behavior at Synanon.[44] The rationale behind this vicious cross-examination is that the fundamental causes for becoming and remaining a drug addict are emotional faults for which a variety of subterfuges and defenses are devised to cover up. Once the secondary symptom of chemical addiction has been cured, the brutal exposure of the synanon sessions is used to uncover the primary emotional pathology. Catharsis is obviously an important mechanism in the treatment. Social support is even more significant.

Consider, for example, Charlie Hamer's "treatment." He was among the first to come to Synanon in 1959, weighing 118 pounds rather than his natural 170, and carrying a life-long heavy habit. Upon entering he met three junkies, all old friends, who were "clean" (free of drugs) and very enthusiastic about Synanon. Charlie couldn't believe it. He spent the first several days on a divan, sick as a dog, trying vainly to persuade some of the other junkies to get him some dope. Two women nursed him day and night, giving him bed baths and wiping up his vomit. Every day Dederich stopped by to shake his hand and taunt him that he could not stick it out.

44 Yablonsky, *op. cit.*, pp. 379–85.

But he did, because he was afraid of his habit and sick of the demoraliza-
tion it caused him. Within a week he kicked the habit and took his first
job, as breakfast cook, but reluctantly. He hadn't bought Synanon; he just
figured to stay thirty days so when he got back to the streets the habit would
cost only about half as much as before. But before long Dederich astonished him by entrusting him with $3 or $4 of the organization's precious
little money to buy groceries and get a meal together. It was a terrific challenge and an important milestone when Charlie managed to get past the
drugstore on that first errand. Within a few months he was chosen as a
director of Synanon. He didn't know what to do about that. He was
flattered and pleased, of course, but also frightened about the responsibility it would entail, and he still was bent on leaving soon. After considering the matter for a few days, a seemingly trivial incident convinced
him of his course of action. He was walking down the hallway on the
second floor, on his way to the toilet, when he saw a cigarette butt on the
floor. He reached down to pick it up and put it in the butt can, and that
started him thinking. If he had acquired such a sense of proprietorship
that he was now picking up butts off the floor, then he must have decided
already to stay at Synanon. The next morning he went downstairs with a
clear look in his eye and started acting like a director, poking his nose into
things he didn't know anything about, like other people's responsibilities.
Charlie Hamer has remained "clean" at Synanon ever since. He has been
in charge of the young-adult group and for a time directed the Synanon
House in Reno, Nevada. Understandably, he has been an outstanding role
model for younger members, who could derive hope for themselves from
the example of his personal success.

The Synanon treatment, which is best characterized as rehabilitation,
has been emulated elsewhere, for example, at Daytop Village in New York
City. There are limitations to such programs. Obviously, not every drug
addict can find a good job like Charlie Hamer's. And unfortunately many
cannot be persuaded that they want to be rehabilitated or to give up drugs.
Either voluntarily or by court commitment, many are treated at federal
hospitals in Lexington, Kentucky, and Forth Worth, Texas, but success has
been limited for involuntary patients.

Decriminalizing Drug Dependence

In an unusual sense, laws are one of society's forms of treatment for
drug dependence. In the opinion of some experts, our present stringent
laws have failed to control drug abuse but caused several undesirable side
effects.[45] Criminal penalties make addicts reluctant to seek help and also
add to the grief of their families. Confiscation and ultimate shortage of
drugs keeps their price high, by the laws of supply and demand, and thus

[45] T. J. Stachnik, "The Case Against Criminal Penalties for Illicit Drug Use," *American
Psychologist*, XXVII (1972), pp. 637–42.

encourages crime to support the habit and fosters aggressive recruitment of new users as the safest way to raise money. Legal prohibition makes illegal traffic more profitable, raises the chances of police corruption, and diverts law enforcement from other crucial crime protection. Felony conviction subjects users to the dehumanizing effects of imprisonment and hampers job rehabilitation, which is critical. And the penalties fall mostly on poor minority groups, who use drugs for escape from the unpleasant realities of their lives, for which the affluent white "establishment" is partly at fault.

Stachnik offers a radical counterproposal that merits careful attention: that we remove the present criminal penalties and treat psychoactive drugs like any other potentially harmful substance (medicine, cigarettes, alcohol). He would treat drug dependence as a medical problem by offering users a choice of heroin or methadone [46] or any other drug in maintenance dosages at community clinics for minimal cost or nothing. Several advantages of this procedure are cited. It would reduce the amount of urban crime, more than half of which is presently committed to support heroin habits. Clean equipment would reduce hepatitis and other illnesses caused by non-sterile injection. Overdose deaths and murders associated with criminal traffic in drugs would be reduced. Moreover, this would provide the first benign contact between the "establishment" and the heroin subculture, which could be followed with careful attempts to shift heroin habits to methadone, initiate rehabilitation, and so on.

Radical as it sounds, such a program has already been tried in Britain, with encouraging initial results. It used to be that every physician in the United Kingdom could use his discretion about prescribing narcotics for addicts, with the result that known heroin and cocaine users tripled in number from 1964 to 1967.[47] Thereafter authorization to prescribe for narcotic addicts was restricted to specialized clinics attached to major teaching hospitals. As long as the addict remains registered with a Drug Dependency Center, he may receive prescriptions for any drug at a standard cost of 52¢ (or free if he cannot afford to pay). A special effort is made to switch heroin addicts to methadone and, if possible, to give up drugs altogether. A number of rehabilitation programs are available if the addict wishes to participate. Most of Britain's registered heroin addicts are now being supplied with methadone. In the first three years of the program the number of British addicts has declined slightly, while during a comparable period the number has more than doubled in the United States.[48]

[46] Methadone is a highly addictive drug that is antagonistic to heroin. It prevents heroin-induced euphoria as well as the excruciating symptoms of heroin withdrawal. The main advantages of methadone are that it does not induce a tolerance necessitating steadily increased dosages, as heroin does, and it produces only mild abstinence symptoms, even with rapid withdrawal. Methadone is the most widely used of several "alternatives" to heroin currently offered on an experimental basis to addicts who want to kick the habit.

[47] J. H. Jaffe, "The Maintenance Approach to the Management of Opioid Dependence," in Zarafonetis, *op cit.*, p. 163.

[48] Whitten and Robertson, *op. cit.*, pp. 38–39.

Though the matter is extremely controversial in this country, a consensus is growing among drug treatment experts that some kind of maintenance programs must be tried out, at least experimentally. We must keep in perspective that maintenance programs only treat the peripheral symptoms of a profound disorder, both in individuals and in society at large. Without simultaneous efforts at prevention and rehabilitation, maintenance programs could at best only mark time. The least that can be said is that experimental maintenance programs are no less reasonable than the recent American agreement to pay a $35 million subsidy to Turkish poppy growers to stop raising their crops by the end of 1972, a scheme that defies the laws of both economics and reason.[49]

Prevention

It is ironic that in handling pressing social problems, efforts at prevention often come last, after programs for relief of symptoms and the rehabilitation of past victims, whereas logic would seem to dictate the reverse priority. Prevention may also come last because to be effective it requires the most knowledge about causes. Though we know little about the precise patterns of etiology for drug dependence, it appears that primary prevention must begin in the family home. A recent questionnaire study of 8,865 high school students in Toronto suggests that the drug-use patterns of parents may influence their children's.[50] Fewer students reported using tobacco, marihuana, barbiturates, heroin, speed, LSD, and other psychoactive drugs if the parents used neither tobacco nor alcohol. Mothers who frequently smoked and drank were most likely to have their children turn to illicit and stronger drugs. These findings might be discounted as showing only that ascetic parents produce ascetic offspring while indulgent parents produce indulgent offspring, a plausible result without very profound implications. However, students whose parents were regular users of tranquilizers were twice as likely to smoke marihuana, three times as likely to use hallucinogens, and eight times as likely to follow the example of drug use set in their households. On the one hand, this might implicate some kind of genetic vulnerability to drug dependence. It also may mean that children learn their attitudes and behavior with respect to drugs from parental role modeling.

Prevention has mainly been attempted through a variety of public education campaigns. Perhaps the most visible of these is one sponsored by the U. S. Public Health Service which features popular sports starts in one minute videotape clips shown as a public service during intermissions of various televised sports programs.[51] For example, Willie Mays, the black

49 *Ibid.*, p. 40.

50 R. G. Smart and D. Fejer, "Drug Use Among Adolescents and Their Parents: Closing the Generation Gap in Mood Modification," *Journal of Abnormal Psychology*, LXXIX (1972), pp. 153–60.

51 G. N. Kurtz, "Putting People in the Communications Process: A National Drug Abuse Education Campaign," in Wittenborn *et al., op. cit.*, pp. 335–56.

baseball player, exhorts the viewing audience not to mess around with drugs and advises them to write to the National Institute of Mental Health for free booklets with the facts about drugs. It is hoped that identification with Willie Mays and a knowledge of the dangers of drugs from the booklets will dissuade youngsters from turning to drugs in the first place. This program is still relatively new, so we can look for some evaluation of its impact, and others like it, in the near future.

CHRONIC ALCOHOLISM

We consider last the drug that is abused more and costs society more than all other drugs combined: alcohol. This is partly because the use of alcohol is legalized almost everywhere and two thirds of American adults drink at least occasionally.[52] It is estimated that nine million people in the United States, or 7 per cent of the adult population, abuse alcohol. Excessive use of alcohol is a contributing cause of 28,000 traffic fatalities, half of the total each year, a third of the suicides, more than half of the criminal homicides, 40–50 per cent of all police arrests, and 60 per cent of all commitments to mental hospitals. Alcohol costs our economy $15 billion a year for time lost from work, health and welfare services for alcoholics and their families, property damage, and medical expenses.[53] Like the other forms of drug dependence, alcohol can be woven into the texture of almost any kind of disorder. Therefore it is impossible to specify a particular developmental history or physiological predisposition for the disorder. Still, some broad regularities have been established.

The Effects of Alcohol

Alcohol is a natural substance formed by the reaction of fermenting sugar with yeast spores. The colorless, inflammable liquid is a major ingredient in beers, wines, and liquors, with varying degrees of distillation or concentration. Although we often speak of its stimulating effects, alcohol is actually a central nervous system depressant. This is clear enough when a person is quite drunk, with failing locomotion and incoherent speech. The initial stimulating effect results from its selective action on neural mechanisms. Its depressant effect touches first the most recently

---

[52] U. S. Public Health Service, *Alcohol and Health,* First Special Report to Congress from the Secretary of Health, Education and Welfare (Washington, D. C.: Government Printing Office, 1971), p. 22. This observation may seem to compromise the proposal to decriminalize drug use, which was warmly presented earlier. It is indeed powerful evidence against *legalizing* the use of psychoactive drugs. Stachnik's proposal is to remove criminal penalties for drug use and to authorize the provision of addicting drugs under government control, but *not* to legalize them or allow their open distribution and use according to individual discretion. We shall see below that the proposal to remove criminal penalties has equal merit for alcohol use, except of course for serious non-victimless crimes such as drunken driving.

[53] *Ibid.,* pp. vii–viii and 41–42; R. Richard, "Alcoholism," *Boston Sunday Globe,* February 2, 1969, p. 2.

evolved areas of the cerebral cortex, which have a predominantly inhibitory function. Disinhibition produces a sense of well-being and relaxation, freedom of thought, and pleasant affect. It is conducive to conversation, hence the wide use of alcohol as a social lubricant.

As intoxication increases, events take a fairly regular course. There is some difference of opinion about this course, depending upon whether or not the observer participates. To a slightly intoxicated judgment it will be apparent that everyone is talking with great zest, wit, and wisdom. The world is full of glowing possibilities; the heart is full of warm, friendly, and expansive feelings. But a sober observer will be apt to see the picture a little differently. He will agree on the zest and expansive feelings, but he may have some reservations about matters of judgment and intellectual keenness. It will occur to him to question whether the gentleman who is informing the company how to construct outdoor fireplaces is really an authority on that subject, and he will doubt whether the great plans for world reform being loudly developed in another part of the room will prove practicable in the cold light of morning reality. If he stays around long enough, he will observe further signs of deterioration as sedation progresses to other parts of the nervous system. Speech, hand coordination, and locomotion become increasingly impaired until finally a state of stupor is reached.[54]

It is commonly observed that people behave more amorously after drinking, so alcohol is often thought to be an aphrodisiac. The truth is that alcohol influences sexuality in the same indirect ways that many psychoactive drugs do. Moderate amounts release inhibitions and can help to overcome lack of confidence or feelings of guilt about sex, which may facilitate sexual activity. But concerning larger amounts, Shakespeare was right: drink "provokes the desire, but it takes away the performance."[55]

Normal and Abnormal Drinking

There are many people who use alcohol frequently but never to excess. In some circles moderate drinking is part of the routine of life, though immoderate drinking is regarded as reprehensible. These facts make it possible to speak of *normal drinking* and to look for some kind of a line beyond which drinking can be called *abnormal*. Such a line might be drawn according to external signs: drinking in the morning, being unable to face any important situation unless "fortified," being unable to drink socially without getting drunk, etc. All of these external criteria, however, get their meaning from the strength of motivation toward alcohol. The

---

[54] Studies of the effects of alcohol on behavior are summarized in H. J. Eysenck, ed., *Handbook of Abnormal Psychology: An Experimental Approach* (New York: Basic Books, Inc., 1961), pp. 664–70.

[55] *Macbeth*, Act II, Scene 3.

crucial question is how urgently and for what the alcohol is needed. The mild disinhibition that is obtained from one or two drinks, with its relaxation, sense of well-being, freedom from restraint, and easy flow of conversation, is a temporary benefit that most people can appreciate. A person who needs alcohol for this benefit and for nothing more is a normal drinker and is likely to remain so. He is under no serious temptation to drink beyond the point where this benefit is obtained, and it is not worth it to him to wake up next morning with a hangover. Furthermore, he is not so dependent on this benefit that he cannot forego it when circumstances so require. The normal drinker, in short, has no strong further motive for using alcohol beyond the enjoyment of its mild disinhibitory effects.[56]

Alcohol has further potentialities, however, and these constitute its appeal for the person who becomes an abnormal drinker. As intoxication increases, as restraint and judgment dissolve, impulses may come to expression which are in no way satisfied in everyday life. Take the case of a college student whose outward personality was marked by a tendency toward derogatory verbal criticism and a certain aloofness from all but his closest friends. Under the influence of sufficient alcohol he became extremely belligerent, picking quarrels and coming to blows with men in bars. His friends often had to rescue him because, although he fought like a demon, his slight physique was really unequal to these encounters. At mixed parties he regularly passed through the belligerent stage to expressions of a different character. He would lay his head on a girl's lap and weep piteously for her loving care, describing himself as a lonely outcast. The following day he would dimly remember his aggressive adventures but his extreme show of dependence would be safely wrapped in amnesia.

This is the sort of case that is likely to progress from normal to abnormal drinking. There is a *repressed* but still active craving for loving maternal care. There is also a very strong aggressive need, *suppressed* by circumstances to the extent that it comes to expression only in verbal form. Alcohol does a lot for these two needs. It permits the young man to act as aggressively as he really feels, without forcing him to assume full responsibility for his actions. It permits him to gratify his dependent cravings without forcing his sober consciousness to become aware of them. Alcohol thus allows him to satisfy strong needs without disturbing the protective organization that ordinarily keeps them in check. One can easily see the fatal attraction of alcohol for a personality organized on these lines.

On the basis of experimental studies, McClelland argues that *men* drink primarily to feel stronger, to increase the feeling of personal power, with

---

[56] A similar "exoneration" could be claimed for the great majority of marihuana users who smoke only occasionally under the same circumstances and for the same reasons. The legal implications differ, of course, but that has little to do with the psychological motivation for drug use.

less feelings of social responsibility, reality orientation, time concern, or social influence.[57] In this way the drinker savors the subjective feelings of potency and invincibility without the necessity to render full social account for their expression.

Abnormal drinking sets in when alcohol fits into personal motivations in some such way as those described. When it temporarily alleviates conflict by allowing expression to otherwise blocked needs, especially when its amnesic properties are utilized to prevent realization of the needs that have been expressed, alcohol is likely to become irresistibly attractive. In such a case the charm of mild disinhibition is but a minor part of the motive for drinking. The major goal is relief from conflict and the expression of cravings that cannot be satisfied in real life.

Alcohol Addiction

With habitual drinking the body develops some tolerance for alcohol, and definitely becomes physically dependent on it. The withdrawal symptoms can be quite severe. Recurrent in the literature is the suspicion that some people have an unusual physical vulnerability. In circles where social drinking is encouraged, it is quite easy to observe individual differences in responsiveness and enjoyment. However, the evidence of a constitutional basis for alcoholism is equivocal, at best, and much more attention has focused on psychological and cultural causes.[58] The disorder is most closely associated with alienation, neurotic tendencies, and impulsivity, traits with which we are familiar from our study of psychoactive drug abuse. It is found most commonly in men of minority races who have experienced exceptional hardships: limited job opportunities, unequal housing and schooling, inadequate medical care, childhood stress, and parental drinking problems. We already know that most serious psychological disorders fall on the disadvantaged, but the last point underscores again that young people learn methods for coping with stress, including maladaptive ones, from imitation and identification with adults. Alcoholism occurs most frequently among those aged 35 to 55, when the stresses of work (or lack of it) and family responsibilities are most acute, and usually evolves slowly from problem drinking over many years.[59]

The prevalence of alcoholism is lowest in cultures where drinking customs and sanctions are unambiguous, widely known, and congruent with other cultural values. In these cultures people drink in a definite pattern. "The beverage is sipped slowly, consumed with food, taken in the company of others—all in relaxing, comfortable circumstances. Drinking is taken for granted. No emotional rewards are reaped by the man who shows

[57] D. C. McClelland, W. N. Davis, R. Kalin, and E. Wanner, *The Drinking Man* (New York: The Free Press of Glencoe, 1972), pp. 332–36.

[58] U. S. Public Health Service, *Alcohol and Health, op. cit.*, pp. vii–viii, 35, and 62–64.

[59] T. F. A. Plaut, *Alcohol Problems*, A Report to the Nation by the Cooperative Commission on the Study of Alcoholism (New York: Oxford University Press, 1967), p. 47.

prowess of consumption. Intoxication is abhorred." [60] On the other hand, maladaptive drinking, drinking without food, and intoxication are most common in those populations where attitudes toward alcohol are ambivalent. The United States is unfortunately one of these. We assign special significance to the use of alcohol, consume increasing quantities of it,[61] but feel guilty about it, perhaps because of our strong Puritan heritage. The result is that we have a high prevalence of alcoholism.

The medical complications of alcohol addiction are extremely serious. It shortens the life span by ten to twelve years and is a primary or related cause of brain damage, cirrhosis of the liver and other digestive organs, heart and nutritional disease, and endocrine disorders.[62]

Treatment of Alcoholism

The treatment of alcoholism offers at least one peculiar difficulty. The patient's main symptom is so available and so attractive that he often cannot resist it. At any point where treatment proves emotionally costly, he is under a terrific temptation to escape into drunkenness. Alcohol constantly offers him an easy solution to the problems both of life and of treatment. Most patients stubbornly cling to the idea that after being cured they will become normal drinkers. Most therapists, on the other hand, believe that only total abstinence will work in a person who has been alcoholic. Once the patient has been in love with the easy solutions offered by intoxication, he can rarely be so fortified against them that he learns to stop after the second drink. Records of treatment are full of relapses which begin when the patient decides that his improved condition has made him capable of normal drinking.

Special methods therefore have to be employed to block a relapse into drinking. Many drugs have been tried, with limited success, to reduce the craving for alcohol. Clearly the best results have been obtained with *disulfiram* (Antabuse), which causes violent vomiting when combined with alcohol.[63] Antabuse must be taken daily and voluntarily by the alcoholic in order to prevent reverting to drinking. The patient is carefully instructed about the extremely adverse physical reaction caused by alcohol when taking Antabuse, or he may be exposed to a mild demonstration reaction himself. The chief value of the drug is that it relieves the patient

---

[60] U. S. Public Health Service, *Alcohol and Health, op. cit.*, p. 3. Incidentally, the same casual attitude is taken by South American natives toward chewing coca leaves (cf. p. 352 above), which explains in part why that form of drug dependence is seldom pathological there.

[61] *Ibid.*, p. 14. The average annual consumption of alcohol in the United States has increased steadily since Prohibition ended, from .97 gallon per person in 1934 to 2.61 gallons in 1970.

[62] *Ibid.*, pp. vii and 54.

[63] E. C. Hoff, "The Use of Pharmacological Adjuncts in the Comprehensive Therapy of Alcoholics," in E. D. Whitney, ed., *World Dialogue on Alcohol and Drug Dependence* (Boston: Beacon Press, 1970), pp. 248–52.

from the worry that he may drink impulsively, because its effects last several days, providing a "temporal cushion" during which any craving for alcohol is checked by knowledge of the unpleasant consequences. The decision to take Antabuse, and the practice of taking it, are closely related to the alcoholic's motivation to abstain. It is usually chosen by younger and less deteriorated patients who are the most highly motivated. Some older patients cannot be given the drug because of physical deterioration, but otherwise it is considered relatively harmless. Because motivation is so critical, Hoff recommends that the patient take the medication unsupervised, without reporting to a member of his family or his employer. He is advised to take the drug in the quiet of his room and specifically re-express his own acceptance of the fact that he cannot drink, and that he has chosen to accept another day of abstinence. In this way, taking the medication serves to reinforce and sustain his own motivation for abstinence, and his own recognition that he is unable to drink safely. Used in this way, Hoff reports improvement for 76 per cent of Antabuse-treated alcoholics.

Some success has also been claimed for aversive conditioning. As mentioned earlier, the patient is given alcohol together with a strong emetic that causes prolonged nausea and vomiting. The desired result is that the patient acquire a conditioned avoidance response to alcohol.[64] These methods, like hospitalization itself, should be regarded as technical aids to treatment. The real work has to be done on the problems of maladjustment that have made the patient an abnormal drinker in the first place.

Alcohol abuse rates as one of our most serious public health problems, surpassed only by cancer and heart disease. Major efforts are now being made, especially as a result of the passage of the "Comprehensive Alcohol Abuse and Alcoholism Prevention, Treatment and Rehabilitation Act of 1970," to treat alcohol abuse as a health problem rather than using traditional, punitive, legal methods that don't work. One of the provisions of the Act was to set up the National Institute on Alcohol Abuse and Alcoholism, which among other duties is charged with public education about the dangers of alcohol abuse. Brief videotape clips will soon be presented on television designed to dissuade people from driving after drinking and from coaxing reluctant guests to drink more than they want.

One of the most successful methods of dealing with alcoholism is by the movement known as Alcoholics Anonymous.[65] This movement was

[64] These techniques are described, with references, in Hunt, *op. cit.*, Vol. II, pp. 1145–47. Since the influence of Pavlov has been strong there, the Russians have developed these techniques assiduously. The story—perhaps apocryphal—is told that a World Health Organization representative on a tour of hospitals in the Soviet Union was shown an experimental ward for the treatment of alcoholics. A group of patients who had completed the cure were lined up to meet the distinguished visitor. Without warning, the physician-in-charge pulled out of his pocket the paper label from a vodka bottle and displayed it to the patients, whereupon they began vomiting right on cue. Less dramatic results than this are usually reported elsewhere.

[65] *Alcoholics Anonymous* (New York: A. A. World Service, Inc., 1955).

originated by a group of cured alcoholics. It is now represented in a great many American cities. The nucleus is a local voluntary association. The meetings are given over to discussions of the common problem, sometimes with testimonials from members who have been cured, and to a sort of leaderless group therapy. When a new member is added, very likely still deeply alcoholic but genuinely desirous of changing, he is at once given some responsible task in the society so that he will more readily become identified with the group. In short, every attempt is made to provide an immediate sense of fellowship and group support as a counterpoise to the member's old haunts and drinking companions. The new life must be more attractive than the old. Another feature of the program consists of providing strong individual support when a member is in the grip of his old temptation. Other members will spend considerable time with him, perhaps even staying with him for days on end, to keep him from relapsing into drink. The success of such maneuvers naturally depends on the fact that every member has had his own troubles with alcohol. When a patient is really struggling to overcome his addiction, he welcomes the help of someone who has been through it all himself. In certain respects a fellow-sufferer can be a better therapist than a trained person who has never been alcoholic. The success of Alcoholics Anonymous gives testimony to the healing power of both group membership and sympathetic insight.

SUGGESTIONS FOR FURTHER READING

"Must" reading, even for the layman, is the excellent report of the Advisory Committee to the Surgeon General, *Smoking and Health* (Washington, D. C., U. S. Department of Health, Education and Welfare, 1964). A more recent report of a similar nature was published by the Royal College of Physicians of London, *Smoking and Health Now* (London, Pitman Medical, 1971). Collections of papers presented at national research conferences have been published by E. F. Borgatta and R. R. Evans, *Smoking, Health and Behavior* (Chicago, Aldine Publishing Co., 1968), and by S. V. Zagona, *Studies and Issues in Smoking Behavior* (Tucson, University of Arizona Press, 1967). *Smoke Screen: Tobacco and the Public Welfare* (Englewood Cliffs, N. J., Prentice-Hall, Inc., 1963) is a discussion by former U. S. Senator Maurine B. Neuberger of the political and economic aspects of the tobacco problem. W. I. Skinner speaks for the defense in *Tobacco and Health: The Other Side of the Coin* (New York, Vantage Press, 1970). His being in the tobacco industry does not discredit his case for tobacco, but the logic of his argument does.

In an area of psychopathology with the epidemic possibilities and rapid changes in scientific knowledge of the psychoactive drugs, it is difficult and important to keep up with the latest research advances. Useful for this purpose are a number of brief publications available from the National Clearinghouse for Drug Abuse Information, Washington, D. C. 20013, and from the Bureau of Narcotics and Dangerous Drugs, U. S. Department of Justice, Washington, D. C. 20537. Among these, a booklet prepared by the Justice Department, *Fact Sheets* (Washington, D. C., Government Printing Office, 1970) contains useful information about drugs and a contemporary bibliography on each of the drug groups discussed in the present chapter. A similar booklet oriented to educating students is a U. S. Public Health Service booklet, *Students and Drug Abuse* (Washington, D. C., Government Printing Office, 1969). Broad representation of viewpoints is included in the first and second Rutgers Symposia on Drug Abuse, edited by J. R. Wittenborn *et al., Drugs and Youth* and *Communication and Drug Abuse* (Springfield, Ill., Charles C Thomas, 1969 and 1970). More up-to-date and useful for a medical perspective is the International Conference on Drug Abuse at Michigan, edited by C. J. D. Zarafonetis, *Drug Abuse: Proceedings of the International Conference* (Philadelphia, Lea and Febiger, 1972). J. C. Ball and C. D. Chambers present a collection of their papers on epidemiology in *The Epidemiology of Opiate Addiction in the United States* (Springfield, Ill., Charles C Thomas, 1970). Legal issues are considered in depth by The President's Commission on Law Enforcement and Administration of Justice in *Task Force Report: Narcotics and Drug Abuse* (Washington, D. C., Government Printing Office, 1967). For a history of Synanon and an account of the more human side of drug dependence and rehabilitation the reader should not miss L. Yablonsky's *The Tunnel Back: Synanon* (New York, The Macmillan Co., 1965).

A comprehensive and very readable summary of all aspects of alcohol abuse is the First Special Report to the U. S. Congress from the Secretary of Health, Education and Welfare, *Alcohol and Health* (Washington, D. C., Government Printing Office, 1971). Also very useful is an earlier volume, *Alcohol Problems: A Report to the Nation by the Cooperative Commission on the Study of Alcoholism* (New York, Oxford University Press, 1967), prepared by T. F. A. Plaut. *World Dialogue on Alcohol and Drug Dependence* (Boston, Beacon Press, 1970), edited by E. D. Whitney, is a collection of papers by experts in the field from throughout the world. *Modern Trends in Drug Dependence and Alcoholism* (New York, Appleton-Century-Crofts, 1970), edited by R. V. Phillipson, is a similar collection with mainly British and American viewpoints. *Alcoholics Anonymous* (New York, A. A. World Service, Inc., 1955) tells the story of a most interesting experiment in treatment. An unusually illuminating case history of a chronic alcoholic who was later cured by Alcoholics Anonymous has been written by Eugenia Hanfmann, "The Life History of an Ex-Alcoholic," *Quarterly Journal of Studies on Alcohol,* 1951, Vol. 12, pp. 405–43. A study of social and family backgrounds is given by W. and J. McCord in *Origins of Alcoholism* (Stanford, Calif., Stanford University Press, 1960).

11

Sexual Disorders

In this chapter we take up a group of disorders specifically in the realm of sexual behavior. Considering the frequency with which sexual problems are involved in neurotic and other kinds of disorder, it may seem arbitrary to single them out for separate consideration. This procedure is justified, however, by the fact that sexual abnormality sometimes occurs in people who in most other respects lead relatively unburdened and productive lives. It is thus possible to think of sexual deviance as a separable form of disorder even though it is more commonly caught up in larger patterns of troubled living.

Since the start of the century, when Freud shocked respectable Western society by disclosing the far-reaching subterranean activity of sexual urge and fantasy, there has been a change amounting to a revolution in the cultural attitude toward sex. The patients from whom Freud derived most of his information had been brought up in an atmosphere conducive to a suppression of sexuality so powerful that whole tracts of experience were sometimes banished from consciousness. Sexual impulses, too insistent to be fully contained, were thus forced into devious channels and might sometimes break through in overt aberrant behavior. Psychoanalytic findings made it possible to believe that sexual disorders had their roots in excessive repression. Evidence was brought in by anthropologists that such disorders were more frequent in societies where sex was culturally suppressed.[1] These ideas contributed to a widespread loosening of sexual constraints both in expressed values and in actual behavior, and it was hoped that the new freedom would eventually put an end to deviance in the sexual sphere. Possibly the revolution is still too young, not yet widely enough diffused,

[1] B. Malinowski, *Sex and Repression in Savage Society* (New York: Harcourt Brace Jovanovich, Inc., 1927); G. H. Seward, *Sex and the Social Order* (New York: McGraw-Hill Book Co., 1946).

to have this effect. But there is also the possibility that there are intrinsic problems in human sexual development which cannot be made to vanish simply by unrestrained expression. Be this as it may, sexual disorders continue to be of frequent occurrence, and much can be learned from their study.

VARIETIES OF SEXUAL DISORDER

In an earlier chapter we took up the normal course of sexual development and the various points at which adaptive difficulties might occur.[2] Sexual excitability and sexual interests exist in childhood. They take the form of masturbation, curiosity about the genitals, self-display, mutual investigation with other children, and crushes and affectionate relationships sometimes accompanied by possessiveness and jealousy. For the most part the sexual tendencies of children are such as would be called perverted if they persisted into adult life. An extensive process of relearning goes on at puberty, colored by the new level of genital excitability and aided by surrounding social expectations. The usual result is that childish object choices and childish modes of satisfaction are put aside in favor, sooner or later, of sexual relations with someone of opposite sex.

This was the picture drawn by Freud in an influential paper published in 1905.[3] Here he advanced the idea that the various forms of deviant sexual behavior should be regarded as developmental disorders rather than expressions of constitutional abnormality; further, that they represented continuations of childhood sexual tendencies. Normally the diffuse "partial impulses" that constitute the child's sexuality are gathered into a new pattern at puberty, submerged by the excitability of the genitals and contributing to the central goal of copulation. If for some reason this integration cannot be achieved—if "genital primacy" remains incomplete—one or more of the earlier patterns may persist and become the preferred mode of sexual expression. On this basis Freud classified sexual aberrations under two headings: deviations of sexual *object* and deviations of sexual *aim*. To cover the clinical varieties of sexual disorder it is necessary to add a third category, wherein object and aim are normal but there is trouble with sexual *performance*.

The chief disorders of sexual performance are *impotence* and *premature ejaculation* in the male and *frigidity* in the female. The most common disorder of object choice is *homosexuality*, the choice of an object of the same sex. In this category belong also the peculiarities known as *fetishism*, in which some small part of the object, such as a hand, a shoe, or a lock of hair, captures special power of sexual arousal. Disorders of sexual aim

---

[2] See above, pp. 184–90.

[3] S. Freud, "Three Essays on the Theory of Sexuality," in *The Standard Edition of the Complete Psychological Works of Sigmund Freud,* Vol. VII (London: Hogarth Press and The Institute of Psycho-Analysis, 1953), pp. 130–243.

include such phenomena as *exhibitionism* and *voyeurism*. In the former, displaying the genitals or the naked body becomes the essential element in obtaining a satisfactory sexual experience. In the latter, observing the bodies and sexual acts of others plays the same indispensable part. These can be regarded as exaggerated perpetuations of childish display and curiosity. *Sadism* and *masochism* have similar counterparts in childhood when the relation between sexual and aggressive feelings is often misunderstood and confused. The sadistic deviation makes violence and giving of pain an indispensable condition for sexual satisfaction. The masochistic deviation similarly associates sex and the receiving of pain.

Readers of the daily press are acquainted with another category, that of "sex fiend." This is a journalistic classification rather than a scientific one. The expression is likely to be used about males whose behavior exhibits a confusion of sex and aggression, as in combined rape and murder; in other words, for acute examples of sadism. It is also employed for adults who direct sexual behavior toward children, a deviation in object choice. Another everyday expression, "sex offenders," designates a legal category rather than a psychological one. In an institution for sex offenders there are likely to be inmates with sexual disorders, but there are others who are not deviant with respect to performance, object, and aim. They are there because their sexual behavior has been so immoderate as to arouse complaint.

DISORDERS OF SEXUAL PERFORMANCE

If a man seeks advice on troubles with sexual intercourse, his complaints are likely to be either that he cannot secure an erection, or that he cannot sustain it long enough for successful insertion, or that he reaches ejaculation so quickly that his partner remains unsatisfied. If a woman seeks advice, her complaint is likely to be that she cannot relax physically or mentally, that she does not feel pleasurably aroused, that intromission is uncomfortable if not painful, and that she does not reach the point of orgasm, all of which means that neither she nor her partner is satisfied. From these common complaints it is easy to deduce that mutually satisfactory sexual intercourse requires whole-hearted abandonment to the bodily sensations and feelings that carry it to completion. This abandonment can be blocked by conflicting feelings such as anxiety, disgust, or guilt.

Sexual intercourse improves with experience, and novices can hardly be expected to perform like seasoned veterans. Episodes of impotence and frigidity are common while the sexual act is still novel, unfamiliar, perhaps a little awesome. Anxiety about one's adequacy as a sexual partner is entirely natural, but anxiety is precisely one of the feelings that can interfere with sexual arousal. Even a tense concentration on technique, on how best to bring about mutual arousal and appropriate timing, can interfere with the involuntary aspects of the experience, although novices can hardly be expected to avoid it. Shortcomings of performance that are due to inexperience cannot be considered disorders, but this designation becomes appropriate if poor performance persists too long or appears at some later point as a falling off from a level previously achieved.

Contributing Causes

Improvement in sexual performance is a learning process that requires reinforcement, and conceivably a person's initial ineptitude may be perpetuated by an unfortunate pattern of reinforcement contingencies. If a young man on his first attempt is impotent because of anxiety, he may be more anxious on the second attempt. Desires for success and enjoyment will be on the side of persisting, but if his partner gives no help, expresses disappointment, and adds to his humiliation, he may well develop a settled conviction of inadequacy. If a young woman in her first experiences is more tense than aroused and thus has more discomfort than satisfaction, and if her partner unhelpfully proceeds to his own consummation, she may well develop a settled conviction that she is naturally frigid. The partner's response is an important part of the reinforcement contingencies, and if the partners encountered in early experience tend to strengthen a sense of inadequacy it becomes hard to build up the confidence requisite for satisfactory intercourse.

Residues of past experience likewise make a significant contribution. Sexual experience is approached with preconceptions and attitudes built up throughout the personal past. One set of preconceptions has to do with the sense of competence. The vigorous boy athlete, successful in a number of different sports, may anticipate sexual experience as another of those physical accomplishments at which he is bound to be great. The awkward, clumsy boy may approach the same situation with a firm expectation that here, too, he will be awkward and clumsy. Similarly a popular girl, accustomed to feeling that she pleases boys, will enter this new branch of experience more confidently than a girl who has come to doubt her charm. A second set of preconceptions is derived from cultural and family attitudes toward sex. Less often than in the past, but still often, children gather from their parents' attitudes and warnings that sex is dangerous, degrading, dirty, and disgusting. These briefings may occasionally be so effective that sex with a partner is never attempted. The more common consequence is to surround intercourse with negative affects that interfere with arousal and good performance; whatever pleasure is obtained tends to be spoiled by subsequent feelings of guilt or shame. Such attitudes may be outgrown, but sometimes they persist throughout life. Contemporary parents occasionally swing to the opposite extreme and constitute themselves a cheering section for their adolescent children's sexual initiatives. This may build up such high expectations that at first the reality seems tame by comparison. As one newly experienced adolescent put it, "Is that all that has to happen to make me mentally healthy?"

An important part in disorders of sexual performance is sometimes played by hostility. This is most clearly seen in marriages that have begun to go wrong. Poor sexual performance has the effect of disappointing the partner. It reduces physical satisfaction and at the same time communicates a message that the partner is no longer an attractive, arousing object. In such cases, of course, the sexual disorder does not stand alone; it is part of a deteriorating human relation, and it may be confined to that relation. When hostility is an habituated part of a person's attitude toward others, its spoiling effect can be general. Competitive feelings, jealousy, chronic resentment, self-preoccupation all interfere with the generous spirit that is implicit in a mutually satisfying act. In some cases of impotence, furthermore, the sexual act is interpreted as destructively aggressive, and the anxiety aroused by one's own hostility has an inhibitory effect on performance.

Treatment

Recent developments in treating disorders of sexual performance have produced decidedly encouraging results. Reporting on work that has had widespread publicity, Masters and Johnson find that 80 per cent of their 790 cases of sexual dysfunction were essentially cured and remained so throughout a five-year follow-up period.[4] Admittedly their patients had a better than average prognosis. For the most part they were married couples who valued their marriage, hoped to improve it, and especially wanted to eliminate the sexual difficulties that seemed to be its only flaw. Few of these subjects showed signs of other forms of disorder.[5] Masters and Johnson acted on the assumption that the sexual disorder could be treated directly without reference to other possible factors. In their view, the marital relationship is the "patient," and the cure consists of each partner's learning how to achieve, and how to help the other partner achieve, sexual satisfaction. Part of the program involves getting the partners to feel comfortable together in sexual situations: relaxed, frank, able to communicate freely. This is best accomplished if they can spend some time away from home near the treatment center, free from domestic distractions, having a sort of second honeymoon. It is further favored by not having complete sexual relations for the first several days, to avoid the anxiety over performance that has been plaguing the partners. The other part of the program consists of detailed instruction in the art of lovemaking with practice by the couple in private. This starts with what might be called "sensuous exercises," an extended sexual foreplay without going any further, designed to allow the partners to rediscover and enjoy the pure pleasure of sexual arousal. From this beginning the couple advances by slow degrees to complete intercourse, no new step being taken until

---

[4] W. H. Masters and V. E. Johnson, *Human Sexual Inadequacy* (Boston: Little, Brown & Co., 1970).

[5] W. L. Maurice and S. B. Guze, "Sexual Dysfunction and Associated Psychiatric Disorders," *Comprehensive Psychiatry*, XI (1970), pp. 539–43.

there is full confidence about the preceding steps. In effect the married pair, caught in an habitually tension-ridden sexual performance, is told to back off and learn the whole thing over again.

This direct approach to treatment can properly be called behavior modification, and it is similar to the principles described by Wolpe.[6] In treating impotence and premature ejaculation, assumed to occur because anxiety is strong enough to inhibit full arousal, Wolpe recommends rearranging the situation so that sexual excitement can gain the upper hand over anxiety. The technique for doing so is much like the one employed by Masters and Johnson, consisting of foreplay alone until anxiety disappears, then gradual approximations to complete intercourse, each step being taken only when it no longer raises anxiety. When patients do not seek treatment in pairs, there is always the practical problem of finding a female collaborator with the kindness, patience, and frustration-tolerance to help a man through the many sessions, maybe as many as 15 or 20, during which he cannot yet give her any real satisfaction. Wolpe reports that of a series of 31 patients treated under relatively favorable circumstances, 21 became wholly satisfactory performers, 6 were improved, and only 4 received no benefit. For the treatment of frigidity a different method is used. Assuming frigidity to be a conditional inhibition resulting from frightening events and frightening parental attitudes in early life, it is treated like a phobia by means of systematic desensitization, as described above in Chapter 7.[7] If the frigidity is specifically with the husband, his collaboration greatly increases the probability of a successful result.

In using these direct methods it is assumed that the sexual disturbance is either the whole trouble or at least sufficiently separable to be treated by itself. Considering what we have learned about the growth of personality the assumption seems too simple to have wide generality. Disturbances of sexual performance have often been studied by psychoanalytic methods, almost always with the result of disclosing both a complex history and a complex interaction with other aspects of personality. A spread of this kind is found in a case described by Lazarus, in which the patient, a man of 33, announced on his first visit: "I have come to you in order to prove to myself that our social values are depraved." [8] It was a long journey from this pronouncement through a tangle of social judgments derogatory to women before the patient disclosed that he was sexually impotent. Being a behavior therapist, Lazarus organized the treatment around systematic desensitization, but anxiety had to be reduced for four different situations: sexual initiative, assertiveness toward women, physical violence, and social

    6 J. Wolpe, *The Practice of Behavior Therapy* (New York: Pergamon Press, 1969), chap. 6.

    7 See above, pp. 245–48.

    8 A. A. Lazarus, "The Treatment of a Sexually Inadequate Man," in L. P. Ullmann and L. Krasner, *Case Studies in Behavior Modification* (New York: Holt, Rinehart & Winston, Inc., 1965), pp. 243–45.

rejection. In this case, impotence did not stand alone; it was part of a whole system of anxiety-laden attitudes toward other people. Lazarus reports that treatment required 57 desensitization sessions over 8 months, but the final result was wholly satisfactory.

From such considerations it might seem that treatment concentrated too heavily on sexual performance might send patients away with improvement in one sector but unchanged with respect to other important personal problems. Presumably this happens, but it does not necessarily constitute an argument against using direct methods. Psychoanalytically oriented treatment, usually requiring a long time, is apparently less successful than behavior modification, very likely because it does not concentrate enough on teachable skills and practical devices for controlling anxiety. Psychological treatment, as we have seen, must often be directed not at everything that conceivably might be done but at some one point where there is a good possibility of initiating a beneficent change. When the patient complains chiefly of a disorder of sexual performance this is surely the place to start, and it is conceivable that improvement in this sphere will have a favorable effect on confidence in other spheres.

HOMOSEXUALITY

The most common disorder of sexual object choice is a preference for members of one's own sex. In the recent past, until the advent of psychoanalysis, homosexuality was widely believed to be a biological abnormality. In the writings of Havelock Ellis, for example, great importance was attached to the fact that many homosexuals reported having preferred members of their own sex as far back in childhood as they could remember.[9] In view of what has since been learned about early childhood sexuality and about repression, the meaning of this evidence has to be reconsidered. Following Freud, emphasis shifted to the psychological side of the problem, and homosexuality was interpreted as a developmental abnormality. Recently the study of sex roles and of gender identity has added substantially to the developmental picture. Most plans for treatment are based on the assumption that the homosexual object choice has been learned somewhere along the way, and that it is not too late to learn to be heterosexual.

Biological Aspects

The part played by biological abnormality has been reviewed by Money.[10] It is not particularly impressive. At one time the belief was held that homosexuality might be related to an abnormal balance in the secretion of

[9] H. Ellis, *Studies in the Psychology of Sex* (3rd ed.; Philadelphia: F. A. Davis Co., 1928), Vol. II, chap. 3.
[10] J. Money, "Sexual Dimorphism and Homosexual Gender Identity." *Psychological Bulletin*, LXXIV (1970), pp. 425–40.

androgen and estrogen, the male and female sex hormones, but subsequent research has substantiated this only in a minority of cases. Statistics on inheritance have spoken but feebly for a genetic basis, and the newly developed techniques of chromosome counting have not yet disclosed any significant average differences between homosexual and heterosexual individuals. Only in certain rare cases has a genetic abnormality been demonstrated. Males with Klinefelter's syndrome, a eunuchoid body build with late and weak virilization at puberty, prove to be endowed with an extra female sex chromosome; this leads often, but not inevitably, to homosexual object choice.

In a series of detailed case studies, Stoller has made a cautious argument for a basic biological influence on object choice. He cites instances, including Klinefelter's syndrome, in which the sex assigned by the obstetrician to the child at birth, based on the appearance of the external sex organs, has been wrong, the internal structures and genetic constitution proving later to be those of the opposite sex. Some persons thus miscast and brought up in the wrong role report always having felt like members of the other sex. In spite of their training, they have never experienced sexual impulses appropriate to what they were supposed to be. Such cases are essentially homosexual, and from their ranks come those individuals called *transexuals* who request surgery to change their sex.[11] A follow-up study of boys referred to a clinic because of markedly effeminate behavior showed that many more than average were bachelors. homosexuals, or transexuals.[12]

The weight of evidence, however, is heavily in favor of learning rather than biologically determined preference. This is nowhere more dramatically revealed than in studies of hermaphrodites by Money and the Hampsons. One form of female hermaphroditism, the adrenogenital syndrome, which if untreated produces a somewhat virilized woman, leads sometimes to assignment at birth as male, sometimes as female. If the assignment passes unquestioned during childhood in the minds of the parents, the child grows up without apparent conflict to be the boy or the girl he is expected to be. Surgical and biochemical treatment can then be used to make the genital organs more masculine or feminine as the case may be, and sexual life can in many respects approximate the normal.[13] Genetic sex is the same in all such cases, but environmental expectations and training can take the child's gender identity in either direction and plant it firmly.

Homosexual object choice does not, of course, necessarily imply the full range of feelings considered appropriate for the opposite sex. Some male

11 R. P. Stoller, *Sex and Gender* (New York: Science House, 1968), especially chap. 7.
12 P. S. Lebovitz, "Feminine Behavior in Boys: Aspects of its Outcome," *American Journal of Psychiatry*, CXXVIII (1972), pp. 1283–89.
13 J. Money, J. G. Hampson, and J. L. Hampson, "Hermaphroditism: Recommendations Concerning Assignment of Sex, Change of Sex, and Psychologic Management," *Bulletin of the Johns Hopkins Hospital*, XCVII (1955), pp. 284–300; J. Money, *Sex Errors of the Body* (Baltimore: Johns Hopkins Press, 1968).

homosexuals are active and assertive toward their partners, preferring them younger and perhaps aspiring to be their heroes. The attitude is traditionally masculine, there is no tendency toward feminine interests, and the abnormality is wholly confined to object choice. The female counterpart is a traditionally feminine woman who stipulates only that her partner be of the same sex. These instances differ from the common stereotypes of effeminate "fairies" and masculine "Lesbians," and it would be less appropriate to invoke a biological factor behind a preference so largely confined to the visual appearance of the object.

Developmental Aspects

If sexual object choice is the result of experience, one hypothesis might be that homosexual seduction during late childhood or early adolescence was responsible for the unusual conditioning. Two reasons make this simple logic unimpressive. The first of these came to light in the Kinsey reports, which revealed an unexpectedly high incidence of homosexual experience in the population at large.[14] Of the total male sample in the Kinsey studies 37 per cent, nearly 2 out of every 5, had some form of overt homosexual experience during the course of life; the figure was 50 per cent for males who remained single until the age of 35. The figures do not disprove the seduction hypothesis, but they show that homosexual experience is more common than had been supposed, and they suggest that it does not necessarily have a strong emotional impact and can coexist with heterosexual interest. Exclusive and permanent homosexuality was reported in only 4 per cent of the total male sample.

The second and more telling reason for doubting the importance of seduction at or after puberty is the undeniably strong evidence that the preference starts much earlier in life. This is widely noticed in clinical cases, where the patient is likely to state that he preferred his own sex from as far back as he can remember, fortifying the statement with recollections from childhood long before the onset of puberty. An early origin is also reported by homosexuals of both sexes who have accepted their preference and made it a way of life, never seeking psychological help. In a study of the natural history of homosexuality, Saghir and Robins selected for intensive interviews 89 male and 57 female homosexuals, secured through homophile organizations, who met the criteria of being productive members of the community, never having been in prison, and never having sought psychiatric help.[15] In contrast to heterosexual control groups, a majority of the homosexual subjects "show during their childhood a cross-over of role preferences and identification." The boys typically lack contact

14 A. C. Kinsey, W. B. Pomeroy, and C. E. Martin, *Sexual Behavior in the Human Male* (Philadelphia: W. B. Saunders Co., 1948).

15 M. T. Saghir and E. Robins, "Male and Female Homosexuality: Natural History," *Comprehensive Psychiatry*, XII (1971), pp. 503–10.

with other boys, shun rough games, and prefer girl playmates and feminine interests. The girls "have mainly boy playmates, are actively involved in sports, and express a dislike for dolls and domestic activity." The unusual role preferences appear to be stably fixed well before puberty, and they become transformed into overt sexual interest in a way that is analogous to the normal heterosexual awakening described by the control subjects.

The early development of preference for the opposite gender identity might suggest that the choice turned on the characteristics of available models. If the father's role seems vastly superior, the little girl may like it better; likewise, the boy may be attracted to superior qualities of the mother in contrast to a worthless masculine model. This explanation, however, is not specific enough. Absent parents and inadequate models are common findings in many kinds of disordered behavior and indeed in normal life histories. Homosexual object choice must depend upon a more specific influence in early childhood, one that invests heterosexual choice with strong anxiety or some other negative affect. In the classic psychoanalytic formulation, much importance was attached to anxiety over the anatomical differences between the sexes. A boy's discovery of the female genitals, Freud believed, might suddenly elevate his fear of castration, while a girl might be driven to acute inferiority and envy by the sight of male genitals.[16] This explanation has been widely criticized as too specific, making too much of the perception of anatomical differences, but it has stimulated research into other ways in which normal gender identity could be blocked by anxiety and defense.

Long-term psychoanalytic treatment was chosen by Bieber and associates as being most likely to illuminate this problem.[17] They called upon a large number of their colleagues to fill out a detailed questionnaire about male homosexual patients they had recently had in treatment, the items being designed to bring out whatever had been revealed about early memories and family experience. The investigators were impressed by a frequent, though not universal, pattern of relations among father, mother, and boy child. The relation between father and mother was not satisfactory; the mother became maternally overprotective of the son but also transferred to him her thwarted marital love; the father, like a defeated rival, treated the son with some combination of criticism, rejection, and sulky withdrawal. In half or more of the homosexual patients the mothers were "dominant wives who minimized their husbands," had "a close-binding intimate relationship" with the sons, preferred the sons and allied with them against the husbands, and were either "explicitly seductive" or had a closeness with the sons that "appeared to be in itself sexually

16 O. Fenichel, *The Psychoanalytic Theory of Neurosis* (New York: W. W. Norton & Co., Inc., 1945), pp. 328–41.

17 I. Bieber *et al.*, *Homosexuality: A Psychoanalytic Study of Male Homosexuals* (New York: Basic Books, Inc., 1962).

provocative." These influences were already at work when the sons were 3 to 5 years old, the time when sexual arousability undergoes an increase and also when male and female social roles are being learned. One might suppose that the chief consequence would be premature heterosexual interest; but the mothers, though seductive up to a point, frustrated and thus surrounded with guilt the more open signs of erotic feeling, while frequently making clear their contempt for the male role as exemplified by the husbands. Thus the boys remained attached, dependent, gratified yet frustrated, and nudged toward the feminine role.

There is evidence from other sources that this family constellation occurs with marked frequency in the histories of male homosexuals. To check on its generality, Evans made a questionnaire study using a sample of men who had not sought psychiatric treatment; the men themselves, rather than their doctors, provided the information on family life.[18] In spite of the difference in method and in the sample the replies confirmed the Bieber studies; the same pattern was found in a large number of the cases. Evidently there is something in this constellation that predisposes to a homosexual outcome, but in a comment on this paper Hooker sounds a timely warning against too tight a linkage of cause and effect.[19] In all the relevant research, she points out, the supposedly pathological family pattern occurs more frequently in homosexuals than in controls, but never in all cases; moreover, it appears sometimes in controls and is similar to a pattern often detected in the childhood of schizophrenic patients. Once again the explanation would be too specific if this family constellation were interpreted as a necessary and sufficient cause of male homosexuality.

Female homosexuality provides additional evidence on the developmental background. Exclusive homosexual object choice occurs, according to the Kinsey report, only a third to a half as often in females as in males.[20] In a study of female homosexuals using reports from the same psychoanalysts who provided the Bieber group with 106 male cases, there were only 24 female cases.[21] This study disclosed a partial converse of the constellation described for males. A good many of the fathers answered the description of having been overintimate and close-binding, and the mothers tended to be puritanical and hostile, but they also emerged as dominant, which was not at all a quality shown by the fathers of male patients. A study made on a contrasting social–economic group brings out a somewhat different picture. Kremer and Rifkin directed their attention

18 R. B. Evans, "Childhood Parental Relationships of Homosexual Man," *Journal of Consulting and Clinical Psychology*, XXXIII (1969), pp. 129 35.

19 E. Hooker, "Parental Relationships and Male Homosexuality," *Journal of Consulting and Clinical Psychology*, XXXIII (1969), pp. 140–42.

20 A. C. Kinsey, W. B. Pomeroy, C. E. Martin, and P. H. Gebhard, *Sexual Behavior in the Human Female* (Philadelphia: W. B. Saunders Co., 1953).

21 H. E. Kaye *et al.*, "Homosexuality in Women," *Archives of General Psychiatry*, XVII (1967), pp. 626–34.

to 25 high school girls, 12 to 17 years old, in a low status neighborhood, whose inclinations were at least in some degree homosexual.[22] Many of the subjects came from disorganized and broken homes: the fathers, far from being close-binding, were "hostile, exploitative, detached," and often absent, while the mothers, "mainly overburdened and hardly adequate for their responsibilities," could not be characterized either as rejective or as dominant. But one point came out sharply: "The caretaking women, mother or surrogate, held or expressed strong negative attitudes toward their own mates and much skepticism about men generally. Warnings to the girls about men were frequent. The girls in turn expressed many negative attitudes toward their fathers and about men."

These findings are no model of consistency. Perhaps one can assume that the most critical influence for both sexes may be an attitude inculcated by the mother that sex is dangerous, disgusting, and contemptible, something to be avoided at all costs. Boy and girl alike would thus grow up in an atmosphere in which pleasing mother meant steering wide of wicked sexual feelings, and this could be construed as steering wide of the whole sex role. But the evidence is by no means clear. No psychogenic formulation thus far proposed seems entitled to generality, and the problem still awaits decisive research.

Not to be overlooked in this connection is the nature of homosexual attraction. Just as heterosexual people find certain members of the other sex especially attractive, so that they enjoy looking at them, want to draw closer, and possibly fall in love, so homosexuals may be drawn to certain members of their own sex who appear to them especially beautiful. More can be learned about this topic by looking briefly at another disorder, *fetishism,* in which the object choice is far more deviant.

Comparison with Fetishism

In its extreme form, fetishism involves being attracted and sexually aroused by some small stimulus that most people would regard as an insignificant part of the whole. The fetishist is not fascinated by another person but by locks of hair, shapely hands, beautiful shoes, fur garments, articles of adornment. There are intermediate degrees, in which one feature is of major interest but sexual intercourse may follow. In the fully developed case, however, the fetish gains exclusive possession of the field, and collection of the desired objects may take the place of physical satisfaction. Vernon Grant in a theoretical paper gives two examples to illustrate these possibilities.[23] The first, drawn from an early paper by Alfred Binet, is the case of a man who preferred a beautiful hand above every-

[22] M. W. Kremer and A. H. Rifkin, "The Early Development of Homosexuality: A Study of Adolescent Lesbians," *American Journal of Psychiatry,* CXXVI (1969), pp. 91–96.

[23] V. W. Grant, "A Fetishistic Theory of Amorous Fixation," *Journal of Social Psychology,* XXX (1949), pp. 17–37.

thing else in the opposite sex.[24] Contemplation of such a hand gave him great pleasure and an erection, and he remembered in minute detail every hand that he had thus enjoyed. "He pretended to a knowledge of palm reading as an excuse for the minute examination of women's hands." Much as he was fixated on hands, however, he was still responsive to the woman as a whole, and the fetish "offered no obstacle to normal sexual relations." The second case comes from Wilhelm Stekel.[25] It is summarized as follows by Grant.

The stimulus consists of aprons, of certain well defined colors and patterns; the susceptibility dates from a very early age. The fetishist has an extensive collection of those aprons that meet the requirements of his taste. He is never sexually excited by the aprons, nor does he use them in masturbation. He is strongly attracted at sight of an apron of the proper design and feels an urge to possess it. At night he takes the apron which is "dearest" to him to bed; at other times he may stroke and kiss the aprons. He has never had sexual intercourse, even during several years of marriage; his attachment to the aprons, he states, makes such a relationship impossible, and has itself functioned as an erotic outlet.[26]

If the study of abnormal psychology were intended for entertainment, like a trip to the zoo, fetishists would provide some of the most amusing exhibits. But Grant brings us back to sober reality by pointing out that there are fetishistic elements in even the most normal sexual attractions.[27] Men who cast an appreciative eye at women's legs or the shape of their breasts should recognize a certain cousinship with the patient who pretended he was a palmist; mild focusing of sexual interest on certain anatomical features, far from being an abnormality, is not in the least uncommon. Furthermore, it is characteristic of sexual object choice to be highly selective in accordance with individual preference and taste. We do not call it a disorder if men prefer blondes, or if they prefer brunettes, or if they reserve their real interest for redheads; we do not even chide them if they choose girls in smart clothes or, vice versa, in ragged shawls and worn dungarees. Sexual attraction is guided to a surprising extent by properties that we experience as aesthetic qualities inherent in the object, and there are great individual differences in what thus allures us. In fetishism this selectivity is carried to an extreme. The fetish can become the exclusive condition for erotic arousal, or its possession can substitute for genital erotic satisfaction. By comparison, preference for a person of the same sex is a less wide deviation in object choice.

The theoretical problem posed by fetishism is how to explain the extraordinary narrowing and focalizing of the erotic stimulus. That such a

24 A. Binet, "Le Fetichisme dans l'Amour," *Revue Philosophique*, Paris, XXIV (1887), pp. 143–67, 252–74.

25 W. Stekel, *Sexual Aberrations* (New York: Liveright Publishing Co., 1930).

26 Grant, *op. cit.*, pp. 25–26.

27 V. W. Grant, "Preface to a Psychology of Sexual Attachment," *Journal of Social Psychology*, XXXIII (1951), pp. 187–208.

result could be produced wholly by uncomplicated conditioning seems hardly plausible, especially in cases like the apron fetish. One can reason that the choice represents an evasive action, erotic feeling being displaced from sexual ideas that arouse anxiety to peripheral and therefore safer images, but this again lacks credibility, especially in cases like the fetish of shapely hands. In psychoanalytic thinking it is proposed that through unconscious associations the fetishistic object serves as a symbol of repressed wishes. The wish that the love object has a penis could thus be symbolized in a hand fetish, while the wish that the partner be a mother could lie behind the fascination with aprons. These possible connections, too, stand in need of convincing proof. The chain of events that leads to homosexual object choice is difficult enough to understand; the one that leads to fetishism is a good deal more obscure.

Treatment of Homosexuality

Through most of the history of abnormal psychology homosexuality has been regarded as hard to treat. When deviant object choice was attributed to a biological defect, treatment was not even attempted. Freud and his followers made much of the developmental aspects, but rates of improvement following psychoanalytic treatment were reported to be not as good as those obtained with neuroses. A somewhat more optimistic view is taken by current workers who use variants of psychoanalysis or who favor the techniques of behavior modification. If homosexuality depends hardly at all on biological peculiarities, if it is almost entirely consequence of learning, then relearning, the essence of psychological treatment, ought to be effective. But the relearning of sexual object choice turns out to be not as simple as it sounds.

The first problem has to do with the patient's motivation. There are many homosexuals, of course, who do not want treatment, who build their sexual preference into a way of life which they consider to be worth the practical difficulties. As our society grows increasingly tolerant on the subject of sex, the legal and social handicaps of homosexuality become appreciably less severe, though still heavy. Sometimes a person who has more or less accepted the deviant orientation while young begins in the course of time to have second thoughts. With youth vanishing, a stable life with marriage and a family looks increasingly attractive. Progress in one's vocation and a growing place in the community may make a person feel more vulnerable to possible scandal and adverse social judgments. Thus a patient may come for psychological treatment with curiously mixed motives. The desire to change sexual orientation may be wholly sincere, but there is lingering reluctance to surrender an important source of satisfaction. Giving up the sexual objects to which one feels spontaneously drawn is a profound sacrifice; resentment is understandable that such a price must be paid to obtain what comes naturally to other people.

Motivation is more favorable if the patient does not accept his deviant preference, has perhaps just discovered it, regards it as a weakness or a vice, and wants to be rescued from its grip. Self-respect, an important ally, is then on the side of a successful outcome, but sexual inclination is still stubbornly on the other side.

Considered as a problem in learning, treatment can be broken down into a number of processes to which the several techniques of behavior therapy appear to be applicable. To reduce the strength of homosexual behavior it is possible to use aversive methods. Lowering the anxiety connected with heterosexual behavior seems a proper place to apply systematic desensitization. Encouraging the patient to attempt heterosexual activity might call for assertiveness training, and if difficulties of performance are encountered there are the methods already described for dealing with impotence and frigidity. Schematically, everything can be covered by those straightforward techniques for behavior modification, but it must be remembered that the therapist's resources—the rewards, punishments, and response contingencies within his power to arrange—are not unlimited, and that the conditionings he is trying to change are likely to be deeply entrenched.

Of these several methods, aversive treatment has proved to be the most controversial. The best known method is a pictorial technique worked out by Feldman and MacCulloch.[28] As used with male patients, pictures of males, some clothed and some nude, are shown on a screen and associated with a painful electric shock. The patient controls the disappearance of both slide and shock by means of a switch, but he is supposed to leave the slide on the screen as long as he finds it sexually attractive. In a later stage female slides appear when male ones are switched off, receiving positive reinforcement through the cessation of pain. Contrived as this sounds, the authors claim considerable success, and report that of 25 patients successfully treated 52 per cent were still normally heterosexual a year later, while 48 per cent had to a greater or less extent relapsed. Wolpe, referring to this as a "gratifying finding," nevertheless concludes that "it does not justify the use of aversion as the primary treatment of homosexuality." He considers it more important to deal first with the anxiety surrounding heterosexual behavior, and cites a case in which the lowering of social anxiety produced a spontaneous change from homosexual to heterosexual interests.[29] It would seem in any event an obvious therapeutic blunder to try to block homosexual behavior before the patient had made progress toward the heterosexual alternative.[30]

[28] M. P. Feldman and M. J. MacCulloch, "Aversion Therapy in the Management of Homosexuals," *British Medical Journal*, I (1967), pp. 594–99.

[29] J. Wolpe, *The Practice of Behavior Therapy* (New York: Pergamon Press, 1969), pp. 208, 255–62.

[30] Aversive treatment has been used also with fetishism; see, for an example, M. Kushner, "The Reduction of a Long-Standing Fetish by Means of Aversive Conditioning," in L. P. Ullman and L. Krasner, eds., *Case Studies in Behavior Modification, op. cit.*, chap. 14.

Systematic desensitization is considerably less hazardous and is especially appropriate when strong anxiety is focalized on the anatomy of the other sex' and on the act of intercourse. In the male homosexuals studied by Bieber's group the female genitals were objects of fear or disgust in a majority of the cases. When this feature is prominent, the condition resembles a phobia, the type of disorder with which desensitization has its best results.[31] However, a good outcome is not likely to be obtained by concentrating the treatment too narrowly. Homosexuality involves more than an attitude toward genitals and intercourse. Gender role preferences, interests, interpersonal relations, even the whole self-concept may form part of the pattern, and the spread of anxieties may be fairly wide. Some workers who started with highly focused techniques of behavior modification have moved toward a broader conception of treatment, drawing upon some of the older traditions of psychotherapy.[32]

Treatment that is psychoanalytically oriented takes more time, but it affords more insight both into what lies behind the deviant object choice and what happens during the process of change. This can be illustrated by a case described by Ovesey, who emphasizes the interpersonal attitudes entangled with homosexual inclinations, especially those having to do with dependence and power.[33]

An Illustrative Case

The patient was a 30-year-old unmarried businessman who complained of severe and increasing anxiety in his work. He reported being strongly competitive and hostile toward male colleagues, whose counter-hostility made him acutely anxious, and he felt that his position was in peril. In the course of history-taking he disclosed that he led an active homosexual life and had only once had heterosexual intercourse, more or less under duress. He had not thought of deviance as curable, and was surprised, pleased, yet somewhat anxious at the therapist's assurance that it might be treated. That night he dreamed that the lobby of the building in which he lived had been reconstructed overnight, transformed into new strength and elegance; he saw the dream as a symbol of his own awakened hopes.

The patient's family background partly fitted the pattern described by Bieber. The father, a moderately successful professional man, was "weak, inadequate, and totally intimidated by the mother, who was the dominant member of the household." The mother was "sharp-tongued, aggressive,

---

[31] W. G. Lamberd, "The Treatment of Homosexuality as a Monosymptomatic Phobia," *American Journal of Psychiatry*, CXXVI (1969), pp. 512–18.

[32] B. Fox and W. J. DiScipio, "An Exploratory Study in the Treatment of Homosexuality by Combining Principles from Psychoanalytical Theory and Conditioning," *British Journal of Medical Psychology*, XLI (1968), pp. 273–82.

[33] L. Ovesey, *Homosexuality and Pseudohomosexuality* (New York: Science House, 1969), pp. 126–37.

self-willed, and obviously brighter than the father," but the patient was fond of her and felt only contempt for his father. Throughout childhood the patient felt that he was not manly. He was the youngest of three brothers and was physically small; moreover, his mother, disappointed at not having a daughter, kept him too long in girls' clothes and long hair and made him do chores of sewing, cleaning, and cooking. Although he dated girls during high school, he began to be plagued by homosexual thoughts. At 19 he was drafted into the Army, where most of his companions were bigger, tougher, and not above taunting him because of his small stature and gentleness. It was at this time, "when he felt particularly unmanly," that he had the first of what became a long series of homosexual relationships. He preferred an assertive role in these encounters, practicing anal intercourse; "in this way, he not only satisfies himself sexually, but also enhances his deflated masculinity by making a woman out of his partner."

During the second month of treatment the patient began to date girls. Even though he made no sexual advances, these meetings caused him constant anxiety. Talking about it to the therapist, he kept harping upon his father's weakness in the face of his mother's strength. When asked what this could possibly have to do with his current difficulties, he gradually recognized his own "fears of standing up to the mother" and "anger with the father for failing to protect him." His conception of the heterosexual relation was so heavily dominated by his early experience in the family circle that he could not yet construe it afresh and was still victimized by the old emotions. But he persisted in his direct attempts to overcome anxiety. He undertook sex play with his dates, even though he felt more anxious than excited, and presently he began to attempt intercourse. Several times he was impotent, but eventually, encouraged by the therapist not to give up, he was successful and began a gratifying sexual life with his partner of that occasion. Six months from the start of treatment he believed himself cured, ready to marry the girl, no longer bothered by homosexual feelings, free of the troubles that had bothered him in his job.

Had the patient been dismissed at this point, his case would doubtless have been recorded as a complete success obtained in a relatively short time. In fact the therapist did not consider him out of the woods and construed his rapid improvement as a "transference cure." This expression refers to a "cure" in which pleasing the therapist, borrowing strength from his encouragement, and earning his respect produces a degree of initiative that temporarily suppresses anxiety, but that cannot survive the ending of the therapist's support. The reader will perceive here a moot point that is actually more factual than theoretical, but the facts are hard to ascertain. The therapist might have judged that although the patient's anxiety of women was not fully deconditioned he could safely terminate treatment, trusting that sexual gratification and feelings of self-respecting manliness—important positive rewards—would progressively circumscribe the power of the old alarms. He might reason that he should let well enough alone and have time for another patient. He might question the wisdom of further exploration as tending to stir up problems that could safely be let lie. In fact, the therapist decided to continue, and what happened next undoubtedly assured him that he was still needed.

After a favorable start, the patient's relations with his girl rapidly deteriorated. As bickering increased, the girl emerged as an aggressive person not unlike the patient's mother, and in the heat of quarrels she presently began to taunt him and impugn his manhood. Once more he found himself thinking about sex as if it were dirty, aggressive, and certain to lead to emasculation by the angry woman. The patient disengaged himself from his girl, gave up the company of women, and thought longingly of resuming his homosexual life. He complained once more about competition with other men at the office. For the moment, he was right back where he started, and he might have stayed there without the therapist's continuing encouragement to keep trying.

Resuming the struggle, the patient entered a period during which he compulsively tried to seduce every attractive woman he met, but he felt no lasting interest in these partners. His assertiveness at the office continued, and he exhibited competitive and hostile feelings toward the therapist. While thus attempting to be the dominant male on all fronts, he became aware of the dependent tendencies against which he was fighting. As a small boy he had been fond of his father and dependent on him as well as on the mother; this presently led into an Oedipal situation from which he emerged fearing the anger of both parents. That the lure of dependence was still strong is shown in an incredible piece of folly: he tried to resume the relation with his first girl, only to discover almost at once the same frictions and anxieties as before. Once out of this trap, the patient gradually learned "that he need not look upon all men as his father, any more than he need look upon all women as his mother," and that "his ultimate answers lay neither in compensatory aggression with men, nor in passive dependence, nor in homosexuality." In the course of time his behavior lost its compulsive extremes, his life became happier, and he found and married a woman with whom his relation could be congenial.

This course of treatment took a long time. Therapist and patient met on 347 occasions in the course of three years. Such length, as we have seen, is the frequent by-product of a technique that gives wide scope to free association and the uncovering of early childhood cognitions. The case shows, however, that an improvement promptly achieved may not be final; anxieties surrounding intimate personal relations, early ingrained and stimulated in a variety of subtle ways, are all too easily reawakened after apparently successful inhibition. When seen in follow-up the patient believed that his ability to discriminate among his own reactions, to perceive the occasions when current stimuli tended to touch off anachronous responses, had helped him to remain steady through situations of potential stress.

DISORDERS OF SEXUAL AIM

In a historically important book on juvenile delinquency, William Healy showed that certain cases of stealing result from an association between this act and sexual excitation.[34] Such association occurs most readily before puberty, when sexual excitation is still diffuse and none too clearly understood. Healy's cases include many like the following. A girl of eight went around with older girls who taught her to steal in shops and who also aroused her interest by free talk about sex. Presently this girl began compulsive stealing accompanied by unmistakable sexual excitement. A boy of eleven often went to the beach with other boys who would steal from shops along the way and later, when undressed, practice mutual masturbation. Before long the boy felt an irresistible impulse to steal whenever he heard talk about sex. These examples are not too serious cases, but they shed a certain light on those which become more serious. There is a plastic quality to the sexual urge, especially in childhood. Under a peculiar combination of circumstances, presumably involving serious anxiety, stealing might become the only stimulus to sexual excitement; it might even crowd out any normal form of consummation.

The clearest cases of disorder in sexual aim are those in which some other aim has totally displaced the normal one. More commonly, however, the aim of heterosexual intercourse is still present, but associated with some condition without which it is mechanical and unexciting. The typical *sadistic* pattern, for instance, calls for inflicting pain during sexual foreplay, and it is this that produces thrilling excitement and fully gratifying coitus. The reverse is true of *masochism*, which in its restricted meaning as a sexual disorder requires the experience of pain as a prelude to fulfillment. In the disorders that involve looking and being seen, *voyeurism* and *exhibitionism*, the substitute aim more easily attains a kind of autonomy, so that, for example, a chronic Peeping Tom may obtain excitement and orgasm on his perch on the fire escape if a suitable scene lies in his field of vision. In the disorder called *transvestism* there may be a similar autonomous thrill to dressing oneself and appearing in public in clothes appropriate to the other sex. All of the behaviors designated by these technical terms occur in casual and playful forms in everyday life, and some of them more openly during sexual foreplay. They become disorders only through excess, and through serious interference with heterosexual behavior. Experienced as irresistible impulses, they can put the patient in serious conflict with the police and the courts.

[34] W. Healy, *Mental Conflicts and Misconduct* (Boston: Little, Brown & Co., 1917), chap. 14.

Treatment of a Case of Exhibitionism

An actual case will be more useful at this point than general statements to make vivid what is involved in such disorders and their treatment.[35] The patient was a married man of 25 who had already run up a police record that included 24 charges of indecent exposure, 11 convictions, and 9 prison sentences mostly of only a few months' duration. The first remembered occurrence of his symptom was at age 13 when he engaged in sex play with a girl of 10, became angry at her indifference, and exposed his erect penis to her. In general he suffered from feelings of inferiority which included the size of his penis, and the gesture of exposing himself sounds like a reassurance, a moment of desperate courage. During adolescence the tendency developed out of all bounds. When he saw an attractive girl in the park, on the streets, even in a department store, he would experience an irresistible sexual excitement along with dread, leading to what he called "a grim determination to expose, come what might." Becoming erect and extremely tense, he would expose himself, but "the spell would be broken" by the shocked response and, trembling with anxiety, he would attempt flight. Several efforts at treatment had been of no avail, so it was decided to undertake a program of systematic desensitization, the patient being brought to the sessions by his wife lest he err on the way.

The patient proved capable of deep relaxation and strong visualization of scenes. Out of the initial interviews a hierarchy of scenes was constructed which involved, with various degrees of closeness, women of the type who appealed to him in locations like streets and stores where he was likely to become excited. The patient imagined each scene in turn until it no longer excited him, the theoretical assumption being that the relaxed state would inhibit the tense condition that always preceded his exposures. In the course of 46 sessions, interrupted twice by lapses that caused his arrest, he reached a point of complete control over his symptom. If momentarily attracted by a woman he told himself to relax, and the sequence of rising tension was stopped at its source. For the next 13 months the patient was free of trouble, and his life, including his relations with his wife, became much happier.

Like the homosexual patient previously described, however, this patient suffered a relapse. This happened after he lost his job and was for some months unemployed and short of money. This situation was a blow to his sense of adequacy and self-respect; it revived the inferiority feelings of his previous life. Three episodes now occurred in which he followed a woman into a public toilet and exposed himself there. It is of interest

---

[35] I. K. Bond and H. C. Hutchison, "Application of Reciprocal Inhibition Therapy to Exhibitionism," in L. P. Ullmann and L. Krasner, eds., *Case Studies in Behavior Modification, op cit..* chap. 24.

that toilets had not been included in the deconditioning hierarchy, so that the patient, still immune on streets and in stores but now again beset by feelings of inferiority, found women in toilets an irresistible stimulus. Further treatment had to be undertaken to close this avenue of stimulation. It seems plain, however, that an improvement in the patient's precarious sense of adequacy would provide more lasting insurance against future relapses.

An Example of Multiple Perversions

While it is convenient to describe sexual disorders one by one, several may occur together in a single patient. The strange complications in such cases can be illustrated by an example that in its time had wide publicity. A seventeen-year-old student was found guilty of three brutal murders and a large number of burglaries.[36] On the wall of one apartment, in which he killed a young woman, was found written with lipstick, "For heaven's sake catch me before I kill more; I cannot control myself." Sexually deviant behavior began in his case at the age of nine and took the form of fetishism and transvestism. He repeatedly stole women's underclothing, took it to his room, and dressed himself in it with great sexual excitement. At thirteen he began securing the desired objects by going into houses through windows. Sexual excitement gradually became concentrated on this act. He often struggled to prevent himself from leaving home at night, but sometimes desire would break down his resolutions. At the sight of an open window at a place that might be burglarized, he experienced sexual excitement with erection. Usually as he passed through the window he experienced orgasm. If so, he generally left without taking anything. The impulse to kill came only if he was startled in the act of burglary. On one occasion, however, he experienced orgasm when he hit a woman who interrupted him, and he left at once without hitting her again.

Reports on this case do not disclose the sequence of events and fantasies that led the sexual need into such peculiar channels. They do show, however, that there were severe blocks on normal channels. At first he indignantly denied that he had ever practiced masturbation, but he later admitted having tried it twice without being able to secure any sexual excitement. With equal reluctance he admitted occasional petting with girls, but reported the experience to be so upsetting and repulsive that he usually burst into tears. The pattern of guilt feeling could hardly be stranger. He was much less upset in speaking of his brutal murders than he was when questioned about normal sexual behavior.

---

[36] F. Kennedy, H. R. Hoffman, and W. H. Haines, "A Study of William Heirens," *American Journal of Psychiatry,* CIV (1947), pp. 113–21; Lucy Freeman, *"Before I Kill More": The William Heirens Story* (New York: Crown Publishers, 1955).

CONCLUSION

It is clear from this survey that sexual disorders are for the most part the result of unfortunate patterns of learning. Biological factors play a part that is decisive only in cases of fairly gross bodily abnormality, and even then they are sometimes overruled by learned gender identity. The conclusion follows that what is learned can also be unlearned, but in practice most sexual disorders do not yield easily to therapeutic endeavors. It is a common finding, when exploration of the past is thoroughly carried out, that the learning relevant to later disorders began early in life and took place in relation to mother, father, and their relation to one another. During the first five years of life there are several hazards to the learning process: global reactions, cognitive misunderstandings, and the force of feeling in the young child's love, dependence, assertiveness, hate, shame, and above all anxiety. Early mislearnings about sexuality, however the child construes it, thus stand a good chance of being stamped in. Furthermore, because no other relations before puberty are likely to have quite the intimate character of parental ones there may be little chance at re-learning through experience before the start of adolescent sexual relations. By this time, as an additional factor, deviant objects and aims may have become strongly reinforced because they provide sexual gratifications. When the disorders are further entwined with anxieties, defenses, identifications, sex role learnings, and sense of personal adequacy, it is no matter for surprise that what has been learned may indeed be difficult to unlearn. Methods of intervention that are traditionally long often take longer with sexual disorders; methods that seek economy of time do not economize as successfully; and all must expect that unsuccessful results will be a little more frequent than in the treatment of neuroses. Nevertheless, sexual disorders are in principle treatable. Relearning is possible, and an optimistic view of the outcome is justified when motivation, patience, and persistence are adequate.

SUGGESTIONS FOR FURTHER READING

Freud's monograph, *Three Contributions to the Theory of Sex* (1905), represents the first attempt to understand deviant sexual behavior as a developmental disorder. It is to be found in *The Standard Edition of the Complete Psychological Works of Sigmund Freud,* Vol. VII (London, Hogarth Press and the Institute of Psycho-Analysis, 1953), and also separately in paperback. The classic psychoanalytic theory of these disorders is given by O. Fenichel, *The Psychoanalytic Theory of Neurosis* (New York, W. W. Norton & Co., Inc., 1945), Ch. 16. Two important works on homosexuality, based on psychoanalytic treatment but with a theory somewhat more adaptational than Freud's, are by I. Bieber and others, *Homosexuality: A Psychoanalytic Study of Male Homosexuality* (New York, Basic Books, Inc.,

1962), and L. Ovesey, *Homosexuality and Pseudohomosexuality* (New York, Science House, 1969). The methods of treatment described by Ovesey form an interesting comparison with those of behavior modification advocated by H. J. Eysenck and S. Rachman in *The Causes and Cures of Neurosis* (San Diego, Robert Knapp, 1965), especially Ch. 10. Disorders having a biological basis, and the complex relation between this and gender identity, are discussed by J. Money in *Sex Errors of the Body* (Baltimore, Johns Hopkins Press, 1968) and by R. J. Stoller, *Sex and Gender: On the Development of Masculinity and Femininity* (New York, Science House, 1968), the latter paying special attention to transexualism and transvestism. A strictly behavioristic method of treating inadequate sexual performance was first described by J. Wolpe in *Psychotherapy by Reciprocal Inhibition* (Stanford, Calif., Stanford University Press, 1958), Ch. 8. Recent work along somewhat similar lines is described by W. H. Masters and V. E. Johnson, *Human Sexual Inadequacy* (Boston, Little, Brown & Co., Inc., 1970). A small book now in paperback, prepared for the Group for the Advancement of Psychiatry, *Sex and the College Student* (Greenwich, Conn., Fawcett Publications, Inc., 1968), deals with sexual development and with campus sexual issues, including college policies and the regulation of sexual conduct.

12

Psychosomatic Disorders

Up to this point we have been concerned primarily with the psychological side of abnormal behavior. Maladjustment, neurosis, delinquency, drug dependence, and sexual disorders were construed mainly as problems in psychological development, or, to put it another way, as problems of motivation, learning, anxiety, and defense. The same can be said of psychotherapy, which is usually an attempt to remove the inner obstacles that interfere with psychological development. We have touched briefly on somatic compliance in neurosis, potential brain dysfunction in psychopaths, somatic effects of drugs, and some physiological factors in sexual disorders, but our study thus far has not attached much significance to the body and the nervous system. This is not because of an inclination to regard people as disembodied spirits. It is because we know very little about the neural changes that accompany learning.

Our attention must now be turned to a group of disorders in which the somatic complications are fully as important as the psychological. Disorders of adjustment are linked up with bodily processes in such a way as to produce real organic illness. The patient complains of stomach trouble or heart trouble; perhaps it is asthmatic attacks or skin diseases or excessive fatigue that bring him to the physician's office. His ailments are not in the least imaginary. Examination discloses serious malfunctioning in the organs about which he complains, sometimes even tissue changes such as ulcers in the stomach or eruptions on the skin. The somatic disorders require treatment in their own right. Ulcers must be dealt with by rest and diet or by surgical means; acute asthma attacks must be checked with

396

adrenalin. But there is a growing body of evidence that disorders of this kind do not always result from organic weakness or from purely local tissue changes. Sometimes the bodily disorder is the end-product of emotional stress. Medication can temporarily relieve it, but recurrence is almost certain unless the emotional stress can be set right.

Disturbances in which emotional stress leads to chronic dysfunction in some organ system are nowadays referred to as *psychosomatic disorders*. As so often happens, the title is not particularly suitable. The term appears to include every disorder in which psychological and somatic factors both play a part, but in practice no one intends to give it such a sweeping meaning. It is best to limit it to those disorders in which chronic maladjustment is the primary process and somatic dysfunction the result or by-product. One might keep in mind the opposite term, *somatopsychic disorders*—though it is not widely used—for those cases in which bodily disorder is primary and psychological changes secondary. Such a term could be applied to head injury or encephalitis, for example, in which dysfunction of the cerebral cortex produces the result of impulsiveness and poor control so that the person has difficulty in accepting social restraints.

In practice, the term *psychosomatic disorders* is further limited to cases in which the somatic dysfunction is in organs controlled by the autonomic nervous system. This serves to exclude hysteria, which otherwise qualifies perfectly as psychosomatic but which long custom classifies as a neurosis. The bodily symptoms of hysteria—the sensory and motor symptoms such as paralysis and anaesthesia—occur in organs innervated by the cerebrospinal portion of the nervous system. Psychosomatic disorders occur in such regions as the gastro-intestinal tract or the circulatory and respiratory systems, which are under the control of the autonomic division.

Prevalence

There has been a great increase in frequency of psychosomatic disorders. Figures on neuropsychiatric breakdowns during military service show a relatively smaller incidence of hysteria and anxiety neurosis in World War II than in World War I, but a much greater frequency of psychosomatic disturbances. Before World War II the incidence of peptic ulcers in the U. S. Army was 1.6 per 1,000 soldiers. In 1941 it rose to 3.2 and in 1942, after the war began, it was 5.8 per 1,000.[1] Thus there is evidence of sharp increases as a result of acute stress as well as a more gradual increment over time. Similar trends are clear in statistics based on civilian populations.[2] To some extent, changes of this sort result from fashion

[1] M. Treisman, "Mind, Body and Behavior: Control Systems and Their Disturbances," in P. London and D. Rosenhan, eds., *Foundations of Abnormal Psychology* (New York: Holt, Rinehart & Winston, 1968), p. 499.

[2] J. J. Schwab, N. H. McGinnis, L. B. Norris, and R. B. Schwab, "Psychosomatic Medicine and the Contemporary Social Scene," *American Journal of Psychiatry*, CXXVI (1970), pp. 1632–42.

in diagnosis. Some disorders are now called psychosomatic which would have been classed as hysteria two generations ago. To a certain extent, moreover, increase in the frequency of a given disease may reflect the advances of medicine in treating other diseases. For instance, in the United States death rates for cardiovascular disorders increased from 287 (per 100,000 population) in 1910 to 520 in 1966. Meanwhile the rates for influenza and pneumonia dropped from 196 to 33 and deaths from miscellaneous other causes dropped from 776 to 146.[3] The greater frequency of cardiac disorders may partly reflect the increasingly hard pace of modern life, but it also arises from the fact that a larger proportion of the population now survives acute respiratory infections, for example, that would have been fatal half a century ago. Consequently more people live to the middle and later decades when cardiac disorders are in any event more common.

These reasons, however, do not wholly explain the increase of psychosomatic disorders, and the social implications of the trend are disturbing.[4] Especially ulcers, heart disease, and diabetes have been occurring with increasing frequency among younger age groups. Sex ratios have changed. Peptic ulcer used to be four times as prevalent in men as in women, but now the ratio is only two-and-one-half to one. On the contemporary social scene, as women participate more actively in the occupational and social arena, they are exposed to added stresses, with greater conflict and ambiguity in their social roles. As a result we can expect an acceleration in ulcers, heart disease, and the like among career women and working mothers. The prevalence of psychosomatic disorders is two or four times as great in lower social classes as in other classes. Death from hypertension is seven times more common in nonwhites as in whites. This may reflect genetic disposition in part, but discrimination and segregation also induce psychological stress and frustrations that can contribute to this outcome as well. There is increasing susceptibility to psychosomatic disorders in urban centers and among mobile people. Experiments have shown that aggregating and mixing induce hypertension in mice: apparently there is similarity in this respect between mice and men.

There may be still other contributing influences, but it is clear that these ambiguous maladies constitute an active focus of contemporary research, and we must set ourselves to understand them.

EMOTION AND BODILY CHANGES

Emotion is obviously related to certain bodily states. There are many common phrases in which this is recognized. The heart is said to ache or to be broken; in its more turbulent moments it can be in one's mouth or

---

[3] U. S. Department of Health, Education and Welfare, *Health, Education and Welfare Trends*, 1966–67 Edition, Part 1 (Washington, D. C.: Government Printing Office, 1968).

[4] Schwab *et al., op. cit.*

go down to one's boots. The color of the face can change over a wide range from white as a sheet to purple with rage. We say that we have no stomach for a job or that we haven't the guts to do it. In China it is appropriate for a man to say to his lady love that his intestines tie themselves in knots while she is away. Language would hardly have become so replete with psychosomatic phrases without some kind of factual basis.

Everyday Observations

Turning from metaphor to observed fact, we still need not set up an experimental situation in order to find examples of psychosomatic relationships. Everyday observation teaches us quite a few lessons on this subject. As a first example we can take the nervousness that many people feel when they have to make a speech or appear in some other capacity before an audience. Stage fright carries with it a number of well-known bodily reactions. For the last meal preceding the public appearance there is poor appetite, possibly even a complete inability to eat. As the great moment approaches, the heart beats rapidly, the mouth becomes dry, the hands tremble and grow cold, and there is a strong desire to urinate and move the bowels. The upset state of mind is reflected in an upset state of body. A contrasting example is offered by the emotion of joy. This will show itself not only in erect posture, springy step, bright eyes, and smiling face, but also in systems under autonomic control. The joyous person usually shows a good color, has a strong deep pulse, breathes deeply, has a good appetite, enjoys his food, and digests and eliminates well. His viscera share in his mental well-being. For a third example we can take grief, which is usually accompanied by marked somatic distress.[5] There is apt to be an aching tightness in the throat, sometimes a choking sensation, shortness of breath, and a frequent need for sighing, all of these being related to a feeling of wanting to cry. Another element is a feeling of weakness and easy exhaustion, so that the bereaved person can scarcely summon energy to climb the stairs or walk for any distance. Disturbances of eating are highly characteristic: appetite is extremely poor and there are complaints such as that all food tastes like sand. Grief ramifies throughout the body, affecting a large number of functions controlled by the autonomic nervous system. We have no reason to doubt that other feelings and emotions besides nervousness, joy, and grief have a widespread influence on the whole bodily economy.

Hypnotic Experiments on Psychosomatic Processes

Hypnosis offers a means of extending the study of psychosomatic reactions. By suggesting various emotional states rather than waiting for them to arise in the course of life it is possible to observe the somatic reactions under well-controlled conditions.

[5] E. Lindemann, "Symptomatology and Management of Acute Grief," *American Journal of Psychiatry*, CI (1942), pp. 141–48.

An experiment by Wolberg illustrates this kind of study and at the same time affords an interesting comparison between neurotic and psychosomatic mechanisms.[6] In hypnotically susceptible subjects it is possible to create a state of post-hypnotic conflict. This is done by giving contradictory suggestions which are to be executed post-hypnotically with amnesia for the fact that suggestions were given. Wolberg's instructions to the hypnotized subject were as follows:

When you awaken you will find next to you a bar of chocolate. You will have a desire to eat the chocolate that will be so intense that it will be impossible to resist the craving. At the same time you will feel that the chocolate does not belong to you and that to eat it would be very wrong and very bad. You will have no memory of these suggestions when you awaken, but you will, nevertheless, react to them.

Wolberg reports the results with three different subjects. One was a patient under treatment for conversion hysteria, and the reaction was a characteristic hysterical symptom: a psychogenic blindness. Although he saw everything else, the patient simply could not see the bar of chocolate that lay beside him. Even when the investigator picked it up and tossed it down, the patient asserted that he saw no chocolate bar. Conflict was avoided by not perceiving the stimulus that would have set it off. The patient maintained his negative hallucination for twenty minutes; thereafter, he saw the candy but refused to eat it. Another subject reacted to the post-hypnotic conflict with symptoms of anxiety and neurocirculatory collapse. Though he tried to avoid looking at the chocolate bar, this defense was insufficient. He complained of dizziness and faintness, proved unable to walk, became pale and cold, then broke out in violent tremor. When his pulse was taken it was found to be rapid and thin. So distressing was his anxiety attack that it became necessary to rehypnotize him and remove the conflict. Very different was the reaction of the third subject, who maintained complete outward composure but showed the effect of conflict by a psychosomatic symptom. At first he talked loquaciously about food and eating, remarked that visitors were expected to accept food when it was offered, and started to eat the chocolate with gusto. Before he finished, his face showed sudden surprise and he remarked that the chocolate tasted bitter. A moment later he complained of stomach pains and nausea, then went to the bathroom and vomited. In this last case one of the conflicting impulses utilized psychosomatic channels. The impulse to eat was not resisted, but the feeling that this act was "very wrong and very bad" came to expression through reversed gastric peristalsis.

On the basis of intensive clinical interviews Graham and his associates[7]

---

[6] L. R. Wolberg, "Hypnotic Experiments in Psychosomatic Medicine," *Psychosomatic Medicine*, IX (1947), pp. 337–42.

[7] W. J. Grace and D. T. Graham, "Relationship of Specific Attitudes and Emotions to Certain Bodily Diseases," *Psychosomatic Medicine*, XIV (1952), pp. 243–51; D. T. Graham, J. A. Stern, and G. Winokur, "Experimental Investigation of the Specificity of Attitude Hypothesis in Psychosomatic Disease," *Psychosomatic Medicine*, XX (1958), pp. 446–57.

discerned specific attitudes associated with different psychosomatic disorders: for example, hives and Raynaud's disease. They hypothesized that the emotional correlates of these attitudes might contribute, via physiological processes, to the somatic pathologies observed. Hives sufferers felt mistreated and were preoccupied with what was happening to them, but had no wish to retaliate. Patients with Raynaud's syndrome, on the other hand, felt a strong wish to take some direct, usually hostile, action. The clinical symptoms of these two disorders are as different as the specific attitudes linked with them. In hives the skin becomes hot and swells up in wheals or patches that itch intensely. In Raynaud's disease the skin of the extremities, especially the hands and fingers, becomes cold and moist and numb. You have probably experienced this in very mild form while watching your favorite athletic team playing in overtime in a championship game. Physiologically, Raynaud's syndrome is produced by constriction of blood vessels in the skin, hives by dilation of these vessels.

To test their hypothesis, Graham *et al.* hypnotized a group of normal young men and suggested to them the attitudes specific to hives and Raynaud's disease while monitoring continuously their skin temperature. For the hives attitude the subject was told that Dr. X was going to burn his hand with a match and he would feel very much mistreated, but would be unable to do anything about it or even think of anything to do. He would think only of what was happening *to* him. To simulate Raynaud's disease, the subject was given the same suggestion but told in addition that he would feel so mistreated that he would want to hit Dr. X as hard as he could, to choke him and strangle him. He could think *only* about how much he wanted to hit Dr. X. The "hives-specific attitude" produced a sustained rise in skin temperature, while the "Raynaud's-specific attitude" produced a steady decline. If suggested attitudes can produce such distinct somatic effects, real ones, especially when long sustained, might well contribute to psychosomatic illness.

Hypnotic suggestion has also been used to suppress allergic skin reactions.[8] Allergens such as pollen extract were injected into the skin of the forearm of allergic subjects in the normal waking condition, and then again under hypnosis with the following suggestion: "You will have the same injection again, but this time there will be no response; there will be no heat, no redness, no swelling, no itching, no reaction. Your arm will no longer respond to the fluid as it did before. It will be just as if water had been pricked in." The allergic response, as measured by the swelling of the skin and increase in skin temperature, could be reduced by this hypnotic suggestion.

As we saw in the historical introduction, Charcot and Janet, and afterwards Freud, came to believe that the mysterious symptoms of hysterical neurosis could be both caused and cured by *ideas* alone. We see here an interesting parallel: that ideas, and feelings, can contribute to and can

[8] S. Black, "Inhibition of Immediate-Type Hypersensitivity Response by Direct Suggestion under Hypnosis," *British Medical Journal*, I (1963), pp. 925–29.

remedy psychosomatic symptoms. Experiments of this kind are often classed with the wonders of hypnotism. It is more accurate to class them with the wonders of psychosomatic processes. The contribution of hypnotism is not uniquely important—it consists merely in heightening the imaginative processes and giving direct suggestions. It evokes stronger somatic reactions, perhaps because the trains of thought suggested under hypnosis are not opposed by competing mental activities that normally occur in the waking state. Similar effects can be obtained by imagination without hypnosis. Digestive secretions can be provoked merely by talking about thick juicy streaks or other relished foods. For our present purposes the important thing is the close relation between psychic and somatic processes. States of conflict, feelings of relish or disgust, thoughts and fantasies about eating are all closely linked to bodily processes governed by the autonomic nervous system. This is the basic fact that lies behind psychosomatic disorders.

The Autonomic Nervous System

The autonomic nervous system, sometimes called the "involuntary" or the "vegetative" nervous system, is a system of motor nerves governing what Cannon has called "the domestic affairs of the interior of the organism." It is intimately connected with the cerebrospinal system, having centers in the medulla, midbrain, hypothalamus, and cerebral cortex, yet it is to some extent set apart both anatomically and functionally. In general, the axons of autonomic neurons do not proceed from the central nervous system directly to muscles or glands; instead they pass to outlying ganglia which serve as relay stations on the way to the final goal. In contrast to the cerebrospinal system which innervates the striated muscles responsible for movement and posture, the autonomic system acts upon the glands and smooth muscles of the viscera and blood vessels.

The autonomic is divided into two subsystems which have somewhat antagonistic effects. The *sympathetic* system is mainly concerned with mobilizing the resources of the body for use in work or in emergencies. Anatomically it is well designed to act more or less as a whole: the sympathetic ganglia lie in an interconnected chain so that excitation at any one level is likely to spread upward and downward to reach all the organs affected by the system. The *parasympathetic* division is mainly concerned with conserving and storing the body resources. Its action is less unified, the ganglia not being interconnected, but some of its nerves branch in such a way as to reach several organs. The vagus nerve, for example, reaches the heart, the bronchi, the stomach, and the intestine. Thus both divisions of the autonomic act with less precision and more diffuseness than the cerebrospinal system.

It is easy to exaggerate the antagonism between the two divisions. Cannon originally conceived that all strong emotions such as anger and fear activated the sympathetic, suppressed the effects of the parasympathetic, and thus put the organism on an emergency footing.[9] The studies of Gellhorn and others have shown that this conception of an emergency reaction is somewhat too simple.[10] If the organism is to react effectively in a crisis, a rise in parasympathetic activity must closely follow the initial burst of sympathetic discharge. The interaction between the two divisions proves to be quite complex; reciprocal action is necessary to maintain an effective bodily state either in emergencies or in quieter times. For our present purposes it is probably better to emphasize not the two parts but the action of the autonomic system as a whole in managing the domestic economy of viscera, blood vessels, and glands.

The autonomic response to a danger signal brings about a marvellously complete preparation for fight or flight. Consider, for example, a deer grazing contentedly in a clearing when a leopard emerges from the forest some distance away. Upon perceiving movement along the edge of the forest, alarm registers immediately in the deer's brain. Involuntarily the deer freezes into immobility, its ears are pricked, its head is turned straight in the direction of the danger, and it sniffs the wind. Meanwhile its body goes through the emergency preparations to flee. Its muscles tense because then they can contract faster and with more power than if they are relaxed. Its liver releases into the bloodstream a large supply of sugar which will be needed as fuel for the muscular effort during flight. Its heart beats faster and its blood pressure rises so that the blood can deliver sugar and oxygen to the muscles faster. The hunger that led it out into the clearing disappears in a flash, because a species as poorly armed to fight as the deer would not survive long if they continued eating in such circumstances.[11] In a sudden attack of diarrhea the deer empties its bowel so that it can run faster, much as men jettison the cargo of a plane that is in danger of losing altitude. Now the deer is prepared for the tumultuous exertion that will be required to save its life if that movement off in the distance turns out to be a leopard.

It is easy to see that psychosomatic disorders in man involve the same physiological functions as these emergency mechanisms. Rheumatoid arthritis results from chronic involuntary muscle tension. Peptic ulcers and colitis are disturbances in the timing and intensity of digestive functions. Essential hypertension and cardiovascular disease result from dysfunctions

9 W. B. Cannon, *Bodily Changes in Pain, Hunger, Fear, and Rage* (2nd ed.; Appleton-Century-Crofts, 1929).

10 E. Gellhorn, *Autonomic Regulations: Their Significance for Physiology, Psychology, and Neuropsychiatry* (New York: Interscience Publishers, Inc., 1943), especially chaps. 14 and 15.

11 Dogs and large cats, on the other hand, growl or roar when threatened during feeding and they eat faster if danger increases. Fear does not destroy their appetite because they are armed well enough to survive by fighting. In this respect man is like the deer: fear wipes out hunger because he is better equipped to flee than to fight. These observations and the illustration of the deer and leopard are drawn from A. T. W. Simeons, *Man's Presumptuous Brain* (New York: E. P. Dutton & Co., 1962).

in blood pressure and heart rate. Diabetes is a disorder in the regulation of blood sugar. Asthma is a respiratory disorder. Hives and Raynaud's syndrome are disturbances in skin function and the regulation of body heat. As a general statement we can say that psychosomatic symptoms result when emergency reactions of the autonomic nervous system are chronically invoked in circumstances in which physical survival no longer depends on them.

Normally the autonomic nervous system maintains an effective equilibrium. Strong emotion is accompanied by overactivity in some part of the system, but strong emotion is usually transient. Anger subsides, and heart rate and blood pressure go back to normal levels. Acute grief passes, and appetite returns to its customary state. The healthy digestive tract, heart, circulation, and respiratory system are equal to quite a large amount of overactivity if occasion demands. Naturally there are limits, beyond which prolonged overactivity tends to create serious dysfunction and even permanent injury. In order to explain psychosomatic disorders it is necessary to show why certain patterns of autonomic discharge remain persistently active in the absence of what appear to be suitable circumstances.

Chronic Autonomic Stimulation

Curiously enough, it is upon our capacious brains that we must lay the responsibility for psychosomatic disorders. The human cerebral cortex, vastly developed in comparison with the deer's, must be reckoned a great evolutionary success, but some of its side effects are troublesome. As Simeons points out, the cerebral hemispheres developed initially to discriminate incoming sensory stimulation, so that mammals need not respond instinctively to all of them.[12] This function was better performed if the brain could maintain a large storehouse of memories readily available to guide behavior in new situations. But this requirement eventually led to the possibility of reflecting about the past and imagining the future. This placed additional burdens on autonomic mechanisms, which were now often called into action by imagined and symbolic threats. In Selye's formulation the adaptive reaction to stress occurs in three stages: an *alarm reaction* that quickly mobilizes the body's defensive forces, a *stage of resistance* to sustain the response to continued stress, and, if the stress continues too long, a *stage of exhaustion* in which protective reactions fail and the animal succumbs.[13] A tough and healthy creature can sustain a long hard fight or flight, but there is a time limit to the internal protective reactions, and if pressed close to this limit they begin to produce destructive tissue change in the organs that are involved.

Animals respond mainly to situations immediately present and do not,

12 *Ibid.*, pp. 7–59.
13 H. Selye, "General Adaptation Syndrome and Diseases of Adaptation," *Journal of Clinical Endocrinology*, VI (1946), pp. 117–28.

as far as we know, worry about the future. They may have hot wars but they do not have cold wars. Emergencies in the lives of modern men are quite commonly of longer duration. They are the autonomic reaction patterns designed for hot wars in those more extended emergencies that are analogous to cold wars. Future events may be the subject of worry long before they happen; past deeds may be regretted long afterwards; resentments may simmer for a long time. Despite the adages, we *do* cross bridges before we come to them and cry over spilled milk. Since man must use what he has, he adapts "for long-term purposes devices designed for short-term needs." [14] And if the term lasts too long, destructive tissue changes may happen in the organs that participate in the physiological protective reaction.

The protective reactions may be used not only for too long a time but in a way that is not appropriate to the actual situation. Thus the body may be mobilized to fight—to engage in strenuous muscular activity—when the real provocation to anger has been of a social or symbolic kind. Perhaps the source of annoyance is a child's misbehavior which must be dealt with by verbal punishment; perhaps it is a slur cast by an acquaintance which must be countered by repartee or an intelligent argument; or perhaps it is an insult by the boss which you dare not repay for fear of losing your job. In the ensuing behavior if the mobilized bodily resources are not used for muscular exertion, as they were originally intended, there may be a long delay in restoring the internal physiological balance. When such symbolic provocations occur repeatedly, even continuously, then the body remains in a continual state of emergency and those are the conditions that lead to psychosomatic breakdown.

Hypotheses Concerning the Location of Disorder

What principles govern the selection of the organ system that becomes disordered? The simplest hypothesis would be that each person breaks down at his weakest point. Serious disturbance occurs first in the organ that happens to be weakest or most vulnerable. The person with a sensitive digestive tract has gastritis or ulcers, the one with a sensitive skin has eczema or some other inflammation, the one with inherent breathing difficulty has asthma. If this hypothesis is used alone, as an attempt at complete explanation, it makes no use of the possibility that different emotions are associated with different autonomic patterns. It can be founded upon the idea of innate differences in the sensitivity of organs, or it can be widened a little by the assumption that the afflicted organ has been weakened by illness or injury. The argument for constitution has a persuasive advocate in George Draper, who for many years, starting before the current interest in psychosomatic medicine, followed the tradition established by Hip-

[14] H. G. Wolff, quoted by S. Cobb, in *Emotions and Clinical Medicine* (New York: W. W. Norton & Co., Inc., 1950), p. 138.

pocrates in pointing out associations between disease and physical type. These associations cannot be overlooked, although they are rarely so close and inevitable as to support a purely constitutional theory.[15]

At the opposite extreme is the so-called "specificity hypothesis," which makes a maximum use of the idea that different emotional states have different patterns of autonomic discharge. Radically stated, the hypothesis would run as follows: Each variety of psychosomatic disorder results from a specific emotional constellation. As Franz Alexander expressed it in an early statement: "Just as the nature of the chronic unrelieved emotional state varies, so also will the corresponding vegetative disturbance vary." [16] In order to justify the hypothesis of specificity it is necessary to demonstrate a close correlation between type of somatic disorder and type of emotional maladjustment. The argument becomes much stronger if it is possible to go further and show a rationale for the correlation, a credible chain of processes leading from the unrelieved emotional state to the end result of organic dysfunction. Occasionally it has seemed that both points could be carried as regards some particular disorder, but Alexander himself finally concluded that the specificity hypothesis would not stand alone.[17] As so often happens, a simple hypothesis that seemed adequate in an early stage of research became discredited when the problems were more intensively studied.

A theory that is sufficient to encompass what we know today about psychosomatic disorders must be more complex than either the constitutional or the specificity hypothesis. These two, however, can guide us for the time being, and we shall be in a better position to improve our formulations when we have looked more closely at some of the disorders. We shall concentrate our attention on three primary groups of disorders: gastrointestinal, cardiovascular, and respiratory. Among these we shall focus for illustrative purposes mainly on peptic ulcer, chronic hypertension, and asthma.

GASTRO-INTESTINAL DISTURBANCES

Formation of Peptic Ulcers

It has been estimated that one out of ten Americans develops a stomach ulcer at some time.[18] The formation of ulcers usually comes after a prolonged period of chronic gastric distress. Discomfort is felt about two hours

15 G. Draper, C. W. Dupertuis, and J. L. Caughey, *Human Constitution in Clinical Medicine* (New York: Paul B. Hoeber, Inc., 1944).

16 F. Alexander, "Fundamental Concepts of Psychosomatic Research: Psychogenesis, Conversion, Specificity," *Psychosomatic Medicine*, V (1943), pp. 205–10.

17 F. Alexander, *Psychosomatic Medicine: Its Principles and Applications* (New York: W. W. Norton & Co., Inc., 1950).

18 J. C. Coleman, *Abnormal Psychology and Modern Life* (3rd ed.; New York: Scott, Foresman and Co., 1964).

after eating and can be alleviated by taking food. During the day the patient can keep fairly comfortable by frequent snacks, but at night his distress is likely to increase. Ulcer formation results from chronic overactivity and oversecretion by the stomach. Under normal circumstances the stomach becomes active when a meal is to be digested. With the accomplishment of this task and the passing of the meal into the intestines, the stomach comes to rest and its acid secretion stops. Severe stress or protracted emotional conflict can work in several ways to upset the normal digestive cycle.[19] First, the alarm system may shut down the blood supply to the stomach, just as if a predator were approaching. If this is mild it strangles the thin-walled veins and blocks the drainage of blood from the stomach, which produces congestion (gastritis or stomach irriation). But if the constriction is strong, it shuts down even the strong-walled arteries. This, in turn, causes the uppermost cells of the stomach lining to lose their oxygen supply and die, exposing the lower layers to erosion by the gastric acid. These lower cells are endowed with less resistance than the upper cells, so they succumb easily to the powerful acid and leave small incipient ulcer craters in the lining. Under normal circumstances such sores would heal very quickly, even in a few hours. However, psychological stress can thwart this natural therapy by activating the parasympathetic system and increasing the secretion of stress hormones, both of which make the stomach secrete more acid, even after the food has left the stomach. Since there is no food to absorb the acid secretions, they only irritate and inflame the mucous lining of the stomach and the upper part of the small intestine (duodenum). This makes the small ulcers even larger, and the continuing hyperacidity makes it difficult for them to heal.

Various experiments with animals have shown that prolonged acid secretion in the stomach elicited by stress eventually produces ulceration.[20] These results are sufficiently conclusive, but hardly as dramatic as those obtained with a human patient by Wolf and Wolff.[21] The patient at the age of nine had drunk some scalding soup which seriously burned his esophagus so that it became closed with scar tissue. In order to feed him, a surgical opening (gastric fistula) was made directly into the stomach through the abdominal wall. At the age of fifty-six the man was in excellent health and rarely suffered digestive difficulties. The fistula was in regular use; it was sufficiently large to permit observation of the stomach walls, and, to make matters perfect for science, a collar of gastric mucosa

[19] This account of the physiological processes in the pathogenesis of ulcers is based on Simeons, op. cit., p. 99; Treisman, op. cit., p. 500; and E. Weiss and O. S. English, Psychosomatic Medicine (3rd ed.; Philadelphia: W. B. Saunders Co., 1957), pp. 292–95. These sources draw mainly on the original work of H. Cushing, "Peptic Ulcers and the Interbrain," Surgery, Gynecology and Obstetrics, LV (1932), pp. 1–34, and S. Wolf and H. G. Wolff, Human Gastric Function (New York: Oxford University Press, 1947).

[20] W. L. Sawrey and J. M. Sawrey, "Conditioned Fear and Restraint in Ulceration," Journal of Comparative and Physiological Psychology, LVII (1964), pp. 150–51.

[21] Wolf and Wolff, op. cit.

had grown out to surround the fistula, thus exposing to direct view a small amount of tissue essentially similar to that which lines the stomach. We shall have more to say about this man in a moment. What is important here is the experimental demonstration that gastric juice produces ulceration. A small erosion occurring on the exposed gastric mucosa, where the supply of mucus was poor, was artificially kept moist with gastric juice for four days. The erosion increased in size, resembled in every way a chronic ulcer, and was painful when touched. When a dressing was placed so as to protect the ulcer from gastric juice, the area healed completely in three days, leaving no trace of a scar.

We know then that ulcers result from increased motility and acid secretion in the digestive tract, which are stimulated by the parasympathetic division of the autonomic nervous system, acting through the vagus nerve. Various studies have shown that gastric ulceration is produced by chronic vagal stimulation, resulting from injuries in the midbrain, drugs, or the shock caused by serious burns. Now we can consider what constellation of factors in everyday life conspire to create the conditions for peptic ulcers to develop. Maher lists three principal determinants that we shall follow in our discussion: (1) prolonged stress, (2) predisposing biological or constitutional factors, and (3) certain kinds of personality patterns.[22]

Prolonged Stress

The level of gastric acid is readily affected by the emotions, especially unpleasant ones like tension, anxiety, or anger. Brady has demonstrated that such stress can cause peptic ulcers in animals if sufficiently prolonged.[23] Pairs of monkeys were placed in restraining chairs and subjected to brief electric shocks every twenty seconds for six hours of every twelve. One of them (the executive) was provided a lever which, when pressed, prevented the shock to either animal. If he failed to press it in time, both monkeys received the shock. The control monkey also had a lever but it was useless, so the executive monkey was responsible for the welfare of both partners. They shared the same amount and frequency of punishment and the same degree of restraint, but the executive had the additional burden of repeatedly making decisions and taking action to prevent unpleasant events. Naturally he learned very well how to avoid shocks by pressing the lever, so both monkeys received relatively few shocks. However, within a few weeks the executive monkeys died of perforating ulcers, while the control monkeys remained healthy.

A natural human experiment concerned a Dr. Hoelzel, a Chicago scientific specialist in the physiology of the stomach who regularly monitored

---

22 B. A. Maher, *Principles of Psychopathology* (New York: McGraw-Hill Book Co., 1966), p. 250.

23 J. V. Brady, "Ulcers in Executive Monkeys," *Scientific American*, CXCIX (1958), pp. 95–100.

his own gastric juices.[24] In January of 1928 his landlady was shot dead during an attempted robbery. Hoelzel was responsible for the arrest of the culprits, and for ten days following their apprehension he was acutely anxious that he would be killed in revenge. On the morning of the shooting, his gastric acid was 100 per cent higher than the highest level it reached normally, and it remained more than 30 per cent above the normal level until he moved to a safer place.

Finally, we shall illustrate the close connection between gastric hyperacidity and psychological stress with the following dream of a man with a history of chronic, mild irritation of the digestive tract (gastritis, colitis):

He was in his childhood home with his family when they were accosted by a strange gang of hoodlums. In the ensuing fight he and several others in his family were wounded by pistol fire. The hoodlums fled through the back alley in the family's car. After lying low for a few minutes, the family left the house to seek help from the neighbors. But just as they emerged from the front door they spied the hoodlums returning through the back way. Thinking they must have returned "to finish the job" so no witnesses would be left to testify against them, the family hurried back into the house to lock the doors and call the police. The man himself realized that this was not a very safe defense because the hoodlums could quickly cut the telephone line, force their way into the house and have the family at their mercy. Therefore, as soon as the rest were locked inside the house he made a break for the neighbor's house next door. He realized this was risky because he was the most seriously wounded, bleeding profusely from gunshot wounds in the lungs and elsewhere. If no one were home next door, he might not have the strength for a longer chase to other houses further down the street. But it appeared that he had no other choice. The others in his family were too horrified to think clearly and it was certain death for all of them to be trapped in the house. The hoodlums saw him as they came out of the garage and they began to give chase. Now he realized that his neighbor would be in the same jeopardy as his own family. Therefore, his only chance was to alert as many neighbors as possible before he was caught so that at least one of them could get a phone call through to the police before their lines were cut. But the hoodlums were not far behind and he was already beginning to get dizzy. . . .

At this point the man awoke, understandably in a state of intense anxiety. He was sweating, breathing heavily, passing gas, and feeling extreme pressure to urinate. He felt a painful tingling and soreness about the walls of his whole abdomen that was similar to what he felt after a severe bout of indigestion. He had to drink several glasses of water before the discomfort was relieved. Upon inquiry about the dream, he immediately associated it with a meeting of top level staff in his company that was held the previous day. He had only recently joined the firm and was already beginning to feel "very much at home with his new family," thinking he might want to stay there permanently. At the meeting a policy issue was discussed which he considered to have far-reaching implications

[24] S. Wright, *Applied Physiology* (8th ed.; New York: Oxford University Press, 1945).

for the future direction of the company and his role in it, which would influence greatly how happy he could be with his work if he stayed there. Consequently, he took a strong stand on the issue in order to persuade his colleagues to his way of thinking. However, he was opposed by a small, but very vocal, group of junior employees, whom he easily identified as the hoodlums in his nightmare. The decision of his colleagues went against him, leaving him angry about their poor judgment and depressed about the long-term viability of the firm. Apparently no one else shared his sentiments.

This case illustrates man's pernicious capacity to symbolize potential threats and to magnify their future significance, often without full awareness. Unfortunately, the human body does not come equipped with a thermostat that adjusts the physiological responses for degrees of psychological abstraction.

Predisposing Constitutional Factors

We introduced the concept of somatic compliance when studying the formation of hysterical symptoms. Constitutional predisposition is even more important in psychosomatic disorders. From our discussion of the mechanics of ulcer formation we can infer that people with low cell resistance in the stomach or high levels of acid secretion are more prone to peptic ulcers. There is no definitive evidence on the first hypothesis but it is known that the resistance of body tissues in general depends upon hormone levels and there are wide individual differences in these. The second hypothesis has been confirmed by Mirsky and co-workers.[25] They measured levels of gastric secretion in 2,073 army inductees at the beginning of basic training. They selected for follow-up 8–16 weeks later 63 with pepsinogen levels in the top 15 per cent of the total distribution and 57 from the bottom 9 per cent. Four draftees had duodenal ulcers to start with and five more developed an ulcer by the second examination. All nine were in the group with the highest rates of gastric secretion. Psychological testing indicated that the draftees with ulcers had strong underlying needs to be fed and supported. They were anxious about expressing hostility for fear of losing desired support. But when support was withheld, they were unable to express the anger they felt. From this we can see that stress, level of gastric secretion, and personality all contribute to the etiology of peptic ulcers.

The hypothalamus is extremely important in controlling the autonomic nervous system. It regulates the rage and flight responses and can influence the motility of the gut and the supply of blood to the muscles. For this reason regular stimulation by electrodes implanted in the hypothala-

25 H. Weiner, M. Thaler, M. R. Reiser, and I. A. Mirsky, "Etiology of Duodenal Ulcer: I. Relation of Specific Psychological Characteristics to Rate of Gastric Secretion (Serum Pepsinogen)," *Psychosomatic Medicine*, XIX (1957), pp. 1–10.

mus can produce ulcers in animals.[26] The hunger center is also located there and these drive systems interact. We tend to be irritable when hungry, perhaps because our ancestors had to be prepared to hunt and fight for their food when they were hungry. Ask any housewife about the mood of their children just before suppertime and you will understand why so many are grateful that *Sesame Street* and *Electric Company* are scheduled at that time. On the other hand, we are more contented and agreeable when well fed. Not much is known about individual differences in hypothalamic function, but therein lie almost certainly many of the keys to the causes of ulcers.

It has also been found that blood of type O predisposes to duodenal ulcer, although the mode of action is not understood.[27]

At a more clinical level, it has long been noticed that ulcer patients tend to the linear, lanky type of physique.[28] Male ulcer patients are generally of slender build, a little above average height but below average in weight. Head and face tend to be narrow, features small, the chest particularly narrow and of small circumference. Their physique tends to be somewhat feminine in character, though not so markedly as in certain other disease groups. Draper points out that not all ulcer patients conform to this physical description. Yet the trend is so marked that it cannot be considered a chance phenomenon. Thus it appears that a linear physique is connected in some way with a proneness to ulcers, although the mode of connection cannot yet be precisely specified.

Personality Patterns in Cases of Peptic Ulcer

Brady chose to call his ulcer-prone monkeys "executives" because ulcers occur frequently in ambitious, hard-driving business executives and others in responsible positions. Peptic ulcers once had the nickname of "Wall Street stomach." Alexander psychoanalyzed several such patients and found a very different emotional constellation beneath the surface.[29] Consciously they saw themselves as efficient, active, and productive. They liked to assume responsibilities, have people depend on them, be the effective leader and the self-sufficient, even aggressive personality. But their unconscious thinking revealed a very strong craving for love and a need for dependence and help. It was clear that they felt ashamed of their dependence. They wanted to fit the American masculine prototype. Sometimes they even assumed more responsibilities than were required of them. But these strenuous efforts did not eliminate their dependent needs. Longings for rest, care,

26 Treisman, *op. cit.*, p. 500.

27 W. K. Cowan, "Blood Groups and Disease. ABH Antigens on Human Duodenal Cells," *British Medical Journal*, II (1962), pp. 946–48.

28 Draper, *et al.*, *op. cit.*, p. 117.

29 F. Alexander, "The Influence of Psychological Factors upon Gastro-Intestinal Disturbances," *Psychoanalytic Quarterly*, III (1934), pp. 501–39. Reprinted in Tomkins, *op. cit.*, chap. 8.

and affection came out in their fantasies and dreams. Could it be that the same longings came out in chronic parasympathetic stimulation of the digestive processes?

The last question is the crux of the psychosomatic problem. The conflict between active assertion and dependent longings is readily understandable, especially in a competitive business society which places a high value on the former trend. The crucial point that requires explanation is the relationship between dependent longings and the process of digestion. On this point Alexander offered the following hypothesis. When dependent longings are severely suppressed either by reaction formation or by the pressure of external circumstances, they receive no gratification and hence remain in a more or less chronic state of tension. This tension activates the digestive processes because of a long-standing associative link between the receiving of loving care and the receiving of food. In infancy these benefits are received all at once: the baby is taken up, cuddled, stimulated, fed, loved, then put down again to go to sleep. Being fed is the predominant element in this complex of affectionate care, and a conditioned response is formed which links anticipatory digestive activity with all the rest of the complex. Very likely, Alexander admitted, this linkage exists in everyone. Most people, however, either sufficiently outgrow their dependent longings so that no great tension accumulates on that score, or at least do not react violently against them, allowing them sufficient indulgence to reduce the tension. It requires a quite special situation to evoke chronic stimulation of digestive processes. The situation must be such that dependent longings persist strongly but are denied any overt satisfaction. As an added support for his thesis Alexander pointed out that ulcer patients sometimes recover without medication when they go to bed or go to the hospital. Recovery could not occur unless parasympathetic stimulation ceased, relieving the digestive tract of its acid excess. The fact of his illness removes the patient from strenuous activity. He can now legitimately relax and accept the attentive ministrations of nurses or members of the family. At last his dependent longings are satisfied and do not have to expend themselves in chronic stimulation of the digestive process.

The medical measures used to cure peptic ulcers include rest, a bland diet to minimize irritation of the stomach and duodenum, and frequent feeding in order to utilize the acid excess. If the ulcers do not heal under this regimen it becomes necessary to remove them surgically. Occasionally the vagus nerves are severed at the stomach in order to prevent further hypermotility and hypersecretion, but this is an operation of last resort. With the exception of the last operation, these measures would not be expected, according to Alexander's hypothesis, to prevent a recurrence of the disorder. When a strenuous reaction formation plays an important part in the genesis of ulcers, the only permanent cure is psychotherapy. The aim of this therapy is to relax the patient's defenses against the dependent longings. When he is able to admit them and ease his overdriving reaction formation, he alters the crucial situation that kept his digestive tract ceaselessly active. He learns to permit himself a certain amount of passive gratification without shame, and he avoids the extremes of activity that only serve to build up dependent longings. In short, he learns to conform to an emotional regimen that suits his personal patterns of motives and that likewise suits his autonomic nervous system. In many cases this opens the way to a further outgrowing of dependent longings.

Other investigators believe that resentment and hostility play a central part in the genesis of peptic ulcer. Mittelman and Wolff, for example, induced emotional states in ulcer patients and in normal subjects by discussing with them various emotionally charged situations in their lives.[30] When these discussions gave rise to anxiety, hostility, and resentment, there was increased motility and acidity in the stomachs of all ulcer patients and some normal patients. Acidity and motility could be reduced by inducing feelings of contentment and well-being. The man with the gastric fistula reported by Wolf and Wolff behaved in a similar fashion. Pathogenic changes came at moments in his life when he was dominated by feelings of anger and resentment. They were particularly acute when he was discharged from a small outside job on grounds of inefficiency, and when a man who lent him money tried to meddle in his affairs. When he experienced fear or sadness, on the contrary, the gastric mucosa became pale and motility and acidity dropped.

In his studies Draper worked out with great care the history of the patient's attacks of gastric pain and ulceration. Many times an acute attack was precipitated by conflict with a mother figure in which the patient felt rejected. Quite frequently the wife's pregnancy and the withdrawal of her interest from the patient to a newborn child provoked gastric difficulties. Often the patient had an extreme sense of guilt over sexual relations, but his guilt revolved chiefly around pleasing or not pleasing his partner. Sometimes the precipitating cause was an event that created a sense of failure. It happened not infrequently that anger and aggression were the outstanding emotions just prior to an attack. These findings argue against a specific emotional constellation as the cause of the gastric conditions that lead to ulceration. All of the emotions discussed here bear a plausible relation to gastric dysfunction because of what we have learned about their connection with the hypothalamus and its mediation of the digestive processes. The evidence is less clear about any regularities in *learned connections* between specific emotional states and gastric function, especially if it involves infantile learning and unconscious learning. That is not surprising since one is then moving over into the sphere of *personal meanings*, a realm always marked by great diversity.

[30] B. Mittelman, H. G. Wolff, and M. Scharf, "Emotions and Gastro-duodenal Functions," *Psychosomatic Medicine*, IV (1942), pp. 5–61.

Anorexia Nervosa

We turn next to a disorder characterized by a highly negative attitude toward food. Appetite and eating is suppressed to such an extent that much weight is lost, in some cases until death by starvation occurs. The disorder is far more common in women than in men and usually occurs during adolescence, in connection with the onset of puberty, sexual relationships, and marriage. Typically, a teen-age girl stops eating and begins to lose weight. The menstrual periods cease and people close to her become quite concerned, urging her to eat. But she deviously evades the matter or dismisses it cavalierly as unimportant, while maintaining a level of vigorous physical activity that is quite astonishing for someone so emaciated. The disorder may be medically confused with severe pituitary disease because of the regression in sexual function and lowered basal metabolism, but it is generally agreed that anorexia nervosa is primarily a psychogenic, rather than an endocrine, disorder.[31] Obviously, serious endocrine imbalance is brought about, probably by the extreme loss of weight, but if treatment is successful the return of normal sexual functions often follows improvement in nutrition.

Distortion in body image, anxiety, and obsessional neurotic symptoms occur in many cases, and severe anorexia is a prodromal stage of schizophrenia in a few cases, being followed within a few months by florid psychotic symptoms. Usually the core of the problem is a severe crisis in psychological maturation.[32] Sometimes the motivation seems to turn on the desire to remain thin, flat-breasted, and sexually unattractive; there is anxiety connected with becoming sexually mature. In other cases the anxiety arises from an unconscious fear of oral impregnation, the association between food and impregnation being based on a childhood misconception of how babies are conceived. In still other cases anorexia has the significance of an aggressive resistance to parental demands or a refusal to become like the same-sexed parent. The attitude most commonly observed in anorexia is disgust (etymologically, the opposite of taste). Often the disgust is focused on food, but that is usually symbolic of distaste for other aspects of one's life. One patient reported that the disgust "can spread out from eating to the whole world, to the whole of life." [33] Many patients can talk freely about the central problem: not wanting to grow up, not wanting to become like their mother. It is easy to see that eating is closely associated with developmental advances throughout childhood, from nursing to drinking from a cup, from being fed to feeding oneself, and "you must eat well

[31] K. Oberdisse, H. G. Solbach and H. Zimmerman, "Die Endokrinologischen Aspekte der Anorexia Nervosa," in J. E. Meyer and H. Feldmann, eds., *Anorexia Nervosa* (Stuttgart, Germany: Georg Thieme Verlag, 1965), pp. 21–33.
[32] J. E. Meyer, "Anorexia Nervosa of Adolescence," *British Journal of Psychiatry*, CXVIII (1971), pp. 539–42.
[33] Meyer, *op. cit.*, p. 541.

in order to grow up to be big and strong like your parents." The natural concern of parents about their children's eating makes it an obvious symbol for expressing resistance to any frightening or mysterious aspect of growing up. The diversity of personal meanings associated with the refusal to eat makes it necessary to study each case individually in order to understand the etiology of the disorder in that instance.[34]

Disorders of Elimination

Let us recall the deer that was literally "scared shitless" by his perception of the leopard. The physiological mechanism that evacuated his bowel was an instinctively triggered contraction of the muscles that surround the colon. In humans the same mechanism can be invoked by perpetual emotional arousal. Chronic overaction of the parasympathetic pathways causes excessive secretion of mucus in the colon and spasm in the muscles, which impedes the circulation of blood and leads to congestion. In mild cases this results in chronic constipation which later passes over into diarrhea, generally of a painful character because the colon is irritated. Experimental stimulation of parasympathetic fibers does not produce *colitis,* but there is strong evidence for their overactivity. White, Cobb, and Jones studied sixty mucous colitis patients and found that the three emotions most commonly associated with their tension were anxiety, resentment, and guilt.[35] The patients were generally overconscientious, dependent on the opinion of others, easily thrown into a state of guilt. Acts of injustice to themselves or others filled them with resentment which brought guilt in its train. Of particular importance was the tendency toward rigid, obsessive thinking which led to long periods of brooding preoccupation. This constant preoccupation was presumed to be responsible for the prolonged tension and hence for the action of the parasympathetic system on the colon.

In more extreme cases the muscle spasms strangle the arteries that feed the inner surface of the colon, causing the death of the cells lining the gut. This condition is called *ulcerative colitis.* Movements are very frequent, as many as twenty times a day, but they consist mostly of blood, mucus, dead bits of tissue, and very little fecal matter.[36] Like peptic ulcers, ulcerative colitis is peculiarly resistant to medicinal treatment. Drugs, folk remedies, and surgery may be tried, but the condition will persist unless the underlying emotional tension is relieved, usually by psychological means.

[34] For a discussion of this disorder, with case illustrations, see S. Cobb, *Emotions and Clinical Medicine* (New York: W. W. Norton & Co., Inc., 1950), chap. 9. For a recent analysis of the emotional roots, see B. C. Meyer and L. A. Weinroth, "Observations on Psychological Aspects of Anorexia Nervosa," *Psychosomatic Medicine,* XIX (1957), pp. 389–98; and on treatment, J. A. Wall, "Diagnosis, Treatment, and Results in Anorexia Nervosa," *American Journal of Psychiatry,* CXV (1959), pp. 997–1001.

[35] B. V. White, S. Cobb, and C. M. Jones, "Mucous Colitis: A Psychological Medical Study of Sixty Cases," *Psychosomatic Medicine Monographs,* I (1939), p. 95.

[36] Simeons, *op. cit.,* pp. 137–38.

Psychoanalytic theorists have pointed out for years the close connection in Western society between toilet training and early emotional exchanges like giving or retaining, conforming or rebelling.[37] Just as the desire for affection and support retains in later life the power to activate the digestive process, so the desire to express angry contempt, for instance, keeps its power to affect eliminative functions.

CARDIOVASCULAR DISORDERS

In the United States 54 per cent of all deaths are due to cardiovascular disorders, and probably half of these deaths result from essential hypertension.[38] That is, one in four people dies from the effects of hypertension in one or another of the vital organs, usually the heart, brain, or kidney. We shall see that cardiovascular disorders are not unlike gastro-intestinal disturbances in their etiology, but they present the gravest threat to life, not even excepting cancer. Moreover, heart conditions and hypertension account for 22 per cent of the chronic disorders that cause restriction of activity, e.g., work, housekeeping or going to school.[39] Our primary purpose here is to describe some distinctive features of cardiovascular disorders that bring up important new points.

To understand cardiovascular disorders let us begin, as before, with a brief synopsis of the system's normal function.[40] In a sudden emergency an immediate increase in arterial blood supply is required by the heart and body muscles, the brain, kidneys, and many other organs, but not the intestinal tract. To bring this about quickly the sympathetic division of the autonomic nervous system constricts the peripheral arteries through little muscles in the arterial walls. This increases blood pressure through the body just as squeezing on a hose increases the force of water from a lawn sprinkler. Meanwhile, the chemical systems gradually increase the pace of the heart until the volume of blood pumped is adequate to the increased needs of the body's musculature. When that is accomplished, the peripheral arteries relax, lowering the pressure, because the volume of blood fed into the organs is sufficient for the exertions of fight or flight. This secondary relaxation of the arteries and the normalization of blood pressure causes the phenomenon called colloquially "second wind," the feeling of renewed strength and vigor after the initial exertion has apparently used up one's physical resources. But second wind can occur only if the additional blood supply is actually used in muscular effort. If not, blood pressure remains high; the autonomic system continues to react as if further preparation were

---

37 Alexander, "The Influence of Psychological Factors Upon Gastro-Intestinal Disturbances," *op. cit.*

38 U. S. Department of Health, Education and Welfare, *op. cit.*, p. 4. Weiss and English, *op. cit.*, p. 225.

39 U. S. Department of Health, Education and Welfare, *ibid.*, p. S–23.

40 Simeons, *op. cit.*, pp. 145–46.

still needed for fight or flight, prolonging the emergency constriction of arteries.

Essential Hypertension

The term "hypertension" does not refer to general tenseness but rather to the specific symptom of high blood pressure. Chronic elevation of blood pressure can result from various organic conditions. Hypertension is called "essential" only in those cases which prove to be free from organic disease initially. Hypertension can create unpleasant symptoms such as headache and dizziness; if prolonged, it may lead to fatal vascular accidents or cardiac failure. It can be effectively controlled medically with tranquillizing drugs or in severe cases by radical surgery that cuts the sympathetic fibers to the heart. This operation allows the patient to lead a fairly normal life, but he has to observe certain restrictions in regard to effort; his heart rate may not be much increased to meet extra demands.

Organic factors are apparently not the primary cause for essential hypertension. Constant vasoconstriction and acceleration of the heart result rather from an enduring state of emotional tension. The emotion of anger is obviously implicated, inasmuch as rage produces precisely this effect on the circulatory system. Therefore it is not surprising that many studies have found difficulties in the management of hostility and aggression among chronically hypertensive patients.[41] A series of patients studied by Saul were gentle in their outward manner, but inside they boiled with rage. This intense and chronic anger was strongly inhibited, but it was in no sense repressed. All the patients were well aware of their rebellious hostility, recognizing it clearly even though they controlled it. They found themselves in a unique psychological impasse where they could neither express the hostility more openly nor suppress it entirely. This curious midway position of hostile impulses, neither expressed nor repressed, seems to be a recurrent feature of essential hypertension. In itself there is nothing unique about a conflict between dependent submission and hostility. The conflict can be solved in various ways, such as avoiding situations that evoke submissive behavior, expressing the rebellion more openly, or repressing the hostility more deeply so that it manifests itself, if at all, in neurotic symptoms rather than a psychosomatic disorder. It is only this particular constellation that is found associated with essential hypertension: a double blocking in which the patient submits but is never reconciled to submitting, feels furious but never discharges his fury.

Experimental evidence confirms the validity of this rationale.[42] Normal

[41] Graham *et al.*, 1962, *op. cit.* L. J. Saul, "Hostility in Cases of Essential Hypertension," *Psychosomatic Medicine,* I (1939), pp. 153–61.

[42] J. E. Hokanson and S. Shetler, "The Effect of Overt Aggression on Physiological Tension Level," *Journal of Abnormal and Social Psychology,* LXIII (1961), pp. 446–48. J. E. Hokanson and M. Burgess, "The Effects of Three Types of Aggression on Vascular Processes," *Journal of Abnormal and Social Psychology,* LXV (1962), pp. 232–37.

subjects were angered deliberately by the experimenter while their blood pressures were being recorded. A control group was treated courteously. Later, half of each group was given an opportunity to administer electric shock to the experimenter. In the angry group, venting the anger in this way brought the blood pressure back to normal, but pressure remained high in that half of the angry subjects who had no chance to shock the experimenter.

Constitutional Factors in Essential Hypertension

Although emotional tension is the primary cause of essential hypertension, there is reasonably strong evidence that a constitutional predisposition for vascular and endocrine hyper-reactivity can be inherited.[43] With marked predisposition, little emotional stress is required to cause hypertension.

Hypertension usually develops in two stages. Keeping angers and conflicts from open expression may repeatedly provoke rises in blood pressure, but in the earlier phase this is brought back to normal by a homeostatic mechanism controlled by the *baroreceptor* nerves. However, high blood pressure throws a strain on blood vessels, kidneys, and other organs, which may gradually produce changes in them that cause the pressure to be maintained at a high level for physiological reasons, even if the original emotional causes no longer operate. In this later phase of *chronic hypertension*, psychological intervention alone may not be sufficient to prevent the malignant effects of the disorder.

Lest we think that constitution tells most of the story, we should keep in mind a study by Winklestein, who found elevated blood pressure in nonrelated persons living in the households of hypertensive patients.[44] This suggests an element of social contagion that underlines the significance of interpersonal factors in the etiology.

A Case of Essential Hypertension [45]

Weiss and English report a case that illustrates dramatically many of the points discussed here. A 29-year-old truckdriver was treated for rather severe hypertension. His father suffered from valvular heart disease and his paternal grandfather died of a stroke after the age of 60. Both of these cardiovascular conditions point to the hereditary vulnerability of the young patient. His father had worked for the same firm and was killed

---

[43] L. C. Mills, "Psychodynamic Factors in Hypertension," in J. H. Nodine and J. H. Moyers, eds., *Psychosomatic Medicine* (Philadelphia: Lea & Febiger, 1962), pp. 122–28. W. E. Miall and P. D. Oldham, "The Hereditary Factor in Arterial Blood Pressure," *British Medical Journal*, I (1963), pp. 75–80. G. Pickering, "Hyperpiesis: High Blood Pressure without Evident Cause—Essential Hypertension," *British Medical Journal*, II (1965), pp. 959–68, 1021–26.

[44] Schwab *et al., op. cit.,* p. 1638.

[45] Weiss and English, *op. cit.,* pp. 237, 246–49.

in an accident, but the family was denied compensation. The patient was "burned up" about that. He wanted to get involved in union activities where he would have an opportunity to avenge his father. He had previously been denied this opportunity because it meant too much work and excitement. Given permission now, he became an organizer and worked hard for the union, six hours a day, in addition to his regular eight hours on the job. Still he actually improved during the two years he was engaged in union activities. His symptoms got better and his blood pressure was normal. Then the union broke up. Again he was "choked with rage" and his blood pressure went up. This continued until his death at 38 of malignant hypertension. It seems clear that his body was relieved of internal tension as long as the union provided an effective outlet for channeling his frustrated aggressive impulses. When he was deprived of that outlet, his body resumed the burden and quite prematurely succumbed.

Coronary Heart Disease

The most common malignant effect of chronic hypertension is coronary heart disease (CHD). In an extraordinary series of studies Rosenman, Friedman, and their associates in the Western Collaborative Group not only investigated the causes of CHD but predicted its occurrence with some success.[46] In their initial studies they found that the people most prone to CHD have top levels of occupational responsibility, a family history of parental CHD and a personal history of high blood pressure, but they were less likely than average to have had peptic ulcers. The two most distinctive features of CHD victims were a characteristic personality constellation which the investigators labeled *behavior pattern A* and high levels of lipids (fat) in the blood. The characteristics of behavior pattern A were: (1) intense, sustained drive for achievement, recognition, and advancement, (2) extraordinary mental and physical alertness, (3) busy involvement with diverse responsibilities and an acute sense of urgency about deadlines for completion, (4) competitive, aggressive, and hostile feelings toward others and toward the clock. Behavior pattern B showed the opposite characteristics. Far more people of the A type than the B type suffered from CHD, though fewer than one in five knew of their heart condition. Starting in 1960 the authors measured the overt behavior pattern, blood lipids, and other aspects of 3,500 men, 39–59 years old, em-

46 M. Friedman and R. Rosenman, "Association of Specific Overt Behavior Pattern with Blood and Cardiovascular Findings," *Journal of the American Medical Association,* CLXIX (1959), pp. 1286–96. R. Rosenman and M. Friedman, "Association of Specific Behavior Pattern in Women with Blood and Cardiovascular Findings," *Circulation,* XXIV (1961), pp. 1173–84. R. Rosenman, M. Friedman, R. Strauss, M. Wurm, R. Kositchek, W. Hahn, and N. Wethessin, "A Predictive Study of Coronary Heart Disease," *Journal of the American Medical Association,* CLXXXIX (1964), pp. 15–22. R. Rosenman, M. Friedman, C. Jenkins, R. Strauss, M. Wurm, and R. Kositchek, "The Prediction of Immunity to Coronary Heart Disease," *Journal of the American Medical Association,* CXCVIII (1966), pp. 1159–62.

ployed in California industries, in an attempt to predict CHD. Over the next two years three times as many A-type men incurred coronary diseases as B-type men. Moreover, the assessment of the behavior pattern was more useful than the blood lipid method for predicting CHD, involving less predictive error.

BRONCHIAL ASTHMA

The suggestion that asthma may sometimes be a psychosomatic disorder is often met with immediate opposition. Asthma is one of the fields in which medicine has in recent years scored a triumph. Many chronic asthmatics have been given allergy tests, found allergic to certain common substances, and cured by regular inoculation with these substances. When there is chronic asthma without discoverable allergic sensitivity, it is at least as reasonable to suggest that an undiscovered allergen is provoking the attacks as it is to assume emotional factors. It is sometimes observed, moreover, that a tendency to asthma runs in families, suggesting an inherent structural weakness or innate sensitivity of the breathing apparatus. In the face of these facts one should not assume that asthma is ever psychogenic unless the claim can be supported by very strong evidence.

There is certainly no ground for assuming psychogenesis in all or even in a majority of asthma cases. Evidence exists, however, that in certain cases the breathing difficulty has become curiously linked to emotional problems. The central piece of evidence is that asthmatic attacks occur in these cases in a specific type of stressful situation. When the attacks are thus regularly associated with a certain emotion, a psychosomatic basis for the disorder is justifiably assumed. It is also known that emotional factors can contribute to, or intensify, asthmatic attacks of primary allergic origin.

Physiological Basis of Bronchial Asthma

The parasympathetic nervous system controls weeping and the respiratory defenses against airborne allergens. These responses include the secretion of tears by the eyes, the dilation of small blood vessels in the nose that causes nasal congestion, and the constriction of the bronchial passages in the lungs. The last response serves to restrict the amount of allergens inhaled but it also hinders breathing, especially exhaling, and in severe asthmatic attacks this hindrance approaches suffocation. These parasympathetic responses may be activated reflexively by local irritation of bronchial tissue or by direct innervation from the hypothalamus. The latter is the mechanism by which emotional states probably bring about asthma attacks. Various pollens, certain food proteins, and animal hairs cause the same result by the reflex mechanism in people who are allergic to them. In either case the asthmatic attack is characterized by extreme breathing difficulty, choking, and wheezing.

Asthma tends to run in families, although many asthmatics have essentially negative family histories.[47] Therefore a certain organic vulnerability may be inherited, more likely in the reactivity of the respiratory tract than in the sensitivity to specific allergens.

Prevalence and Course of the Disorder

At least one in forty persons in the United States suffers from bronchial asthma. About 60 per cent of asthmatics are children under 17, with twice as many boys as girls, although the sex ratio evens out during the adult years.[48] However, improvement is the rule in most cases: 71 per cent of asthmatic children improve considerably, usually during or soon after adolescence.[49] Asthma can be a very serious condition. In this country it causes 4,000 to 7,000 deaths annually,[50] and it accounts for more of the chronic conditions that restrict necessary everyday activities than peptic ulcer (5.1 per cent vs. 2.4 per cent).[51] Asthma is estimated to be responsible for nearly one fourth of the school days missed because of chronic illness in children.

Emotional Precipitation of Asthma Attacks

Early attention was focused on the extreme dependent attachment of psychoanalyzed asthmatics to their mothers.[52] Outwardly they presented a wide variety of personality patterns, but the common feature was a deep unconscious fear of being separated from the mother. In these cases an asthmatic attack was interpreted as the equivalent of a repressed cry for the lost mother. The physiological basis for such a connection is plausible enough and other investigators have been struck with the dependent attachments of asthmatic patients, but subsequent evidence has not confirmed the hypothesis of a specific personality constellation or nuclear conflict, and Purcell has pointed out that either conscious or unconscious attempts to suppress weeping may be avoidance responses because crying in itself can provoke an attack.[53]

Rather than speak of specific types of personality or interpersonal needs, it is more accurate to say that asthmatic attacks can be precipitated or

[47] K. Purcell and J. H. Weiss, "Asthma," in C. G. Costello, ed., *Symptoms of Psychopathology* (New York: John Wiley & Sons, Inc., 1970), p. 598.

[48] *Ibid.*, p. 599.

[49] F. H. Rackeman and M. D. Edwards, "Medical Progress: Asthma in Children: Follow-up Study of 688 Patients after 20 Years," *New England Journal of Medicine*, CCXLVI (1952), pp. 815–58.

[50] P. M. Gottlieb, "Changing Morality in Bronchial Asthma," *Journal of the American Medical Association*, CLXXXVII (1964), pp. 276–80.

[51] U. S. Department of Health, Education and Welfare, *op. cit.*, p. S–23.

[52] T. M. French and F. Alexander, "Psychogenic Factors of Bronchial Asthma," *Psychosomatic Medicine Monographs*, IV (1941), No. 1.

[53] M. Stein, "Etiology and Mechanisms in the Development of Asthma," in Nodine and Moyer, *op. cit.*, p. 153. Purcell and Weiss, *op. cit.*, p. 603.

intensified by emotional states, like anger, excitement with pleasurable feeling, anxiety or worry, and depression. Various kinds of stress may give rise to these emotional states. The manner in which this happens will depend on the needs and personal experience of each individual; wide diversity must be expected. In one case, separation anxiety may be the common precipitant. In another, it may be fear of having an attack when the medicine has been left at home. In still another, it may be resentment against parental restrictions.

An experiment reported by Stein illustrates how the personal meanings an individual applies to a situation can provoke an asthmatic attack, even in the absence of allergenic irritants.[54] A 32-year-old man with a history of asthma and severe eczema was locked in a small allergen-free chamber with a door about as thick as the usual bank vault. His initial remark was, "I'll be locked in a box and what will happen if you two suddenly collapsed and died?" The situation made him extremely apprehensive and led shortly to severe asthmatic symptoms. At the height of the attack he complained, "This is the worst I have felt in weeks." At this point an attempt was made to relieve the attack using suggestions and a nebulizer filled with saline.[55] When this placebo had no effect, the attack was promptly terminated by substituting the appropriate medicine for the saline.

A case reported by Metcalfe illustrates how a particular kind of social situation repeatedly provoked asthma attacks.[56] A young single woman kept a detailed diary of her activities for 85 days, during which time she was a patient in a hospital but free to come and go as she pleased. She suffered asthma attacks on 15 days, about one each week. Metcalfe plotted the time relations between those attacks and the patient's contacts with her mother. Nine of the 15 attacks (60 per cent) occurred within 24 hours of being with her mother, whereas only 14 of 70 (20 per cent) asthma-free days were preceded by a visit with her mother. Looked at another way, asthma attacks followed about two contacts of every five (39 per cent) with her mother although they occurred only once every ten days (10 per cent) otherwise. The degree of association between the attacks and the visits was statistically highly significant. Moreover, further analysis showed that the attacks were substantially more likely to occur if the meeting took place at home rather than outside the home. Clearly the combination of meeting with her mother and being at home was the principal psychosocial impetus for the attacks. A study of the patient in depth would be required to ferret out precisely which psychodynamic aspects in that situation were stressful for her.

54 Stein, *op. cit.*, p. 151.
55 A nebulizer is a small oral inhalator which usually emits an epinephrine mist or other stimulant that relieves the bronchial constriction by way of the sympathetic nervous system.
56 M. Metcalfe, "Demonstration of a Psychosomatic Relationship," *British Journal of Medical Psychology*, XXIX (1956), pp. 63–66.

Treatment of Bronchial Asthma

In treating asthma one must keep in mind that allergens and emotional factors can *both* contribute to an attack, regardless of which is the primary causative agent. For this reason an investigation of the causes in Metcalfe's case should not overlook the possibility that the mother may keep a favorite flower in her home to which the patient is sensitive. Obviously, where allergens are involved prevention may be possible through insight and avoidance of the irritants or through injections to increase the body's tolerance. Symptomatic relief may be obtained with antihistamines in mild attacks, regardless of the cause. More severe attacks may require epinephrine or another stimulant by oral inhalation or injection. A few extreme cases can only be treated by intensive hospital care.

Both medical and psychological methods have been used with some effectiveness to treat the psychological causes of the disorder.[57] Hypnosis and tranquilizers can facilitate relaxation and inhibit extreme emotional reactions to stress. Counseling, psychoanalysis, and family therapy usually seek some insight into the complex interpersonal transactions that habitually trigger the attacks and attempt to remedy them with appropriate role changes. Behavior therapy has attempted to desensitize patients to the psychological and social stimuli that cause anxiety or excitement, on the assumption that diminished responsivity will alleviate the severity of the attacks. While no single type of personality disturbance is characteristic of all asthmatic patients, disturbance of some kind is the rule.[58] Appropriate psychological treatments aimed at correcting those disturbances can reasonably be expected to alleviate the respiratory symptoms as well.

PROBLEM OF SYMPTOM PLACEMENT

Having examined several varieties of psychosomatic disorder, we are in a position to reconsider the difficult and critical problem of symptom placement. In a way the problem is similar to that of the choice of neurosis, but in psychosomatic disorders the chain of events is longer, extending into the domain of the autonomic nervous system and of bodily physiology. The earlier work in this field centered, as we saw, around two relatively simple hypotheses concerning the location of psychosomatic symptoms. One of these hypotheses invoked constitutional differences, stating that a disorder would make its appearance in the weakest or most vulnerable organ system. On the other hand, the specificity hypothesis held that each variety of psychosomatic disorder resulted from a specific emotional constellation which affected the autonomic system in a partic-

---

[57] Purcell and Weiss, *op. cit.*, pp. 612–20.

[58] P. H. Knapp and S. J. Nemetz, "Acute Bronchial Asthma: I. Concomitant Depression and Excitement, and Varied Antecedent Patterns in 406 Attacks," *Psychosomatic Medicine*, XXII (1960), pp. 42–56.

ular way. More recent research has clarified a great deal, especially about the physiological processes that mediate between psychological events and somatic disruptions. The facts we have examined make it clear that there is some truth in both hypotheses but neither one can stand in simple and sovereign form. The easy models that appeal to our need for simplification do not seem to fit this particular segment of reality.

Take first the specificity hypothesis. Certain connections of a quite general nature have been confirmed by several different researches, but the attempt to correlate highly specific emotional constellations with particular disorders has led to little agreement. There is much support for the view that suppressed hostility is the leading emotional problem in essential hypertension and that passive dependent feelings are prominent in peptic ulcer and bronchial asthma. These general associations, however, do not carry us far toward explaining the location of symptoms. As we include more kinds of disorder we begin to run out of broad emotional constellations to distinguish them. Anxiety, dependence, passivity, guilt, and aggression recur with monotonous frequency, so much so that Ruesch has proposed to simplify the whole problem by regarding all psychosomatic patients as immature, inadequate people who have failed to achieve independence and an adult channeling of aggression.[59] The explanatory power of these general associations is further weakened by such contrary evidence as that hostile feelings as well as dependent ones can activate the digestive processes that lead to ulcers.

While the early formulations of the specificity hypothesis have not been confirmed, a reduced version of it has been rather widely accepted. For each individual the kinds of stress, emotion, and autonomic response are reasonably regular, and the pattern of association among them can usually be understood by careful study of the personal meanings attached to them. These personal meanings and their autonomic associations seem to originate quite early in life and are extremely diverse across individuals. Thus, unless there is some built-in connection, as between anger and elevated blood pressure, no universal association can be assumed between emotional constellation and somatic disorder. The connection is an individual matter determined by experience and personal meaning.

The constitutional hypothesis has fared somewhat better. The evidence for an association between physique and type of disorder is rather thin; however, a limited but reliable hereditary predisposition has been found in most of the psychosomatic disorders. Various experimental studies bear on the question of individual differences in the patterns of autonomic response. Of particular relevance is a report by Lacey and Van Lehn, who

---

[59] J. Ruesch, "The Infantile Personality—the Core Problem of Psychosomatic Medicine," *Psychosomatic Medicine*, X (1948), pp. 131–44. This argument, however, neglects the fact that "all psychosomatics" includes a very substantial portion of the entire population and that many of them are quite mature and adequate in other respects. Here, too, knowledge permits us to be more discriminating nowadays.

studied a group of normal children at the Fels Institute.[60] Each child was given the cold pressor test, in which a lively autonomic response is evoked by immersing the hand for one minute in painfully cold water. Autonomic activity was measured in several ways, including blood pressure, heart rate, and perspiration. It was found that the children exhibited characteristic individual profiles of autonomic reaction, and that these profiles could be reproduced through a later administration of the test. There seems to be, in other words, a hierarchy of autonomic responses which is stably characteristic of each individual so that it can be referred to as his "autonomic constitution." With one child the response to stress may be most conspicuous in heart rate, with another in peripheral blood pressure, with another in perspiration, and so on.[61] Research with adult psychosomatic patients does not supply such telling evidence of early individual differences, but it yields results of the same kind. Cardiovascular patients, for example, respond to laboratory stress situations with predominant cardiovascular changes and little change in muscular tension, whereas patients complaining of head and neck pains react to the very same stress with marked muscular tension and little change in the cardiovascular system.[62]

There is no reason to doubt the existence of individual differences in the pattern of autonomic responses under stress, and there is no reason why we should hesitate to believe that some of them are innately determined. Constitution, however, does not operate in a vacuum. Almost at once it manifests itself in the child's behavior and affects the responses of others to him. This point has been worked out by Mirsky in connection with differences in the general level of gastric activity.[63] If an infant has very intense oral needs, his feeding demands may seem exorbitant even to a normally nurturing mother, especially if she has had other less greedy babies, and a relationship may be set up in which oral satisfaction is never complete. Constitution, in short, exerts much of its effect on the transactions that take place between the child and his early human environment.

It will be observed that both lines of our inquiry have arrived at the same point. On the one hand, we have been forced back from adult emotional constellations to the early childhood conditioning of autonomic

[60] J. I. Lacey and R. Van Lehn, "Differential Emphasis in Somatic Response to Stress," *Psychosomatic Medicine*, XIV (1952), pp. 71–81.

[61] E. L. Lipton, A. Steinschneider, and J. B. Richmond, "Autonomic Function in the Neonate. II. Physiological Effects of Motor Restraint," *Psychosomatic Medicine*, XXII (1960), pp. 57–65; A. Thomas, S. Chess, H. Birch, and M. E. Hertzig, "A Longitudinal Study of Primary Reaction Patterns in Children," *Comprehensive Psychiatry*, I (1960), pp. 103–12.

[62] R. B. Malmo, C. Shagass, and F. H. Davis, in *Life Stress and Bodily Disease* (Baltimore: The Williams & Wilkins Co., 1950), pp. 231–62. J. Schachter, "Pain, Fear and Anger in Hypertensives and Normatensives," *Psychosomatic Medicine*, XIX (1957), pp. 17–29.

[63] I. A. Mirsky, S. Kaplan, and R. Bro-Kahn, "Pepsinogen Excretion (Uropepsin) as Index of Influence of Various Life Situations on Gastric Secretions," *Proceedings of the Association for Research in Nervous and Mental Disease*, XXIX (1950), pp. 628–46.

patterns; on the other hand, we have been forced forward from innate differences to the effect these differences may have on the conditioning of autonomic patterns in the child's early environment. The spotlight turns to the first year or two of life, and this is exactly where we should look, according to Grinker, if we hope to unravel the secrets of psychosomatic disorders.[64]

Grinker's exposition of this theme starts from the observation that the newborn child shows very little differentiation of responses to stress. The frustrated infant "functions with everything it has available": crying, salivating, regurgitating, defecating, thrashing, becoming red in the face. The first protective response is a mass response. Differentiation of autonomic patterns soon starts, however, and may have advanced a long way before the child emerges from his preverbal life of feeling into more organized psychological patterns. Sometimes early infections or enzyme deficiencies begin the process of accentuating some and suppressing other parts of the autonomic repertory. This process is in any event strongly influenced by the atmosphere of the nursery, the circumstances of feeding, the manner in which training is carried out, the use of diets, laxatives, enemas, and special medications, in fact by anything that tends to subdue some functions and overload others. The result of all this early conditioning can be observed in many ways, but the adult anxiety response furnishes a particularly good example. Each individual has his own particular way of feeling anxious, no matter what the nature of the threat. With some people there are sinking abdominal sensations, with others shortness of breath, with others diarrhea, with others vomiting, with others palpitations, and so on through hundreds of variations. The general protective reaction has become individualized through conditioning in early childhood.

On this basis it becomes possible to explain the wide variety of organ systems that becomes involved in psychosomatic disorders. As a consequence, illness finally occurs in those elements of the bodily reaction that have been most accentuated in the course of early childhood conditioning. This explanation differs from the hypothesis of specific emotional constellations in attaching less psychological weight to the current symptom. Today's asthmatic attack does not mean that the patient is in conflict precisely over the issue of acting on an impulse or confessing it to his mother. It means that this was once a vital issue, that bronchial constriction became an accented part of the reaction to stress, and that now any prolonged reaction to stress is likely to culminate in asthmatic symptoms. Specific emotional constellations may have existed in childhood at the time when autonomic patterns were being differentiated and conditioned. Present problems *may be* very similar to the original ones, but they *do not have to be* in order to produce the symptoms. All that is needed is prolonged stress. The historically conditioned autonomic patterns will do the rest.

It is not surprising, in view of this, that rather modest therapeutic results

[64] R. R. Grinker, *Psychosomatic Research* (New York: W. W. Norton & Co., Inc., 1953), especially chaps. 5–7.

have been reported when standard psychoanalysis was used. The alteration of childhood autonomic patterns cannot really be expected. They are something with which the patient must learn to live. Marked benefit can result from freeing blocked impulses like the hypertensive's simmering anger; furthermore, the patient can learn to perceive threats in a more conscious, discriminating way that makes them less threatening. It is probably through such changes that the reported cures by psychotherapy actually come about. This does not require a deep "uncovering" technique, but it does call for a skilled and sensitive use of more superficial measures. In a program of this kind the boon of relief from symptoms can be expected for about two patients out of three.[65]

IMPLICATIONS FOR GENERAL MEDICINE

Psychosomatic research raises far-reaching problems and carries radical implications as regards the general practice of medicine. How many of the supposed bodily ailments that bring patients to the office of the general practitioner are really based on emotional maladjustment? There is no telling, but many conservative observers are putting their estimates as high as 50 per cent. A new meaning is being given to the old ideal of a sound mind in a sound body. Two generations ago the implication of this phrase was that you could not have a sound mind unless you had a sound body. Today we begin to wonder whether it is possible to have a sound body unless you have a sound mind—or, as we would be more likely to say, unless you have attained sound adaptation. For the general practitioner and family physician this is a startling change. Possibly half the time he is dealing with emotional disturbances that have come to some kind of bodily focus.

If is foolish to exaggerate the psychogenic point of view. A doctor would be stupid to diagnose a case of high blood pressure as psychogenic without making thorough tests for kidney, vascular, and other possible organic disorders. Equally foolish would be a recommendation of psychotherapy for asthma without making skin tests or taking a history of seasonal and geographical variations in the attacks. When we speak of psychosomatic disorders we do not mean that the somatic part of the disturbance has ceased to be important. The phrase implies only that the psychological aspects may also be important.

The general practitioner is at present neither well trained nor well situated to practice psychotherapy. Patients do not currently expect their physician to advise in other than strictly bodily matters and might well resent it if he seemed to be meddling in their "private affairs." These expectations will change slowly, and the doctor must always respect them. Furthermore, the training of physicians does not generally include a sufficient background in psychology to warrant their meddling in the realm of emotional adjustment. More harm than good is done by the doctor who, having excelled in chemistry and learned to regard a patient as a complex piece of machinery, leans back in his chair and tells the piece of machinery how to lead its life. Psychotherapy is a difficult art that calls for practiced skill. Some workers believe, however, that it is both possible and necessary to train the general physician along this line. In any event it is important that he recognize emotional complications and show the patient that bodily changes can be closely related to emotions. He must not, as so often happens now, encourage the psychosomatic patient to sink into a routine of invalidism and medication if there is a chance that his emotional adjustment can improve. The physician must be capable of psychosomatic diagnosis. He must know when and how to refer a patient for psychotherapy, just as he knows when to send him for any other kind of specialized treatment. He should be able to understand not only his patient's bodily economy but also his economy of happiness.

Psychosomatic medicine opens up the area where mind and body overlap, where it is no longer possible to distinguish between them. The physician of the future, whether he be general practitioner, specialist, or research worker, must be a psychosomatic physician. He must be able to describe with equal precision the tissue changes in organs, the neural pathways, and the emotional constellations that may have sent traffic over the neural pathways. The physician will be forced more and more to take account of man's emotional nature.

SUGGESTIONS FOR FURTHER READING

A stimulating, brief summary of current knowledge in this field is the chapter by Michel Treisman, "Mind, Body and Behavior: Control Systems and Their Disturbances," in P. London and D. Rosenhan, eds., *Foundations of Abnormal Psychology* (New York, Holt, Rinehart and Winston, 1968). A. T. W. Simeons' book, *Man's Presumptuous Brain: An Evolutionary Interpretation of Psychosomatic Disease* (New York, E. P. Dutton, 1962), is a fascinating little essay written for lay readers. It is beautifully and audaciously written, full of sound medical insights (and a few unsound ones) that are palatably interpreted. If you must choose only one book to read and you can do without scientific documentation—this has none—pick this one and enjoy yourself. More serious readers will find E. Weiss and O. S. English, *Psychosomatic Medicine* (3rd ed., Philadelphia, W. B. Saunders, 1957) an authoritative and useful medical textbook. More recent compendia are J. H. Nodine and J. H. Moyer, eds., *Psychosomatic Medicine* (Philadelphia, Lea and Febiger, 1962), and C. G. Costello, ed., *Symptoms of Psychopathology* (New York, John Wiley & Sons, Inc., 1970. E. Gellhorn and G. N. Loufbourrow, *Emotions and Emotional Disorders* (New York, Hoeber-Harper, 1963) gives thorough treatment of the physiological basis of psychosomatic disorders. An interesting array of cases is brought together by H. H. W. Miles, S. Cobb, and H. C. Shands in *Case Histories in Psychosomatic Medicine* (New York, W. W. Norton & Co., Inc., 1952). An important monograph on heart disorders is M. Friedman's *Pathogenesis of Coronary Heart Disease* (New York, McGraw-Hill Book Co., 1969).

13

Schizophrenic Disorders

Schizophrenia is the most common form of psychosis. One person out of five admitted for the first time to a mental hospital is given this diagnosis. Starting early in life, often during adolescence and still more often in the decade of the twenties, it can wreck the person's whole adult career and prevent him from making any useful contribution to society. If spontaneous recovery does not occur, or if treatment is not successful, the patient may become a public charge for forty or fifty years. Because the disorder has a chance to last so long, schizophrenics accumulate in mental hospitals and constitute something like 50 per cent of the inmates at any given time. The disorder must be considered highly costly, whether we reckon the cost in dollars spent or in the more important coin of human lives gone wrong.

The prevalence rate usually cited for schizophrenic disorders is one per cent although 1.5 per cent is probably more accurate.[1] This means that there are about 3,000,000 schizophrenics in the United States today. The question that may be of more direct interest than these rather abstract statistics is: What are the chances that I or someone I know will become schizophrenic? The answer is that about 3 per cent of people reaching age 15 years develop schizophrenia during their subsequent lifetime.[2] There is a common misconception that most schizophrenics reside in

[1] A. B. Hollingshead and F. C. Redlich, *Social Class and Mental Illness* (New York: John Wiley & Sons, Inc., 1958), p. 236.
[2] S. F. Yolles and M. Kramer, "Vital Statistics," in L. Bellak and L. Loeb, eds., *The Schizophrenic Syndrome* (New York: Grune & Stratton, Inc., 1969), pp. 78–79.

mental institutions, but some simple calculations can show that this is not so. In 1970, there were 457,000 patients hospitalized in state, country, private, and VA hospitals.[3] Half of them, or 228,500, can be assumed to be diagnosed schizophrenic. Obviously, more than ten times as many schizophrenics live in the community as live in mental institutions. This might seem frightening because schizophrenics are known to do unpredictable and dangerous things, such as attempting to assassinate presidential candidates.[4] However, such dangerous individuals are even less common among schizophrenics than schizophrenics are in a general population, and it is unwarranted to characterize any class of people by its extreme constituents. Moreover, we shall see that there are good reasons—economic, humanitarian, and psychiatric—why schizophrenics should not be "locked away" any longer than is absolutely necessary for the welfare of all concerned. Surely the best reason was given by Harry Stack Sullivan: everyone, even such a disorganized person as a schizophrenic, is much more simply human than otherwise.[5] Mankind required several centuries to grasp the full implications of that idea.

The term *schizophrenia* was introduced by Bleuler in 1911. It now supersedes the name *dementia praecox* originally coined by Morel in the middle of the nineteenth century and made popular by Kraepelin around the turn of the century. The older title reflected the belief that dementia, starting early and running a slow progressive course, was characteristic of all cases. We know now that the disorder does not always start early, true dementia seldom follows, and many people recover (most, if the diagnostic formulation is broad), so the term is no longer appropriate. Bleuler's term means a splitting of the personality but is not meant to suggest such gross "splits" as occur in hysterical dissociations and multiple selves. Bleuler had in mind a general loosening of associative connections and disorganization in thought and behavior. He considered this fragmentation of integrated behavior to be the truly central disorder of schizophrenia.

The different forms of schizophrenia exhibit a tremendous diversity of symptoms, leading some to question Kraepelin's historic step of classifying these divergent pictures under a single heading. The majority of experts, however, agree with Kraepelin that the different varieties have enough in common to warrant giving them a common name, but the basic nature of the disorder is not thereby established. Most cases have obvious psychodynamic features, the psychosis coming as the culmination of a history of

---

[3] U. S. Bureau of the Census, *Statistical Abstracts of the United States: 1970* (91st ed.; Washington, D. C., 1970).

[4] Sirhan Sirhan, who killed Senator Robert Kennedy in 1968, was diagnosed paranoid schizophrenic. Early indications point to a probable schizophrenic pattern in the life of Arthur Bremer, who in 1972 stalked President Nixon for some time in Canada and then shot and seriously wounded Governor George Wallace.

[5] H. S. Sullivan, *Schizophrenia as a Human Process* (New York: W. W. Norton & Co., Inc., 1962), p. 224. The most general statement of his "one genus postulate" is in H. S. Sullivan, *The Interpersonal Theory of Psychiatry* (New York: Norton, 1953), p. 32.

unsuccessful adjustments. On the other hand, certain of the phenomena are so bizarre and so extravagant that it has seemed impossible to explain them without resort to biogenic hypotheses. Over half a century ago Kraepelin wrote: "The causes of dementia praecox are at the present time still wrapped in impenetrable darkness."[6] Despite massive research efforts in the intervening years, we still don't know what goes wrong in schizophrenic disorders or what causes them. Like the six blind men who set about to identify an elephant,[7] investigators have studied schizophrenia with exhaustive thoroughness from virtually every perspective—constitution, physiology, biochemistry, the nervous system, intellectual functions, emotions, adjustment and defense, early experience, social environment—and not arrived at a compelling portrait of "the nature of the beast." Since the darkness has not been dispelled, our account here must reflect the same inquisitive bewilderment.

KRAEPELIN'S VARIETIES OF SCHIZOPHRENIA

Because it was the first, Kraepelin's system for classifying schizophrenic disorders was the one used most widely for many years. It is obvious that three of his four subgroups (paranoid, hebephrenic, and catatonic) represent aberrations in the faculties of thinking, feeling, and will or volition, respectively, which were the most popular divisions in the organization of psychology in the nineteenth century. Subsequent research has shown that these groupings are not mutually exclusive, but overlap, with the predominant symptoms changing markedly in the course of the illness, requiring a shift in diagnosis. It is clear now that this is because the subgroups have no *functional* coherence. For this reason they have fallen into disuse during the last two decades and been replaced by more useful classifications which we will consider later.[8] Nevertheless Kraepelin's categories offer a convenient format for describing schizophrenic disorders.

[6] E. Kraepelin, *Dementia Praecox and Paraphrenia,* trans. R. M. Barclay (New York: Robert E. Krieger Publishing Co., 1919, reprinted with an historical introduction, 1971), p. 224.

[7] J. G. Saxe, "The Blind Men and the Elephant: A Hindoo Fable," *The Poems of John Godfrey Saxe* (Boston: James R. Osgood and Co., 1873), pp. 135–36. These were the "six men of Indostan to learning much inclined, who went to see the Elephant (though all of them were blind)." Each found a different part of the animal: the side, tusk, trunk, knee, ear, and tail. And each reached a different conclusion about what it was like: a wall, spear, snake, tree, fan, and rope. "And so these men of Indostan disputed loud and long, each in his own opinion exceeding stiff and strong, though each was partly in the right, and all were in the wrong!" The moral is worth quoting for students of schizophrenia: "So oft in theologic wars, the disputants, I ween, rail on in utter ignorance of what each other mean, *and prate about an Elephant not one of them has seen!"*

[8] Indeed, one writer reports that a search of first admission records over a recent five-year period at one large mental hospital found not one case of hebephrenic or catatonic schizophrenia. P. London, "The Major Psychological Disorders," in P. London and D. Rosenhan, eds., *Foundations of Abnormal Psychology* (New York: Holt, Rinehart & Winston, 1968), p. 412.

The Simple Form

The positive symptoms of the simple form are a gradual loss of interest and general ineffectiveness in meeting social demands. Instead of expanding his social horizons and increasing his participation as he passes through adolescence and early adulthood, the person drifts into a simple and rather solitary way of life. Many simple schizophrenics can be found leading a marginal existence in hobo jungles, brothels, and rundown sections of urban areas. Others live like hermits in rural areas. They are usually apathetic and sometimes irresponsible, but generally satisfied with an outwardly routine existence, showing no ambition for personal advancement in the world of their contemporaries. No type of patient is more colorless nor more unlike the popular stereotype of a lunatic. On the whole, schizophrenics of the simple type are quiet, although they may be occasionally irritable or grouchily refuse to accept pressure or suggestions from outside. Their thinking and attention are not particularly good and their withdrawn manner is easily taken for stupidity, so they may be considered mentally retarded. Their intelligence usually *is* rather low, but memory is seldom impaired and there is loss of mental capacity only in deteriorated cases. Affective life is outwardly shallow and uneventful. They do not seem to want or need strong feeling. A simple and restricted life appears to suit them.

Simple schizophrenics are not in any general sense out of contact with reality. Most characteristic is lack of assertiveness, which prevents them from making a good sexual adjustment, from expressing anger, from standing up for their rights, and even from making friendly overtures toward the people around them. In part, the diagnosis is established negatively, by systematically excluding the more severe schizophrenic symptoms. Except for the fact that some cases develop delusions, hallucinations, and other florid symptoms, the simple form might not be considered a psychosis at all. Such individuals might be classified as *schizoid personality* types or some other form of personality disorder.

The Hebephrenic Form

This is the least clearly defined and increasingly the rarest type of schizophrenia, in part because the principal defining symptoms are various forms of regression that can now be prevented by drugs and improved hospital management. The chief symptoms are silliness, inappropriate smiling and laughter, bizarre disorganized ideas, and an incoherent stream of talk studded with words made up out of the blue (neologisms). There are scattered delusions and hallucinations which have little continuity and no organization. Some hebephrenics are infectiously good natured. One man frequently laughed ostentatiously during ward meetings and when asked why he disturbed the meeting with his outburst he would eagerly relate the story of how he bought that laugh for $50 from a fellow in Chicago back in 1945. A young psychiatrist chose to live as a patient on his ward for two weeks for the announced purpose of "seeing what it was like"; at the end of the second day the same patient came over to the doctor, put his hand protectively on his shoulder and confided with mock earnestness, "You know, Doc, I think you're much better already." If deterioration occurs the patient may be found eating with the fingers, neglecting dress and toilet habits, smearing feces, and otherwise dropping the restraints of socialized living.

The disorganization and fleeting strange ideas are well illustrated in the following piece of ward conversation.[9] The doctor addresses the patient, a Negro, with a standard question to which he receives a surprising answer.

"How old are you?"
"Why, I am centuries old, sir."
"How long have you been here?"
"I have been now on this property on and off for a long time. I cannot say the exact time because we are absorbed by the air at night, and they bring back people. They kill up everything; they can make you lie; they can talk through your throat."
"Who is this?"
"Why, the air."
"What is the name of this place?"
"This place is called a star."
"Who is the doctor in charge of your ward?"
"A body just like yours, sir. They can make you black and white. I say good morning, but he just comes through there. At first it was a colony. They said it was heaven. These buildings were not solid at the time, and I am positive this is the same place. They have others just like it. People die, and all the microbes talk over there, and prestigitis you know is sending you from here to another world . . . I was sent by the government to the United States to Washington to some star, and they had a pretty nice country there. Now you have a body like a young man who says he is of the prestigitis."
"Who was this prestigitis?"
"Why, you are yourself. You can be a prestigitis. They make you say bad things; they can read you; they bring back Negroes from the dead."

In this conversation the hebephrenic jumps from image to image and merely returns now and then to a theme. Everything is jumbled. Even the feelings seem jumbled and pulled out of coherent relation to events. The patient may weep when explaining how well he feels or laugh foolishly when describing an attack on his mother, as Kathi Hermann did. She was diagnosed hebephrenic, although she was quite young and obviously not at an advanced stage of the disorder. Still one can see in her

9 W. A. White, *Outlines of Psychiatry* (New York: Nervous and Mental Disease Publishing Co., 1932), p. 228.

case inappropriate emotions, presumptuous behavior toward ward personnel, and incipient elements of social restraints dropped or neglected.

A combination of paranoid and hebephrenic characteristics appears in the following excerpt from an essay written by a patient. The attempt at system is typical of the paranoid form. The use of language, however, is a nice example of what a French writer has called "word salad," a phenomenon that is particularly well developed in the hebephrenic form. The essay is entitled "Mother of Man" and begins with this paragraph.

This creation in which we live began with the Dominant Nature as an Identification Body of a completed evolutionary Strong Material creation in a Major Body Resistance Force. And is fulfilling the Nature Identification in a like Weaker Material Identification creation in which Two Major Bodies have already fulfilled radio body balances, and embodying a Third Material Identification Embodiment of both; which is now in the evolutionary process of fulfillment but fulfills without the Two Parents' Identification Resistances, therefore shall draw the resistances and perpetuate the motion interchanging of the whole interrelationship; thus completing this Creation in an interchanging Four in Three Bodies in One functioning self-contained, self-controlled and self-restrained comprising the Dominant Moral Nature and consummating a ratio balanced Major Body of maximum resistance, in a separated second like Weaker Material Major Body Functioning Counter Resistance Force to the Strong Material Major Body Resistance Force, the beginning of this creation; and the Dual Force Resistances then as a Major Body and Major Body Functioning completes a University in material balance functioning the preservation of all things.

The reader may experience difficulty in grasping the patient's thought, but to the patient herself it was full of significance. She had gone over her typescript with great care, correcting the punctuation and inserting words or phrases to clarify any possible obscurity in her meaning. Her paragraph is not without a theme. One can infer that she is writing about the creation of new life by the union of two bodies, though she is careful to keep her subject at a metaphysical plane. But the language gets completely out of hand. Words are strung together in incongruous chains, happily liberated from their usual task of conveying precise ideas. Whatever the patient had in mind, one cannot say that she achieved successful communication. To communicate with others, either through speech or writing, is a social act, and it is in the sphere of social acts that the schizophrenic disorder is most apparent.

The Catatonic Form

In the catatonic variety of schizophrenia the focus of the disorder is on motility. There are peculiar postures and gestures, curious grimaces, and stereotyped actions that are repeated endlessly. More dramatic are the phases, sometimes alternating, of catatonic stupor and catatonic excitement. The excited episodes are usually of short duration, but while they last they are often extremely violent with real danger of both homicide and suicide. Sometimes the frenzy is accompanied by delusions, hallucinations, and feelings of great power; at other times it looks more like a wild, disorganized outbreak of energy. Much of the activity, however, has symbolic significance that can be related to the patient's personal problems and fantasies. The stupors are of longer duration, going on sometimes for weeks and months. The patient sits in one position and does not speak. His immobility may extend to the point that urine and feces are not passed until they move involuntarily and that saliva is not swallowed so that it accumulates and falls from the mouth. The patient has to be dressed and undressed, moved in bed, and fed through a tube. This state of exaggerated immobility may start suddenly and may disappear in an instant. Older theories which posited degenerative changes in the nervous system were discredited by these abrupt onsets and remissions.

Careful study of catatonic stuporous states has shown that they are less passive than they appear. It is usually more accurate to say that the patient is in a state of active immobility. If anyone attempts to change his position, there will be strong muscular resistance. The patient is not in a limp state, and he is also not in a state of mental stupor. He refuses to react, but his mind is alertly observant of what is going on. Often a patient can afterward report in great detail the things that happened and were said around him while he was in apparent stupor. He is in a state of acute negativism, so acute that it invades the whole motor system, but his vigilance is not suspended. It can be inferred that rumination and fantasy go forward during the stuporous periods. Sometimes the stupor ends in response to an hallucinated command, evidently the climax of a silent inner drama.

The Paranoid Form

This is by far the most common form of schizophrenic disorder. Mild elements of paranoid symptoms are frequently found in other disorders, as we saw in Benton Child's unfounded (premature) belief that his wife was unfaithful to him and in Kathi Hermann's feelings of persecution by her clique of acquaintances. In paranoid schizophrenia the delusions are usually more richly developed. The delusions are typically changeable, numerous, fantastic, and accompanied by hallucinations. Delusions are nothing more than distorted or unrealistic personal beliefs, but they may be exaggerated to preposterous dimensions. The person does not rest content with thinking that people are persecuting him; he hears them murmuring against him, sees them lurking at the windows, feels the electric ticklings they are directing at his skin, tastes the poison that they have slipped into his food. He does not stop with the mere belief that he is Christ or Napoleon or Hitler or George Washington; he hears voices announcing his fame and bringing him important messages of state. In the early stages of the illness it is generally possible to see the connection between the patient's misinterpretations of reality and his personal wishes, needs, and fears. As time goes on, however, the delusions may spread out in a disorganized fashion. Magical forces and mystical powers come into the picture, and strange influencing machines are supposed to exist which the person may draw in great detail. The whole universe created in his mind becomes increasingly bizarre.

To illustrate, let us consider two cases which would both be diagnosed paranoid schizophrenic, though the outlook for the two would obviously be very different. The first, a man of 38, was admitted to a Veterans' hospital in an acutely anxious and depressed state. He was an extremely conscientious and hard-working family man, with three children, who until recently had considered himself happily married. He had been working under a lot of pressure, putting in long hours on the job. At home he had several run-ins with his neighbors, particularly the man next door. To complicate matters he and his wife had not been getting along well, especially in their sexual relations. (Experienced clinicians would wonder here which problem came first.) Over the last several months he had begun to wonder what the neighbors had against him. This was coupled with his observation that his wife increasingly displayed herself naked with casual abandon in the bedroom, in full view of the neighbors. To his accusations, his wife replied impatiently that the curtains were drawn and the lights were out, so no one could see in. But he insisted on pulling the blinds as well, and now he began to keep an eye on the neighbors. His suspicious behavior eventually drew some complaints to the police, and this convinced him that they, too, were involved in the plot. One day he came home from work exhausted and frustrated, to find the *front door open* and *his wife's underpants lying on the bedroom floor. That* convinced him that his wife was having an affair with the man next door. His work was suffering noticeably because he heard voices at work talking about his domestic problems, so he lost his job. Shortly thereafter he was admitted to the hospital.

His recovery was amazingly rapid. With rest, intensive drug treatment, and individual and group psychotherapy he gradually began to distantiate himself from the delusional system. He was helped to understand that the pressure he felt on the job was primarily attributable to his own intense desire to provide well for his family, and not intrinsic to the job itself, as his employer made clear. He was persuaded that his neighbors were no more covetous of his possessions or his wife than most people are, but that any attentions they showed were magnified out of all proportion by his own insecurity, for which he compensated in part by extreme industriousness at work. He began to see, though reluctantly at first, that his wife's provocative sexual behavior was really directed at him, and stemmed from their increasing alienation from one another over the past several months. He was released from the hospital in much improved condition after six weeks and was welcomed back at home and by his previous employer. On follow-up a year later he was free of symptoms and doing well.

The second case is a pleasant spinster in her fifties who was encountered at a convention of the American Psychological Association in San Francisco. Without introduction she struck up a conversation in a coffee shop at one of the convention hotels, explaining that she attended all the conventions although she herself was not *formally* trained in psychology. She had always been fascinated with the mysteries of the mind, extrasensory perception, mysticism, and occult matters. Through her reading and travels she had learned a great deal of psychology. She sponsored popular seminars at her home in New York City. Timothy Leary, the professor-turned-psychedelic-specialist, had given a presentation and several Indian mystics of world renown. Her psychiatrist encouraged her to do this because it was good for her. She obviously could easily afford these seminars and it gave her something to do. Upon learning that her listener was from Harvard, she immediately dropped the names of Henry Murray, Gordon Allport, and others of her close friends there. Harvard, of course, is where a cyclotron is located, the one that exploded a few years ago. That was the machine that was used to burn out the pineal gland in her brain. It was done by remote control many years ago. That started all the trouble that led to her being hospitalized so many times, prevented her from achieving the level of recognition for which her talents entitled her, and caused her to lead an eccentric and lonely existence.

The delusions of persecution in the first case were much more comprehensible in the context of the patient's recent history. This was his first major psychological disturbance and his distorted belief system had fortunately not become stabilized. In the second case the delusional system was much more extensive and implausible. We can guess that this patient had quite a long history of serious psychological disturbance, which had now stabilized at a tolerable level of eccentricity.

There is a form of psychosis, paranoia, in which the symptoms are confined to the development of a delusional system. This psychosis is generally assigned independent status outside of schizophrenia. The clearest distinguishing feature is the absence of hallucinations. Falsification of reality is restricted to misinterpreting events; what happens is correctly perceived, but peculiar inferences are drawn from it. Except for the delusional system, the patient is perfectly oriented and perfectly normal in his conduct. The personality does not become disorganized, and interest in the environment is substantially preserved. One might say that paranoia is a restricted psychosis, sufficiently circumscribed so that it does not invade and disintegrate the personality as a whole. We shall consider presently the nature and origins of paranoiac thinking. The disorder is mentioned here because of its similarity to the paranoid form of schizophrenia. Both show an extensive use of the mechanism of *projection*. In paranoid schizophrenia, however, there is a more far-reaching loss of interest, loss of contact with reality, and general disintegration of personality.

By means of projection a person may spare himself intolerable anxiety by attributing certain of his tendencies not to himself but to other people. He transforms his wishes and fears into external facts for which he himself is not in the least responsible. When a patient claims that God has chosen him to lead mankind to its salvation, he is expressing an extremely grandiose wish but he is assuming no responsibility for it. When he claims that pursuers and unseen forces are preventing him from achieving great things, as the pleasant spinster did, he is expressing both a grandiose wish and a fear of his incompetence to fulfill it, but he is again avoiding responsibility for this conflict. One man voluntarily entered a hospital because he was being followed by five FBI agents, and he pointed to the five trees in front of the hospital behind which they were now hiding. When asked why they were following him, he explained that somehow the rumor had gotten around that he was a homosexual. He vehemently disclaimed any truth to the rumor, but he was sure that was the reason because he had recently been the victim of homosexual advances in several bars which, admittedly, were known as homosexual haunts, but he had as much right to drink there as anyone else. It was clear that he was getting vicarious sexual gratification from these encounters, while neatly disclaiming any homosexual inclinations in himself because that was anathema to a man of his conventional background. Unfortunately, the guilt this created in him was too overwhelming. The delusional and hallucinatory aspects of paranoid schizophrenia are thus intelligible in terms of desire, anxiety, and defense. Further principles of explanation, however, are needed to understand the more strictly schizophrenic aspects of the disorder: the loss of interests, the growing confusion, and the gradual deterioration of thought and conduct.

Is Schizophrenia a Unity?

What common features are to be found which justify the placing of these diverse symptom pictures under a common heading? One thing that can be said about all of them is that they show a disturbance of relationship with people. Even in the simple form there is failure to interact effectively with others, and this failure is much greater in the other three forms, where sometimes the attempt to communicate seems to be altogether abandoned. It is often said that the schizophrenic withdraws from social participation and retires into himself, living more and more in the world of his thoughts and fantasies. It seems clear, however, that this process of withdrawal does not explain all the strangeness of schizophrenic behavior. Just as we cannot explain depression as the uncomplicated result of discouragement or loss, so we cannot understand the bizarre character of schizophrenia as a direct outcome of social withdrawal. In all but the simple form there is a degree of disorganization that goes beyond anything we might reasonably ascribe to lack of human contact. The patient's contact with his inanimate surroundings also becomes seriously impaired. Jenkins has expressed the view that although "schizoid withdrawal is a typical precursor of schizophrenia" it is not the essential psychotic process. Jenkins reminds us that "withdrawal from empathic contact with the human environment is a stable long-term characteristic of many personalities who never show schizophrenic disorganization." What turns withdrawal into a disorder is a "progressive personality disorganization," a breakdown of integrated thinking and integrated adaptive behavior.[10] It is perhaps here that one can make the strongest case for the unity of the several forms of schizophrenia.

This was the central point of Bleuler's theory of schizophrenia, advanced in 1911 and now regarded as a historical milestone.[11] Bleuler believed that disorganization reflected the root disorder. It appeared with fewest complications in schizophrenia simplex, where it consisted of "a particular type of alteration in thinking, feeling, and relation to the external world." The more dramatic symptoms—the delusional systems, the word salads, the catatonic excitements—were to be regarded as secondary developments. Bleuler believed that the central disorder could exist in various degrees of severity and that it could run a variety of courses. With some patients there would be steady deterioration, with others, intermittent attacks; the disease might take a chronic downward course, but it might be subject to arrests and remissions. Because of these variations in onset, course, and prospects, he often referred to the "group of schizophrenias." On the basis of 515 cases admitted to the Swiss hospital where he worked, he reported that 22 per cent advanced to severe deterioration and that 60 per cent recovered sufficiently to be capable of earning a living. He did not regard the recovered patients as completely well, and some of them eventually relapsed, but others apparently remained free from incapacitating illness.

How far have we been able to advance beyond Bleuler's view of schizophrenia? We can specify much more precisely the prognosis of a case in advance, as we shall see in the next section. And the length of hospitalization for schizophrenic disorders has been greatly reduced. A study in West Germany found that the average hospital stay was 1,033 days during the period 1929–1931 (before electroshock therapy was introduced), but was down to 353 days in 1949–1951 (before tranquilizing drugs were discovered), and 113 days in 1959–1961 (when drugs were the primary mode of treatment).[12] However, almost a fourth of hospitalized schizophenics are still destined for severe deterioration; and the number of satisfactory, though perhaps not permanent or complete, recoveries still hovers around 60 per

[10] R. L. Jenkins, "The Schizophrenic Sequence: Withdrawal, Disorganization, Psychotic Reorganization," *American Journal of Orthopsychiatry*, XX (1952), pp. 738–48.

[11] E. Bleuler, *Dementia Praecox or the Group of Schizophrenias*, 1911, trans. J. Zinkin (New York: International Universities Press, Inc., 1950).

[12] J. E. Meier, personal communication, 1967.

cent.[13] Such evidence seems to indicate a disorder of a fundamental character that is still beyond the reach of current knowledge of psychodynamics, neurophysiology, and biochemistry. This impression is further strengthened by evidence of an entirely different sort. Cross-cultural studies show that in all parts of the world and in all varieties of culture, it is possible to recognize certain individuals whose behavior has the typical earmarks of schizophrenia. Within the American culture it has been shown, for example, that Irish and Italian schizophrenics reflect their subcultural background: the Italian patients are more overtly aggressive and more given to motor expression, whereas the Irish are more compliant, restrained, and imaginative. Yet both alike are schizophrenic.[14]

THE PROCESS-REACTIVE DIMENSION

Bleuler's observation of the variations in onset and course of illness has given rise to a much more fruitful classification that offers some promising connections with etiology and with prognosis, which Kraepelin's categories did not. Some cases of schizophrenia develop slowly over many years with gradually increasing withdrawal and signs of disorganization, until the person's maladjustment can no longer pass unrecognized and he is sent for help. Other cases develop much more rapidly, as in the case of the 38-year-old paranoid schizophrenic man described earlier. Usually such rapid onset occurs at a time when the person is under serious psychological stress, such as a major vocational setback, a domestic crisis, or the loss of a loved one. Adolph Meyer, a contemporary of Bleuler, construed schizophrenia in such cases as a reaction to severe social circumstances and hence considered it more susceptible to recovery.[15] This implied a direct connection between present psychotic behavior and previous social experience and opened the way to a whole new approach to schizophrenia, from the viewpoint of social and psychological development. Sullivan extended this viewpoint, concentrating his own attention on the early adolescent years of development. There followed a vast amount of research designed to isolate the cardinal characteristics that distinguish *reactive schizophrenias* with good prognosis from *process schizophrenias* with poor prognosis. The results have been remarkably consistent.[16] Good prognosis is associated

13 F. A. Freyhan, "Eugen Bleuler's Concept of the Group of Schizophrenias at Mid-Century," *American Journal of Psychiatry*, CXIV (1958), pp. 769–79.

14 M. K. Opler, "Cultural Perspective in Research on Schizophrenics: A History with Examples," *Psychiatric Quarterly*, XXXIII (1959), pp. 506–24.

15 A. Meyer, "Fundamental Conceptions of Dementia Praecox," *British Medical Journal*, II (1906), 757–60.

16 G. E. Vaillant, "The Prediction of Recovery in Schizophrenia," *Journal of Nervous and Mental Disease*, CXXXV (1962), pp. 534–43; R. E. Kantor and W. G. Herron, *Reactive and Process Schizophrenia* (Palo Alto: Science and Behavior Books, Inc., 1966), pp. 17–23; E. Robins and S. B. Guze, "Establishment of Diagnostic Validity in Psychiatric Illness: Its Application to Schizophrenia," *American Journal of Psychiatry*, CXXVI (1970), pp. 983–87.

with acute onset, obvious precipitating stresses, good premorbid adjustment, confusion, prominent depressive symptoms, and a family history of affective disorders. Poor prognosis is associated with gradual onset, schizoid premorbid adjustment, emotional blunting ("flat affect"), relatively clear thinking, and a family history of schizophrenia. In short, the chances for recovery are less if there is clear evidence of a genetic predisposition for schizophrenia rather than depression, if schizoid withdrawal seems to be an established way of life and if the psychotic experience seems neither very disturbing nor different from the person's customary behavior.

The most convincing demonstration of the validity of the process-reactive concept was made by Stephens and Astrup, although a number of other investigations have achieved similar results.[17] They classified 143 schizophrenics as either process or non-process types while in the hospital, and compared the two groups on independent ratings of improvement at discharge and on follow-up 5–13 years later. The results were as follows:

Follow-up of Process and Non-Process Schizophrenics *

Clinical Rating	At Discharge		At 5–13-Year Follow-Up	
	Process	Non-Process	Process	Non-Process
Recovered	7%	17%	10%	38%
Improved	38	51	41	59
Unimproved	55	32	49	3

* Stephens and Astrup, 1963; see footnote 17.

The risk of deterioration, which was the principal defining characteristic of the disorder in Kraepelin's work, was very slight in the non-process schizophrenics but about 50 per cent in the process cases. This opens the encouraging prospect that schizophrenic disorders may be reliably classified for probable outcome, not so much on the basis of salient clinical symptoms as on pertinent social and life historical criteria.

Organic vs. Psychogenic Etiology [18]

Bleuler described reactive schizophrenia as a morbid reaction to an affective experience, whereas process schizophrenia is conditioned by a morbid process in the brain, although the two forms cannot be distinguished clinically because the symptoms intermingle.[19] There is some empirical support for this attractive hypothesis. In a variety of studies process schizo-

[17] J. H. Stephens and C. Astrup, "Prognosis in 'process' and 'non-process' schizophrenia," American Journal of Psychiatry, CXIX (1963), pp. 945–54; G. Nameche, M. Waring, and D. Ricks, "Early Indicators of Outcome in Schizophrenia," Journal of Nervous and Mental Disease, CXXXIX (1964), pp. 232–40; G. E. Vaillant, "Prospective Prediction of Schizophrenic Remission," Archives of General Psychiatry, XI (1964), pp. 509–19.

[18] An extensive review of this issue is provided in N. Garmezy, "Process and Reactive Schizophrenia: Some Conceptions and Issues," Schizophrenia Bulletin, II (1970), pp. 30–74.

[19] E. Bleuler, Textbook of Psychiatry (New York: The Macmillan Co., 1924).

phrenics have shown more impairment of abstract thinking, greater deficit in physiological responsiveness, more "organic" signs on the Rorschach, and so on, but it is impossible to determine from these studies whether the defects reflect *causes* or *consequences* of the disorder. More compelling evidence is based on data gathered prior to the onset of psychotic symptoms. Ricks and Nameche found that "soft signs" of neurological impairment (rigidity, speech abnormalities, abnormal gait, poor coordination, impaired attention span, enuresis, hyper- and hypo-activity) were the best predictors for chronicity in the guidance clinic records of adolescents later hospitalized for schizophrenia.[20] Other investigations have implicated pregnancy and birth complications as potential contributors to chronic outcome.[21]

Another source of convergent evidence is the recent study in Denmark that traced the biological family histories of adopted children who were hospitalized for schizophrenia as adults.[22] Schizophrenic disorders were found among the biological relatives of the adoptees who developed chronic schizophrenia and borderline schizophrenia, but none were found among the relatives of the acute (reactive) schizophrenics. This suggests that genetic predisposition is significant for chronic and borderline schizophrenias, both of which can be considered process types because they constitute general life styles, but not for the more episodic reactive schizoprhenics. Winokur and his associates take the argument a step further.[23] They found more schizophrenia in the relatives of poor prognosis schizophrenics and more affective disorders in the relatives of good prognosis schizophrenics; they concluded that the latter (reactive) form of the disorder is genetically related to affective psychosis rather than schizophrenia. This of course ties reactive schizophrenia to an organic cause, albeit a different one than for process schizophrenia, but is consistent with the view that situational and psychological factors can play a primary role in the etiology of depressive disorders. However, we shall see later that there are real limits to the power of genetic evidence for explaining any form of psychosis.

An alternative view is offered by Phillips, who considers the process-reactive dimension as a continuum of psychological development.[24] Reactive schizophrenics achieve demonstrably higher levels of social com-

[20] D. Ricks and G. Nameche, "Symbiosis, Sacrifice and Schizophrenia," *Mental Hygiene,* L (1966), pp. 541–51.

[21] S. A. Mednick, "Breakdown in Individuals at High Risk for Schizophrenia: Possible Predispositional Perinatal Factors," *Mental Hygiene,* LIV (1970), pp. 50–63.

[22] S. S. Kety, D. Rosenthal, P. H. Wender, and F. Schulsinger, "The Types and Prevalence of Mental Illness in the Biological and Adoptive Families of Adopted Schizophrenics," in D. Rosenthal and S. S. Kety, eds., *The Transmission of Schizophrenia* (Oxford: Pergamon Press, 1968), pp. 345–62.

[23] M. S. McCabe, R. C. Fowler, R. J. Cadoret, and G. Winokur, "Familial Differences in Schizophrenia with Good and Poor Prognosis," *Psychological Medicine,* I (1971), pp. 326–32; R. C. Fowler, M. S. McCabe, R. J. Cadoret, and G. Winokur, "The Validity of Good Prognosis Schizophrenia," *Archives of General Psychiatry,* XXVI (1972), pp. 182–85.

[24] L. Phillips, *Human Adaptation and Its Failures* (New York: Academic Press, 1968), pp. 153–57.

petence prior to breakdown and have for this reason greater adaptive potential after the acute phase has passed. Differences in genetic predisposition or other organic factors are not incompatible with this view, but they would be significant etiologically only insofar as they affect the whole course of the person's social and psychological development. There is an important departure here from most conceptions, which emphasize the regressive aspects of schizophrenic disorder. Phillips argues that the disorder represents a continuous process in which the premorbid, intermediate, and ultimate stages are meaningfully related. Knowing the level and modes of adaptation prior to onset makes seemingly anomalous aspects of the psychosis comprehensible, and, most importantly, explains the variations in outcome.

It is still too soon to place these hypotheses and empirical facts definitely in a theory of etiology. Clearly Kraepelin's system of classification is being superseded by other systems based more on personal history than on clinical symptoms. From many viewpoints reactive forms of schizophrenia are coming to be distinguished from process forms, despite their similar symptoms. This may lead ultimately to a formal revision of diagnosis for the functional psychoses, perhaps along the lines suggested by Astrup and Noreik.[25] These workers would classify as *schizophrenia* only the process psychoses that have a high risk of schizophrenic deterioration. The cases with a significant mixture of "true" schizophrenic indications and depressive signs would be called *schizoaffective psychoses;* they would carry a medium risk for long-term defects. Reactive psychoses would be grouped along with mania and depression as *affective psychoses,* and would carry low risk of deterioration.

Acute Schizophrenic Episodes with Recovery

The outbreak of unmistakable schizophrenic behavior sometimes occurs under circumstances that illuminate the nature of the patient's inner turmoil. A girl of eighteen returned from a year in Europe in an acute schizophrenic condition, withdrawn, guilt-ridden, frightened, preoccupied with delusions of persecution. The year abroad was her first time away from home and she had always been sheltered and restricted by her overprotective father. While in Europe she became acquainted with boys for the first time, and became infatuated with one in particular. They had lain together in bed and kissed, so now she was certain that she was pregnant! She knew that her father would have disapproved of her behavior, and this made her feel doubly guilty. She was certain that everyone knew about her sinfulness, even the garbage collectors, so she was afraid to go outside alone. This young woman was helped by some fundamental sexual information. Her parents and older sister were advised to reassure her about

25 C. Astrup and K. Noreik, *Functional Psychoses* (Springfield, Ill.: Charles C Thomas, 1966), p. 139.

the presumed "transgressions" and to encourage her to more active social participation. In this case the natural sexual experiences were interpreted as great personal shortcomings and abnormalities because of misinformation and misguided moral attitudes. The immediate cause of breakdown was a sharp blow to self-esteem that may well have been already precarious. This was mirrored in her belief that everyone "knew about her" and led to her withdrawal and rather serious disorganization of behavior.

French and Kasanin have published a detailed analysis of recovery from schizophrenia.[26] They make two points: (1) that an acute psychosis can sometimes be regarded as a temporary episode that marks the transition from an old to a new adjustment, and (2) that in his delusions the patient may foreshadow the means he is going to employ in achieving the new adjustment. A woman of twenty-four had a critical breakdown soon after she left home to make an independent life for herself and soon after she accepted for the first time sexual attentions from a man. Both steps were radical ones, especially the second, which was sharply at variance with the severe moral standards of her parents. Apparently these steps were at first too much for her. A typical schizophrenic psychosis developed with many strange and incoherent delusions. The theme of most of these delusions was punishment and suffering for what she had done. She felt that she was dead and that she was being transformed into a snake which was loathsome to everyone. In these delusions she probably expressed in a symbolic way her inability to take the steps toward sexual expression. Another set of delusions made no sense at first, but afterwards appeared to foretell the mechanism of her recovery. She was being kidnapped and transported to Italy, this being the land of her ancestral home, and in addition she had become a Catholic, this being her ancestral faith but not the faith of her parents. As time went on her delusion of having become a Catholic increasingly took the form of a desire to confess her sins and receive absolution. This desire eventually brought her back into contact with the hospital staff and especially with the psychiatrist, who could function in a role not unlike that of a priest. It would seem an unwarrantable piece of interpretation to say out of hand that the patient's delusion about Italy and the church meant that she wanted to resume her growth, but needed the guidance and support of someone whose attitude would be kindly and forgiving. Yet this was precisely the means by which the patient recovered. At first leaning heavily on the psychiatrist for advice at every step, then with steadily increasing independence, she gradually achieved the new learning that brought her to vocational and sexual adulthood. Follow-up over several years showed distinctly superior adjustment in marriage.

[26] T. M. French and J. Kasanin, "A Psychodynamic Study of the Recovery of Two Schizophrenic Cases," *Psychoanalytic Quarterly*, X (1941), pp. 1–22. Reprinted in S. S. Tomkins, ed., *Contemporary Psychopathology* (Cambridge: Harvard University Press, 1943), chap. 27.

These transient schizophrenias can be described as retreats from reality. When viewed in the light of their later outcome, however, they can better be characterized as tactical retreats having the function of a delaying action until the patient can gather himself together for a fresh attack on the problem of new adjustment. A prominent aspect of the clinical symptoms in both of these cases was guilt, which Phillips considers a good prognostic sign because "turning against the self" in time of stress, in contrast to "turning against others" or "avoiding others," reflects a high level of psychological development.[27]

Gradual Onset with Progressive Disorganization

In cases where the onset is more gradual it is sometimes possible to detect warning signs that something more than withdrawal is taking place. During childhood the person gives evidence of "clinging to the mother's apron string" and avoiding rough, competitive play. Very often there is early success with schoolwork and a continuing interest in studies. Thus far the pattern cannot be called morbid, though it may lack something of assertiveness. Before long, however, it becomes possible to observe something more serious: a general retraction of interest. Outside observers may sense that the youngster's interests are becoming less intense and less numerous. The individual himself may feel that he is growing more passive in his attitude and that outside events are losing their meaning for him. He ceases to make new friends, even older or younger friends, and his interest in schoolwork declines into dreamy inattentiveness. This change for the worse is likely to occur at puberty. So long as interest is maintained in some form of constructive activity—art or writing, for example—there may be a chance that the person will find his way back, along the lines of his specialty, to social acceptance and participation. But if interests are retracted to the point of listlessness and apathy, so that fantasy reigns without further correction by real experience, then the condition must be regarded as ominous.

Ideas of reference may tend to creep gradually into the picture without at first assuming the status of delusions. The incipient patient is keenly aware of outside stimulation even though he does not overtly respond to it. For a long time he recognizes that the source of his difficulties is in himself. Nevertheless he cannot help feeling that the world is a little hostile, or at least inconsiderate, and that other people take a derogatory attitude toward him. Highly aware of his own fantasies, he wonders what other people would think if they knew what was going on in his head. It is a short step to occasional fleeting delusions. The patient half believes that people are actually saying derogatory things and behaving in a hostile fashion. In this borderland of half belief he may remain for some time, only gradually slipping over to the point where insight is lost. It is when he is already

[27] Phillips, *op. cit.,* pp. 146–47.

in this borderland, we may suppose, that any downward slipping of self-esteem is likely to precipitate overt psychosis.

The general retraction of interests can be considered a first sign of impending disorganization. It is not a logical consequence or natural extension of defensive withdrawal from people. The patient now seems to be giving up the attempt to move forward even along unsocial lines. Sometimes the retraction of interest finds expression in ideas that the world has changed and that everything is dying. The affective change in the patient is perceived as a physical change in the world.

The following case illustrates both the gradual appearance of disorganization and the way in which events can progressively deepen a schizophrenic reaction. A boy in high school was considered by his friends to be sensitive, solitary, and a little eccentric. They knew that he was an orphan and lived with an elderly, somewhat peculiar foster mother. The boy was good in his studies, especially in history and literature. His English teacher, who constantly read his literary productions, noted distinct talent but many eccentricities of content. Themes of death and decay, images of dilapidated castles and gardens gone to seed, scenes of an ancient glory now crumbling to dust—these and similar gloomy ideas dominated his beautifully written verses. Although the boy spent a good deal of time alone, he had several friends among the students who were preparing for college. At graduation he was separated from his chums, he himself being unable to go to college. Occasionally he visited them, but it was clear that he resented his inferior position and the interruption of his own education. His friends now began to suspect that he was building up fictions about himself. He showed them an application blank that he had received from an art school. They believed that he had prepared it on his own typewriter. He also discoursed at length on his distinguished French ancestry, a theme which he was able to fill out convincingly from his knowledge of history. He repeatedly mentioned that his real mother, a countess, was now living in the city, and that he was in frequent communication with her. The friends began to feel that he was a liar, and they laid plans to expose him. One day they confronted him with numerous fatal inconsistencies in his stories and accused him of fabrication. He thereupon admitted that his stories were not true, but explained that he had been forced to disguise himself in this way in order to elude a hostile power known as the Third Element. He now claimed that he and his mother, the countess, had collaborated in preparing a set of disguising fictions to keep the Third Element off their trail. He told his accusers that the situation was growing increasingly serious. Most of his friends had turned against him, and only three remained on his side.

It is clear that this boy's history showed signs of schizophrenic disorganization before he graduated from high school. That event, with separation from his circle of friends, gave his adjustment a downward jolt and sharply increased his symptoms. He now began to lose track of the line between fantasy and fact, speaking of his fantasies of noble lineage as if they were true. The motive behind these fabrications was pathetically clear: if he could not go to college, he would at least have some form of distinction to keep him on a footing with his friends, and while he was at it he provided himself with a mother. Unfortunately his attempts at compensation only irritated his friends and their unsympathetic action constituted a second, more direct, and more personal rejection. This event threw him into deeper psychosis. His delusions about hostile friends and a hostile Third Element reflected the real feeling of hostility that he sensed in his accusers. Unfortunately the delusions now began to assume a generalized form which made him more and more inaccessible to friendly advances from others.

In general it can be said that sharp downward steps on the path to schizophrenia occur in connection with events that lower the patient's already feeble self-esteem or challenge in some way his adequacy. Anything that makes him feel more different from others, or less competent than he already thinks himself to be, has a devastating effect upon his contact with reality. The sexual changes of puberty, and such major challenges as engagement, marriage, childbirth, or heavy vocational responsibilities, often serve as precipitating events. Each step toward fuller independence and maturity stands like a threat and may deepen the schizophrenic reaction.

Early Identification

A natural outgrowth of the growing recognition that schizophrenia does not just happen all of a sudden is an expansion of efforts to identify children at risk for schizophrenia before the onset of psychosis. Retrospective studies based on records from child guidance clinics and schools have isolated a number of likely indications of vulnerability. Preschizophrenic children have been found to have lower intelligence, on the average, than their classmates and siblings.[28] They have an unusually high frequency of parental death during childhood, and there is some indication that the risk is more extreme if the death occurs before the child reaches eight years of age.[29] Examining the cumulative school records of preschizophrenic children, Watt found sharp sex differences in social adjustment; teachers described the boys as abrasive, defiant, and emotionally unstable, whereas the

---

28 E. Lane and G. Albee, "Childhood Intellectual Differences between Schizophrenic Adults and Their Siblings," *American Journal of Orthopsychiatry*, XXXV (1965), pp. 747–53; A. W. Lubensky, *Childhood Intelligence and Scholastic Performance of Adult Schizophrenics*, Unpublished Doctoral Dissertation, Harvard University, 1972.

29 I. Gregory, "Studies of Parental Deprivation in Psychiatric Patients," *American Journal of Psychiatry*, CXV (1958), pp. 432–42; N. F. Watt, "Childhood Roots of Schizophrenia," in M. Roff, D. Ricks, and A. Thomas, eds., *Life History Research in Psychopathology*, vol. III (Minneapolis: University of Minnesota Press, in press); H. Barry, Jr., "Significance of Maternal Bereavement before Age Eight in Psychiatric Patients," *Archives of General Psychiatry*, LXII (1949), pp. 630–37.

girls were primarily inhibited, sensitive, and introverted.[30] Slight deviation was apparent during the primary school years, but the sharpest behavioral abnormalities were manifest in junior and senior high school, which suggests that the social maladjustments begin to accumulate in early adolescence for many preschizophrenics until they culminate in breakdown in young adulthood.

A major obstacle to studying children prior to the onset of schizophrenia is that the disorder occurs so rarely in a general population. However it is well established that about 10 per cent of the children of schizophrenic parents will become schizophrenic themselves. Therefore Mednick seized upon the ingenious idea of studying adolescent children of process schizophrenic mothers.[31] His group of 207 such children was considered to have a "high risk" for schizophrenia; "low risk" controls were 104 children of normal mothers. When initially tested around 15 years of age in 1962 there were already pronounced differences between the groups. The high-risk children were more nervous, withdrawn, passive, easily upset, and poorly adjusted socially. Their performance was lower on arithmetic and coding subtests of intelligence, which required sustained concentration and effort, and their word associations tended to drift. On psychophysiological measures they were more easily and quickly aroused by mild stress, indicating highly labile autonomic responsivity. On follow-up five years later 20 of the high-risk children had already suffered psychiatric breakdown. These 20 (the "Sick" Group) were compared with 20 other high-risk children whose initial adjustment level was comparable but who were still functioning adequately (the "Well" Group). The Sick Group had been separated earlier from their mothers, who were rated more severely ill. The Sick Group were described by their teachers as more disturbing in class and more easily upset, which is remarkably consistent with the retrospective school record studies reported above. They also showed more associative drifting on a continuous word association test. Thus there are consistent early indications of associative disturbance, autonomic liability and social maladjustment years before the onset of psychotic symptoms. Mednick plans to follow all these children for 20 years, through the period of maximum psychiatric risk. As the results of the first five-year follow-up indicate, we can expect from this project and others like it[32] important new leads to the etiology of schizophrenia.

[30] N. F. Watt, *op. cit.*; N. F. Watt, R. D. Stolorow, A. W. Lubensky, and D. C. McClelland, "School Adjustment and Behavior of Children Hospitalized for Schizophrenia as Adults," *American Journal of Orthopsychiatry*, XL (1970), pp. 637–57; N. F. Watt, "Longitudinal Changes in the Social Behavior of Children Hospitalized for Schizophrenia as Adults," *Journal of Nervous and Mental Disease*, CLV (1972), pp. 42–54.

[31] S. A. Mednick and F. Schulsinger, "Some Premorbid Characteristics Related to Breakdown in Children with Schizophrenic Mothers," in Rosenthal and Kety, *op. cit.*, pp. 267–91.

[32] E. J. Anthony, "A Clinical Evaluation of Children with Psychotic Parents," in R. Cancro, ed., *The Schizophrenic Syndrome* (New York: Brunner/Mazel, 1971), pp. 244–56.

DISORGANIZATION IN SCHIZOPHRENIC THINKING

From the descriptions already given it will be clear that the problem of schizophrenia can be approached from several directions. As in the neuroses, emotional problems crop out at every turn: difficulties with sex and aggression, with love and hate, with competence and self-esteem are everywhere apparent in the case histories. This leads our thoughts toward the family circle and the interaction of parents and child during the early years. We notice also a weakening of social interest and a progressive failure of communication with others, suggesting unusual difficulties in the process of social adaptation. Thus far we might be dealing with another variety of neurosis; but then we are confronted everywhere by signs of disorganization, a seeming breakdown in the very structure of thinking that has no counterpart in the neuroses and is somewhat like what we shall study in connection with brain injuries. Perhaps such fundamental disorganization can be understood in psychodynamic terms, though it is hard to conceive of it happening without some biochemical changes in the brain. Whatever the ultimate explanation turns out to be, we must try to understand this central aspect of the disorder.

It is extraordinarily difficult to follow the thought processes of a schizophrenic patient. With other types of patients the observer can usually establish empathy and follow the course of thought even though it appears somewhat strange. It is not difficult, for instance, to comprehend a deluded paretic who offers us a pleasant weekend at his country estate, or to understand a manic patient when he lays vast plans for humanitarian reform. These patients are crazy, but somehow the schizophrenics seem crazier. Their thinking falls to pieces, it defies logic, it contains weird constructions like prestigitis, the Third Element, and the Strong Material Major Body Resistance Force. Nevertheless it is not always impossible to understand what is going on in schizophrenic thought. What we have to realize is that the thought processes are autistic, like dreams and daydreams; more than that, they are full of conceptions that seem quite immature. We shall try to learn why this should be so.

The Development of Paranoid Thinking

The study of schizophrenic thought is most easily begun at the point where it is least abnormal. We shall therefore begin by considering delusions. A delusion is essentially a misinterpretation of experience. It does not, like an hallucination, entail a distorted registering of experience or a false perception of what is going on. An hallucinated patient hears voices in the ventilating system that loudly discuss his faults and denounce his sins. A merely deluded patient proceeds with more respect for reality. He correctly perceives a number of people talking, and although he does not overhear them he infers that they are discussing his faults and denouncing his sins. In delusions the disorder is localized at the point where inference or the interpretation of experience begins. Otherwise the contact with reality is correctly maintained.

Delusional thinking is primarily a disorder of communication. Children acquire an image of themselves by noticing how others react to them.[33] Their criticism of their own behavior contains a distillation of the criticisms they have received from others. Gradually the child learns to see himself and his conduct in different perspectives: as his mother sees them, or as his brother or his teacher or his chum or his rival sees them. By shifting perspectives he can take different attitudes toward his behavior. By taking the role of others, the child incorporates their perspectives in his own behavior. Role taking is an acquired skill, and there are great individual differences in the extent to which it is acquired. "The adult who is especially vulnerable to paranoid developments is one in whom this process of socialization has been seriously defective." [34] Like everyone else he draws inferences from what he observes, but unlike others he remains an amateur in realizing how these inferences might appear to someone else.

Now suppose that a person whose limited social experience deprives him of that flexibility of perspective becomes involved in emotional difficulties. More specifically, suppose that his internal economy of aggression, sense of competence, and self-esteem suffer a serious setback. The effect of this is to sensitize him to any impressions that have to do with his standing in relation to others. Then, like the playwright on opening night, he scrutinizes the audience for clues to their reaction, selecting fragments of behavior, many of which may be totally irrelevant, and weaving them together into a fictitious critique. The problem is especially serious for the person whose self-esteem has been shattered. Everything that happens seems related to this consuming problem. In this condition the conclusions he reaches about other people's judgments may be completely fictitious. They correspond only to what the person is thinking about himself. As we saw earlier in the paranoid schizophrenic homosexual, everyone *else* had to think he was homosexual because he couldn't tolerate that repugnant thought himself.

The critical point in the development of delusions, however, is the *failure of correction*. Weak in habits of role taking, accustomed to puzzle and brood alone, the person becomes trapped in his own single perspective and shares his misgivings with no one. The result is cumulative misinterpretations; "the lone individual lacks the usual checking over with other persons which might modify and correct them." Before long he has built up what Cameron calls a "pseudo-community." He ascribes imaginary attitudes and functions to the real people in his environment. They are detectives,

[33] R. D. Laing, *The Divided Self* (London: Tavistock Publications, 1960).
[34] N. Cameron, "The Paranoid Pseudo-Community Revisited," *American Journal of Sociology*, LXV (1959), pp. 52–58.

they are gansters, they are pursuers who mean harm. The more he organizes this pseudo-community, the more it becomes necessary for him to take action in it. Eventually he does something in the way of protective or aggressive behavior. He takes action in the real social field, and is judged by the other persons in that field to be insane.

Despite these distortions of reality and the social withdrawal that follows, the person often attempts to regain contact with other people. He may try to reconstitute his human environment and lay a new basis for social behavior. It is important to bear this general principle in mind in our study of schizophrenia. In many cases psychosis involves not only disorganization but also a peculiar or psychotic reorganization of experience. We can learn something more about this by examining an instance of abrupt break with reality.

The Changed World in Schizophrenia

A case of catatonic schizophrenia reported by Angyal is of unusual service at this point because the initial break with reality was clearly recalled by the patient after his recovery.[35] The characters in the story are the patient, B, a 22-year-old electrician; the girl, D, to whom he was engaged; and a music teacher, K, a man twice B's age who was very much attached to him. B lived at home in a stormy relation with his incompetent widowed father, for whom he had no respect. His engagement to D, a girl from a lower middle-class background like his own, was the culmination of a typical history of normal interest in girls. The unsatisfactory character of his life at home lent special significance to his friendship with K, who gave him free singing lessons, guided his reading, took him to the theater, and opened the door upon a world of culture and refinement to which he had always been attracted. K became a good father to him and a man in whom he could confide. One would assume a homosexual interest on K's part, but this was never openly manifested; however, it is not without significance that K, who wished to monopolize B, was jealous of D and declared that she was too crude and unrefined for B. A situation thus developed in which D and K became conflicting goals: D meant heterosexuality, marriage, and an independent but unrefined life; K meant music, culture, emotional support, but a dependent relationship and unconsciously a threat of homosexuality. This problem was completely unsolved when B was inducted into the Army. Some seven weeks later, without warning or preliminary signs of illness, he awakened one morning to a new world.

Outwardly B's new world looked like the old one, and he behaved the same way in it, but everything had assumed a new meaning. B knew for a certainty that he was selected to serve as an FBI agent in the camp, that

[35] A. Angyal, "The Psychodynamic Process of Illness and Recovery in a Case of Catatonic Schizophrenia," *Psychiatry*, XIII (1950), pp. 149–65.

K was the person in charge who had selected him, and that he was being tested as to his fitness for a special secret assignment. He was very proud and happy. He realized that everything happening around him had a significance for his new position. If the coffee tasted bad, it was doped with a narcotic as a test of his ability to keep a secret even though drugged. When people spoke, an assignment was being conveyed to him surreptitiously; by carefully piecing together a word here and a phrase there he could decode his orders. After several preliminary assignments which got him into no trouble he received the final order: he was to take a new name and report home to K for the next phase of his career. The attempt to carry out this order was viewed with disfavor by his officers, and when they found him insisting upon a new name they referred him to the station hospital.

This example of the sudden onset of a delusional system can best be understood by means of the concepts introduced by Jung and further developed by Sullivan. Jung in 1906 made the first serious attempt to understand the content of schizophrenic thinking. Studying schizophrenic productions and associations in much the same way that Freud had studied the associations of neurotic patients, Jung reached the conclusion that emotional conflicts played the decisive part. The patient was completely absorbed in his "complexes" and had no energy left over for adjustment to reality. "The separation of the schizophrenic patient from reality," Jung wrote, "the loss of interest in objective happenings, is not difficult to explain when we consider that he persistently stands under the ban of an invincible complex. He whose whole interest is chained by a complex must be like one dead to all surroundings. He dreams with open eyes and psychologically no longer adapts himself to his surroundings." [36]

Sullivan carried the matter further by pointing out the historical connection between a "complex" and infantile ways of thinking. Grave anxieties in early childhood lead to the formulation of *dissociated systems of motives*—Sullivan's equivalent for Jung's "complex" and the Freudian concept of repression. A dissociated system is thereafter kept out of the self system; the motives it represents are felt as abhorrent and foreign to the self. These motives, therefore, can find expression only in autistic, dreamlike ways and are never channeled into adult logic and realistic thinking. When circumstances stimulate a dissociated system to the point where it begins to control behavior, autistic thinking also takes control and has a disintegrating effect on the regular forces of government. The intruding system commands only autistic and infantile processes, with which equipment it undertakes to operate the personality when it finally prevails over the reigning self. The revolution, of course, is never complete. As Sullivan put it, "A dissociated system which has broken cover in this way can only very briefly continue to be free from complication by what remains of the

36 C. G. Jung, *The Psychology of Dementia Praecox*, trans. A. A. Brill (New York: Nervous and Mental Disease Publishing Co., 1936), p. 89.

self system." [37] It is the struggle between rationality and intruding primitive logic that makes schizophrenic thought so confusing to the observer.

Sullivan's account is well illustrated in the case of B. Through some drama of inner forces B was tempted to solve his problems by going over completely to K. In realistic terms this could have meant allowing K to be his mentor and direct his life, and it would further have meant turning his back on D and independent adulthood. Behind this solution, however, one can infer a dissociated system of motives compounded of dependence and passive homosexual desires, and it was this system which brought forward the primitive ideas of omnipotence, mysterious communication, and magical practices like changing oneself into a different person.

Nature of the Intellectual Disorder

It is natural to suppose that the disorganization in schizophrenic thinking will be accompanied by a drop in level of intelligence. In point of fact the deficit on intelligence tests is smaller than might be expected. Schooler and Feldman have abstracted 28 studies published in this area between 1950 and 1965.[38] They show a consistent but moderate deficit in over-all intelligence. The impairment is general rather than specific to any particular domain and seems to be related to understandable aspects of the patient's life situation, such as education, length of hospitalization, age, and severity of current distress. In most comparisons the schizophrenics were less impaired than patients with known brain damage. The conclusion is unmistakable that the poor performance of schizophrenics is as much attributable to social inaccessibility as to intrinsic (organic) pathological processes. Performance is worst on tasks requiring sustained attention and effort, and even these improve if the patient's clinical condition gets better.

One way to understand schizophrenic thought is to suppose that infantile, preverbal conceptions are pushing their way forcibly into the fabric of adult logic and rationality. Resemblances between schizophrenic thought processes and those of children were pointed out in detail by Werner, and have been summarized in a paper by Goldman.[39] It is certainly true that schizophrenic thinking is structurally much like that of young children. It shows similar characteristics of simplicity and concreteness; it tends to be stimulus-bound, overgeneralized, distractible, weakly governed by sets and principles of relevance. This similarity, however, does not lead us to an easy explanation. The concept of regression seems badly stretched if it must include a literal return to childhood forms of thought, and often enough patients alternate rapidly between adult thought patterns and

---

[37] Sullivan, 1953, *op. cit.*, p. 327.

[38] C. Schooler and S. E. Feldman, *Experimental Studies of Schizophrenia* (Goleta, Calif.: Psychonomic Press, 1967), pp. 58–63.

[39] H. Werner, *Comparative Psychology of Mental Development* (New York: International Universities Press, Inc., 1948); A. E. Goldman, "A Comparative-Developmental Approach to Schizophrenia," *Psychological Bulletin*, LIX (1962), pp. 57–69.

primitive ones. Regression would seem to apply metaphorically rather than literally.

More significant is the clue provided by the weakness of sustained effort and attention. It is almost as if the patient could not regularly summon the mental energy necessary for the organization of thought of which he is still capable. Frankl has called attention to a very general characteristic of schizophrenic experience which he calls the "passivizing of the psychic functions." [40] The patient feels helpless, observed, photographed, influenced, the passive object of things happening around him. Patients complain that the world has become shifting and kaleidoscopic; this perhaps betokens a kind of perceptual passivity in which all stimuli have a claim on attention and nothing can be excluded. They perform poorly on complex learning tasks with many alternatives because they cannot maintain the learner's active role of selecting the relevant and excluding the irrelevant. They fail in sustained abstract thinking because they do not muster the necessary degree of active control over intellectual processes. The passivizing of thought may be the most telling description of the change that characterizes schizophrenic mental operations. It is this that a biochemical or psychodynamic hypothesis must explain.

SCHIZOPHRENIA IN CHILDHOOD

Of late years there has been a great deal of interest in childhood schizophrenia; and a great deal of research has been conducted, mostly through the medium of attempts at psychotherapy. Considering the substantial difficulties of diagnosis, the many varieties of clinical picture, and the different ages of the children studied, it is not surprising that some rather different formulations have appeared in print. What is overwhelmingly clear, however, is that serious disorders having a resemblance to adult schizophrenias make their appearance early in life.

Early Infantile Autism

One fairly clear category, *early infantile autism,* was established by Kanner in 1943 and seems to have passed the test of time at least up to the present.[41] This disturbance is seen as early as the first two years of life. It is readily distinguished from feeble-mindedness by the facts that the infant's face has an "intelligent and pensive" expression and that he shows normal if not superior skill in dealing with his inanimate environment. The difficulty shows itself in a serious lack of contact with people, a backwardness in the use of language for communication, and "an obsessive

40 V. E. Frankl, *The Doctor and the Soul* (New York: Alfred A. Knopf, Inc., 1955), pp. 247–57.
41 L. Kanner, "Autistic Disturbances of Affective Contact," *The Nervous Child,* II (1943), pp. 217–50.

desire for the preservation of sameness."[42] This last trait conveys the impression that the child cannot tolerate anything new; his sense of security depends upon keeping the environment constant and free from surprises. If we imagine these traits as remaining throughout the course of development it is clear that the end result would correspond in many respects to the unassertive adult schizophrenic who faces hesitantly each new stage of growth, communicates poorly with his fellowmen, and has no strong affective contact with anyone around him. By calling this condition *early infantile autism* Kanner hoped to avoid a premature assumption that such children supplied recruits for later schizophrenia, but most workers are inclined to view it as the start of at least a strong trend in that direction.

Early infantile autism is a rare and relatively specific symptom syndrome with a prevalence of about 2 cases per 10,000 population.[43] It should not be confused with childhood schizophrenia as a whole. The distinguishing marks are early appearance and the central symptom of unresponsiveness to the human environment. The baby is usually unresponsive from the very beginning, even when attempts are made to mother, cuddle, and play with him. Observational studies confirm that the child cannot be coaxed into interactive play, such as pat-a-cake or rolling a ball back and forth.[44] More than simply not responding, the child seems to actively resist the human environment, in a fashion not unlike what is seen in catatonic stupor. The child looks past or through his adult would-be playmate, turns his back, or occupies himself with something else. His impairment is less marked when dealing with the inanimate environment. Here he seems to establish some of the sense of competence he is unable to feel with people.

The parents of autistic children are reported to have higher intelligence and socioeconomic status than average, although these reports have been challenged on the grounds that wealthier, better educated, and more intelligent parents are more likely to seek psychiatric help.[45] Kanner describes the mothers as cold, distant, obsessive, and mechanical in their handling of their babies. Because many are well educated and successful women it can be argued that they reject the maternal role, suppress the associated feelings, and experience the care of their children as a routine, unrewarding duty. The fathers were similarly found to pay no attention to babies and evince no desire to give them a place in their lives.[46] The family

---

[42] L. Kanner, "The Conception of Wholes and Parts in Early Infantile Autism," *American Journal of Psychiatry*, CVIII (1951), pp. 23–26.

[43] D. A. Treffert, "Epidemiology of Infantile Autism," *Archives of General Psychiatry*, XXII (1970), pp. 431–38.

[44] S. Ritvo and S. Provence, "Form Perception and Imitation in Some Autistic Children: Diagnostic Findings and Their Contextual Interpretation," *The Psychoanalytic Study of the Child* (New York: International Universities Press, Inc., 1953), Vol. VIII, pp. 155–61.

[45] B. Bettelheim, *The Empty Fortress* (New York: The Free Press of Glencoe, 1967).

[46] L. Eisenberg, "The Fathers of Autistic Children," *American Journal of Orthopsychiatry*, XXVII (1957), pp. 715–24.

picture is thus one of intellectual, controlled, preoccupied parents whose particular form of adjustment is disturbed and threatened by the child's presence.[47] One might say that the autistic child responds in kind to the treatment he receives. But these unflattering descriptions of the parents have been challenged by other workers who point out, thinking in more interactional terms, that an initial unresponsiveness on the infant's part would make the mother's role unrewarding and at the same time fill her with anxiety. Furthermore, as we have already seen so many times, the disorganization of the child's behavior has to be understood; and it is not altogether easy to derive it from the parental relation.

We have no evidence of gross brain disorder in autistic children, but a number of biogenic hypotheses have been offered. Their behavior has a good deal in common with certain rare cases in which autopsy revealed an early degenerative brain disease.[48] Rimland has collected evidence for the idea that autistic children have organic defects in the reticular formation of the brain stem, and Mirsky has extended this argument to include all of schizophrenia.[49] Rimland's thesis is that the reticular formation co-ordinates and integrates sensory input with memory content; hence the autistic child is impaired in his ability to link new stimuli with remembered experience. Thus the child is virtually divested of the means for deriving meaning from his experience. He cannot form a comprehensive perception of the world, so it tends to remain kaleidoscopic for him; boundaries between himself and others cannot be made firm; hence relationships are vague and unmanageable. He is therefore destined for affective isolation.

Noting the exceptional intellectual abilities of many autistic children and their parents and some similarities between autistic children and sensorily deprived subjects, Moore and Shiek offered the intriguing hypothesis that as a fetus the autistic child was neurologically advanced and developmentally ready for primary socialization *while still in the womb*.[50] They argued that the result is that the fetus imprints prematurely to the personless womb, the heartbeats of itself and its mother, and its hands—the only objects available to it before birth. Having passed through the critical period for imprinting too soon, the child cannot develop the human attachments of the normal infant.

[47] L. Kanner, "Infantile Autism and the Schizophrenias," *Behavioral Science*, X (1965), pp. 412–20; I. Kaufman, E. Rosenblum, L. Heims, and L. Willer, "Childhood Schizophrenia: Treatment of Children and Parents," *American Journal of Orthopsychiatry*, XXVII (1957), pp. 683–90.

[48] C. Benda, "Childhood Schizophrenia, Autism and Heller's Disease," in P. W. Bowman and H. V. Mautner, eds., *Mental Retardation*, Proceedings of the First International Congress on Mental Retardation (New York: Grune & Stratton, Inc., 1960), pp. 469–92.

[49] B. Rimland, *Infantile Autism* (New York: Appleton-Century-Crofts, 1964), pp. 193–94; A. Mirsky, "Neuropsychological Basis of Schizophrenia," *Annual Review of Psychology*, XX (1969), pp. 321–48.

[50] D. J. Moore and D. A. Shiek, "Toward a Theory of Early Infantile Autism," *Psychological Review*, LXXVIII (1971), pp. 451–56.

Childhood Schizophrenia

It is usual to reserve the term *childhood schizophrenia* for disorders that make their appearance after the first four or five years. There are various symptom pictures, but on the whole they cannot be interpreted simply as autism of later onset. This is most sharply shown in a pattern described by Margaret Mahler as *symbiotic psychosis*.[51] In contrast to autism, where the child displays no attachment to the mother or anyone else, in this group of cases there is a termendously strong relationship between mother and child. The term *symbiosis,* which is in general use in biology, refers to close mutual dependence between two organisms, each requiring the other for its continued existence, as bees require flowers for honey and flowers require bees for fertilization. The symbiotic psychosis may be said to exist when the mother–child relationship has been so close that the infant fails to differentiate his mother from himself and thus stumbles over the whole process of distinguishing himself and his thoughts from external realities. Any threat of separation throws the child into disorganized panic, which is the central aspect of his numerous more acute symptoms. Mahler's description is built on direct study of young child patients, but a moving autobiography by a patient of Frieda Fromm-Reichmann shows how the underlying schizophrenic potential can remain latent until late childhood, when the new stresses of adolescence reactivate the earlier confusion in reality testing.[52]

At somewhat older ages, in the juvenile era and later childhood, the diagnosis of schizophrenia can usually be made on the strength of behavior which is more openly and obviously bizarre. A six-year-old boy described by Ross, for example, rummaged through women's purses whenever he got a chance, entered rest rooms to examine the pipes under bathroom fixtures, got on his hands and knees to look at women's legs, hit other children on the head, was deeply preoccupied with the daily mail delivery, crawled under parked trucks to examine fender aprons, frequently swung his arms around in purposeless movements, was acutely anxious in games with other children, and tried to keep his mother at his side as much as possible.[53] If we reduce these eccentricities to the formula of aggression, anxiety, dependence, and curiosity about anatomy, they are not different in kind from the interests of normal younger children and from continuing unconscious trends in older ones, but we do not expect them to be expressed so openly, controlled so poorly, or pursued with such repetitive intensity that no energy is left over for general enjoyment or constructive growth. It is in

51 M. Mahler, "On Child Psychosis and Schizophrenia," *The Psychoanalytic Study of the Child* (New York: International Universities Press, Inc., 1952), Vol. VII, pp. 286–305.

52 H. Green, *I Never Promised You a Rose Garden* (New York: Holt, Rinehart and Winston, Inc., 1964).

53 A. B. Ross, "A Schizophrenic Child and His Mother," *Journal of Abnormal and Social Psychology,* LI (1955), pp. 133–39.

fact this "lack of nuance and proportion" that strikes one observer, Anne-marie Weil, as a central characteristic in many cases: "these children hardly ever hit the middle line; they react in extremes." [54] Their attacks of anxiety illustrate these extremes, reminding one of "states of anxiety in very young children, before the ego emerges and consolidates." On the whole it seems appropriate to say that there is in these cases a retardation of ego development. Instead of flexible control and a wholesome respect for reality there is impulsiveness, explosive behavior, overintense pursuit of certain goals, and also passivity and fear. Weil points out that the diagnosis of schizophrenia in middle and late childhood is best made not on the strength of any one pathological feature but with reference to a generally "inadequate progression" toward a level of development appropriate to the child's age.

There are about 10,000 psychotic children in state hospitals, residential treatment, day care centers, and outpatient clinics; estimates of the total number of schizophrenic children in this country range from 100,000 to 500,000.[55] One cannot help having the highest respect for professional workers who have addressed themselves to the task of treating autistic and schizophrenic children. Their work is slow and discouraging; it requires infinite patience and persistence, and it must often go unrewarded by responsiveness and improvement on the child's part. Substantial recovery is claimed for only 20 to 25 per cent of child patients, and those who remain unchanged or deteriorate run from 23 to 33 per cent.[56] Schizophrenias that are already crippling in childhood can be presumed to be unusually serious, so perhaps the thing we should emphasize in the figures is that something like a quarter of these severely disordered children can be rescued.

PSYCHODYNAMIC ASPECTS OF THE DISORDER

With these facts before us we can turn directly to a consideration of causes. In this section we shall look at things from the psychodynamic point of view, emphasizing the child's experience in the family circle. It should be kept in mind that a fully adequate theory must account not only for emotional problems but also for schizophrenic disorganization.

Parent–Child Interactions

It is already clear that parents, especially mothers, play a vital part in those events of infancy which are assumed to be the starting point for

---

[54] A. P. Weil, "Clinical Data and Dynamic Considerations in Certain Cases of Childhood Schizophrenia," *American Journal of Orthopsychiatry*, XXIII (1953), pp. 518–29.

[55] B. B. Wolman, *Children without Childhood* (New York: Grune & Stratton, Inc., 1970), p. 1.

[56] L. Eisenberg, "The Course of Childhood Schizophrenia," *A. M. A. Archives of Neurology and Psychiatry*, LXXVIII (1957), pp. 69–83; P. Errera, "A Sixteen-Year Follow-Up of Schizophrenic Patients Seen in an Outpatient Clinic," *A. M. A. Archives of Neurology and Psychiatry*, LXXVIII (1957), pp. 84–88; M. J. Boatman and S. A. Szurek, "A Clinical Study of Childhood Schizophrenia," in D. D. Jackson, ed., *The Etiology of Schizophrenia* (New York: Basic Books, Inc., 1960), chap. 14.

schizophrenic developments. Therefore it is not surprising that the parents of schizophrenics have been the object of close psychological scrutiny. They have been mercilessly criticized by clinical researchers and there has been some name-calling (e.g., "schizophrenogenic") that borders on scapegoating. Hill suggests that this flaw in the observer is a natural consequence of his excellence as a therapist.[57] Partisanship is understandable. Clinical work with schizophrenics requires exceptional capacity for empathy and it is extremely difficult to remain impartial to the anguish and hostility of the client, much of which is bound up with, and directed at, his parents. Nevertheless, we shall see that there is also objective substance to the characterization of the parental role in some schizophrenic cases.

The essence of the psychodynamic approach is that schizophrenic experience and behavior, which in adult clients usually appear to be senseless, often make more sense when they are examined in their original family context.[58] It is presumed that, even though schizophrenic *breakdown* may be quite abrupt, the unconventional patterns of thinking and relationship have a long and intelligible history of learning. Therefore this approach looks for characteristic patterns of socialization from which a child might acquire the mental and emotional habits exemplified in schizophrenic disorder. From this perspective, in this social context, crazy behavior must be in some sense appropriate. Typically the focus of research is on faulty relationship or role learning,[59] faulty thinking and communication,[60] or both.[61]

Most of the theory in this area was derived from clinical studies, but increasingly these observations are being refined by objective empirical studies. Using Strodtbeck's *revealed differences* procedure for studying verbal interaction among three family members, Farina found more conflict between the parents of schizophrenics than between parents of controls (hospitalized tuberculosis patients).[62] The schizophrenics were further divided on the basis of premorbid adjustment into good premorbid and poor premorbid groups. The mothers of the poor premorbid schizophrenics were distinctly more dominant than the fathers, whereas the fathers of the good premorbid schizophrenics were more dominant than

[57] L. B. Hill, *Psychotherapeutic Intervention in Schizophrenia* (Chicago: University of Chicago Press, 1955), p. 104.

[58] R. D. Laing and A. Esterson, *Sanity, Madness and the Family* (2nd ed.; New York: Basic Books, Inc., 1971), pp. viii–ix.

[59] T. Lidz, S. Fleck, and A. R. Cornelison, *Schizophrenia and the Family* (New York: International Universities Press, 1965), pp. 424–28.

[60] L. C. Wynne and M. T. Singer, "Thought Disorder and Family Relations of Schizophrenics: I. A Research Strategy; II. A Classification of Forms of Thinking," *Archives of General Psychiatry*, IX (1963), pp. 191–98 and 199–206.

[61] G. Bateson, D. D. Jackson, J. Haley, and J. H. Weakland, "Toward a Theory of Schizophrenia," *Behavioral Science*, I (1956), pp. 251–64. Reprinted in D. D. Jackson, ed., *Communication, Family and Marriage* (Palo Alto: Science and Behavior Books, Inc., 1968), pp. 31–54.

[62] A. Farina, "Patterns of Role Dominance and Conflict in Parents of Schizophrenic Patients," *Journal of Abnormal and Social Psychology*, LXI (1960), pp. 31–28.

the mothers. Since most of the conflict was observed in the parents of poor premorbids, this suggests that both parental conflict and inverted parental dominance may have contributed to their inadequate social functioning and presumably poor psychiatric prognosis.

Waring and Ricks studied the parents of children treated at a child guidance clinic.[63] Some were subsequently hospitalized for schizophrenia and later released; some were hospitalized for schizophrenia and remained there permanently; the controls were never hospitalized for psychiatric disorder. On almost all counts there was greater parental pathology among the schizophrenics than the controls, and in most respects greater parental disturbance among the chronic than the released schizophrenics. The chronics had more parents who were themselves psychotic or seriously disturbed, a finding of ambiguous significance for psychogenic hypotheses because of the established genetic connection discussed earlier. Still we cannot dismiss the pathogenic potential of a close relationship with a seriously disturbed parent, especially in genetically predisposed offspring. There was more evidence of *emotional divorce*[64] between the parents and more symbiotic unions involving the schizophrenic child in the families of the chronics. At first glance these two findings might appear to be contradictory, implying that the chronics were exposed both to too much and too little close relationship. But closer examination shows that the results may be complementary, depending upon the constellation of alliances within the family. It is frequently found, for example, that as the parents grow further apart from one another, one of them (often the mother) compensates for this with an all too strong investment in the child. The child may then become an instrument for coping with the father or an overvalued and overprotected object of love. If such a relationship becomes a way of life for the child, this presents enormous obstacles to his separating himself and emerging at the appropriate stage of development to a sense of independent selfhood. Studies of withdrawn children in later childhood sometimes show that the central problem is to protect oneself from a demanding, interfering, overwhelming mother.[65]

Waring and Ricks also found that the released schizophrenics were more often openly rejected and forced to leave home and the control group families showed more open conflict. From this we can infer that open hostility and rejection are damaging for the child but temporary in their effects. Covert forms of emotional conflict are clearly more pernicious. Surprisingly, there were more "classic schizophrenogenic" mothers in the control

---

[63] M. Waring and D. Ricks, "Family Patterns of Children Who Became Adult Schizophrenics," *Journal of Nervous and Mental Disease,* CXL (1965), pp. 351–64.

[64] This is an expression coined by Murray Bowen to characterize marriages in which the partners have grown so distant and hostile toward one another that they are divorced in reality if not in fact, while continuing to live together. M. Bowen, "A Family Concept of Schizophrenia," in Jackson, *The Etiology of Schizophrenia, op. cit.,* p. 354.

[65] L. Nagelburg, H. Spotnitz, and Y. Feldman, "The Attempt at Healthy Insulation in the Withdrawn Child," *American Journal of Orthopsychiatry,* XXIII (1953), pp. 238–52.

and released families. Perhaps that singular creature is more ubiquitous than most people think. (And that, of course, is a major problem with the concept.)

The Double Bind

Probably the most stimulating and influential conception of the psychodynamic etiology of schizophrenia is the *double bind* hypothesis of Bateson *et al.*[66] This work grew out of the earlier views of Sullivan on the significance of interpersonal communication. Basing their observations on the interactions of schizophrenics with their families, the Bateson group reasoned that ambiguous communication by the parents could be a primary cause of schizophrenia. A principal means of socialization is through communication with parents, first because it gives the child an orientation to language and thought, and, perhaps more importantly, because it establishes his basic approach to human relationships. The Bateson group observed that the parents of schizophrenics characteristically expressed double messages that disqualified or contradicted each other, often at different levels of abstraction. They offer the following illustration of the double bind.

A young man who had fairly well recovered from an acute schizophrenic episode was visited in the hospital by his mother. He was glad to see her and impulsively put his arm around her shoulders, whereupon she stiffened. He withdrew his arm and she asked, "Don't you love me any more?" He then blushed, and she said, "Dear, you must not be so easily embarrassed and afraid of your feelings." The patient was able to stay with her only a few minutes more and following her departure he assaulted an aide and was put in the tubs.

The authors point out that this kind of treatment, extrapolated over many years of impressionable childhood, would teach the child a peculiar kind of intellectual deception ("What you say is not what you mean at least not unequivocally"). More importantly, since interpersonal relations are based fundamentally on communications between people and you can't trust those unequivocally, the child learns to avoid a definite relationship with other people. It is safer than committing oneself to a particular kind of relationship and being whip-sawed in the middle. Given such a developmental history it is not surprising that a schizophrenic person is confused or confusing in his thinking and abnormally cautious in his approach to relationships with other people.

A particularly insidious aspect of the double bind illustrated above is that the mother controls every aspect of their relationship, even the boy's thoughts about it. A natural reaction to her duplicity would be to point out the contradictions in her behavior, but the boy's intense dependency and previous training prevents him from doing this, though she interprets his behavior, even his unexpressed feelings, and forces him to accept them,

[66] Bateson *et al., op. cit.*

on pain of losing her love. The boy's dilemma is clear: she expresses ambiguous or downright contradictory messages about their relationship. He is punished if he discriminates accurately what she means and responds appropriately to one of the messages, e.g., withdrawing his arm when she stiffens. On the other hand, he is also chastised for not responding to the other message, of love. And finally it is the boy who is at fault for being uncertain of his feelings rather than the mother for being ambivalent. Is it any wonder that his thinking would be confused or his approach to other people cautious and supersensitive?

We saw elements of the double bind pattern in the case of Kathi Hermann. Her mother often boasted of her own non-conformity and tacitly supported her daughter's escapades, but she nagged incessantly when Kathi became a beatnik, dressed and acted in sexually provocative ways, and *really* let herself go. She was very proud and supportive of Kathi's wide social interests, but often interfered with her friendships, driving away the "wrong kind" of companions. Finally, she would not relinquish control of her daughter, even though she shipped her off to boarding schools and families in Europe. One has to wonder about the motives of a woman who needs such a close relationship with her daughter, spoils and protects her, and intrudes constantly in her life, but still chooses to have her reared somewhere else. "Of course" she always read Kathi's letters and diaries. Obviously Kathi had to fight for her independence, though perhaps not so literally as she did. Given this perspective, we can see the wisdom of the decision to release Kathi from the hospital to the custody of a responsible family friend. We may even indulge in a bit of optimism about her future prospects, once the War of Independence has been waged and won.

Mishler and Waxler [67] carried out a highly systematic laboratory study of the verbal interactions of 32 families with a schizophrenic child and 17 normal control families. The "schizophrenic" families were selected to include cases of both sexes, some with good and some with poor premorbid adjustment, and each with a non-schizophrenic sibling of the same sex. The most significant finding was that the normal families were the most expressive and responsive to the communications of others in the family. This did not mean that the normal families had fluent, orderly conversations. On the contrary, there were frequent interruptions and fragmentations in their speech but despite this they were highly responsive to what the others said and felt, especially in the opinions they expressed, so their communication was quite effective and adaptive. The families of the good premorbid schizophrenics were more controlled and rigid, making their conversations rather abstract and impersonal. The families of the poor premorbid schizophrenics were the least responsive, showing more confusion and a lack of orientation. The normal families had conventional role

[67] E. G. Mishler and N. E. Waxler, *Interaction in Families* (New York: John Wiley & Sons, Inc., 1968).

structures; there was typically a parental coalition with the parents attending mostly to each other, the father highest in status or power and the children lowest. Despite the clear hierarchy of power and authority, the parents did not exercise authoritarian or coercive control; while the members of these families did make more direct attempts to control or influence one another, this was also done by the low status children. By contrast, the schizophrenic families, especially the "good premorbid" ones, had unconventional authority structure, with the mother more powerful than the father, often in coalition with the schizophrenic child against him, and the exercise of power was more impersonal and indirect. Thus the parents provided poor role models of identification. There were virtually no behavioral differences between the schizophrenic cases and their normal siblings, and the parents treated them similarly, exaggerating their characteristic styles only slightly with the schizophrenic child. Therefore it appears that the interaction patterns were more characteristic of the family than specific to the afflicted child. Although the schizophrenic parents communicated very differently than the normal parents, most of the comparisons showed great overlap between the family types. If anything, there was somewhat more conflict and subterfuge in the families of the good premorbid schizophrenics than in those of the poor premorbids.

Limits of Psychodynamic Explanation

These analyses of emotional conflicts in the family, and of the subtle communication of irrationality to the child, represent a great advance over earlier studies of the "schizophrenogenic" mother. They are impressive, but they have by no means stilled the voices of controversy. It is prudent to remember that psychodynamic explanations of the neuroses and of delinquent behavior generally imply no small amount of emotional stress in the family, leading, however, to quite different outcomes in the child. When one tries to isolate what might be peculiar to the family of the schizophrenic—the irrational methods of dealing with conflict and the "double-bind" type of communication—one can hardly avoid misgivings about the specificity. It has certainly not been demonstrated that parental behavior is less pathological and communication less irrational in the families of neurotics and delinquents. We may even suspect, listening to the average level of communication in the fast-moving daily events of family life, that a goodly portion of irrationality and "double-bind" is universal in childhood. It is important not to contrast the "schizophrenogenic" family with a wholly fanciful image of normal rationality. In addition it must be kept in mind that not every child in a family is likely to be schizophrenic. There is no reason to doubt that each child will be treated a little differently, but if we want the psychogenic hypothesis to be completely adequate we must be prepared to show how the well children escaped the fate of the sick one.

Psychodynamic studies thus continue to leave open the possibility that there is something unusual about the child who, earlier or later, succumbs to the schizophrenic disorder. We must now consider what progress has been made toward detecting a somatogenic component.

SOMATOGENIC ASPECTS OF THE DISORDER

It seems clear that one cannot conceive of schizophrenia as a somatic disease that is analogous to general paresis. It does not follow a course or have a character that is consistent with gross cerebral pathology. The schizophrenic disorder is consistent, however, with such possibilities as a generalized vulnerability, an oversensitive disposition, or even a subtle biochemical deviation. It is possible that psychodynamic processes of the kind we have discussed serve as necessary but not sufficient causes of schizophrenia. The disorder cannot occur without them, but it does not occur simply as their consequence. Other ingredients are required, some element of somatic disposition, which might plausibly take the form of an innate temperamental peculiarity or neurophysiological deviation that would have an insidious but cumulative effect.

Genetic Evidence

Certainly no other research area in schizophrenia has yielded more advance and refinement of knowledge than this one. Much of the refinement has consisted of moderating the early and over-zealous estimates of the magnitude of the genetic contribution by such pioneers as Franz Kallmann.[68] For example, a prime focus of research has been the *concordance rates*[69] of identical vs. fraternal twins, because higher concordance among identical twins would confirm a genetic factor in the disorder. A survey of such concordance studies from 1928 to 1967 shows that the median rates reported before 1954 were 68 per cent for monozygotic (identical) and 18 per cent for dizygotic (fraternal) twins. However, the studies after 1960, which were based on much improved experimental designs and better procedures for discerning zygosity, reported median rates of 38 per cent, and 9 per cent for MZ and DZ twins, respectively.[70] While the rate differential is still impressive and strongly implicates a genetic determinant, the over-all reduction in the estimates indicates how much the earlier work was biased by the preconceptions of the investigators.

Similar confirmation comes from studies of family histories. Heston followed up 47 children who had been permanently separated from their

[68] F. J. Kallmann, *The Genetics of Schizophrenia* (New York: Augustine, 1938).

[69] Twins are concordant if both share a particular physical or behavioral attribute or if neither manifest it. Twins are discordant for schizophrenia, for example, if one becomes schizophrenic but the other does not.

[70] B. P. Dohrenwind and B. S. Dohrenwind, *Social Status and Psychological Disorder* (New York: John Wiley & Sons, Inc., 1969), p. 34.

schizophrenic mothers at birth. He found five (11 per cent who became schizophrenic, as contrasted with none of the control children of normal mothers.[71] The recent family history studies in Denmark, one of which has been discussed already, show remarkably consistent results. Kety *et al.* studied the incidence of schizophrenia in the biological relatives of adopted children who became schizophrenic.[72] Thirteen of 150 relatives (9 per cent) had psychiatric disorders "in the schizophrenic spectrum," although only seven (5 per cent) were explicitly schizophrenic. This was contrasted with one per cent of the control relatives with schizophrenic tendencies, none of whom was explicitly schizophrenic. These investigators carried out a companion study, using the same basic pool of subjects, which essentially replicated Heston's study.[73] Like Heston, they examined the frequency of schizophrenia among adopted children whose biological parents had been schizophrenic. Eleven of the 34 offspring of schizophrenic parents (32 per cent) had psychiatric disorders "in the schizophrenic spectrum," although only 9 (26 per cent) were explicitly schizophrenic and only 3 (9 per cent) were chronic or true schizophrenics. We can tell that these figures are unusually high because 15 per cent of the control adoptees had diagnoses in the schizophrenic spectrum and 2 per cent were diagnosed explicitly schizophrenic. These diagnoses were based on direct psychiatric interviews and the interviewers probably made their diagnoses liberally so as not to overlook any signs of pathology. Nevertheless, the large differential in the rates can be trusted because the interviews were conducted "blind": the interviewers did not know to which group the subjects belonged.

All of these findings taken together mean that a schizophrenic psychosis is more likely to develop in individuals who carry a certain inherited predisposition. The number of schizophrenics in whom such hereditary "loading" is manifest in the family history is not large, probably no more than one in five and possibly as few as one in eleven. But the contribution of genetic determinants, even if it be a small one, is incontrovertible. Moreover, we can specify that the genetic disposition for schizophrenia is distinguishable from that for affective psychosis.[74] There remains some ambiguity about genetic factors in the reactive or remitting schizophrenias, where the evidence for inheritance is either equivocal or nonexistent, as discussed before.

Modes of Genetic Transmission

Explaining the mode of genetic transmission has been devilishly difficult because the disorder is so rare and the family pedigrees do not conform to

[71] L. L. Heston, "Psychiatric Disorders in Foster Home Reared Children of Schizophrenic Mothers," *British Journal of Psychiatry*, CXII (1966), pp. 819–25.

[72] Kety *et al., op. cit.*

[73] D. Rosenthal, P. H. Wender, S. S. Kety, F. Schulsinger, J. Welner, and L. Østergaard, "Schizophrenics' Offspring Reared in Adoptive Homes," in Rosenthal and Kety, *op. cit.,* pp. 377–91.

[74] Astrup and Noreik, *op. cit.,* p. 82.

simple Mendelian formulas. Almost certainly the earliest investigators believed in a straightforward dominant mechanism. Kallmann realized that familial incidence was too low for that and argued for a recessive mechanism with incomplete manifestation of the disorder in schizoid personalities. Böök postulated a dominant mechanism with *reduced penetrance* and Karlsson concluded from his studies in Iceland that a dominant gene is required with a recessive modifier.[75] However, no genetic theory remains tenable if it postulates a low level of penetrance because it becomes untestable and indefinite. Moreover, as each new study further reduced the incidence of schizophrenia in the families of schizophrenics, the viability of a Mendelian model of transmission became more and more doubtful.

Many investigators are now turning to a *diathesis-stress* model of etiology for schizophrenia which presumes a *polygenic* mode of genetic inheritance.[76] This means that a constitutional defect determined by several genes is inherited by many people, whom Meehl calls *schizotypes*. They will have many of the schizoid traits, avoidance of others, inability to experience pleasure, and so on, but most of them will not become manifestly schizophrenic except under very unfavorable circumstances of personal history and psychological stress. If the mode of transmission is polygenic, then the person's genetic vulnerability would depend on the number of defective genes he inherited. This model assumes a far larger number of *potential* schizophrenics in our society than most theories do, but it also assigns a much greater weight to the significance of personal history in potentiating the manifest disorder. This should make it a more acceptable vehicle for reconciling the genetic evidence with the impressive clinical data on psychodynamic causes.

Biochemical and Neurophysiological Evidence

Kraepelin advanced a chemogenic theory of schizophrenia. He believed that the root of the difficulty lay in disordered secretions of the sex gland. This might produce a chemical state in the body (autointoxication) that in some way disturbed the proper functioning of the nervous system. When the importance of endocrine glands was first appreciated, there was reason to expect some support for Kraepelin's view. Research soon discredited the theory, however, and the complexity that was found characteristic of endocrine functions discouraged any attempt to specify a single process.

[75] J. A. Böök, "Schizophrenia as a Gene Mutation," *Acta Genetica*, IV (1953), pp. 133–39; J. L. Karlson, *The Biological Basis of Schizophrenia* (Springfield, Ill.: Charles C Thomas, 1966), pp. 45–46. Penetrance is a term used by geneticists when a genetic factor is thought to be present but for some reason does not become manifest in the person carrying it. The concept has been much criticized because it is hypothetical, not observable, and hence cannot be measured. It is discussed by Böök in "Genetic Aspects of Schizophrenic Psychoses," in Jackson, *The Etiology of Schizophrenia, op. cit.*, pp. 29–30.

[76] P. E. Meehl, "Schizotaxia, Schizotypy, Schizophrenia," *American Psychologist*, XVII (1962), pp. 827–38; D. Rosenthal, "Genetic Research in the Schizophrenic Syndrome," in R. Cancro, ed., *The Schizophrenic Reactions* (New York: Brunner/Mazel, 1970), pp. 245–58.

It was one of Kraepelin's hopes that the nature of the chemical alternation would one day be illuminated by experiments on the effects of drugs. If a drug could be found which produced temporarily the symptoms of schizophrenia in normal people, analysis of its properties would point the way to the chemical secret of the disorder. Recently it has been found that a number of chemicals called psychotomimetics (because they mimic psychosis) comes fairly close to having this effect. Typical results with lysergic acid (LSD–25), concordant with studies of mescaline and other chemicals elsewhere, have been published by Rinkel and others.[77] The effect on normal subjects is startling alike to themselves and to the observers. It is in many respects closely analogous to a moderately acute psychotic episode with considerable turmoil and confusion. In all cases there are marked disturbances of thinking, perceiving, and feeling. Some of the subjects show catatonic reactions, others hallucinations, other paranoid suspiciousness and delusions. Several subjects reported losing their sense of personal identity and experiencing their bodies in peculiar ways, such as the legs walking of their own volition. People around them look different, sometimes hostile and sinister, sometimes changed in size, sometimes as if transparent or behind a glass partition. The subjects suffer a loss in sociability; more of their behavior than usual is avoidant, hostile, or dependent. In tests of intellectual processes they show an impairment in concentration and consecutive thinking. Attention wanders and is often caught by minute features of the physical environment. Needless to say, the psychotic-like episode lasts for only a few hours, and normal subjects are usually none the worse for their brief visit to insanity. After all, there were no crazier than we all are in our night dreams.

It was soon discovered that mescaline, LSD–25, and most of the other hallucinogens are methylated compounds that are structurally similar to *dopamine* and *serotonin,* neurochemicals known to be centrally involved in the normal functioning of the brain. Therefore it was hypothesized that some forms of schizophrenia might be caused by an alteration in the metabolic process of methylating normal neurochemicals so that abnormal compounds similar to mescaline were produced.[78] This view was supported by the demonstration, several times replicated, that psychotic symptoms were made worse in some schizophrenics by administering methionine, which is known to stimulate the methylation process. It is plausible that methionine and the psychotomimetic drugs produce their abnormal effects by inhibiting or changing these necessary neurochemicals in some way. Pursuit of these leads, however, has turned up a number of contradictory

77 M. Rinkel, R. W. Hyde, H. C. Solomon, and H. Hoagland, "Experimental Psychiatry II: Clinical and Physio-Chemical Observations in Experimental Psychosis," *American Journal of Psychiatry,* CXI (1955), pp. 881–95.

78 S. S. Kety, "The Hypothetical Relationships between Amines and Mental Illness: A Critical Synthesis," in H. E. Himwich, S. S. Kety, and J. R. Smythies, eds., *Amines and Schizophrenia* (Oxford: Pergamon Press, 1967), pp. 272–74.

and puzzling findings, leaving investigators with the feeling that although serotonin and dopamine are essential for normal functioning, they have not yet fathomed the manner of their disturbance.[79] Indeed, one of the leading experts in this field recently confessed that there is not one lead in the area of biochemical research which, if pursued, he would expect to lead to a greater understanding of schizophrenia.[80] Obviously, genetic factors, to which Kety has now mainly turned his attention, must operate at a biochemical level at some point, but their effects might be on the anatomy or electrical connections in the brain, and a simple biochemical approach is hardly likely to elucidate much about them.

Similar enthusiasm and disappointments have attended Heath's discovery that *taraxein,* a protein substance found in the blood of schizophrenics, could produce psychotic symptoms in nonpsychotic subjects.[81] Other workers have failed to reproduce Heath's results, and the biochemical analysis on which they were based seems open to a good deal of question.[82]

On the whole it is fair to say that the biochemical investigations have thus far made no breakthrough with respect to schizophrenia. We must remember, however, that the biochemical secrets of the brain are well guarded and that research in this complex domain is bound to proceed through many trials and many errors. Difficulties of proof beset the somatogenic hypothesis as they do the psychogenic. Assuredly the facts are not yet all at hand. The hypothesis must be kept open that an abnormal biochemical condition may contribute to the disorganization and primitiveness of schizophrenic thinking.

A great deal of related research has centered around the hypothesis of abnormal physiological arousal in schizophrenics.[83] Broen develops the argument that excessively high arousal in some schizophrenics may activate inhibitory homeostatic processes which are known, for example, to affect sensory receptivity. Because schizophrenics are often overloaded with stimulation beyond their capacity to organize and assimilate, they may learn methods to reduce their stimulability. These defenses may manifest themselves in the idiosyncrasies of inattention, avoidance of people, and autistic thinking that we associate with schizophrenia.

[79] S. S. Kety, "Recent Biochemical Theories of Schizophrenia," in Jackson, *The Etiology of Schizophrenia, op. cit.,* pp. 134–37.

[80] S. S. Kety, panel discussion, in Cancro, *The Schizophrenic Reactions, op. cit.,* pp. 281–82.

[81] R. G. Heath, A. F. Guschwan, and J. W. Coffey, "Relation of Taraxein to Schizophrenia," *Diseases of the Nervous System,* XXXI (1970), pp. 391–95. Reprinted in Cancro, *The Schizophrenic Syndrome, op. cit.,* pp. 414–21.

[82] S. S. Kety, in Jackson, *The Etiology of Schizophrenia, op. cit.,* chap. 4.

[83] W. E. Broen, *Schizophrenia: Research and Theory* (New York: Academic Press, 1968), pp. 215–16; P. J. Lang and A. H. Buss, "Psychological Deficit in Schizophrenia. II. Interference and Activation," *Journal of Abnormal Psychology,* LXX (1965), pp. 77–106.

Limits of Somatogenic Explanation

We must be careful to keep within legitimate bounds our ideas about the role of biological factors. Wonder-drug reasoning has led some enthusiasts to believe that once we find the magic substance, schizophrenia will be eliminated by the simple process of injection. Unfortunately, this is a little like supposing that a drug can blast a man out of his lifelong habits and convictions. Wondrous as the effects of tranquilizing drugs have been, as we shall see in the next section, they promise no such panacea. Let us say that a patient's nervous system has operated under a biochemical handicap; nevertheless, it has operated, and the resultng pattern of life cannot be undone in a moment. Whatever else it may be, schizophrenia is certainly a cumulative disorder, rooted in the habits and attitudes built up through a long individual history. It is not a temporary poisoning that clears up and leaves the patient in perfect health.

To illustrate the point let us imagine that the middle-aged spinster described earlier has been given a drug that cures schizophrenia. The medication could not greatly clarify her thinking processes, which are already quite normal except on the subject of her reputation and the assault on her brain. It could not remove her lifelong anxious feelings of inferiority, and it would therefore have little effect on her compensatory delusions of grandeur or her solitary way of life. This was, of course, an older woman whose disorder had become consolidated. If we take an example of incipient psychosis in a younger person whose life is still in the making, we can suppose that the imaginary drug would be more helpful, though still not omnipotent. The electrician B, for instance, whose psychotic episode began so suddenly, might have been restored to greater immediate clarity of thought, although the emotional crisis that precipitated his breakdown would not be dissolved by the drug. We saw how rapidly Kathi Hermann's acute psychotic symptoms responded to medication, but no drug can resolve her crises of identity and independence. One must earnestly hope that the biological mysteries will soon be solved, but this happy event would not eliminate the need for skilled personal treatment of schizophrenia.

TREATMENT OF SCHIZOPHRENIA

It may seem incongruous to report great improvements in the treatment of schizophrenia after depicting such bewilderment about the classification and causes of the disorder and citing the Hindoo fable about groping in the dark. But there is a good deal of precedent for this in medical history. In the Maternity Hospital of Vienna in 1858, medical students' maternity cases showed an average over a period of six years of 99 deaths per thousand from puerperal fever; almost one in ten mothers died in childbirth. Semmelweiss, who was the physician in charge of the hospital at that time, believed the cause to be something arising within the hospital and made his students wash their hands in a solution of chloride of lime. In one year the death rate in his wards tumbled from 18 per cent to 3 per cent and soon after to one per cent. It was not until 1866 that Lister published his work on antisepsis, giving us the first knowledge of the causal *agents* of infection, but the treatment Semmelweiss devised on a hunch was no less effective because of his ignorance of specific etiology. We shall see that the treatment of schizophrenia has proceeded historically by a series of similar trial-and-error experiments and a few accidents with far-reaching effects.

Before 1930 schizophrenic patients received only the most minimal treatment. For the most part they were committed to mental hospitals which were overcrowded and chronically understaffed. Nothing more was attempted than to keep them in good physical health and comfort. "Treatment" usually consisted of sedation, physical restraint, or ice packs to cool a patient down if he got upset or assaultive, and plenty of latitude for the patient to do what he liked, which more often than not was nothing. It was not understood at that time that such purely custodial incarceration contributed in itself to the deterioration and regression which were considered prominent symptoms of schizophrenic disorder.

Shock Treatment

The insulin coma method discovered by Manfred Sakel was one of those chance discoveries that for a while promised a revolution in treatment. Insulin was injected intramuscularly to produce a deep coma that was interrupted after an hour or so by administering glucose. After repeated treatments the patient's mental state sometimes improved sufficiently to allow a clinician to establish rapport and initiate psychotherapy. However, there were many problems with insulin shock therapy. It was expensive because of the amount of medical supervision and nursing care required. Often the treatment lasted several months and the patients typically gained enormous amounts of weight because of the tampering with their sugar metabolism. Moreover, the frequency of relapse after improvement proved to be high.[84] The enthusiasm aroused in the late 1930's by this first treatment that really seemed to have an impact subsided rapidly in view of the modest results.

Insulin shock treatment soon gave way to electroconvulsive therapy (ECT) and has had little use since World War II. Initially the procedures for administering ECT were primitive, but refinements have been made over the years. Nowadays a patient receives prior injections of a sedative

[84] L. Salzman, "An Evaluation of Shock Therapy," *American Journal of Psychiatry*, CIII (1947), pp. 669–79.

to induce loss of consciousness, and curare or a similar drug to relax the muscles and inhibit the violence of the convulsive response. Before the introduction of the latter precaution patients and even those attending them sometimes sustained serious injuries from the uncontrolled thrashing of the body and limbs. This violent convulsion is produced by passing a powerful jolt of electric current between electrodes attached to the head. When the seizure has run its course, the patient sleeps or rests for a few minutes until his head clears and his aroused somatic functions return to normal, and then he may go about his business as usual. The procedure has been so streamlined that some private physicians offer the treatment to outpatients in their offices.

ECT had many of the same effects as insulin shock (quieting, amnesia, social accessibility) but few of the unpleasant side effects, and was less expensive. It enjoyed a similar boom of enthusiasm and remained a primary mode of treating psychoses until largely displaced by tranquilizing drugs in the mid-1950's. Research soon showed, however, that it was of doubtful value for schizophrenics: many who improved quickly relapsed.[85] It had a better record in treating affective disorders, though even here its main benefit was to speed up the process of recovery rather than to increase the rates of improvement.[86] ECT today occupies a minor place in treating schizophrenia. A recent survey of patients admitted from 1920–1971 suggests that it may be almost as effective as tranquilizing drugs for treating catatonics.[87] This may be explained, in part, by the fact that catatonic symptoms are quite similar to the symptoms of affective psychosis.

Tranquilizing Drugs

The most effective tranquilizers proved to be a group of phenothiazine chemicals whose amazing effects were first discovered accidentally by Deschamps and Laborit in 1952 as they were trying to develop a powerful sedative for use in sleep therapy. Delay and Deniker capitalized on this happy accident by employing *chlorpromazine* as a therapeutic agent in schizophrenia and other psychoses with psychomotor agitation.[88] The results were so dramatic that they initiated a revolutionary breakthrough in psychiatric treatment. The phenothiazines were called *ataractic* or tran-

---

85 T. Rennie, "Present Status of Shock Therapy," *Psychiatry,* VI (1943), 127–37.

86 P. E. Huston and L. M. Locher, "Manic-Depressive Psychosis: Course when Treated and Untreated with Electric Shock," *Archives of Neurology and Psychiatry,* LX (1948), pp. 37–48; A. B. Szalita, "Psychodynamics of Disorders of the Involutional Age," in S. Arieti, ed., *American Handbook of Psychiatry* (New York: Basic Books, 1966).

87 J. R. Morrison, "The Syndrome of Catatonia: Results of Treatment," in M. Roff, D. F. Ricks, and A. Thomas, eds., *Life History Research in Psychopathology,* vol. III (Minneapolis: University of Minnesota Press, 1973).

88 J. Delay and P. Deniker, "Le Traitement des Psychoses par une Methode Neurolytique Dérivée de l'Hibernotherapie. (Le 4560 RP Utilisé Seul en Cure Prolongée et Continuée)." In *Congrés de Mèdecins Aliénistes et Neurologistes de France et des Pays de Langue Francaise. Compte Rendu.* Luxembourg (1952), p. 514.

quilizing drugs because their most obvious effect was to reduce tension and anxiety. However, it also became clear that they could directly affect perception, attention, and mood, so they are widely regarded now as antipsychotic drugs. To gain some impression of their impact, one need only consult the statistics on resident populations in U. S. public mental hospitals. From 1945 to 1955 the year-end population increased at a rate of two per cent per year, reaching its peak of 559,420 in 1955, one year after the use of tranquilizers became widespread.[89] Since then it has declined steadily until in 1968 it was 399,152.

How the tranquilizers achieve their effects on the nervous system is not precisely known, but it is generally believed that they inhibit the transport or absorption of amines in the brain, such as serotonin, which presumably are otherwise produced in excess or metabolized in a faulty way.

Like most forms of treatment, tranquilizers are most successful with cases having a recent onset of relatively abrupt character. Results are poorer with patients who have made their peace, so to speak, with a psychotic condition. It is generally conceded that the drugs alleviate symptoms but do not cure the basic disorder, so patients improved by drugs may relapse if treatment is discontinued. Here, however, the drugs have a practical advantage: patients can be kept on maintenance doses even after they have been discharged. In fact, more and more cases are being treated in Community Health Centers and outpatient clinics without being hospitalized at all. The only hazard is that the drugs may have harmful side effects when taken in large doses or over a long period of time, a point that is under close scrutiny in pharmacological research.

Psychotherapy

The earliest attempts at psychotherapy encountered what seemed to be an insuperable obstacle. Try as he might, the therapist could almost never break through the wall of the patient's reserve to establish a trustful working relationship. It has been pointed out that whereas a neurotic must learn to accept repressed *psychological* facts, the psychotic must learn to accept rejected *external* facts. This difference is vitally important when it comes to establishing the initial therapeutic relationship. The therapist can be the ally of the patient whose task it is to accept repressed psychological facts. It is much more difficult to occupy this role with a psychotic patient because the clinician himself is among the rejected external facts. The schizophrenic is often remarkably aware of his inner life, so it may be of no great value to have him learn more about it. In fact, it may even do harm, deepening his preoccupation and increasing his disturbance.

[89] M. Kramer, E. S. Pollack, and R. W. Redick, "Studies of the Incidence and Prevalence of Hospitalized Mental Disorders in the United States: Current Status and Future Goals," in P. H. Hoch and J. Zubin, eds., *Comparative Epidemiology of the Mental Disorders* (New York: Grune & Stratton, Inc., 1961), p. 73.

The therapeutic task is rather to help him discover that reality can be bearable and even rewarding. This fact may first be discovered in his relation to the therapist.

Fromm-Reichmann pointed out that a schizophrenic enters a withdrawn state as a means of protecting himself from the frustrations of reality, with its constant reminders of his inadequacy.[90] Suspicious and distrustful of everyone, he is particularly upset by any attempt to intrude into his isolated world and personal life. For this reason she made it abundantly clear to her clients that they need not take her into their world or give up any part of their "sickness" until they were completely ready to do so on their own accord.[91] Yet she was convinced that every schizophrenic has some dim notion of the unreality and loneliness of his substitute delusionary world. A part of him still longs for contact and understanding, and once he has managed to accept the therapist his attachment becomes unbelievably strong. He is so sensitive that almost anything that happens may wound his self-esteem. One patient responded twice with catatonic stupor when the hour of appointment had to be changed; both times it was immediately dispelled when the therapist explained the reasons for the change.

For our purposes the most important feature of Fromm-Reichmann's work is her convincing demonstration that the schizophrenic is capable of developing strong relationships of love and hatred toward his therapist. Once a relationship is established, it is of vast importance to the patient and it is charged with strong emotions. Nothing could show more clearly the nature of the schizophrenic disorder. Having been injured many times, the schizophrenic has learned the art of protective withdrawal, but the flame of feeling proves not to be extinguished.

In some cases, especially with the helpful adjunct of tranquilizers, it is possible to establish the necessary contact by daily conversation, expressions of consistent interest, and a tactful policy of waiting for the patient to build up confidence in his therapist. The patient is treated as an adult, though a very sensitive one. This process may take a long time, however, and it may be quite impossible if the patient is much disturbed or extremely regressed. In such cases more direct and vehement methods must be used to establish contact. Sometimes this may require directly gratifying infantile needs or entering into the patient's regressed world, using the kind of language and symbols that dominate his own disorganized thought processes. Both elements are utilized in John Rosen's "direct analysis," which has sometimes been successful in restoring contact with patients in extremely severe schizophrenic states.[92] Rosen's method includes mothering the patients, sitting with them for hours, feeding them,

90 F. Fromm-Reichmann, *Principles of Intensive Psychotherapy* (Chicago: University of Chicago Press, 1950).

91 H. Green, *I Never Promised You a Rose Garden, op. cit.* This is an autobiographical account of a recovered schizophrenic girl treated by Fromm-Reichmann.

92 J. Rosen, *Direct Analysis: Selected Papers* (New York: Grune & Stratton, Inc., 1953).

helping them, expressing affection for them. It also involves grasping the meaning of their behavior, gestures, silences, and streams of incoherent conversation, all of which are taking place at a regressed, infantile level. When meaning is perceived it is at once interpreted to the patient. These interpretations, with their blunt references to bodily functions, sucking needs, sexual perversions, and primitive hostilities, are often quite shocking to outside observers, but they achieve a very direct kind of communication. The patient at last feels that somebody understands him. Somebody realizes that he is in a panic because his mother's milk is poisoning him or a monster father is going to cut him up. If the doctor understands this, then it is possible to trust the doctor and believe him when he says he will protect the patient from this harm. Rosen's method requires rare skill in grasping the meaning of highly confused productions, and a power of becoming dramatically involved in the patient's plight.

This method of establishing contact is not a complete method of treatment. It serves to bring the patient out of acute psychosis and thus restores sufficient organization so that a more rational psychotherapy becomes possible. It shows the rescuing power of love, sympathy, and understanding, but the patient must eventually become able to lead his life without depending upon such a bounty of parental devotion.

Increasingly in recent years psychotherapy has been directed toward the adult rather than the infantile aspects of the personality. The purpose is to promote the patient's sense of his own identity and enhance his self-esteem. These more ego-oriented approaches concentrate on the person's evasive adjustment patterns, his retreats in the face of difficulty and his inclination to let others make his decisions and solve his problems. However, conventional goals of social adjustment and extroversion are often uncongenial to former schizophrenics, and may constitute a hazard for future health. It may be better for some to find their own sources of satisfaction and security, irrespective of the approval of their neighbors, of their families, and of public opinion. Toward this end the therapist may be more helpful if he himself is a champion of individuality rather than conventionality. This may explain, in part, the great popularity, especially among young schizophrenics, of the views of R. D. Laing, who lays the blame for much of madness squarely on the doorstep of the family home and encourages his patients to savor their acute psychotic experience as an inner voyage of personal discovery, from which one should expect to profit and grow.[93]

The Hospital as Therapeutic Milieu

We examined in Chapter 8 the widespread changes that have occurred in transforming the mental hospital from a custodial institution to a therapeutic milieu. Schizophrenic patients are among the chief beneficiaries

[93] R. D. Laing, *The Politics of Experience* (New York: Pantheon Books, 1967).

of this change. Withdrawal and regression, it is now realized, did not just happen in the custodial hospital as a result of disease; they were actively encouraged by an environment in which there was nothing for the patient to live for, nothing to do, nothing to arouse interest and create an atmosphere of rewarding participation. When a ward is organized as a therapeutic milieu every attempt is made to reverse these conditions, creating an environment designed to promote interest, friendly interaction, usefulness, and self-esteem. The appeal, as in individual therapy, is to the adult in the patient rather than to his dependent needs. The reader should not imagine that milieu therapy quickly transforms the ward into a scene of merriment and lively social life. Schizophrenics become socially responsive, if at all, at their own very slow pace, and life on the ward would seem tame indeed to an extrovert from the outside world. But it is a distinct forward step when a detached, confused schizophrenic dares to make a sympathetic remark to another patient, agrees to help make sandwiches for a ward party, gets dressed without reminder in time for a meal in the cafeteria, ventures to speak up in a patient government meeting—and these are steps that point in the direction of resuming a normal place in the world.

An Experimental Comparison of Treatment Methods

May and his associates carried out a very careful study comparing the effectiveness of five treatment programs at a large state hospital in California.[94] They assigned randomly 228 first admission schizophrenics from the middle third of prognostic range to one of five treatment conditions: (1) individual psychotherapy alone, (2) tranquilizing drugs alone, (3) individual psychotherapy plus tranquilizing drugs, (4) electroshock, and (5) milieu. All patients were treated in one of these programs until release or one year after admission and then followed up for two years subsequently. In terms of release rates, drugs plus psychotherapy and drugs alone were the most effective methods, whereas milieu and psychotherapy alone were the least effective. The rates were 96 per cent for drugs plus psychotherapy, 95 per cent for drugs, 79 per cent for ECT, 64 per cent for psychotherapy, and 59 per cent for milieu. Drugs reduced the length of hospital stay by 20 per cent, whereas psychotherapy extended it by 14 per cent, perhaps because of the complications of terminating the therapeutic relationship. By most of the clinical criteria drugs seemed to have the best effect, but drugs plus psychotherapy led to the most insight. From a practical point of view, the analysis of comparative cost was a matter of importance. The cost of treatment from admission to release was least for drugs alone ($2,700) and most for psychotherapy alone ($4,480). The costs for the other programs fell in between: ECT ($2,820), drugs plus psychotherapy ($3,260) and milieu ($3,380).

[94] P. R. A. May, *Treatment of Schizophrenia* (New York: Science House, 1968).

The poor results for psychotherapy alone have been sharply challenged on the grounds that the therapists were inexperienced residents under supervision.[95] Karon and Vandenbos report that psychotherapy with experienced clinicians in their project reduced length of hospitalization and improved psychiatric condition significantly regardless of whether drugs were used adjunctively. Therapy with inexperienced clinicians led to *longer* hospitalization without drugs but *shorter* hospitalization with drugs. They conclude that May's findings must be limited to treatment by inexperienced therapists.

A similar question could logically be raised about the poor results of milieu treatment. If the milieu program was being run by inexperienced therapists, student nurses, and attendants in training, it might be expected to fare badly, for a ward can be run on a truly therapeutic basis only if there is a happy combination of training, talent, experience, and seasoned wisdom. The tribute to tranquilizing drugs that is implicit in these results is undoubtedly deserved, but it is worth noting that the surprising benefit attributed to ECT is out of line with other findings concerning its value in schizophrenia. These questions and paradoxes illustrate the extraordinary difficulty of doing comparative research on therapeutic outcomes in a way that controls all relevant factors.

May's results thus far are limited to short-term measures of outcome. One of his consultants is inclined to believe that the long-term outcomes for the five groups would not differ significantly, presuming apparently that this would be determined primarily by other factors (genetic disposition, premorbid adjustment, etc.) rather than treatment during the acute phase of the disorder.[96] However, Astrup and Noreik have found that drug treatment does seem to prevent the development of schizophrenic defects over the long term.[97] Clearly, May's follow-up studies will be of great interest.

SUGGESTIONS FOR FURTHER READING

Probably the first thing that should be undertaken by a student who wants to read further about schizophrenia is to get a better idea of how things look to the patient. Ideal for this purpose is the collection edited by B. Kaplan, *The Inner World of Mental Illness* (New York, Harper & Row, 1963), and the one by C. Landis, edited by F. A. Mettler, *Varieties of Psychopathological Experience* (New York, Holt, Rinehart and Winston, Inc., 1964). A shorter work with the same intent has been published by V. W. Grant, *This is Mental Illness* (Boston, Beacon Press, Inc., 1963). A. A. Stone and S. S. Stone show the phenomenology of mental illness with

[95] B. P. Karon and G. R. Vandenbos, "Experience, Medication and the Effectiveness of Psychotherapy with Schizophrenics," *British Journal of Psychiatry*, CXVI (1970), pp. 427–28.

[96] M. Leavitt, "Open Forum," in May, *op. cit.*, p. 303.

[97] Astrup and Noreik, *op. cit.*, p. 102.

literary excerpts written by disordered people in *The Abnormal Personality through Literature* (New York, Prentice-Hall, Inc., 1966). H. Green's *I Never Promised You a Rose Garden* (New York, Holt, Rinehart and Winston, Inc., 1964) is an extraordinarily lucid and moving autobiography of a schizophrenic girl who recovered without extravagant promises from her therapist, Frieda Fromm-Reichmann.

Collections of case studies are available by R. D. Laing and A. Esterson, *Sanity, Madness and the Family* (2nd ed., New York, Basic Books, 1971) and by C. G. Schulz and R. K. Kilgalen, *Case Studies in Schizophrenia* (New York, Basic Books, 1969).

For a survey of research on schizophrenia and theories about its origin, *The Etiology of Schizophrenia,* edited by Don D. Jackson (New York, Basic Books, 1960) is to be recommended. A superb selection of research papers culled from the world literature on schizophrenia by a distinguished panel of international investigators is reprinted in R. Cancro's *The Schizophrenic Syndrome: An Annual Review* (New York, Brunner/Mazel, 1971). Since this is an annual review, new volumes can be expected each year. For detailed consideration of the problems of schizophrenic thinking, the best references are still E. Hanfmann and J. Kasanin, *Conceptual Thinking in Schizophrenia* (New York, Nervous and Mental Disease Publishing Co., 1942), and S. Arieti, *Interpretation of Schizophrenia* (New York, Robert Brunner, 1955), Chs. 10–13.

R. E. Kantor and W. G. Herron review the process-reactive concept and research literature in *Reactive and Process Schizophrenia* (Palo Alto, Calif., Science and Behavior Books, 1966), and C. Astrup and K. Noreik have written an exceptional monograph on prognosis in *Functional Psychoses* (Springfield, Ill., Charles C Thomas, 1966). The most comprehensive summary of the literature on childhood schizophrenia and autism is B. Rimland's *Infantile Autism* (New York, Appleton-Century-Crofts, 1964). A research scholar will find very useful a compilation of abstracts of published articles from 1950–1965 by C. Schooler and S. E. Feldman, *Experimental Studies of Schizophrenia* (Goleta, Calif., Psychonomic Press, 1967).

The important ideas of Harry Stack Sullivan can be gleaned from his posthumously published lectures, *Schizophrenia as a Human Process* (New York, W. W. Norton & Co., Inc., 1962). An unusually fine introduction to the topic of psychotherapy is Lewis B. Hill's *Psychotherapeutic Intervention in Schizophrenia* (Chicago, University of Chicago Press, 1955), which also has much to say on childhood origins and the general nature of the disorder. As a further step along the same line there is the symposium edited by E. B. Brody and F. C. Redlich, *Psychotherapy with Schizophrenics* (New York, International Universities Press, Inc., 1952), which contains papers by several workers, comments on the papers, and good introductory chapters by the editors. Collections of papers bearing on family communication and the double bind have been published by Don D. Jackson, *Communication, Family and Marriage* and *Therapy, Communication and Change* (Palo Alto, Science and Behavior Books, 1969). T. Lidz, S. Fleck and A. R. Cornelison offer an alternative view in *Schizophrenia and the Family* (New York, International Universities Press, 1965).

Papers with a longitudinal perspective are collected in a continuing series of volumes edited by M. Roff and others, *Life History Research in Psychopathology,* vols. 1 and 2 (Minneapolis, University of Minnesota Press, 1970 and 1972).

D. Rosenthal and S. S. Kety's *The Transmission of Schizophrenia* (Oxford, Pergamon Press, 1968) contains papers mainly on genetic research from leading investigators throughout the world.

E. Goffman wrote a devastating critique of mental hospitals in *Asylums: Essays on the Social Situation of Mental Patients and Other Inmates* (Chicago, Aldine Publishing Co., 1962). The best window upon the transformation of mental hospitals from places of custody to therapeutic milieux is provided by O. von Mering and S. H. King in *Remotivating the Mental Patient* (New York, Russell Sage Foundation, 1957). The book edited by M. Greenblatt, D. J. Levinson, and R. H. Williams, *The Patient and the Mental Hospital* (New York, The Free Press of Glencoe, 1957) contains a large number of reports given at an important conference on this theme. A valuable new work on the whole subject by J. and E. Cumming is entitled *Ego and Milieu: Theory and Practice of Environmental Therapy* (New York, Atherton Press, 1962). An experimental comparison of treatment methods is reported in P. R. A. May, *Treatment of Schizophrenia* (New York, Science House, 1968).

14

Depressive and
Manic Disorders

Melancholia and mania have been recognized as forms of mental disorder for more than two thousand years. In some respects they seem to be opposites, but long before modern times it was observed that in certain patients mania and melancholia succeeded each other. On the whole the opinion prevailed that these were cases in which one disease transformed itself into another. Toward the middle of the last century, however, there were frequent suggestions that mania and melancholia belonged together in a single disease process, both being exaggerations in the sphere of mood. Designations such as "cyclical insanity" were from time to time proposed. Finally, in 1899, Kraepelin introduced the term *manic-depressive insanity,* including under this heading not only the alternating forms but the simple manias and melancholias as well. "In the course of years," he wrote, "I have been more and more convinced that all of these pictures are but forms of a single disease process. Certain fundamental features recur in these morbid states notwithstanding manifold external differences." [1] Thus the concept of *manic-depressive psychosis* became firmly established in psychiatric thought.

Whatever the ultimate nature of these disorders turns out to be, they rank as a profoundly serious form of affliction. Depressed states typically mean prolonged and seemingly senseless suffering for the patient. Manic states, which appear excitedly happy, may lead to unwise decisions and to

[1] Quoted by S. Jelliffe, "Some Historical Phases of the Manic-Depressive Synthesis," *Journal of Nervous and Mental Diseases,* LXXIII (1931), pp. 353–74, 499–521.

ultimate exhaustion, and they impose heavy burdens on the environment. It is this seriousness that justifies classifying the disorders under *psychosis*. The distinguishing mark of psychosis is a loss of contact with reality. Roughly speaking, a disorder is called a psychosis if the patient's condition meets the legal criteria of *insanity:* the patient is either unable to take care of himself, or is dangerous to others, or both. These criteria are met in severe depressed states and highly manic states, for both of which it is essential that the patient be hospitalized. On the other hand, patients are constantly seen at clinics or in private practice who show marked mood changes, generally along with other symptoms, yet who are not disoriented, "out of their heads," or in need of hospital care.[2] There is substantial disagreement among psychiatrists as to whether these cases should be labeled mild psychosis or placed in some other category such as neurosis or psychophysiological disorder.

These initial remarks about classification can hardly be said to start us on a nicely charted course. It is all the more important, therefore, to begin our account at a descriptive level, considering depressed states and manic states in their own right. If we can lay a reasonably solid factual foundation we may be able to straighten out some of the confusion which seems to prevail in the study of depressed and manic disorders.

DEPRESSED STATES

In a carefully designed factor analysis of the clinical symptoms of depression, as recorded by the hospital staff in daily observation of a series of 96 patients, Grinker and associates found four partially independent clusters or patterns of behavior and feeling.[3] The first pattern, in which the patient feels dismal, hopeless, and painfully low in self-esteem and in which action, speech, and thought are laboriously slow, corresponds fairly well to what has previously been called a *retarded depression*. The second factor, involving high anxiety, guilt feelings, and hopelessness together with agitated behavior and clinging demands for attention, sounds much like the older idea of an *agitated depression*. The other two patterns are less sharply distinguished. Both entail the typical depressive affects of gloom and hopelessness, but in both the behavior is more assertive, described by such terms as "demanding," "angry," and "provocative." These observable distinctions warn us not to oversimplify the problem of depression. The idea of a single "typical" form is a fiction.

[2] J. D. Campbell, *Manic-Depressive Disease* (Philadelphia: J. B. Lippincott Co., 1953), pp. 2–5; A. T. Beck, *Depression: Clinical, Experimental, and Theoretical Aspects* (New York: Harper & Row, Hoeber Medical Division, 1967), pp. 64–86.

[3] R. R. Grinker, Sr., J. Miller, M. Sabshin, R. Nunn, and J. C. Nunnally, *The Phenomena of Depressions* (New York: Harper & Row, Hoeber Medical Division, 1961).

Retarded Depressions

The typical symptoms of retarded depression can be grouped under the headings of underactivity and a dejected mood. In their mildest form they shade imperceptibly into a normal state of discouragement. The underactivity shows itself in slowness of movement and speech. Exertion is experienced as difficult; the patients prefer to sit in one place with folded hands, and cannot summon the energy to perform the simplest errands. If questioned they speak slowly, in a low tone, with great economy of words, and they prefer not to speak at all. There is a similar retardation in the sphere of thought. Ideas do not come to mind and a great inertia seems to block the solving of problems. As one patient described it, "At these times my brain feels paralyzed; I have not the strength or ambition to do anything. . . . I have the impulse to act, but it seems as if something shuts down and prohibits action." [4] Illustrative of the retardation in thought is the patient's reaction to reading. What is read seems to call up no associations; it is not assimilated, and the whole business of keeping up continuous attention is felt as painfully exhausting.

The dejected mood may take the form simply of unrelieved sadness. Everything looks gloomy; if the patient talks about his troubles he paints a picture of utter hopelessness. Some patients concentrate their woes on bodily complaints, feeling sure that they have an incurable disease. Others concentrate on the theme of poverty and deprivation, believing that their money is gone and that there is no hope for the future. The one theme on which the patient has strength enough to converse is that of his worthlessness and wickedness. The mechanism of projection appears to be unavailable to depressed patients. Their minds are full of self-blaming, and they do not lift this burden by transferring the blame to outside persecutors. If they think the tax collector or the police will come for them, such action is perceived as entirely justified. In severe cases the hopelessness is so profound that the possibilities of suicide cannot be discounted.

That this ideation deserves to be called psychotic becomes clear if any attempt is made to influence it. The obvious social response to declarations of despair and worthlessness is to try to cheer up the patient. Such efforts are of no avail. There is no answering smile, no look of relief, if one tells the patient that he is loved and valued or reminds him of creditable past performances. The conviction of poverty does not yield even to such objective evidence as a bank statement. The depressed mood seems to be firmly in command, and nothing but frustration awaits the person who tries to bring about a more dispassionate testing of reality.

4 W. A. White, *Outlines of Psychiatry* (13th ed.; New York: Nervous and Mental Disease Publishing Co., 1932), p. 161.

Example of Retarded Depression

In our historical chapter we mentioned the autobiography of Clifford W. Beers, a book which did a great deal to establish the mental hygiene movement. Beers was in a psychotic condition with ups and downs for three years. The seriousness of his condition first became fully apparent when he tried to commit suicide by throwing himself out the window of his bedroom. For the next two years he was in a depressed state, complicated in various ways by hallucinations and other less usual features. At the end of this time he changed rather quickly to a manic condition. His account of his experiences will provide us with illustrations for both conditions.[5]

Because of injuries sustained in his jump from the window, Beers was first taken to a general hospital in his home city. He conceived that he was under a criminal charge for attempted suicide, and that his crime must be known to everyone in the city. "The public believed me the most despicable member of my race. The papers were filled with accounts of my misdeeds." The hospital was located on the street that led to the university athletic field, and a crowd of students and graduates went by on their way to a class-day game. Beers was sure that every one of these people loathed him for having disgraced his alma mater. "When they approached the hospital on their way to the athletic field, I concluded that it was their intention to take me from my bed, drag me to the lawn, and there tear me limb from limb." Some time later he was taken to a sanatorium in another community. "The day was hot, and, as we drove to the railway station, the blinds on most of the houses in the streets through which we passed were seen to be closed. I thought I saw an unbroken line of deserted houses, and I imagined that their desertion had been deliberately planned as a sign of displeasure on the part of their former occupants. I supposed them bitterly ashamed of such a despicable townsman as myself."

Nearly two years later Beers was still convinced that he was to go on trial. His brother, who visited him often, was apt to comment favorably on his health and to add, "We shall straighten you out yet." To Beers this was an ambiguous phrase "which might refer to the end of the hangman's rope, or to a fatal electric shock." He interpreted his improving physical health as a sign that the doctors were fattening him for the slaughter after his trial which, of course, could have but one outcome. Suicide seemed a preferable fate, and for many weeks he devised a series of schemes to bring about this result. Everything that happened only served to remind him of his misery. He could take no pleasure in his daily walks with his attendant, for example, because he was sure that everyone knew his black record and impending punishment. "I wondered why passers-by did not revile and stone me. It was not surprising that a piece of rope, old and frayed, which someone

[5] C. W. Beers, *A Mind That Found Itself* (Garden City, N. Y.: Doubleday & Co., Inc., 1931). The depressed phase of the illness is described on pp. 11–87, the manic phase on pp. 87–189.

had carelessly thrown on a hedge by a cemetery that I sometimes passed, had for me great significance."

These examples show the pervasive effect of the dejected mood. Even quite incidental impressions receive a distorted meaning which fits them into the patient's depressed state of mind. His sense of sin and worthlessness is so dominating that he can no longer interpret experience in any other terms. This is the characteristic that has led to the description of depressive and manic conditions as *affective disorders* or disorders in the sphere of moods.

Agitated Depressions

The second clinical pattern disclosed in Grinker's research includes depressive affect without retardation of action or thought. There is the same mental content of hopelessness and worthlessness that appears in the retarded depressions, but there is likely to be a stronger emphasis on sin, guilt, responsibility for surrounding evils, and dire punishments that must be in store. Thoughts of death are prominent and suicide is a real danger. But instead of sitting silently in an attitude of despair, the patient is extremely active and talkative. He cannot keep still, he cannot sleep, he can only pace up and down with moans and sighs and wringing of the hands. The existence of this variant form of depression makes it clear that dejected mood and underactivity do not necessarily go together. As a matter of fact patients are sometimes found who combine mood and activity in the reverse pattern: action and thought are seriously retarded, but the mood is one of exultation. In the case of agitated depressions the patient's behavior reflects a combination of depressed mood and anxious tension.

The following example can be considered a fairly typical case.[6] A fifty-three-year-old woman of apparently healthy ancestry and good educational background was admitted to the hospital in a highly agitated and deeply depressed condition. As a young woman she had been quiet, conscientious, and self-sacrificing, but distinctly sociable, well-liked by her friends, and a capable manager of the house. At twenty-five she married a man who proved to be a hopeless alcoholic and drug addict. This was the beginning of a life that grew more and more difficult. The patient was constantly worried about her husband, her children, and the family finances. When the husband's deterioration made further home life impossible, she separated from him and took to running a rooming house in order to support herself and the children. For five years before her illness she had been unable to secure help and was constantly exhausted by the work of the house. As a result she had severe attacks of grippe every winter and was in a badly run down condition. The psychosis came on suddenly. She began to moan, pace up and down, and wring her hands. She felt herself a wicked sinner

[6] E. A. Strecker and F. G. Ebaugh, *Practical Clinical Psychiatry* (5th ed.; Philadelphia: The Blakiston Co., 1940), pp. 356–60.

for having left her husband; she ought never to have been born because she brought such trouble on the whole world.

In this condition she arrived at the hospital. She was in a state of almost ceaseless activity, squirming in her chair, walking rapidly about, pulling at her hair, pinching her cheeks, biting her fingers. Her deeply lined face bore an expression of unutterable woe. At times she was frankly terrified; at other times she shrank from the nurse's hand because she felt herself unworthy to be touched. She believed that all her family had been killed because of her wrongdoing. "Oh, what have I done!" she would exclaim. "Can't I be saved? What is in store for me?" Then she would get started on her poverty: "Not a cent left, not a cent." She made one unsuccessful attempt at suicide. In spite of her miserable state and violent self-accusations, she was not disoriented or hallucinated nor were there any discernible gaps in her memory. As the end of a year she was well on the way to recovery, with the beginnings of insight into the distorted nature of her previous ideas.

MANIC STATES

Characteristics of Mania

In its mildest stages, often called hypomania or subacute mania, a manic state is difficult to distinguish from a normal state of good spirits and high efficiency. There is a certain amount of overactivity, expressing itself both in motor channels and in a free flow of ideas and speech. There is also a show of confidence and enterprise that may drift over into boastful self-assertion. Ordinary people are apt to envy a patient in this stage, and business offices consider him ready for promotion. The signs that all is not well do not show themselves in single actions but rather in the continuity of one action or idea with another. It will be apparent that the patient flies from one idea to a different one, makes a plan one moment only to cancel it the next, and is unduly irritated if the least frustration lies in his path. Subacute mania bears some resemblance to mild alcoholic intoxication. The patient is lively, witty, and jolly, free in speech and high in self-confidence. He is full of plans and not bothered by the thought of difficulties or risks in carrying them out. Just as in alcoholic intoxication, his efficiency may be lowered but his illusion of efficiency raised. He may be having a wonderful time and see not the slightest reason why anyone should be concerned about him.

The true hallmarks of the disorder can be more clearly perceived in acute mania. Outstanding is the stream of talk, which seems never to abate. Taken in short units, it is perfectly coherent, but change from topic to topic is constantly taking place. These changes reveal the patient's distractibility. Whatever he sees or hears may divert his attention completely, and may cause him to make personal remarks that take visitors aback: "My, how gray your hair is," or "Look at those holes in your sweater." In the motor sphere there is constant restlessness. The patient is always busy, never tired. He sleeps little at night and is eager for action long before sunrise. If he cannot find enough ways to use up his energy, he may burst into shouts and song, smash furniture, or do setting-up exercises. The need for action amounts to an irresistible pressure. Continued over many days and through sleepless nights it presently begins to tell on the patient's health. Physical restraint and continuous hot baths were formerly in frequent use to keep manic patients quiet. Tranquilizing drugs are now more commonly used for the same purpose, but fairly large supervised doses are usually needed to produce appreciable results.

The prevailing mood is one of joyous elation. The patient is full of confidence and is quite willing to carry his enterprises to the White House, to Wall Street, to Hollywood, or wherever he believes they will be most rapidly dispatched to their splendid conclusions. The confident mood easily rises to domineering arrogance, especially toward those in authority. Very inconsiderate of those around him, the patient is easily aroused to anger and fury if his activities are in any way curbed. If his thoughts take a sexual turn, he will show a similar lack of restraint. All impulses come to immediate expression in words and in acts insofar as these are permitted. Any kind of restraint is extremely uncomfortable because of the pressure to activity.

Disturbances of thought and loss of contact with reality are incidental results of the overactivity and overconfidence. The patient is too distractible to perceive the environment with accuracy, too changeable to turn his flight of ideas into consecutive thinking, too elated to take account of facts that run counter to his mood. Delusions of great wealth or accomplishment readily develop, but the distortion of reality rarely extends to hallucination. In a way a manic patient does not strike an observer as being as crazy as a schizophrenic or general paretic. The effect is rather of a person abnormally speeded up and thus seriously disorganized, but not unintelligible. The patient is highly incompetent to carry on his own affairs and needs to be hospitalized for his own good and for the sake of his health. But he does not seem as far away from the normal as is the case with other psychotics.

Just as it is impossible to encourage a really depressed person, so it is impossible to discourage a manic one. There is the same implacable dominance of mood over the testing of reality. It is of no use to ask the patient to sit still, take some rest, or stop talking and give others some rest. Attempts to sidetrack a proposed telephone call to the White House will be answered, "But I know the President is just waiting to hear from me." Well-meaning intervention is bounced off by the manic patient just as effectively as by the depressed.

Example of Manic Behavior

We turn to the third year of Clifford Beers' psychosis for a concrete example of the manic state. While there were many preliminary signs that Beers' depression was lifting, the decisive change of mood came quite suddenly. The sensation was like the lifting of a cloud, and at once his mind began to be flooded with ideas for a vast program of humanitarian reform. The following day he attended a church service. Instead of discovering gloomy forebodings and veiled threats in the service, he now heard every word as if it were a personal message from God. Phrases from the psalms clearly referred to the great projects that were coursing through his mind, and to his own role as the instrument chosen to carry them out. "My heart is inditing a good matter," he heard, "my tongue is the pen of a ready writer." This surely referred to his heart and his tongue, so he began writing letters about everything that had happened to him. Soon exhausting his supply of stationery, he arranged to secure large quantities of wrapping paper which he cut in strips a foot wide and pasted together into vast rolls. "More than once, letters twenty or thirty feet long were written, and on one occasion the accumulation of two or three days of excessive productivity, when spread upon the floor, reached from one end of the corridor to the other—a distance of about one hundred feet. My hourly output was something like twelve feet. . . . Under the pressure of elation one takes pride in doing everything in record time. Despite my speed my letters were not incoherent. They were simply digressive, which was to be expected, as elation befogs one's 'goal idea.' "

The writing of colossal letters soon proved an insufficient means of using up his energy. "I proceeded to assume entire charge of that portion of the hospital in which I happened at the moment to be confined. What I eventually issued as imperative orders were often presented at first as polite suggestions. But, if my suggestions were not accorded a respectful hearing, and my demands not acted upon at once, I invariably supplemented them with vituperative ultimatums." Beers soon determined to conduct a complete investigation of the hospital. This proved very trying to the staff and resulted in serious friction. It led to his being placed in a small cell in the violent ward where for want of paper he proceeded to write all over the walls. Angered at his treatment, he rigged up a fake scene of suicide to frighten the attendants—a striking contrast to his serious and persistent attempts to take his life when depressed. Before long his mind turned to inventions. Characteristically, these were not of a minor order; he decided "to overcome no less a force than gravity itself." Tearing a carpet into strips, he managed to suspend his bed with himself in it between the window and a transom over the door. "So epoch-making did this discovery appear to me that I noted the exact position of the bed so that a wondering posterity might ever afterward view and revere the exact spot on the earth's surface whence one of man's greatest thoughts had winged its way to immortality."

The successful overcoming of gravity seemed to open endless possibilities. Great wealth would soon be in his hands. And with this he planned to transform his home city into a veritable garden spot and center of learning. Scores of parks would be dotted with cathedrals, libraries, art galleries, theaters, and great mansions, the whole scene to be crowned by the most magnificent and efficient university in the world. But his mind was presently recalled from these splendid prospects by the more immediate problem of correcting the abuses in state hospitals. With great ingenuity he smuggled a long letter to the governor, who was sufficiently impressed by the tales of violent treatment to interrogate the staff of the institution.

It is interesting to observe the continuity between Beers' intentions at this time and his career following recovery. So lasting was the impression made upon him by his treatment in mental hospitals that he dedicated his life to what presently became the mental hygiene movement. He became instrumental in bringing about reforms that were much needed and highly constructive. His scientific experiments were discontinued and his plans for improving his home city fell by the wayside, but one at least of the goals conceived at the height of his illness was capable of realistic fulfillment. Again one is impressed with the fact that the manic patient is less basically confused than other psychotics. He is overdriven, speeded up, and expansive, and this results in a distorted relation to reality, but the radical change of tempo takes place in a fundamentally sound mind. When normal tempo and normal mood are restored, mental function shows not the slightest trace of impairment.

NATURE OF DEPRESSIVE AND MANIC DISORDERS

Most people can read descriptions of depressed and manic behavior with a feeling of at least partial empathic understanding. The emotions of joy and sadness are familiar in everyday experience; we all know what it is like to feel elated and to be plunged into discouragement. It is a fairly common experience, although there are large individual differences in this respect, to undergo changes of mood over short intervals of time, even in the course of the day. External demands coming in a steady stream often conceal our natural rhythms; we must go on working whether or not we feel like it. But everyone is aware to some extent of his better and poorer times of day. For some, morning is the time when ideas flow freely, when many things seem possible, and when action is energetic and full of zest. With afternoon comes fatigue, drowsiness, a dulling of the bright morning prospects, a need to put everything aside. Others experience the diurnal rhythm in reverse, reaching their peak of zestfulness in the evening. We are no strangers to mood. If required to do so, as were groups of college students in a research by Wessman and Ricks, we can keep a daily diary of our mood states, even rating ourselves by means of check lists on highly specific aspects of affective experience. The subjects in this research differed widely with respect to stability of mood. Everyone, however, was aware of some degree of variation between different self-rating periods.[7]

---

[7] A. E. Wessman and D. F. Ricks, *Mood and Personality* (New York: Holt, Rinehart & Winston, Inc., 1966).

Everyday experience of moods, however, does not quite prepare us for the extremes of manic and depressive behavior. Even if we recall our most vivid experiences—the joy of a hard-won triumph, the misery of a bereavement, the gloom of a far-reaching failure—our behavior does not fully correspond to that of a manic or depressed patient. Our extreme moods may seem to flood us, but not to the extent of subverting our judgment and making us impervious to the influence of others. Pathological depression and mania imply something more than sorrow and joy. Their onset, their duration, and their frequently spontaneous remission often bear no obvious relation to circumstances, and they interfere gravely with realistic judgment. The suffering of depressed patients is painfully real, yet disproportionate and senseless. Real also is the elation of manic patients, but unlike pure joy it is compulsive, overdriven, and again senseless.

Melancholia and mania owe their age-long recognition as mental disorders to this excess, this something more beyond sorrow and joy. This has led many observers to believe that depressed and manic states are analogous to drugged and intoxicated conditions. Some peculiarity of metabolic regulation, it is argued, makes the patient's mood shoot down or up as if he had taken a strong drug or a strong drink. This is essentially the theory proposed by Kraepelin and favored by those who prefer a somatogenic explanation for depressed and manic conditions. We shall see presently that the evidence for something of this kind is considerable, but this does not exempt us from searching for the psychological meaning of the two states. Even if we suppose that depressions and elations come from autonomous fluctuations in the metabolic system, we must examine all the available evidence, including what the patient experiences and how he behaves, for clues as to the nature of this fluctuation. We shall therefore turn our attention first to the psychological aspects of the problem.

PSYCHOLOGICAL ASPECTS

As a first step toward greater psychological understanding it is worthwhile to examine more closely the content of the two conditions as shown in patients' behavior and conversation. Is it possible to discern in these disordered states an adaptive attempt, a struggle to cope with human difficulties? Can we perceive any intelligible relation between manic states and depressions?

Psychological Content of Manic States

The first thing to notice is that the two states are at opposite poles with respect to self-esteem. In depression there is an utter collapse of self-esteem. The patient can hardly find words strong enough to express the depth of his degradation and worthlessness. In manic states, on the other hand, self-esteem is joyfully boundless. All things seem possible, and the patient's feeling of competence extends in every direction. There is often a sensation of being flooded by plans for today, tomorrow, and the distant future, yet the patient is not bothered by the thought that time and resources may prove to be limited. To an observer who does not share the manic mood there is something false about this high level of self-esteem. It is different from the expansive planning of a person whose self-confidence is founded on a record of real achievement. It is maintained by two devices: speed and change of direction. Like a good broken-field runner in football, the patient's mind races forward at top speed and dodges sharply whenever it is in danger of being tackled by a hard fact. Records of manic conversation show that there is tremendous distractibility, but the distractions are not entirely at random. They achieve the purpose of avoiding thoughts that would be detrimental to self-esteem.

The deduction has been made from such observations that the manic patient is making heavy use of the primitive mechanism of denial.[8] He denies the existence of every fact and every thought that might make him feel depressed. His overactive behavior can also be considered to constitute a *reaction-formation* against the possibility of being depressed. It is the heavy use of these two mechanisms that gives to the patient's buoyancy its element of falseness. A similar pattern of behavior is sometimes seen in response to sudden tragedy. To a particularly tragic bereavement, for instance, the person may respond by immersing himself at once in work, business plans, activities, even amusements, his whole behavior constituting a daily assertion that he is not deserted, grief-stricken, or helpless. Occasionally it happens that a true manic attack develops as the first response to a situation that involves loss and a threat to self-esteem. Especially in such instances manic behavior seems to have the character of an attempt to control and counteract depression and thus escape the pains of blasted self-esteem.

The Adaptive Attempt in Depressed States

On the face of it there is no parallel adjustive attempt in depressions. These states seem rather to represent breakdown and collapse with little sign of a struggle to rectify the situation. While it is true that certain extreme disorders—for example, the disorganization that goes with total panic—represent pure breakdown, we must always be on the watch for signs of attempted repair and restoration. Can we detect a purpose in depressed behavior, a struggle to accomplish something that will improve the patient's situation and reduce the force of his distress?

An affirmative answer to this question is given by Rado, who has devoted many years to the psychoanalytic study of depressed patients.[9] Rado inter-

---

[8] B. D. Lewin, *The Psychoanalysis of Elation* (New York: W. W. Norton & Co., Inc., 1950), chap. 3.

[9] S. Rado, "Psychodynamics of Depression from the Etiological Point of View," *Psychosomatic Medicine*, XIII (1951), pp. 51–55.

prets the depressed spell as a reaction to loss. Perhaps a loved person dies or deserts the patient. Perhaps the patient loses the moral support of a congenial group. Perhaps the loss is of a more subtle and symbolic nature, as when the patient senses a cooling of interest on the part of his spouse or a reduction of applause on the part of audiences formerly enthusiastic. Whatever the current nature of the loss, Rado believes that its extraordinary significance for the patient lies in the fact that it reanimates terrible childhood experiences of loss of the mother's affection. Some part of a depressed person's behavior can be understood as a cry for love: a display of helplessness and a direct appeal for the affection and security that have been lost. But the whole reaction is greatly complicated by the presence of angry hostility toward the deserting person and by guilty fear that this hostility has actually caused the desertion. Early in a depressed spell there may be signs that the patient is trying to vent aggression directly and force some return of affection. The verbal equivalent for this behavior—"you are wicked to desert me, you must now love me"—reveals at once the tactical weakness of this move, especially when we imagine it as taking place in the relationship of a small child to its mother. As a consequence, repentance soon gains the upper hand and the rage becomes directed against the self. The patient's unending self-criticism is intended as an act of expiation. He fully accepts the blame for his anger, confesses his unworthiness, and attempts thereby to deserve again and win back the lost affection. Rado points out elsewhere that these tactics, too, are likely to miscarry. The pain of self-punishment and the despair caused by the constant downgrading of self-esteem may become unbearable, even driving the patient to suicide, before the attempted expiation brings any sense of restored love.[10] But there is still a method in the madness, and the depressive spell can be conceived as an attempt, however misguided, to repair the situation created by serious loss of supporting love.

Adding to this description another element, Bonine argues that depressed behavior contains essential hostility directed toward the environment as well as toward the self.[11] The effect of a depression on the people with whom the patient lives is in fact frustrating, even punishing. The stubborn refusal to be cheered up, the quick rejection of any hopeful suggestion as if it were utterly stupid, keeps putting those around the patient in a position of helpless incompetence. Behavior that contains in one package a cry for love, a plea for forgiveness, an expiatory but tiresome self-criticism, and an implacable rejection of attempts to be helpful, hardly constitutes a workable pattern, and the adaptive effort not surprisingly produces no coherent result.

10 S. Rado, "Hedonic Control, Action-Self, and the Depressive Spell," in P. H. Hoch and J. Zubin, eds., *Depression* (New York: Grune & Stratton, Inc., 1954), chap. 11.

11 W. Bonine, "The Psychodynamics of Neurotic Depression," in S. Arieti, ed., *American Handbook of Psychiatry*, Vol. III (New York: Basic Books, Inc., 1966). See also M. M. Weissman, G. L. Klerman, and E. S. Paykel, "Clinical Evaluation of Hostility in Depression," *American Journal of Psychiatry*, CXXVIII (1971), pp. 261–66.

Coping with Affect

These views on the adaptive attempt in manic and depressed states obviously do not point to rational and well-considered ways of dealing with
human relations and problems of self-esteem. It is possible to view the
behavior in a different light simply as an attempt to cope with extreme
mood states. This is consistent with a somatogenic interpretation of the
moods: if they arise from internal biochemical events they simply flood the
patient with either positive or negative affect which has no intelligible relation to past or present experience. The mood developed in this way enjoys
pre-emptive strength, so that every event and every thought is invested either
with gloom or with exuberant elation. The patient tries to account for the
change in his experience. When he is manic, everything feels so wonderful
that he must be a wonderful person capable of doing anything that comes to
mind. When he is depressed, everything feels so dreadful that he must indeed be a dreadful person, sinful and worthless, for whom there can be no
hope. Depressed behavior and conversation fit this alternative explanation
fairly well. The patient cannot be cheered because every supposedly hopeful communication is at once drowned in negative affect and thus interpreted as not really hopeful. Feeling so badly, the patient accounts for it
by blaming and criticizing himself, but it is not inconsistent that a cry for
help, and anger because nothing does help, should be woven into the pattern.

The Theme of Loss

Clinical observers who lean more toward a psychogenic explanation have
been impressed by a recurrent theme of loss in depressed states. They find
in the patient's complaints a sense of loss and of the collapse of self-esteem
occasioned by loss. This makes possible the supposition that adult depressions recapitulate reactions to loss that first took place in childhood, very
likely as the result of early separation from the mother. According to this
conception, both the force and the irrationality of depressed states can be
attributed to a *regressive* process: "Adult depression is precipitated by a
current loss (real or symbolic) that recapitulates the original loss and causes
the adult to regress to the emotional state he was in when the original loss
occurred." [12] This idea was first put forward by Freud and Abraham, who
proposed that the psychoses represent an especially deep regression; that is,
the reactivated dangers lie in early infancy, and ways of perceiving and
dealing with them have the earmarks of a truly primitive stage in mental
development. [13] Infantile trauma conceivably establishes vulnerability to
later loss and freezes primitive patterns for dealing with it.

[12] J. Mendels, *Concepts of Depression* (New York: John Wiley & Sons, Inc., 1970), p. 61.
[13] S. Freud, "Mourning and Melancholia," in *Collected Papers* (London: Hogarth Press,
Ltd., 1925), Vol. II; see also O. Fenichel, *The Psychoanalytic Theory of Neurosis* (New
York: W. W. Norton & Co., Inc., 1945), chap. 17.

This is not an hypothesis that is easily proved or disproved. There is, of course, no doubt that reactions resembling depression occur in infancy. As mentioned earlier in this book, Spitz has described depressive reactions in infants during the second half of the first year of life.[14] The occasion for these reactions is a loss or diminution of the "emotional supplies" provided by the mother or her substitute. When the child is shifted from a mothering to an impersonal environment, he may soon begin to show signs of withdrawal, anxiety when approached, loss of appetite, and loss of weight. In the course of time the picture is further complicated by loss of motility, difficulty in sleeping, and a general slowing down of mental development. When one thinks of the adult depressive patient's losses of appetite and weight, insomnia, and motor and mental retardation, it seems possible that Spitz's observations point to the kind of experiences in infancy that can set the stage for later depressive reactions. Many features of the depressive state seem to be borrowed directly from the infantile reaction to a loss of "emotional supplies." But it is obviously difficult to demonstrate that such traumatic events have regularly occurred in the histories of patients who become depressed in adult years. The patients themselves cannot remember so far back, and their relatives are not likely to be able to supply reliable information.

The hypothesis of acquired vulnerability to loss would be helped by a showing that depressed and manic states are reactions to losses in the patient's current life. Even this more limited undertaking runs into research difficulties. Malmquist examined the records of patients admitted to a mental hospital with acute disorders, comparing depressed patients with a matched group showing no depressive symptoms.[15] The main hypothesis to be tested was simply that the depressed group would have a larger number of losses than the nondepressed group in the time preceding their illness. The results were negative; there was no significant difference in the frequency of current losses. But the measures were necessarily crude. Current losses were defined as death of a family member or loss of a significant relationship, as by divorce, abandonment, or breaking of an engagement, and they were considered current if they had occurred at any time during the year preceding admission. Objective criteria of this kind cannot be true measures of the experience of loss. Not all bereavements, divorces, abandonments, and broken engagements carry the personal meaning of a devastating desertion. Thus the research is not conclusive, but it certainly does not strengthen the case for a special role of loss in depression.

The theme of loss has been approached in a different way by considering the personality pattern of people liable to depressions and elations. It

[14] R. Spitz, "Anaclitic Depression: An Inquiry into the Genesis of Psychiatric Conditions in Early Childhood," *The Psychoanalytic Study of the Child*, II (1946), pp. 313–42.

[15] C. P. Malmquist, "Depression and Object Loss in Acute Psychiatric Admissions," *American Journal of Psychiatry*, CXXVI (1970), pp. 1782–87.

has been noticed that in their periods of remission, and reportedly also before the first onset of their disorder, manic-depressive patients show a characteristic pattern of traits. This pattern, known technically as the *cyclothymic* pattern, is not one that suggests weakness or maladjustment; on the contrary, it contains many elements that are generally associated with psychological health. Cyclothymic people are apt to be energetic, lively, and full of interests. They are warmly responsive to others and are often esteemed as delightful companions. In their closer relationships they are affectionate, loyal, and strongly attached. When in good health they function well, often leading rich and highly satisfying lives. Yet there is a vulnerable point in the organization of their personalities. Beneath the surface they are acutely dependent upon their principal love-objects and cannot tolerate frustration or disappointment from this source. As Edith Jacobson expresses it, "What they require is a constant supply of love and moral support from a highly valued love-object." This love-object is usually a person, "but it may be represented by a powerful symbol, a religious, political, or scientific cause, or an organization of which they feel a part." [16] The weak spot in these otherwise healthy personalities is this specific overdependence on one principal person as a source both of love and of self-esteem.

There is a natural tendency for strong dependence to create a weak spot in a person's feeling of competence. He may be effective in all other respects, but when it is a question of securing his central supply of supporting love he faces a problem that cannot be handled by direct, assertive measures. Love cannot be commanded; it has to be won. But this is an issue on which the cyclothymic individual cannot afford to lose, or even to be moderately frustrated. An intensive study of manic-depressive patients brings to light one of the adjustive techniques whereby they try to compensate for the weak spot. This technique is described as gratifying one's dependency by a skillful manipulation of others, maneuvering them into positions where they either want or feel obliged to express devotion and give emotional support.[17] Along such lines the patient may feel some competence, but this kind of maneuvering is at best an uncertain business. If the patient fails in one of his vital manipulations there is nothing else he can do, and his self-esteem falls precipitously. The importance of this drop in self-esteem has been emphasized by Bibring, who believes that depression occurs when the patient is swept by "a feeling of powerlessness and helplessness with regard to his loneliness, isolation, weakness, in-

[16] E. Jacobson, *Depression: Comparative Studies of Normal, Neurotic, and Psychotic Conditions* (New York: International Universities Press, Inc., 1971), p. 232.

[17] M. B. Cohen *et al.*, "An Intensive Study of Twelve Cases of Manic-Depressive Psychosis," *Psychiatry*, XVII (1954), pp. 103–39; R. W. Gibson, M. B. Cohen, and R. A. Cohen, "On the Dynamics of the Manic-Depressive Personality," *American Journal of Psychiatry*, CXV (1959), pp. 1101–7.

feriority, evilness or guilt." [18]   Bibring's account takes the emphasis off the specific experience of loss and restores it to the inescapable clinical fact of changes in the level of self-esteem.

The Theme of Guilt

Depressive states, as we have seen, often show a heavy content of guilt, expressed as feelings of sinfulness and a conviction that one deserves to be punished. To understand this feeling it is possible to hypothesize a sequence of events analogous to those postulated for loss. The stage would be set by one or more traumatic experiences in early childhood in which the child expressed rivalrous and aggressive impulses only to discover from the parents' response that this behavior branded him as evil. This would create vulnerability to future situations capable of reanimating the original feelings and it would dispose the person to interpret events in this light. When the patient's anger is mobilized by things going wrong in his life he has more than an average tendency to flip over into blaming himself and become depressed. The sequence seems especially clear in depression following the death of a person of whom the patient was fond but toward whom he also harbored hostile feelings. As Freud originally pointed out, the patient may blame himself not only for his own faults but for faults he had previously found in the lost person.[19] The process appears curiously global and primitive, as if the patient had to find himself bad in all possible ways; this, however, is explicable if we assume a reanimation of early childhood ways of thinking.

The theme of guilt sometimes emerges clearly in depressions in men on military service following the death of a comrade. The patient may constantly blame himself for the comrade's death even when he had not the least part in it. When it is possible to probe carefully into the meaning of the comrade's death a curious mixture of feelings may be uncovered. In one case, for example, that of a depressed airman, much was heard at first about the dead friend's virtues, his generosity, his wonderful qualities of companionship. Only later did it come out that there was another side to the relationship, less clearly conscious: the two men were also keen rivals in matters of prowess and had been competing intensely for the position of flight leader. On the mission which proved fatal to the friend, the patient had been designated flight leader. Near the target the friend had drawn his plane out of formation and tried to take the leader's position, but the patient refused to yield. It was at this point that the friend's plane had been struck by ground fire and gone down in flames. The patient's childhood history had left him with strong competitive feelings, behind which there is always a good deal of hostility toward rivals. His

[18] E. Bibring, "The Mechanism of Depression," in P. Greenacre, ed., *Affective Disorders: Psychoanalytic Contribution to Their Study* (New York: International Universities Press, Inc., 1953), p. 42.

[19] S. Freud, "Mourning and Melancholia," *op. cit.*

anger must have been unbounded when his friend on a dangerous mission refused to play fair and stay in formation. The outcome must have seemed a perfect piece of justice, but for a person in whom jealous hostility is repressed it is a terrific threat to have a death wish come true. The case of Bert Whipley has taught us how shattering this can be in early childhood. In the present case the patient berated himself for his friend's death and for many other incidents in which his conduct had actually been blameless. He experienced the overwhelming guilt of a child whose aggressive naughtiness has had serious and irreparable consequences.[20]

PROBLEMS OF CLASSIFICATION

Our study of the psychological aspects of depressive and manic disorders has raised a number of possibilities without leading us to fully attested explanations. If the problem consisted merely of explaining the content of depressed and manic states, little would need to be added to what we have reviewed under the headings of loss, guilt, and adaptive attempts. There is, however, more to explain. It is necessary to account for the intensity of the reactions, for the pre-emptive force of the moods, that prevents the patients from appraising reality and responding to social influence. This problem of excess has been approached, as we have seen, in two main ways. One hypothesis attributes the excess to the moods themselves, considered to be products of an abnormality in biochemical regulation. They happen because of somatic events that are not mainly determined by situations and stresses in personal life. Depressed or manic moods thus descend upon the patient like mysterious visitations, and the resulting behavior represents an attempt to understand and cope with the unshakable wretchedness or the startling sense of well-being. The other hypothesis attributes the excess to reanimation of reactions that first occurred early in life. Traumatic situations involving loss, separation, and guilt set off in the young child an overwhelming depressive reaction, physical and psychological, that creates a lasting vulnerability to similar experiences in later life. The person becomes too well tuned, so to speak, to loss and guilt, tries to avoid them by strong attachments to people, but reacts violently when they do occur, either with depression or with a manic reaction-formation. These mood states are thus explained as global, unmodulated infantile reactions to current stresses of a particular kind.

When two alternatives are presented, our natural tendency is to wonder which one is right. With respect to human behavior, however, it is often impossible to make such sharp decisions. In the present instance one can picture a continuum extending from purely somatogenic to purely psychogenic forms of manic-depressive disorder. The extremes of this con-

[20] R. R. Grinker, Sr., and J. P. Spiegel, *Men Under Stress* (Philadelphia: The Blakiston Co., 1945), pp. 281–88.

tinuum are not imaginary. There are cases in which depressive and manic states occur in a regular cycle, perhaps every spring and fall, perhaps every eight weeks, perhaps even in shorter sequences of a few days' duration. It is hardly plausible that life stresses should occur on such a regular schedule. At the other extreme is the patient who is depressed just once in the course of his life, in direct response to a grievous loss. He presently recovers, perhaps with the help of treatment whereby he learns to understand his emotional reactions more fully. The great majority of cases, lying between these extremes, can then be considered to represent different mixes of constitutional and acquired vulnerabilities.

This formulation is undoubtedly too simple and schematic. Yet something like it runs through all recent attempts at classification. There seems to be agreement that somatogenic and psychogenic factors can be present in different proportions. The classification adopted by the American Psychiatric Association in 1968, in line with the one developed by the World Health Organization, places depressive and manic disorders under three main headings, as follows:

A. *Major Affective Disorders.* The chief sub-category is *manic-depressive illness,* divided into manic type, depressed type, and circular type. Under this heading is placed any disorder of mood "that dominates the mental life of the patient and is responsible for whatever loss of contact he has with his environment. . . . These disorders are marked by severe mood swings and a tendency to remission and recurrence. . . . The onset of the mood does not seem to be related directly to a precipitating life experience." Included as another subcategory is *involutional melancholia,* depression occurring at the involutional period of life, especially in women between 45 and 55, but "opinion is divided as to whether this psychosis can be distinguished from the other affective disorders."

B. *Psychotic Depressive Reaction.* "This psychosis is distinguished by a depressive mood attributable to some experience. Ordinarily the individual has no history of repeated depressions or mood swings. The differentiation between this condition and the next depends on whether the reaction impairs reality testing or functional adequacy enough to be considered a psychosis."

C. *Depressive Neurosis* (also described as *reactive depression*). "An excessive reaction of depression due to an internal conflict or to an identifiable event such as the loss of a love object or cherished possession." [21]

If the reader finds these distinctions less sharp than he would like, he should bear in mind that a classification of mental disorders is a human product, the result of compromises among many different workers. It is adopted to bring provisional order to complex phenomena before their

[21] American Psychiatric Association, *Diagnostic and Statistical Manual of Mental Disorders* (2nd ed.; Washington, D. C.: American Psychiatric Association, 1968).

real underlying nature is fully understood. Problems of classification take care of themselves when facts are clear and undisputed. No such clear scene yet exists with respect to the phenomena of depressive and manic disorders.

SOMATIC ASPECTS

Turning now to the somatic side of the problem, the central task is to search for the physiological correlates of extreme moods and their fluctuations. To the extent that affective disorders are somatogenic, to the extent that depressed and manic moods arrive like visitations without situational cause, the hypothesis is appropriate that abnormal internal events are taking place which affect the functioning of the nervous system. Unregulated moods should be correlated with erratic tendencies in biochemical regulation. Is it possible to detect a constitutional tendency of this sort in manic-depressive patients?

Possible Genetic Factors

Statistical studies show that there is a significant tendency for manic-depressive disorders to run in families. While figures reported by different investigators do not perfectly agree, they regularly show an incidence of disorder in the relatives of manic-depressives that is well above chance. The incidence of this disorder in the population at large varies in different studies between one per cent and one half of one per cent. Incidence in the parents of patients, however, is much greater, ranging from 7.5 per cent to 25 per cent in different studies, and similar figures for siblings run between 14.1 and 29 per cent. Incidence in identical twins of patients is still higher; several reports come close to a figure of 60 per cent.[22] These findings leave little doubt that a genetic factor is involved in the occurrence of depressive and manic disorders. Recent advances in genetics improve the chances of eventually identifying this factor. Winokur and Reich, for example, present evidence for the thesis that two different genes are involved, one making for a tendency to depression and the other adding a predisposition to mania.[23]

Genetic predisposition is part of the picture, but it cannot stand alone as the cause of affective disorders. If its sway were absolute, so to speak, the rate of occurrence in identical twins would be 100 per cent and the other figures probably higher than they are. What would we expect of children both of whose parents had suffered from manic-depressive illness?

[22] See reviews by A. T. Beck in 1967, *Depression: Clinical, Experimental, and Theoretical Aspects, op. cit.,* pp. 128–32; and by J. Mendels in 1970, *Concepts of Depression, op. cit.,* pp. 90–93.

[23] G. Winokur and T. Reich, "Two Genetic Factors in Manic-depressive Disease," *Comprehensive Psychiatry,* XI (1970), pp. 93–99.

Mendels calls attention to a European study in which the investigator found 20 married couples both members of which had been diagnosed as manic-depressive. Of the 47 adult offspring of these parents, 14 had developed a psychotic illness, 10 being diagnosed as manic-depressive, but 33 appeared to be entirely normal. "This suggests that whatever the genetic mechanism may be," Mendels concludes, "it does not have 100 per cent penetrance; that is, it does not operate invariably." [24]

An equally restricted interpretation must be applied to another line of evidence based on the study of physique. Half a century ago Kretschmer pointed out an association between manic-depressive psychosis and the so-called *pyknic* physique.[25] This meant that the disorder was more likely to occur in people of broad and solid frame, deep-chested and with relatively large trunk and viscera, and was less likely in small-muscled, small-boned, slender people. Both Kretschmer and later workers reported associations between the pyknic physical type and traits of personality that correspond to the cyclothymic pattern mentioned earlier in this chapter. In a highly detailed review of this topic up to 1960, Rees considered the correlation to be confirmed, but with much smaller figures than Kretschmer had supposed.[26] The findings again point to a constitutional element predisposing to affective disorder, but again the connection is far from invariable. More often than the average, but not always, manic-depressive patients are of pyknic physique.

Biochemical Factors

We come now more directly to Kraepelin's idea of a metabolic instability. Both the activity and the sense of well-being shown by manic patients suggest a high rate of speed in vital processes, whereas the depressed mood and general retardation seem to imply that the whole bodily system has slowed down. It was doubtless this contrast which led Kraepelin to frame his hypothesis around the idea of metabolism—the rate of vital activity in the tissues as a whole. Better methods of examination have since shown, however, that Kraepelin's formulation requires certain changes. As regards bodily functions mania and depression are not polar opposites. Cameron early pointed out that there is no evidence for biological opposition between the two states.[27] If one takes measurements such as basal metabolism, blood pressure, blood sugar level, rate of blood flow, etc.,

[24] Mendels, *op. cit.*, p. 92.

[25] E. Kretschmer, *Physique and Character,* trans. W. J. H. Sprott (London: Routledge and Kegan Paul, Ltd., 1925), chap. 2.

[26] L. Rees, "Constitutional Factors and Abnormal Behavior," in H. J. Eysenck, ed., *Handbook of Abnormal Psychology: An Experimental Approach* (New York: Basic Books, Inc., 1961), chap. 9.

[27] N. Cameron, "The Place of Mania Among the Depressions from a Biological Standpoint," *Journal of Psychology,* XIV (1942), pp. 181–95.

there are no important differences between manic and depressed patients. Wherever significant differences have been found, they have proved to be related to activity level rather than mood. At the biological level, therefore, agitated depressions and manic states are very much alike, both differing significantly from retarded depressions. "It is the general activity of the person," says Cameron, "rather than his particular mood that seems to correlate with whatever metabolic changes are found."

Research on this problem is made difficult by the enormous complexity of biochemical processes. When the importance of the endocrine glands was first recognized, early in this century, the hope dawned that each gland controlled a particular function the nature of which would quickly be discovered. Such reasoning soon proved to be far too simple. The glands constitute a regulatory system, constantly influencing one another and producing their results through elaborate teamwork. Complex systemic functioning seems to be characteristic of all biochemical processes, including those that affect the activity of the nervous system. Furthermore, events taking place in nervous tissue and in its biochemical milieu are not open to ready inspection; they must usually be inferred from indirect measures such as the concentration of particular substances in the blood or urine, measures which are not specific to brain physiology but to the body as a whole. It is not surprising that Kraepelin's hypothesis of metabolic instability remained for many years indefinite and controversial. Even the discovery that treatment by electric shock could be helpful did not at first point to any plausible somatic mechanism. But the introduction of antidepressant drugs produced a sudden burst of research interest, and the decade of the 1960's was marked by striking progress in understanding and treating the affective disorders.

Research has moved forward along several lines. For a while it appeared that the adrenal glands might be major culprits. Among the many functions of those glands is the secretion of a number of steroid hormones the concentration of which in the body can be measured in the urine. One of these hormones, *cortisol,* was shown to be overproduced in depressed patients; it was even possible to demonstrate a close connection in time between increased cortisol production and the onset by episodes of depression.[28] Other work has shown, however, that increased cortisol production is not peculiar to depressions. It occurs in other disorders and in normal responses to stressful circumstances; it therefore seems best considered a nonspecific response to stress. This explanation is consistent with results obtained by Sachar in the course of psychotherapy with depressed patients. Cortisol levels, most of the time within normal range, became elevated on those days on which the patient attained sudden up-

---

[28] W. E. Bunney, Jr., J. W. Mason, and D. A. Hamburg, "Correlations Between Behavioral Variables and Urinary 17-hydroxycorticosteroids in Depressed Patients," *Psychosomatic Medicine,* XXVII (1965), pp. 299–308.

setting insights into aspects of his problems and experienced marked distress.[29]

A second line of work, pointed more directly at the functioning of the nervous system, deals with *electrolyte metabolism*. Electrolytes, or electrically charged atoms, have a vital part in the activity of nerve cells and the transmission of neural impulses. They are unevenly distributed on either side of the cell's membrane; in particular, there is normally a higher concentration of sodium ions on the outside of the membrane and of potassium ions on the inside. This arrangement maintains an electrical balance or equilibrium which determines the cell's resting potential, and it is restored after the passage of a nervous impulse. Several investigations have turned up evidence that in depressed patients, and still more in manic patients, there is an abnormally high concentration of sodium ions inside the cell membrane, which changes the normal balance in the direction of greater excitability. In a paper reviewing the topic, Whybrow and Mendels propose the hypothesis that there is "an unstable state of central nervous system hyperexcitability in depression, and probably also in mania." [30] It may seem paradoxical to invoke overexcitability for retarded depressions, though the concept seems appropriate for agitated depressions and manic states. But the research on electrolyte metabolism is still in its early stages, and the hypothesis of neural hyperexcitability needs considerably more confirmation.

A third line of research is directed toward *biogenic amine metabolism*. Biogenic amines are hormones that have important effects on the functioning of the central nervous system. Among them are the so-called catecholamines, which include epinephrine and norepinephrine, known for some time to be produced by the adrenal glands in emergency reactions but now recognized as arising from other sites as well; and the *indole amines* of which serotonin and histamine are representative. Experiments with animals have shown that drugs that increase the level of amines in the brain produce alertness and overactivity, whereas those that deplete brain amines result in sedation and inactivity. The maintenance of effective amine concentrations is a constant metabolic process. Amines are used up, so to speak, by activity in nerve cells but are also steadily produced to make up for the loss, so that in normal circumstances homeostasis—a steady state—is maintained. It is conceivable, however, that the delicate balance might be upset, that precisely at this point there might be defects in regulation leading to episodes of underproduction and overproduction of brain amines and thus to sharp changes of activity and mood. It is even possible that such defects would manifest themselves chiefly in connection with life stress, the upset in amine regulation occurring only when there were heavy

---

[29] E. J. Sachar, "Corticosteroid Responses to Psychotherapy of Depressives," *Archives of General Psychiatry*, XVI (1967), pp. 461–70.

[30] P. C. Whybrow and J. Mendels, "Toward a Biology of Depression: Some Suggestions from Neurophysiology," *American Journal of Psychiatry*, CXXV (1969), pp. 1491–1500.

demands upon the central nervous system. The rationale is strengthened by the fact that drugs which are effective in treating depression and mania are known to have primary influence on amines in the brain.

Research attention has thus far been concentrated mainly on one amine, norepinephrine. In 1965 Schildkraut, surveying a large amount of evidence, proposed a catecholamine hypothesis to account for affective disorders, to the effect "that some, if not all, depressions are associated with an absolute or relative deficiency of catecholamines, particularly norepinephrine, at functionally important receptor sites in the brain. Elation conversely may be associated with an excess of such amines." [31] Possibly the hypothesis will need to be broadened to include serotonin, which seems to play a somewhat similar part.[32] But in any event biogenic amine metabolism now seems to be established as the most probable site of somatogenesis in depressive and manic disorders. Kraepelin's guess about metabolism has been brought closer to a specific target.

It is not yet possible, of course, to account fully for the biochemical abnormality. Erratic regulation of amine metabolism might occur for a variety of reasons; the precise mechanism has by no means been laid bare. Kraines has put forward a theory, worked out in great detail, that pushes the explanation to a particular brain center, the hypothalamus, which is known to have a strong influence upon emotional expression and which is also an important source of norepinephrine. His thesis is that "a persistent, intensifying inhibition of hypothalamic function is the mechanism of a depressive syndrome and that a gradually increasing excitation of this area produces the manic state." [33] Even so, we do not quite catch up with the initial abnormality; we are bound to ask what causes the unusual inhibition and excitation of the hypothalamus. Clearly the topic is not closed, but this should not obscure the progress that is being made in biochemical research nor the more optimistic attitude that has come to prevail with respect to treatment.

METHODS OF TREATMENT

Depressive and manic disorders do not usually manifest themselves early in life, although a few cases of their occurrence in childhood are on record.[34] The most frequent period of onset is the decade of the thirties. The disorders are somewhat more common in women than in men. On the whole,

---

[31] J. J. Schildkraut, "The Catecholamine Hypothesis of Affective Disorders: A Review of Supporting Evidence," *American Journal of Psychiatry,* CXXII (1965), pp. 509–22.

[32] A. H. Glassman, "Indoleamines and Affective Disorders," *Psychosomatic Medicine,* XXXI (1969), pp. 107–14.

[33] S. H. Kraines, "Manic Depressive Syndrome: A Physiologic Disease," *Diseases of the Nervous System,* XXVII (1966), pp. 573–82, 670–76.

[34] J. D. Campbell, *Manic-Depressive Disease* (Philadelphia: J. B. Lippincott Co., 1953), chaps. 9 and 10.

spontaneous recovery is the rule. From a half to two thirds of hospitalized patients with manic and depressive states are discharged in good health and do not have a later recurrence of illness important enough to require a return to the hospital. In some cases, however, the attacks recur and repeated hospitalization is necessary, and in a very small proportion of cases recovery is not sufficient to warrant discharge from the hospital. The expectation of at least temporary spontaneous recovery is so high that it is difficult to evaluate the effects of therapeutic measures. Most of the patients get well anyway, regardless of what is done. Therapeutic goals cannot be set up in terms simply of recovery, but must include considerations such as shortening the period of illness, reducing the recurrence, and freeing the patient's life from unnecessary psychological burdens.

Hospitalization

The specialized care provided by a mental hospital is clearly needed in severe depressed and manic states such as those described earlier in this chapter. Manic patients are disturbing and exhausting to those around them, and with their indiscriminate self-confidence they may get themselves into a lot of trouble, including laying a trail of unpaid bills that far exceeds their actual financial resources. Depressed patients are disturbing in a different way, and the danger of suicide hangs in the air even though taking one's life is talked about more often than it is tried. The decision to use the services of a hospital must rest on a weighing of relevant considerations: the extent of the patient's disturbance and irrationality, the kinds of treatment probably needed, the risk of suicide, the amount of friction that is being generated between the patient and his family, the protection of children from a parent's irrationality. The hospital can often do a better job than would be possible by a grim attempt to ride out the storm at home.

Hospitalization is less quickly and less often recommended today than was the case in the recent past. There is growing reluctance to send people out of the community to institutions that may be some distance away. If community mental health agencies exist, such as an outpatient clinic or psychiatric services in the local hospital, adequate care can be provided for patients who continue to live at home. Most of the less severe depressed and manic states can be handled on an outpatient basis. Even the somatic methods of treatment—electroconvulsive therapy and the use of drugs—do not necessarily call for hospitalization; they can be adapted to both office and outpatient practice. It is no longer the inevitable fate of a manic-depressive patient to be sent away.

Psychological Methods

Patients in severe depressions or manic states are almost wholly unresponsive to psychological treatment. Suggestion and persuasion are dramatic failures in both states; the depressed patient automatically considers them useless, the manic barely listens. Treatment that involves interpretation of psychological problems may make a depressed patient perceive new grounds for his feeling of worthlessness; the manic patient finds the interpretation brilliant and skips on to his next thought. Behavior therapists who undertake to reward and reinforce more desirable behavior may discover that they are not in possession of rewards of real value to the patients. The extreme moods seem to capture the reward mechanism itself, so that the depressed patient feels little reward in the therapist's favorable attention, while the manic finds everything else that happens equally rewarding. The burden for some depressed patients can be slightly lightened by calm assurance that the depression will ultimately pass. Beyond this, not much can be accomplished while mood is in such complete command.

In milder states and during periods of remission the situation is more favorable for psychological work. A minimum goal might be to assist the patient in learning to live with his illness, adapting his life to the possibility of recurrent episodes. Setting the sight a little higher, the patient might be helped in coping with difficulties of living that put him under stress. This is of value even if these difficulties are not specific causes of the affective disorder. Whether or not anything more should be attempted depends upon one's judgment of the relevance of psychodynamic problems in the particular case. Undoing the vulnerabilities and strategies created by early traumatic losses is in all probability an inherently difficult therapeutic problem, but success in dealing with it is sometimes reported.[35]

Electroshock

This method of treatment, already described in the last chapter, continues to be widely used for depressions, where it often produces definite movement toward a more cheerful outlook. It is sometimes reported to have a calming influence on manic patients, but tranquilizing drugs have largely supplanted it for this purpose.

The wide use of electroshock has made it possible to accumulate a good deal of information about results. There is diversity in the reported figures, but complete remission seems to be obtained in from 40 to 80 per cent of patients in depressed states, somewhat less in patients having manic attacks. The involutional depressions generally show the highest rate of improvement. Of course the rate of spontaneous remission is high in the affective disorders, but electroconvulsive therapy (ECT) serves to hasten

[35] Goals and methods are discussed by R. W. Gibson, "Psychotherapy of Manic-depressive States," *Psychiatric Research Reports, American Psychiatric Association*, XVII (1963), pp. 91–102, and by W. Bonine, "A Psychotherapeutic Approach to Depression," *Contemporary Psychoanalysis*, II (1965), pp. 48–53. E. Jacobson, in *Depression: Comparative Studies of Normal, Neurotic, and Psychotic Conditions* (New York: International Universities Press, 1971), reports a certain number of good results from extended psychoanalysis.

the remission and spare the patient many unpleasant and expensive weeks of hospitalization. On the question of recurrence the reports strike a less cheerful note. Shock-treated patients in the manic-depressive category are a little more likely to reappear in the hospital, and to reappear sooner, than patients who regained their health without shock.

The results can be pictured more clearly by considering a specific study from the Pennsylvania Hospital in Philadelphia.[36] Comparisons are made between 567 depressed or manic patients in the years 1925–1934, before ECT was available, and 563 patients in the years 1940–1946, when ECT was regularly available but drugs were not yet in use. In recovery rate the second group shows a definite though not very large advantage, 72 per cent as against 59 per cent. With patients where a five-year follow-up study could be completed the difference largely disappears, the lasting recovery figures being 66 per cent and 64.5 per cent respectively, but the figures for the ECT group are based on a much reduced sample of the original 563. Most striking is the difference found for average length of stay in the hospital: 4.5 months in the earlier period, 2.3 months in the years after the introduction of ECT. Recurrence of disorder occurred more often in the shock-treated cases. At the end of one year, 16 per cent of the earlier cases had broken down again, 28 per cent of the later group, and this difference seemed to be sustained through several more years.

It is clear from these figures that ECT performs its greatest service in reducing the length of attacks. Particularly with depressions, where its benefit is largest, it can spare the patient many days of despair, acute suffering, and expense. On the other hand it clearly cannot rank as fundamental therapy in the sense that it reduces the likelihood of future attacks, and the evidence seems to show that it protects the patients even less than a spontaneous recovery. There have always been misgivings about its use. Patients dislike it and often become anxious about it. The very efficiency of the treatment has led to indiscriminate use and an attitude on the part of the physician that has suggested the phrase, "push-button psychiatry." Some workers were troubled that no acceptable hypothesis emerged concerning the mode of action of ECT. Even psychiatrists who warmly advocated its use admitted that its action was "shrouded in mystery."[37]

Antidepressant Drugs

Tranquilizing drugs, which as we saw in the last chapter produced something of a revolution in the care of schizophrenic patients, have played a less dramatic part in the affective disorders. Though helpful in manic states and agitated depression, they are clearly inappropriate for dealing with depressed moods. Effective antidepressant drugs were developed a little

36 E. D. Bond, "Results of Treatment in Psychoses—with a Control Series," *American Journal of Psychiatry*, CX (1954), pp. 881–87.
37 L. B. Kalinowsky and P. H. Hoch, *Shock Treatments, Psychosurgery, and Other Somatic Treatments in Psychiatry* (2nd ed.; New York: Grune & Stratton, Inc., 1952).

later, but they were quickly adopted and to a considerable extent, though not entirely, have supplanted ECT. This does not necessarily imply that they work better. Flat comparisons between standard ECT and a standard drug treatment show that ECT produces good, if not better, results.[38] But drugs are easier and more pleasant; moreover, doses can be regulated and changed, and combinations can be worked out to suit patients' individual needs. This flexibility has improved treatment "to the point where management of the affective disorders is among the most gratifying aspects of clinical practice." [39]

It might be supposed that a stimulant like amphetamine would be perfect for depressions, but this drug has proved to be of no value. Two other classes of drugs, however, have shown antidepressant properties: the *tricyclic* drugs, of which imipramine is the most studied representative, and the *monoamine oxidase inhibitors*. These two classes are significantly different in chemical structure and presumably operate through different biochemical mechanisms, but both appear to produce the result of increasing the quantity of biogenic amines available for use in the central nervous system. Recently a third substance, *lithium,* has become the object of intensive experimentation. In this case it is more plausible to assume that electrolyte metabolism is affected; lithium salts may play a part analogous to sodium and calcium, affecting the electrical balance on the two sides of the nerve cell membrane. Lithium is chiefly used to bring down manic attacks, but there are claims that it also helps to level out depressions.[40]

The current literature is full of conflicting reports of the effectiveness of these several drugs and their variants. Conclusions range all the way from miraculous to worthless. Final evaluation is out of the question until more is known. The problem of evaluation is greatly complicated by the emerging probability that there are large individual differences in the response to different drugs. We can perhaps picture the day when it will be possible through criteria not yet known to prescribe what is best for each patient, ECT for some, just the right drug for others, for still others just the right combination of drugs. Pending the arrival of such a day we must be satisfied with a provisional conclusion and some cautions. The antidepressants should not be regarded as "wonder drugs." The reported results are always, to coin a medical-sounding term, submiraculous: the effects are somewhat irregular, and only some of the patients are substantially benefited by any one preparation. Nevertheless, it seems likely that antidepressant drugs do some good, and this justifies the hope that further use, experimenting carefully with dosages and combinations, will show how they can do more good. But it must always be kept in mind that drugs powerful

[38] Beck, *op. cit.,* pp. 305–10.

[39] M. A. Lipton, "Affective Disorders: Progress, But Some Unresolved Questions Remain," *American Journal of Psychiatry,* CXXVII (1970), pp. 357–58.

[40] National Institute of Mental Health, *Lithium in the Treatment of Mood Disorders* Washington, D. C.: Government Printing Office, 1970).

enough to relieve depression are likely to have other effects, possibly harmful and even dangerous. Some preparations produce side-effects of drowsiness and dizziness, some interfere with motor coordination, and some tend to have too great an effect on, for example, heart rate or liver function. Such consequences set limits to the dosage and especially to the continued use of antidepressant drugs on a maintenance basis. These limitations should be borne in mind even while we recognize the progress that has been made in lightening the burdens of depressive and manic disorders.

SUGGESTIONS FOR FURTHER READING

Ideal as a first step toward increasing one's knowledge of depressions is a small but clear and well-balanced survey by J. Mendels, *Concepts of Depression* (New York, John Wiley & Sons, Inc., 1970). The literature on the same subject is gathered up in considerable detail by A. T. Beck in *Depression: Clinical, Experimental, and Theoretical Aspects* (New York, Harper & Row, Hoeber Medical Division, 1967), with possibly an overemphasis on how little of our knowledge has actually been proved. The somatogenic position is warmly espoused in J. D. Campbell's *Manic-Depressive Disease* (Philadelphia, J. B. Lippincott Co., 1953) which otherwise surveys the disorder quite fully. Excellent for its clinical descriptions is E. Kraepelin's *Manic-Depressive Insanity and Paranoia* (trans. by R. M. Barclay; Edinburgh, Livingstone, 1921). The psychoanalytic contribution is summarized by O. Fenichel in *The Psychoanalytic Theory of Neurosis* (New York, W. W. Norton & Co., Inc., 1945), Ch. 17; more recent contributions are contained in *Affective Disorders,* a series of papers edited by P. Greenacre (New York, International Universities Press, Inc., 1953) and in E. Jacobson's *Depression: Comparative Studies of Normal, Neurotic, and Psychotic Conditions* (New York, International Universities Press, 1971), a gathering together of her many influential papers on this subject.

In addition to C. W. Beers' *A Mind That Found Itself* (Garden City, N.Y., Doubleday & Co., Inc., 1931) which is used in the text to provide illustrations of depressed and manic states, there are other interesting inside accounts of manic-depressive psychosis: for instance, *Reluctantly Told* by J. Hillyer (New York, The Macmillan Co., 1927), and *A Mind Restored* by E. Krauch (New York, G. P. Putnam's Sons, Inc., 1937). Some cases of this kind are contained in a collection edited by B. Kaplan, *The Inner World of Mental Illness* (New York, Harper & Row, 1963); other first-hand accounts will be found in C. Landis and F. A. Mettler, *Varieties of Psychopathological Experience* (New York, Holt, Rinehart & Winston, Inc., 1964), Chs. 12 and 13.

15

Injuries and Abnormal Conditions in the Brain

In our clinical introduction we made the acquaintance of a patient with a severe brain disorder. The case of Martha Ottenby formed a contrast with those patients whose disorders arose from personal difficulties in living. She was the victim of a disease, an impersonal affliction that struck her without the slightest discernible relation to current life stress or to changes in her economy of happiness. In studying psychosomatic disorders we saw that it is possible for a bodily dysfunction to come as the result of chronic emotional problems. With the disorders now to be examined the situation is chronologically reversed. The trouble starts in neural tissue or in biochemical abnormalities that directly affect neural tissue. Disorders of behavior, feeling, and cognition follow, but as consequences of pathological influences on the operation of the nervous system.

The study of somatogenic disorders lies by no means outside of the province of abnormal psychology. Historically this province has always included the mental and behavioral changes that result from injuries or other unusual conditions in the nervous system. How the brain works has been for many years the object of intensive research in laboratories all over the world. A recently published review confined to the topic of recovery of function following brain injury includes no less than 223 references.[1] Most of the

[1] B. S. Rosner, "Brain Functions," *Annual Review of Psychology*, XXI (1970), pp. 555–94.

research, of course, is done with animals, and therefore cannot include certain peculiarly human capacities such as speech and sustained thought. But diseases and accidental injuries in the human brain have added to the store of knowledge and given us fascinating insights into what is involved in complex activities like speaking, writing, linguistic understanding, planning, and the organization of behavior. One is likely to end with great respect for the infinitely complex organ that at its best manages such striking accomplishments, not the least of which is the study of itself.

VARIETIES OF PATHOLOGICAL PROCESS

What mishaps can befall the central nervous system, especially the brain? Encased within bony walls, the brain, like the spinal cord, is protected against certain obvious hazards. But it is by no means immune to injury or to internal conditions that impair its proper functioning. By way of initial orientation we shall quickly survey the pathological processes that affect brain activity.

Survey of Pathological Processes

The first possibility is an inadequate development of brain tissue, technically called *aplasia*. Occasionally a child is born with almost no development of the cerebral cortex, a truly rudimentary brain. In cases of less severe defect the brain may be completely formed but of smaller than average size and with less well-marked convolutions, suggesting a primitiveness of structure. One variety of severe mental defect, microcephaly, is characterized by a greatly diminished size of the upper skull; within this constricted space the brain is small and poorly developed. In mongoloid deficiency the abnormality in the shape of the head is less marked, though still distinctive, and the brain shows few obvious structural defects, but mental performance is sluggish and seriously deficient. Mental retardation will be taken up in detail in Chapter 16.

Next on the list of cerebral mishaps is *trauma*, some direct physical injury to brain tissue. The head and the underlying cerebral tissue may be traumatized at the time of birth if the labor is extremely prolonged and difficult, so that the head is exposed to severe pressure. Any severe blow on the head may produce swelling and injury of brain tissue. Most children, of course, fall on their heads from time to time without damage, but occasionally one of these accidents produces temporary or even permanent brain injury. If the skull is fractured, and especially if brain tissue is penetrated as is the case in bullet or shrapnel wounds, a marked change in mental performance may result. Even when the wounds heal there may be atrophy and scar formation in the brain which impairs its normal functioning. Another form of direct injury is caused by *cerebral tumors*. As a tumor grows, it crowds and distorts the surrounding brain tissue. Up to a certain point, especially if the growth is slow, the brain tissue can adapt itself to the change without functional impairment, but eventually the crowding prevents normal metabolism in the nerve cells.

The nervous system may become the seat of *infection* by microorganisms. Certain not very common forms of illness such as encephalitis lethargica (epidemic "sleeping sickness") represent an inflammation of cerebral tissue resulting from infection. In the first chapter of this book we used another infectious disease, general paresis, as an example of the somatogenic disorders. Although resistant to most varieties of infection, brain tissue has certain susceptibilities that may lead to serious damage.

The functioning of the brain can be disturbed by unfavorable alterations in its internal environment. The maintenance of an internal condition that is optimal for cerebral functioning is part of the general process of homeostasis. *Metabolic disorders* may throw out the balance in one way or another so that optimal functioning is impaired. Certain endocrine disorders, for instance, especially those affecting the thyroid gland, bear a direct relation to mood, initiative, and intelligence. Furthermore, recent research has shown that vitamin deficiency plays a part in certain kinds of mental disorder. In the last chapter we learned of the importance of electrolyte metabolism and of biogenic amines in nervous activity, especially in relation to mood level. The internal environment can also be altered by the action of *toxins* or poisons. The toxic effects of excessive alcohol come under most frequent observation, but analogous changes result from other drugs, certain metals like lead, and certain gases like carbon monoxide. *Shortage of oxygen* has a marked effect on mental activity and may permanently injure the nervous system. *High fever* produces a gross though temporary interference with normal brain activity that is reflected in the mental state of delirium.

Finally, the central nervous system is subject to *degenerative changes*. Usually these are associated with old age, but sometimes, as in Pick's disease (from which Martha Ottenby suffered) and the rather similar Alzheimer's disease, changes of an apparently degenerative character begin in middle life. Sometimes a thickening and hardening of the arterial walls is at fault (cerebral arteriosclerosis), so that the supply of blood to the brain cells becomes progressively less adequate. A nutritional deficiency in brain tissue can probably be assumed even when the arteries are not radically hardened. Much remains to be learned about the cerebral changes that go with old age, but there is little doubt that these changes play the predominant part in the mental disorders of later life.

Plan of the Chapter

If this book were a textbook in neuropsychiatry, intended to train medical specialists to meet their professional obligations, it would be necessary at this point to embark upon a detailed description of the organic psychoses.

There are many varieties, subvarieties, and cross-varieties of these disorders. Most of them occur infrequently, but the neuropsychiatrist must be in a position to recognize them and establish a differential diagnosis. The student of abnormal psychology is in a more fortunate position. It is his privilege to select those disorders which are most instructive, which have the most to teach him as regards mental processes and their cerebral correlates. Not yet in professional training, he can afford to concentrate on topics that will most effectively contribute to his understanding of disordered personal reactions, thus ultimately to his understanding of human nature.

This privilege is reflected in the plan of this chapter. We shall first examine in some detail the effects of *localized* brain injury, especially in those areas that seem to serve fairly complex functions. Although local brain injuries are not especially common, they have been investigated with unusual care, and the use of brain surgery for certain types of disorder has yielded further information. Then we shall turn to the *general* consequences of abnormal conditions in the brain, examining the effects of oxygen deprivation, the mental state of delirium, and the intellectual changes believed to result from a diffuse lowering of cerebral efficiency. Next we shall give attention to brain injury in children, considering especially the over-all effects on behavior and the problems inherent in training and schooling. One special form of disorder, epilepsy, will repay examination as a problem both of cerebral function and of adaptation to the fact of illness. Finally we shall survey the disorders of old age, placed against the background of the changed abilities and psychological situation of older people.

EFFECTS OF LOCALIZED CORTICAL INJURY

In war and in civilian accidents the brain is sometimes the site of direct physical injury. This injury is chiefly to the cerebral cortex, which lies directly beneath the skull, although it may reach the thalamus and lower brain centers as well. Occasionally the cortex is the site of disease such as brain tumor or a degenerative process, so that parts of the tissue have to be surgically removed. These accidents and interventions have contributed a good deal to our knowledge of the human brain.

One possible idea about the cerebral cortex would be that each bit of it governed some particular process or activity. We know that in the spinal cord there is clear localization of this kind, and that in lower brain structures such as medulla, cerebellum, and thalamus it has been possible to find centers for fairly specific functions. In 1861 the French surgeon Broca made a discovery that suggested precise localization in the cortex itself. He had the opportunity to examine carefully and later to do an autopsy on a patient who for many years had been unable to speak. There were no defects in the muscles involved in speech, and the patient could communicate by signs in a way that indicated unimpaired intelligence. The autopsy showed a small circumscribed lesion, apparently of long standing, in the left cerebral hemisphere. This led Broca to conclude that he had located the center for speech. His discovery inspired subsequent investigators to try to map the functions of the rest of the cortex. Most of the research was done with animals, but there were occasional opportunities to make parallel observations with human subjects. On the whole the results have not been what Broca would have expected. Some areas, to be sure, have a certain specificity. It can be predicted, for instance, that injury to the occipital poles, at the very back of the head, will cause an interference with visual functions but not affect auditory or motor processes; similarly, that injury to the temporal lobes, in the temples, is likely to affect auditory functions but leave vision undisturbed. The largest part of the cortex, however, seems to have very little specificity of function; and its injury has often produced fewer identifiable consequences than might have been expected.

Findings of this kind have led some workers to believe that the functions of the cerebral cortex are of a highly general nature. In the most radical form of this theory, it is claimed that the various parts are largely equipotential: defects will be in proportion to the amount of tissue that is damaged, more or less regardless of its location. In effect this assigns to the cortex a generalized organizing power, leaving to lower centers the specifics of what is to be organized. Comparing the two views, the student will recognize one of those situations where the truth is more likely to lie somewhere in the middle than at either extreme. There is certainly some localization in the cortex, but it is equally certain that we would miss important information if we were not alert to the general consequences of abnormal conditions in the brain.

We shall consider first the effects that seem to be closely connected with location. The cortex has been mapped by Brodmann into forty-six areas distinguished by the architecture of the cell layers. Part of this scheme is represented by the numbers on the accompanying figure (Figure 1) which shows the left cerebral hemisphere as it would be seen from the left side. These structurally different areas, however, correspond in only a few cases to areas having known specific functions. The diversity of architecture is not matched by diversity of functions.

The main sensory receiving stations in the cortex occupy a relatively small space. Area 17 is the center for vision, area 41 for hearing, areas 1, 2, 3, and 5 for touch and pressure from skin and deep end organs. The areas immediately surrounding these centers probably have a somewhat restricted function; area 18, for instance, is believed to be limited to the perceptual elaboration of visual impressions. Area 4 is the motor area which when stimulated gives rise to specific muscular movements, and area 6 seems closely related to the motor sphere. This is about as far as one can go with specific localizations. Of the remaining parts of the cortex, two large zones are of particular interest. One of these is the *frontal* area, represented by the numbers 9, 10, 11, and possibly 45. It is the elaborate development of the frontal cortex that gives man his high forehead and

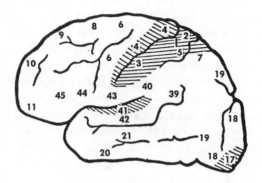

Figure 1

Schematic drawing of the left lateral aspect of the human cortex. The numbers are those assigned by Brodmann on the basis of cellular architecture. The shaded areas are those having fairly definite functions, as described in the text. Areas 9, 10, 11, and 45 together constitute the prefrontal area. The parietotemporal area is represented by the numbers 39, 40, 42, 43, and 44 (From S. Cobb, *Foundations of Neuropsychiatry* [Baltimore: Williams & Wilkins Co., 1941], p. 72.)

intelligent appearance in comparison with chimpanzees and monkeys, so that in popular thought the frontal areas are associated with the distinctively human attainments. The other area, the *parietotemporal*, represented on the diagram by the numbers 39, 40, 42, 43, and 44, turns out in fact to bear a special relation to the distinctively human attainments of language and the meaning of symbols. Curiously enough, this complex array of skills is dependent only on the leading or dominant hemisphere, the left in right-handed and the right in left-handed people. Injury to the parietotemporal area in the dominant hemisphere is a disaster. Injury to the corresponding area in the other hemisphere has somewhat less curious consequences, having no effect, for instance, on language. To this extent there is localization of function between the two hemispheres. Research on penetrating head wounds indicates that the areas in the left hemisphere governing the right hand do not exactly correspond to the areas in the right hemisphere controlling the left hand, which suggests that the whole organization of the two sides of the brain may be different.[2]

Many difficulties beset the investigator of localized injuries. Even when lesions can be fairly precisely located, account must be taken of the character of the injury. It has been shown that focal and diffuse lesions on the same site produce detectably different effects; that static and progressive lesions have different results; and even that it is possible to discern different consequences of lesions due to tumor, vascular disease, inflammation, and degenerative disorders.[3] Furthermore, the same kind of lesion in the

[2] J. Semmes, S. Weinstein, L. Ghent, and H. L. Teuber, *Somato-sensory Changes After Penetrating Brain Wounds in Man* (Cambridge: Harvard University Press, 1960).

[3] R. M. Reitan, "Psychological Deficit," in *Annual Review of Psychology*, XIII (Stanford: Annual Reviews, Inc., 1962), p. 421.

same place will produce effects that differ from one person to another. The results of individual learning are represented in the brain, but since no two histories of personal experience are exactly alike we cannot expect that they will be registered in a standard manner in standard locations. Each brain becomes unique through the process of learning.[4] The effect of an injury is also influenced by the time of life at which the lesion occurs. Younger and older brains, differing in the amount and organization of experience, are differently affected by the same disease.

Injury in the Parietotemporal Area

Injury to the parietotemporal area in the dominant hemisphere produces an effect chiefly on language. This area lies between the centers for vision, the centers for hearing, and the motor centers. The use of language involves vision (apprehending the written word), hearing (apprehending the spoken word), and the motor acts of speaking and writing. It is not surprising, therefore, that injury to the parietotemporal cortex disturbs the language function in one way or another. The resulting conditions are known by the general name of *aphasia*.

The results of injury are extremely complex. At first sight the disorders seem highly selective and highly restricted. Thus one patient may display only an inability to read, his understanding of spoken language and his speech and writing being uninjured. Another may have a specific inability to find words, especially nouns, to express the thoughts he has in mind. Such a patient may show by gestures and fragments of speech that he remembers perfectly the details of a walk he has just taken, but he is unable to bring out the proper words to describe the objects he has seen along the way. A patient described by Hollingworth used almost no substantives, but inserted the automatisms "seriat" and "feriat" in their place.[5] When asked where he lived, he said, "I come from seriat." When asked his occupation, he said, "I am a feriat." He drew a picture of an anvil, which he called a "seriat," and remarked that he worked at it. When the examiner called it an anvil he brightened and said, "That's it, you said it, it's a seriat." When he tried to read aloud he pronounced practically every word "seriat." Sometimes the disorder is even more narrowly selective. A foreign language is lost but the native tongue is unaffected. The extreme is represented in the case of a patient formerly able to read music who after his injury could read music in the key of C, with some difficulty in the key of G, and not at all in other keys. In all these cases it is apparent that general understanding is not greatly injured. The patient seems to grasp much more than his injured language function is able to represent.

The high specificity of some of these losses has tempted many workers

---

[4] W. Penfield and P. Perot, "The Brain's Record of Auditory and Visual Experience: A Final Summary and Discussion," *Brain*, LXXXVI (1963), pp. 595–696.

[5] H. L. Hollingworth, *Abnormal Psychology* (New York: The Ronald Press Co., 1930), p. 455.

to think that the different aspects of language are localized in small specific parts of the cortex. Injury at one spot causes word blindness, at another spot word deafness, at another spot the comprehension of sentences, at still another spot the speaking of nouns, etc. The parietotemporal cortex has even been compared to a typewriter keyboard, to a complex piece of electrical wiring, and to a computer. There may be something to these analogies, though they seem a little too metallic to explain the workings of an organ made up of living cells. The work of Penfield and his associates at Montreal certainly indicates that there is some specialization among the cortical areas that subserve language. These workers have investigated the cortex very carefully in the course of brain surgery conducted with local anaesthesia of the scalp. The patients were comfortable and fully conscious, hence able to report upon their experiences. Electrical stimulation somewhere in the region of areas 43 and 44 produced an arrest of speech: the patient knew what he wanted to say but could not say it. A little further back the effect of stimulation was to prevent the finding of names and nouns as in the case mentioned above.[6] Such findings leave no doubt that there is an appreciable division of labor within the area responsible for language.

Two points are of especial importance here for the understanding of aphasic disorders. In the first place, the effect of electrical stimulation in the parietotemporal area appears to be inhibitory rather than excitatory. It does not, like stimulation in the motor area, produce involuntary overt movement. It does not cause the patient to speak aphasically or to make incorrect writing movements. The patient must be engaged in conversation and must speak on his own initiative in order to reveal the consequences of the stimulation. These consequences can be understood only as a suppression of accustomed behavior patterns. In the second place, what is suppressed can best be considered not as specific elements of speech but as larger linguistic functions such as the finding of words appropriate to express one's thoughts and the placing of words in grammatical arrangement. Penfield's experimental findings on speech are therefore consistent with the ideas of Hughlings Jackson, who in the nineteenth century conceived of the aphasias as disturbances of "propositional thinking," and of Henry Head, who after much experience with brain injuries in World War I reached the conclusion that the central disorder was of "symbolic formulation and expression." It is not parts of speech that are lost through injury; it is rather some part of the symbolizing activity that goes on in the understanding and use of language.[7]

These reflections make it possible to grasp more clearly the process of recovery from aphasia. Good results are often obtained by a process of re-

[6] W. Penfield and L. Roberts, *Speech and Brain Mechanisms* (Princeton, N. J.: Princeton University Press, 1959).

[7] C. E. Osgood and M. S. Miron, *Approaches to the Study of Aphasia* (Urbana: University of Illinois Press, 1963).

training. Sometimes a portion of language behavior is gone beyond repair, so that it is necessary to teach the patient some roundabout method of overcoming the defect. This is illustrated in a case reported by Gelb and Goldstein, in which the patient had become unable to recognize any objects through visual experience.[8] It was impossible to retrain his visual recognition, but he learned to read again by a combination of eye movements and finger movements. He traced the letters with his fingers and followed them with his eyes, providing himself in this way with the cues necessary for recognition. More typically, however, retraining does not involve new learning; it involves the reappearance of old learning which had been suppressed by the injury.[9] It may take a long time to bring about some use of the suppressed function, but once it has begun to operate again it may soon be restored as a whole. If our aphasic ironworker, for example, could be brought to use a few appropriate nouns instead of "seriat" and "feriat," he might presently recover the complete use of substantives. That a resurgence of old learning is taking place, rather than new learning, is shown in the following incident. A Southerner with total aphasia was trained for a year by a New England teacher. The training was successful, and it was noteworthy that the patient resumed talking without any impairment of his southern accent.[10]

Injury to the Frontal Areas

It was long supposed that the frontal lobes were the seat of the highest intellectual functions. Studies soon began to show, however, that the effects of injury were not large in the intellectual sphere. In fact, the trend of recent thought has been in the opposite direction, emphasizing the smallness of deficit in intellectual functions. One of the best older studies was made by Rylander, of Stockholm, who reported on 32 cases in which the frontal area was surgically removed on one side.[11] In the majority of the cases there was deficit in respect to memory, concentration, and speed of thought. But there was also an exaggerated sense of well-being (euphoria) in 20 cases, restlessness in 14, loss of initiative in 12, depression in 8, these changes being distinctly of nonintellectual character. By and large, unilateral excision of the frontal area does not produce extensive changes.

More radical consequences might be expected to follow extirpations involving both frontal lobes. Reviewing the literature in 1945, however, Hebb found little evidence of intellectual impairment and no satisfactory demon-

8 The case is described briefly in K. Goldstein, *Aftereffects of Brain Injuries in War* (New York: Grune & Stratton, Inc., 1942), pp. 149–52, and in more detail in W. D. Ellis, *A Source Book of Gestalt Psychology* (New York: Harcourt Brace Jovanovich, Inc., 1938), pp. 315–25.

9 J. M. Wepman, *Recovery from Aphasia* (New York: The Ronald Press Co., 1951).

10 H-L. Teuber, review of Wepman's *Recovery from Aphasia*, in *Journal of Abnormal and Social Psychology*, XLVII (1951), pp. 610–11.

11 G. Rylander, *Personality Changes After Operation on the Frontal Lobes* (Fair Lawn, N. J.: Oxford University Press, 1939).

stration of localization of specific functions.[12] Fifteen years later, after a great deal more research, the evidence still told in the same direction. Meyer reached the conclusion that "frontal lobe lesions, compared with lesions elsewhere, are not more disruptive of complex intellectual performance," and that "the research so far available has not conclusively established the dependence of any function on this area." [13]

This does not imply that the frontal lobes are a mere luxury without functions. It means that the functions are general, hard to measure, and perhaps not mainly intellectual in character. A clue to their possible nature is suggested in a case studied with great care and reported in a book by Brickner.[14] The patient, a successful broker, was operated for cerebral tumor in 1930. The growth was extensive so that it proved necessary to remove from the left side most of area 8 and all of areas 9, 10, 11, and 45; from the right side a slightly larger area was excised. At the time of operation the patient was forty years old. Prior to his illness he had been an energetic, intelligent businessman, but in other respects a rather mild and submissive individual. As a child he was quiet and shy, dependent on his mother. When he married, following a courtship in which the girl took the active part, he expressed the desire to continue living in his parents' home. He rarely displayed aggression except in the form of facetious and somewhat boastful stories. Such was the man upon whom the operation was performed. The effect of removing the frontal lobes was sufficiently great so that the patient was never able to go back to work. Initiative was impaired, memory was imperfect, distractibility was increased, and the patient showed a clear deficit in judgment and logical reason. More striking, however, was the change in his self-criticism and self-restraint. After the operation he experienced considerable euphoria and appeared to lose all restraint over his previous mild boastfulness. He proclaimed himself the best of all businessmen, the man whom nobody could fool, and he told stories of youthful sexual exploits and of playground fights in which he knocked down all comers. Along with boastfulness and aggression his dependent tendencies were also exaggerated. He allowed others to bathe and dress him and care for all his wants. The constructive organization of personality was more markedly injured than the intellectual processes.

Prefrontal Lobotomy

It was this general picture of frontal lobe functions that prompted the Portuguese surgeon Moniz in 1935 to make the bold experiment of trying to relieve certain serious mental symptoms by brain surgery. He reasoned

[12] D. O. Hebb, "Man's Frontal Lobes: A Critical Review," *Archives of Neurology and Psychiatry (Chicago)*, LIV (1945), pp. 10–24.

[13] V. Meyer, "Psychological Effects of Brain Damage," in H. J. Ensenck, ed., *Handbook of Abnormal Psychology: An Experimental Approach* (New York: Basic Books, Inc., 1961), p. 542.

[14] R. M. Brickner, *The Intellectual Functions of the Frontal Lobes* (New York: The Macmillan Co., 1936).

that patients who showed a tremendous excess of control, with constant tension, anxiety, and anguish, might be relieved and placed in a more relaxed frame of mind by deliberate interference with the frontal lobes. Prefrontal lobotomy does not involve the removal of nervous tissue, and the cerebral cortex is touched only to the extent that may be required for introducing the instrument. The purpose of prefrontal lobotomy is to sever some of the neural connections between the frontal lobes and other parts of the brain, particularly the thalamus and hypothalamus. It might be described as an attempt to reduce the action of the frontal lobes upon the rest of the system, and it actually effects a partial isolation of the prefrontal cortex—areas 9, 10, 11, and 45. Although surgery of any kind is naturally frightening, the operation itself is not unusually difficult for the patient. It can be carried out under local anaesthesia with the patient fully conscious and able to talk.

The immediate effect of the operation is a stuporous and mildly confused state, but this passes in the course of time. Given standard intelligence tests after recovery, the patients perform nearly as well as they did before surgery. There is some impairment in accuracy, generalizing, profiting from past mistakes, and planning ahead.[15] These deficits, however, are neither great nor widespread, and the findings as a whole are consistent with the belief that the functions of the frontal lobes are not primarily intellectual. The main changes in behavior are in the direction of those described in Brickner's patient, though less extreme. Petrie called attention to a weakening in social restraint and to a less adequate sense of responsibility as shown in such matters, for instance, as keeping promises.[16] Greenblatt and Solomon were perhaps showing the brighter side of much the same coin when they reported that in the hospital ward the patients interacted more freely with other patients and showed more friendliness and positive affect.[17] Jenkins and associates have compared the responses of chronic schizophrenics on a sentence completion test before and after lobotomy. The following samples are completions of the sentence fragment, "The best thing about old age is . . . ." One patient before operation completed the sentence with the gloomy thought "that one doesn't have long to live"; afterwards, the completion was "social security." Another patient changed from "a person is more tolerant and mellow" to "rich cake Grandma used to bake." Still another changed from "more knowledge" to "comfort." Such changes support the authors' conclusion that "lobotomy simplifies the world for the patient," leading him to think of "the more tangible, even sensual enjoyments of social security benefits, rich cake, and ease." [18]

15 A. Petrie, *Personality and the Frontal Lobes* (Philadelphia: The Blakiston Co., 1952). 16 *Ibid.*, pp. 111–13.

17 M. Greenblatt and H. C. Solomon, *Frontal Lobes and Schizophrenia: Second Lobotomy Project of Boston Psychopathic Hospital* (New York: Springer Publishing Co., Inc., 1953).

18 R. L. Jenkins, J. Q. Holsopple, and M. Lorr, "Effects of Prefrontal Lobotomy on Patients with Severe Chronic Schizophrenia," *American Journal of Psychiatry*, CXI (1954), pp. 84–90.

The most persistent attempt at theoretical explanation of these changes has been made by Freeman, who starts with the hypothesis that the frontal lobes are concerned with what might be described as foresight. Broadly speaking, this means the person's projection of himself into the future: his planning of what he desires to accomplish, his recognition of the means to be employed, his awareness of the extent to which he reaches this goal. Of course, the patient can still make plans, perceive means to ends, and make judgments about himself, but somehow these processes no longer come together into an effectively functioning whole. Robinson and Freeman have shown by means of special tests that lobotomized patients have a reduced feeling of self-continuity and of concern about the self.[19] Similarly they are less concerned about the attitudes of others toward them. The patients become a little obtuse to the impression they are making on others, and they are less restrained by images of making themselves ridiculous. For patients who are highly overconcerned and self-conscious this can be regarded as a shift in the direction of health. In Freeman's words, "The problem in surgery is therefore to reduce the function of self-regard and of sensitivity to limits that can be tolerated by sick persons, without sending them too far in the other direction." [20]

Not surprisingly, in view of the kind of results produced and the finality of a surgical procedure, there was a good deal of opposition to prefrontal lobotomy on grounds both practical and ethical. Was the brain surgeon justified in deliberately lowering a person's capacity for judgment, foresight, and self-criticism? The operation, of course, was used only as a last resort in cases that entailed great suffering. "Some clinicians took the view that even if permanent personality changes and intellectual deterioration did occur, this would be a reasonable price to pay for relief from continuing torment from obsessional or delusional ideation associated with tension and agitation that were resistant to other therapeutic procedures." [21] During the period between 1935 and 1952 many thousands of patients the world over received prefrontal lobotomy, and favorable though not remarkable results were widely reported. The most extensive evaluation, a British Ministry of Health report, was based on 10,365 patients operated upon during the period from 1942 to 1954. It showed that 46 per cent of these patients were eventually well enough to be discharged from hospital.[22] That more than half the patients never got well enough to leave the hospital shows that the operation was less than miraculous, but the recovery

[19] M. F. Robinson and W. Freeman, *Psychosurgery and the Self* (New York: Grune & Stratton, Inc., 1954).

[20] W. Freeman, "Psychosurgery," *American Journal of Psychiatry*, CXI (1955), pp. 518–20.

[21] J. M. C. Holden, T. H. Itil, and L. Hofstatter, "Prefrontal Lobotomy: Stepping-stone or Pitfall?" *American Journal of Psychiatry*, CXXVII (1970), pp. 591–98.

[22] G. C. Tooth and M. A. Newton, "Leucotomy in England and Wales, 1942–54," *Ministry of Health Reports on Public Health and Medical Subjects* (London: H. M. Stationery Office, 1961), No. 104.

rate must be read against the probability that virtually none of these seriously disturbed patients would have recovered without prefrontal lobotomy.

Then suddenly the surgical method was displaced by tranquilizing drugs, which put into the physician's hands a quicker, safer, far less expensive means of quieting patients who were tense, agitated, and anguished. The decline of prefrontal lobotomy as a therapeutic method was even more rapid than its rise, and it is used today only very rarely.[23] Its chief legacy is an increase of knowledge about the functions of the frontal cortex, and the findings support in a general way what had previously been inferred from more gross forms of surgery.

GENERAL EFFECTS OF ABNORMAL CONDITIONS IN THE BRAIN

Research on abnormal functioning in the human brain often has to be done without knowing which localities are most affected. It is only through localized injuries, accidental or surgical, that the somewhat different functions of the parietotemporal cortex and the frontal cortex have come to light. The abnormal conditions created by oxygen lack, fever, and drugs may not affect all nervous tissue alike, but so far we have no direct evidence of such selectivity. Furthermore, many workers believe that brain impairment, whatever its locus, produces a weakening of certain over-all functions having to do with the organization of behavior. It is worthwhile to study these postulated general changes, partly for what they suggest about cerebral functions, partly for what they disclose about the normal organization of behavior, a subject about which we know all too little.

Effects of Anoxia

Nervous tissue is highly dependent upon oxygen. Complete deprivation of oxygen, even for a few seconds, causes irreparable damage to nerve cells, especially to those in the brain. Partial deprivation produces less drastic effects which are nevertheless of great practical importance to mountain climbers and airmen who operate at altitudes where the supply of oxygen is markedly reduced. Experiments on the effects of anoxia have been conducted at high altitudes and, more conveniently, in specially built chambers in which the concentration of oxygen can be controlled. As the oxygen content of inspired air is diminished, a fairly regular sequence of changes takes place. According to McFarland and his associates, these are as follows.[24] First comes a loss of self-criticism and judgment. Sometimes

[23] Holden, Itil, and Hofstatter, op. cit., describe a modified form of the operation which they consider appropriate in certain cases.

[24] R. C. McFarland, "The Psychophysiological Effects of Reduced Oxygen Pressure," Research Publications of the Association for Research in Nervous and Mental Diseases, XIX (1939), pp. 112–43.

this is accompanied by feelings of exhilaration similar to those produced by mild alcoholic intoxication. Attention and concentration then begin to show impairment, and the speed and accuracy of mental work decline; score on mental tests fall off. Motor and sensory performances resist some- what longer, but as the anoxia increases there is a loss in such skilled acts as handwriting and an impairment of visual and auditory perception. Ultimately there is loss of consciousness.

The effects of long-continued low-grade anoxia are less clearly estab- lished. People who live for a long time at high altitudes usually become acclimatized, but there are individual differences in this compensation. Certain individuals become irritable, get along badly with their companions, suffer mild feelings of depression, and experience difficulty in concentrating on mental tasks.[25] With a return to lower altitude the symptoms disappear. These changes have a familiar ring. They have much in common with the effects of alcoholic intoxication, as described in Chapter 12, and of injuries to the frontal lobes. The early vulnerability of self-criticism and judgment, and the lowering of attention and concentration, are alike in all three abnormal conditions.

Delirium

It might be supposed that an attempt to analyze delirious states would produce only confusion. The task has been attempted, however, by Cameron and Magaret, who point out that there are many common features in delirious behavior no matter what its cause.[26] A delirious person is typically restless, confused, and disoriented. He misidentifies people and things, shows marked defects of recent memory, and appears to be at the mercy of dreamlike and often terrifying images. It is difficult to catch and hold his attention, and sometimes even a simple question is answered in groping, rambling speech that quickly drifts away from the point. Cameron and Magaret summarize the characteristics of this behavior under four heads. It shows (1) *incoordination,* best illustrated in the staggering gait, fumbling manipulation, and slurred speech; (2) *interpenetration,* when one sequential act invades another, as in the case of a man who starts to change his clothes for dinner and ends up in pajamas; (3) *fragmentation,* when actions and even sentences are broken off before they are completed; and (4) *overinclusion,* shown in the failure to keep one's behavior from being constantly influenced by momentary impulses and surrounding im- pressions. All of these defects come from a disturbance of "attitude or- ganization." "The delirious patient is deprived of his ability to maintain

25 R. C. McFarland, "Psychophysiological Studies at High Altitudes in the Andes," *Journal of Comparative Psychology,* XXIII (1937), pp. 191–258, and XXIV, pp. 147–220.
26 N. Cameron and A. Magaret, *Behavior Pathology* (Boston: Houghton Mifflin Co., 1951), pp. 452–77.

habitual anticipant and supporting attitudes in the presence of competing and discordant stimulation." [27]

This analysis should give us a new respect for what the normal intact brain accomplishes even in the ordinary affairs of life. A tremendous task of ordering, selecting, and excluding goes on throughout our waking hours. The necessary control and direction is provided by certain attitudes, the nature of which can be made clear by an illustration. When a physician interviews a patient he gives selective attention to the story of the illness, the symptoms, the probable cause and probable remedy, excluding all stimuli which are not relevant to this purpose. The guiding principle is provided by an anticipant attitude—to try to understand this particular case—behind which lies a general set of supporting attitudes—to fulfill the role of physician, to be of service, etc. What the delirious brain seems unable to accomplish is the maintaining of these directive attitudes. Without them, behavior simply falls to pieces and loses its organized plan. Memory depends upon organization, and it is therefore easy to understand how little a person can recall of the events of delirium.

Although the brain-injured patient is inclined to be apathetic rather than excited, it is possible to detect certain similarities between his general impairments and those seen in delirious patients. *Overinclusion,* for instance, is highly characteristic of the brain-injured, who are readily distracted by external impressions, and a *fragmentation* of behavior is often the consequence. Probably we can assume that there is a similar difficulty in maintaining directive attitudes, but the wild disorder of delirious behavior is counterbalanced in the brain-injured by a tendency toward rigid perseveration. Attention sometimes becomes riveted on some object of interest, and if the patient manages to solve some difficult problem he keeps trying to repeat this solution on new tasks.

Perceptual Peculiarities

Abnormalities in perception are often associated with local injury, a case in point being the changes in the apprehension of language that go with parietotemporal injuries. Many workers, however, attach importance to a perceptual peculiarity that seems to be a consequence of many forms of cerebral dysfunction. This is described as a blurring of the boundaries between figure and ground. It is very obvious in normal perception, especially visual perception, that a certain portion of what is perceived constitutes a clearly defined figure, the remainder being a less clearly defined ground. In certain ambiguously drawn pictures it is possible to make figure and ground reverse themselves in rapid succession, but ordinarily the two can be clearly discriminated. This characteristic of perception applies also to any complex process in the nervous system. An action

[27] *Ibid.,* p. 474.

such as raising the arm constitutes figure, but is accompanied by a ground of readjustments in other muscles which keep the body in equilibrium. In brain injury, then, especially in injury to the cortex, the relation of figure and ground is disturbed and leveled.

This phenomenon can be illustrated by performance on a test devised especially for brain-injured children by Werner and Strauss.[28] The examiner takes an ordinary marble board having 100 holes arranged in 10 rows. He places marbles in some of the holes, making some kind of a figure, for example two overlapping hollow squares. He then gives the child an empty board and marbles and asks him to copy the arrangement. It may be noticed in passing that this is a type of test which permits the examiner to observe the whole course of the patient's performance, with all its pauses, errors, and false starts. Tests in which the subject merely gives answers, without revealing how he got them, are all but valueless in the study of brain injuries. The marble board experiment proves particularly difficult for brain-injured children. Inspection of their performance shows the source of the difficulty. Unlike normal children, and unlike mentally retarded children without brain injury, these children are unable to separate figure from ground—the figure made by the marbles from the ground made by all the rest of the holes. They place their marbles in a random, disorganized fashion, and even if they get the placements approximately right they show no sign of realizing that the stimulus consisted of figures such as the two squares. Children with neurological injury likewise take more time and make twice as many errors as normals when given the task of copying geometric designs with sticks.[29] This perceptual abnormality is peculiar to brain-injured subjects, who in comparison with other psychiatric patients are more sharply disrupted when required to copy figures on paper that already has a background design.[30] Brain injury makes it difficult to keep figure from getting mixed up with ground.

Loss of the Abstract Attitude

Goldstein attempted to conceptualize an important general consequence of brain injury as a loss of the abstract attitude. With this notion we are already somewhat familiar because it was well illustrated in the case of Martha Ottenby. In describing how she got lost when returning from the hospital workroom, how she determined whether it was winter or summer, and how she ran into the street to talk with her brother who was actually dead, we reached the conclusion that her behavior was bound by immediate

28 Cf. A. A. Strauss and L. E. Lehtinen, *Psychopathology and Education of the Brain-Injured Child* (New York: Grune & Stratton, Inc., 1947), pp. 31–49.
29 J. H. Wise, "Performance of Neurologically Impaired Children Copying Geometric Designs with Sticks," *Perceptual and Motor Skills*, XXVI (1968), pp. 763–72.
30 A. Canter, "A Background Interference Procedure to Increase Sensitivity of the Bender-Gestalt Test to Organic Brain Disorders," *Journal of Consulting Psychology*, XXX (1966), pp. 91–97.

and concrete impressions.[31] She was unable to detach herself from these impressions or to think about her behavior in abstract terms. Even in test performances she was blocked by the simplest abstraction, although she could perform quite well with concrete problems.

Goldstein conceived of the abstract attitude broadly. He saw it not as an acquired mental set or specific aptitude but as what he called "a capacity level of the total personality." [32] In contrast to the concrete attitude, which is realistic, immediate, and unreflective, the abstract attitude includes in its scope more than the immediately given situation. The real stimulus is transcended and dealt with in a conceptual fashion. Objects before us are seen as members of a class or category, or they are apprehended in a framework of wider implications. To take a very simple example: a patient shows great skill in throwing balls into boxes that are located at different distances from him, but he is unable to say which box is farthest away or how he manages to aim differently. He is able to function concretely but not to manage the abstract idea of distance, and he can give no account of throwing harder or less hard. The importance of loss of the abstract attitude becomes even clearer when we consider the following limitations: the patient cannot keep in mind several aspects of a situation at one time, cannot readily grasp the essentials of a given whole, cannot plan his actions ahead in ideational fashion. Even with so simple a task as copying a clear, unambiguous figure in reverse, the patient is blocked by the abstraction that is involved.[33]

Shortcomings in the capacity for abstraction make themselves apparent in tests that require sorting and classification, for example the picture-object test used by Strauss and Werner.[34] Two pictures are put up, one showing a house on fire, the other a boy struggling in water. The child is then asked to put in front of each picture those toy objects lying on the table which go with the picture. A brain-injured boy of twelve put some appropriate objects, such as a fire engine, in front of the house on fire, but also added some very peculiar items. Wrench and pliers were supplied to repair the car in case it was burned; a "slow" sign was set up to keep people from running into the fire; a black train was introduced to match the black suits of people watching the fire; a fork was added because one of the witnesses thought he saw food in the burning building; an envelope was put in place so that the firemen could read the address and find their way to the fire. To a mind that finds these groupings appropriate, it is evident that the world might become at times a little confusing.

Not all workers agree with Goldstein that the described changes arc

31 See above, pp. 73–80.

32 K. Goldstein and M. Scheerer, "Abstract and Concrete Behavior: An Experimental Study with Special Tests," *Psychological Monographs,* LIII (1941), pp. 1–31.

33 G. G. Haydn and A. Rutsky, "Figure-reversing Ability in Chronic Brain Syndrome and Controls," *Journal of Nervous and Mental Diseases,* CXLII (1966), pp. 168–71.

34 Cf. Strauss and Lehtinen, *op. cit.,* pp. 54–74.

best interpreted in terms of concreteness and abstractness. There is little doubt, however, that we are dealing with a loss of organization, a kind of flattening of mental activity which makes it hard to exclude the irrelevant, to subordinate associative processes to consecutive thought, and to govern behavior in the direction of steadily imagined future goals. Though less dramatically exaggerated, the picture overlaps a good deal with the loss of habitual anticipant and supporting attitudes noticed in delirium.

Symptoms Expressing the Struggle with Defect

Whatever the merits of the concept of abstract attitude, we owe to Goldstein an illuminating recognition that the brain-damaged patient is a person who is trying to adapt himself to the limitations imposed by injury. Many curious forms of behavior become explicable as adaptive attempts of this kind. In various ways the patient tries to find or make an environment in which demands that are beyond his resources will not occur. Brain injury makes it difficult to deal with anything that is unexpected. It is sometimes observed that patients start violently when they are addressed. One means of protection against the unexpected is excessive orderliness. All the patient's belongings are kept in the most meticulous arrangement, so that everything can be found and used with a minimum of mental exertion. Another means of protection is to be constantly busy. By concentrating on a particular activity the patient protects himself from dreaded social stimulation and surprise. The activity may not be important in itself, but the patient cherishes it because of its protective character. Holzberg describes a man who had suffered severe concussion and lasting brain damage in a motor accident. At a certain point in his convalescence "he assumed responsibility for sweeping his ward and, when doing so, would become oblivious to everything around him for hours. . . ." He apparently "found much safety in his ward cleaning," becoming upset only when he was interrupted by other patients. This useful activity won him a certain commendation, but its main function was to keep him from being "continually harassed by practically every stimulus about him." [35] Orderliness and persistent work are clearly not direct consequences of brain damage. They are adaptive strategies designed to prevent confusion, distraction, and surprise.

BRAIN DYSFUNCTION IN CHILDREN

Until recently it was assumed that brain disorders in children were of relatively rare occurrence. They were chiefly known through examples in which there was gross impairment of behavior or severe limitation in mental capacity. As we shall see in the next chapter, some forms of mental retarda-

---

[35] J. D. Holzberg, "A Carpenter with Traumatic Brain Damage." in A. Burton and R. E. Harris, eds., *Clinical Studies of Personality* (New York: Harper & Row, 1955), chap. 20.

tion are associated with visible physical abnormalities and have been shown to depend upon structural defects in the brain. Other disorders which clearly imply dysfunction in the central nervous system are known by dramatic behavioral manifestations like the convulsions or "fits" of epilepsy or the jerky spastic movements of cerebral palsy. Brain disorder thus occupied the position of a rare but drastic affliction which was expected to show itself in marked behavioral disorder. Neurological examination, consisting of a systematic series of small behavioral tests, would clinch the diagnosis by revealing a large number of abnormal signs such as tremor, poor motor control, perceptual irregularities, and changes in reflex patterns. Little could be done to correct the failings of the nervous system, and treatment consisted of training to get around the handicaps and live with them.

Cerebral Palsy

An example of a disorder that fitted this conception is provided by cerebral palsy. This term refers to a group of disorders that depend upon injuries to lower brain centers rather that the cortex, injuries that are presumed to occur either prenatally or as a consequence of difficult birth. The effects appear most prominently in motor control; intelligence is typically spared and is superior in a proportionate number of cases. The motor handicaps may be severe and are of such a nature as to attract unfavorable notice. Lomotion may be extremely slow and awkward, the arms may jerk and the hands twitch uncontrollably, and frequent involuntary grimaces may sweep across the face. Obviously a child thus handicapped is unlikely to profit from indiscriminate interaction with other children, who tend to find a "spastic's" behavior either terrifying or hilarious until they become fully accustomed to it. Much can be accomplished through special programs of training during childhood. Signs of disability are likely to remain, but the person can learn to some degree how to get around the handicap and lead a relatively normal life. There are many "spastic" adults who lead normal and even highly productive lives in spite of a permanent disorder of motor control. These are, however, the relatively fortunate ones. About a third of the children born with cerebral palsy are so handicapped as to require permanent custodial care, and another third become trained and minimally educated only through close personal supervision.[36]

Brain Injury

Sometimes following a severe head injury, and sometimes following an attack of encephalitis (which is known to injure brain tissue at least temporarily), the behavior of a previously well-adjusted child will undergo a sharp change. There is a conspicuous rise in the level of motor activity.

36 E. Denhoff and I. P. Robinault, *Cerebral Palsy and Related Disorders* (New York: McGraw-Hill Book Co., Blakiston Division, 1963).

The child seems to be constantly restless, continually in motion, unable to sit still, creating annoyance by getting into everything. The restraint of sitting still at table or in the school classroom becomes suddenly more difficult; the teacher complains that her pupil keeps leaving his desk and wandering around the room. Attention is unfavorably affected; there is great distractibility, and power to stick to a task is damagingly reduced. There is also loss of control over impulse and temper. Delay of gratification cannot be brooked, and outbursts of emotion and irritation occur with increased frequency. Probably the symptom of hyperactivity is more prominent in children; otherwise, this pattern differs hardly at all from what we have seen to be characteristic of adult brain dysfunctions.

The difficulties experienced and created by brain-injured children can be illustrated from one of the case reports given by Strauss and Lehtinen.[37] The boy in question had suffered a birth injury which was presumed to have lastingly injured brain tissue. His I.Q., tested on various occasions, averaged somewhere in the 60's, and his performance on the marble board test was extremely disjointed, indicating severe blurring of figure and ground. When given tests he showed the typical distractibility; "at times, despite repetition of questions, it was difficult to know whether or not he had actually heard because his attention wandered and his interest span was so short." Constant restlessness was also prominent in test situations. "He moved around continually, leaning back in the chair or yawning or handling material on the desk." When admitted to the training school at the age of ten he had to be constantly reminded of routine requirements, partly because his distractibility prevented him from remembering them, partly because he defiantly disregarded them. He "liked to fuss around with odd jobs to keep busy." Perhaps this was an outlet for his restlessness, but it may also have been an attempt to avoid catastrophic situations by constant activity. Though often "friendly and good-humored," he was "insistent about his likes and dislikes," and "made himself very unpopular with the group because of his continued interference in the business of others." On one occasion he tore down decorations for a party as fast as they were put up. On another he decided that the furniture should be moved around, shouted to the other boys to move desks and chairs, and himself seized a large table, knocking down other furniture in his path. He was frequently in fights, apparently over trifles. His best adjustment was to work in the shop, where in spite of his "enthusiastic and 'slam-bang' abandon" he was capable of functioning as a good worker. Returned to his family at sixteen, the boy made a good adjustment, handling merchandise on a shipping dock of a large hotel. He took pride in his responsibilities and in his ability to earn an independent living.

This boy was living under a grave handicap. It was very hard for him to keep still or to resist whatever impulses or emotions presented them-

[37] *Psychopathology and Education of the Brain-Injured Child, op. cit.,* pp. 35–38.

selves. Thus, without having particularly hostile intentions, he was constantly at odds with the group. The reader should imagine himself in the position of having to discipline this boy, either at school or at home. Even with the best intentions in the world it would be almost impossible not to get furious with him. Ideas of awaiting his turn, sharing with others, remembering obligations, taking pains and doing things slowly would have little effect on a person so restless, impulsive, concrete, and disorganized. Small wonder that friction almost always exists between such a child and his mentors. Overactivity alone can be exasperating, but even more trying is the resistance to attempts at helpful intervention. As if he did not listen and did not try, the child seems to disregard socializing influences and keeps creating in his mentor a feeling of helpless incompetence.

It is fair to ask, however, whether a child with brain damage is capable of listening and trying. The boy just described exhibited an almost total disregard for the rights and feelings of others. On what does consideration for others depend? Studies of the development of moral insight have shown that it depends to a large extent on being able to see things from another person's point of view.[38] It calls for multiple perspectives. One of the traits used explicitly by Goldstein to define the abstract attitude is the ability to hold simultaneously in mind various aspects of a situation. If brain injury renders a child incapable of taking the abstract attitude, it also makes him virtually incapable of being considerate of others. Such a child cannot transcend moral realism. His failure to become a socialized member of groups comes partly from an intellectual inability to grasp what it means to be a considerate group member.

Training programs have to be adapted to the limitations imposed by injury. Strauss and Lehtinen described some of the measures devised to improve school performance.[39] Everything possible must be done to minimize distraction. The schoolroom must be undecorated, bare, removed from outdoor noises, its windows painted so that the children cannot see out. Desks should be far apart, perhaps even facing the walls, so that the children will not distract each other. Gloomy as this sounds, it is often welcomed with great appreciation by the children themselves, who suddenly find themselves able to keep their minds on their tasks. Restlessness and hypermotility must be met by a program which includes many activities, and by devices which link learning with motor action. To overcome the leveling of figure and ground it is often necessary to prepare the teaching materials with a sharp outlining of the essential figures in color. All of these devices are used only to get the children started on a better educational performance; as rapidly as possible they are trained to participate in a more traditional school routine.

[38] E. Lerner, "The Problem of Perspective in Moral Reasoning," *American Journal of Sociology,* XLIII (1937), pp. 249–69.
[39] *Ibid.,* chap. 9; A. A. Strauss and N. C. Kephart, *Psychopathology and Education of the Brain-Injured Child* (New York: Grune & Stratton, Inc., 1955), Vol. II, chap. 8.

Minimal Brain Dysfunction

During the 1960's two developments took place that put certain child-hood disorders in a new light and at the same time held out greater hope of improvement for children with brain dysfunction. In the first place, the expansion of clinical facilities for children made it possible to document the fact that the pattern of traits hitherto attributed to brain damage and encephalitis was relatively common. One of the most frequent reasons for referring a child, especially a boy, to a mental health clinic is the familiar combination of restless hyperactivity, inconsiderate and aggressive behavior, low attention span, and poor performance in school work. In the second place, experiments were tried with some of the new drugs that had proved helpful with other types of disorder, and the startling discovery was made that this pattern of symptoms responded favorably to ampheta-mine. This drug rates as a stimulant, and it seemed paradoxical that it should benefit behavior already so overactive and impulsive.

We must first notice the diagnostic dilemma resulting from these dis-coveries. Many of the young patients referred for the brain-damage be-havior patterns have no histories of birth injury, head trauma, or en-cephalitis; furthermore, when given a neurological examination they do not necessarily reveal a sufficient number of abnormal signs to justify a traditional positive diagnosis. In such cases the evidence for cerebral dys-function is wholly indirect, an inference from the over-all pattern of be-havior. Classification might be made, of course, on the basis of the effects of amphetamine, but this principle fits no better with neurological signs. The drug is not effective in all cases. It works well in some cases with clear signs of brain damage, but fails in others; it works well in some cases with no direct evidence of brain damage, but fails in others. The reason behind such findings has yet to disclose itself.

As a best guess, however, child psychiatrists have gone ahead and in-troduced a diagnostic category called *minimal brain dysfunction*. It is applied to children who show all or most of the hyperactive, impulsive, distractible pattern of behavior and to children with special difficulties in school learning. Readers who find this solution arbitrary should bear in mind that the classification of disorders is not an emanation of pure reason but serves practical purposes in clinical work. To talk of minimal brain dysfunction, instead of concentrating on human relations and attitudes, suggests at once that treatment should be somatic rather than psychological. Prior to the use of amphetamine the hyperactive, distractible, impulsive pattern in children with no direct signs of brain damage was considered to be psychogenic. The child was seen as a victim of parental rejection who because of anxiety and resentment had failed to acquire the internal controls needed for socialized living either at home or at school. This sug-gested psychological treatment, sometimes on a one-to-one basis with the child, more often in some joint form involving the parents. The results were poor; the children all too often made scant progress in developing the desired controls. The diagnosis of minimal brain dysfunction announces the physician's preference for a somatic approach. The child's behavior may resist influence because it proceeds from some condition in the brain that makes anything else impossible. The first step in treatment should therefore be biochemical, designed to alter the cerebral abnormality that makes the child's behavior so difficult.

When amphetamine produces a good result, it often does so in a surprisingly short time. Instances are cited by Wender in which substantial change of behavior occurs in a matter of weeks.[40] One boy of 7, who in addition to the typical pattern had been steadily stealing and had twice set fire to the house, changed during the first week so that his mother wrote: "He is behaving like an angel . . . he is a different child." A week later she specified in detail his accomplishments, which included reading and drawing quietly by himself, helping around the house without being asked, and complete cessation of tantrums, stealing, and fire-setting; she added, "For the first time in four years he is enjoying life instead of fighting it." [41] In another case two weeks was enough to bring about a sharp change of behavior at home, and at three weeks the mother reported with surprise: "He has friends. . . . Children come to the house for him. . . . He does what he is told. . . . He's never been so good for so long in his whole life before." [42] Of a third case, a boy of 8, his teacher wrote after three months: "Mike has improved considerably. . . . He feels he's taking the 'magic' pill and so he can do no wrong while under the influence of it. Consequently his whole self-image appears to have changed. He is now considered by *himself* and his *classmates* to be the *new* Mike, a 'good' Mike, the Mike who helps everyone." Formerly a bully, he now stopped other children from bullying. Simultaneously, his reading comprehension score took a remarkable upward jump and his schoolwork as a whole became satisfactory.[43]

Dramatic results of this kind are not, of course, obtained in every case. Sometimes amphetamine is ineffective and in rare instances it seems to make things worse. But the good results, especially when they occur quickly, make a strong case for somatogenesis. It is hard to understand the rapid emergence of the good new Mike if we think of the bad old one as frozen by resentment or as stamped in by a long history of reinforcement in an unfortunate family situation. The boy had little trouble understanding and enacting a different pattern of behavior; he seemed only too glad to try it once he could slow down and keep his attention from chasing

---

[40] P. H. Wender, *Minimal Brain Dysfunction in Children* (New York: John Wiley & Sons, Inc., 1971).
[41] *Ibid.*, pp. 205–6.
[42] *Ibid.*, pp. 200–1.
[43] *Ibid.*, p. 198.

every stimulus. Children with this syndrome often report bewilderment at their own bad behavior and inability to control it. They describe the effects of amphetamine in such phrases as "I am a lot more relaxed," "my head feels clearer," and "I can concentrate better." The assumption seems justified that the drug corrects a biochemical condition that prevents optimal cerebral efficiency, lowering the functional level in a way analogous to brain damage. Seen in this light, the paradox vanishes that amphetamine, a stimulant, should produce behavior that is outwardly more tranquil. Control and organization are important cerebral functions, and it is perhaps these, perhaps specifically the frontal cortex, that are especially stimulated. Clear-headedness and better reasoning are reported by adults who have used amphetamine, along with a kind of alertness that makes them respond with more interest to other people. The good new Mike was ready to emerge as soon as the cerebral basis was made right.

There is an air of magic about dramatic good results, and a broader clinical view is needed to restore balance. Wender, a strong advocate of amphetamine medication, makes clear in the following words the limits of its action.

Drug treatment is of great importance, but it must be emphasized that there are several things medication cannot accomplish. Once the syndrome has remained untreated for any length of time, psychological deficits accumulate. Obviously, medication cannot compensate for educational and experiential deficits. Medication can facilitate learning, not provide compensation for several years in which a child may have been severely handicapped in learning. It can help a child learn to read, but it cannot teach him. Drugs can make the child more amenable to discipline and more lovable, but they cannot provide the experience of having been loved, trusted, admired, and accepted in the past. . . . New experience will be necessary for the child to learn that which he has not learned and to experience that which he has been prevented from experiencing.[44]

In order to improve the chances that this new experience will be constructive, Wender advocates a program of "psychological management" that includes explanations to parents, advice on how to make the home environment more predictable and appropriately rewarding, help in softening parental attitudes built up by the child's past annoying behavior, explanation to the child in terms not injurious to his pride why he needs pills when others do not, and other practical advice as occasion may require. More than this, however, may often be required. The parents may find it difficult to change the attitudes engendered by months and years of mingled anxiety and frustration in trying to manage an unmanageable child. The child's peers may be slow to accept a new version of the pest who has so often spoiled their fun. The teachers may view with distrust the unaccustomed calm and expect at every moment a renewal of restless mischief. Change in one person's behavior spreads its influence widely.

44 *Ibid.*, p. 109.

To produce a new set of interactions with others, and to develop an expectation that these interactions will continue, may require more than a little psychological help.

As now used, the category of minimal brain dysfunction applies to cases of unusual learning difficulty even when hyperactivity is not part of the problem. That this classification is justified is indicated in a study by Hertzig, Bortner, and Birch, who conducted neurological examinations on 90 children aged 10 to 12 with conspicuous learning disabilities.[45] These children were classed as "brain-damaged" merely on educational grounds; the problem was to see whether or not independent evidence of cerebral dysfunction could be obtained. The results were clear: in contrast to educationally normal controls, this group of children showed a substantial number of signs indicative of cerebral abnormality. These included abnormal reflex responses, motor discoordination as shown in a certain clumsiness of gait and balance, difficulties in executing fine motor processes, mild disorders of speech, and tremor and small involuntary movements. Only 5 per cent of the 90 cases were wholly free from such signs, as compared to 67 per cent of the controls. These findings, the authors conclude, justify the label of brain dysfunction in severe learning difficulties. There is "primary atypicality in the organization of the central nervous system," a basic handicap that affects many other aspects of behavior.[46]

The most likely point of origin for minimal brain dysfunction is shortly before, during, or after birth. In two studies Pasamanick and Knobloch have shown a significant association between this type of disorder and a number of unfavorable circumstances surrounding birth, such as toxemia, infection, premature birth, or anoxia during long and difficult labor.[47] These complications, writes Eisenberg, occur more frequently "among the poor, the black, the unmarried, the underaged, and the overaged mothers" and appear to result "from an interaction between inadequate diet, poor prenatal care, poor housing, and gross stress, each of which is associated with pregnancy outcome." [48] Steps that might be taken to prevent minimal brain dysfunction thus belong in the broad realm of public health and environmental betterment.

[45] M. E. Hertzig, M. Bortner, and H. G. Birch, "Neurologic Findings in Children Educationally Designated as 'Brain Damaged,'" *American Journal of Orthopsychiatry,* XXXIX (1969), pp. 437–46.

[46] *Ibid.,* p. 445. The research findings are confirmed by a similar study, A. Wikler, J. F. Dixon, and J. B. Parker, Jr., "Brain Function in Problem Children and Controls: Psychometric, Neurological, and Electroencephalographic Comparisons," *American Journal of Psychiatry,* CXXVII (1970), pp. 634–45.

[47] B. Pasamanick and H. Knobloch, "Retrospective Studies on the Epidemiology of Reproductive Casualty: Old and New," *Merrill-Palmer Quarterly of Behavior and Development,* XII (1966), pp. 7–26; H. Knobloch and B. Pasamanick, "Prospective Studies on the Epidemiology of Reproductive Casualty: Methods, Findings, and Some Implications," *ibid.,* pp. 27–43.

[48] L. Eisenberg, "Child Psychiatry: The Past Quarter Century," *American Journal of Orthopsychiatry,* XXXIX (1969), pp. 389–401.

Treatment of children with amphetamine has aroused considerable opposition both within and outside the mental health professions. This drug, once widely used in low dosages as a "pep pill" and a means of keeping awake while cramming for examinations, has recently been classified as dangerous, and its prescription by physicians is strictly limited to certain disorders, one of which, however, is minimal brain dysfunction. Taken in large doses for "kicks," amphetamine is undoubtedly dangerous, leading occasionally to psychotic episodes, possibly to brain damage, and always to a bad subsequent let-down. This is the usage that justifies stricter legal control, but small doses taken even over long periods of time have not been shown to produce harmful side-effects. The trouble is that the drug produces no permanent alteration in brain chemistry and must therefore be taken every day. Does this imply that medication must go on forever and that the brain-damage syndrome will immediately reappear if the pills are stopped? Two points are worth mentioning. (1) There is evidence that some of the symptoms, especially overactivity, tend to fade out as puberty approaches, making possible a tapering off of medication. (2) Educational and interpersonal gains made during the period of treatment are not abruptly wiped out if medication is stopped. There may be some loss of efficiency and concentration, but their effects will be far less damaging if in the meantime behavior has become more habitually mature and stably organized. These two points, however, still require research confirmation, as does the nature of the biochemical reaction produced by amphetamine.

EPILEPSY

Epilepsy is based on a disordered condition of the brain which leads to periodic seizures. The most distinctive feature is a temporary loss of consciousness, but this may be accompanied by varying degrees of motor and autonomic perturbation. It occurs in something like one half of one per cent of the general population. This figure seems small, but it means that about 700,000 persons in the United States are afflicted with epilepsy. Although the disorder is not continuous, and the person is in a perfectly normal state between attacks, it constitutes even in its milder forms a serious handicap in living.

Varieties of Epileptic Attack

There are three main types of epileptic seizure or fit. Most dramatic and most frequent of occurrence are the *grand mal* attacks, which correspond to the idea most people have of an epileptic fit. The second variety, *petit mal,* is not badly described as a smaller fit limited to a brief loss of consciousness with few motor accompaniments. The third variety, the least common of the three, has not yet been stably christened. It is variously known as *psychic seizures, psychic equivalents, psychic variants,* or *psychomotor seizures.* The reader will easily deduce from this fumbling with names that the third class of epileptic phenomena is still but little understood. The condition is an interesting one, however, and it may prove to be of considerable importance.

Grand Mal

Grand mal attacks are often preceded by warning symptoms generally called the *aura.* These may consist of dizziness, tingling, numbness, peculiar sensations in the head, discomfort in the abdomen. They last for but a few seconds and often do not give the patient time enough to prepare for the fit. The seizure itself is introduced by sudden muscular rigidity. Respiration is suspended so that the face turns dark, and if not supported the patients falls heavily to the ground. Almost at once the tonic phase (with muscular rigidity) gives place to the clonic phase of the seizure, characterized by rapid jerking movements of the muscles. The jaws are included in the jerking movements so that the tongue is often bitten and frothy saliva gathers on the lips. Autonomic disorganization is shown in involuntary urination and sometimes defecation. Within a few minutes the clonic phase gives place to coma. Consciousness may be regained almost at once or only after a matter of hours. Some patients have grand mal attacks very infrequently, perhaps once or twice a year. Usually the attacks occur more frequently, and in severe cases there may be several convulsions a day.

Petit Mal

The petit mal attack is of shorter duration and is limited to loss of consciousness, perhaps with a few small twitchings of the eye and face muscles. No mental confusion attends these attacks; there is simply a "mental black-out," starting and stopping suddenly and lasting from a few seconds to a minute or two. The effect may be so transient that other people set it down to a mere moment of absent-mindedness. Petit mal attacks may occur with great frequency, many times a day. While not as disturbing either to the patient or to those around him, they may constitute almost as severe a handicap as the grand mal attacks.

Psychomotor Attack

The third variety of seizure is characterized by at least a partial loss of consciousness without suspension of organized motor activity. There may be slight signs of tonic rigidity for a moment, but thereafter the patient continues to perform purposeful acts. But he is completely out of touch with his environment, pays no attention to what is said to him, and presently returns to normal consciousness with no recollection of the attack. Psychomotor seizures may last for as much as an hour or even longer. Conceivably a person might commit acts of a violent and criminal nature during the course of an extended psychomotor epileptic attack. This possibility has to be considered when there is genuine confusion and amnesia for the period during which the offense was committed.

About one half of the victims of epilepsy have only one type of seizure. The other half have two and even three types, sometimes mixed in the same fit. The three varieties of attack are thus not three different kinds of disease. They can be assumed to spring from similar conditions in the brain.

The Electroencephalogram in Epileptics

At no point has electroencephalography proved of greater value than in the study of epilepsy. Whatever the nature of the underlying neural disturbance, it reflects itself with extraordinary clearness in the electrical activity of the cortex. The *electroencephalogram* (EEG) is a graphic recording of the electrical activity of the cortex. When electrodes are attached to the scalp and connected with an amplifier it is possible to record fluctuations in voltage, popularly known as "brain waves," which arise from activity in cerebral tissue. Under basic conditions—that is, with the subject awake but resting quietly with closed eyes—the normal adult record shows a predominance of slow waves, *alpha rhythms,* averaging about 10 cycles per second. Superimposed on these waves are the faster *beta rhythms* with a frequency anywhere up to 40 cycles per second. Waves of less than 8 per second, sometimes called *delta waves,* are rare in the records of normal adults. They are typical of infants in the first year of life, and their frequency of occurrence decreases with age. One form of EEG abnormality is a distinctly greater frequency of very slow waves (less than 8 per second) than is characteristic for the person's age. This is the abnormality often found in cases with known brain damage and in minimal brain dysfunction. For such disorders, however, the EEG is a crude and somewhat unsatisfactory diagnostic tool. Abnormal EEG's of this type are obtained in something like 20 to 30 per cent of the population, including many people with no signs of disordered behavior.[49]

During epileptic seizures, however, the EEG becomes abnormal in an entirely different way, and the pattern of abnormality is different for each of the three varieties of attack. The accompanying diagram (Figure 2) shows four tracings which are typical for grand mal, petit mal, a variant form of petit mal, and the psychomotor seizure. Each tracing begins with a section of normal record, affording a sharp contrast with the record during seizure. The tonic phase of grand mal is accompanied by very fast waves of high voltage. These give place in the clonic phase to waves still of high voltage having a characteristically erratic form. In petit mal attacks there is a typical association of slow waves with spikes, each pair coming at the

[49] H. Strauss, *Diagnostic Encephalography* (New York: Grune & Stratton, Inc., 1952).

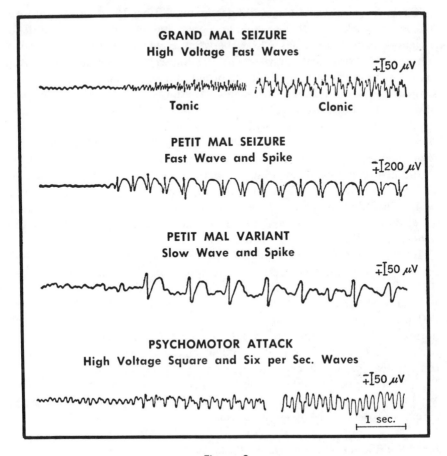

GRAND MAL SEIZURE
High Voltage Fast Waves

$\mp$[50 μV

Tonic   Clonic

PETIT MAL SEIZURE
Fast Wave and Spike

$\mp$[200 μV

PETIT MAL VARIANT
Slow Wave and Spike

$\mp$[50 μV

PSYCHOMOTOR ATTACK
High Voltage Square and Six per Sec. Waves

$\mp$[50 μV

1 sec.

Figure 2

Representative electroencephalograms of four patients to show records taken before, and during, four different types of seizures: grand mal, two forms of petit mal, and a psychomotor attack. At the right is the perpendicular deflection made by a 50-millionth or 200-millionth volt potential, and at the bottom the time marked by one second. The left of each tracing is a portion of the person's normal record. The rest of the tracing was made during a seizure. The uppermost record is the tonic, and then, after an interval, the clonic phase of a grand mal convulsion. The second tracing is the three-a-second alternate wave and spike of petit mal. The third tracing is of the relatively rare two-a-second wave and spike called petit mal variant. The fourth tracing was taken during two phases of a psychomotor seizure. The tracings are about one-third their natural size. (From F. A. Gibbs, E. L. Gibbs, and W. G. Lennox, *Archives of Neurology and Psychiatry*, XXXVIII [1939], p. 1112.)

rate of three a second. Sometimes the rate is even slower: at two a second it is called petit mal variant and is not usually associated with an overt seizure. The waves are shaped quite differently in psychomotor attacks. Voltage is abnormally high, and the waves frequently have square tops. They occur at the rate of between four and eight a second.

These findings were originally made by Gibbs, Davis, and Lennox.[50] The same workers were also able to show that 85 per cent of epileptic patients showed abnormal EEG's between seizures. These abnormalities consisted of short bursts of waves having higher than normal voltage and taking a form similar to those recorded during seizures. The evidence suggests that what is going on during the attacks is an abnormal discharge of energy by the neurones of the brain, and that the patient's brain has a tendency toward excessive discharge even between attacks. If this conclusion is correct we learn a new and interesting fact about the brain: consciousness and the coordinating functions depend upon a level of activity in the neurones that is less than the maximum of which they are capable. When the discharge level is too high, the so-called higher functions disappear. They disappear also in electroshock therapy, which involves passing an electrical current through the brain and which results in loss of consciousness and a convulsive seizure.

It has been shown that about 10 per cent of normal people have abnormalities in the EEG that are similar to those found in epileptic patients.[51] This points to the possibility of a predisposition toward overdischarge, with only about one predisposed person out of twenty actually becoming epileptic. A further finding is of great importance, namely, that abnormal EEG's are found with great frequency in the relatives of epileptic patients.[52] Taking a group of over 200 relatives, it was found that 53 per cent (instead of the general average of 10 per cent) had abnormal records. Even more impressive is the fact that in only 10 per cent of epileptic patients were the records of both parents normal. Clearly the epileptic carries an hereditary predisposition to his disease.

Facts Bearing on the Causes of Epilepsy

There is an unmistakable relation between convulsive seizures and brain injuries. While by no means all epileptics have a history of brain injury, in a certain number of cases the onset of symptoms follows head trauma or some other likely cause of cerebral damage. Tumor of the brain is particularly likely to be accompanied by seizures, and gunshot wounds in the head produce the same result in from 5 per cent to 20 per cent of cases. Almost any gross injury to the brain seems capable of leading to seizures, though it may be that predisposition must also be present to bring about this result.

The way in which brain injuries lead to convulsions has been the object

[50] F. A. Gibbs, H. Davis, and W. G. Lennox, "The Electroencephalogram in Epilepsy and in Conditions of Impaired Consciousness," *Archives of Neurology and Psychiatry*, XXXIV (1935), pp. 1133–48.

[51] L. C. Kolb, *Noyes' Modern Clinical Psychiatry* (7th ed.; Philadelphia: W. B. Saunders Co., 1968), chap. 17.

[52] W. G. Lennox, E. L. Gibbs, and F. A. Gibbs, "Inheritance of Cerebral Dysrhythmia and Epilepsy," *Archives of Neurology and Psychiatry*, XLIV (1940), pp. 1155–83.

of special study by Penfield and Erickson.[53] In certain cases of epilepsy it can be shown that the attacks always begin with excessive neuronal discharge in a particular region of the brain, spreading from there to involve the cerebrum as a whole. This form of the disorder is called "focal epilepsy" in contrast to the many cases in which no local point of origin can be detected. Focal epilepsy sometimes permits surgical intervention with removal of the offending tissues, an operation for which Penfield and his associates became famous. The first step in locating the focal point is to make a careful study of the aura, which is actually a part of the attack even though it precedes the loss of consciousness. If the aura always contains certain sensations or motor actions, this constitutes presumptive evidence for a focus in the corresponding sensory or motor area of the cortex. If there are repetitive dream-like images in the aura the temporal lobes are likely to be involved. The second step in the search is to refine the location by means of the EEG. The electrodes are placed on different parts of the head until the spot is found that most regularly yields an abnormal record. If these steps point to a fairly circumscribed area—which is by no means always the case—a direct investigation of the cortex is made. Under local anaesthesia a flap of bone and skin is cut and turned back, exposing the suspected area. It is then possible to explore by means of electrical stimulation until the precise spot is found that produces an aura, if not actually a convulsion, and the pathological tissues can be examined and removed.

In these focal cases there is pretty certain to be evidence of an old injury, very likely the consequence of some internal mishap such as a hemorrhage rather than a trauma from outside. In the area of injury part of the tissues will be dead, but dead tissues are not responsible for fits. Penfield and Erickson often found that the crucial tissues were those on the edge of a dead area, alive but insufficiently supplied with blood to permit normal functioning. They proposed the hypothesis that these nerve cells suffered from anemia "due to periodic impairment of blood flow through one or other of the small local blood vessels," and that a certain degree of anemia is "irritative in the sense that greater activity occurs in local neurones." [54] Perhaps there is an analogy here to the frantic struggle of a drowning man or of a person partly asphyxiated; the deprived cells, struggling to stay live, fire with everything they have. However this may be, the hypothesis has virtue in explaining the facts discovered about epilepsies with a highly focalized point of origin in the cortex. Excessive discharge in one area can eventually overload the whole system and provoke the generalized over-discharge that constitutes the seizure.

What we do not know, of course, is whether this hypothesis can be ex-

53 W. Penfield and T. C. Erickson, *Epilepsy and Cerebral Localization* (Springfield, Ill.: Charles C Thomas, 1941).
54 *Ibid.*, pp. 198–99.

tended to encompass the commoner cases in which no local starting point for the convulsive seizures can be detected. Recent evidence suggests that there may be widespread small areas of injury with constricted blood supply, but the possibility remains open that dysrhythmic overdischarge by cerebral neurones can also result from other conditions.[55]

Psychological Aspects

The influence of psychogenic factors seems to be distinctly secondary in epilepsy. It is true that the individual attack is often precipitated by a situation involving emotional stress, but stress cannot be considered a primary cause. The claim once advanced that there is a characteristic epileptic personality type has not received convincing research support.[56] Furthermore, some of the traits often mentioned in this connection, such as distractibility and inattentiveness, sound like those of minimal brain dysfunction, while others can be readily understood as reactions to handicapping illness. Having an affliction so overwhelming and meaningless is not conducive to taking life in a calm and joyous spirit. Especially if the patient has grand mal attacks, he knows that every so often he is likely to pass into a state of unconsciousness which is terrifying to others, which makes people want to avoid him, which precludes the holding of most jobs and such activities as driving a car—in short, which handicaps him severely in leading a satisfactory life. That a person should become morose and oversensitive under such circumstances, that he should appear self-centered, emotionally shallow, a little antagonistic toward others, is a most natural outcome of his psychological situation.

Treatment of Epilepsy

Although the surgical procedures used by Penfield and others are often successful when there is a highly focalized cortical lesion, it is obvious that they cannot be used with the majority of epileptic patients. Early efforts at treatment took the form of diets and medication that had been shown to reduce the frequency of seizures. Starting about thirty years ago, good results began to be obtained with phenobarbital, with dilantin sodium, and with a combination of the two. Very great improvement can often be obtained by means of these drugs, and the recently burgeoning research with new drugs now gives the physician a considerable choice of medications that can be adapted to individual needs.[57] In many cases seizures can be suppressed entirely, in others brought to a degree of control that greatly reduces the interference with normal living. Proper medication

[55] F. C. Redlich and D. X. Freedman, *The Theory and Practice of Psychiatry* (New York: Basic Books, Inc., 1966), chap. 18.

[56] B. Tizard, "The Personality of Epileptics: A Discussion of the Evidence," *Psychological Bulletin,* LIX (1962), pp. 196–210.

[57] Kolb, *op. cit.,* chap. 17.

can give to a substantial proportion of epileptics, probably 75 per cent, the chance to lead satisfactory lives, with no marked intellectual handicaps at school or occupational impairments in adulthood.

Psychological treatment can be an important adjunct, though obviously not with the goal of curing the brain condition. In the first place, it can be helpful in reducing conflicts and tensions in general, and this in itself is sometimes found to diminish the frequency and severity of seizures. In the second place, it can help the patient to work out the worst of his anxiety and resentment over the fact of being handicapped, enabling him to meet his frustrations with something closer to equanimity. In the third place, it can help him to overcome the warping that may have occurred in his development through the bewilderment and anxiety of his parents. Cobb cited the case of a young man of 17 who had suffered from convulsive seizures since infancy. His father, disgusted with him, was morosely uncompanionable, and his mother was so oversolicitous that she became practically his jailer. Social experience and a feeling of independence were simply absent, and it became the task of therapy to encourage and watch over these developments as they belatedly occurred. Medically the patient progressed to the point of having no more than occasional petit mal attacks; "socially he became a changed human being." [58]

MENTAL CHANGES AND DISORDERS OF OLD AGE

One person out of five entering a mental hospital suffers from a disorder associated with old age. The frequency of such disorders is steadily increasing. This is an indirect consequence of the general advance of medical science. As fewer people die of such disease as tuberculosis, diphtheria, and pneumonia, more survive into their sixties and seventies when senile changes begin to take place. It is to be expected that this trend will continue. If medicine succeeds in conquering such enemies as cancer and heart disease, an even greater part of the population will live into their seventies. In 1850 only 2.6 per cent of the population lived beyond 65; in 1950, 7.6 per cent exceeded that age. Whether this will mean a steadily increasing incidence of senile mental disorders depends upon our ability to understand and alleviate these afflictions of later life. The senile psychoses can be looked upon as exaggerated forms of the changes that are inseparable from aging. Some of these changes are bodily, others are psychological. We shall first consider the normal course of change with advancing years, thus establishing a background for the understanding of senile disorders.

58 S. Cobb, *Borderlands of Psychiatry* (Cambridge: Harvard University Press, 1943), pp. 112–13. For a systematic account see C. Bagley, *The Social Psychology of the Epileptic Child* (Coral Gables: University of Miami Press, 1967).

The Decline of Abilities

As age advances, there is a marked decline of physical energy. One after another the more vigorous forms of physical exertion have to be avoided. Even for a person who takes his physical limitations good-naturedly, it is hard to avoid a feeling of growing helplessness. The decrease in motor capacity is matched by a weakening of sensory acuity. Less sharpness both in vision and hearing is characteristic of the older years. There is also a decline in the speed of response. Studies of reaction time show a steady decrease, beginning in the second or third decades of life, and proceeding at a faster rate in the later decades. There are wide individual differences, but the general trend is clear. An older person registers his environment less keenly, responds to it less quickly, and is able to respond in less varied and energetic ways.

A similar decline is observed in those functions that are measured by intelligence tests. This is partly but not wholly a function of speed. In tests where speed is not important the decrease is less marked but still present. Not all types of performance are equally affected. Tests of vocabulary and tests of general information show the smallest losses with advancing years, whereas tests requiring ingenuity in new performances are particularly vulnerable. The effects of age may be markedly resisted in the case of knowledge and skills that continue in active use. Thus an elderly scholar who keeps steadily at work may show a minimum of impairment in his special field of expertness, remembering details in a way that startles younger people who do not share his interest in the field. There are also great individual differences in the amount of loss; plenty of people in their eighties, and a few in their nineties, remain keen and productive. Nevertheless, intellectual competence undergoes on the average a definite decline comparable to the falling off of sensory and physical prowess.[59] There is evidence that the decline is associated with a variety of more direct signs of impairment in cerebral function.[60]

Failing memory is one of the most obvious symptoms of aging. The inability to remember names is often extremely frustrating to the person himself. Although tests of rote memory do not show much impairment until after the age of eighty, the assimilation of memories and the power to act upon them appear to decline somewhat earlier. It is a generally observed fact that the memory loss of older people is greatest in respect to recent events. They may remember current happenings so poorly as to seem almost disoriented, yet remain completely clear about the earlier events of their lives, even of their childhood. There is no fully satisfactory

[59] D. Wechsler, *The Measurement and Appraisal of Adult Intelligence* (4th ed.; Baltimore: Williams and Wilkins Co., 1958); J. Botwinick, *Cognitive Processes in Maturity and Old Age* (New York: Springer Publishing Co., 1967).

[60] H. S. Wang, W. D. Obrist, and E. W. Busse, "Neurophysiological Correlates of the Intellectual Function of Elderly Persons Living in the Community," *American Journal of Psychiatry*, CXXVI (1970), pp. 1205–12.

explanation for this fact, which is also found in cases of brain deterioration caused by general paresis and chronic alcoholism. It is possible that attention and initial registration are more at fault than recall. In any event the net result is a weakening of memory, especially for recent and current happenings.

The decline of abilities can be measured at even more basic levels than those just discussed. Behind the weakening physical and mental capacity it is possible to conceive of a more generalized impairment which affects the cells of all tissues, including those in the central nervous system. In old tissues there is an increase of inert material, chiefly fibrin and collagen. This inert material surrounds many cells and simply by mechanical blocking impairs the delivery of oxygen and nutrient materials to the still active or metabolizing cells. There is, furthermore, a diminution of the number of functioning cells in older tissues. In addition, the flow of blood may be less adequate and regular, especially if the artery walls have hardened and thickened. The result of these changes is to interfere with normal cellular metabolism. Changes of this kind probably affect the cells of the body but are of especial importance for those in the central nervous system. Reviewing a large amount of evidence from research, Hicks and Birren conclude that deterioration in lower brain centers, rather than in the cortex itself, best explains at least the psychomotor slowing that occurs in old age.[61]

The effect of this general lowering of cellular efficiency is an increasing difficulty in maintaining homeostasis. The body becomes less capable of maintaining the constancy of its internal environment and has to work harder to achieve this goal. Reserve capacities and emergency reactions must be drawn upon more freely, leaving less surplus energy for other activities. Stress continues to occur, and a greater proportion of available energy has to be devoted to restoring equilibrium. If we consider the maintaining of homeostasis as the first demand on any organism, it becomes clear that a general restriction will necessarily be felt in all activities not directly concerned with that central demand.

Psychosocial Situation of the Aged

When family units are large, as is still the case in some societies and perhaps in rural areas generally, older people remain in the family circle. Grandparents continue to play an essential though reduced part in the life of the family. The situation is different in the small urban family unit which at least in the United States is rapidly becoming the standard pattern. The family unit typically consists of but one pair of parents and their children, and a grandparent living in the home is quite generally felt to be a burdensome intrusion. Many older people face the alternative

[61] L. H. Hicks and J. E. Birren, "Aging, Brain Damage, and Psychomotor Slowing," *Psychological Bulletin,* LXXIV (1970), pp. 377–96.

of being an unwelcome visitor in the household of one of their children or of living by themselves in restricted and lonely circumstances. In either case they are likely to feel themselves useless and superfluous. Whereas in simpler times grandfather might putter around the farm with relatively useful results, he is now more likely to be distinctly retired and out of a job. If grandmother wants to help in the kitchen or with the children, she is likely to be told that her ideas on psychology are old-fashioned and that she must be careful not to break the kitchen appliances. The fact that our times are rapidly changing has the effect of decreasing the utility of older people. The wisdom of the aged is less wise in a time of rapid change.

A second feature of our society that tends to create problems for older people is its powerful "accent on youth." The young do not want to look middle-aged, but the middle-aged want to look young, and they spend millions of dollars every year trying to create this illusion. In this cultural climate the old tend to be pushed aside much as used to be the case with mentally defective children. For reasons both technological and cultural, old people have thus dropped out of a position of significance in their society. They are likely to be treated with condescension, even by youthful psychologists and social workers bent on helping them to adjust. Small wonder that senior citizens, when asked what they want, say that they would like a voice in their own retirement and that they want somehow to remain an active part of the community, doing some kind of purposeful and productive work. They do not want to be put away on a shelf.[62]

Old age thus involves for many people a variety of serious threats. Sometimes it is necessary to move to a new home in a new neighborhood, producing a sense of isolation from friends and old associations. If the older people remain in the same home, the situation is only relatively better. They are likely to experience loss of friends by death, and they are not in a good position to make new ones. For those who have had regular outside employment, retirement may bring a shrinking of both agreeable interactions with others and a sense of personal significance. The desire to be loved and valued may encounter the further frustration that younger people are often impatient with the limitations of the elderly. The difference in tempo alone can be irritating. To wait for slow movement, slow speech, slow comprehension can indeed be frustrating, and such surface irritations may obstruct the expression of liking and esteem. Failure of communication between young and old can be caused also by the difference in time perspective. In youth, most of life lies ahead; the future may be unformulated, but many splendid achievements are within the range of possibility. Young people have little interest in hearing how things used to be before they were born, especially if there is some sugges-

62 J. E. W. Wallin, "The Psychological, Educational, and Social Problems of the Aging as Viewed by a Mid-Octogenarian," *Journal of Genetic Psychology,* C (1962), pp. 41–46.

tion that things have ever since been going to the dogs. An older person's life is mostly behind him. What he has achieved and what he has become as a person are both matters of history, capable of no further change. What sometimes appears to be an obstinate conservatism can represent a determined effort to preserve self-respect by reaffirming the worth of what one has done and valued.

Attempting to conceptualize the over-all direction of change in later life, Cumming and Henry have described it as a process of disengagement.[63] The older person deals with his own diminished resources by disengaging himself from the commitments and social activities that were central earlier in his life. There is "a realignment of the relation of inner events to outer events in such a manner that the former take on an increasing centrality, that interiority becomes increasingly important." The older person becomes less shaped by social expectations, more like "his own inner events, the sameness and continuity of which now have every opportunity to be maximized." [64] But the generality of this formula has been challenged. As Kastenbaum puts it, "the basic problem for the aging individual is how to find meaning and satisfaction in life as he becomes increasingly less able to keep everything going at once." [65] There are a great many different ways of meeting this challenge, ways determined both by the external situation and by individual adaptive patterns. Here as elsewhere, allowance must be made for human diversity.

Before considering disordered responses to the problems of aging, we should notice that many people succeed in growing old gracefully, usefully, and happily. In a study of men and women over 65 in a midwestern community, it was found that 75 per cent considered themselves happy, 79 per cent considered themselves healthy, only 6 per cent were homebound, and many were continuing to lead a fairly active life.[66] In another study, of men close to and after retirement, several different ways were observed of achieving a satisfactory life.[67] The pattern rated most successful by the observers, who labelled it *mature,* represented a nice balance between maintaining an active, interested life and accepting inevitable limitations. "People ought to take their age for granted," said one of these men; "they're not young any more. If people call me an old goat, I just laugh and say, 'Well, I am an old goat!' " [68] Characteristically, self-respect was not shaken by becoming old; the men partici-

[63] E. Cumming and W. Henry, *Growing Old* (New York: Basic Books, Inc., 1961).

[64] W. Henry, in R. Kastenbaum, ed., *Contributions to the Psychobiology of Aging* (New York: Springer Publishing Co., 1965), pp. 19–36.

[65] Kastenbaum, *ibid.,* p. 17.

[66] R. J. Havighurst and R. Albrecht, *Older People* (London: Longmans, Green & Co., Ltd., 1953).

[67] S. Reichard, F. Livson, and P. G. Peterson, *Aging and Personality* (New York: John Wiley & Sons, Inc., 1962).

[68] *Ibid.,* p. 127.

pated appropriately in the life around them and enjoyed having more time to see friends and pursue hobbies. For another group of men contentment was reached quite differently. The *rocking-chair* pattern was favored by relatively passive, dependent men who tended to lean on others. "Unambitious men who found little satisfaction in work, they were glad to take it easy when retirement came." Said one of these subjects, "I'm not dissatisfied with the way I've lived my life. Of course, my success hasn't been great compared to some people that I know of, but it takes care of my tastes and my habits and those of my wife." [69] For this group, happiness was found in the opportunity to sit and talk and enjoy freedom from pressure. A third group, which the observers chose to call *armored*, found their contentment in continuing, perhaps a little strenuously, to be active after retirement. There was latent anxiety in these men about becoming helpless and dependent, but this was successfully counteracted by finding a part-time job or by self-initiated projects such as repairing the house, thus continuing the satisfaction involved in being busy. The elderly continue to be individuals who deal with their problems not in some standard fashion, but in their own particular ways.

Old age nevertheless has its difficulties, both psychological and somatic, and it can give rise to various forms of disordered personal behavior.

Neurotic Tendencies

Sometimes the inherent threats connected with aging are met by neurotic reactions. The two most common forms are *hypochondria* and *reactive depression*.[70] The realistic basis for hypochondria lies in the actual aches, pains, and ailments that become more frequent in later years. Concern with health is natural, but when it becomes preoccupying, so that the person thinks and talks of little else, restricts himself unduly, and cannot stop pestering his physician, the behavior has the overdriven character that suggests neurotic anxiety and defense. Conceivably, worry about health in such cases acts to divert and conceal worries about isolation, boredom, dependence, and crumbling self-esteem. Fancied ill health can also serve as an excuse for not taking initiatives that come harder as the years go by. Depressions in older people are often rather clearly connected with events that entail loss. They are doubtless made more common by the time perspective of the later years: losses are final, unlikely to be compensated, and improved conditions are hardly to be expected. Therapeutic goals in treating such cases must be modest, but the therapist's interest may somewhat repair self-esteem and his encouragement may help the patient to resume interest and participation in whatever is still possible.

---

[69] *Ibid.*, pp. 129, 135.

[70] E. W. Busse, "Psychoneurotic Reactions and Defense Mechanisms in the Aged," in P. H. Hoch and J. Zubin, eds., *Psychopathology of Aging* (New York: Grune & Stratton, Inc., 1961), chap. 16.

Senile Psychoses

When a chronic mental disorder occurs in an elderly person and is accompanied by signs of mental deterioration, it is called either senile psychosis or senile dementia. Both terms are in a way correct. These conditions are really a combination of senile deterioration with special reactions that still further increase the loss of contact with reality. Depressed states, agitated states, delirious and confused states, or paranoid reactions may add themselves to the general picture of impairment. The onset is gradual, sometimes almost imperceptible. The patient becomes a little more egocentric and conservative, inefficient and forgetful, sad, disturbed, or suspicious, until it seems to everyone that he can no longer take care of himself outside the hospital. Perhaps forgetfulness crosses the line into confusion: he goes for a walk and cannot find his way home. Perhaps querulous complaints about his food and digestion slip over into delusions that his daughter-in-law is trying to poison him. Sometimes a physical illness or some situational stress marks the boundary a little more sharply. Perhaps the family home has to be sold and the old person moved to new surroundings. Sickness or ailments of a lasting sort may suddenly restrict the range of available activities. In all such cases the person is called upon rather suddenly to make a whole series of readjustments, and he proves unequal to the strain. But deterioration has been in progress and the onset is never really sudden.

Senile patients are apt to be restless and sleepless. Often they wander in the night and at such times are likely to be particularly confused. Irritation is frequent, judgment is poor, attention is erratic, and the registration of impressions decidedly irregular. On top of this general picture of impairment go the depressed, agitated, or paranoid reactions. As the disorder advances, intellectual deficit increasingly dominates the picture. Speech becomes rambling and incoherent, and failing memory may be pieced out with fabrications. The patient may fail to recognize his relatives. In the course of time, episodes of confusion, occasionally with hallucinations, occur with greater frequency. Social amenities and courtesy are preserved almost to the last, but the end point is a state of helplessness and vegetation in which the patient becomes oblivious to his surroundings. It is obvious that not much can be done for senile patients except to make them comfortable, keep them in physical health, provide occupations that are within their powers, and protect them from unnecessary difficulties.

The changes in the brain that underlie senile psychoses are of a degenerative character the causes of which are not fully understood. Autopsy findings include a general shrinkage of brain tissue, a reduction in the number of nerve cells, and a thickening in the intercellular tissues. All the changes are diffuse; they are not concentrated in any one spot sufficiently to alter the cortical architecture. The signs of degeneration are not peculiar to senile psychoses, being found with lesser severity in normal older people and with greater severity in Alzheimer's and Pick's diseases.[71]

Psychoses with Cerebral Arteriosclerosis

When there is a considerable degree of arteriosclerosis, the changes in the brain are of a more devastating character. Hardening and thickening of the walls of the blood vessels, including not only the large arteries but also the small arterioles and capillaries, reduces the supply of blood to all tissues. The effect of this reduction is especially serious in the brain, where the tissues are peculiarly dependent on an adequate supply of oxygen and nutrient materials. The brains of arteriosclerotic patients at autopsy show a variety of severe focal lesions in which the cerebral structure is completely destroyed, although surrounding nervous tissue may be in a state of good preservation. Softened and disintegrated tissue is found at the points of lesion. The temporal and occipital areas seem to be particularly vulnerable. While the cause of these focal softenings is not definitely known, the best hypothesis seems to be that they occur as a result of restricted blood supply.

There are usually various premonitory symptoms prior to the development of full psychosis. Physical and mental letdown may be noticed, along with headaches and dizziness. In more than half the cases the onset of the acute psychosis is sudden, differing in this respect from senile psychoses. It takes the form of an attack of confusion with clouding of consciousness, incoherence, great restlessness, and complete loss of contact with the environment. The confused state may last for weeks or months. In about half the cases it subsides, leaving the patient with considerable senile impairment but in a much less confused condition. Later attacks are the rule, however, and cure is not to be expected.

The condition of the brain caused by cerebral arteriosclerosis is fairly similar to the condition found in general paresis. The mental changes are of a somewhat similar order. It is therefore interesting to notice certain differences in the content of the symptoms and the psychological processes which they imply. Occasionally there are delusions of grandeur and persecution in psychoses with cerebral arteriosclerosis, but these are far less characteristic and less extravagantly developed than is the case in general paresis. This difference seems to be attributable to the age of the patients, or more directly, to the general level of vitality at which they are living. An old person already physically handicapped and living within shrunken horizons having no perspective toward the future typically becomes confused, perhaps with a touch of depression or agitation, when his brain reaches a point of damage that is no longer consistent with integrated action. A person in middle life, still relatively vigorous, ambitious, with

---

[71] J. E. Birren, *The Psychology of Aging* (Englewood Cliffs, N. J.: Prentice-Hall, Inc., 1964), chap. 11.

considerable strength of drive, reacts to brain damage with symptoms of a more compensatory kind. His thoughts may be delusions, but they are delusions that place him in satisfying and glorious situations or that use the mechanism of projection to free him from any sense of personal shortcoming. Thus even in the study of brain diseases it is impossible to overlook psychological factors, even though these are not responsible for initiating the disorder. The disease happens to the man, and the man puts his stamp on the standard symptoms that result from the disease.

SUGGESTIONS FOR FURTHER READING

For the student who wants to review the anatomy and functions of the nervous system, the concise but clear book by Stanley Cobb is recommended: *Foundations of Neuropsychiatry* (5th ed., Baltimore, The Williams & Wilkins Co., 1952). Most of the disorders taken up in this chapter are described in more technical detail in textbooks of psychiatry such as F. C. Redlich and D. X. Freedman, *The Theory and Practice of Psychiatry* (New York, Basic Books, Inc., 1966) or L. C. Kolb, *Noyes' Modern Clinical Psychiatry* (7th ed., Philadelphia, W. B. Saunders Co., 1968).

The student with a serious interest in the functioning of the brain should familiarize himself with D. O. Hebb's book, *The Organization of Behavior* (New York, John Wiley & Sons, Inc., 1949) in which is constructed a working hypothesis based on the type of facts discussed in this chapter.

Kurt Goldstein's important contributions to the study of brain injury can be gleaned from his chapter, "Functional Disturbances in Brain Damage," in S. Arieti, ed., *American Handbook of Psychiatry* (New York, Basic Books, Inc., 1959), Ch. 39. Probably the best introduction to aphasia is still J. M. Wepman's *Recovery from Aphasia* (New York, The Ronald Press Co., 1951). P. H. Wender's *Minimal Brain Dysfunction in Children* (New York, John Wiley & Sons, Inc., 1971) is a thorough review marked by an enthusiasm for biochemical methods of treatment.

Important historically and still valuable as an introduction are two books on epilepsy: *Science and Seizures* by W. G. Lennox (New York, Harper & Row, 1941), and *Convulsive Seizures* by T. J. Putnam (Philadelphia, J. B. Lippincott Co., 1943). Penfield's work and reflections appear in a large work entitled *Epilepsy and the Functional Anatomy of the Human Brain* by W. Penfield and H. Jasper (Boston, Little, Brown & Co., 1954). The human problems encountered by epileptic children are discussed by C. Bagley, *The Social Psychology of the Epileptic Child* (Coral Gables, University of Miami Press, 1967).

A standard informative work on the problems and disorders of the older years is J. E. Birren, *The Psychology of Aging* (Englewood Cliffs, N. J., Prentice-Hall, Inc., 1964). Commendable for its descriptions of different adaptive patterns is the report by S. Reichard, F. Livson, and P. G. Petersen, *Aging and Personality: A Study of Eighty-Seven Older Men* (New York, John Wiley & Sons, Inc., 1962).

16
Mental Retardation

A first visit to a home for mentally retarded children is likely to be full of surprises. Those who are unfamiliar with the subject have in mind a dismal scene with children sitting around like vegetables, lethargic, expressionless, peculiar looking, and destined to stay there forever. Visitors who in their personal lives have attached great importance to intellectual brilliance may even imagine that the children must be dreadfully unhappy because of their handicap. So it is startling to be greeted at the door by a self-appointed receptionist who, though short of stature, odd of countenance, and husky of voice, takes evident pleasure in making the visitors welcome and showing them around. Looking out the window toward the play yard, the visitors may be further surprised to see three healthy-looking youngsters vigorously engaged in the cooperative task of building a snow fort. Presently a child will be encountered who is not only physically perfect but almost incredibly beautiful; the visitors will be astonished when they learn that this Adonis is incapable of any kind of restraint and happily destroys everything within reach. Elsewhere the face of a somber child may light up responsively with a beatific smile that the visitors will remember with delight for many days. Of course some of the sights are sadder. Some of the children are lethargic, some are unattractive and even deformed, a few give the impression of taking in little of what goes around them. But the visitors are likely to come away with a far less dismal conception of life at the home, and they will have stored up another valuable lesson about the vast range of human individual differences, which show so dramatically even among the mentally retarded.

Having a retarded child is almost inevitably a tragedy for the parents, but it need not be seen in this light for the children. Retardation by no means necessarily interferes with being happy and affectionate or with enjoying life, and one can well argue in our time that a mental horizon too limited to understand the state of the world qualifies as something of a blessing. In the recent past mental retardation, like mental illness, carried undertones of shame and was mentioned as little as possible. It has shared, however, in the recent revolutionary change of attitude. Parents have organized to secure better opportunities for special education, and services for the retarded have won a place in community mental health programs. Retarded children thus stand a better chance than ever before to develop their full potential and make the most of their lives, even though the scale of these lives be small.

Measurement and Varieties of Retardation

A milestone in the history of psychology was established early in this century when Binet devised his first test for the measurement of intelligence. The practical request which prompted this venture was to find some way of sorting out beforehand those school children who could not keep up with their classes. The unprecedented success of Binet's scales led to a close association between intelligence tests and the whole concept of mental retardation. In some places mental retardation was even legally defined as a Binet intelligence quotient of less than 75, and the criterion of the I.Q. was considered sufficient for placement in special classes or in state schools for the feeble minded. The same basis was used in making the division of mental retardation into three grades: mild subnormality (moron) with I.Q. from 69 to 50 and adult mentality on the level of children of eight to twelve years; moderate subnormality (imbecile) with I.Q. from 49 to 20 and mental age of three to seven years; and severe subnormality (idiot) with I.Q. of 19 or less and mental age no higher than two years.

Eventually the flood tide of enthusiasm for the I.Q. began to recede, making possible a more balanced and realistic conception of intelligence. The tests were too much like school tasks and placed too much emphasis on verbal and intellectual skills. They were not always successful in predicting the adequacy of behavior in the practical concerns of everyday life. It was in order to meet this difficulty that Edgar Doll worked for many years to perfect the Vineland Social Maturity Scale.[1] This is a scale to be filled out by observers of the child's daily behavior, and it includes motor performances and social adjustments as well as linguistic development. The criterion of social incapacity can thus be added to the result of tests, and mental retardation comes to have the more reasonable meaning of a lack of "common sense" or of general adaptability. This is reflected in the recent definition of mental retardation by the American Association on Mental Deficiency as "subaverage general intellectual func-

[1] E. A. Doll, *Measurement of Social Competence* (Vineland, N. J.: Educational Publishers, 1953), especially chaps. 1–3.

tioning which originates during the developmental period and is associated with impairment in adaptive behavior." [2] Nowadays it is preferred to classify retarded children more practically in terms of general adaptive potential, as "educable," "trainable," or "totally dependent." [3] An educable child may achieve a fourth- or fifth-grade scholastic level, a moderate level of social adjustment, and a satisfactory degree of self-support through occupations not requiring abstract thought. A trainable child may attain an acceptable level of self-care, social adjustment to home and neighborhood, and a degree of economic usefulness in a home; residential facility, or sheltered workshop. A totally dependent child needs assistance in personal care, makes little adaptation to the environment and usually requires permanent institutionalization.

It has been estimated that over six million people in the United States, i.e., about 3 per cent, are mentally subnormal.[4] However, 4 per cent of the 18–27-year-old men screened for military service in World War II were rejected for intellectual inadequacy.[5] The actual prevalence of subnormality may be even higher than that. By far the largest part of those called mentally subnormal are only mildly retarded. They are clearly educable and capable of leading productive lives. Most of them are classified as cultural-familial because they typically come from families and cultural backgrounds where retardation is common.

About 200,000 retarded individuals reside in institutions, 82 per cent of which are designed for people below the educable or mildly retarded level of intelligence.[6] It has been proposed to reserve the term *mental deficiency* for these more extremely retarded children because their handicaps are more pronounced and are presumably related to brain damage.[7] In such cases there is almost always clear evidence of gross developmental abnormality. Structural defects are apparent both in the nervous system and in other organs. For most of these disorders there is strong evidence against simple inheritance of low intelligence, as in sociocultural retardation; they commonly occur in families of average intelligence and sometimes in the offspring of highly gifted parents. There are several

[2] R. F. Heber, "A Manual on Terminology and Classification in Mental Retardation," *American Journal of Mental Deficiency*, LXIV (1959), Monograph Supplement (rev. ed., 1961).

[3] "Report of the American Medical Association Conference on Mental Retardation," *Journal of the American Medical Association*, CXCI (1965).

[4] H. F. Dingman and G. Tarjan, "Mental Retardation and the National Distribution Curve," *American Journal of Mental Deficiency*, LXIV (1960), pp. 991–94.

[5] E. Ginzberg and D. W. Bray, *The Uneducated* (New York: Columbia University Press, 1953).

[6] M. M. Klaber, "The Retarded and Institutions for the Retarded—A Preliminary Research Report," in S. B. Sarason and J. Doris, *Psychological Problems in Mental Deficiency* (New York: Harper & Row, 1969), p. 148.

[7] H. B. Robinson and N. M. Robinson, *The Mentally Retarded Child* (New York: McGraw-Hill Book Co., 1965), p. 218.

recognized varieties of severe mental deficiency, but most of them occur quite rarely.[8]

In this chapter we shall describe in some detail three illustrative forms of retardation and mention briefly several others to give some impression of the variety of possible causes for mental retardation. The principal illustrations are *mongolism,* a genetic disorder, *phenylketonuria,* a metabolic disorder, and *cultural-familial* retardation, which will introduce us to the effect of sociocultural influences in the development of intelligence.

DOWN'S SYNDROME (MONGOLISM)

Nearly a century ago Langdon Down, a British physician, gave the name of *mongolism* to a form of mental deficiency in which it struck him that the child had the facial characteristics of the Mongolian races. The alleged resemblance is actually found only in the eyes, which especially during the first few years are almost almond shaped and slope upward toward their outer corners. Mongolism is a severe form of mental deficiency in which the trainable level is rarely surpassed. But it is more than a mental deficiency; in view of the many associated physical symptoms, it must be considered a form of general developmental arrest. The whole head is peculiarly shaped, quite flat on the back and with depression of the nasal bridge. The tongue is large and coarsely fissured; in many patients it protrudes from the mouth a good deal of the time. The hands and feet are stubby and square, and there is often a wide separation between the big toe and the other toes. Stature is small for age, the musculature tends to be hypotonic or rubbery, and gait is awkward and shambling. The appearance of mongoloid children is decidedly odd and becomes only more so if they grow to adulthood. Their adjustment to society would be no easy matter even if intelligence were normal.

On post-mortem study, mongoloid brains are found to be clearly abnormal, showing signs of widespread interference with the growth of brain cells. Investigators differ as to how to characterize and explain this defect, but Benda believes that asphyxiation of nerve cells is one of the most important features.[9] He speculates that a metabolic deficiency may prevent the brain cells, as well as other tissues, from developing normally.

Down's syndrome accounts for 10 per cent of the cases institutionalized for mental subnormality.[10] The proportion is undoubtedly smaller among retardates who live at home since mongoloid children usually fall in the lower ranges of ability and are therefore less readily managed at home. A few children with Down's syndrome will advance to the point of master-

[8] For descriptions, see Robinson and Robinson, *ibid.,* chaps. 4–6.
[9] C. E. Benda, *Down's Syndrome* (New York: Grune & Stratton, Inc., 1969), p. 164.
[10] *Ibid.,* p. 6.

ing simple speech and doing simple chores. One study rated only 4 per cent of the mongoloids living at home as educable.[11] More typically, speech is absent or confined to a few hoarsely spoken sounds, and activities consist of rather repetitive play. Despite their limited equipment, mongoloid children are not usually sluggish or unhappy. Institutional workers find them more friendly, happy, and affectionate than other severely handicapped children. A small minority are aggressive and hostile.[12] However, the frequency of emotional disturbance is no greater than in other groups, even of normal children. Menolascino found abnormal EEG tracings in half of his disturbed mongols, suggesting that additional cerebral abnormalities may be responsible for their deviation from the "sunny disposition" stereotype.[13]

Physical health in Down's syndrome is poor. It has been found that 30 per cent die before one month, 53 per cent by one year, and 60 per cent by ten years.[14] Few mongoloids live very far into adulthood. The most common causes of death are bronchopneumonia and congenital heart disease. Noting the high frequency of death by tuberculosis, Down attributed the cause of mongolism to an inherited disposition to tuberculosis.[15] It now appears that having a large tongue protruding from a small mouth induces mouth breathing and susceptibility to all sorts of upper respiratory infections. With the recent discovery of the true cause of the disorder, a basic genetic flaw that is reproduced throughout the body, it is now understandable that such children would be exceptionally vulnerable to physical disease.

The birth rate for Down's syndrome is approximately one in 700 live births. However the rate increases sharply as the age of the mother goes up. For mothers under 25 the risk is less than one in 1,500 births, but it increases to one in 150 births for mothers over 35 and to one in 38 for mothers over 45.[16] There is as yet no certain explanation for this correlation with maternal age. Some workers have pointed out that the diverse physical symptoms of Down's syndrome make a certain sense when one considers them as lying in those organs which undergo crucial differentiation during the second and third months of embryonic life. The foetus with Down's syndrome shows during this period a deceleration of normal development which is not compensated in the later months before birth. It is noteworthy that at precisely this period there is a fairly radical

11 W. L. Wunsch, "Some Characteristics of Mongoloids Evaluated at a Clinic for Children with Retarded Mental Development," *American Journal of Mental Deficiency*, LXII (1957), pp. 122–30.

12 *Ibid.*

13 F. J. Menolascino, "Psychiatric Aspects of Mongolism," *American Journal of Mental Deficiency*, LXIX (1965), pp. 653–60.

14 B. H. Kirman, "The Patient with Down's Syndrome in the Community," *Lancet*, II (1964), pp. 705–14.

15 J. L. Down, "Observations on an Ethnic Classification of Idiots," *London Hospital Reports* (1866).

16 Robinson and Robinson, *op. cit.*, p. 97.

readjustment in the maternal hormone pattern in order to sustain the further development of the foetus. Conceivably in older mothers, near the end of reproductive capacity, hormonal changes give rise to the genetic fault that initiates the mongoloid deviation, though it would seem likely that so fundamental a defect would have its origin earlier in the reproductive cycle.

Genetic Fault

Because of the striking physical abnormalities it has been suspected for a long time that genetic aberrations might cause Down's syndrome. Only recently have the technical means been developed to discern this aberration specifically. One of the great breakthroughs in modern mental health was the discovery in 1959 that the body cells of mongoloid children contain 47 chromosomes rather than the normal 46.[17] In the course of normal reproduction the egg cell from the mother and the sperm cells from the father separately undergo cell division to reduce the chromosome count in each from 46 to 23, so that when the two unite during fertilization the offspring will possess the normal complement of 46 chromosomes, half from each parent. Lejeune and his colleagues found that mongoloid children have three, rather than two, number 21 chromosomes, and labelled this pattern *trisomy 21*. They inferred that the fault lay in the failure of the two chromosomes of pair number 21 to separate (nondisjunction) in the egg cell prior to ovulation. If such an ovum with 24 chromosomes is fertilized by a normal sperm with 23 chromosomes, the offspring with 47 chromosomes will be mongoloid. It is possible that the extra chromosome could come from the father. In the fruit fly, however, nondisjunction is greatly influenced by maternal aging, and considering the correlation between maternal age and mongoloid birth rate, it seems most likely that the egg bears the extra chromosome. It is still not known precisely what causes the faulty maturation of the egg.

Down's syndrome caused by nondisjunction is very rarely familial. It is a *genetic* disorder but not an *inherited* one, because the reproductive error produces a genetic makeup unlike that of the parents. There is a rare form of Down's syndrome, about 4 per cent of all cases, that can be inherited. On the whole, however, parents of a mongoloid child need not fear passing on a genetic liability through their normal children, and if they are still young and want to have more children they are usually advised to do so.

Treatment

Children with Down's syndrome are not destined for substantial improvements in intelligence. Thyroid and other medications produce no

[17] J. Lejeune, M. Gautier, and R. Turpin, "Le Mongolisme: Premier Exemple d'Aberration Autosomique Humaine," *Annales Genetiques*, I (1959), p. 41.

more than a slight improvement in general alertness. For a while great hopes were entertained for glutamic acid, which seemed to produce an immediate rise in the I.Q.'s of mongoloid and other severely deficient children. Some workers believe that these gains are genuine and lasting, though others are quite skeptical; in any event the gains are simply not large enough to make any real change in the patients' prospects.[18] This is understandable in the light of the genetic etiology, which is probably irreversible.

Most children with Down's syndrome are placed in institutions at an early age and live out the remainder of their lives there. However, Sarason and Doris [19] offer a spirited critique of "instant institutionalization" unless it is medically necessary (e.g., when the child has congenital heart defects) or otherwise required by social considerations. In increasing numbers families have decided to raise the children at home. The decision is fraught with difficulty. Probably it is better for the child to be at home, but the parents may overestimate their own capacity to be tied down by continuous intensive care, and the effects on their normal children may be far from desirable. If they decide for home rearing, they will do well to seek such help as can be obtained from community mental health agencies.

It is possible that the recent genetic discoveries will lead eventually to prevention. Experiments in progress are aimed at securing a chromosome count in tissue samples taken from the foetus. If this technique should become practicable, therapeutic abortion could be recommended to prevent the birth of a child with Down's syndrome.

PHENYLKETONURIA (PKU)

Phenylketonuria is a rare form of mental retardation. It occurs about once in 10,000 live births [20] and accounts for about one per cent of the cases in institutions for the retarded.[21] However, it has great theoretical significance because it is one of the most thoroughly understood forms of retardation, it can be effectively treated if discovered early, and it serves as a prototype for investigating a whole class of metabolic disorders that have been discovered recently.

PKU was first recognized in 1934 by Asbjorn Følling, a Norwegian biochemist and physician, when the parents of two retarded children brought

18 F. T. Zimmerman and B. B. Burgemeister, "Permanency of Glutamic Acid Treatment," *Archives of Neurology and Psychiatry,* LXV (1951), pp. 291–98; A. P. Astin and S. Ross, "Glutamic Acid and Human Intelligence," *Psychological Bulletin,* LVII (1960), pp. 429–34.

19 Sarason and Doris, *op. cit.,* pp. 378–81.

20 Robinson and Robinson, *op. cit.,* p. 109.

21 R. Heber, *Epidemiology of Mental Retardation* (Springfield, Ill.: Charles C Thomas, 1970), p. 62.

to his attention a musty odor in the urine of both children. Upon chemical analysis he ascertained that the odor was caused by phenylpyruvic acid, which was excreted in the urine because the children lacked a basic enzyme that is necessary to metabolize phenylalanine, an amino acid. Surveys of institutions for the retarded in several countries turned up many other cases and quickly made it clear that the disorder is transmitted genetically in recessive Mendelian fashion. It has been estimated that one person in 100 carries the gene,[22] but more recent prevalence figures would indicate that carriers may number twice that many. A retarded child results only when one carrier mates with another carrier, which accounts for the fortunately low prevalence of the disorder. However, the risk increases considerably when relatives marry because if one mate carries the gene the other is more likely to carry it also. The danger is highest, of course, in any family which already has a phenylketonuric child; this constitutes clear evidence that the gene is carried on both sides of the family. One in four siblings of a child with PKU will also predictably have the disorder.

Nearly all affected children are blond and blue-eyed with fair skin that is susceptible to eczema. They usually are of small stature and have rather small heads. Their teeth are broad and widely spaced. Their reflexes are accentuated and they may be somewhat humpbacked, which causes them to move and walk peculiarly. Sometimes they sweat excessively. About 90 per cent of untreated cases develop severe or moderate mental retardation, which is probably associated with the degenerative changes in the brain found on autopsy. Recent studies of PKU infants have found the most common symptoms to be vomiting, eczema, urine odor, irritability, and unpredictable behavior like rocking movements, grinding of teeth, arm waving, and over-all aimless behavior; several of these lead to occasional misdiagnosis as early childhood schizophrenia.[23] PKU children usually enjoy good physical health and many are quite attractive in facial appearance, which is unusual in severe forms of retardation.

The most telling symptom is still the presence of phenylpyruvic acid in the urine. Very simple tests with ferric chloride reveal the presence of the acid, usually in the first few weeks of life. However, in some cases the acid may not be detected in the urine until as late as five weeks. Early detection is vital to early treatment and to genetic counseling regarding future pregnancies. More complicated and expensive tests can be made for excessive phenylalanine in the blood serum after the fifth or sixth day of life, even before the infant leaves the newborn nursery. In this way siblings of known PKU victims or the offspring of two known carriers of the gene can be monitored carefully from birth onward for signs of the disease. Several states in this country now sponsor massive screening pro-

[22] L. S. Penrose, *The Biology of Mental Defect* (3rd ed.; New York: Grune & Stratton, Inc., 1963), p. 154.
[23] R. Koch, P. Acosta, K. Fishler, G. Schaeffler, and A. Wohlers, "Clinical Observations on Phenylketonuria," *American Journal of Diseases of Children,* CXIII (1967), pp. 6–15.

grams in hospitals[24] and through routine pediatric follow-up. It is possible (though not yet foolproof) to identify carriers of the recessive gene by feeding them very large amounts of phenylalanine and measuring how fast it disappears from the blood.[25]

Dietary Control

The reason so much attention has been concentrated on diagnosing PKU early is that proper dietary control may greatly lessen or prevent altogether the damaging effects of the metabolic error.[26] Special diet preparations are now available which contain all the necessary nutrients and the minimum essential amount of phenylalanine. The synthetic foods are supplemented with natural foods of low phenylalanine content and sufficient milk to prevent blood levels of phenylalanine from falling too low; if that happens the child's growth and neurological development are impaired in another way. Like most amino acids, some phenylalanine is vital for growth.

Dietary treatment should begin as early as possible because the ultimate I.Q. a child attains is very highly correlated ($r = .67$) with age at which treatment is begun.[27] Knox estimated an average I.Q. loss of nearly five I.Q. points for each ten weeks' delay in treatment. Improvements in intellectual levels are dramatic for most children if treatment begins early, and many attain normal I.Q.'s. It appears that all of the intellectual damage is done during the first two or three years, when brain development is most rapid. Therefore dietary treatment can be discontinued after about six years of age.[28] Apparently, after that point the central nervous system is sufficiently mature to tolerate the elevated phenylalanine levels without further damage or intellectual deterioration. The special diet may also result in behavioral improvement for older children without previous treatment, but I.Q. gains are very limited.

Finding ways to limit the transmission of a recessive gene would meet enormous practical and ethical obstacles. First it would be necessary to identify all of the unaffected carriers of the gene, who may number over four million in the United States alone. Naturally such screening could omit all people over or under the child-bearing age, but that would still

[24] R. Guthrie and S. Whitney, "Phenylketonuria Detection in the Newborn Infant as a Routine Hospital Procedure," U.S. Department of Health, Education and Welfare, Children's Bureau, Publ. No. 419 (1964; rev. 1965).

[25] D. Y. Hsia, K. W. Driscoll, W. Troll, and W. E. Knox, "Detection by Phenylalanine Tolerance Tests of Heterozygous Carriers of Phenylketonuria," Nature, CLXXVIII (1956), p. 1239; H. Berry, B. Sutherland, and G. M. Guest, "Phenylalanine Tolerance Tests on Relatives of Phenylketonuric Children," American Journal of Human Genetics, IX (1957), pp. 310–16.

[26] Robinson and Robinson, op. cit., pp. 110–11.

[27] W. E. Knox, "An Evaluation of the Treatment of Phenylketonuria with Diets Low in Phenylalanine," Journal of Pediatrics, XXVI (1960), p. 1–11.

[28] Sarason and Doris, op. cit., pp. 352–53.

leave tens of millions of Americans to be tested. With present techniques that would be exorbitantly expensive. However it is conceivable that in the next few years the screening procedures will be streamlined enough to permit a PKU carrier test for all couples who apply for a marriage license, in the same way that the Wasserman test for syphilis is now required. How would the knowledge of those results be utilized to help eliminate PKU? Presumably, a couple that learned they were both carriers of the recessive gene might find the 25 per cent risk of conceiving a defective child was too great and decide to adopt children instead. But by what logic would society impose that decision on them if they were unwilling? Or consider the less threatening case of a carrier marrying a noncarrier. Could society justify prohibiting that couple from procreating, merely on the ground that this would perpetuate a latent potential for the disorder in subsequent generations?

It seems clear that such a eugenic program would not be tolerated. We are left with the prospect of living with the latent threat. But fortunately we are not without some tools to cope with phenylketonuria in its manifest form. It is already feasible now to identify most infants with the disorder, at modest cost, by means of the ferric chloride urine test and/ or the Guthrie blood serum test. Once identified, the severe effects of the disorder can be limited in most cases by careful dietary treatment during the first few years of life. And in the not too distant future, with improved actuarial and technical procedures, it may be possible to carry out the pedigree studies necessary to pinpoint the matings and the childbirths that require the closest surveillance.

CULTURAL–FAMILIAL RETARDATION

Only 4 per cent of the retarded reside in institutions; the rest live at home.[29] By far the largest part of these are only mildly retarded. Most are capable of some self-care and may be able to work. There is seldom evidence for gross structural defect in the brain. The majority do not have an abnormal electroencephalogram (EEG) and do not, if they come to autopsy, show distinctive peculiarities in cerebral tissues. On psychological tests they do not make the sort of performance errors that are characteristic of brain-injured patients. In contrast to Down's syndrome and phenylketonuria, no single somatic agent is presumed to cause this sort of retardation. Affected children are normal in physical appearance, health, and longevity. We shall here use the term *cultural-familial retardation* to cover this milder form of backwardness. The diagnosis is usually made when the child enters school and often is dropped when

[29] "Report of the American Medical Association Conference on Mental Retardation," *op. cit.*, p. 67.

he leaves, suggesting that intellectual retardation is more conspicuous than deficiencies in social adaptation. The real trouble is that the child is slow in schoolwork and seems perhaps a little dull in general understanding.

These children usually do not differ much from their parents in I.Q. We might infer that they are simply inheriting limited intellectual capacities, a fact no more startling than that the children of gifted intellectual people tend to be bright. The prevalence of retardation is greatest for the nearest relatives of retarded persons.[30] This could signify that the milder forms of retardation are a consequence of polygenic inheritance. Although no single dominant or recessive gene accounts for the inheritance of intelligence in general, it is now believed that a number of related genes in combination do so. This conception of the genetic aspect would lead us to expect that if two itinerant farm hands or two slum dwellers of limited intelligence produce offspring, their children will likewise be of limited intelligence.[31] Just as bright parents have bright children, dull parents have dull children—so goes the strictly genetic reasoning.

Recent studies of intelligence, however, put the question in a somewhat different light. Expressed in a nutshell, these studies show that intelligence, as measured at any point, depends significantly on past experience and past stimulation; whatever the natural potential, it has to be developed by exercise.[32] This means that environment plays a part in what we refer to as level of intelligence. New significance at once appears in the fact that mildly retarded children come so often from families with poor education living in depressed neighborhoods. To quote from a national report on retardation:

Epidemiological data from many reliable studies show a remarkably heavy correlation between the incidence of mental retardation, particularly in its milder manifestations, and the adverse social, economic, and cultural status of families and groups of our population. These are for the most part the low income groups—who often live in the slums and are frequently minority groups—where the mother and the children receive inadequate medical care, where family breakdown is common, where individuals are without motivation and opportunity and without adequate education. In short, the conditions which spawn many other health and social problems are to a large extent the same ones which generate the problems of mental retardation. To be successful in preventing mental retardation on a large scale, a broad attack on the fundamental adverse conditions will be necessary.[33]

30 E. W. Reed and S. C. Reed, *Mental Retardation* (Philadelphia: W. B. Saunders Co., 1965), p. 31.

31 A. Jensen, "How Much Can We Boost IQ and Scholastic Achievement?" *Harvard Educational Review*, XXXIX (1969), pp. 1–123.

32 J. McV. Hunt, *Intelligence and Experience* (New York: The Ronald Press Co., 1961); see also his *The Challenge of Incompetence and Poverty* (Urbana: University of Illinois Press, 1969).

33 The President's Panel on Mental Retardation, *A Proposed Program for National Action to Combat Mental Retardation* (Washington, D.C.: Government Printing Office, 1962), pp. 9–10.

Sociocultural Deprivation

The adverse social conditions mentioned above are those commonly associated with poverty as Miller lists them: "economic privation, social and economic discrimination, inadequate and overcrowded housing, substandard nutrition, low parental education attainment, unskilled laboring vocations, usually large families, and often, minority group membership." [34] That they are related to mental retardation is shown in estimates of retarded intelligence at various socioeconomic class levels. Over 11 per cent of children in the lowest class (of five) have I.Q.'s below 75, as compared with 4 per cent in the middle class and less than one per cent in the highest class.[35] Similarly, over 25 per cent of black men were excused from military service in World War II because of deficient intelligence, as compared with less than 3 per cent of white men.[36]

Sociocultural deprivation contributes to mental retardation in two physical ways: birth complications and malnutrition. Obstetrical mishaps are disproportionately frequent among the economically disadvantaged, and the incidence of mental retardation is significantly greater when pregnancy or delivery are complicated. Consider, for example, some facts concerning premature births. Substantially more premature babies are born to lower-class parents than to middle- or upper-class parents.[37] Incidence of physical and mental abnormalities increases as birth weight decreases. On Gesell developmental examinations at forty weeks after birth, 17.6 per cent of very small babies were judged to be retarded or borderline in intellectual potential, as compared with 1.8 per cent of the moderately small babies and 1.6 per cent of the control babies with average birth weight.[38] It is clear that mental retardation is more common among deprived classes because they have more premature births, which in turn is explained by a number of interrelated circumstances. They have more pregnancies at a very early age, inadequate and tardy prenatal medical care, small maternal stature, and poor nutrition and general health.

Malnutrition is a common condition in the large rural areas of the southeastern United States, in crowded urban slums, and especially where the black population is large. Women in these areas have diets that are poor, especially in the proteins that are essential for the development of the central nervous system. They also have the highest rates of congenital malformations in their children, particularly those affecting the central

34 J. O. Miller, "Cultural Deprivation and Its Modification: Effect of Intervention," in H. C. Haywood, ed., Socio-Cultural Aspects of Mental Retardation (New York: Appleton-Century-Crofts, 1970), p. 457.

35 Heber, Epidemiology of Mental Retardation, op. cit., p. 17.

36 Ginzberg and Bray, op. cit., p. 43.

37 Heber, Epidemiology of Mental Retardation, op. cit., pp. 91–99.

38 H. Knobloch, R. Rider, P. Harper, and B. Pasamanick, "Neuropsychiatric Sequelae of Prematurity: A Longitudinal Study," Journal of the American Medical Association, CLXI (1956), pp. 581–85.

nervous system. It is well known that malnutrition can impair mental development. Beginning six months before birth and lasting until six months after birth, cell division causes rapid growth of brain tissue. Nutritional deprivation during this period can severely retard that growth, and this may be irreversible unless treatment begins before cell division ends. From six months through the second year of life, the rate of brain growth is still very rapid, mainly through protein synthesis, but nutritional rehabilitation still can be partially effective. Beyond this point the rate of brain growth is much slower so the effects of treatment on I.Q. scores are negligible after the age of four.[39] Harrell *et al.* demonstrated convincingly the effect of good nutrition on intelligence by giving daily dietary supplements to pregnant mothers of poor socioeconomic status in Virginia.[40] Children whose mothers had received supplements of thiamine, riboflavin, niacin, and iron during pregnancy had significantly higher I.Q.'s at three years of age than those whose mothers had been given only inert material. Such results are encouraging because they indicate that inexpensive and expedient intervention *can* increase the intellectual potential of large numbers of deprived children.

Sociocultural deprivation affects mental retardation by another route. Disadvantaged children make a poor start in school. Initially they score substantially lower on intelligence tests and the gap increases with age.[41] They come to school without the skills necessary to profit from first grade work. In their language skills, both written and spoken, they are less advanced than other children. Visual discrimination is poorly developed. They fall two years behind in scholastic achievement by the sixth grade and almost three years behind by the eighth grade. Not surprisingly, they are more likely to drop out of school before completing a secondary education. Even those socioculturally deprived children who have adequate ability are less likely to go to college.[42] As a result of abortive schooling the employment prospects for such children are bleak, and getting worse. Advances in technology displace mostly people from unskilled jobs while creating new positions for people with high levels of education and technical skill. Over-all employment in this country expanded steadily from 1953 to 1963 but jobs for those without high school education declined by 25 per cent. Two thirds of the unemployed in 1963 had failed to complete high school. Meanwhile jobs for registered nurses, auto mechanics, carpenters, computer operators, and machinists went begging.[43] When cul-

---

[39] B. Waitzkin, "Malnutrition and Mental Deficiency," *Psychological Bulletin,* in press.

[40] R. F. Harrell, E. Woodyard, and A. I. Gates, *The Effects of Mothers' Diets on the Intelligence of Offspring* (New York: Teachers College, 1955).

[41] R. F. Heber and R. B. Dever, "Research on Education and Rehabilitation of the Mentally Retarded," in Haywood, *op. cit.,* pp. 419–24.

[42] R. D. Hess and V. C. Shipman, "Early Experience and Socialization of Cognitive Modes in Children," *Child Development,* XXXVI (1965), pp. 869–70.

[43] J. Tizard, "The Role of Social Institutions in the Causation, Prevention and Alleviation of Mental Retardation," in Haywood, *op. cit.,* pp. 289–90.

turally deprived children grow up, their horizons remain limited because their lack of education and skills leaves them no leverage for economic and social advancement. Consequently their children enter school with the same cultural handicaps that their parents had, and the cycle begins again.

Stimulation and Motivation

Two important reasons for the scholastic and social limitations of deprived children are their lack of early intellectual stimulation and their failure to acquire the values and motives of the dominant culture in our society. Numerous studies have shown that their parents read less to them in the preschool years; they have less variety of visual and other sensory exposure; and verbal interchanges with their parents are restricted. Their physical and social environments are relatively unresponsive to their natural urges to explore and "do things" because they live in drab settings with few novel objects and their parents are too preoccupied with managing daily life to return a smile or to engage in entertaining play. Behavior patterns that produce a result tend to be repeated, and getting results, as we have seen, is prerequisite to acquiring a sense of competence and mastery over the environment. It seems reasonable to infer that discouraging exploratory behavior through nonresponse leads to the apathy and incompetence so often seen in these children. Similarly, deprived children receive less parental encouragement for their natural efforts in self-care and independence. There are fewer rewards to make them strive for achievement in school, learn aesthetic and technical skills, develop personal control, or delay gratification.[44] These are obvious handicaps to success in school and later in the job market.

Orphanages, hospitals, and schools for the retarded are special kinds of deprived environments and, unfortunately, they have the same adverse effects on intelligence and social adaptation.[45] Skeels and Dye have measured substantial rises in the I.Q.'s of retarded children after transfer from a dull orphanage to an institution where they became the objects of much affection and encouragement.[46] After two years in the new setting the children gained more than 28 I.Q. points on the average while a control group that remained in the orphanage lost 26 I.Q. points. Most of the

[44] I. C. Uzgiris, "Sociocultural Factors in Cognitive Development," in Haywood, op. cit., pp. 39–46.

[45] Evidence of declining I.Q. scores during institutional upbringing has been summarized by J. Bowlby, Maternal Care and Mental Health (New York: Schocken Books, 1966). Effects on social development are reported by R. A. Spitz, "Hospitalism: An Inquiry into the Genesis of Psychiatric Conditions in Early Childhood," Psychoanalytic Study of the Child, I (1945), pp. 53–74.

[46] H. M. Skeels and H. B. Dye, "A Study of the Effects of Differential Stimulation on Mentally Retarded Children," Proceedings of the American Association on Mental Deficiency, XLIV (1939), pp. 114–36.

experimental group were placed in adoptive homes and maintained their earlier gains in intelligence. Follow-up study 21 years later showed that the two groups maintained their divergent patterns of ability as adults. All of the experimental group were self-supporting; their average education was through twelfth grade and their average income was $5,220; almost all of them had married and their children had an average I.Q. of 104. By contrast, a third of the control children remained wards of institutions and one had died during adolescence in an institution; their average education was through third grade and their average income was only $1,200; only two had married, one having four normal children and the other having a retarded child.[47] Had the experimental children remained in the orphanage or similar institutions, it seems clear they would not have approached their full intellectual and social potential, and quite possibly that constriction might have extended to their children and beyond.[48]

Some public schools resemble these custodial institutions in their effects on children's growth. It is well known that the quality of education is poorest in "racially imbalanced" school systems (where there are few or no white children), in isolated rural areas like Appalachia, in urban slum areas, and in other places where poverty is extensive. There are obvious reasons for this. Good teachers, equipment, and school buildings are expensive commodities, and competing demands for public service have a claim on tax dollars. The quality of public education is determined in part by the pressure for improvement exerted by citizens and parents. Here again the effects of deprivation are self-perpetuating. Well-educated parents place a high value on their children's education and readily translate that desire into political and social action. Should their efforts be frustrated, they resort to private education. Less educated parents, on the other hand, typically exert less pressure to improve schools, perhaps because they are less aware of their value or because they doubt the efficacy of their efforts to bring about change. Finally, teachers and parents and the children themselves tend to *expect* poor scholastic performance from culturally deprived youngsters. Early belief on the teacher's part that a child is untalented is likely to drain her attention and interest to pupils who seem more gifted, whom she thus unwittingly gives a better education. It may well be that lower-class children are prevented from reaching their full potential by the discouraging attitudes of their teachers. The happy counterpoint to that is that changing attitudes toward their capacity to learn may pay off handsomely.

[47] H. M. Skeels, "Adult Status of Children with Contrasting Early Life Experiences," *Monographs of the Society for Research in Child Development,* XXXI (1966), no. 3, ser. no. 105.

[48] Even more systematic evidence of the potential effectiveness of removing children from institutions is provided by S. A. Kirk, *Early Education of the Mentally Retarded: An Experimental Study* (Urbana: University of Illinois Press, 1958), and by A. D. B. Clarke and A. M. Clarke, "How Constant is the I.Q.?" *Lancet,* II (1953), pp. 877–80.

Summary

Cultural–familial retardation is by far the most common form of mental retardation. Typically such retardates are only mildly impaired and have no obvious organic pathology. They usually come, however, from families of low intelligence and from social classes that are poor and underprivileged. It is plausible to presume that genetic endowment may set some upper limit on their intellectual and social capacities. But it is also clear that a variety of environmental circumstances can contribute to that impairment. Mental development can be limited by sociocultural deprivation through inadequate prenatal and infant medical care, malnutrition, lack of intellectual stimulation and parental encouragement, and the discouraging attitudes of teachers and others. Deprivation is perpetuated from one generation to the next in insidious ways, making it extremely difficult to break into the vicious cycle of retarded parents begetting retarded offspring. Custodial institutions and even some public schools contribute to the problem through lack of stimulation, challenge, and personal encouragement.

Fortunately, intervention works. The progressive retardation associated with lower-class or institutional living can be substantially offset by early removal from the depriving environment, by improved nutrition and medical care, and through carefully constructed preschool and elementary school programs aimed at scholastic and social enrichment. Encouragement can be found in the apparent success of *Sesame Street,* the public television program, in teaching culturally deprived preschoolers (and privileged children, too) how to read, spell, and count.

Recent evidence indicates that the earliest years of life may be critical for determining ultimate intellectual capacity. One investigator estimated that 50 per cent of mental development takes place between conception and age four, 30 per cent between four and eight, and 20 per cent between eight and seventeen.[49] This is consistent with Kirk's view that special educational programs are most effective if begun in the earliest years, preferably at one or two years.[50] Many educational programs have not produced sustained improvement in academic achievement, perhaps because they started too late in the child's development. At a later age, vocational habilitation is a valuable method of treatment. Many retardates can now find employment and job success if their attitudes and other personal qualities are favorable. Though most of these jobs are unskilled (thus offering little opportunity for economic advancement) people of limited I.Q. can perform and hold them about as well as nonretarded persons doing the same work.[51] But a great deal more is required to pre-

[49] B. Bloom, *Stability and Change in Human Characteristics* (New York: John Wiley & Sons, Inc., 1964).
[50] S. A. Kirk, "The Effects of Early Intervention," in Haywood, *op. cit.,* pp. 490–95.
[51] Heber and Dever, *op. cit.,* p. 397.

vent sociocultural factors from having their deleterious effects. As recommended by the President's Panel on Mental Retardation, this will require a broad attack on the adverse social conditions which tend to keep intelligence depressed: poverty, ignorance, and discrimination. This is an ambitious undertaking, and success depends on the willingness of the public to make it possible.

OTHER FORMS OF RETARDATION

The brief synopses that follow might lead to some confusion about how various forms of mental retardation are classified. The labels for some refer to a cardinal symptom of the disorder, as microcephaly, for example, denotes small head size. Other labels designate the persons who discovered or publicized the disorder, e.g., Tay and Sachs. Still others name the cause, e.g., maternal rubella. This inconsistency is partly to be understood by considering how we come to know about disorders historically. Ideally in medicine disorders are classified according to fundamental causes which thus at once suggest the methods of treatment. Initially, however, and in the early stages of investigation of a newly discovered disorder, enough may not be known to single out the fundamental causes. In that case the disorder may be labeled and classified according to a particular theory, as Langdon Down did with *mongolism* because of a quaint theory about racial evolution. Or it might be called *Down's syndrome* by others who accept Down's description but doubt his theory. Finally, as our knowledge about it increases we may classify it as a genetic disorder of specifiable origin, and we may possible relabel it as *trisomy 21* to indicate what went wrong and where.

In part the inconsistencies in classification reflect real irregularies in the disorders themselves. It would be difficult to classify microcephaly according to causes because it has been shown to result from a variety of causes. On the other hand it could be misleading to classify maternal rubella (German measles) by its symptoms because it may cause a number of different symptoms or no damage at all, depending upon the stage of foetal development when the infection occurs. We must tolerate a certain amount of ambiguity in classification until our knowledge of these disorders is as advanced as our knowledge about Down's syndrome and phenylketonuria.

Maternal Rubella (German Measles)

Following an Australian epidemic of rubella in 1941 it was discovered that many defective babies were born to mothers who had the disease during the first three months of pregnancy.[52] Recent studies have reported

[52] Penrose, *op. cit.*, p. 236.

congenital defects in about 10 per cent of such pregnancies, although almost half of the infants are abnormal if the infection occurs in the *first month* of pregnancy. The children show a variety of defects, including deafness, blindness due to cataracts, heart malformation, and mental retardation. When retardation occurs it is usually moderate to severe and is frequently accompanied by cataracts or deafness. Mothers of a substantial proportion of deaf-mutes report rubella in pregnancy. Many of the pregnancies affected are complicated or aborted and many of the babies die. The risk of defect diminishes greatly if the infection occurs after the first trimester of pregnancy. The foetus is protected from many infections during pregnancy, but rubella is obviously one of those which can cross the placental barrier via the blood supply.

Congenital defects can also be caused by other maternal infections, such as syphilis and Asian flu, and by drugs taken during pregnancy. The latter possibility was illustrated in 1962 by the shocking example of thalidomide, a seemingly innocent tranquilizer which when taken during pregnancy produced the side-effect of gross abnormality in the developing foetus. Although some of the symptoms of these disorders can be treated after the baby is born, there is no known antidote for structural damage occurring *in utero*. However, they can be prevented by shielding expectant mothers from exposure early in pregnancy. Effective prevention requires widespread dissemination of information about the dangers of infection and drugs in pregnancy.

Microcephaly

This disorder is diagnosed when the head circumference is very small. In rare cases it is carried by a single recessive gene, but more commonly it results from maternal infections, massive irradiation in pregnancy, or birth complications. In the inherited form the skull is small and conically shaped. The back of the head is flattened and the jaw and forehead recede, which makes the scalp wrinkle as though it were too big for the skull. The face and ears are about normal in size, so they stand out prominently, giving the head a bird-like appearance. The child is short and has a curved spine and apparently long extremities, which cause him to walk in a stooped position or hop rather like a monkey. The majority are severely retarded, never develop speech, and are completely dependent on others for feeding and toilet care. Visual defects and convulsions are common.

In the secondary form of microcephaly, which is acquired after conception, the clinical picture is more variable. Any of the foregoing symptoms may be present in varying degrees, a markedly reduced head circumference being the critical sign. The best documented cause is radiation exposure in pregnancy. There were seven microcephalics among eleven children born to mothers who in the first 20 weeks of pregnancy were exposed at close hand to the atomic blast at Hiroshima.[53] The proportion of defective children was much smaller for pregnant women who were some distance from the center of the blast. Massive therapeutic X-rays during pregnancy have also been found to produce serious abnormalities in half of the babies born, microcephaly being the most frequent.

It is obvious why microcephalic children are mentally retarded. The small size of the skull indicates small size of the brain, especially in the upper cortical regions that are essential to the higher intellectual processes. In fact, an estimate of the weight of the cortex provides a reasonably accurate approximation to the degree of intellectual retardation to be expected in adulthood. Some microcephalics have virtually no cortex at all, which renders them entirely helpless. As might be expected in such a severe structural deficiency, there is little that can be done to recapture the lost intellectual potential once the initial damage has occurred. If a microcephalic survives infancy he does not usually have poor health, although he seldom lives to very old age and almost never can have children of his own. Most are institutionalized although some could be kept at home if the family had the resources to provide the extensive personal care required.[54]

Hydrocephaly

This is another skull malformation that occurs approximately once in 2,000 live births. It may be caused by a sex-linked recessive gene, maternal infection, birth injury, tumor, and a number of other factors that influence the amount of cerebrospinal fluid within the skull. In some cases the normal channels for draining fluid from the brain are blocked, causing fluid to accumulate in the skull and pressure to increase within the brain. In other cases the accumulation is caused by overproduction or under-absorption of the fluid. As fluid accumulates, the cerebral cortex may be stretched until it is paper thin and the skull may expand in a globular shape, often to prodigious size. The head of one seven-year-old child weighed 27 pounds. The upper part of the face expands so that the eyes become widespread and the bridge of the nose flattened. In advanced cases one often finds visual impairment, epilepsy, and spastic paralysis of the lower limbs. In such cases body growth is severely limited; the child is bedridden and usually dies before adulthood. However the severity of symptoms varies widely. In mild cases the child may participate in normal activities and be only slightly retarded. If the condition is arrested before the cortex is permanently damaged, there may be no intellectual deficit at all.

[53] G. Plummer, "Anomalies Occurring in Children Exposed in Utero to the Atomic Bomb in Hiroshima," *Pediatrics*, X (1952), pp. 687–93.

[54] The synopses of microcephaly and hydrocephaly are abstracted primarily from Robinson and Robinson, *op. cit.*, pp. 142–46 and 162–67, and Penrose, *op. cit.*, pp. 170–74 and 197.

Like Down's syndrome and other malformations of the central nervous system, the incidence of hydrocephaly increases dramatically with maternal age, the reasons for this being unknown. Mothers over 40 have five times as many hydrocephalic babies as those between 20 and 35.[55]

Blockage of the drainage channels can sometimes be corrected by surgically inserting drainage tubes at the base of the brain to *shunt* the excess fluid directly into the heart for recirculation. If the operation is performed early enough, brain damage and the accompanying retardation can be prevented or mitigated, but there is a high mortality risk from the operation itself. Drug treatment has had some success in slowing the accumulation of the fluid.

Blood-Type Incompatibility

Many jokes are told about man's unconscious desire to return to the womb, where all his earthly needs were met and life was uncomplicated. It must have been quite a shock for many to learn around 1941 that in some rare instances the womb is the most dangerous place for a baby to be. At that time it was discovered that blood-type incompatibilities of mother and foetus may be harmful, even lethal, to the foetus. There are several types of incompatibility possible, but the one that is best known and most frequently associated with mental retardation is *Rh-incompatibility*. Blood type is inherited. The *Rhesus factor* is transmitted as a dominant characteristic, so that 87 per cent of white persons are classified as *Rh-positive*. When a baby inherits both recessive genes, he has the *Rh-negative* blood type. If an Rh-negative mother conceives an Rh-positive child, the conditions are set for a dangerous clash between the blood systems of the two, which are separate but connected. Components of the child's blood may be absorbed through the placental barrier into the mother's bloodstream, causing the mother's blood to become sensitized to the Rh factor. Her body retaliates by producing an antibody to combat the foreign intruder, and that antibody can enter the baby's bloodstream and destroy its red blood cells. This results in oxygen deprivation in the foetus and death or abortion. In less extreme cases the child may be born with severe anemia and jaundice, permanent brain damage, paralysis of limbs, deafness, and mental retardation.

The danger to the baby is greatest if the mother has already developed antibodies in her blood. For this reason first-born children are less likely to be affected than later children. Not too long ago popular reaction to the dangers of Rh-incompatibility was so extreme that many believed Rh-incompatible mates should not conceive any children at all, but now it is known that only about 5 per cent of Rh-negative mothers become sensitized during pregnancy. Even more reassuring has been the great success of blood

55 R. L. Masland, "The Prevention of Mental Subnormality," in R. L. Masland, S. B. Sarason, and T. Gladwin, *Mental Subnormality* (New York: Basic Books, Inc., 1958), p. 61.

transfusions during the first day or two of life. By replacing all the baby's blood with new blood free of the antibodies, the threat to the baby's health is terminated. Follow-up studies have shown that such children retain a slight intellectual handicap (5 to 10 I.Q. points) compared to their own unaffected siblings, which is probably attributable to the damage done *in utero*. Severely affected children, by contrast, have a handicap of more than 20 I.Q. points. In 1944 it was estimated that blood-type incompatibility accounted for 3 to 4 per cent of institutionalized retarded cases, but by 1963 that figure was less than one per cent.[56] With advanced knowledge it is now possible to monitor carefully the pregnancies of Rh-incompatible parents and, if need be, to induce early labor should maternal sensitization become so extreme as seriously to threaten the baby.[57]

Cretinism

All forms of cretinism stem from a lack of the thyroid hormone *thyroxin,* which stimulates metabolic processes throughout the body. In about a third of the cases the disorder is inherited through receipt of one of several recessive genes that interfere with the production and metabolism of thyroxin. The genetic forms usually produce an enlargement of the thyroid gland, known as *goiter,* which distinguishes them from the more common nongenetic forms, where atrophy of the thyroid gland usually precludes goitrous growth. *Endemic* cretinism occurs mainly in the mountainous regions like the Rocky Mountain area because the soil, water, and air contain unusually low concentrations of iodine, which is essential for the production of thyroid hormone. The incidence of endemic cretinism has been effectively reduced by the addition of iodine to table salt and by careful regulation of maternal diet during pregnancy.

The typical clinical features are severe mental retardation, sluggish behavior, dwarfed stature, coarse dry skin and hair, a large protruding tongue, and not infrequently deafness. In some respects cretins resemble Down's syndrome children, but it is easy and important to distinguish between them because prompt, controlled thyroid medication works wonders in cretinism. The physical symptoms respond favorably to thyroid medication in almost all cases. Mental retardation is also moderated, although normal intelligence is seldom achieved. Damage done to the central nervous system before birth is, of course, irreparable. Cretinism has always been relatively rare in institutional populations, and with improved diet and medical treatment its prevalence has been greatly reduced.

---

[56] Heber, *Epidemiology of Mental Retardation, op. cit.,* p. 33.

[57] The synopses of blood-type incompatibility and cretinism are abstracted primarily from Robinson and Robinson, *op. cit.,* pp. 116, 140–41, and 159–62, and Penrose, *op. cit.,* pp. 160–61 and 237–38.

Tay-Sachs Disease

This is the best known of several disorders of fat metabolism that are caused by a recessively inherited enzyme deficiency. Tay-Sachs is the infantile form of a group of such disorders that used to be called *amaurotic familial idiocy* because of the profound retardation and total blindness (amaurosis) that was invariably present. Due to the faulty enzyme, fatty substances accumulate in the central nervous system and cause progressive deterioration of the brain and optic nerve. The child usually appears normal until six months of age, when motor coordination begins to decline, vision deteriorates, and apathy sets in. Spastic paralysis, convulsions, and death ensue, usually within one to three years. Similar forms of the disorder that have onset later in childhood have different names but very similar features, course, and outcome.

Tay-Sachs disease is more prevalent among Jewish families than others. The historical ostracism of Jews has probably led to a disproportionately large number of marriages between blood relatives, which tends to increase the frequency with which a recessive genetic disease becomes manifest. An ambitious project is currently underway in the Baltimore–Washington area, aimed at blood-testing thousands of Jews of child-bearing age. Among the first 8,000 tested, about one in 30 has been found to carry the recessive gene and four couples have been found in which both partners are carriers. In such cases one in four offspring will predictably have the disease. It is now possible—though not without some danger—to test sample extracts from the amniotic fluid during pregnancy for evidence of the critical enzyme. If it is missing, the baby will almost certainly have the disease, and therapeutic abortion can be performed, there being no known treatment for the Tay-Sachs syndrome. This project is an exciting experiment in mass education and genetic counseling. Surely it will prove useful for all the carriers to know this fact about themselves, and the information gathered from such large numbers should provide valuable knowledge about the disorder.[58]

CONCLUSION

There has been much tangible progress during the last thirty years in understanding and treating mental retardation. It is worth pointing out that most of the breakthroughs in knowledge concern etiology and prevention as well as pathology and remediation. Most severe types of retardation are first of all physical disorders of the brain that secondarily entail disruptions of mental processes. The causes are frequently genetic or biological, centering around the processes of reproduction and early development. Prevention or treatment may be as simple as changing a diet or having a

---

[58] This synopsis is drawn mainly from Robinson and Robinson, *op. cit.*, pp. 113–14; Penrose, *op. cit.*, pp. 163–64, and *Time* (September 13, 1971), p. 54.

routine blood test. There are indications throughout that severe mental retardation is a field of abnormality about which we can *do* something. In this respect it is gratifying to tie together the lessons to be learned from our study. Indeed it is tempting to write such a summary in a humorous vein, as *A Layman's Guide to Having Healthy Babies* or *Prescriptions for the Amateur Parents (As If There Were Any Other Kind)*. But there are too many sober sides to mental retardation to allow for such amusement: physical deformities, wasted human potential, parental anguish and guilt, and enormous social cost. In part, though, these tragic undercurrents create a zeal in research workers to keep on pressing their search.

Family Planning

Planning a family actually begins with selecting a mate. It is clear that much genetic mischief has resulted from relatives marrying. The majority of the forms of retardation reviewed in this chapter *may* be inherited recessively, and the pairing of recessive genes is much more frequent in consanguineous marriages. If relatives do marry, they should at least be aware of the measure of danger to their offspring. Penrose has found that more than 18 per cent of their children are retarded, as compared with a norm of 4 per cent.[59] Simple blood and urine tests can determine the risk of the most common forms of defect, but this is not at all foolproof. There may be recessive disorders that are still unknown. Stern estimates that each of us carries more than 10 recessive genes that are potentially detrimental.[60] All of these potential threats are more likely to be actualized in consanguineous marriages. It would be unusual but by no means frivolous for *any* enlightened couple to request thorough medical and laboratory examinations before conceiving children. This is especially recommended if defective children have previously been born in either family.

There is a decided correlation between maternal age and maldevelopment of the central nervous system in babies. This is particularly significant for women over 35 although the risk is reduced if they have had babies previously. Risk is also greater for very young mothers. For this reason Penrose encourages prospective mothers to have their offspring between the ages of 22 and 30.[61] Many individuals and religious groups remain opposed to birth control and abortion on moral grounds, and these objections must be respected. There is no question, however, that the improvements in these procedures and their increased availability have made family planning more feasible and more effective. The means for birth control are now legally available in most states in the United States. Abortion is an accepted practice in many countries and has recently been offered upon

[59] Penrose, *op. cit.*, p. 287.

[60] C. Stern, *Principles of Human Genetics* (2nd ed.; San Francisco: W. H. Freeman and Co., 1960), p. 396.

[61] Penrose, *op. cit.*, p. 291.

request, at modest cost, in New York and other states in this country. Liberalized abortion has recently been seized as a major objective of Women's Liberation campaigns, which will probably help to produce wider acceptance of the practice.

Prenatal Care

In the field of mental retardation an ounce of prevention is worth *several* pounds of cure. Anyone who has planted seeds knows that the most crucial period for survival and healthy development is the very first period of life. The situation is no different with human beings. Neither is the sort of care very different. Like plants, human seedlings require a balanced diet with adequate amounts of necessary nutrients, minerals, and vitamins. They must be shielded from unnecessary exposure to infection, extreme irradiation, and drugs, especially in the first three months of life. For human beings the mother's body provides the first environment for growth. For this reason competent prenatal medical supervision is extremely important, starting as soon as conception is suspected, in order to regulate the mother's diet, monitor the baby's development, and handle any emergencies that may arise.

Early Childhood Care

Regular medical supervision is also essential from birth until school age. As we have pointed out, many of the initial signs of mental retardation are apparent to the trained observer or laboratory technician during the first week of life. Others can be picked up in routine pediatric follow-up through blood tests and periodic charting of the developmental milestones. Most of the special treatments for retardation must be prescribed, executed, or monitored by physicians. But many of the childhood needs of retardates are the same as other children's: security, discipline, stimulation and challenge, good example, and affectionate care. If the family is not too burdened by poverty, ignorance, and cultural deprivation, and if the parents are capable of psychological generativity, much can be done to lighten the effects of intellectual handicap.

Attitudes Toward Mental Retardation

Not so long ago the public attitude toward mental retardation was one of looking away and forgetting. Institutions were poorly financed, research was weakly supported, special training opportunities were provided on a most inadequate scale. Even the parents of severely retarded children sometimes fell in with this attitude, placing the child in an institution and pretending that he did not exist. The problem for parents, however, was always much complicated by the inadequacies of institutions. Most state training schools do not admit children under five years, and most have a long waiting list which delays admittance two or three years longer. Furthermore, financial and emotional considerations often conspire to favor rearing even severely retarded children at home, sometimes against professional advice and at considerable cost to the happiness and adjustment of normal siblings.

Today there are signs of a decided change in the public attitude. For this change the parents of retarded children are largely responsible. They have formed influential organizations all over the world that work for improvement of state institutions, cooperative nursery schools, more and better special classes in the public schools, and informational and group therapy programs for themselves. The members provide moral support for one another in that they share a common plight, either the frustration and disturbance of having a retarded child at home or the guilt they feel for having placed their child in an institution. Their morale is further strengthened by the discovery that something can be accomplished through joint effort. Similar developments have occurred with respect to cerebral palsy and epilepsy. In the long run it may prove to be not the least of the services rendered by these movements that they awakened interest in research and stimulated financial support for it.

SUGGESTIONS FOR FURTHER READING

To gain some perspective on the recent advances in mental retardation the reader might skim through A. F. Tredgold's *A Textbook of Mental Deficiency* (6th ed., Baltimore, Wm. Wood & Co., 1937). For decades this text, in various editions, was consistently the most authoritative source. The sixth edition was published before most of the important breakthroughs in genetics, blood chemistry, epidemiology, and the psychological effects of deprivation. While an excellent book, it illustrates nicely the state of our ignorance only a quarter of a century ago. There have been several more recent editions, the latest being R. F. Tredgold and K. Soddy, *Tredgold's Text-book of Mental Deficiency* (11th ed., Baltimore, The Williams & Winkins Co., 1970).

For thoroughness and readability the best modern textbook is H. B. Robinson and N. M. Robinson, *The Mentally Retarded Child* (New York, McGraw-Hill Book Co., 1965). In addition to treatments of all the major syndromes, upon which the present chapter relied heavily, it includes a basic introduction to the concepts and theories of intelligence, retardation, and human genetics. A third of the book is devoted to the practical clinical problems of diagnosis and treatment, which clinicians will find useful.

One cannot read very far in this field before discovering the immense influence of L. S. Penrose, *The Biology of Mental Defect* (3rd ed., London: Sedgwick & Jackson, 1963). For four decades Penrose has been the leading authority on genetic aspects of birth defects. American readers may find a certain archaic quality in his thinking about retardation, giving rather short shrift to the social and psychological aspects, but there is nowhere a more comprehensive account of the genetic and biological aspects. Balance for this can be found in H. C. Haywood, ed.,

Socio-Cultural Aspects of Mental Retardation (New York, Appleton-Century-Crofts, 1970), a report of the proceedings of a major conference at George Peabody College, with contributions from 38 leading investigators from throughout the world.

S. B. Sarason and J. Doris, *Psychological Problems in Mental Deficiency* (4th ed., New York, Harper & Row, 1969), offers a valuable historical review of the field and quite extensive accounts of Down's syndrome, phenylketonuria, and sociocultural retardation. The book contains a good deal of explicit social advocacy. Coverage of the field is less systematic than Robinson and Robinson or Tredgold.

R. Heber, *Epidemiology of Mental Retardation* (Springfield, Ill., Charles C Thomas, 1970) is a small book (99 pages) that compiles succinctly, though not very systematically, a wealth of quantitative facts about mental retardation and birth defects. W. K. Estes presents a systematic review of literature on mental retardation from a learning theory perspective in *Learning Theory and Mental Development* (New York, Academic Press, 1970). To be recommended for parents of retarded children as well as those interested in work with the retarded is Edward L. French and J. Clifford Scott, *Children in the Shadows* (Philadelphia, J. B. Lippincott Co., 1960).

17

Community Mental Health

The problems created by disordered personal reactions cannot be solved without reference to the society in which they occur. Treating and caring for people whose behavior is disturbed, still more preventing their reactions from becoming disordered in the first place, imply a high level of social effort and social organization. In the preceding chapters of this book we have often discussed the diverse problems of abnormal psychology as if they were simply problems in scientific understanding. It is now time to give up this artificially narrowed focus and let the picture expand to its full dimensions. What does it take to deal effectively with the problems of mental health? How great are those problems, what institutions are needed to cope with them, what forms of training and varieties of manpower are requisite, and how much will it all cost? Clearly the huge task of improving mental health cannot be borne by professional workers alone. We shall therefore also consider the contributions that can come from anyone who cares to make his behavior as a parent and a citizen count in this direction.

In the historical introduction we took note of a recent major revolution in the public attitude toward mental health. As lately as 1948 it was possible to think of professional mental health workers and their civilian supporters as a tiny band struggling for existence, unable to attract interest or financial support, working almost in vain to overcome a public tendency to look away from the problems rather than confronting them. But the time was evidently ripe for a drastic change. Within a few years mental health came to be regarded as a concern of the whole community and a suitable object for community action.

SIZE OF THE PROBLEM

In 1955 an act of Congress called the Mental Health Study Act ordered the formation of a Joint Commission on Mental Illness and Health which was charged with the task of evaluating needs and resources and making recommendations for a national mental health program. The Commission made its study in great depth and submitted its final report in 1960, published the next year as *Action for Mental Health*.[1]

The Problem of Numbers

The most general estimate is that 17 million people in the United States suffer at one time or another from relatively serious mental disorder. At any given moment the number of sufferers will be around 700,000. Half the hospital beds in the nation, the report further points out, are occupied by mental patients—a vivid reminder of the relative size of this medical problem.[2] The same facts have been expressed a little differently by saying that at any given time one out of every 250 people will be resident in a mental hospital.[3] It has also been estimated that mental illness in a form serious enough to require hospital care "strikes about 1 in 5 families and about 1 in 13 people in the course of a lifetime." [4] These last estimates sound so gloomy that they should not stand without a reminder that patients leave mental hospitals as well as enter them. In 1950 some 340,000 patients were discharged, not all fully recovered but at least in a considerably improved condition. Furthermore, since 1956 the rate of discharge has crept ahead of the rate of admission. The Joint Commission's report shows that between 1956 and 1960 there was a decline of 3 per cent in mental hospital populations.[5] In subsequent years this trend has increased so that mental hospitals, traditionally overcrowded, are in some instances no longer used to capacity.

Hospital patients are easy to count, but the true extent of mental health needs can be uncovered only through community surveys. In the Midtown Manhattan Study, for instance, needs were estimated through extensive interviews with 1,660 people, a carefully chosen representative sample from a circumscribed population of 110,000 in New York City.[6] Only 18 per

[1] Joint Commission on Mental Health and Illness, *Action for Mental Health* (New York: Science Editions, Inc., 1961).

[2] *Ibid.*, p. 4.

[3] D. Blain, K. E. Appel, A. E. Scheflen, and R. L. Robinson, "The Current Picture of Mental Health and Psychiatry in the U. S.: Pertinent Statistics," *American Journal of Psychiatry*, CXII (1955), pp. 53–54.

[4] S. K. Weinberg, *Society and Personality Disorders* (Englewood Cliffs, N. J.: Prentice-Hall, Inc., 1952), p. 361.

[5] *Action for Mental Health, op. cit.*, p. 7.

[6] L. Srole, T. S. Langner, S. T. Michael, M. K. Opler, and T. A. C. Rennie, *Mental Health in the Metropolis: The Midtown Study*, Vol. 1 (New York: McGraw-Hill Book Co., 1962); T. S. Langner and S. T. Michael, *Life Stress and Mental Health* (New York: The Free Press of Glencoe, 1963).

cent of the sample were rated as really "well," that is, free from psychiatric symptoms, whereas 23 per cent were judged to be seriously impaired by their symptoms. The latter group stood in real need of mental health care, but in fact only a quarter of these people had received any kind of treatment. Large as is the current demand for mental health services, the *potential* demand would seem to be still larger by a considerable margin.

Community surveys have also thrown light on the distribution of different disorders in different sections of the population. The New Haven study brings out the fact that the neuroses tend to be concentrated in the middle and upper social classes, whereas psychoses have a sharply disproportionate frequency of occurrence at the lowest class level.[7] The prevalence of schizophrenia, for example, is thus greatest where the effects of poverty, unemployment, malnutrition, and alienation are most severe. Indeed it has been demonstrated by Langner and Michael that the proportion of psychotics in the lower classes is directly related to amount of social and environmental stress in childhood, as shown by indicators such as poor physical health, poor health of parents, and broken homes. The New Haven studies show that members of the lowest class tend to lead isolated lives with little participation in organized endeavors, even in the labor unions that stand for their interests. They see the world as hostile and uncontrollable, and they tend to think of mental and emotional disorders as afflictions of external origin. The same point is made in the Stirling County studies in Nova Scotia, where the people of the "depressed areas" are found to have little sense that they can influence the decisions and policies of those who have power in the community. This suggests the possibility that being always on the receiving end and having no control over your destiny may encourage the use of psychotic mechanisms such as projection. At all events it is in the "depressed areas" that psychosis occurs with greatest frequency.[8]

The Financial Problem

In its report the Joint Commission estimated the direct cost of mental and emotional disorders at one billion dollars a year and the indirect cost at two billion more.[9] It is hard to make figures in billions convey more than a vague sense of vast magnitude. The point of importance here is that mental disorder is by all odds the most costly of the nation's health problems. Even if we said nothing about the loss of happiness and effectiveness, the financial loss would be a problem in its own right.

Before World War II, when mental illness was still a shunned topic, it was almost impossible to find voluntary sources of money to stimulate better care and research. This situation presently changed, so that in 1959 the

[7] A. B. Hollingshead and F. C. Redlich, *Social Class and Mental Illness: A Community Study* (New York: John Wiley & Sons, Inc., 1958).

[8] C. C. Hughes, M.-A. Tremblay, R. N. Rapoport, and A. H. Leighton, *People of Cove and Woodlot* (New York: Basic Books, Inc., 1960).

[9] *Action for Mental Health, op. cit.*, p. 4.

annual campaign for mental health raised $5.5 million. Although this was a striking increase over the sum collected, for instance, in 1950, it was still a tiny share of what was contributed for health as a whole. In the same year $31.3 million was raised for poliomyelitis, $31.0 for cancer, $26.0 for tuberculosis, $24.0 for heart, $10.3 for crippled children, and $9.5 and $4.6 respectively for cerebral palsy and muscular dystrophy, both of which are vastly less common than mental disorders.[10] The generosity of the public with respect to physical ailments is not to be criticized, but mental health even today does not receive the share of the voluntary health dollar that its importance warrants.

Mental health care, however, is such a large operation—a "major American industry," as David Mechanic has called it—that its main financial support must come from public sources. Federal participation channeled through the National Institute of Mental Health rose from $100 million in 1961 to nearly $400 million in 1969,[11] and large increases also appeared in state budgets. Even so, the mental health enterprise continues to suffer from short financial rations. Rising costs and rising expectations are partly responsible, but a more important source of increased expense is the intent to make services available to the whole population, regardless of ability to pay.

COMMUNITY MENTAL HEALTH CENTERS

One of the most striking features of the Joint Commission's report in 1960 was the recommendation of a major shift of emphasis in mental health care from the existing mental hospitals to the community. Early in 1963 President Kennedy sent a special message to Congress in which he urged the establishment of community mental health centers. One aim of the proposed program was to reduce by half within the next twenty years the number of patients under custodial care in mental hospitals, this to be accomplished by early treatment and facilities near home. But the purpose was much broader: the President envisioned community centers as providing comprehensive service for all mental health needs, with special emphasis on prevention. Congress passed the necessary legislation the same year, and Federal funds became available to assist the establishment of community mental health centers.

The Ideal

The stated goal of the national program was to set up a fully staffed community mental health center for every 100,000 of population, obviously a goal that could be realized only over many years. The legislation states

10 *Ibid.*, pp. 7, 15.
11 D. Mechanic, *Mental Health and Social Policy* (Englewood Cliffs, N. J.: Prentice-Hall, Inc., 1969).

that a center must provide, at a minimum, these services: (1) inpatient care, (2) outpatient care, (3) partial hospitalization including especially day care, (4) 24-hour emergency service, and (5) consultation and education with agencies in the community. Other services are encouraged, including aftercare of patients discharged from mental hospitals, services for the mentally retarded, and special classes for children with unusual disabilities. Occasionally a community mental health center has been started from scratch, with a complex of buildings providing for the whole array of services. But this is expensive; more often, the attempt is made to utilize or enlarge existing facilities and, if they were previously separate, to join them in a single comprehensive organization. In one community, for instance, there already existed, in widely scattered buildings, a psychiatric outpatient clinic for children and adults, a family counseling service, an association for retarded children, and a mental health society doing educational work. These separate enterprises turned into a mental health center when the general hospital opened a psychiatric ward capable of meeting the inpatient and emergency requirements, when the four existing agencies moved to a building on the hospital grounds, and when an administrator was appointed to see that they all operated in reasonable concert.

We can most quickly understand the potential value of a community mental health center by imagining how it might work in a particular case. John Doe's family, let us suppose, labors under a series of handicaps. There is John's elderly father living in the home, who is beginning to have difficult episodes suggesting senile psychosis. John's son, always a disciplinary problem, is now, in early adolescence, experimenting with drugs and delinquent adventures. John's daughter performs badly at school, seems socially inept, and may possibly be mentally retarded. His wife, overwhelmed by so much trouble, has fits of weeping and is becoming too lethargic to manage the housework. And John himself, clinging desperately to his ill-paid job, feels mounting resentment and recognizes that his marital relation is deteriorating. If the date is 1940 there is a strong chance that this situation will simply go from bad to worse. The old father will be committed to a mental hospital fifty miles away. The son will be caught by the police and sent to a reform school forty miles in another direction. The daughter will drift along, become an early dropout, and perhaps land in an institution for the retarded sixty miles in a third direction. Mother will be told that she needs a psychoanalysis, but no one will take her for the small amount she could pay. She and John become further estranged and reach emotional if not actual divorce.

If we shift the date to the mid-1970's and place the family in a community with a well-organized mental health center, there is a chance of a better outcome. In the first place, the problems will be seen not as individual disorders but as part of family relations; in the second place, there will be facilities at hand for each special need. Partial hospitalization or short periods in the local psychiatric ward may keep father at home without his being in everybody's hair. The adolescent son can receive individual or group treatment at the outpatient clinic. The daughter's attitude in school may be helped through talks between the teacher and a mental health consultant. If her difficulties appear to be emotional, the center can provide both individual counseling and special classes for the emotionally disturbed; if retardation proves to be genuine, there is a sheltered workshop for the handicapped. The wife can receive psychotherapy regardless of capacity to pay, and John himself can be drawn into family treatment that may put the marital relation on a firmer footing. Neighbors may notice that the Doe family, in spite of its multiple problems, seems to be getting along rather well.

To tell the story in this fashion no doubt makes the whole thing sound easy. In actuality nothing of the kind could happen without long preparation and an extensive deployment of human resources. If John Doe is going to commit his family to the center's care, he must have formed a favorable opinion of what it can accomplish. Such an opinion is not indigenous. Even today, even in relatively advantaged communities, it may take five years or so of educational work to produce confidence in "this psychology stuff" and conviction that there is a real local need. Then there is the question of expense. A good deal of professional time, it will be noticed, is being devoted to the John Doe family. Implicit in the story is a large corps of trained experts: psychiatrists and other psychotherapists, nurses and occupational therapists on the psychiatric ward, a consultant to the schools, a teacher of special classes, a supervisor of the sheltered workshop, a family counselor. All of this is costly, as is the general staff required to run such an organization and keep the necessary records. As a public service the center must be open alike to rich and poor, and clients' fees can never be expected to meet more than a small fraction—perhaps 10 or 15 per cent—of the costs. Those in charge thus find themselves constantly scrounging to balance the budget, continually involved in appeals to a reluctant community, an economy-minded legislature, and federal granting agencies whose funds are not unlimited. Even those citizens who are most convinced of the value of a community mental health center may sometimes wonder, as taxpayers, whether they can afford to pay for it.

In point of fact, a good many centers, though nowhere near the projected number, have been opened under the federal policy of 1963 and under related policies adopted by the states. Enough time has gone by and enough experience has accumulated to show that merely opening a center does not guarantee that it will meet all expectations. First enthusiasms have now given place to critical scrutiny.

The Actuality

One of the most insistent themes in the criticism is that professional workers have failed to adapt to the new conditions implicit in community centers. They have tended to perceive these centers as opening new slots in which to continue their traditional activity. Thus they may initiate prolonged one-to-one treatment even though this seriously limits the number of clients who can be served. Continuing the familiar procedures of office practice, workers have failed to look outward at the community, to see their clients as members of a society, and to utilize or develop community resources which might extend the effects of their own therapeutic endeavors. Every professional person who has been obliged in the course of his life to work under radically changed conditions will realize that it is no small matter to shift one's style, redirect one's skills, and risk one's habituated sense of competence. But community mental health has somewhat the character of a new deal. Many more clients must be served in many more ways, using a variety of new resources. Flexibility and a spirit of innovation are much needed, and those always seem to be in short supply.

A second point of criticism is the failure of community mental health centers to reach the wider population for which they were intended. In a survey made in Boston, a city unusually rich in psychiatric manpower, Ryan points to a long list of unmet needs.[12] He mentions in particular the needs of multi-problem families, one of whose problems is likely to be poverty. He further specifies a shortage of mental health service to seriously disturbed children and adolescents, the aged, and people returning to the community from mental hospitals. Only a small part of Boston's psychiatric manpower is engaged in community work; most of the effort is still directed to patients seen in private practice. Commenting on this study, Albee remarks: "The settlement houses are helping more disturbed children than the child psychiatry clinics, and the clergy are seeing more disturbed people for counseling than are psychiatrists." [13] But the difficulty is not wholly on the side of the professionals. When a mental health center is established in the middle of a poverty area its existence may be scarcely noticed by the surrounding population. Social workers visiting homes may recommend using the service, but perhaps in no more than one case in four will this advice be followed. As we have already noticed, the very concept of mental health may be foreign to people of limited education and outlook. Thus one can have the spectacle of a costly mental health center, set down by legislative fiat in a city slum, which for some time does not draw enough clients to keep its staff busy.

It is possible to look upon these troubles as the growing pains of a new movement. Community mental health is a more drastic innovation than anyone at first realized; time will be required to make the whole idea effective. Allowing for this, however, it would still be a mistake to assume

12 W. Ryan, *Distress in the City* (Cleveland: Case Western Reserve University Press, 1969).

13 G. W. Albee, "Through the Looking Glass," *International Journal of Psychiatry,* IX (1970–71), pp. 293–98.

that time alone will set everything right. In all candor we must recognize that the dream of universal mental health care through community centers may be impossible to fulfill. Trying to do for many people what has been done with less than perfect success for a few may turn out to be impracticable—we do not yet know. Success will certainly not come without radical rethinking. Three questions in particular deserve the most careful scrutiny.

1. What changes in existing institutions and what kinds of new facilities are needed to implement community mental health care?
2. What sources of manpower must be drawn upon and what new methods of training must be devised to meet the expanding need for services?
3. What expectations are reasonable and realistic with respect to the prevention of disordered personal behavior? We shall take up these questions in turn.

DEVELOPING FACILITIES FOR MENTAL HEALTH CARE

In the new outlook the mental hospital is no longer the pivot of mental health care. Even the psychiatric ward of the local general hospital is an auxiliary rather than the central service. The doorway through which the prospective client enters should be that of a counseling center and outpatient service, where his troubles can be heard and his footsteps guided toward whatever service seems most appropriate. Sometimes a mental hospital that already runs an outpatient service refurbishes it to meet this need. If there is already an independent counseling center or outpatient clinic, this institution is well-suited to take the central position in the mental health enterprise. Among other things, the center should be a mine of information. Familiarity with all the facilities in the community and in the region is essential for maximal effectiveness. The client may need some service that is not a part of local resources but can be obtained in a neighboring community. At all events he should feel that the center is a place where they know how to get things done and can put you in touch with what you need.

Child Guidance Clinics

Services offered to children are perhaps the most quickly appreciated functions of a community mental health center. Many adults are more willing to seek help for their children's problems than for their own; furthermore, there is the hope that timely ministering to the needs of children will prevent the evolution of more serious disorders. In their original form, child guidance clinics were customarily staffed by psychiatrists, clinical psychologists, and psychiatric social workers. There was a rough division of functions according to which the psychiatrist was responsible for

diagnosis and treatment, the psychologist for diagnostic testing and appraisal of the child's capacities, the social worker for securing the parents'
version of the history and carrying out such measures as advising the
parents and changing the child's activities. These functions became blurred
as thinking developed in the direction of family psychotherapy. The whole
team became co-therapists in attempting to deal with the complex of
family relations that usually lies behind a child's problems. A children's
service often proves to be the means whereby adult emotional problems
and mental disorders are brought to the surface for treatment.

Other Services for Children

In recent years it has been increasingly recognized that children's mental
health needs often require more than can be provided through individual
and family psychotherapy. This is clearly apparent when *mental retardation* is part, or perhaps all, of a child's difficulty. Separate training schools
for the retarded still perform an essential function when the disability is
large, but for those children classed as "educable" it is an advantage for
all concerned to have facilities in the community. These may well consist
of kindergartens, special classes in the public schools, and sheltered workshops for those who have finished their formal education. The first and
third facilities gain something by proximity to the community mental
health center: they need from time to time the diagnostic and appraisal
services and the family counseling resources that are to be found there.
Benefiting also from close contact with other services are special classes for
emotionally disturbed children. These are children who cannot prosper
in the ordinary school system because they are too anxious, too impulsive,
too excitable, or too lethargic and withdrawn; they can learn only in a very
small group where instruction can be individualized and wide latitude
allowed for idiosyncrasies. Such classes require specially trained teachers
and readily available consultation with a child psychiatrist. A third desirable and appropriate form of service is the *day center* especially for disturbed adolescents. A day center makes it possible to take upset adolescents
out of their homes, where they are usually experiencing great friction, and
put them in quarters pleasantly furnished where there are opportunities
for crafts, reading, rapping, music, games, preparing snacks, and perhaps
a bit of group psychotherapy, all under the supervision of skilled leaders.
The treatment of adolescent patients in mental hospitals has been shown to
have rather poor outcomes.[14] The day center is certainly a better way to
start, even if its results are less than magical.

Psychological Services in Schools

School systems today generally consider their services to pupils incomplete if counseling is not included. The main functions of a school guid-

[14] E. Hartman, B. A. Glasser, M. Greenblatt, M. H. Solomon, and D. J. Levinson,
Adolescents in a Mental Hospital (New York: Grune & Stratton, Inc., 1968).

ance department are typically educational counseling, the appraisal of abilities, and vocational advice, but maladaptive patterns of personal behavior often come to the counselors' attention. Usually the guidance staff lacks training to deal with these difficulties if they do not respond to nondirective counseling, and it is at this point that the community mental health center can make a useful contribution. This help may take the form of a consultation service for members of the school staff. A psychiatrist, social worker, or psychologist holds regular conference hours each week at which teachers or counselors can discuss problems they may be having with particular children. Under this arrangement the mental health worker does not see the disturbed child, but he can often assist a teacher by pointing out the possible significance of some of the behavior and suggesting how the teacher, without herself trying to play psychiatrist, can best adapt her behavior to be helpful to the trouble-giving child. If these measures prove to be unsuccessful it may be necessary, of course, for the child to be seen at the mental health center. But sometimes this step, a little upsetting in itself, can be avoided, and the mental health consultant will hear the good news that the problem child is doing much better and that the teacher is feeling more competent.

Partial Hospitalization

One of the services that must be offered by a mental health center in order to qualify for federal support goes under the name of partial hospitalization. The image that springs to mind of a patient standing in the door with one foot in and one foot out is not correct: the patient's time is divided between hospital and home. Under certain conditions the patient may spend nights in the hospital and days at home or at work. This is especially appropriate with older patients who sleep badly and become confused during the night, and with those given to nocturnal attacks of anxiety. In the main, however, partial hospitalization signifies care during the day, with the patient returning home for the night.

The day hospital plan is unsuitable for patients who are highly disturbed or too apathetic to follow the routine, but it is entirely practicable with many whose condition is less severe. An early experiment carried on for several years at the Massachusetts Mental Health Center in Boston led to half of the patients being on day care, and many of these were admitted directly to it, without any period of full-time residence in the hospital.[15] The rationale and problems of partial hospitalization are discussed by Glasscote, who includes a number of "case studies" of particular programs.[16] The saving in beds, space, and night care commends the experiment on financial grounds, but the strongest arguments in its favor are psychological.

[15] B. M. Kramer, *Day Hospital: A Study of Partial Hospitalization in Psychiatry* (New York: Grune & Stratton, Inc., 1962).

[16] R. M. Glasscote, *et al.*, *Partial Hospitalization for the Mentally Ill* (London: Garamond Pridemark, Ltd., 1969).

Provided there is a hospital or psychiatric ward in the community—otherwise the experiment is unworkable—the patient is not taken wholly out of his neighborhood, the relatives are not wholly relieved of their responsibility for him, the role of the sick person is not sharply established, and the regressive attractions of bed care are not added to the patient's other difficulties in facing the conditions of his life. When the time comes to end daily visits to the hospital, the transition does not have the character of an abrupt shock.

The Mental Hospital

The movement for community mental health has put traditional mental hospitals on the defensive. Emphasizing services near at hand, including psychiatric wards in general hospitals, the community movement makes a virtue of keeping patients out of mental hospitals; this goal was explicit in the original act of Congress. In historical perspective this can be seen as an injustice to a type of institution to which we owe most of our knowledge of the more serious mental disorders. The leading mental hospitals have unquestionably played an outstanding part in the advancement of knowledge and in the training of professional workers. Why have they been so suddenly given the role of villain in the mental health drama?

The shortest answer is that over the years they turned in a poor therapeutic record. Originally called asylums, they gave shelter and protection to mental patients but accomplished too little in the way of rehabilitation. They served the custodial function demanded by the public but put too little effort into sending patients home again in an improved condition. Considering how little was known about treatment for so long, and considering also the meager financial support provided by the taxpayers, it is not remarkable that many hospitals did not go beyond their custodial functions. Furthermore, we should remember that the better ones were pioneers in the development of shock treatments, drug therapy, group psychotherapy, and therapeutic milieux, and recovery rates have been steadily moving up. Even so, the mental hospital, often remote from the community and exhibiting some of the rigidity of a long-established institution, has become the target of a great deal of criticism.

Soon after World War II there was a rapid growth of research into the mental hospital as a social organization. Staff roles and staff tensions were investigated, also the informal interactions of patients among themselves. One study of this interaction used the technique of participant observation: the observer assumed the role of a patient and lived for two months on the ward, his true status being known only by two senior staff members.[17] It was clear that an informal but definite social organization pre-

[17] W. Caudill, F. C. Redlich, H. R. Gilmore, and E. B. Brody, "Social Structure and Interaction Processes on a Psychiatric Ward," *American Journal of Orthopsychiatry*, XXII (1952), pp. 314–34. See also W. Caudill, *The Psychiatric Hospital as a Small Society* (Cambridge, Mass.: Harvard University Press, 1958).

vailed among the patients, who as a group tried to meet many of the problems of hospital life "by developing a shared set of values and beliefs translated into action through a system of social roles and cliques." Included in the interactions were many examples of help and support, as when one patient sat up all night with another who was experiencing anxiety. Further observations of this kind have recently been added by Rockwell, who considers the "living in" experiment so illuminating that it ought to be a part of every psychiatrist's training.[18] A more extensive study was published in 1954 by Stanton and Schwartz, who describe with striking detail some of the relationships between staff administrative policies and the social and emotional climate of a ward for disturbed patients.[19] Disagreement among staff members, even when it is not brought to open expression, can communicate itself to patients and cause no small amount of disturbance in the ward. It is profitable, for reasons both practical and theoretical, to study the hospital as a system of hierarchical positions, to grasp the inherent conflicts of different roles in this system, and to give thought to the problem of communication among the different parts of the system. Just as we had to analyze what is communicated in parent–child interactions, so we have to understand what is communicated from doctors to nurses, from doctors to patients, and from nurses to patients. Steinfeld points out that double-bind communication is not restricted to the families of schizophrenics; something much like it occurs in messages from staff to patients, especially when an attitude prevails that patients are recalcitrant children rather than sick adults deserving respect.[20]

Studies of this kind have contributed to the lowered repute of mental hospitals. Removing patients from their communities, forcing them to adapt to a wholly unfamiliar social milieu, treating them most of the time with professional impersonality, may have damaging effects that offset the possible benefits of treatment.[21] But these disclosures do not mean that mental hospitals have to be abandoned. "The psychiatric hospital need not be a social anachronism," says a report prepared by a committee of the Group for the Advancement of Psychiatry; "it has unique functions that can complement community mental health programs." [22] There are always cases in which constant observation and supervision are necessary, in which

[18] D. A. Rockwell, "Some Observations on 'Living In,'" *Psychiatry,* XXXIV (1971), pp. 214–23.

[19] A. H. Stanton and M. S. Schwartz, *The Mental Hospital: A Study of Institutional Participation in Psychiatric Illness and Treatment* (New York: Basic Books, Inc., 1954).

[20] G. J. Steinfeld, "Parallels Between the Pathological Family and the Mental Hospital: A Search for a Process," *Psychiatry,* XXXIII (1970), pp. 36–66.

[21] The plight of the hospital patient has been dramatized by Erving Goffman in *Asylums: Essays on the Social Situation of Mental Patients and Other Inmates* (New York: Anchor Books, 1961). The picture drawn should be balanced by reading an article by L. S. Linn, "The Mental Hospital from the Patient Perspective," *Psychiatry,* XXXI (1968), pp. 213–23, who took greater pains in ascertaining the facts.

[22] Group for the Advancement of Psychiatry, "The Crisis in Psychiatric Hospitalization," *International Journal of Psychiatry,* IX (1970–71), pp. 565–603.

community resources have proved unequal to the strain, or in which hospitalization can serve as a useful retreat permitting the patient to "remarshall his forces." Five definite indications for hospitalization are specified in the report:

1. When supportive measures have been unsuccessful in halting or reversing the regressive process.
2. When the magnitude of regressive, depressive, or aggressive behavior is no longer tolerable to the patient and/or society.
3. When the management of special treatments, somatic procedures, and psychopharmacologic drugs requires continuous observation.
4. When a controlled environment is essential for the use of psychotherapy.
5. When medication or drugs on which the patient has become dependent must be withdrawn.[23]

The authors of the report further urge that when any of these conditions are found to prevail, hospitalization should be recommended as a positive step rather than as a reluctant last resort. They caution against haste in sending the patient home. Returning to the community is a difficult step, and it is no service to bring pressure to take it before careful preparations have been made both at home and in the patient's own expectations.

The Patient's Return to the Community

When a patient is discharged from a mental hospital, he does not return to an unchanged situation at home. The behavior that led up to hospitalization may have been disturbingly noticeable in the community and at his place of work. It is certain to have been seriously upsetting to the members of the family. The family has probably been under great strain during the course of the breakdown and has felt no small sense of relief when responsibility could be turned over to doctors and nurses. In many ways the homecoming may be joyful, but we cannot be surprised that everyone has certain misgivings about the returning patient. Will he be able to resume his former place and take up his usual activities? Must he be treated in a special way? Will he break down again?

It is increasingly recognized that cure does not end at the hospital and that the patient's chances of continued improvement depend to some extent on his reception in the community. To a degree the community has lost confidence in him, just as he may have lost confidence in himself. To a degree it may be advisable for him to lead a less strenuous life than before, to be given more care and more privileges. Thus the return to the community is bound to require adjustments, and the former patient can be either much helped or much hindered by the attitudes of those around him. Strictly speaking, mental patients cannot be sent home well. The

23 *Ibid.*, p. 569.

best that can be done is to send them home in a condition sufficiently improved to justify the hope that they can re-establish themselves satisfactorily in their families and in the community.

Realizing this, progressive workers in the hospitals have tried to reverse the common older attitude that patients' relatives are a nuisance to be kept away. Visits by relatives are encouraged, including talks with the patient's doctor; and the patient is likely to be sent home for short trial visits before final discharge. In some cases doctor, patient, and relatives together work out decisions as to the time of discharge and the immediate plans for the patient's life.[24] Attempts may be made to talk with former or future employers concerning the patient's chances of success. Measures of this kind not only help the former patient to find understanding but also serve to modify some of the anxious attitudes toward mental disorder that prevail in the community. Not until the late 1950's were there signs that these attitudes were undergoing favorable modification.[25]

Sometimes the situation is more difficult. After a long and severe illness, for instance, the patient's confidence in his ability to live again in the community may be deeply shaken, his contact with other people still painfully fragile. Former patients thus burdened may profit greatly if they can live for a while in an environment purposely made easy for them. This is sometimes accomplished by foster family care. Another method is the so-called "halfway house," a boarding house the occupants of which ideally include patients, a certain number of understanding people who are not patients, and a trained person in charge or at least supervising the operation. In such a setting the former patient can go out to his work every day but return to the house either to mingle with the others or not, as he pleases; and the step of adapting again to his family and old acquaintances is postponed to a later time. Raush and Raush have drawn a composite portrait of both halfway houses and their residents.

The modal resident of the modal halfway house is an ex-hospital patient, at one time diagnosed as schizophrenic. Directly or shortly after leaving the hospital, he came to the house, perhaps after some visiting. He finds the house very different from the hospital ward. For one thing, it is in a residential area of the city. It is a many-roomed place, dating from the twenties or thirties, in town rather than in the suburbs. It is a house, and it looks like a house and not like a hospital. Aside from staff, there are only about ten other residents. The resident has his own room or he shares a room with just one other person; also, unlike the hospital, the house has no locked rooms. While there are lots of things to do at the house, he has to go outside for any special entertainment. Moreover, he pays for his room and board.

24 O. G. Simmons, J. A. Davis, and K. Spencer, "Interpersonal Strains in Release from a Mental Hospital," *Social Problems*, IV (1956), pp. 21–28.

25 H. E. Freeman and O. G. Simmons, *The Mental Patient Comes Home* (New York: John Wiley & Sons, Inc., 1963); S. Olshansky, S. Grob, and I. Malamud, "Employers' Attitudes and Practices in the Hiring of Ex-Mental Patients," *Mental Hygiene*, XLII (1958), pp. 391–401.

At the modal house the resident receives no written rules. Still, he finds out that there are some things he must not do, such as drink on the premises, and some things that he must do, such as tell staff when he goes out, come to meals promptly, keep himself and the premises clean and obey his doctor's orders. He must care for his own room and he is usually expected to do some extra work of his own choice around the house. If he doesn't live up to these requirements, considerable social pressure will be placed on him and he may even be threatened with having to leave the house. In some ways, then, it isn't like living independently at a boarding house; it is much more closely supervised, and there is much more interaction with staff and other residents. . . .

The modal resident will stay at the house from four to eight months.[26]

The halfway house differs also from a boarding house in its provision of services. Conspicuous among these is helping ex-patients to find jobs and to manage their own finances. In a true sense these houses are halfway between the hospital and independent living, and they seem to serve as a valuable stepping stone for patients unable to make the transition in one stride.

Another scheme to ease the return is the establishment of community centers or clubs for former patients. These might be nicknamed "three-quarters houses" on the ground that the ex-patient has returned to his usual residence but still needs certain periods of extra social support. With the help of initiative by the staff, these centers can become scenes of great activity, with regular meetings, amateur shows, dances, concerts, outings, even a weekly newsletter, all of which implies planning and committee work which in the end is mostly accomplished by the former patients. The fact that all the members are familiar with mental illness creates a feeling of unusual comradeship and understanding.[27] Somewhat different in emphasis is a scheme reported by Fairweather and associates whereby a group of mental patients was removed from an open hospital ward, established in a disused motel, and set to operate, at first under supervision, a private, commercially competitive janitorial service. Conditions being favorable, the experiment was successful; the small subsociety implanted in the community took root, the service prospered, and the former patients progressively took over the management, with great benefit to their self-respect.[28]

All of these facilities perform a valuable service and show that by careful management it is possible to do a better job in restoring mental patients to normal existence. Optimism, however, should be tempered. A recent research done under relatively favorable conditions showed that six months after discharge from a mental hospital 21.6 per cent of the patients had

26 H. L. Raush with C. L. Raush, *The Halfway House Movement: A Search for Sanity* (New York: Appleton-Century-Crofts, 1968), pp. 190–91.

27 V. Goertzel, J. H. Beard, and S. Pilnick, "Fountain House Foundation: Case Study of an Ex-patient's Club," *Journal of Social Issues,* XVI (1960), pp. 54–61.

28 G. W. Fairweather, D. H. Sanders, D. L. Cressler, and H. Maynard, *Community Life for the Mentally Ill: An Alternative to Institutional Care* (Chicago: Aldine-Atherton, Inc., 1969).

been readmitted; at the end of a year, 37.4 per cent.[29] Further, it appears that readmission is not closely correlated with adverse external factors such as uneasy employers, unsympathetic neighbors, and destructive attitudes on the part of family members.[30] An ex-patient's behavior can continue to be difficult even when circumstances seem favorable. Mental disorders, after all, entail deeply rooted maladaptive tendencies that interfere with flexible response to the environment immediately present. When these tendencies persist after discharge, as happens all too often, there are bound to be disappointing failures in even the most skillful work of rehabilitation.

THE MANPOWER PROBLEM

A close look at unmet needs in mental health shows that the difficulty is not wholly financial. There is a serious manpower shortage in the related professions. In a survey of state and county mental hospitals, Albee reported in 1959 that 25 per cent of the positions budgeted for psychiatrists and psychologists, and 20 per cent of those budgeted for social workers and nurses, remained unfilled because nobody could be found to take them.[31] Budgeted positions, of course, do not necessarily reflect the number needed for high quality service. As against the standards formulated by the American Psychiatric Association for the adequate staffing of mental hospitals and clinics, a survey in 1958 showed that these institutions had in fact only 57 per cent of the physicians needed, 75 per cent of the psychologists, 40 per cent of the social workers, and 23 per cent of the registered nurses.[32] The shortage contributed to a most unequal distribution of mental health work throughout the nation. With most workers having choices of jobs, there was a high concentration in large cities of the North, East Coast, and West Coast; and the problem of staffing services in smaller communities and rural areas was already severe.

The movement for community mental health centers was bound to increase these shortages. To meet the goal of a fully staffed center for every 100,000 people it would be necessary to open hundreds of new centers and to increase the staffs of many more that were in operation on a part-time basis. The demand for trained professionals was clearly going into a steep upward curve. How could such a demand be met?

The answer that first springs to mind is that training institutions should drastically increase their output, trebling or quadrupling it if necessary to

---

[29] W. M. Michaux, M. M. Katz, A. A. Kurland, and K. H. Gansereit, *The First Year Out: Mental Patients after Hospitalization* (Baltimore: The Johns Hopkins Press, 1969), p. 66.

[30] S. S. Angrist, S. Dinitz, M. Lefton, and B. Pasamanick, *Women after Treatment: A Study of Former Mental Patients and Their Normal Neighbors* (New York: Appleton-Century-Crofts, 1968).

[31] G. W. Albee, *Mental Health Manpower Trends* (New York: Basic Books, Inc., 1959).
[32] *Action for Mental Health, op. cit.,* p. 8.

meet the rising need. The National Institute for Mental Health put its weight behind increased output by providing federal training stipends for graduate students preparing for the mental health professions. At the height of its policy in the late 1960's NIMH was granting 10,000 stipends a year, though this rate has since declined somewhat as pressures increased for economy in federal welfare agencies. There has been in fact a substantial increase of manpower in the mental health professions, but it is still far from sufficient to meet current demands, and by all indications the discrepancy is likely to continue. Why this is so will become clear if we consider what is involved in professional training of this kind.

Professional Training

The complexity of the manpower problem comes out with striking clarity in the case of psychiatry. A *psychiatrist* is first of all a physician. He has gone through medical school, taking whatever training in psychiatry is offered during the four-year course, received his M.D. degree, and specialized in psychiatry in his subsequent internship. It is incorrect to call anyone a psychiatrist who does not have the M.D. degree. Psychiatry is a medical specialty.

Implicit in this training is a huge institutional backing. To the facilities of the medical school itself are added those of teaching hospitals and clinics where first-hand experience has to be found. Much of the learning of one's specialty takes place during internships and residencies, and it may be several years beyond the M.D. degree before board examinations are taken to become a certified specialist. If psychoanalytic training is sought, which is offered by independent psychoanalytic institutes, the young doctor may remain partly in the status of a trainee for three or four more years. Of course, interns and resident physicians start giving service as well as being trained, but they still make demands on the time of older doctors to teach and supervise them. A crash program designed to increase the output of physicians would put impossible demands on the personnel and institutions now responsible for training. There is no way to increase quickly the number of senior physicians and other seasoned experts who would have to teach the enlarged cohort of new students.

There are thus inherent difficulties in stepping up the output of physicians. But two further facts are relevant. In the first place, the popularity of medicine as a profession has dropped considerably in recent years. From a peak of popularity after World War II, when competition for places in medical school was intense, applications have steadily fallen off to a degree that has created alarm about meeting future health needs. In the second place, the expansion of medical education has moved slowly, held back by the conservation that so often develops in a profession with a long history of success and prestige. Writing bluntly in 1970, Albee said: "Our nation's supply of physicians is shrinking in proportion to population. We are not now embarked on a course of action that promises to change this situation for the foreseeable future. As a consequence, our nation's supply of psychiatrists is also shrinking." [33] It looks as if the complaints from outlying community mental health centers that they cannot find medical directors will continue to be heard for some time.

Stepping up manpower is only a little less difficult in the case of the *clinical psychologist*. The ranks of this professional group have swelled considerably during the last quarter-century, though not yet enough to meet the current need. A fully trained clinical psychologist typically holds a Ph.D. degree granted by a university faculty of arts and sciences. His training is thus somewhat more academically oriented than that of a psychiatrist. It includes supervised practice and a year's clinical internship, but it also includes training in research and a doctoral dissertation that is intended to make a contribution to scientific knowledge. In practice today the clinical psychologist is likely to perform a variety of duties including psychotherapy, counseling, consultation, and the appraisal of abilities, but he can be of special value in planning and guiding research on, among other things, the effectiveness of different clinical procedures. Again the necessary training is of a character that does not permit doubling the output overnight. It requires the support of clinical and research facilities, both notably expensive, and it makes large demands on senior staff for individual supervision. There is active debate among clinical psychologists about training and the future shape of their profession.[34] Attachment to academic departments of psychology, with their single-minded scientific ideals and lack of interest in application, has caused a great deal of friction. Experiments with training are being tried and can be expected to increase.

The professional group that has grown most rapidly is that of *psychiatric social worker*. Originally a social worker was a person who visited homes and brought helpful advice and services to needy inhabitants. The role had no connection with psychiatry until certain psychiatrists began to see that their work with office patients could be helped by direct knowledge of the social and family background. In due course the psychiatric social worker evolved from being the psychiatrist's social investigator to being a co-therapist in work with the whole family. This professional group is taking an increasingly important part in community mental health.

The psychiatric social worker typically completes a course of training that leads to a Master's degree. The academic side of the training consists of courses in psychiatry and psychology, child development, community organization, and social statistics. Great emphasis is placed on supervised field training, which occupies at least half of the two-year program. The students are placed at clinics or hospitals where they participate increasingly

[33] G. W. Albee, "Through the Looking Glass," *International Journal of Psychiatry*, IX (1970–71), pp. 293–98.

[34] I. Iscoe and C. D. Spielberger, eds., *Community Psychology: Perspectives in Training and Research* (New York: Appleton-Century-Crofts, 1970).

in the work and thus learn their trade at first hand under careful supervision. Direct experience with research has gradually been given greater emphasis. Increasingly the social worker takes part in institutional research programs and needs familiarity with the impersonal rigors of research method.[35] The output of psychiatric social workers can be more easily increased merely because the training takes a shorter time. Supporting institutions and senior supervisors, whose number rises slowly, play a large part in that training.

Shortage of personnel in the chief mental health professions is thus real, severe, and not subject to rapid correction. Does this mean that the movement for community mental health will have to stop short of its goals, leaving many communities without this type of service?

Non-professional Aides

Rather than accept such a frustrating conclusion, mental health leaders have considered the possibility of using larger numbers of people not trained to the professional level. Such a move always produces anxiety, raising direful images of well-meaning blunderers making clients worse rather than better. Nevertheless, when the question is examined closely it seems sensible that some of the work of community mental health might be done by interested nonprofessionals, provided they are carefully chosen, receive practical training, recognize limits in what they attempt, and work under close professional supervision. These provisos are of the utmost importance. If they are not met, the nonprofessional worker is indeed a well-meaning blunderer who would be wiser not to tinker with mental health.

Beginning in the mid-1950's, college students began volunteering to serve as aides in mental hospitals. Experience with these volunteers, now quite extensive, illustrates both the possibilities and the problems of lay helpers in mental health work. Students were drawn to this work partly because of the glaring need: many patients in hospitals which had a custodial orientation were badly neglected, receiving no treatment and minimal attention from the overworked staff. In what are called Companion Programs each volunteer is assigned to a particular patient whom he visits at least once a week. At these meetings the volunteer tries to engage the patient in conversation, which may not be easy, and seeks to be friendly and helpful. Perhaps the patient has wants or grievances that can be called to the attention of the staff; perhaps communication with relatives has broken down and can be restored through the efforts of the volunteer; perhaps the patient can be sent home if the volunteer takes initiative and helps in making the necessary arrangements. Even if none of these is possible, the patient may be pleased and perceptibly brightened by the attention. The program can work, however, only if it is supervised by some-

[35] J. Wax, "Psychiatric Social Work," *American Journal of Psychiatry*, CXVIII (1962), pp. 627–29.

one who selects and knows the students, who knows and selects the patients, who runs a weekly group meeting for the volunteers, and who is available for individual conferences and advice. Sometimes the volunteers become bewildered by the peculiarities of psychotic conversation. Sometimes they try to push the patient too fast toward behavior that takes confidence and initiative. Sometimes they become discouraged when there are no signs of improvement, perhaps piqued that their own good intentions are ineffective. Sometimes they feel hurt and rejected by behavior which a more seasoned observer would attribute to mood changes or internal dramas having little to do with the actual visitor. The supervisor's help is constantly needed to sustain the volunteer's morale and to interpret the interactions with the patient. The students' work may be harder than expected, the gain smaller than was hoped. Yet the enterprise is worthwhile on both sides. Several reports strongly suggest that visited patients, compared to others in the same hospital, are more likely to show improvement, and more of them reach the point of discharge.[36] The students, on their part, report valuable changes in themselves. They believe that "they learned a great deal from the case-aide experience," that they "gained insight into their own personalities and problems through their relationships with the patients and their own group," and that identity formation and vocational choice were often favorably affected.[37]

Housewives constitute another source of nonprofessional help in mental health work. In one program, for instance, it proved possible after fairly brief training to use housewives as mental health counselors working directly with clients.[38] The women chosen for such programs are generally well-educated, and their activities are circumscribed in the sense that they work with assigned clients and report frequently to their professional supervisor. In another program, at the University of Rochester, housewives are trained to serve as teacher aides in public schools.[39] The women chosen may be of any age and often have limited education, but are judged to have been effective mothers, genuinely interested in young children and potentially capable of relating to them warmly and comfortably. Their job is to work with children screened from regular classes because of emotional dif-

[36] G. G. Gruver, "College Students as Therapeutic Agents," *Psychological Bulletin,* LXXVI (1971), pp. 111–27; H. A. Buckey, G. A. Muench, and B. M. Sjoberg, "Effects of a College Student Visitation Program on a Group of Chronic Schizophrenics," *Journal of Abnormal Psychology,* LXXV (1970), pp. 242–44.

[37] C. C. Umbarger, J. S. Dalsimer, A. P. Morrison, and P. R. Breggin, *College Students in a Mental Hospital* (New York: Grune & Stratton, Inc., 1962); J. D. Holzberg, R. H. Knapp, and J. L. Turner, "Companionship with the Mentally Ill: Effects on the Personalities of College Student Volunteers," *Psychiatry,* XXIX (1966), pp. 395–405.

[38] M. J. Rioch, C. Elkes, A. A. Flint, B. S. Usdansky, R. G. Newman, and E. Silber, "National Institute of Mental Health Pilot Study in Training of Mental Health Counselors," *American Journal of Orthopsychiatry,* XXXIII (1963), pp. 678–89.

[39] M. Zax and E. L. Cowen, "Research on Early Detection and Prevention of Emotional Dysfunction in Young School Children," in C. D. Spielberger, *Current Topics in Clinical and Community Psychology* (New York: Academic Press, 1969), pp. 67–108.

ficulties. The training of these women is limited to five weeks; it consists of orientation to basic aspects of mental health, personality development, behavior problems, and the nature of the school system. They are paid for their work, but not at a rate that would attract fortune hunters. Ministering to the emotional needs of children and fostering their educational development can be construed as both currently therapeutic and preventive of later disorders. The housewives are well suited to this work; indeed, their experience as effective mothers may be a more relevant credential than a formal certificate of professional training.

There is a large pool of potential mental health manpower among people having a strong personal interest in a particular form of disorder. Starting with Clifford Beers, whose personal trials with mental hospitals led him to initiate the mental health movement, there is a long tradition of private effort such as Alcoholics Anonymous, founded by cured alcoholics, Synanon established by former drug addicts, and associations for retarded children created by parents of such children. One such organization, called Widows for Widows, started oddly when a recent widow persuaded the management of a cemetery to hire her to develop a program for widows of men buried there. The bereaved are recognized as a population at risk for physical and psychiatric illness up to a period of eighteen months.[40] Our social support system, including support from religious institutions, stops too soon; the widow in question realized the need for much more extended support. Widows for Widows, staffed by widow volunteers, seeks out people who have recently been bereaved and offers them a variety of counseling and personal services. These include advice about legal matters and taxes, help with practical problems, and attempts to prevent impulsive decisions like selling a house or changing a job until the storm of grief and depression has been weathered. Or the service may consist merely of visits to provide companionship and solace, which can be done with special empathy because of the visitor's own experience of grief.

It is evident from these examples that nonprofessional aides can be of great value in forwarding community mental health. We can be optimistic about the existence of manpower and of eagerness to take part. But we must be careful not to exaggerate the part that can be taken by those who are not professionally trained. What must especially be avoided is lack of communication with professional experts. Unexpected problems are always likely to crop up for which only a broad professional experience can provide answers. A well-organized community mental health center offers the best possibility that communication will stay open among all those who are cooperating in the work.

40 W. D. Rees and S. G. Lutkins, "Mortality of Bereavement," *British Medical Journal,* IV (1967), pp. 13–16; D. Maddison and W. L. Walker, "Factors Affecting the Outcome of Conjugal Bereavement," *British Journal of Psychiatry,* CXIII (1967), pp. 1057–67.

PREVENTION OF DISORDERED BEHAVIOR

Sensible readers, familiar with the adage that an ounce of prevention is worth a pound of cure, should now be asking how much we can expect of community mental health in forestalling disordered personal behavior. If mental health services are made widely available in the community, can we hope that preventive programs, early recognition of risks, prompt treatment, and the spread of information will decisively lower the future incidence of mental disorders and maladaptive behavior?

Prevention is, of course, a recognized goal of community mental health centers. But if we let our minds run over the many topics discussed in this book it will be apparent that prevention means a great many different things. Much of the needed effort does not lie within the traditional field of mental health. As we have seen, schizophrenic disorders occur with highest frequency at low socioeconomic levels. There is a clear relation between poverty and such troubles as juvenile delinquency and drug abuse. Even mental retardation, once thought to be wholly a matter of inheritance, turns out to be influenced by cultural deprivation. We would presumably have a lower incidence of schizophrenia, juvenile delinquency, crime, drug abuse, and cultural-familial retardation if poverty were ameliorated and society more humanely organized. Whose job is this? How is it to be carried forward? The improvement of society is not a task that can be accomplished by a small group of professionals. It cannot happen at all unless there is widespread support among citizens of voting age.

Another important part of prevention has its locus in general medical care. One of the most obvious ways of reducing later maladaptive behavior according to Huessy, is "to see to it that no pregnant mother does without an adequate protein diet, that no expectant mother does without adequate prenatal and perinatal care, and that no infant goes through its first year with inadequate nutrition." We would certainly have a lower incidence of disorders such as cerebral palsy, minimal brain damage, and several forms of severe mental retardation if these public health measures were more effectively performed. This again is not the usual sphere of direct mental health intervention, but Huessy urges that "a mental health program worth its salt should be turning heaven and earth to see to it that whoever is responsible or able to do this job gets it done. One must give them all the support possible." [41]

These examples serve to show that the task of preventing disordered personal behavior cannot be assigned to any one compartment of human effort. Some disorders can be decreased only by changes in social organi-

[41] H. Huessy, "Community Mental Health: Fact and Fiction," *Mental Health in Western Massachusetts: Issues in Training* (Amherst, Mass.: Department of Psychology, University of Massachusetts, 1971), pp. 7–23.

zation; some belong in the province of the healer of bodily ills. The prevention of many others, however, can be considered the special responsibility of the mental health professions.

Preventing Psychogenic Disorder

The most obvious contribution that a community mental health center can make to prevention is to intervene more promptly in the lives of people likely to become disordered. Providing local services, at low cost if necessary, is a step in this direction. Services for children and consultations in the schools are designed to locate maladaptive behavior early and provide such redirection as may be possible. Especially when family psychotherapy has a successful result, the hope seems justified that a situation otherwise destined to go from bad to worse has been turned around to permit further growth. We shall not be able for some time, of course, to assess the results of earlier intervention, but the policy certainly deserves a thorough trial.

Strictly speaking, however, early intervention is still corrective rather than preventive. It occurs only after maladaptive behavior has begun to show itself. More fundamental prevention would mean trying to keep such behavior from happening in the first place. Our study of psychological development has shown the importance of the early years of life and of the family and neighborhood that constitute the social environment of these years. The concepts of anxiety and defense were of particular service in understanding maladaptive learnings, and the attitudes of parents often seemed to be implicated in the genesis of pathological reactions. The prevention of disorders arising out of the personal history of learnings would seem to require as its first step the changing of parental attitudes so as to produce less anxiety and give more encouragement to positive growth. Such changes can be effected only through parent education.

Only to a small extent is the educative task analogous to the usual public health program. Certain ideas about child rearing, such as feeding practices and the best times for weaning and cleanliness training, qualify as factual information which can be directly communicated, but these form a small part of the message. When it comes to parental attitudes of a more general kind one must recognize that the teaching situation is of an entirely different nature. In the first place, the expert who possesses the specialized knowledge cannot do any part of the job of applying it. It is the parents who must put it into practice, who must use the information to become in some sense experts themselves. In the second place, what has to be taught is a whole way of feeling and behaving, a general attitude toward children which will quietly but consistently steer the parents' behavior through all the vicissitudes of daily contact.

Two disquieting questions are raised by this view of the matter. (1) How sound is the information that the psychological professions are currently prepared to convey? (2) What educational methods are suitable for conveying information of this kind?

Limitations of Knowledge

Our knowledge of the effects of parental attitudes on children's development is largely limited to the effects that have been harmful. We have developed a long list of parental evils: emotional deprivation, overt rejection, covert rejection, cold mechanical handling, overprotection and absorption of the child's life, capricious punishments, severe and crushing discipline. The experts are voluble in telling parents what not to do. On the positive side the message has been thin and perhaps a touch sentimental: the atmosphere of the home must be one of unconditional love, acceptance, permissiveness, democracy; the climate must always be warm. One may well feel surprised that so much of this advice, supposedly based on scientific predictability, is expressed in metaphors of the weather. Yet the vagueness can hardly be avoided in view of the essentially negative character of what we know. No doubt there is a certain inherent difficulty in working out the positive side. As we saw in our study of development, maladjustment can often result from either too much or too little of something: for example, too much discipline or too little discipline. Middle grounds and golden means are always more difficult to describe than pathological extremes. Still it is true that our knowledge is gravely incomplete and takes a form where the "do's" are badly snowed under by the "don't's."[42] The main difficulty is that studies of disordered people have not been well balanced by studies of people whose development came out well.[43]

As a consequence of this situation we do not really know how much weight to attach to parental attitudes as causes of unhealthy development. Occasional studies suggest that normal growth can occur in a family circle that seems full of psychological evils. If further work should substantiate this impression, mental health education would have to become more discriminating in its account of what produces disordered behavior. Another thing we do not know much about is the effect of later experience—during the juvenile period, later childhood, adolescence, and even adulthood— in counter-balancing the early influence of the family circle. When breakdown occurs there is regression, and one gets the impression that early childhood influences are all-powerful. What of the children with equally troubled infancies whose later development takes a healthy turn so that they never break down? Such children never show up in clinics or hospitals, so we simply do not know whether they exist, or, if they do, what factors were important in salvaging their development. Lack of all this

[42] P. V. Lemkau, B. Pasamanick, and M. Cooper, "The Implications of the Psychogenetic Hypothesis for Mental Hygiene," *American Journal of Psychiatry,* CX (1953), pp. 436–42.

[43] R. W. White, *Lives in Progress: A Study of the Natural Growth of Personality* (2nd ed.; New York: Holt, Rinehart & Winston, Inc., 1966), pp. 22–25, 366–74.

essential information means that the mental health message first reached parents in an extremely alarming form. Children can be ruined by their parents early in life, ruined by behavior and attitudes of which the parents are not fully conscious, after which only the expert can save them. This is all that many parents could make of what they were told ten or twenty years ago.

Difficulties in Communication

Further trouble was encountered in finding the right manner of conveying information. The educative task was naturally assumed by psychiatrists, social workers, and psychologists, who seem to have approached it at first without much foresight as to all that might be involved. Through books, lectures, and magazine articles parents were told what not to do and warned of the dreadful things that would happen if they did not follow the advice. A great deal of parent education was conducted in a spirit that hardly qualified as warm, accepting, and democratic. Undoubtedly a factor in this difficulty was the tendency of professional workers to side with patients against parents and to perceive parents, either in the present or through their past influence, as the chief obstacles to therapeutic success. It is small wonder that parents sometimes felt they were being berated rather than helped.

After a while it was recognized that parent education was producing unfortunate consequences. Some of these were examined in a paper by Bruch, author of a book significantly entitled *Don't Be Afraid of Your Child*.[44] Bruch pointed out that "the enumeration of all the possible acts and attitudes that might injure a child creates an atmosphere of uncertainty and apprehension." Instead of being helpfully informed, parents and future parents are in too many cases simply intimidated. Clearly the production of anxiety in parents will defeat the purpose of reducing it in their children. Teaching which makes parents hesitant, self-conscious, and fearful of doing the wrong thing cannot be expected to bring children a feeling of security. Bruch pointed out another undertone in parent education which might be considered even more sinister. The parents are given an illusion of omnipotence, a supposedly scientific reason for believing that their influence upon the child is paramount, so that they can set "the goal of manipulating him into becoming a perfect adult." This opens the way for the parent to feel not only guilt and anxiety over the child's faults but also a most unbecoming vainglory over his excellencies. Sometimes when a child does something particularly well one hears his parents receiving congratulations for having done a fine job of bringing him up. Can we be surprised that the product of this fine job shows resentment when he

---

[44] Hilde Bruch, "Parent Education or the Illusion of Omnipotence," *American Journal of Orthopsychiatry*, XXIV (1954), pp. 723–32; *Don't Be Afraid of Your Child: A Guide for Perplexed Parents* (New York: Farrar, Straus & Co., Inc., 1952).

senses "that he is supposed," as Bruch puts it, "to prove something about the parents, and not about himself?" Bruch's work was symptomatic of a change of heart that presently steered parent education into new channels.

Newer Trends in Parent Education

Parents do not select their attitudes voluntarily, nor do they assume them simply out of ignorance. Attitudes toward children are deeply embedded in the personalities of parents and may be complexly involved with the parents' own problems. The only way to have a beneficial effect on unfortunate attitudes is to make it possible for the parents to have corrective experiences such as are the goal of psychotherapy. They must themselves be motivated to change, they must go at their own pace, they must not be made resistant by untimely interpretations, they must feel that the atmosphere is one of understanding and respect. If these conditions prevail, parents can reach real working insights into how they interact with their young, while at the same time not losing their sense of the child's part in the interaction. They can become better parents without sacrificing the naturalness and individuality of their behavior at home.

This goal can best be accomplished not by the lecture method but by group discussion. Success seems to be greatest when the discussion is conducted with a minimum of direction, so that the topics introduced come straight from the actual problems of individual parents. There is a certain advantage in keeping the experts out of sight. Parent groups can be successfully conducted by volunteers from the community provided these lay workers have received brief training in mental health concepts and in methods of facilitating group discussion. The absence of an expert encourages the participants to go further in seeking their own solutions to the problems that have brought them together.

A first attempt at evaluating the results of such methods was made in 1959 by Brim.[45] Although adequate measurement is extremely difficult, it appeared that there were usually small gains, showing more, however, in parental knowledge than in changed parental behavior. Small results should not be interpreted to mean worthless ones: even small bits of insight may set things moving in a more satisfactory way between parent and child. Here again, however, we cannot expect miraculous results; if family psychotherapy does not always work, it is not likely that parent education groups will quickly produce impressive changes. Moreover, discussion groups have a readier reception among people at least moderately well educated. In deprived neighborhoods the approach must usually be different, most likely in the form of highly practical advice.

Education is always most successful when the learner feels a strong need for what is offered. Parents of nursery school children, uneasy about the

[45] O. G. Brim, Jr., *Education for Child Rearing* (New York: Russell Sage Foundation, 1959).

early separation and the child's capacity to flourish in the new environment, are often unusually receptive to counsel. In an experiment on community mental health Caplan has sought opportunities to intervene at significant points in people's lives, such as pregnancy, bereavement, adaptation to a defective child, or adjustment to an incurable illness in a family member.[46] These are moments, he maintains, when ounces of prevention will have their traditionally large effects: moments when stress is high and the need for help may be strong.

THE CITIZEN'S CONTRIBUTION

Many readers of this book will not be planning a professional career in which knowledge of abnormal psychology is generally deemed essential. Their relation to public health, mental hospitals, and community mental health centers will be no closer than that of an intelligent citizen. They will properly ask themselves what part the citizen can play in alleviating the burden of disordered personal reactions. They will want to know whether abnormal psychology, in addition to its special professional uses, adds anything to the leaven of thought by which the world is changed for the better. The subject is, to be sure, a relatively specialized field of knowledge. In one respect, nevertheless, the knowledge and insight that can be most readily gained by studying it reaches out beyond the bounds of a specialty and becomes significant for anyone who wants to play an enlightened part in human betterment. For the task of preventing disordered personal reactions penetrates deeply, as we have seen, into public and private life.

The most direct form of service consists of volunteering as a nonprofessional aide. Earlier this meant what we might call civilian duty in a mental hospital, analogous to the volunteer service which has proved so valuable in operating general hospitals. The community mental health movement has greatly expanded the opportunities for civilian duty and stands in great need, as we saw, of varied nonprofessional manpower. Another form of service, decidedly challenging to those who like to take part in community affairs, is the civilian management of mental health facilities. Although public funds and professional direction play a large part in the community centers, citizens' boards have a role in securing additional monies, providing buildings and equipment, supervising the practical side of the operation, and enlarging community contacts. A mental health center that does not have this kind of community cooperation operates at a great handicap.

The citizen's contribution can be of a much less direct but hardly less important kind. In his personal life he interacts with many other people,

[46] G. Caplan, *An Approach to Community Mental Health* (New York: Grune & Stratton, Inc., 1961).

and his effect upon them may or may not be conducive to mutual adjustment. We are all familiar with people who have a gift for stirring up
trouble. They cannot enter the most harmonious group without throwing
it into violent discord, and they seem adept at making the anxious people
more anxious, the guilty more guilty, the angry more angry. Other people seem generally to have the opposite effect; things go better when they
are around. This desirable effect is not achieved simply by being a peace-
maker. There may be strong partisanship and a vehement espousal of
ideas, but the person is able to do this without rancor, without implying
that every other viewpoint is stupid, without resentment when others disagree or even outvote him. This is one aspect of the many-sided quality
which we call emotional maturity. A person can often improve his own
maturity when he becomes interested in reflecting on his feelings and noticing his interactions with others. He is not likely to change overnight,
but it is part of the citizen's contribution to do what he can in the direction of personal maturity.

It need hardly be mentioned that the citizen in his role of parent can
contribute importantly toward mental health. The fallacy of parental omnipotence should be avoided, but the parent is still a significant item in the
child's environment. Interest plays an important part in the success of
parent–child relationships. When parents are interested in their children
and can take them in a spirit that combines affection with a humorous
sense of perspective, many excellencies follow as a matter of course. Interest
guarantees that they will at least not ride roughshod over the child's strivings and preoccupations. Then there is the matter of respect. While realizing the child's inexperience and immaturity, parents should recognize
accomplishments as they appear and let the child know that they appreciate his initiative and growing competence.

One of the obstacles that prevent parents from guiding their children
to a healthful development is the social order in which they are compelled
to operate. Individual parents are usually wiser and better than the society
in which they live. They have outgrown, let us say, any personal inclination to keep up with the Joneses, but they cannot resist the pressure when
somebody ridicules their children for not keeping up with the Joneses' children. Perhaps they do not want their children to be prudes, but they cannot resist the prudish atmosphere of the neighborhood. Again they may
hope that their children will not be snobs, but they cannot prevent them
from absorbing this social poison if it is in the air. Thus even the best
parents are the victims of the culture and social organization in which they
live.

Our society has evolved in such a way as to present many startling contradictions. Its standards of socially desirable behavior are both conflicting
and confusing. We believe in being gentle, considerate, kindly, and forgiving, but we also believe in competitive success. A child who listens to
the voice of the culture will hardly know whether to share his toys with

other children or to hoard them and prevent their value from being depreciated. He will scarcely be able to decide whether to turn the other cheek on the playground or to hit first before the other fellow gets his guard up. Some of our ideals necessarily entail disappointment for all but a few. The glittering life of the advertising pages and the screen is within the reach of but a tiny number of people; all the rest are given a good chance to feel inferior because they cannot attain it. We sing the praises of individual freedom, but actually the great majority is seriously hemmed in by circumstance. Cooperative and kindly ideals, the individualism of the frontier, the materialistic values of competitive business, the aggression that is inherent in nationalism, the equality of the Declaration of Independence, the class and caste distinctions that go with great differences in wealth, all mix with the utmost confusion in our stew of values. Diversity of ideals in a free society is to be admired, but flat contradictions make the adjustive task of the child hopelessly difficult. There is a lot of straightening out to be done.

Adjustment is a process of learning, and learning cannot take place advantageously when the cognitive field is not clear. Many intelligent adults would be hard put to it to state the kind of world in which they want their children to grow up. This being the case, it is very hard for them to present a clear cognitive field to their children. Victims of the confused ideals which pervade our culture, they cannot put before their children a series of consistent guides or signposts pointing toward social adjustment. Anything which clarifies the nature and purposes of our society is likely to have a beneficial effect on psychological health. A parent or future parent who seriously tries to think out his system of values, deciding what he really wants to stand for, may be making an important contribution to the emotional health of himself, his children, and the people around him.

It is clear that the task of preventing abnormal behavior is one in which every citizen can participate. To the extent that such behavior arises out of the process of socialization, everyone can be of some help in its prevention. As parent and as teacher, everyone can learn to guide more wisely the steps by which children adapt themselves to the requirements of living together. As voter and citizen, everyone can throw his influence in favor of a social and moral order intelligently fashioned to encourage the best possibilities in human nature.

SUGGESTIONS FOR FURTHER READING

A pivotal point in the history of mental health care is occupied by *Action for Mental Health* (New York, Science Editions, Inc., 1961), the final report of the Joint Commission on Mental Health and Illness. This report, covering finances, facilities, programs, and manpower, was the document that set in motion the national policy of establishing community mental health centers. There is currently an outpouring of publications on community mental health. Public policies with regard to the more serious mental illnesses are discussed in a brief book by David Mechanic, *Mental Health and Social Policy* (Englewood Cliffs, N. J., Prentice-Hall, Inc., 1969). Much longer, because they consist of collections of papers by different authors, but therefore more varied in content, are Leopold Bellak, ed., *Handbook of Community Psychiatry and Community Mental Health* (New York, Grune & Stratton, Inc., 1964), and D. Adelson and B. Kalis, eds., *Community Psychology and Mental Health* (Scranton, Pa., Chandler Publishing Co., 1970). While it is too soon to expect a thorough evaluation of mental health centers, R. Glasscote and associates have prepared *The Community Mental Health Center: An Interim Appraisal* (Washington, D. C., American Psychiatric Association, 1969). Bellak and H. H. Barten edited in the same year *Progress in Community Mental Health*, Vol. 1 (New York, Grune & Stratton, Inc., 1969).

A standard older work on the social aspects of disorder is S. Kirson Weinberg's book, *Society and Personality Disorders* (Englewood Cliffs, N. J., Prentice-Hall, Inc., 1952), which "views the disordered person as an emergent of his social relations within the cultural setting." One of the first books to take this point of view was James S. Plant's *Personality and the Cultural Pattern* (New York, The Commonwealth Fund, 1937), based on studies of personality disorder in relation to disorder in the immediate social environment. The theme was pursued further in James L. Halliday's *Psychosocial Medicine: A Study of the Sick Society* (New York, W. W. Norton & Co., Inc., 1947).

For readers who are curious about innovations in the care of mental patients there is an interesting book by H. L. Raush with C. L. Raush, *The Halfway House Movement: A Search for Sanity* (New York, Appleton-Century-Crofts, 1968). Valuable also is R. M. Glasscote *et al.*, *Partial Hospitalization for the Mentally Ill* (London, Garamond Pridemark, 1969). A valuable and straightforward guide toward helping former patients back into the family is the book by K. R. Beutner and N. G. Hale, Jr., *Emotional Illness: How Families Can Help* (New York, G. P. Putnam's Sons, Inc., 1957).

An experiment in the use of college students as group leaders to help in the treatment of chronic hospitalized mental patients is reported by J. Rappaport, J. M. Chinsky, and E. L. Cowen, *Innovations in Helping Chronic Patients: College Students in a Mental Institution* (New York, Academic Press, 1971). One of the first experiments with a companion program, carried out over several years, is described by C. C. Umbarger, J. S. Dalsimer, A. P. Morrison, and P. R. Breggin, *College Students in a Mental Hospital* (New York, Grune & Stratton, Inc., 1962). A companion program of college students with troubled fifth- and sixth-grade boys is reported by Gerald Goodman, *Companionship Therapy: Studies in Structured Intimacy* (San Francisco, Jossey-Bass, 1972). The use and training of nonprofessionals in mental health work is the subject of a collection of essays edited by C. Grosser, W. E. Henry, and J. G. Kelly, *Nonprofessionals in the Human Services* (San Francisco, Jossey-Bass, 1969).

Name Index

Abeles, M., 216
Abraham, K., 491
Ackerman, N. W., 163, 288, 290, 310
Acosta, K., 555
Adams, J. E., 92, 93
Adelson, D., 603
Adler, A., 32, 44, 57, 133, 144, 164, 165, 167, 212, 237, 267, 274
Adorno, T. W., 157
Agros, S., 207
Aichhorn, A., 163
Ainsworth, M. D., 165
Albee, G., 447
Albee, G. W., 580, 589, 590
Albrecht, R., 543
Alexander, F., 185, 237, 240, 256, 262, 406, 411–12, 415, 421
Allen, C., 44
Allen, F. H., 287
Allport, G. W., 144, 191, 197, 344
Angel, E., 274, 285
Angrist, S. S., 589
Angyal, A., 216, 237, 451
Ansbacher, H. L., 44, 165, 237, 267
Ansbacher, R. R., 44, 165, 237, 267
Anthony, E. J., 448
Antonitis, J. J., 137
Appel, K. E., 575
Argyris, C., 305
Arieti, S., 330, 471, 477, 547
Aronfreed, J., 330
Arthurs, R. G. S., 331
Asch, S. E., 109
Ashby, M. C., 331
Astrup, C., 441, 443, 465, 476, 477
Averback, A. H., 222
Averill, J. R., 93
Ayllon, T., 105, 250

Bach, G. R., 299
Bagley, C., 539, 547
Baker, B. L., 251
Baldwin, A. L., 159, 165
Ball, J. C., 358, 372
Ban, T. A., 99
Bandura, A., 109, 132, 139, 163, 165, 264, 319, 338
Barclay, R. M., 431
Baron, A., 137
Barry, H., 447
Barten, H. H., 603
Bateson, G., 459, 460
Beall, L., 290
Beard, J. H., 588
Beck, A. T., 497, 505, 506
Becker, W. C., 160
Beers, C. W., 11, 19, 44, 482, 506, 594
Beier, E. G., 272
Bell, N. W., 164
Bellak, L., 603
Benda, C. E., 456, 551
Benedek, T., 428
Bergin, A. E., 280
Berlynne, D. E., 237
Berne, E., 300, 310
Bertrand, A., 22
Bettelheim, B., 455
Beutner, K. R., 603
Bibring, E., 493
Bieber, I., 382, 388, 394
Binet, A., 384, 549
Bini, L., 20
Binswanger, L., 273–74
Bion, W. R., 300
Birch, H. G., 148, 232, 424, 531
Birk, L., 302
Birren, J. E., 541, 546, 547
Black, S., 431
Blackwell, W. E., 357
Blain, D., 575
Bleuler, E., 430, 439
Bloom, B., 563
Blos, P., 177

Blum, G. S., 165
Boatman, M. J., 458
Bockoven, J. S., 19
Bond, E. D., 504
Bond, I. K., 392
Bonine, W., 493, 503
Book, J. A., 466
Borgatta, E. F., 237, 371
Bortner, M., 531
Boss, M., 274
Bossard, J. H, 186
Botwinick, J., 540
Bowen, M., 460
Bowlby, J., 164, 561
Brady, J. V., 408, 411
Bray, D. W., 550, 558
Brecker, R., 344
Breger, L., 254
Breggin, P. R., 593, 603
Bremer, A., 430
Brendtro, L. K., 155
Brenner, J. H., 349
Breuer, J., 225
Brickner, R. M., 516, 547
Brim, O. G., Jr., 599
Briscoe, O., 332
Broca, P. P., 14, 510
Brodman, K., 511
Brody, E. B., 477, 584
Broen, W. E., 468
Bro-Kahn, R., 425
Bromberg, W., 8, 10, 44
Bronfenbrenner, U., 159
Brown, R., 336
Bruch, H., 598
Buckey, H. A., 593
Burchard, J., 324
Burgemeister, B. B., 554
Burgess, M., 417
Burmey, W. E., 499
Burton, A., 89, 284, 310, 524
Buss, A. H., 165, 468
Busse, E. W., 540, 544

Cadoret, R. J., 442

Cahoon, E. B., 331
Cameron, D. C., 352
Cameron, N., 450, 498, 520
Campbell, J. D., 480, 501, 506
Cancro, R., 466, 468, 477
Cannon, W. B., 402
Canter, A., 522
Caplan, G., 600
Capote, T., 326, 328, 339
Caudill, W., 584
Caughey, J. L., 406
Cautela, J. R., 250
Cerletti, V., 20
Chambers, C. D., 358, 372
Charcot, J. M., 23–24, 39, 202, 225, 229, 277, 401
Chess, S., 148, 232, 424
Cleckley, H., 325, 339
Cobb, S., 404, 415, 427, 512, 539, 547
Coelko, G. V., 96
Cohen, A. A., 321
Cohen, M. B., 493
Cohen, R. A., 493
Cohen, S., 352, 354
Coleman, R. W., 141
Colombier, J., 7
Coolidge, J. C., 170
Cooper, C. L., 310
Cooper, M., 597
Cornelison, A. R., 447, 459
Costello, C. G., 428
Cottrell, L. S., 323
Cowan, W. K., 411
Cowen, E. L., 593, 603
Crafts, M., 334
Cressey, D. R., 313, 338
Cressler, D. L., 588
Cumming, E., 478, 543
Cumming, J., 478

Davis, F. H., 425
Davis, J. A., 587
Davis, W. N., 368
Dederick, C., 359, 361
Delay, J., 471
Dell, S., 332
Denhoff, E., 525
Deniker, P., 471
Denker, D. G., 281
De Reuck, A. V. S. de, 332
Deschamps, A., 471
Deutsch, A., 10, 11, 44
Deutsch, H., 182
Dever, R. B., 560, 563
Dicks, H. V., 204, 229, 295
Dingman, H. F., 550
Dinits, S., 589
Di Scipio, W. J., 388
Diven, K., 101, 209

Dix, D. L., 10, 12
Dixon, J. F., 531
Dohrenwind, B. P., 464
Dohrenwind, B. S., 464
Doll, E., 549
Dollard, J., 146, 152, 165, 237, 264, 285
Dolsinen, J. S., 593, 603
Domino, E. F., 348
Doob, L. W., 152, 165
Doris, J., 554, 556, 573
Down, L., 551–52
Draguns, J. G., 48
Draper, G., 405, 411, 413
Driscoll, W., 556
Drolette, M., 131
Dubois, P., 36, 39
Dupertuis, C. W., 406
Dye, H. B., 561

Ebaugh, F. G., 483
Edwards, M. D., 421
Ehrlich, S. K., 331
Eisenberg, L., 171, 455, 531
Eissler, K. R., 242
Elkes, C., 593
Ellenberger, H. F., 274, 285
Ellingson, R. J., 331
Ellis, H., 379
English, O. S., 428
Enneis, J. M., 310
Erickson, T. C., 537
Erikson, E. H., 139, 147, 161, 165, 169, 183, 194, 196, 198, 201
Errera, P., 458
Escalona, S. K., 162
Esquirol, J. E. D., 15
Esterson, A., 459, 477
Estes, S. G., 272
Estes, W. K., 572
Evans, J., 156
Evans, R. B., 383
Evans, R. R., 371
Eysenck, H. J., 208, 233–34, 237, 278, 332, 366, 395, 498, 516
Ezriel, H., 298, 300

Fagan, J., 275
Fairbain, W. R. D., 226
Fairweather, G. W., 588
Farina, A., 459
Feldman, M. P., 387
Feldman, S. E., 453, 477
Feldman, Y., 460
Fenichel, O., 152, 165, 236, 237, 382, 394, 491, 506
Ferreira, A. J., 291

Fiedler, F. E., 267
Filstead, W. J., 310
Finney, J. C., 332
Fischer, D. E., 133
Fishler, G., 555
Fiske, D. W., 137
Fleck, S., 459, 477
Fliess, W., 344
Flint, A. A., 593
Folling, A., 554
Ford, D. H., 274, 285
Foulkes, S. H., 299
Fournier, A., 16
Fowler, R. C., 442
Fox, B., 388
Fox, R. E., 276, 282
Frank, J. D., 277, 284
Frank, J. M., 243
Frankl, V. E., 454
Fraser, H. F., 347
Freedman, D. Y., 538, 547
Freeman, H. E., 587
Freeman, W. W., 518
French, E. L., 573
French, T. M., 240, 262, 421, 444
Frenkel-Brunswik, E., 157
Freud, A., 118, 121, 133
Freud, S., 26–28, 39, 44, 115, 118, 125, 149, 152, 165, 167, 184, 202, 207, 210, 225, 229, 239, 240, 255, 267, 277, 284, 287, 344, 373, 386, 394, 401, 491, 494
Freyhan, F. A., 440
Friedman, S., 329
Fries, M. E., 161
Fromm, E., 180
Fromm-Reichmann, F., 267, 284, 310, 457, 473, 477
Funkenstein, D., 154

Galanter, E., 110
Galen, 6
Gansereit, K. H., 589
Gardner, G. E., 89
Gareluk, E. L., 259
Garmezy, N., 441
Gates, A. I., 560
Gautier, M., 553
Gelb, A., 515
Geleerd, E. R., 222
Gelhorn, E., 403, 428
Gendlin, E. T., 269, 273
Ghent, L., 512
Gibbens, T. C. N., 332
Gibbs, E. L., 536
Gibbs, F. A., 536

Gibson, R. W., 493
Gilmore, H. R., 584
Ginzberg, S., 550, 558
Glaser, D., 338, 339
Glasscote, R. M., 583, 603
Glasser, B. A., 582
Glasser, W., 275
Glassman, A. H., 501
Goertzel, V., 588
Goffman, E., 478, 585
Goldberg, C., 306
Goldfarb, W., 139
Goldman, A. E., 453
Goldstein, K., 111, 515, 522–23, 524, 526, 547
Gonen, J. Y., 298
Goodman, G., 603
Gottlieb, J. S., 331
Gottlieb, P. M., 421
Gottschalk, L. A., 307
Grace, W. J., 400
Graham, D. T., 400-1
Granger, C., 334
Grant, J. D., 317
Grant, M. Q., 317
Grant, V. W., 89, 384, 385, 476
Green, A., 102
Green, H., 457, 473, 477
Greenacre, P., 494, 506
Greenblatt, M., 307, 309, 478, 517, 582
Greene, B., 310
Gregory, I., 447
Griesinger, W., 14
Grinker, R. R., 426, 428, 480, 483, 495
Grinspoon, L., 349
Grob, S., 587
Grosser, C., 603
Grunebaum, M. G., 172
Gruver, G. G., 593
Guthrie, R., 556
Guttmacher, J. A., 302
Guze, S. B., 377

Hacker, F. J., 222
Haggard, E. A., 259
Hahn, P. B., 170
Hahn, W., 419
Haines, W. H., 393
Hakanson, J. E., 417
Hale, N. G., Jr., 603
Haley, J., 289, 459
Hall, C. S., 104, 132, 237
Halliday, J. L., 603
Hamburg, D. A., 92, 93, 96, 499
Hampson, J. G., 380
Hampson, J. L., 380

Handel, G. F., 163, 165
Hanfmann, E., 216, 237, 372, 477
Hare, R. D., 333, 335, 337, 339
Harkins, E. B., 297
Harlow, H. F., 137, 138
Harlow, M. K., 138
Harrell, R. F., 560
Harris, R. E., 89, 542
Harris, W. C., 354
Hart, J. T., 269, 284
Hartman, E., 582
Haslam, J., 15
Haughton, E., 105
Havighurst, R. J., 543
Hayden, G. G., 523
Haywood, H. C., 572
Head, H., 514
Healy, W., 391
Heath, R. G., 468
Hebb, D. O., 515, 547
Heber, R. F., 550, 554, 559, 560, 563, 568, 573
Heidegger, M., 273
Heine, R. W., 284
Heins, L., 456
Hendrick, I., 258, 260, 284
Henry, G. W., 8, 13, 17, 44
Henry, J., 162
Henry, W., 543
Henry, W. E., 603
Herling, J., 313
Heron, W., 137
Herron, W. G., 309, 477
Hertzig, M. E., 232, 424, 531
Hess, R. D., 163, 165, 560
Heston, L. L., 464
Hicks, L. H., 541
Hill, D., 332
Hill, G., 10
Hill, L. B., 459, 477
Hillyer, J., 506
Himwich, H. E., 467
Hippocrates, 6, 13, 14
Hire, A. W., 89
Hirsch, S. J., 98, 196
Hoagland, H., 467
Hobbs, N., 298
Hoch, P. H., 472, 504
Hoelzel, 408
Hoff, E. C., 369, 370
Hoffman, H. R., 393
Hofstatter, L., 518, 519
Holden, J. M. C., 518, 519
Hollingshead, A. B., 276–77, 429, 576
Hollingworth, H. L., 513
Holsopple, J. W., 517
Holzberg, J. D., 524, 593
Hooker, E., 383

Horney, K., 32, 124, 125, 133, 149, 156, 158, 186, 267
Horper, P. 558
Horton, P., 223, 224
Howels, J. G., 310
Hsia, D.-Y., 556
Huessy, H., 595
Hughes, C. C., 576
Hughes, J. R., 332
Hunt, J. McV., 171, 370, 558
Husserl, E., 273
Huston, P. E., 471
Huswitz, I., 172
Hutchinson, H. C., 392
Hyde, R. W., 467

Imboden, J. B., 226
Iscoe, I., 591
Itil, T. H., 518, 519

Jackson, D. D., 458, 459, 466, 468, 477
Jackson, H., 514
Jacobson, E., 493, 503, 506
Jaffe, J. H., 363
James, W., 36, 144
Janet, P., 22, 24–26, 36, 37, 39, 44, 225, 229, 231–32, 236, 401
Jasper, H., 547
Jelliffe, S., 479
Jenkins, R. L., 315, 329, 439, 517
Jensen, A., 558
Johnson, J. A., 310
Johnson, V. E., 377–78, 395
Jones, C. M., 415
Jones, H. E., 89
Jones, M., 307, 333
Jones, M. C., 103
Jones, R. M., 216, 237
Jung, C. G., 181, 233, 267, 452

Kagen, J., 232
Kalb, L. C., 536, 538, 547
Kalhorn, J., 159
Kalin, R., 368
Kalinowsky, L. B., 504
Kalis, B., 603
Kallman, F. J., 464, 466
Kanfer, F. H., 249–51, 284
Kanner, L., 454
Kantor, R. E., 309, 477
Kaplan, B., 89, 212, 476, 506
Kaplan, S., 425
Karlson, J. L., 466
Karon, B. P., 476
Kasanin, J., 444, 477
Katz, M. M., 589
Kaufman, I., 456

Kaye, H. E., 383
Kelley, J. G., 603
Keniston, K., 98, 196
Kennedy, F., 393
Kennedy, J. F., 577
Kennedy, R. F., 430
Keogh, R. P., 331
Kephart, N. C., 527
Kesey, K., 308
Kety, S. S., 442, 465, 467, 468, 478
Kierkegaard, S., 273
Kilgalen, R. K., 477
Kimball, B., 172
King, S. H., 308, 478
Kinsey, A. C., 188, 381, 383
Kirk, S. A., 562, 563, 564
Kirman, B. H., 552
Kish, G. B., 137
Klaber, M. M., 550
Klapman, J. W., 298
Klerman, G. L., 490
Knapp, P. H., 423
Knapp, R. H., 593
Knoblock, H., 531, 558
Knott, J. R., 331
Knox, W. E., 556
Koch, R., 555
Kohl, R. N., 294
Kohler, W., 108
Korn, S., 232
Korner, A. F., 232
Kositchek, R., 419
Kostenbaum, R., 543
Kraepelin, E., 17, 46, 77, 430, 440, 466, 479, 488, 498, 506
Krafft-Ebing, R. von, 16
Kraines, S. H., 501
Kramer, B. M., 583
Kramer, M., 429, 472
Krasner, L., 208, 250, 392
Krauch, E., 506
Kremer, M. W., 383
Kretschmer, E., 228, 498
Kris, E., 141
Krishner, M., 387
Kurland, A. A., 589
Kurtz, G. N., 364

Laborit, H., 471
Lacey, J. I., 424
Lacey, J. R., 102
Laing, R. D., 275, 450, 459, 474, 476
Lamberd, W. G., 380
Lambert, W. W. 237
Landis, C., 89, 281, 476, 506
Lane, E., 447
Lang, P. J., 468

Langner, T. S., 575, 576
Lazarus, A. A., 248, 250, 254, 279, 284, 378
Leary, T., 351, 437
Leavitt, M., 476
Lebovitz, P. S., 380
Lefton, M., 589
Lehtinen, L. E., 523, 526, 527
Leighton, A. H., 576
Lejerine, J., 553
Lenkau, P. V., 597
Lennox, W. G., 536, 547
Leonard, W. E., 112–13, 211
Lerner, E., 150
Lessac, M. S., 330
Lessler, K., 276, 282
Leventhal, H., 345
Levin, H., 150, 165
Levinson, D. J., 307, 332, 478, 582
Levy, D., 141, 160, 165, 335
Lewin, B. D., 489
Lewis, O., 156
Lidz, T., 459, 477
Lindemann, E., 93, 339
Lindzey, G., 104, 132, 237
Linn, L. S., 585
Lippitt, R., 177
Lipton, E. L., 425
Lipton, M. A., 505
Lipton, R. C., 138
Lister, J. L., 17, 470
Livson, F., 542, 547
Locher, L. M., 471
Locke, E. A., 254
London, P., 397, 428, 431
Lonfbourrow, G. N., 428
Lorr, M., 517
Louria, D. B., 352, 355, 358
Lovibond, S. H., 245
Lubensky, A. W., 448
Luborsky, L., 222
Lutkins, S. G., 594

Maccoby, E. E., 150, 165
MacCulloch, M. J., 387
Maddi, S. R., 137
Maddison, D., 594
Magaret, A., 520
Magnan, V., 14
Maher, B. A., 330, 335, 408
Mahler, M., 456
Maier, N. R. F., 113
Main, T. F., 295
Malamud, I., 587
Malamud, W., 226
Malinowski, B., 373
Malmo, R. B., 425
Malmquist, C. P., 492
Mangham, I. L., 310

Marcia, J. E., 195
Martin, M. F., 222
Mason, J. W., 499
Masserman, J. H., 114
Masters, W. H., 377–78, 395
Maurice, W. L., 377
May, P. R. A., 475–76, 478
May, R., 274, 285
Mayhew, C., 350
Maynard, H., 588
Mays, W., 364, 365
McArthur, C. C., 164
McCabe, M. S., 442
McClelland, D. C., 367, 448
McCord, J., 318, 329, 339, 372
McCord, W., 318, 329, 339, 372
McCurdy, H. G., 224
McDougall, W., 222
McFarland, R. C., 519, 520
McGaugh, J. L., 254
McGinnis, N. H., 397
McGuire, L. E., 354
Mead, G. H., 193
Mechanic, D., 577, 603
Mednick, S. A., 448
Meehl, P. E., 466
Meier, J. E., 439
Mendels, J., 491, 497, 498, 500, 506
Menolascino, F. J., 552
Mering, O. von, 308
Merrill, M. A., 315
Meserve, W. G., 342
Mesmer, A., 22–24, 35, 39, 44, 277
Metcalfe, M., 422, 432
Metter, F. A., 89, 476, 506
Meyer, B. C., 415
Meyer, E., 231
Meyer, J. E., 414
Meyer, V., 516
Miall, W. E., 418
Michael, S. T., 575, 576
Michaux, W. M., 589
Miles, H. H. W., 428
Miller, D. R., 165, 223, 224, 317
Miller, G. A., 110
Miller, J., 480
Miller, J. O., 558
Miller, N. E., 102, 146, 152, 165, 237, 264, 285
Miller, W., 321
Mills, L. C., 418
Mintz, E. E., 310
Miron, M. S., 514
Mirsky, A., 456
Mirsky, I. A., 410, 425
Mishler, E. G., 462
Mittelmann, B., 152, 413

Moment, D., 305
Money, J., 379, 380, 395
Moniz, E., 516
Montaigne, M. de, 6
Moore, D. J., 456
Moore, J. W., 16
Morel, B. A., 14, 430
Moreno, J. L., 296, 310
Morrison, A. P., 593, 603
Morrison, J. R., 471
Mosland, R. L., 567
Mowrer, O. H., 114, 152, 165, 244
Mowrer, W. M., 244
Moyers, J. H., 418, 428
Mucha, T. F., 230
Muench, G. A., 593
Munroe, R., 267
Murphey, E. B., 96
Murphy, G., 128, 133, 186, 193–201, 237
Murphy, L. B., 89, 92, 132
Murray, H. A., 110, 120, 146, 258

Nagelburg, L., 460
Nameche, G., 441, 442
Nemetz, S. J., 423
Neuberger, M. B., 371
Newcomb, T. M., 201
Newman, R. G., 593
Newton, M. A., 518
Nichols, W. W., 352
Nixon, R. M., 430
Nodine, J. H., 418, 428
Noguchi, H., 16
Noreik, K., 443, 465, 476, 477
Norris, L. B., 397
Nunn, R., 480
Nunnally, J. C., 480

Oberdisse, K., 414
Obrist, W. D., 540
Ohlin, L. E., 314
Oldham, P. D., 418
Olshansky, S., 587
Oltman, J., 329
Opler, M. K., 440, 575
Osgood, C. E., 514
Ostergaard, L., 465
Ovesey, L., 388, 395

Parens, H., 165
Parker, J. B., 531
Pasamanick, B., 531, 558, 589, 597
Pasteur, L., 17
Pattison, E. M., 307
Paul, C., 36

Pavlov, I. P., 39–40, 99, 207, 208, 234, 244, 254, 370
Paykel, E. S., 490
Pearlin, L. D., 96
Peck, M., 261
Penfield, W., 513, 537, 547
Penrose, L. S., 555, 564, 569, 570, 572
Perls, F., 275
Perot, P., 513
Perry, W. G., 195, 272
Peterson, D. E., 106, 108, 132
Peterson, D. R., 49, 322
Peterson, P. G., 543, 547
Petrie, A., 517
Phillips, J. S., 249–51, 284
Phillips, L., 48, 442, 445
Phillipson, R. V., 372
Piaget, J., 108, 150
Pickens, R., 354
Pickering, G., 418
Pilnick, S., 588
Pinel, P., 8–11, 12, 13, 15, 17, 21
Plant, J. S., 603
Platt, E. P., 331
Plaut, T. F. A., 368, 372
Plummer, G., 566
Polansky, N. A., 177, 297
Pollack, E. S., 472
Porter, R., 332
Powers, E., 323
Prentice, N. M., 172
Pribram, K. H., 110
Prichard, J. C., 324
Prince, M., 223, 230, 236
Provence, S., 138, 141, 455
Purcell, K., 421
Putnam, T. J., 547

Quay, H. C., 332

Rachman, S., 208, 233–34, 237, 247, 280, 395
Rackeman, F. H., 421
Rado, S., 489
Radzinowicz, L., 339
Rapaport, D., 222
Rapoport, R. N., 576
Rappaport, J., 603
Raush, C. L., 587, 603
Raush, H. L., 587, 603
Rayner, R., 100
Redick, R. W., 472
Redl, F., 319, 324, 338
Redlich, F. C., 276–77, 429, 477, 538, 547, 576, 584
Reed, E. W., 558
Reed, S. C., 558
Rees, L., 498

Rees, W. D., 594
Reich, T., 497
Reich, W., 128
Reichard, S., 543, 547
Reinhardt, R. F., 230
Reiser, M. R., 410
Reitan, R. M., 512
Remington, F. J., 317
Rennie, T. A. C., 471, 575
Ribble, M. A., 136, 138
Richmond, J. B., 424
Ricks, D. F., 441, 442, 447, 460, 471, 487
Rider, R., 558
Riesen, A. H., 137
Riesman, D., 180
Riesman, J. D., 242
Riesman, J. M., 285
Rifkin, A. H., 383
Rimland, B., 456, 477
Rinkel, M., 467
Rioch, M. J., 593
Ritvo, S., 455
Roberts, L., 514
Robertson, I., 347, 358, 363
Robinault, I. P., 525
Robins, E., 381
Robins, L. N., 329, 332, 334
Robinson, H. B., 550, 552, 553, 556, 566, 568, 569, 572
Robinson, M. F., 518
Robinson, N. M., 550, 552, 553, 556, 566, 568, 569, 572
Robinson, R. L., 575
Rockwell, D. A., 585
Rodin, S. S., 171
Roff, M., 447, 471, 477
Rogers, C. R., 38–39, 58, 268, 284, 285, 298
Romasco, A., 323
Rosen, J., 473
Rosen, S., 177
Rosenberg, M., 96
Rosenblum, E., 456
Rosenhan, D., 397, 428, 431
Rosenman, R., 419
Rosenthal, D., 442, 465, 478
Rosenzweig, S., 154
Rosner, B. S., 507
Ross, D., 109
Ross, S. A., 109
Ross, T. A., 170, 237, 457
Rossi, J. J., 310
Ruesch, J., 424
Ruitenbeck, H. M., 306, 310, 360
Rush, B., 7
Rutsky, A., 523
Ryan, W., 580

Rylander, G., 515

Sabshin, M., 480
Sachar, E. J., 499
Saghir, M. T., 381
Sakel, M., 19, 470
Salzman, L., 215–16, 470
Sanders, D. H., 588
Sanford, R. N., 157, 300
Sarason, S. B., 573, 554, 556
Sarbin, T. R., 296
Saslow, G., 272
Satir, V., 291, 310
Saul, L. J., 165, 284, 417
Sawrey, J. M., 407
Sawrey, W. L., 407
Saxe, J. G., 431
Schachter, J., 425
Schaeffler, G., 555
Scheerer, M., 523
Scheflin, A. E., 575
Schilder, P., 221
Schildkraut, J. J., 501
Schooler, C., 453, 477
Schreiber, D., 173
Schulsinger, F., 442, 448, 465
Schulz, C. G., 477
Schwab, J. J., 397, 418
Schwab, R. B., 397, 418
Schwartz, M. S., 307, 585
Schwitzgebel, R., 324
Scott, J. C., 572
Sears, R. R., 120, 150, 152, 165
Seevers, M. H., 353
Selye, H., 404
Semelaigne, R., 8
Semmelweiss, I. P., 470
Semmes, J., 512
Shagass, C., 425
Shakespeare, W., 366
Shands, H. C., 428
Shapiro, D., 216, 235, 237
Shaw, C. R., 89, 175
Shephers, I. L., 275
Shetler, S., 417
Shiek, D. A., 456
Shipman, V. C., 560
Short, J. F., 321, 339
Shutz, W. D., 306
Silber, D. A., 96
Silber, E., 593
Silverberg, W. V., 143
Simeons, A. T. W., 403, 404, 415, 416, 428
Simmons, O. G., 587
Singer, E., 285
Singer, M. T., 459
Sirhan, S., 429
Sjoberg, B. M., 593
Skeels, H. M., 561, 562

Skinner, B. F., 104, 132
Skinner, W. I., 341, 346, 371
Slack, C. W., 323
Slavson, S. R., 298, 303
Sloane, R. B., 254
Smart, R. G., 364
Smith, D. E., 353, 356
Smith, R., 355
Smith, R. L., 102
Smythies, J. R., 467
Soddy, K., 572
Solbach, H. G., 414
Solomon, H. C., 467, 517
Solomon, M. H., 582
Solomon, R. L., 113, 330
Spencer, K., 587
Sperry, B. M., 172
Spiegel, J. P., 495
Spielberger, C. D., 591, 593
Spitz, R. A., 136, 138, 492
Spotnitz, H., 460
Srole, L., 575
Stachnik, T. J., 362, 363
Stanton, A. H., 307, 585
Steig, W., 203
Stein, M., 421, 422
Steinfeld, G. J., 585
Steinschneider, A., 424
Steiper, D. R., 243
Stekel, W., 385
Stephen, J. H., 441
Stephenson, G., 334
Stern, C., 570
Stern, J. A., 400
Stern, W., 142
Stevenson, R. L., 192
Stoller, R. P., 380, 395
Stolorow, R. D., 448
Stone, A. A., 476
Stone, S. S., 476
Strauss, H., 534
Strauss, R., 419
Strackey, J., 284
Strauss, A. A., 522, 526, 527
Strecker, E. A., 483
Strodtbeck, F. L., 321, 459
Strupp, H. H., 276, 277, 280, 282
Subotnik, L., 280
Sullivan, C. E., 317
Sullivan, H. S., 168, 176, 177, 183, 201, 267, 430, 440, 452, 460, 477
Sutherland, E. H., 312, 338
Sutherland, J. D., 300
Swanson, G. E., 165
Swinehart, J. W., 342
Sylvester, D., 207
Symonds, P. M., 111
Szalita, A. B., 471

Szasz, T., 48
Szurek, S. A., 458

Tarjan, G., 550
Taylor, W. S., 223
Teuber, H. L., 512, 515
Thackery, W., 346
Thaler, M., 410
Thomas, A., 148, 232, 424, 447, 471
Thompson, W. R., 137
Thorndike, E. L., 103
Thorne, F. C., 273, 334
Thrasher, F. M., 175
Tiffany, T. L., 322
Tizard, B., 538
Tizard, J., 560
Tolman, E. C., 108
Tomkins, S. S., 120, 231, 444
Tomlinson, T. M., 269, 284
Tooth, G. C., 518
Tredgold, A. F., 572
Tremblay, M. A., 576
Trieschman, A. E., 155
Triesman, M., 397, 411, 428
Troll, W., 556
Tuke, W., 9, 12, 13
Tupin, R., 553
Turner, J. L., 593
Turner, L. H., 330
Twain, M., 344

Ullmann, L. P., 208, 250, 392
Umbarger, C. C., 593, 603
Urban, H. B., 274, 285
Usdansky, B. S., 593
Uzgiris, I. C., 561

Vaillant, G. E., 441
Vandenbos, G. R., 476
Van Lehn, R., 424
Vives, J. L., 6
Vogel, E. L., 164
Von Mering, O., 478

Waitzkin, B., 560
Wakefield, J., 345, 346
Waldfogel, S., 170
Walker, W. L., 594
Wall, J. A., 415
Wallen, R., 275
Wallin, J. E. W., 542
Walters, R. H., 109, 132, 139, 163, 319, 338
Wang, H. S., 540
Wanner, E., 368
Ward, M. H., 251
Waring, M., 441, 460
Warson, S., 162
Watson, J. B., 39–40, 100

Watt, N. F., 447
Wax, J., 592
Waxler, N. E., 462
Weakland, J. H., 459
Wechsler, D., 540
Weil, A. P., 458
Weinberg, H., 89
Weinberg, S. K., 315, 575, 603
Weiner, D. N., 243
Weiner, H., 410
Weinroth, L. A., 415
Weinstein, S., 512
Weisch, R., 354
Weiss, E., 428
Weiss, J. H., 421, 428
Weissman, M. M., 490
Welner, J., 465
Wender, P. H., 442, 465, 529, 530, 547
Wepman, J. M., 515, 547
Werner, H., 453, 522
Wessman, A. E., 487
Wethessin, N., 419
Weyer, J., 6
Wheeler, S., 327
White, B. V., 415
White, R. W., 89, 132, 140, 164, 165, 201, 597

White, W. A., 433, 481
Whitney, E. D., 372
Whitney, S., 556
Whittaker, J. K., 155
Whitten, P., 347, 358, 363
Whybrow, P. C., 500
Whyte, W. F., 175
Wikler, A., 357, 531
Wilkins, W., 254
Willer, L., 456
Williams, R. H., 307, 478
Willis, T., 7
Wilson, W., 332
Wineman, D., 319, 324, 338
Winokur, G., 400, 442, 497
Winslow, R. W., 312
Wise, J. H., 522
Wittenborn, J. R., 372
Wohlers, A., 555
Wolberg, L. R., 400
Wolf, S., 407, 413
Wolfenstein, M., 136
Wolff, H. G., 405, 407, 413
Wolfgang, M. E., 339
Wolman, B. B., 458
Wolpe, J., 208, 245, 278, 279, 284, 378, 387
Wolstein, B., 284

Woodworth, R. S., 166
Woodyard, E., 560
Woolf, P. J., 161
Wright, S., 408
Wunsch, W. L., 552
Wurm, M., 419
Wynne, L. C., 113, 459

Yablonsky, L., 310, 338, 359, 360, 372
Yalom, I. D., 310
Yolles, S. F., 429

Zagona, S. V., 371
Zalesznik, A., 305
Zarafonetis, C. J. D., 347, 349, 350, 372
Zax, M., 593
Zeithin, B. B., 310
Ziegler, F. J., 226
Zilboorg, G., 7, 8, 13, 16, 17, 44
Zimmerman, F. T., 554
Zimmerman, H., 414
Zola, I. K., 318
Zorbaugh, H. W., 175
Zubin, J., 472

Subject Index

Ability, 1
  and personality, 95
  at school, 173–74
  Bert Whipley (case), 81
  decline in old age, 540
Abnormal psychology, 45
  perspective, 48–49
  subject matter, 4
Abreaction, 26–31
Abstraction, 79, 109
  in Martha Ottenby, 79
  loss of abstract attitude, 522
Acceptance, parental, 158, 160
Acting out, 303, 311
Acting out neurosis, 322
Activity group therapy, 303–4
Activity level, 160
Adaptation, and competent action, 93
Adaptive process, 90–98
  analysis of, 90–98
  complexity of, 95
  definition, 91
  in early life, 134–65
Adaptive styles, 235
Addiction, 343
Adjustment; *see also* Maladjustment
  adjustive attempt in depression, 489
  and competence, 143
  and social enslavement, 179
  and traits, 125
  as compromise, 91
  as process, 91
  problems and aggression, 153
  sexual, 184, 187
  to brain defect, 524
  to reality, 91
Adolescence, 167–201, 440, 445
  and group membership, 177, 183, 320–21
Adolescent maladjustment, 188 ff.
Adolescent rebellion, Kathi Hermann (case), 59–60
Adrenal gland, 499
Adrenogenital syndrome, 380
Affect
  affective bleaching, 517

coping with, 491
  disorders of, 483
  in psychopathic personality, 326
  in schizophrenia, 430–32, 446
Affective psychosis, 433
Age; *see also* Senile psychosis, 539
  decline of abilities, 540
  psychological situation of aged, 541–44
  senile psychosis, 545
Aggression, 86, 125, 413, 416
  aggressive trend, 124
  ambivalence, 153
  and activity group therapy, 304
  and delinquency, 318
  and introjection, 150
  and essential hypertension, 417
  and frustration, 152, 153
  and maladjustment, 156
  and mania, 485
  and mature reaction, 155
  and need for power, 127
  and neurosis, 125, 127
  and obsessive symptoms, 214
  and projection, 120
  and psychosomatic eliminative disorders, 416
  case of maladjustment, 156
  channeling, 153–55
  children who hate, 319
  conditions favoring repression, 318–19
  definition, 151
  in peptic ulcer patients, 413
  nature of, 151
  sibling rivalry, 154
Air encephalogram, 74
Alarm reaction, 404
Alcohol addiction, 368
Alcoholics Anonymous, 370, 594
Alcoholism, 34, 365–71
  aversive conditioning, 370
  cultural factors, 368
  effects of alcohol, 365
  etiology, 367–68
  incidence, 576
  medical implications, 369

Alcoholism (*Continued*)
  normal and abnormal drinking, 366
  predisposing factors, 367
  treatment, 369–71
Allergy, 420
Alphy rhythm, 534
Alzheimer's disease, 509, 546
Amaurotic familial idiocy, 569
Ambivalence, 153
American Association of Mental Deficiency, 549
American Psychiatric Association, 589
Amnesia, 221
  and alcohol, 368
  and epilepsy, 534
  and hypnosis, 22
  and hysteria, 25
  case of, 221
  for personal identity, 221
  Martha Ottenby (case), 73–80
Amobarbitol, 356
Amphetamine (benzadrine), 352, 355, 360, 505
Anaesthesia, 225
Analytical psychology, 267
Androgen, 380
Anger; *see* Aggression
Animal magnetism, 22
Animal research
  and neurotic paradox, 114
  on deprivation, 137
Anorexia nervosa, 414
Anoxia, 519, 531, 541
Antabuse (disulfiram), 369
Anti-Semitism, 157
Anti-social impulses, 214
Anxiety, 111ff., 148, 396, 457–58
  and aggression, 153
  basic, 125
  and combat, 225
  and criminal behavior, 85
  and drugs, 471
  and frustration, 125
  and hysterical tremor, 225
  and interpretation, 259
  and learning, 111
  and learning theory, 100
  and neurosis, 30, 46, 111–12
  and obsessive symptoms, 213
  and phobia, 206 ff.
  and placement of hysterical symptom, 228
  and projection, 120, 438
  and reaction formation, 121
  and rejection, 158–59
  and schizophrenia, 452
  and sex, 185, 189, 375
  anxious conformity, 148
  psychosomatic disorders, 47, 415, 422
Anxiety states, 203–6, 545

  and phobias, 207
  anxiety attacks and hypnotic suggestion, 400
  case of anxiety attacks, 203
Apathy, 432
Aphasia, and cortical localization, 513
Aphonia, 225
Aplasia, 508
Arteriosclerosis, 509
  psychosis with, 546
Arthritis, 47
Ascendance; *see* Assertiveness
Assertive training, 251–53
Assertiveness, 432
Asthma, 47, 396, 420–23
  and hypnosis, 423
  and infantile frustration, 426
  case examples, 422
  emotional constellation and choice of symptom, 422
  emotional precipitation of attacks, 421
  physiological basis, 420
  prevalence and course, 421
  treatment, 432
Attitude
  classification of, 157
  of children toward parents, 160
Attitudes of parents
  aggression, 154
  dependence, 138
  development, 157–61
  sex, 188
Attitudes of society
  delinquency, 312
  masturbation, 184–85
Attitudes of students
  abnormality, 48–49
  society, 80–82
Aura, 533, 537
Autistic children, 454
Autistic thought, 449
Autonomic constitution, 424
Autonomic nervous system, 402 ff., 408, 424–26
  and central nervous system, 402
  and insulin shock, 470
  and psychosomatic disorders, 396
  and stress, 402, 425–26
  functions, 402–4
  protective reaction, 404, 426
Autonomy
  and overprotection, 160
  and parental attitudes, 158–59
  maladjustment and, 148
Aversion therapy, 250; *see also* Behavior therapy

Barbara (case of client-centered therapy), 270–71
Barbiturates, 356–57; *see also* Sedatives

Baroreceptor nerves, 418
Beauchamp, C. (case of multiple personality), 223
Beers, C. W. (case of manic-depressive psychosis), 482, 485–86
Behavior maintenance, 105–6
Behavior modification, 39–40
  and phobias, 213
  in sexual disorders, 378
Behavior therapy, 39, 244–55
  and anxiety, 245–46
  and autonomic nervous system, 246
  and homosexuality, 387
  and hypnotism, 246
  and punishment, 250
  and reciprocal inhibition, 246
  assertive training, 251–53
  aversion therapy, 250
  comparison to psychoanalysis, 259, 264–66
  criticism of, 254
  cure rates, 253
  enuresis, example of behavior therapy, 244
  evaluation, 253–55
  hierarchy, 245
  limitations, 254
  modification of behavior, 244
  operant conditioning, 249–51
  reinforcement contingencies, 249
  results, 280
  selection of patients, 278
  social anxiety, 252
  social inhibition, 252
Bereavement, 93
Beta rhythm, 534
Big Sur, 305
Biochemistry
  and schizophrenia, 466
  limits of, 468–69
Biogenic hypotheses, and schizophrenia, 431
Birth order, 164
Blindness, hysterical, 225, 400
Blood-type incompatibility, 567–68
Brain injury, 576
  and epilepsy, 536
  and psychopathic personality, 331
  case (child), 526
  effects of anoxia, 519
  in children, 456, 522
  injury in parietotemporal area, 513–15
  injury to frontal areas, 515–16
  loss of abstract attitude, 522
  prefrontal lobotomy, 516–19
  symptoms based on struggle with defect, 524
  symptoms of defect, 524
  training of children, 527
Breuer–Freud case, 27, 225

Brodman's areas, 511
Bronchial asthma; see Asthma
Bryan, H. (case of client-centered counseling), 271

Cannabis, 347–48
Cardiac disorders, 398
Cardiovascular disorders, 416 ff.
Castration anxiety, 382
Catatonic schizophrenia, 434–35
  and drugs, 467
  case, 451
Catecholamine hypothesis, 501
Cerebral cortex; see Cortex
Cerebral dominance, 512
Cerebral localization, 510–11
Cerebral palsy, 525
Cerebral style, 235–36
Cerebral tumors, 508
Cerebellum, 510
Cerebrospinal system, 402
Change
  adjustment to, 91
  and personal tendencies, 191
  and client-centered therapy, 270
Character armor, 128, 259
Character traits, 125
  in obsessive neurosis, 215
Chemogenic disorders, 509
  effects of anoxia, 519
  schizophrenia, 466
Child, Benton (case of multiple disorders), 65–73, 140, 145, 165, 168, 200, 295, 435
  attitude toward school, 60
  children, 71
  diagnosis, 68–69
  family history, 65–66
  hospitalization, 68
  medication, 72
  parental indulgence, 60
  self-doubt, 71
  sexual relations, 66
  symptoms, 67–69
  treatment, 68
  use of alcohol, 66–68
Child guidance; simultaneous treatment of mother and child, 338
Child guidance clinics, 12, 581
Childhood
  and symptom placement, 424–26
  and super-ego development, 149
  autonomy, 141–46
  children's attitudes, 160
  dependence, 135–37
  deprivation, 137–40
  growth problems, 135
  importance of first year, 138
  improvement in child training, 598
  loss of affection and depression, 490

Childhood (*Continued*)
  moral judgment, 150
  origins of mania and depression, 491
  panic and neurosis, 208
  schizophrenia, 454–58
  sexuality, 184–90, 374
  studies of brain injury, 522
Chlorpromazine, 20, 471
Chronic autonomic stimulation, 404
Chronic hypertension, 418
Classification of mental disorders, 12
  difficulties, 13–20
  Kraepelin, 17
  Pinel, 13
Claustrophobia, 207
Client-centered therapy, 38–39, 42; *see also*
    Psychotherapy
  criticism of, 272
  evaluation of, 271–73
  limitations, 272
Clinical psychologist, 591
  and child guidance, 581
  and psychotherapy, 591
  psychological testing, 591
  research, 591
  training, 591
CMT, 349
Cocaine, 352, 359
Coercion, 148
Cognitive development, 108
Cognitive fields, 108
  and treatment, 110–11
Cognitive maps, 108
Cognitive organization, 107–11
Colitis, 403, 409, 415
Communication, 450, 598
Communication theory, 291
Community
  and child guidance clinics, 581
  attitude of, toward mental illness, 574
  patients' return to, 586
Community mental health, 12–13, 38,
    574 ff.
Community mental health centers, 577–82
  criticism, 579–80
  need for, 577–79
  problems, 580
  services, 578
Companion programs, 592
Compensation, 32, 144
Competence, 142
  and adjustment, 143
  and amnesia, 221
  and growth, 143
  and inferiority complex, 143–46
  and self-esteem, 142–43
  decline with age, 540
  in mania, 489
  in social area, 143
Competent action, and adaptation, 93

Competition, 176
Compliant trend, 124
Complexes, 452
Compulsion, 213; *see also* Obsessional
    neurosis
Concentration, 526
Concordance rates, and schizophrenia, 464
Concrete behavior, 78–80, 523
Concussion, 524
Conditioned fear reactions, 100
Conditioned stimuli and response, 99–100
Conditioning, 208
  and alcoholism, 369
  counter-conditioning, 244
  infantile, and peptic ulcer, 412
  of general protective reaction, 426
Conflict, 31, 32, 46, 47
  and alcoholism, 367
  and delinquency, 319
  and hypertension, 417
  and multiple personality, 223
  and placement of hysterical symptom,
    228
  and sex, 188
  Bert Whipley (case), 82
  neurotic conflict, 224
Conformity
  and anti-Semitism, 157
  and dominance, 160
  anxious, 148
  excessive, 179–81
Conscience
  and psychopathic personality, 326
  and super-ego, 149
Conscientiousness, in obsessive neurosis,
    215
Construction of reality, 108–9
Constipation, 415
Constitution
  and mania and depression, 497
  and psychopathic personality, 325
  and psychosomatic disorders, 405, 410 ff.,
    424
  differences in, and choice of symptoms,
    234
Continuity of neurosis and normality, 131
Control
  and inhibition, 120
  and obsessions, 214
  in psychopathic personality, 331, 332
Conversion, 225, 271ff.; *see also* Hysteria
Conversion reaction, 225
  explanation of symptoms, 226
Coronary heart disease, personality factors,
    419
Corrective emotional experience, 240
  in client-centered therapy, 270
Cortex, 402, 510, 516, 537
  in Pick's disease, 74
  injury to, 512

lobotomy, 516–19
localization, 510
Cortisol, 499
Counter-conditioning, 103, 244
Course of disease, 14, 17
Cretinism, 568
Crime
deterrent vs. punishment, 336
society's response to, 335
Criminal behavior, 312–13
Criminal types, psychological differentiation, 336
Criminality, case of Bert Whipley, 80–89
Culture
and attitude toward abnormality, 574
and autonomy, 146
and conflict, 601–2
and personality development, 174
and power, 127
contradictions in, 601–2
Cultural–familial retardation, 551
and IQ, 559, 561–62
and malnutrition, 559–60
and socio-cultural deprivation, 558–61
causes of, 557–58
characteristics, 557–58
importance of stimulation and maturation, 561–62
incidence of, 557, 559
prevention, 560
treatment, 560–62
Curare, and ECT, 471
Curiosity, in children, 184
Cyclical insanity, 479
Cyclothymic pattern, and personality, 493

Day hospitals, 582
Death instinct, 152
Defect
reaction to, 524
symptoms of, 524
Defense, 396
and free association, 256
and interpretation, 258
and loss of personal identity, 221
and obsessive symptoms, 213, 214
and psychotherapy, 258
and schizophrenia, 446
and self-picture, 128–29
and transference neurosis, 260–61
as obstacle to relearning, 117–18
constitutional differences in, 234
Defense mechanisms, 118–22
other defenses, 121
primary defensive process, 118
secondary defensive process, 118, 215
Degeneration, 509
Delay of gratification, 330
Delinquency, 34, 47, 87, 175, 311–24, 396
and deprivation, 316

and immaturity, 316
and indulgence, 318–19
and neurosis, 311, 322
and parental standards, 317
and social organization, 314
as failure to introject parental standards, 318–19
Cambridge–Somerville Youth Study, 318 ff.
children who hate, 319
classification, 312
cultural deviant, 315
delinquency areas, 316
diagnostic system for, 317
gangs, 175, 321
group memberships, 321
treatment, 322–24
Delirium, 520
Delta waves, 534
Delusions
and drugs, 467
case of Martha Ottenby, 73–80
in schizophrenia, 432, 446, 449 ff.
of grandeur, 467, 546
of persecution, 467, 545, 546
sudden onset, 452
Dementia praecox, 18, 430; see also Schizophrenia
Denial, 489
Dependence, 135, 417
and depression, 493
and sibling rivalry, 154
in asthmatic patients, 421
in childhood, 135
in peptic ulcer patients, 411
in schizophrenia, 445, 460
maladjustment and, 140
on group, 179
Depression, 76, 480, 515
adjustive attempt, 489
agitated, 480, 483
and deprivation, 135
attitude toward self, 483
case examples, 482, 483
in infants, 492
infantile origins, 492
methods of treatment, 501–6
psychological meaning, 488
psychosomatic view, 496
reactive, 544
retarded, 480 ff.
Depressive neurosis, 496
Deprivation, 135–40
Desensitization, case of Walter Lilly, 54
Desertion, reaction to, 490
Dextroamphetamine (dexedrine), 352
Diabetes, 404
Diarrhea, 415
Diathesis-stress model, 466
Differential reinforcement, 109

Dilantin sodium, 538
Direct analysis, 473
Discipline, 141ff., 318–19
    and self control, 146–51
Disordered personal reactions, 45
    main varieties, 46–49
    and normal experience, 48–49
Disorganization, 534
    and schizophrenia, 439
    in schizophrenic thinking, 446, 449–54
    social, and delinquency, 316, 319, 326
Displacement, 121
    in phobias, 209
Disruptive effect, 93
Dissatisfaction, chronic, 130–31
Dissociation, 25, 223
    dissociated conditions, 220–24
Distractibility, 161, 485, 526, 538
Dominance, parental, 160
    and overprotection, 160
    and traits of children, 158
Dominant–dependent relationship, 200
Dopamine, 467
Double-bind hypothesis, 461–63
Down's syndrome; see Mongolism
Drama, as aid to psychotherapy, 296–97
Dream analysis, 262
Dreams, 449
    analysis, 261–62
    and neurosis, 130
Dropping out of school, 173
Drug dependence, 340–72
    decriminalizing, 362–64
    prevention, 364–65
    psychological aspects, 359–61
    treatment, 361
Drugs
    ataractic, 471
    anti-depressant, 504–6
    in epilepsy, 538
    in schizophrenia, 467
    tranquilizing, 20–21
    use of, in therapy, 519
Dynamic psychology, 311

Efficacy, experience of, 143
Ego, 182, 190 ff.
    alien, 149
    and client-centered therapy, 272
    and obsessions, 215
    ego strength, 319
    identity, 194
    potential and psychotherapy, 276–77
Ego weakness, 196
Elation, 485–86
Electra complex, 185
Electroconvulsive therapy, 470
Electroencephalogram, 331
    and epilepsy, 534

Electroshock, 19–20
    results with affective disorders, 499
Emergency theory, 403, 500
Emotion
    and bodily changes, 398–400
    and psychotherapy, 259
    and thinking, 450
    autonomic nervous system, 402
    control, 78, 95
    corrective emotional experience, 259
    everyday observation, 399
    experiments, 400
    in epileptics, 538
    loss of emotional supplies, 492
    precipitation of asthma attacks, 421
    specific psychosomatic relationships, 406, 417, 424
Emotional divorce, and schizophrenia, 460
Emotions, and peptic ulcer, 412
Encephalitis, 331, 397, 509, 525
Encounter groups, 42, 305–7
Endocrine glands, 509
    disturbance, 466
    in manic depression, 499
    in schizophrenia, 466
Enslavement, social, 179–81
Environment
    and adjustment, 91
    stress, 83–84
Epilepsy, 510, 532
    case, 539
    causes, 536
    effects on personality, 538
    electroencephalogram, 534
    focal, 537
    incidence, 532, 576
    treatment, 538
    varieties of attack, 532
Epinephrine, 423, 500
Esalen, 305
Essential hypertension, 403
Esteem, 153
    and adolescence, 177
    and depression, 488
    and gangs, 175
    and group memberships, 175
Estrogen, 380
Euphoria, 515
Excitatory process, 234
Exhaustion, stage of, 404
Exhibitionism, 375, 391
    case of treatment, 392
Existential psychoanalysis, 273
Existential psychotherapy, 273–74
Experimental neurosis, 114
Extension of self, 198
Extinction, 102–3
Extra-punitive, 154
Extroversion–introversion, 233

Family
  as environment for growth, 157–61
  as social system, 162
  cohesiveness of, 318
  concepts, 163
  importance for development, 596–97
Family circle, 185
Family psychotherapy, 40–41, 287–94
Family therapy, 287–94
  and communication theory, 291
  case examples, 291ff.
  course of therapy, 291
  defense of families, 290
  family as patient, 289
  family as system, 288–91
  mother–child relationship, 287
  origins, 287
  patient, in family therapy, 289
Fantasy
  and schizophrenia, 435
  and self-picture, 129
Father–son relationship, 319
Fear, 111ff., 189
  and neurosis, 130
  of rejection, 186
  of defecation, 115–16
Feeble-mindedness, incidence of, 576
Feeding problems
  in infancy, 136
  psychosomatic disorders of appetite, 414
Feelings
  expression of, 296
  of worthlessness, 86, 480 ff., 482
Fever, 509
Fits, 538
Fixation
  and autonomy, 148
  and dependence, 140
  and sex, 188
  of the super-ego, 150
Flexibility, principle of, 298
Foresight, 518
Foundling homes, study of, 136
Fragmentation, 520
  in brain-injured patients, 521
  in schizophrenia, 430
Free association, 28 ff., 256, 261, 296
  and dream interpretation, 261
  example, 256
Friendship
  and maladjustment, 183
  and personality development, 182
Frontal lobes, 511
  and abstract behavior, 78–80, 523
  and Pick's disease, 74
  injury, 512, 515
  prefrontal lobotomy, 516–19
Frustration, 152
  and aggression, 153
  and basic threat, 125

and demands of reality, 91
and dependence, 140, 205
and excessive group identification, 179–81
and neurotic pattern of affection, 125
and neurosis, 130
and sibling rivalry, 154
and social isolation, 178
and symptom placement, 425–26
feeding frustration, and peptic ulcer, 412
Fugues, 221–22
Functional psychoses, 46
  comparison to organic psychosis, 77

Galvanic skin response (GSR), 101
Gangs, 175, 321
Gastritis, 407, 409
Generalization, 100–2
Generativity, 197–99
  and maladjustment, 198–99
General paresis, 14–15, 509
  age at onset, 15
  and psychoses with arteriosclerosis, 546
  and syphilis, 16
  course, 15–16
  mode of onset, 16
  neurological changes, 16
  sex distribution, 16
Genogenic disorders
  epilepsy, 536
  schizophrenia, 464
Gephryophobia, 207
German measles, 564–65
Gestalt therapy, 275
Grand mal, 533
Grief, 93, 399
  and mania, 489
Group for the Advancement of Psychiatry, 585
Group membership
  and belongingness, 177
  and delinquency, 175, 320–21
  and maladjustment, 178–82
  and psychotherapy, 303
  and schizophrenia, 446
  and social isolation, 178
  effects of, 174 ff.
  in adolescence, 177
  in adulthood, 178
  in juvenile era, 176
Group psychotherapy, 41–42, 298–307
  activity groups, 303–4
  advantages, 302
  and individual psychotherapy, 303
  as environment for change, 302
  case example, 300–1
  course, 299
  definition, 298
  group-centeredness, 298

Group psychotherapy (*Continued*)
    interpretation, 299
    psychodrama, 296–97
Growth
    autonomy and discipline, 141–46
    dependence and deprivation, 135–40
    problems in early life, 135
    sexual development, 184–90
Guided group interaction, 323
Guilt, feelings of, 82, 85, 121, 182, 189,
        214, 217, 393, 415, 424
    and anorexia nervosa, 414
    and conscience, 149
    and delinquency, 320
    and depression, 482
    and manic-depressive psychosis, 494
    and obsessive symptoms, 214

Habituated interactions, 95
Halfway House, 587
Hallucinations, 449
    and hypnosis, 22
    and schizophrenia, 435, 449
    in depressive states, 482
    in senile psychoses, 545
    Martha Ottenby, 76
    under drugs, 467
Hallucinogens, 349–52
Hans (case of phobia in five-year-old boy),
        185, 210
Happiness, economy of, 95
Hashish, 348–49
Hebephrenic schizophrenia, 432–34
Heirens, W. (case of sexual deviation), 393
Heredity, and epilepsy, 536
Hermann, Kathi (case of adolescent men-
        tal breakdown), 58–65, 433, 435, 462,
        469
    adolescent rebellion, 59
    childhood history, 58–59
    diagnosis, 63
    sexual problems, 60–61
    treatment, 63
Hermaphroditism, 380
Heroin, 354, 357, 358–59
    and crime, 358
    dependence, 358
    physical effects, 358
    psychological effects, 358
    withdrawal from, 358
Hickock, R. (case of psychopathic per-
        sonality), 326–27, 330–31
High-risk populations, and schizophrenia,
        447–48
High-risk research, 447–48
Hives, 401, 404
Homeostasis, 541
Homolophobia, 207
Homosexuality, 374, 379 ff.

    and behavior therapy, 387–88
    and family, 382–83
    and learning, 380
    and schizophrenia, 452
    biological aspects, 379
    comparison with fetishism, 384–85
    developmental aspects, 381–84
    illustrative case, 388–90
    in childhood and adolescence, 188 ff.
    Kathi Hermann, 59–60
    motivation for change, 386
    psychoanalytic view, 382
    psychogenic factors, 381–84
Hospitalism, 137
Hostility; *see* Aggression
Hunger, in childhood, 135, 412
Hydrocephaly, 565–66
Hyperactivity, 526, 528–32
Hypersensitivity, 538
Hypertension, 398, 406, 417–19
    and aggression, 417
    and dependence, 417
    and hostile impulses, 417
    case examples, 418
    constitutional factors, 418
    definition, 417
    specific emotional constellation, 417
    status of hostile impulses, 417
    symptoms, 417
Hypnosis, 35
Hypnotism, 22, 193
    and hysteria, 23, 27
    and multiple personalities, 224
    experiments on psychosomatic processes,
        399–402
    post-hypnotic amnesia, 400
    post-hypnotic conflict, 400
    post-hypnotic suggestion, 400
Hypochondriasis, 544
Hypothalamus, 402, 501, 517
Hysteria, 225–31, 397
    and anaesthesia, 225
    and neurology, 23–24
    and repression, 29
    Breuer–Freud case, 26–29
    case of Irene, 25
    case of Solomon, 288
    changing picture of, 230
    early studies, 21
    in World War I, 397
    mental state, 24
    onset, 24
    placement of symptom, 228
    study of hysterical tremor, 228
    symptoms, 23, 225
    therapy, 27
Hysterical blindness, case of, 226–27
Hysterical fit, 225
Hysterical styles, 235
Hysterical twilight states, 225

Ideals
  and the super-ego, 149
  ego-ideal, 149
Identification, 194
  and children who hate, 319
  and super-ego, 150
  ego-identity, 194
  excessive, with social role, 180
  with father, 197
  with friend, 182
  with group, 174
Identity, and maladjustment, 195
Identity achievement, 195
Identity crisis, 196
Identity diffusion, 195
Identity foreclosure, 195
Identity status, 195
Imagination; see Fantasy
Imitation, and sex roles, 186
Immaturity, 326
Impotence, 229
Imprinting, 456
Impulses
  and aggressive disorders, 320
  and interpretation, 259
  and obsessional neurosis, 214, 215
  blocking, in psychosomatic disorders, 426
  in brain injury, 526–27
  status of, in hypertension, 417
Impulsive style, 235
Impulsiveness, 332
Impunitive reaction, 154
Incoordination, 520
Independence; see Autonomy
Individual differences, in children, 161
Individual psychology, 267
Indole amines, 500
Indulgence
  and delinquency, 318–19
  and overprotection, 160
  and traits of children, 160
Indulgence, parental, 148, 160, 188
  infantile sexuality, 185
  latency period, 187
  Oedipus complex, 185
Infection, 509
Inferiority complex, 143–46, 195
  case of Water Lilly, 57–58
Inferiority, feelings of, 32, 128, 145
  and sex, 189, 392
Influenza, 398
Inhibition, 120
  and alcohol, 366
  and psychodrama, 296–97
  and psychopathic personality, 333
Inhibitory process, 234
Insanity
  and crime, 335
  and psychosis, 46, 480
  as brain disease, 13

fear of, 130
Insecurity, 288
Insight, 46, 108, 300
  and client-centered therapy, 270
  and psychoanalysis, 259
  moral, 527
Institutional care, 584–86
Institutionalization, indications for, 586
Insulin, results with schizophrenia, 470
Insulin shock, 19–20, 470
Integration, and competence, 142, 144
Intellectualization, 121
  in obsessional neurosis, 215
Intelligence
  and aging, 540
  and epilepsy, 539
  and frontal lobes, 515, 517
  in psychopathic personality, 326
  and psychotherapy, 276–77
  and senile psychosis, 545
  disorder in schizophrenia, 453
Intelligence quotient, 549
  and mental retardation, 549
  and PKU, 556
Internal organization, 109
Interest, at school, 173–74
Interaction
  parent–child, 162
  social, 174–75
  with environment, 91, 96
  with groups, 174–84
  with individuals, 182–84
Interpenetration, 520
Interpersonal relationships
  and intimacy, importance of, 182
  and need for power, 127
  and personal maturity, 601
  and self-awareness, 193
  in juvenile era, 176
Interpretation
  in group therapy, 299
  in psychoanalysis, 258–59
  of dreams, 261–62
Intrapunitive reaction, 154
Introversion–extroversion, 233
Introjection, 150
  and delinquency, 318–19
  and psychopathic personality, 325
Irene (case of hysteria), 25
Irrational fears, 100
Isolation, 122, 216
  social, 178 ff.

Jealousy, 154, 185
Joint Commission on Mental Illness and
  Health, 575
Judgment; see Moral judgment, Thinking
Juvenile delinquency, 314–24; see also De-
  linquency
  and adult crime, 314

Klinefelter's syndrome, 380

Language disorder, 434
Latency period, 187
Law of effect, 103
Learning
  and ambivalence, 154
  and brain function, 513
  and criminal behavior, 83–86
  and parental acceptance, 160
  and psychosomatic connections, 414
  and psychotherapy, 239, 276–77
  and sibling rivalry, 154
  and the self, 193
  and the super-ego, 149
  defensive obstacles to relearning, 117–18
  failure in psychopathic personality, 318–
    19
  in infancy, 137
  relearning after fright, 111–17
  relearning at puberty, 187
Learning, principles of, 98–111
  anxiety response, 100
  conditioned fear reactions, 100
  conditioned responses, 99–100
  counter-conditioning, 103
  generalization, 100–2
  irrational fears, 100
  law of effect, 103
  operant conditioning, 103–7
  reinforcement, 104 ff.
Learning theory, and psychotherapy, 244–
    45
Legend of chronicity, 308
Leonard, W. E. (case of phobia), 211
Libido theory, 32
Librium, 356
Life patterns, 199–200
Lilly, Walter (case of adolescent malad-
    justment), 49–58, 106, 145, 155, 178,
    248, 252
  anxiety, 51
  desensitization, 54
  inferiority complex, 57–58
  interaction with father, 55
  loss of self-esteem, 51
  school work, 53
  social situation, 51
  symptoms, 49–51
Lithium, 505
Lobelin, 346
Lobotomy, 516–19
  effects, 517–19
  therapeutic value, 517–18
Localization, 513
Loss, and manic-depressive psychosis, 491–
    92
LSD, 349–52, 355, 360
  case example, 351
  physical effects, 350–52

psychological effects, 350–52
Lysergic acid, 467

Maguire (case of delinquency), 315
Maladjusted personality, 276–77
  case of adolescent maladjustment, 49
Maladjustment, 47
  and aggression, 155
  and autonomy, 147
  and dependence and deprivation, 138 ff.
  and generativity, 198–99
  and group role and membership, 178–82
  and psychosomatic disorders, 397, 427
  and sex, 188–90
  and social enslavement, 179–81
  and social isolation, 178
  arising from discipline, 147
  as failure to become autonomous, 147
  at college, 97–98
Mania, 479, 484
  adjustive attempt, 489
  and psychosomatic interaction, 495
  case example, 485–86
  characteristics, 484
  infantile origins, 491
  psychological meaning, 488
  treatment by drugs, 504–6
Manic-depressive psychosis, 18 ff., 479, 491
  and anti-depressant drugs, 504–7
  and biogenic amine metabolism, 500
  and electrolyte metabolism, 500
  and guilt, 494
  and hospitalization, 502
  and loss, 492
  and psychotherapy, 503–4
  biochemical factors, 498
  chemogenic factors, 495
  genetic factors, 497
  genogenic factor, 491
  problems of classification, 495
  shock treatment, 503
  somatic aspects, 497
  treatment, 501–6
Marihuana, 347–49
  incidence, 347
  laws against, 348–49
  psychological effects, 348
  use, 347
Marketing personality, 181
Masochism, 375, 391
Massachusetts Mental Health Center, 583
Masturbation, 216, 393
  case history, 189
  in childhood, 185, 188
Maternal rubella, 564–65
McNaughten rules, 335
Medulla, 402, 510
Melancholia, 479
  involutional, 496, 503
Melissophobia, 207

Memory
  and frontal lobes, 515
  and simple schizophrenia, 432
  defect, 76, 78
  decline with age, 541
Mental hospitals, 584–86
  as therapeutic milieu, 474–75
  day hospitals, 582
  out-patient service, 586
  social organization, 584
  staffing, 589
  student volunteers in, 592
Mental hygiene, 487
Mental illness as problem for society
  citizens' contribution, 600–2
  finance, 576
  institutions, 584–86
  manpower, 589
  numbers, 575
  prevention, 595–600
  professions concerned, 94
  return of patient to community, 586
  size of problem, 575
Mental retardation, 582
  attitude toward, 571–72
  definition and degrees of, 549–50
  early childhood care, 571
  family planning, 570–71
  incidence of, 550
  labelling, 564
  measurement of, 548–73
  prenatal care, 571
Mescaline, 349, 467
Mesomorphy, 498–501
Metabolic disorders, 509
Metabolism, 494, 509, 541
  instability in manic-depressive psychosis, 18, 498
Methamphetamine (methedrine), 352, 356
Methionine, 467
Methylation process, 467
Microcephaly, 508, 565–66
Midbrain, 402
Midtown Manhattan study, 575
Minimal brain dysfunction, 528–32
  and amphetamines, 528–30, 532
  and anoxia, 531
  and cortical functioning, 530
  and learning difficulties, 531
  and psychological correlates, 530
  and self-image, 529–30
  and social class, 531
  and toxemia, 531
  case examples, 529
  classification, 531
  psychogenic versus somatic factors, 528–31
  treatment, 529–31
Modeling, and psychopath, 330
Mongolism, 551–54

and birth rate, 552
and health, 552
and maternal age, 552–53
characteristics, 551–52
degrees of, 551–52
etiology, 551–53
prevention of, 554
treatment, 553–54
Mongoloid deficiency, 508
Monoamine oxidase inhibitors, 505
Mood
  and electroshock, 503
  changes, 78
  disorders of, 480 ff.
Moral insight, 527
Moral judgment
  and super-ego, 149
  moral realism, 527
Moral knowledge, 336
Moratorium (identity), 195
Mothering, 136–38
  in therapy with schizophrenia, 473
Motivation, 171–72, 396
  and psychotherapy, 276–77, 322–24, 338, 386
  and use of alcohol, 366
Multiple personality, 192, 222–24, 430
Multiple sclerosis, 230
Multiple sexual perversions, 393
Mutism, 225

Narcotics
  incidence of use, 358
  physical effects, 358
  psychological effects, 358
National Institute of Mental Health, 577, 590
Nebulizer, 422
Negative identity, 196
Negativism, in catatonia, 434–35
Neologisms, 432
Neurasthenia, 31
Neurochemicals, 467
Neuropathology; see also Brain injury
  effects of localized brain injury, 510–19
  examples of chemogenic disorders, 519
  incidence, 576
  survey of pathological properties, 508–10
Neuroses, 46, 144, 202–36, 299, 396
  affection, as neurotic pattern, 125
  and adaptive styles, 235
  and anxiety, 203
  and current stress, 235
  and defense, 114
  and difficulties of living, 234–35
  and group therapy, 299
  and learning, 236
  and old age, 544
  and personality traits, 232–33
  and psychopathic personality, 87

Neuroses (*Continued*)
  and repression, 29 ff.
  and sex, 31
  and sexual deviations, 394
  and strivings for superiority, 32
  childhood origins, 492
  choice of, 205, 231–32
  chronic dissatisfaction, 130–31
  comparison with healthy organization,
    131–32
  current research, 232
  dynamics of, 231
  effectiveness of treatment, 278–84
  incidence, 576
  need for power, as neurotic pattern, 127
  neurotic depression, 480
  neurotic paradox, 114 ff.
  neurotic pattern, 122–28
  neurotic protective organization, 122–29
  overdriven strivings, 124, 127, 129, 130,
    205, 219
  phobias, 206 ff.
  predisposition, 232
  problems with terms, 202
  spontaneous remission, 280–82
  tension, 130
  transference, 260
  varieties, 202
Neurotic delinquent, 337
Neurotic styles, 235
Neurotic trends, 124
Neuroticism, 233
New Haven study, 576
Non-commitment, 216
Non-directive counseling, 268–69; *see also*
    Psychotherapy, client-centered
Non-professional aides, 592–94
Norepinephrine, 353, 500–1
Norms
  and super-ego, 150
  in adulthood, 181
  parental, 150
  via group membership, 174–75
Nurturant tendencies, 198

Oberman, Peter (case of obsessive neuro-
    sis), 217–20
Obsession, 213
Obsessive-compulsive state, 31, 235
Obsessional neurosis, 213–20
  case of Peter Oberman, 217–20
  distinctive features, 214
Occipital poles, 511
Oedipus complex, 185, 204, 210
Omnipotence, 219
Onomatophobia, 207
Operant conditioning, 103–7
Orderliness, 148, 214, 215, 527
Organic psychoses, 46
  case of Martha Ottenby, 73–80

Organized crime, 313–14
Orgasm, 391, 393
Orizon, 306
Other-directed persons, 180
Ottenby, Martha (case of Pick's disease),
    73–80, 507, 509
  behavior in hospital, 76
  comparison with functional psychosis, 77
  earliest symptoms, 75
  personal history, 74–75
  reduction of behavior to the immediate
    and concrete, 78–82
  role of personal needs, 77
Outcome of disease, 13, 17
Overachievement, 171–72
Overdriven strivings, 124, 219
  and hysteria, 226–27
Overinclusion, 520, 521
Overprotection
  and dependence, 140
  and social isolation, 178
  maternal, 160, 318–19, 421
Oxygen deprivation, 509; *see also* Anoxia

Panic, 111, 204
  case of W. E. Leonard, 112
Paralysis, 15, 225
Paranoia, 437, 545
  Kathi Hermann, 61
Paranoid style, 235
Paranoid trends, 545
  development of paranoid thinking, 449–
    51
  paranoid schizophrenia, 435
Parasympathetic division of the autonomic
    nervous system, 402, 415, 420
Parent–child relations
  and activity level, 161
  and adjustment, 601–2
  and conformity training, 146
  and delinquency, 315, 318–19
  and formation of super-ego, 149
  and outgrowing autonomy, 142–44
  and psychopathic personality, 329
  and schizophrenia, 443, 458–64
  and school phobia, 170
  and self-esteem, 143
  and sex, 188
  Bert Whipley, 84, 163, 322
  case of hysterical tics, 288
  Peter Oberman, 217–20
Parental attitudes, 157; *see also* Accep-
    tance, Attitude, Rejection
  and depression, 492
  and maladjustment, 156
  and social enslavement, 180
  and super-ego, 150
  dominance–indulgence, 160
  effect on development, 157, 163, 596–97

maternal overprotection, 160, 421
part played by child, 160
Parental control, 146
Parents, education of, 599
Parietotemporal lobes, 512
and aphasia, 513
injury to, 513–15
Parthenophobia, 207
Partial hospitalization, 583
Partial sexual impulses, 374
Passivity, 161, 454
and dependence, 205
Pathological process, varieties of, 508–10
Patient, government, 309
Pedophile, 327
Penis envy, 382
Pepsinogen, 416
Perception, 521
Performance tests, 522, 526
Persistence, and adaptive process, 91
Persona, 181
Personality
and epilepsy, 538
and neurosis, 233
as habituated tendencies, 95
as unity, 191–92
Persuasion (case of Walter Lilly), 56
Peter (case of animal phobia), 40
Petit mal, 533
Peyote, 349
Phenobarbitol, 356, 538
Phenobarbitol sodium, 356
Phenylketonuria (PKU), 551, 554–57
and dietary control, 556
and IQ, 556
characteristics, 554–55
detection of, 555–56
etiology, 555
genetic screening, 556–57
incidence of, 555
treatment, 556–57
Phobias, 203, 206–13
and choice of neurosis, 231
and repression, 209
as conditioned anxiety responses, 208
cases of, 40, 185, 210, 247
definition, 206
element in neurosis, 248
Hans (case), 185, 210
Peter (case), 40
secondary gain, 212
school phobia, 170
treatment, 213
Phobic vulnerability, 210–12
Physique, and manic-depressive psychosis, 498
Pick's disease, 509, 546
case of Martha Ottenby, 73–80
Pioneer House, 324
Plan, concept of, 110

Pneumonia, 398, 403
Power, need for, 127
Prescriptive penology, 338
Primary gain, 212
Primary psychopaths, 325
Proaction, 110
Professions dealing with disordered people,
590–94
clinical psychology, 591
psychiatric social work, 591
psychiatry, 590
Projection, 120–21, 437–38, 576
Protectively burdened personality, 122–29
Pseudo-community, 450
Psilocybin, 349
Psychasthenia, 26
Psychiatric social work and child guidance,
581
Psychiatrist, role and training of, 590
Psychiatry
and child guidance, 581
and psychotherapy, 590
as profession, 589
Psychoactive drugs, and crime, 346–47
Psychoanalysis, 37 ff.
and client-centered psychotherapy, 258
and fetishism, 386
and psychiatry, 590
and recovery, 279
comparison to behavior therapy, 259,
264–66
dream analysis, 261
free association, 256
group therapy, 298–300
illustrative case, 262 ff.
interpretation, 258–59, 261, 287
neo-Freudian techniques, 267–68
standard, 255–66
training, 590
transference neurosis, 260–61
with children, 287
with delinquents, 322–24
Psychoanalytically oriented therapy, 267
Psychodrama, 296–97
Psychodynamics, 32–33
Psychogenic disorders, prevention of, 596
Psychogenic hypothesis, 21, 34, 35, 46, 90,
311, 427
and depression, 491, 498 ff.
and hysteria, 26
and psychopathic personality, 329
and schizophrenia, 463
comparison with somatogenic, 77
Psychological counseling, 268; see also Psychotherapy, client-centered
Psychomotor attack, 533, 534
Psychopathic personality, 47, 87, 324 ff.
and brain injury, 331
and psychological privation, 329
case example, 326

Psychopathic personality (*Continued*)
  central pattern of traits, 325–26
  classification problem, 325
  differential diagnosis of, 325
  psychogenic aspects, 329
  somatogenic aspects, 331–33
  treatment, 333–35
Psychopathology, 17, 21
Psychosis, 46, 196, 480
  and psychopathic personality, 326
  in infancy, 454
  incidence, 576
Psychosomatic disorders, 47, 396–428
  and hives, 401–4
  anorexia nervosa, 414
  bronchial asthma, 420–23
  classification, 397–98
  colitis, 403
  definition, 397
  diabetes, 404
  emotion and bodily changes, 398–406
  essential hypertension, 403, 417–19
  gastro-intestinal disturbances, 406–13
  implications for general medicine, 437
  incidence, 397–98
  problem of symptom placement, 405, 423–27
  Raynaud's disease, 401, 404
  rheumatoid arthritis, 403
  specificity hypothesis, 406, 424
Psychosurgery, 516–19, 537
Psychotherapy, 35–43
  and delinquency, 322–24
  and deviant sexual behavior, 386–88, 392, 394
  and epilepsy, 539
  and general medicine, 427.
  and manic-depressive psychosis, 503–4
  and motivation, 276–77
  and neurosis, 238
  and psychogenic disorders, 239
  and psychopathic personality, 333
  and psychosomatic disorders, 412, 423, 426–27
  and schizophrenia, 472–74
  as behavior change, 240
  as corrective emotional experience, 240, 259, 276
  as relearning, 239
  behavior therapy, 244–55; *see also* Behavior therapy
  changes in client, 270
  choice of patients, 276–78
  client-centered, 258, 268–73
  combined with shock therapy, 470
  course of treatment, 270
  criteria for patient selection, 276–78
  direct methods of establishing contact, 472
  ego strengthening, 474
  encounter groups, 305–7
  evaluation of, 271–73
  examples of abreaction, 26–29
  existential psychotherapy, 273–74
  expression of feeling, 240, 296
  family psychotherapy, 287–94
  family therapy, 287–94; *see also* Family therapy
  gestalt therapy, 275
  goals of treatment, 474
  group methods, 286–310
  group psychotherapy, 298–307
  in epilepsy, 539
  individual, 238–84
  initial steps, 242
  marital counseling, 294–95
  milieu therapy, 307–10
  nature of, 239
  new behavior, 276, 297
  obstacles to, 240
  occupational therapy, 307
  other forms, 266–76
  psychoanalysis, 255–66
  psychoanalytically oriented, 267
  psychodrama, 296–97
  reality therapy, 275
  recognition of feeling, 268
  relationship in, 261, 270
  results, 278–84
  role expectations in, 295
  roles of clinical psychologist and social worker, 591
  specific techniques, 243
  spontaneous remission, 280–82
  standard psychoanalysis, 255–66
  therapeutic milieu, 307–10, 324
  therapeutic relationship, 241
  training for, 590–91
  warmth of therapist, 242
Psychotic depressive reaction, 496
Psychotomimetrics, 467
Puberty, 129, 182, 187, 374
Puerperal fever, 470
Punishment, purpose of, 335
Pyknic physique, 498

Rationalization, 122
Raynaud's disease, 401, 404
Reaction, 110
Reaction formation, 121
  and dependence, 140, 412, 421
  and inferiority complex, 144
  and mania, 489
  and obsessive neurosis, 215
  and sex, 189
  and social isolation, 178
Reaction patterns, 234–35
Reactive depression, 496
Reactive schizophrenia, 440
Reality, 46, 436, 487

and adaptation, 91–92
and schizophrenia, 436, 445, 450, 451, 452
Reality therapy, 275
Recognition, 127
Recovery from fright, 111
Reference, ideas of, 445
Regression, 97, 118, 454
    and schizophrenic thinking, 453
Reinforcement, 104
Rejection, 123, 216
    and asthma, 421
    and dependence, 140
    and group identification, 169, 178
    fear of, 186
    and neurotic need for affection, 126
    parental, 158, 329
    traits of children, 158–59
Relearning; see Learning
Repression, 29 ff., 118–20, 367
    and aggression, 125, 156
    and anxiety, 30, 118–20
    and free association, 256
    and obsessional neurosis, 214
    and phobia, 209
    and sex, 214
    experimental demonstration, 118–20
    of personal identity, 221
Research
    in penology, 338
    on neurosis, 232 ff.
Resentment, 149, 415
Resistance, 29 ff., 256, 404
    example, 256
Resperine, 20
Retardation, in depression, 480–81
Retraining, 114 ff.
Rheumatoid arthritis, 401, 404
Rigidity, 538
Rocco, J. (case), 156
Role expectations, 295
Roles
    and group membership, 174–75
    and maladjustment, 450
    persona, 181
    as skill, 450
Rorschach test, 422

Sadism, 375
Schizoaffective psychosis, 443
Schizoid personality, 432
Schizophrenia, 18 ff., 429–76
    and delusions, 449
    and guilt, 445
    and physiological arousal, 468
    case examples, 443, 446
    causes, 430–31
    changed world in, 451–53
    childhood, 457

classification, 431–38
common features, 438
concordance rates, 464
disorganization, 449–54
early identification, 447
etiology, 448
family history, 442
high-risk populations, 447–48
in childhood, 454–88
incidence, 429–32
insulin shock, 19–20
Kathi Hermann, 69
modes of genetic transmission, 456–66
nature of intellectual disorder in, 453
organic etiology, 441 ff.
parent–child interactions, 458–64
premorbid characteristics, 445–46
process vs. reactive patterns, 440
prognosis, 439 ff.
psychodynamic aspects, 458–64
psychogenic etiology, 441ff.
psychosurgery in, 517
treatment, 469–76
varieties of onset and course, 440–45
Schizophrenogenic mothers, 455, 459
Schizotypes, 466
School difficulties, 34
School phobia, 170
Schools
    and competence, 168
    psychological service in, 582–83
Secobarbital sodium (seconal), 356
Secondary gain, 229
    from phobias, 212
Secondary psychopaths, 325
Secondary rewards, 106–7
Security
    and neurosis, 130
    and neurotic trends, 125
Sedatives, 356–57
    dependence on, 357
    laws against, 357
    physical effects, 356–57
    psychological effects, 356–57
    withdrawal from, 357
Self, 190 ff.
    and ego-identity, 194
    as unifying concept, 191–92
    extension of, 198
Self-attitude
    in depression, 480–81, 482
    in mania, 484
Self-centeredness, 199
Self-consciousness, 518
Self-corrective tendencies, and obsessive symptoms, 214
Self-criticism, 82, 482, 490
Self-esteem, 147, 249, 297
    and competence, 142–43
    and conformity, 180

Self-esteem (Continued)
 and depression, 480, 492
 and inferiority complex, 144
 and mania, 484, 488
 and schizophrenia, 444, 446
 and school work, 168
Self-formation, 192–94
Self-picture
 and conformity, 180
 and need for power, 127
 and protective traits, 128
Self-respect, 84, 195, 262
Semantic dementia, 326
Senile psychosis, 545, 546
Sensitivity training, 305
Serotonin, 467
Sesame Street, 563
Sex, 31–32, 120, 131, 373–94, 443, 444
 and aggression, 152, 375, 414, 485
 and maladjustment, 188–90
 and obsessive symptoms, 214
 and repression, 31–32, 189
 case history, 189
 disorder of glands, 466
 in puberty, 187, 374
 influence of culture, 187, 373
 pre-puberty, 185–87, 373
 roles, in early childhood, 186
 societal attitude toward, 373
Sexual aim, disorders of, 391
Sexual deviations, 47, 325, 373–94
 as developmental abnormality, 373
 case, 393
 homosexuality, 379 ff.
Sexual disorders, 373–94
 and hostility, 377
 and psychoanalysis, 378
 and stealing, 391
 behavior modification of, 378
 contributing causes, 376
 disorders of sexual aim, 391
 exhibitionism, 375, 391
 fetishism, 374, 384–86
 frigidity, 374
 homosexuality, 374; see also Homosexuality
 impotence, 374
 masochism, 375, 391
 multiple perversions, 393
 of performance, 375 ff.
 parental attitudes, 376
 premature ejaculation, 374
 sadism, 375, 391
 transvestism, 391
 treatment, 377–79, 392
 varieties of, 374–75
 voyeurism, 375, 391
Shock therapy, 19–20
 electroshock, 19–20, 503
 insulin shock, 19–20, 470

results with schizophrenics, 470
Sibling rivalry, 85, 304
 and aggression, 154
 and ambivalence, 153
 and inferiority complex, 145
Simple schizophrenia, 432
Skin diseases, 47, 396, 405
Sleep, and tension, 130
Smoking (tobacco), 341–46
 and disease, 341–42
 habit, 343–45
 incidence, 341–42
 reasons for, 343
 treatment, 345–46
Social class
 and minimal brain dysfunction, 531
 and psychotherapy, 276–77
Social development
 intimate relations, 182–84
 relations with groups, 174–81
Social incapacity, 549
Social inhibition, 252
Social relations
 and schizophrenia, 438, 446, 450
Social schizophrenia (case), 296–97
Socialization, 318–19
 and aggression, 153
 and ambivalence, 153
 and brain injury, 331, 526
 and epilepsy, 539
 and lobotomy, 517
 therapy, 322–24
Socialization failure
 and delinquency, 319, 322–24
 and psychopathic personality, 325
 and schizophrenia, 450
 and sexual deviations, 394
Society's response to crime, 335
Sociogenic hypothesis, 34
Somatogenic hypothesis, 13–20
 and depression, 488, 496 ff.
 and hysteria, 26–29
 and manic-depressive psychosis, 496 ff.
 and psychopathic personality, 331–33
 and psychosis, 46
 and schizophrenia, 464–69
 comparison with psychogenic, 77
Somatopsychic disorders, 397
Sophomore slump, 97–98, 173
Spastic behavior, 525
Specificity hypothesis, 406, 424
Speech, and traits, 128
Speed, 353
Spontaneous remission, 280–82
 in schizophrenia, 502
Spontaneous working-through, 115
Stanford–Binet intelligence test, 186
Status, 176
Stealing, and sexual disorders, 391
Stereotypy; see Rigidity

Stimulants, 352–56
  and violence, 354–56
  laws against, 355
  physical effects, 353–54
  psychological effects, 353–54
  use, 352–53
  varieties, 352
Stimulation management, 232
Stirling County studies, 576
STP, 349
Stress
  and autonomic functioning, 402
  and neurosis, 235
  and old age, 542
  and schizophrenia, 440
  and ulcers, 408–9
  in war, 494
Stress diseases; see Psychosomatic disorders
Structuring therapeutic relationship, 270
Subcultural delinquent, 337
Submissiveness, 417; see also Indulgence,
    parental
  parental, 158–59
Suicide, 482
Super-ego, 311
  and conscience, 149
  and delinquency, 311
  fixation, 150
  in children who hate, 320
Superiority, strivings for, 32, 127, 205
Supportive effect, 93
Suppression, 190, 367
  and maladjustment, 156
  of aggression, 155, 157
  of anxiety, 127
Symbiotic psychosis, 457
Symbolic representation, 109
Sympathetic division of autonomic nervous
    system, 402
Symptom, 35–36
  complex, 15, 17; see also Symptom syn-
    drome
Symptom formation
  choice of symptom, 206
  primary gain and secondary gain, 229
  psychosomatic, 405
  symptom placement, 228
Symptom syndrome
  choice of, 231–32
  psychopathic personality, 325
Synanon, 594
Synesthesias, 350
Syphilis, 16
Systematic desensitization, 245

Taraxein, 468
Tay–Sachs disease, 569
Temperament, 125
Temporal lobes, 511

Tendencies
  and parent–child relationships, 459–60
  and personality, 191
  pattern of, 124
Tension, 130
  and drugs, 471
  and psychosomatic disorders, 415
Termination of therapy
  and goals with schizophrenics, 474
  psychoanalysis, 276–77
Tetrahydrocannibal (THC), 348
Thalamus, 510, 517
Thalidomide, 565
Therapeutic milieu, 307–10
Therapeutic relationship, 241
Thinking
  development of paranoid thinking, 449
  disorder produced by drugs, 467
  schizophrenic thinking, 432–38
Thyroid gland, 509
Thyroxin, 568
Tics, 225
  cases of, 262, 288
Toilet training, 146
  and psychosomatic disorders, 416
Toxemia, 531
Toxins, and effect on brain function, 509
Training groups, 42
Traits
  adjustive function, 128
  and self-picture, 128
  protective, 124–29
Transexuals, 380
Transference
  cure, 389
  neurosis, 260–61
  manipulating the transference, 261
Transvestism, 391
Traumatic neurosis, 287
  and symptom placement, 229
Trauma
  to brain, 508; see also Brain injury
Treatment costs, 475
Treatment methods, experimental com-
    parison, 475
Tremor, 225, 228, 525
Tricyclic drugs, 505
Trisomy 21 (and mongolism), 553
Trust, development of, 139
Tumor, brain, 508, 536
Twins, and incidence of manic-depressive
    disorders, 497

Ulcer patients, peptic
  aggression, 413
  constitution, 410 ff.
  dependence, 411, 424
  mechanism of ulcer formation, 406–7
Ulcers, 47, 396, 406–13
  and guilt, 413

Ulcers (*Continued*)
 and personality patterns, 411
 and prolonged stress, 408–9
 prevalence, 406
Unconscious perception, 102
Unconscious strivings
 and neurosis, 38
 and transference neurosis, 260
Underachievement, 171–72
Underlying difficulties in case examples, 89
Undoing, 122, 216
Unemployment, 83
Unity of personality, 191

Vineland Social Maturity Scale, 549
Vitamin deficiency, 509
Voyeurism, 375, 391

Walden Two, 105
War

and depression following combat, 494
brain injury, 515
Whipley, Bert (case of criminality), 80–89,
 114, 139, 140, 150, 163, 168, 322, 495
 abilities, 82
 attitudes encouraged by companions, 85
 attitudes encouraged by parents, 84
 catastrophic childhood event, 85
 classification, 87
 contributory causes, 83–86
 criminal record, 80
 family history, 83–84
 self-defeating behavior, 80–82
White collar crime, 312–13
White collar criminal, 337
Widows for Widows, 594
Withdrawal, 438
 consequences of, 131, 178, 445–46
 from alcohol, 368
Word association test, 101